T
CRICK
WHO'S WHO
2010

Foreword by
PAUL COLLINGWOOD

Edited by
MICHAEL HEATLEY

Statistics by
RICHARD LOCKWOOD

Photographs by
GETTY IMAGES

This edition first published in the UK in 2010 by Green Umbrella Publishing

© Green Umbrella Publishing 2010
www.gupublishing.co.uk

Publisher: Jules Gammond

ISBN: 978-1-907311-39-0

Editor (for Green Umbrella Publishing): Kirsty Ennever
Layout: Alan Kinsman
Assistant editor: Peter Gamble
Picture research: Ellie Charleston
Quiz compiled by Chris Mason
Cover design by David Wildish
Printed by Zrinski, Croatia

ACKNOWLEDGEMENTS

Cover and most inside photographs by
Getty Images, 101 Bayham Street, London, NW1 0AG

The publishers would also like to thank the county clubs, the players
and their families for their assistance in helping to assemble
the information and photographs in this book.

Additional information has been gathered from
cricinfo.com and cricketarchive.com

Thanks also to the following for providing photographs:
Martin Bennett, Derbyshire CCC, Durham CCC, Richard Darwin, Pete Edmondson,
Gloucestershire CCC, David Griffin, Hampshire CCC, Kent CCC, Lancashire CCC,
Leicestershire CCC, MCC, Northamptonshire CCC, Nottinghamshire CCC, Tom
Reilly, Ian Smith, Somerset CCC, Surrey CCC, SWpix, Worcestershire CCC,
www.philbrittphotography.co.uk

CONTENTS

FOREWORD

5

INTERNATIONAL FIXTURES 2009

7

REVIEWING THE SITUATION

8

THE PCA MVP AWARDS

10

THE PLAYERS

17

THE UMPIRES

711

ROLL OF HONOUR 2009

742

FIRST-CLASS AVERAGES 2009

744

INDEX OF PLAYERS BY COUNTY

754

QUIZ ANSWERS

760

Foreword
by Paul Collingwood MBE

Welcome to the 2010 edition of *The Cricketers' Who's Who*. I know many people use this book as their reference point for players – getting to know about us – learning more about us than mere statistics allow.

Cricket is in exciting times. As I write, I am about to fly home from South Africa after an exciting and hard fought Test series and, in less than a month, I will fly to Dubai to play Pakistan, to Dhaka and Chittagong to play Bangladesh, then to India for the IPL, the West Indies for the ICC T20 World Championship before returning to England for the domestic season and Tests and ODIs against Bangladesh and Pakistan. All of this, of course, by way of build-up to our defence of the Ashes in Australia at the end of the year!

Scheduling is a massive issue for international cricketers. In addition to the international schedule, we also want to factor in IPL and the Champions League. These new competitions are squeezing the English domestic season at both ends and I do not envy the schedulers their task in making a coherent structure out of all this cricket. From the top of the game and all the way down to individual counties, administrators are saying the right thing about the primacy of Test cricket. But the reality seems to be drifting away from that and we all bear responsibility to create balance between the formats and to promote Test cricket.

Test cricket is definitely the pinnacle – think back to the nail-biting last ball draws at Pretoria and Cape Town and consider how no other sport and no other format can create such intensity, such tension, such sustained excitement. Undoubtedly, the best way of achieving genuine primacy for Test cricket would be the creation of a World Test Championship – giving every Test match context and meaning – and I urge the ICC to try and achieve that as soon as possible.

The challenges cricket faces in 2010 should not be underestimated, but neither should they detract from the brilliant spectacle that our game provides. The County Championship is in rude health and competition is intense. The new 40-over one-day competition sees all 18 counties challenge for a new trophy and the T20... well, what more is to be said about T20? Not only is it a great competition in its own right, but the finalists now qualify for the Champions League, which was, last year, without doubt the finest competition for domestic clubs ever and, lest we forget, the richest such tournament in cricket history. So, while the challenges are enormous, the progress is rapid and positive and we should all be grateful for that.

Enjoy the summer and enjoy searching through this invaluable book for those titbits of information about me and my colleagues that you just can't get anywhere else.

Paul Collingwood MBE
England and Durham
January 2009

International Fixtures 2010

ENGLAND v BANGLADESH

Test Matches
May 27-31	1st Test	Lord's
June 4-8	2nd Test	Old Trafford

One-day internationals
July 8	Trent Bridge [f]
July 10	Bristol
July 12	Edgbaston

ENGLAND v AUSTRALIA

NatWest Series one-day internationals
June 22	The Rose Bowl [f]
June 24	Sophia Gardens [f]
June 27	Old Trafford
June 30	The Oval [f]
July 3	Lord's

ENGLAND v PAKISTAN

Test Matches
July 29-August 2	1st Test	Trent Bridge
August 6-10	2nd Test	Edgbaston
August 18-22	3rd Test	The Oval
August 26-30	4th Test	Lord's

T20 internationals
September 5	Sophia Gardens
September 7	Sophia Gardens [f]
July 12	Edgbaston

NatWest Series one-day internationals
September 10	Chester le Street]
September 12	Headingley
September 17	The Oval
September 20	Lord's [f]
September 22	The Rose Bowl [f]

[f] = Floodlighting (day-night match)

Reviewing the Situation

Before the coming of the levels of technology we now have in sport, most fans thoroughly enjoyed their hobby of complaining about the decisions of referees, umpires and any other match officials who happened to be there to be blamed. In cricket, it was widely acknowledged by those who understood the game that umpires sometimes had extraordinarily difficult decisions to make – especially regarding LBW (where, apart from anything else, the laws were constantly changing) and with catches by wicketkeepers and slip fielders. Although supporters moaned, most of them believed the majority of umpires did a good job, that they were always honest and could only do their best.

Some would argue that the advent of sophisticated technology has changed all that and umpires have, in certain circumstances, been seen to be rather less competent. Yet when a ball is travelling at over 90 mph it is incredibly difficult for anyone to judge whether it would have hit the stumps, or gone over or past the wicket had it not struck the batsman's pad. If one watches these incidents in real time, it's clear that the poor old umpire, who has only a split second to take all the relevant LBW laws and other matters into account before deciding the fate of the batsman, can be on a hiding to nothing when the incident is shown on an enormous pitch-side screen a few seconds later. It is a similar story with spin bowling and with catches behind the wicket – the umpire may have a fraction of a second longer to ponder, but he has to decide on the likely original destination of the ball, or whether or not the batsman gave it the slightest nick with bat or glove as it passed on its way to the 'keeper.

Various kinds of slow motion photography have been around for a long time, and have been used for the showing of 'action replays' on television. After a while this led to the development of Hawk-Eye, a computerised system which tracks the path of the ball, analysing the statistical probability of where it would have ended up had it not been impeded by a pad or anything else. It also led to the invention of the 'snickometer', commonly known as Snicko, which analyses the various sounds and gives a visual representation of any contact made.

And now there is Hot Spot, a more recent development which involves an infrared imaging system. Two cameras are used, recording continuously, and when the recording is fed into a computer the image shows any heat produced by the ball striking bat, pad, glove or anything else. Taken together, Hawk-Eye, Snicko and Hot Spot would seem to be capable of providing incontrovertible proof of what actually happened out there in the middle.

With all this evidence to hand, some television viewers have become very self-righteous and cross when what they thought had been the wrong decision by the umpire, turned out to have been exactly that. The availability of all this technology led to the idea of a 'referral system' (to be known rather more officially as the Umpire Review System) which would at least cut out the more glaring errors. Both teams would be able to challenge the on-field umpire's ruling by asking the Third Umpire to look at the recorded evidence and decide whether or not the batsman was out.

The system has been in use in some international matches since 2008, the rules governing it having since been tweaked in the light of experience. For example, each side is currently limited to two unsuccessful referrals per innings, rather than the original three, and Umpire's Call, which allows the original decision to stand even though the recorded evidence suggests that the umpire may have been wrong (but only by a very small margin) was introduced when it was decided Hawk-Eye's ability to track the future path of the ball could not be guaranteed. The decision to limit referrals is clearly designed to stop captains challenging every single decision, marginal or not. One criticism of the system is that it causes too many lengthy interruptions to the game, so limiting referrals to two would help prevent this.

There was naturally some opposition to the introduction of the system, although many players were broadly in favour. In January 2008 it received the support of Pakistan captain Javed Miandad, who said that umpires were now more prone to go wrong as they made their decisions in a hurry, and it was also supported by, amongst many others, Zaheer Abbas. Umpires past and present have been generally less enthusiastic, Yorkshire's greatest former umpire, Dickie Bird, claiming recently that referrals belittle the authority of the on-field match officials.

The system was first used, on a trial basis, in the Sri Lanka v India 2008 Test series. Trials continue, and there have been some inevitable controversies. One problem seems to have been that not all umpires or players fully understand the rules. This also applied to one or two TV commentators who referred to 'benefit of the doubt going to batsmen' when this is not actually part of the rules governing referrals.

Sometimes the recorded evidence shows clearly whether or not the on-field umpire's original decision was correct. However clear, or otherwise, the recorded evidence is, the Third Umpire still has to make a decision, or decide it is Umpire's Call. Daryl Harper was much criticised during 2009 for failing to give Graeme Smith out caught behind off Ryan Sidebottom in South Africa in January 2010 when a loud click of what appeared to be bat on ball was heard. It's worth remembering, though, that on-field umpire Tony Hill didn't hear it either – so the decision, right or wrong, would have been the same had the referral system not been in place.

The situation was not helped in South Africa by the fact that not all the technology was available. It is very expensive to set up and is provided courtesy of the TV companies. There are only four Hot Spot cameras in the world, and they were being used in Australia and New Zealand.

It is certainly true to say that the referral system has met with mixed fortunes to date. A lot of people don't like it, but the system is still being developed and many would say the ICC are to be congratulated for giving it a go. It does seem essential, though, that all available technology is used rather than selected pieces. If the system is to be employed on a permanent basis it should be applied in all international matches – or at least in all Test matches. In the longer term, perhaps it will be possible to introduce it to English County games.

While there can be no doubt that some of the glaring umpiring errors of the past are being avoided by the use of technology, it is also clear that, more often than not, umpires do get decisions right. A number of the marginal decisions in South Africa during the winter were clearly shown by the referral system to have been correct. While debate will continue, it seems inevitable that some kind of referral system will eventually become permanently established in international cricket.

The PCA Most Valuable Player Awards

Launched by the PCA for the domestic season 2007, its MVP – Most Valuable Player – Award is the newest benchmark in the game. It is a statistic that for the first time combines all aspects of a player's game and gives him a ranking in relation to his peers. It is unique in sports statistics in being an evaluation of the players, designed by the players. It is their game, their statistic.

MVP is a core concept in American sport and, with its new player ratings, the PCA has seen MVP quickly integrated into the fabric of English cricket.

Overall individual performance

In 2006, the PCA undertook an extensive review of all player-performance related statistics in the game. Our results highlighted that cricket statistics are:
• Too focused on individual elements of the game – averages, run rates, wickets taken.
• Not clear and not relevant to all cricket – ICC rankings and other international stats.
• Not reflective of a player's total contribution to his team.
Cricket is a game that requires players to be skilled at multiple disciplines. To take wickets, to score runs, to take catches, to affect run-outs. The value to a side of a genuine all-rounder cannot be underestimated.

The PCA MVP are calculated by combining a player's overall individual performances. In April 2006, the PCA set up its MVP Committee. During the 2006 season, the Committee carried out the following steps:

• An overview of existing player-related statistics – strengths and limitations.
• The engagement of a cross-section of players to design an outline PCA player rankings concept and its objectives.
• The initial design of a formula to process a player's contribution to any match.
• The in-putting of the first half of the season's scores.
• A mid-season review with 10 current players and a refinement of the formula.
• The completion of the 2006 domestic season's results.
• An end of season review – focusing on comparisons of performances.

Current, past first-class and international cricketers have been involved at every step of the design process. The PCA has invested hundreds of hours in the design and development of the ratings formula. It is truly reflective of the players' view of the game.

The Formula

The PCA MVP is a cumulative points system that rewards players for every run scored, every wicket taken and every catch held – and, how well they do it.

A player achieves bonus points based on certain criteria. An overview of the formula is set out below:

Batting + Bowling + Fielding + Captaincy + Winning = Total MVP points

Batting

• The basis of the batting points takes into acccount runs scored, the rate scored at and the precentage of the team's total.

Batting bonus points are achieved for:
• Reaching a century
• Achieving a benchmark run-rate (varies per tournament, i.e. 1.5 runs per ball in the Twenty20)
• Scoring over 30 per cent of a team's runs

Bowling
• The basis for the bowling points takes into account the number of wickets and economy rates
• Bowlers achieve higher points for getting out higher order batsmen

Bowling bonus points are achieved for:
• Achieving a benchmark economy rate (varies per tournament, i.e. less that 6 runs per over in Twenty20)
• Taking 5 or more wickets in an innings
• Bowling maidens

Fielding
Points are accumulated for:
• Catches
• Run-outs – direct hits
• Run-outs – assists
• Stumpings
• Bonus for 5 fielding dismissals in an innings

Captaincy
A captain of a winning side will receive a points bonus

Winning teams
All members of a winning team receive a points bonus.

Roll of Honour

2009
Overall MVP – Marcus Trescothick (*pictured*)
LV – MVP Marcus Trescothick
FPT MVP – Ed Joyce
T20 MVP – Darren Stevens
Pro40 MVP – Phil Mustard

2008
Overall MVP – Martin Van Jaarsveld (*pictured*)
LV – Dimi Mascarenhas
FPT – Martin Van Jaarsveld
Pro40 – Steve Davies
T20 – Graham Napier

2007
Overall MVP – Ottis Gibson (*pictured*)
LV – Ottis Gibson
FPT – Ottis Gibson
Pro40 – Graeme Swann
T20 – Luke Wright

Editor's Notes

The cricketers listed in this volume include all those who played 1st XI cricket for a first-class county at least once last season, in first-class or one-day (including Twenty20) cricket, and all those registered (at the time of going to press in February) to play for the 18 first-class counties in 2010. The umpires' section contains the officials making up the first-class list for 2010.

All players' statistics are complete to the end of the last English season (the Stop Press section for individual players notes subsequent highlights) and cover first-class, List A and Twenty20 fixtures played that season. Such matches that took place elsewhere in the cricket-playing world during the period do not feature in the players' season statistics but are recorded in their career tables. Test, ODI and Twenty20 International tallies for umpires are up to and including 31 January 2010.

Within the season statistics tables, List A refers to the English domestic one-day competitions and limited-over games such as those between the counties and sides touring England. In addition, just as a player's first-class figures include Test matches, which are also extracted and listed separately, so his List A figures include One-Day Internationals, which are pulled out and appear separately in the same way. Furthermore, in the career tables the List A category contains figures of all the official 'full-length' one-day games in which a player has taken part worldwide. The categories 20/20 Int (Twenty20 Internationals) and 20/20 (all Twenty20 matches) operate in similar fashion to the corresponding first-class and one-day categories.

Numbers of hundreds given in the statistics tables include all multiples (200s, 300s etc.). Tallies of multiple hundreds for players and also of one-day hundreds and one-day five-wicket innings for umpires who are former players are shown in the body of the entry, since these cannot be found in the statistics tables. Statistics for 2009 are not given for players whose appearances that season were only for teams other than a county – e.g. universities (excluding international cricketers on tours to England). These appearances are, however, reflected in their career statistics and reference is made in the Extras section to the team for which they played.

Figures about 1000 runs, 50 wickets and 50 dismissals in a season refer to matches in England only. The figures for batting and bowling averages refer to the full first-class English list for 2009, followed in brackets by the 2008 figures. Inclusion in the batting averages depends on a minimum of six completed innings and an average of at least 10.00; a bowler has to have taken at least ten wickets for inclusion in the averages.

In the Overseas tours section, the layout 'England to Pakistan 2005-06 (one-day series)', for example, indicates that a player was selected for only the one-day portion of the tour; the layout 'England to Zimbabwe (one-day series) 2004-05', on the other hand, indicates that the tour consisted of a one-day series only.

The following abbreviations apply in the text: ODI means One-Day International; Twenty20 Int means Twenty20 International; * means not out. In statistics tables FC means all first-class matches, including figures for Test matches; List A – 'full-length' one-day matches classified as such by the ICC (e.g. Friends Provident Trophy, NatWest Pro40 and limited-overs matches against touring sides), including figures for One-Day Internationals; 20/20 Int – Twenty20 Internationals; 20/20 – all 'official' Twenty20 matches, including figures for Twenty20 Internationals and Twenty20 matches between counties and touring sides. Some further abbreviations appear in the Best batting and Best bowling sections. These identify particular grounds in cities and towns that boast more than one. A list of the abbreviations featured and the grounds to which they refer is set out overleaf.

Please note that Worcestershire ceased awarding caps in 2001 and now present 'colours' to each player who appears for the county in the Championship; that beginning in 2004 Gloucestershire have awarded caps to players on making their first first-class appearance for the county; that Durham ceased awarding caps after the 2005 season, replacing the cap system with grades of player seniority.

A book of this complexity and detail has to be prepared some months in advance of the new cricket season, and occasionally there are recent changes in a player's circumstances or the structure of the game which cannot be included in time. Many examples of facts, statistics and even opinions which can quickly become outdated in the period between the compilation of the book and its publication, months later, will spring to the reader's mind, and I ask him or her to make the necessary commonsense allowance and adjustments.

Michael Heatley
February 2010

GROUND ABBREVIATIONS

Abu Dhabi (SZ) – Sheikh Zayed Stadium
Brisbane (AB) – Allan Border Field
Bulawayo (AC) – Bulawayo Athletic Club
Chittagong (B) – Bir Shrestha Shahid Ruhul Amin Stadium
(Chittagong Divisional Stadium)
Christchurch (VG) – Village Green
Colombo (Bur) – Burgher Recreation Club Ground
Colombo (CCC) – Colts Cricket Club Ground
Colombo (PP) – Police Park Ground
Colombo (PSS) – P Saravanamuttu Stadium
Colombo (RPS) – R Premadasa Stadium
Colombo (SSC) – Sinhalese Sports Club Ground
Delhi (KS) – Karnail Singh Stadium
Harare (A) – Alexandra Sports Club
Harare (T) – Takashinga Sports Club
Johannesburg (WM) – Walter Milton Oval, University of Witwatersrand
Karachi (UBL) – United Bank Limited Sports Complex
Lahore (C) – Lahore City Cricket Association Ground
Melbourne (SK) – St Kilda Cricket Club Ground (Junction Oval)
Paarl (PCC) – Paarl Cricket Club Ground
Portsmouth (BP) – Benjamin's Park
Pretoria (LCD) – LC de Villiers Oval
Pretoria (SCC) – Sinovich Park
Rajkot (MS) – Madhavrao Scindia Cricket Ground
Rawalpindi (KRL) – Khan Research Laboratory Ground
Stellenbosch (US) – Stellenbosch University Ground
Toronto (MSE) – Maple Leaf South-East Ground, King City

THE PLAYERS

KOLPAK

If a cricketer is a national of a country that has an Association Agreement with the EU (such as South Africa or Zimbabwe) and also has a valid UK work permit, he enjoys the same right to work within the EU as an EU citizen and may be eligible to play county cricket as a domestic (that is, non-overseas) player. Cricketers playing in England under this system are commonly referred to as Kolpak players, after the Kolpak ruling, a judgement in the European Court of Justice that found in favour of Maros Kolpak, a Slovakian handball goalkeeper who challenged his status as a non-EU player in Germany.

QUIZ

Throughout the book there are 100 quiz questions relating to Test encounters over the years between England and this year's tourists Pakistan and Bangladesh. Answers can be found on page 760.

ACKERMAN, H. D. Leicestershire

Name: Hylton Deon (<u>HD</u>) Ackerman
Role: Right-hand bat, right-arm medium bowler
Born: 14 February 1973, Cape Town, South Africa
Height: 5ft 11in **Weight:** 13st
County debut: 2005
County cap: 2005
Test debut: 1997-98
1000 runs in a season: 3
1st-Class 200s: 2
1st-Class 300s: 1
Place in batting averages: 73rd av. 41.35
(2008 13th av. 56.60)
Parents: Hylton and Dawn
Wife and date of marriage: Kerryn, 22 March 2008
Family links with cricket: Father (H. M. Ackerman)
played first-class cricket in South Africa and also for Northamptonshire
Education: Rondebosch Boys' High School, Cape Town, South Africa
Career outside cricket: Family business
Overseas tours: South Africa U24 to Sri Lanka 1995; Western Province to Australia
1995-96, to Zimbabwe 1996-97; South Africa A to England 1996, to Sri Lanka 1998,
to Zimbabwe 2004; South Africa to Zimbabwe 2001-02; Leicestershire to Pakistan and
India 2005
Overseas teams played for: Western Province 1993-94 – 2002-03; Gauteng 2003-04;
Lions 2004-05; Cape Cobras 2005-06; Warriors 2006-07; Dolphins 2008-09
Career highlights to date: 'Being picked for South Africa in 1998'
Cricket moments to forget: 'Being dropped from South African team'
Cricket superstitions: None
Cricketers particularly admired: Steve Waugh
Other sports followed: Football (Manchester United), golf (Ernie Els)
Favourite band: Snow Patrol
Relaxations: 'Golf, movies, reading, spending time with friends and family'
Extras: Scored maiden first-class double century (202*) v Northerns at Centurion in
the SuperSport Series 1997-98, in the process breaking Barry Richards's record for the
most first-class runs by a South African in a domestic season (ended 1997-98 with
1373 at 50.85). Scored century (145) for South Africa A v Sri Lanka A at Matara 1998,
winning Man of the Match award. Man of the SuperSport Series 2000-01. His other
domestic awards include Man of the Match v Griqualand West at Kimberley (81) and
v KwaZulu-Natal at Durban (86*), both in the Standard Bank Cup 2003-04. Captain of
Leicestershire 2005. Scored 309* v Glamorgan at Cardiff 2006, setting a new record
for the highest individual first-class score by a Leicestershire player – also scored 62
in second innings to set a new record individual match aggregate for the county (371).

Leicestershire Cricketer of the Year 2006. In 2008, he scored freely in all competitions, amassing almost 2000 runs, including 8 centuries and 7 fifties. Decided to end his county career at the end of the 2009 season. Is not considered an overseas player
Opinions on cricket: 'If a player has an opinion he is considered controversial, so no, no opinions.'
Best batting: 309* Leicestershire v Glamorgan, Cardiff 2006

2009 Season

	M	Inn	NO	Runs	HS	Avg	100	50	Ct	St	Balls	Runs	Wkts	Avg	BB	5I	10M
Test																	
FC	12	21	1	827	180	41.35	1	5	5	-	0	0	0		-	-	-
ODI																	
List A	5	5	1	243	118*	60.75	1	1	-	-	0	0	0		-	-	
20/20 Int																	
20/20	4	4	1	100	66*	33.33	-	1	-	-	0	0	0		-	-	

Career Performances

	M	Inn	NO	Runs	HS	Avg	100	50	Ct	St	Balls	Runs	Wkts	Avg	BB	5I	10M
Test	4	8	0	161	57	20.12	-	1	1	-	0	0	0		-	-	-
FC	220	369	34	14625	309*	43.65	40	75	183	-	102	57	0		-	-	-
ODI																	
List A	226	219	25	6327	139	32.61	4	41	82	-	48	52	0		-	-	
20/20 Int																	
20/20	55	55	7	1811	87	37.72	-	17	13	-	0	0	0		-	-	

ADAMS, A. R. Nottinghamshire

Name: André Ryan Adams
Role: Right-hand bat, right-arm fast-medium bowler
Born: 17 July 1975, Auckland, New Zealand
Height: 5ft 11in **Weight:** 14st 7lbs
Nickname: Dre, Doctor
County debut: 2004 (Essex), 2007 (Nottinghamshire)
County cap: 2004 (Essex)
Test debut: 2001-02
ODI debut: 2000-01
Twenty20 Int debut: 2004-05
Place in batting averages: 184th av. 25.00
(2008 240th av. 13.30)
Place in bowling averages: 36th av. 28.46
(2008 7th av. 19.16)
Parents: Felise du Chateau and Keith Adams

Wife and date of marriage: Ardene, 5 April 2003
Children: Danté, 24 February 2004, and Balian
Family links with cricket: 'Parents West Indian!'
Education: West Lake Boys, Auckland
Overseas tours: New Zealand to Sharjah (ARY Gold Cup) 2000-01, to Australia 2001-02 (VB Series), to Sharjah (Sharjah Cup) 2001-02, to Pakistan 2002, to Africa (World Cup) 2002-03, to Sri Lanka 2003 (Bank Alfalah Cup), to England 2004 (NatWest Series), to Bangladesh 2004-05 (one-day series), to Zimbabwe 2005-06 (Videocon Tri-Series), to South Africa (one-day series) 2005-06
Overseas teams played for: Takapuna, Auckland; Auckland 1997 – 2008; Kolkata Tigers/Royal Bengal Tigers (ICL) 2007-08 –
Career highlights to date: 'Test victory against England in final game (Auckland) in 2002, my Test debut'
Cricket moments to forget: 'Losing to India in 2003 World Cup'
Cricket superstitions: None
Cricketers particularly admired: Viv Richards, Richard Hadlee, Garfield Sobers
Other sports followed: Rugby (Auckland Blues, All Blacks)
Favourite band: Dr Comfort and the Lurid Revelations
Relaxations: Xbox 360
Extras: Member of New Zealand team to 1998 Indoor Cricket World Cup. Leading wicket-taker in 1999-2000 Shell Cup one-day competition (28 wickets – av. 13.50). His ODI match awards include Man of the Match v India at Queenstown 2002-03 (5-22) and v West Indies at Port Elizabeth in the 2002-03 World Cup (35*/4-44). An overseas player with Essex July to September 2004 and in 2005 and 2006. Scored maiden first-class century (91-ball 124) v Leicestershire at Leicester 2004 in his first Championship innings and batting at No. 9. Took Championship hat-trick (Burns, Jayasuriya, Hildreth) v Somerset at Taunton 2005. Was a temporary overseas player with Nottinghamshire during the 2007 season as a replacement for David Hussey, returning in both 2008 and 2009. Nottinghamshire's leading first-class wicket taker in 2009 season. Signed a two-year contract with ICL side Kolkata Tigers (now Royal Bengal Tigers) in 2008
Opinions on cricket: 'Let it be played'
Best batting: 124 Essex v Leicestershire, Leicester 2004
Best bowling: 6-25 Auckland v Wellington, Auckland 2004-05

2009 Season

	M	Inn	NO	Runs	HS	Avg	100	50	Ct	St	Balls	Runs	Wkts	Avg	BB	5I	10M
Test																	
FC	11	13	1	300	84	25.00	-	1	13	-	2454	1224	43	28.46	4-39	-	-
ODI																	
List A	10	6	1	82	30	16.40	-	-	1	-	348	296	5	59.20	2-33	-	
20/20 Int																	
20/20	4	2	0	23	20	1.50	-	-	1	-	78	132	2	66.00	2-34	-	

Career Performances

	M	Inn	NO	Runs	HS	Avg	100	50	Ct	St	Balls	Runs	Wkts	Avg	BB	5I	10M
Test	1	2	0	18	11	9.00	-	-	1	-	190	105	6	17.50	3-44	-	-
FC	101	133	11	2918	124	23.91	3	12	68	-	20057	9582	395	24.25	6-25	13	2
ODI	42	34	10	419	45	17.45	-	-	8	-	1885	1643	53	31.00	5-22	1	
List A	146	106	27	1425	90*	18.03	-	1	37	-	6677	5279	178	29.65	5-7	3	
20/20 Int	4	2	1	13	7	13.00	-	-	1	-	77	105	3	35.00	2-20	-	
20/20	35	26	6	280	54*	14.00	-	1	11	-	726	983	40	24.57	3-35	-	

ADAMS, J. H. K. Hampshire

Name: James (<u>Jimmy</u>) Henry Kenneth Adams
Role: Left-hand opening bat, left-arm medium bowler
Born: 23 September 1980, Winchester
Height: 6ft 1in **Weight:** 14st 7lbs
Nickname: Bison, Nugget, Hippy, HC
County debut: 2002
County cap: 2006
1000 runs in a season: 2
1st-Class 200s: 1
Place in batting averages: 29th av. 51.92
(2008 220th av. 17.16)
Parents: Jenny and Mike
Family links with cricket: 'Dad played a bit for
Kent Schoolboys. Brothers Ben and Tom, Hampshire
age groups'
Education: Sherborne School; Loughborough University
Qualifications: BSc Human Biology, Levels 1 and 2 coaching
Career outside cricket: 'A bit of coaching, and other bits and bobs'
Overseas tours: West of England to West Indies 1995; England U19 to Sri Lanka
(U19 World Cup) 1999-2000; Sherborne School to Pakistan
Overseas teams played for: Woodville, Adelaide 1999-2000; Melville, Perth 2000-
01; Bayswater-Morley, Perth 2004-05
Career highlights to date: 'Maiden hundred and county cap'
Cricket moments to forget: 'Kidderminster, June 2000'
Cricket superstitions: 'Routines more than anything – I like a long breakfast, though'
Cricketers particularly admired: M. Parker, R. Smith, B. Lara
Other sports played: Hockey (Dorset age group when 14). 'Bit of five-a-side, but not
as much in terms of other sport as I'd like'
Other sports followed: 'Most sports' – football (Aston Villa), NFL
Relaxations: 'Music, reading and food'
Extras: Played in U15 World Cup 1996. Hampshire Young Player of the Year 1998.

Represented England U19 2000. Played for Loughborough UCCE 2002-04 (captain 2003), scoring a century in each innings (103/113) v Kent at Canterbury 2002. Represented British Universities 2002-04 (captain 2003). Scored maiden Championship century (168*) as Hampshire scored 404-5 to beat Yorkshire at Headingley 2006

Opinions on cricket: 'Twenty20 pulls the crowds and draws a younger audience which is great, but I think the powers that be may bleed it dry in an attempt to maximise profits. All pretty good in general.'

Best batting: 262* Hampshire v Nottinghamshire, Trent Bridge 2006
Best bowling: 2-16 Hampshire v Durham, Riverside 2004

2009 Season

	M	Inn	NO	Runs	HS	Avg	100	50	Ct	St	Balls	Runs	Wkts	Avg	BB	5I	10M
Test																	
FC	17	30	4	1350	147	51.92	3	10	17	-	108	88	1	88.00	1-49	-	-
ODI																	
List A	13	13	1	575	79	47.91	-	6	6	-	6	17	0		-	-	
20/20 Int																	
20/20	11	11	1	174	68*	17.40	-	1	1	-	0	0	0		-	-	

Career Performances

	M	Inn	NO	Runs	HS	Avg	100	50	Ct	St	Balls	Runs	Wkts	Avg	BB	5I	10M
Test																	
FC	88	157	15	5072	262*	35.71	7	28	74	-	949	657	11	59.72	2-16	-	-
ODI																	
List A	36	33	2	1058	90	34.12	-	8	16	-	79	105	1	105.00	1-34	-	
20/20 Int																	
20/20	24	17	4	222	68*	17.07	-	1	5	-	36	60	0		-	-	

1. What was the series result when Pakistan played their first Tests in England in 1954?

ADSHEAD, S. J.   Gloucestershire

Name: <u>Stephen</u> John Adshead
Role: Right-hand bat, wicket-keeper
Born: 29 January 1980, Worcester
Height: 5ft 8in **Weight:** 13st
Nickname: Adders, Top Shelf
County debut: 2000 (Leicestershire), 2003
(Worcestershire), 2004 (Gloucestershire)
County cap: 2003 (Worcestershire colours), 2004
(Gloucestershire)
Place in batting averages: 76th av. 40.77
Parents: David and Julie
Wife: Becky
Family links with cricket: Father and brother club

cricketers in Worcester, mother a keen spectator
Education: Brideley Moor HS, Redditch
Qualifications: 9 GCSEs, 3 A-levels, Level 2 coaching
Career outside cricket: Coaching
Overseas tours: Leicestershire to Potchefstroom, South Africa 2001
Overseas teams played for: Fish Hoek, Cape Town 1998-99; Witwatersrand
Technical, Johannesburg 1999-2000; Central Hawke's Bay, New Zealand 2000-01
Career highlights to date: 'Winning C&G final at Lord's 2004'
Cricket moments to forget: 'The whole 2002 season was a fairly miserable one'
Cricket superstitions: None
Cricketers particularly admired: Alec Stewart, Steve Waugh
Favourite band: U2
Relaxations: 'Spending as much time as possible with my wife Becky. Gym, eating'
Extras: Scored 187-minute 57* to help save match v Lancashire at Cheltenham 2004.
Played in only one first-class match in 2008 but took nine catches in two innings;
appeared regularly in one day and Twenty20 fixtures. Released at the end of the 2009
season
Best batting: 156* Gloucestershire v Essex, Southend 2009

2009 Season

	M	Inn	NO	Runs	HS	Avg	100	50	Ct	St	Balls	Runs	Wkts	Avg	BB	5I	10M
Test																	
FC	7	10	1	367	156*	40.77	2	-	22	1	0	0	0		-	-	-
ODI																	
List A	18	13	2	367	87	33.36	-	3	16	3	0	0	0		-	-	
20/20 Int																	
20/20	9	9	1	77	17*	9.62	-	-	2	2	0	0	0		-	-	

Career Performances

	M	Inn	NO	Runs	HS	Avg	100	50	Ct	St	Balls	Runs	Wkts	Avg	BB	5I	10M
Test																	
FC	73	118	18	3179	156*	31.79	3	17	192	15	0	0	0	-	-	-	
ODI																	
List A	99	83	18	1566	87	24.09	-	8	103	30	0	0	0	-	-		
20/20 Int																	
20/20	49	35	9	424	81	16.30	-	1	18	17	0	0	0	-	-		

AFZAAL, U.   Surrey

Name: Usman Afzaal
Role: Left-hand bat, slow left-arm bowler
Born: 9 June 1977, Rawalpindi, Pakistan
Height: 6ft **Weight:** 12st 7lbs
Nickname: Saeed, Gulfraz, Usy Bhai, Trevor
County debut: 1995 (Nottinghamshire), 2004
(Northamptonshire), 2008 (Surrey)
County cap: 2000 (Nottinghamshire),
2005 (Northamptonshire), 2009 (Surrey)
Test debut: 2001
1000 runs in a season: 7
1st-Class 200s: 1
Place in batting averages: 21st av. 57.68 (2008 41st
av. 46.42)
Parents: Firdous and Shafi Mahmood
Marital status: Single
Family links with cricket: Older brother Kamran played for NAYC and for
Nottinghamshire U15-U19 ('top player'), younger brother Aqib played for Notts and
England U15. 'Uncle Mac and Uncle Raja were great players'
Education: Manvers Pierrepont School, Nottingham; South Notts College
Qualifications: Coaching certificates
Overseas tours: Nottinghamshire to South Africa; England U19 to West Indies 1994-
95, to Zimbabwe 1995-96; 'the great ZRK tour to Lahore, Pakistan' 2000; England A
to West Indies 2000-01; England to India and New Zealand 2001-02
Overseas teams played for: Victoria Park, Perth
Career highlights to date: 'Playing for England in the Ashes [2001]'
Cricket moments to forget: 'Every time I get out'
Cricketers particularly admired: David Gower, Saeed Anwar, Ian Botham, Clive
Rice, Uncle Raja and Uncle Mac
Other sports played: Indoor football
Other sports followed: Football ('a bit of Man Utd')

Relaxations: 'Praying, spending time with friends and family, listening to Indian music'

Extras: Played for England U15 and U17. Won Denis Compton Award 1996. Took wicket (Adam Gilchrist) with third ball in Test cricket v Australia at The Oval 2001. C&G Man of the Match award for his 3-8 (from four overs) and 64* v Ireland at Clontarf 2002. Left Northamptonshire at the end of the 2007 season and joined Surrey for 2008, where he had an excellent season with the bat. Only Ramprakash and Newman scored more first-class runs during the 2008 season. Scored maiden first-class double century in County Championship match v Northamptonshire at Northampton, June 2009. Had an even better season with the bat in 2009 than 2008, finishing with an average of 57.68 and moving from 41st to 21st in the batting averages table

Best batting: 204* Surrey v Northamptonshire, Northampton 2009
Best bowling: 4-101 Nottinghamshire v Gloucestershire, Trent Bridge 1998

2009 Season

	M	Inn	NO	Runs	HS	Avg	100	50	Ct	St	Balls	Runs	Wkts	Avg	BB	5I	10M
Test																	
FC	16	28	6	1269	204*	57.68	3	7	3	-	527	348	7	49.71	3-51	-	-
ODI																	
List A	15	15	1	341	58	24.35	-	1	4	-	147	134	6	22.33	2-2	-	
20/20 Int																	
20/20	9	9	1	251	98*	31.37	-	2	-	-	60	96	3	32.00	2-17	-	

Career Performances

	M	Inn	NO	Runs	HS	Avg	100	50	Ct	St	Balls	Runs	Wkts	Avg	BB	5I	10M
Test	3	6	1	83	54	16.60	-	1	-	-	54	49	1	49.00	1-49	-	-
FC	222	384	45	13373	204*	39.44	31	70	100	-	8636	4861	90	54.01	4-101	-	-
ODI																	
List A	186	175	24	5367	132	35.54	6	33	49	-	1596	1563	59	26.49	4-49	-	
20/20 Int																	
20/20	50	47	7	928	98*	23.20	-	4	6	-	195	262	8	32.75	2-15	-	

2. How many Test matches did Imran Khan play for Pakistan?

AGA, R. G.   Sussex

Name: <u>Ragheb</u> Gul Aga
Role: Right-hand bat, right-arm medium-fast
bowler; all-rounder
Born: 10 July 1984, Nairobi, Kenya
Height: 6ft 3in **Weight:** 13st 3lbs
Nickname: Rags
County debut: 2007 (one-day), 2008 (first-class)
ODI debut: 2004
Twenty20 Int debut: 2008
Parents: Munawar and Zeenat
Marital status: Single
Education: Hillcrest Secondary School, Kenya;
Brighton University (Eastbourne Campus)
Qualifications: 'Sport and exercise scientist –
specialist area environmental physiology'
Career outside cricket: 'BDM MKK Sports. Eastbourne College hockey coach'
Overseas tours: Kenya U19 to New Zealand (U19 World Cup) 2001-02 (c); Kenya to
West Indies (Carib Beer Cup) 2003-04, to England (ICC Champions Trophy) 2004, to
Europe 2008 (Scotland, Netherlands, Ireland), to Zimbabwe 2009; Kenya VI to Hong
Kong 2004, plus other tours with Kenya U19 and Kenya.
Career highlights to date: 'Man of the Match v India A in Nairobi [2004] – 4-18 to
win match'
Cricket moments to forget: 'First club game, aged 16 – ran out club captain'
Cricketers particularly admired: Jacques Kallis, Chris Cairns, Wasim Akram
Other sports played: Hockey (Eastbourne 1st XI – Player of the Season 2006-07;
Eastbourne U21 captain – Sussex Cup winners 2005)
Other sports followed: Football (Spurs), rugby (Leicester Tigers)
Relaxations: 'Cooking (and eating), reading'
Extras: Made first-class debut for Kenya v Jamaica in Grenada in the Carib Beer Cup
2003-04. Man of the Match v India A in the Kenya Triangular Tournament in Nairobi
2004 (17-ball 16 followed by 4-18). Appointed stand-in captain of Kenya for the semi-
final of the ICC Inter-Continental Cup v Scotland in Abu Dhabi 2004. Brighton
University Sporting Hall of Fame: Achievement in Cricket (with Kenya) 2006.
Eastbourne CC 1st XI Player of the Season 2007. Signed a new two-year contract with
Sussex in October 2008
Best batting: 43 Kenya v Namibia, Nairobi 2004
Best bowling: 4-63 Sussex v Kent, Canterbury, June 2008

2009 Season

	M	Inn	NO	Runs	HS	Avg	100	50	Ct	St	Balls	Runs	Wkts	Avg	BB	5I	10M
Test																	
FC	3	3	1	27	24	13.50	-	-	-	-	264	155	3	51.66	2-8	-	-
ODI																	
List A																	
20/20 Int																	
20/20																	

Career Performances

	M	Inn	NO	Runs	HS	Avg	100	50	Ct	St	Balls	Runs	Wkts	Avg	BB	5I	10M
Test																	
FC	17	27	4	274	43	11.91	-	-	6	-	1578	925	27	34.25	4-63	-	-
ODI	2	2	0	1	1	.50	-	-	-	-	78	87	2	43.50	2-17	-	
List A	12	10	0	72	16	7.20	-	-	3	-	396	420	14	30.00	4-14	-	
20/20 Int	4	4	1	51	28	17.00	-	-	1	-	83	83	3	27.66	2-12	-	
20/20	4	4	1	51	28	17.00	-	-	1	-	83	83	3	27.66	2-12	-	

AHMED, J. S. Essex

Name: Jahid Sheikh Ahmed
Role: Right-hand bat, right-arm medium-fast bowler
Born: 20 February 1986, Chelmsford
Height: 5ft 11in **Weight:** 11st 7lbs
Nickname: J, Jarhead, Jay-Z
County debut: 2005
Parents: Sheikh Faruque Ahmed
Marital status: Single
Education: St Peter's High School; University of East London
Qualifications: GCSEs, A-levels, BSc (Hons) 2:2 in Sports Science
Overseas tours: Essex to South Africa 2006
Career highlights to date: 'Getting 4-32 against Sri Lanka 2006' [List A debut]
Cricketers particularly admired: Brett Lee
Other sports played: Badminton, football, cross country (Essex)
Other sports followed: Football (Arsenal)
Favourite band: 2Pac, The Outlawz
Relaxations: 'Listening to music, going out, chilling with friends, snooker, swimming pool, sauna and jacuzzi'

Extras: Essex Academy 2004. Community award from Bangladeshi channel, presented by the High Commissioner. 'First British Bengali to play first-class cricket in this country.' Played only one first-class match for Essex (against West Indies) in 2009. Released at the end of the 2009 season

Opinions on cricket: 'Standard of the game is very high. Kolpak players good for short term but not long term. One overseas player is good.'

Best batting: 16* Essex v Gloucestershire, Bristol 2008

Best bowling: 3-42 Essex v Gloucestershire, Bristol 2008

2009 Season

	M	Inn	NO	Runs	HS	Avg	100	50	Ct	St	Balls	Runs	Wkts	Avg	BB	5I	10M
Test																	
FC	1	1	0	5	5	5.00	-	-	-	-	66	55	2	27.50	2-55	-	-
ODI																	
List A																	
20/20 Int																	
20/20																	

Career Performances

	M	Inn	NO	Runs	HS	Avg	100	50	Ct	St	Balls	Runs	Wkts	Avg	BB	5I	10M
Test																	
FC	7	6	4	49	16*	24.50	-	-	3	-	733	542	13	41.69	3-42	-	-
ODI																	
List A	6	2	2	1	1*		-	-	2	-	240	202	10	20.20	4-32	-	
20/20 Int																	
20/20	2	0	0	0	0		-	-	-	-	36	56	2	28.00	1-25	-	

3. How many times did Imran Khan captain Pakistan in Tests?

AHMED, M. Worcestershire

Name: <u>Mehraj</u> Ahmed
Role: Right-hand bat, right-arm fast bowler
Born: 5 January 1989, Birmingham
Nickname: Maz
County debut: 2008
Parents: Altaf and Nassim
Marital status: Single
Education: Kingsbury School; Josiah Mason College
Qualifications: Level 1 Maths, Level 2 English
Cricket moments to forget: 'None'
Cricket superstitions: 'I wear my silver chain round my neck'
Cricketers particularly admired: Waqar Younis
Young players to look out for: Aneesh Kapil (Worcestershire)
Other sports played: Football, rugby ('just for college')
Other sports followed: Football (Manchester United)
Favourite band: G-Unit
Relaxations: 'Listening to music'
Extras: Bowling has been clocked at 87mph. Player of the year three times for club. Released by Worcestershire at the end of the 2009 season
Best batting: 0* Worcestershire v Sussex, Hove 2009
Best bowling: 1-28 Worcestershire v Loughborough UCCE, Kidderminster 2008

2009 Season

	M	Inn	NO	Runs	HS	Avg	100	50	Ct	St	Balls	Runs	Wkts	Avg	BB	5I	10M
Test																	
FC	1	2	2	0	0*	-	-	-	-	-	54	73	0	-	-	-	-
ODI																	
List A																	
20/20 Int																	
20/20																	

Career Performances

	M	Inn	NO	Runs	HS	Avg	100	50	Ct	St	Balls	Runs	Wkts	Avg	BB	5I	10M
Test																	
FC	2	2	2	0	0*	-	-	-	2	-	150	143	2	71.50	1-28	-	-
ODI																	
List A	1	0	0	0	0		-	-	-	-	18	34	1	34.00	1-34	-	
20/20 Int																	
20/20																	

ALI, K.   Hampshire

Name: <u>Kabir</u> Ali
Role: Right-hand bat, right-arm medium-fast bowler
Born: 24 November 1980, Birmingham
Height: 6ft **Weight:** 12st 7lbs
Nickname: Kabby, Taxi
County debut: 1999
County colours: 2002
Test debut: 2003
ODI debut: 2003
50 wickets in a season: 5
Place in batting averages: 255th av. 13.50
(2008 212th av. 18.15)
Place in bowling averages: 116th av. 44.09
(2008 6th av. 18.74)
Parents: Shabir Ali and M. Begum
Marital status: Single
Family links with cricket: Father played club cricket. Cousins Moeen and Omar
play for Worcestershire. Cousin Kadeer plays for Gloucestershire
Education: Moseley School; Wolverhampton University
Qualifications: GNVQ Leisure and Tourism, coaching
Overseas tours: Warwickshire U19 to Cape Town 1998; ECB National Academy
to Australia and Sri Lanka 2002-03; England to Australia 2002-03 (VB Series),
to South Africa 2004-05 (one-day series), to Pakistan 2005-06 (one-day series), to
India 2005-06 (one-day series); England VI to Hong Kong 2003, 2004, 2005, 2006;
England A to West Indies 2005-06; England Lions to India 2007-08
Overseas teams played for: Midland-Guildford, Perth; Rajasthan, India 2006-07
Career highlights to date: 'Playing for England'
Cricketers particularly admired: Wasim Akram, Glenn McGrath
Other sports played: Football, snooker
Other sports followed: Football, snooker
Relaxations: 'Playing snooker and spending time with family and friends'
Extras: Warwickshire Youth Young Player of the Year award. Represented England
U19. NBC Denis Compton Award for the most promising young Worcestershire player
2000. Junior Royals Player of the Year 2001. Worcestershire Player of the Year 2002.
PCA Young Player of the Year 2002, 2003. Made Test debut in the fourth Test v South
Africa at Headingley 2003, taking a wicket (Neil McKenzie) with his fifth ball.
Worcestershire Young Player of the Year 2003. Don Kenyon Award 2003. Player of the
Final in the Hong Kong Sixes 2004. Had an excellent 2008 season with the ball, taking
59 wickets at an average of less than twenty. At the end of 2009 season, he agreed a
three-year deal with Hampshire but compensation issues delayed completion of the
move until January 2010

Best batting: 84* Worcestershire v Durham, Stockton 2003
Best bowling: 8-50 Worcestershire v Lancashire, Old Trafford 2007

2009 Season

	M	Inn	NO	Runs	HS	Avg	100	50	Ct	St	Balls	Runs	Wkts	Avg	BB	5I	10M
Test																	
FC	5	8	2	81	30*	13.50	-	-	3	-	702	485	11	44.09	6-68	1	-
ODI																	
List A	1	1	0	11	11	11.00	-	-	-	-	25	24	0		-	-	
20/20 Int																	
20/20	3	1	0	3	3	3.00	-	-	1	-	42	69	1	69.00	1-4	-	

Career Performances

	M	Inn	NO	Runs	HS	Avg	100	50	Ct	St	Balls	Runs	Wkts	Avg	BB	5I	10M
Test	1	2	0	10	9	5.00	-	-	-	-	216	136	5	27.20	3-80	-	-
FC	113	156	23	2319	84*	17.43	-	7	30	-	19228	11520	429	26.85	8-50	21	4
ODI	14	9	3	93	39*	15.50	-	-	1	-	673	682	20	34.10	4-45	-	
List A	156	97	25	1091	92	15.15	-	3	25	-	6653	5713	226	25.27	5-36	2	
20/20 Int																	
20/20	27	20	4	264	49	16.50	-	-	8	-	555	738	33	22.36	4-44	-	

ALI, K.   Gloucestershire

Name: <u>Kadeer</u> Ali
Role: Right-hand opening bat, right-arm medium bowler
Born: 7 March 1983, Birmingham
Height: 6ft 2in **Weight:** 12st 7lbs
Nickname: Kads, Kaddy, Rat
County debut: 2000 (Worcestershire), 2005 (Gloucestershire)
County cap: 2002 (Worcestershire colours), 2005 (Gloucestershire)
1000 runs in a season: 1
Place in batting averages: 116th av. 34.75 (2008 88th av. 35.95)
Parents: Munir Ali and Maqsood Begum
Wife and date of marriage: Naheeda Khanum, 8 October 2009
Family links with cricket: 'Father has cricket academy – "Streets to Arena". Brother Moeen plays for Worcestershire and cousin Kabir for Hampshire'.
Education: Handsworth Grammar; Moseley Sixth Form College
Qualifications: 5 GCSEs, Level 1 coaching

Off-season: Training and coaching for Gloucestershire
Overseas tours: England U19 to India 2000-01, to Australia and (U19 World Cup) New Zealand 2001-02; England A to Malaysia and India 2003-04. 'Streets to Arena' academy to Pakistan
Overseas teams played for: WA University, Perth 2002-03; Lahore Model Town CC, Pakistan 2005; PTCL, Pakistan 2005-06
Career highlights to date: 'Playing in Twenty20 finals day. Playing in the final against Kent at Edgbaston (2007). Playing against Australia and South Africa'
Cricket moments to forget: 'My debut against Glamorgan – got a pair'
Cricketers particularly admired: Graeme Hick – 'Awesome!'
Other sports played: Football, snooker
Other sports followed: Football (Birmingham City FC)
Relaxations: 'Cinema, relaxing with friends and family, Xbox (Pro Evo)'
Extras: Young Player awards at Warwickshire CCC. Represented England U19 2000-02. Scored 111 runs in a record 256-run 2nd wicket partnership with Bilal Shafayat (201*) for England U19 v India U19 at Northampton, 2002. England U19 Player of Series v India U19 2002. NBC Denis Compton Award for the most promising young Worcestershire player 2001, 2002. ECB National Academy 2003-04. Became first player to hit a ball over the Basil D'Oliveira Stand at Worcester, v New Zealanders 2004. Gloucestershire Young Player of the Year and Players' Player of the Year 2007. Scored over 1000 runs for the county in first-class and one-day games in 2008. In January 2009 he committed himself to the county until 2011
Opinions on cricket: 'Changing year by year – new shots, new deliveries…'
Best batting: 161 Gloucestershire v Northamptonshire, Bristol 2008
Best bowling: 1-4 Gloucestershire v Glamorgan, Bristol 2005

2009 Season

	M	Inn	NO	Runs	HS	Avg	100	50	Ct	St	Balls	Runs	Wkts	Avg	BB	5I	10M
Test																	
FC	16	28	4	834	90	34.75	-	4	10	-	24	15	0		-	-	-
ODI																	
List A	14	14	2	241	100*	20.08	1	1	7	-	12	9	0		-	-	
20/20 Int																	
20/20	4	4	1	81	33	27.00	-	-	-	-	0	0	0		-	-	

Career Performances

	M	Inn	NO	Runs	HS	Avg	100	50	Ct	St	Balls	Runs	Wkts	Avg	BB	5I	10M
Test																	
FC	93	168	9	4666	161	29.34	6	24	49	-	480	304	3	101.33	1-4	-	-
ODI																	
List A	62	62	3	1750	114	29.66	3	11	15	-	75	68	1	68.00	1-4	-	
20/20 Int																	
20/20	16	16	3	370	53	28.46	-	1	3	-	0	0	0		-	-	

ALI, M. M. Worcestershire

Name: <u>Moeen</u> Munir Ali
Role: Left-hand bat, right-arm off-spin bowler;
batting all-rounder
Born: 18 June 1987, Birmingham
Height: 6ft **Weight:** 11st
Nickname: Brother Mo
County debut: 2005 (Warwickshire), 2007
(Worcestershire)
County colours: 2007 (Worcestershire)
Place in batting averages: 153rd av. 28.67
(2008 126th av. 30.00)
Parents: Munir Ali and Maqsood Begum
Wife and date of marriage: Firuza Parveen Hussain,
11 October 2008
Family links with cricket: Brother Kadeer plays for
Gloucestershire. Younger brother Omar is also at Worcestershire. Cousin Kabir plays
for Hampshire. Father has 'Streets to Arena' cricket academy
Education: Moseley School
Qualifications: GCSEs and Leisure and Tourism
Overseas tours: 'Streets to Arena' to Pakistan 2002; England U19 to India 2004-05,
to Bangladesh 2005-06, to Sri Lanka (U19 World Cup) 2005-06 (c); England
Performance Programme to India 2007-08
Overseas teams played for: Claremont-Nedlands, Perth 2003-04; St Augustine's,
South Africa, 2008
Career highlights to date: 'Winning Pro40 in 2007. Scoring a hundred off 46 balls
[v Northamptonshire at Kidderminster in the Pro40 2007]'
Cricket moments to forget: 'Don't have any'
Cricket superstitions: None
Cricketers particularly admired: Saeed Anwar, Graeme Hick, Nick Knight
Other sports played: Football ('Worcester YCs – always score a goal!')
Other sports followed: Football (Liverpool)
Favourite band: No Beats Necessary
Relaxations: 'Islam and praying'
Extras: Represented England U15 2002. Won five Warwickshire youth awards from
age of 11. Represented England U19 2004, 2005, 2006. NBC Denis Compton Award
for most promising young Warwickshire player 2004, 2005, 2009. Scored a 56-ball
century against Sri Lanka in 2005 U19 Test
Opinions on cricket: 'Too many days of cricket in the season.'
Best batting: 153 Worcestershire v Yorkshire, Leeds 2009
Best bowling: 4-29 Warwickshire v Hampshire, Worcester 2009

2009 Season

	M	Inn	NO	Runs	HS	Avg	100	50	Ct	St	Balls	Runs	Wkts	Avg	BB	5I	10M
Test																	
FC	17	30	2	803	153	28.67	2	3	4	-	565	461	7	65.85	4-29	-	-
ODI																	
List A	16	13	0	394	125	30.30	1	2	6	-	164	140	5	28.00	3-32	-	
20/20 Int																	
20/20	10	10	0	214	46	21.40	-	-	2	-	42	54	2	27.00	2-15	-	

Career Performances

	M	Inn	NO	Runs	HS	Avg	100	50	Ct	St	Balls	Runs	Wkts	Avg	BB	5I	10M
Test																	
FC	33	54	4	1427	153	28.54	2	9	9	-	1371	1033	10	103.30	4-29	-	-
ODI																	
List A	51	47	2	1124	125	24.97	2	7	12	-	498	460	12	38.33	3-32	-	
20/20 Int																	
20/20	21	20	2	342	46	9.00	-	-	2	-	48	65	2	32.50	2-15	-	

ALLENBY, J.   Glamorgan

Name: James (<u>Jim</u>) Allenby
Role: Right-hand bat, right-arm medium bowler;
county vice-captain
Born: 12 September 1982, Perth, Australia
Height: 6ft **Weight:** 13st 8lbs
Nickname: Jimmy, Jay, Jay Bay, Ducktails
County debut: 2005 (one-day, Leicestershire),
2006 (first-class. Leicestershire)
1000 runs in a season: 1
Place in batting averages: 72nd av. 41.37
(2008 131st av. 29.30)
Place in bowling averages: 32nd av. 27.70
(2008 62nd av. 28.30)
Parents: Michael and Julie
Marital status: 'Unmarried'
Family links with cricket: 'Great-grandfather
played at Yorkshire/Hampshire'
Education: Christ Church Grammar School, Perth
Qualifications: Level 1 coaching
Career outside cricket: 'Hopefully don't have to figure that out for a bit!'
Off-season: 'Playing cricket and coaching at Claremont-Nedlands in Perth.
A lot of beach!'

Overseas teams played for: Claremont-Nedlands CC, Perth 1993 – ; Western Australia 2006-07

Career highlights to date: 'Playing in and winning Twenty20 [2006]. Century (103*) and 68* on Championship debut [Leicestershire v Essex at Leicester 2006]. Century for Leicestershire v Nottinghamshire in Twenty20. Being the leading six-hitter and second highest run-scorer in Twenty20 2009. Moving to Glamorgan. First century for Glamorgan.'

Cricket moments to forget: 'Pro40 match for Leicestershire against Glamorgan, Colwyn Bay [2008]. Some of July and August 2009 didn't make a whole lot of sense, although my golf swing improved!' [*After a disagreement with Leicestershire during discussions about a new contract, he was sidelined for the second half of the 2009 season, and later moved to Glamorgan*]

Cricket superstitions: 'Put gear on same way each time I bat'

Cricketers particularly admired: Steve Waugh, Dean Jones, Paul Nixon, Andrew Flintoff

Young players to look out for: David Brown (Glamorgan)

Other sports followed: Football (Leeds United), rugby (Tigers and Cardiff Blues)

Injuries: 'Side strain. Missed a couple of games.'

Favourite band: Powderfinger, Jack Johnson

Relaxations: 'Playing golf, swimming/surfing at beach'

Extras: Set record individual score for Western Australia in U19 cricket (180) v Northern Territory 2000-01. Played for Durham Board XI in the 2003 C&G. Scored 103* and 68* on Championship debut v Essex at Leicester 2006. Appointed vice-captain of Leicestershire at the end of August 2007. Became first player ever to take 4 wickets in 4 balls in Twenty20 for Leicestershire v Lancashire in June 2008. In 2008, he scored over 1000 runs in all competitions. Leading six-hitter and second highest run-scorer in Twenty20 2009. Left Leicestershire for Glamorgan at the end of the 2009 season. Is not considered an overseas player

Opinions on cricket: 'I hope the push for young players to play does not get used as an excuse for poor performances and sacking older players. I think the best 11 players available should play, regardless of age etc. Younger players will develop quicker if they have to earn their place and can learn from good players.'

Best batting: 138* Leicestershire v Bangladesh A, Grace Road 2008

Best bowling: 5-125 Leicestershire v Gloucestershire, Bristol 2007

2009 Season

	M	Inn	NO	Runs	HS	Avg	100	50	Ct	St	Balls	Runs	Wkts	Avg	BB	5I	10M
Test																	
FC	12	18	2	662	137	41.37	1	6	10	-	1144	471	17	27.70	3-70	-	-
ODI																	
List A	9	8	1	176	60	25.14	-	1	1	-	212	191	6	31.83	2-23	-	
20/20 Int																	
20/20	10	10	1	432	110	48.00	1	3	4	-	168	208	4	52.00	3-25	-	

Career Performances

	M	Inn	NO	Runs	HS	Avg	100	50	Ct	St	Balls	Runs	Wkts	Avg	BB	5I	10M
Test																	
FC	47	71	11	2242	138*	37.36	3	15	44	-	4078	1892	58	32.62	5-125	1	-
ODI																	
List A	51	46	7	1007	91*	25.82	-	5	17	-	1486	1261	46	27.41	5-43	1	
20/20 Int																	
20/20	40	36	8	829	110	29.60	1	6	16	-	477	618	28	22.07	5-21	2	

AMBROSE, T. R. Warwickshire

Name: Timothy (Tim) Raymond Ambrose
Role: Right-hand bat, wicket-keeper
Born: 1 December 1982, Newcastle, New South Wales, Australia
Height: 5ft 7in
Nickname: Shambrose, Freak, Mole
County debut: 2001 (Sussex), 2006 (Warwickshire)
County cap: 2003 (Sussex), 2007 (Warwickshire)
Test debut: 2007-08
ODI debut: 2008
Twenty20 Int debut: 2008
1st-Class 200s: 1
Place in batting averages: 97th av. 37.00 (2008 116th av. 31.25)
Parents: Raymond and Sally
Marital status: Single
Family links with cricket: Cousin played Sydney first grade. Father was captain of local grade D4 team
Education: Merewether Selective High, NSW
Career outside cricket: Greenkeeping
Overseas tours: Sussex to Grenada 2001, 2002; England Performance Programme to India 2007-08; England to New Zealand 2007-08, to West Indies 2009; England Lions to New Zealand 2009
Overseas teams played for: Wallsend, NSW 2000; Nelson Bay, NSW 2001; Newcastle, NSW 2002
Career highlights to date: 'Winning the Championship 2003. Maiden first-class century, 149 v Yorkshire [2002]. Making my England Test debut.'
Cricketers particularly admired: Alec Stewart, Ian Healy, Steve Waugh, Mushtaq Ahmed

Other sports played: Football, squash, golf, rugby league, rugby union, AFL, 'I'll have a go at anything'
Other sports followed: Rugby league (Newcastle Knights), Australian Rules (Sydney Swans), football (Tottenham Hotspur)
Favourite band: Jeff Buckley, Ben Harper, Jack Johnson
Relaxations: 'Guitar, music'
Extras: Captained Newcastle (NSW) U16 1999 Bradman Cup winning side. Played for New South Wales U17. Won NSW Junior Cricketer of the Year three years running. C&G Man of the Match award for his 95 v Buckinghamshire at Beaconsfield 2002. Scored maiden first-class double century (251*) v Worcestershire at Worcester 2007, in the process sharing with Heath Streak (66) in a new Warwickshire record partnership for the sixth wicket (226). Represented England Lions 2007, 2009. Scored 117 in Lions' first innings as they beat the West Indies in May 2009 as well as claiming five victims behind the stumps in the match
Best batting: 251* Warwickshire v Worcestershire, Worcester 2007

2009 Season

	M	Inn	NO	Runs	HS	Avg	100	50	Ct	St	Balls	Runs	Wkts	Avg	BB	5I	10M
Test																	
FC	18	24	2	814	153	37.00	3	4	43	2	0	0	0		-	-	-
ODI																	
List A	15	10	1	180	46	20.00	-	-	15	6	0	0	0		-	-	
20/20 Int																	
20/20	9	8	2	79	18	13.16	-	-	7	2	0	0	0		-	-	

Career Performances

	M	Inn	NO	Runs	HS	Avg	100	50	Ct	St	Balls	Runs	Wkts	Avg	BB	5I	10M
Test	11	16	1	447	102	29.80	1	3	31	-	0	0	0		-	-	-
FC	109	165	15	5266	251*	35.10	9	30	246	16	6	1	0		-	-	-
ODI	5	5	1	10	6	2.50	-	-	3	-	0	0	0		-	-	
List A	103	91	13	2221	135	28.47	3	8	108	18	0	0	0		-	-	
20/20 Int	1	0	0	0	0		-	-	1	1	0	0	0		-	-	
20/20	31	26	6	532	77	26.60	-	2	19	10	0	0	0		-	-	

4. Who replaced Imran Khan as captain of the Pakistan Test and one-day teams, following the 1992 World Cup?

AMLA, H. M.   Nottinghamshire

Name: <u>Hashim</u> Mahomed Amla
Role: Right-hand bat, right-arm medium or
right-arm off-break bowler
Born: 31 March 1983, Durban, South Africa
Height: 6ft
County debut: 2009 (Essex)
Test debut: 2004
ODI debut: 2008
Twenty20 Int debut: 2008
1st-Class 200s: 1
Family links with cricket: Brother Ahmed
plays for Dolphins
Overseas tours: South Africa U19 to New Zealand
2000-01; South Africa to India 2004-05, to Sri Lanka
2006, to Pakistan 2007-08, to India 2007-08, to
Bangladesh 2007-08, to England 2008, to Australia 2008-09
Overseas teams played for: KwaZulu-Natal 1999-00 – 2003-04; Dolphins 2004-05 –
Extras: South African Cricketer of the Year 2006. Signed for Essex mid-2009. Signed
for Nottinghamshire in February 2010
Best batting: 249 Dolphins v Eagles, Bloemfontein 2004-05
Best bowling: 1-10 South Africa A v India A, Kimberley 2001-02

2009 Season

	M	Inn	NO	Runs	HS	Avg	100	50	Ct	St	Balls	Runs	Wkts	Avg	BB	5I	10M
Test																	
FC	3	5	1	410	181	102.50	2	1	2	-	0	0	0		-	-	-
ODI																	
List A	2	2	0	133	111	66.50	1	-	1	-	0	0	0		-	-	
20/20 Int																	
20/20																	

Career Performances

	M	Inn	NO	Runs	HS	Avg	100	50	Ct	St	Balls	Runs	Wkts	Avg	BB	5I	10M
Test	37	65	4	2460	176*	40.32	6	14	34	-	42	28	0		-	-	-
FC	116	193	17	8250	249	46.87	24	41	95	-	309	221	1	221.00	1-10	-	-
ODI	18	17	3	614	140	43.85	1	3	7	-	0	0	0		-	-	
List A	63	62	5	1901	140	33.35	4	10	23	-	16	28	0		-	-	
20/20 Int	2	2	0	52	26	26.00	-	-	-	-	0	0	0		-	-	
20/20	26	25	0	555	57	22.20	-	2	3	-	0	0	0		-	-	

ANDERSON, J. M.   Lancashire

Name: <u>James</u> Michael Anderson
Role: Left-hand bat, right-arm fast-medium bowler
Born: 30 July 1982, Burnley
Height: 6ft 2in **Weight:** 13st
Nickname: Jimmy
County debut: 2001 (one-day), 2002 (first-class)
County cap: 2003
Test debut: 2003
ODI debut: 2002-03
Twenty20 Int debut: 2006-07
50 wickets in a season: 2
Place in batting averages: 244th av. 15.37
Place in bowling averages: 10th av. 22.71
(2008 17th av. 21.04)
Parents: Michael and Catherine
Wife and date of marriage: Daniella (Lloyd), February 2006
Family links with cricket: Father and uncle played for Burnley
Education: St Theodore's RC High School and Sixth Form – both Burnley
Qualifications: 10 GCSEs, 3 A-levels, Level 2 coaching
Overseas tours: Lancashire to Cape Town 2002; ECB National Academy to Australia 2002-03; England to Australia 2002-03 (VB Series), to Africa (World Cup) 2002-03, to Bangladesh and Sri Lanka 2003-04, to West Indies 2003-04, to Zimbabwe (one-day series) 2004-05, to South Africa 2004-05, to Pakistan 2005-06, to India 2005-06, to India (ICC Champions Trophy) 2006-07, to Australia 2006-07, to West Indies (World Cup) 2006-07, to South Africa (World 20/20) 2007-08, to Sri Lanka 2007-08, to New Zealand 2007-08, to India 2008-09, to West Indies 2008-09, to South Africa 2009-10; England A to West Indies 2005-06
Career highlights to date: 'ODI hat-trick. Two five-fors at Lord's'
Cricket moments to forget: 'Ashes 2006-07'
Cricketers particularly admired: Allan Donald, Darren Gough, Peter Martin
Other sports played: Golf (12 handicap), football, tennis
Other sports followed: Football (Burnley, Arsenal), 'interested in all sports'
Favourite band: Oasis, U2
Relaxations: 'Reading, music'
Extras: Represented England U19 2001. Took 50 first-class wickets in his first full season 2002. NBC Denis Compton Award for the most promising young Lancashire player 2002. Took Championship hat-trick (Robinson, Hussain, Jefferson) v Essex at Old Trafford 2003. Recorded a five-wicket innings return (5-73) on Test debut in the first Test v Zimbabwe at Lord's 2003. Became the first England bowler to take an ODI hat-trick (Abdul Razzaq, Shoaib Akhtar, Mohammad Sami) v Pakistan at The Oval in the NatWest Challenge 2003. Cricket Writers' Club Young Player of the Year 2003.

His series and match awards include England's Man of the [Test] Series v India 2007 and two Man of the Match awards in the 2002-03 World Cup. England 12-month central contracts 2007-08, 2009-10. Named as one of *Wisden*'s Five Cricketers of the Year 2009. Had match figures of 9-125 in the England win over West Indies at Chester-le-Street, May 2009. Part of the England team which claimed back the Ashes in 2009. Took five wickets as England beat South Africa in fourth one-day international Port Elizabeth November 2009. Now has well over 100 Test wickets to his name

Opinions on cricket: 'Twenty20 has taken all forms of the game to a new level, but we should be very wary of overkill.'

Best batting: 37* Lancashire v Durham, Old Trafford 2005
Best bowling: 7-43 England v New Zealand, Trent Bridge 2008

2009 Season

	M	Inn	NO	Runs	HS	Avg	100	50	Ct	St	Balls	Runs	Wkts	Avg	BB	5I	10M
Test	7	10	2	114	29	4.25	-	-	3	-	1335	737	23	32.04	5-80	2	-
FC	9	11	3	123	29	15.37	-	-	4	-	1743	886	39	22.71	6-56	5	1
ODI	7	2	1	1	1	1.00	-	-	1	-	349	312	10	31.20	4-55	-	
List A	8	2	1	1	1	1.00	-	-	1	-	385	329	11	29.90	4-55	-	
20/20 Int	6	1	0	0	0	0.00	-	-	-	-	128	159	5	31.80	3-23	-	
20/20	6	1	0	0	0	0.00	-	-	-	-	128	159	5	31.80	3-23	-	

Career Performances

	M	Inn	NO	Runs	HS	Avg	100	50	Ct	St	Balls	Runs	Wkts	Avg	BB	5I	10M
Test	42	56	27	412	34	14.20	-	-	17	-	8453	4883	140	34.87	7-43	7	-
FC	97	112	49	667	37*	10.58	-	-	40	-	17627	9910	345	28.72	7-43	18	2
ODI	117	49	25	146	15	6.08	-	-	30	-	5682	4682	153	30.60	4-23	-	
List A	166	69	41	237	15	8.46	-	-	38	-	7918	6333	223	28.39	4-23	-	
20/20 Int	17	4	3	1	1*	1.00	-	-	2	-	380	500	17	29.41	3-23	-	
20/20	35	7	5	22	16	11.00	-	-	5	-	741	1007	32	31.46	3-23	-	

5. Mushtaq Mohammad made his first Test match appearance for Pakistan in 1959. In which year did he play in his final Test?

ANDREW, G. M.   Worcestershire

Name: <u>Gareth</u> Mark Andrew
Role: Left-hand bat, right-arm fast-medium bowler
Born: 27 December 1983, Yeovil
Height: 6ft **Weight:** 14st
Nickname: G-Train, Brad, Sobers
County debut: 2003 (Somerset), 2008
(Worcestershire)
County colours: 2008
Place in batting averages: 108th av. 35.54
(2008 224th av. 16.58)
Place in bowling averages: 112th av. 43.08
(2008 116th av. 37.70)
Parents: Peter and Susan
Marital status: Single
Family links with cricket: Father and younger
brother club cricketers

Education: Ansford Community School; Richard Huish College, Taunton
Qualifications: 10 GCSEs, 3 A-levels, Level 1 coaching
Overseas tours: West of England U15 to West Indies 1999; England U17 to
Australia 2001; Somerset Academy to Western Australia 2002; 'Aus Academy'
to Perth 2003
Overseas teams played for: Swanbourne CC, Perth 2002-03; Glenelg CC,
Adelaide 2005-06 – 2006-07
Career highlights to date: 'Twenty20 champions 2005, division two winners 2007,
Pro40 promotion 2007 – all with Somerset'
Cricket moments to forget: 'Whenever bowling in the Twenty20'
Cricket superstitions: 'Always put my boots on the right feet'
Cricketers particularly admired: Ian Botham, Andrew Flintoff, Chris Cairns
Young players to look out for: Joss Buttler (Somerset), Rob Travers (Wiltshire)
Other sports played: Football (Bruton Town FC, Yeovil District U11-U16, Castle
Cary AFC)
Other sports followed: Football (Yeovil Town, Manchester Utd)
Favourite band: Red Hot Chili Peppers
Extras: Represented England U19 v South Africa U19 2003. Signed a new two-
year contract in September 2008
Best batting: 92* Worcestershire v Nottinghamshire, Worcester 2009
Best bowling: 5-58 Worcester v Middlesex, Kidderminster 2008

2009 Season

	M	Inn	NO	Runs	HS	Avg	100	50	Ct	St	Balls	Runs	Wkts	Avg	BB	5I	10M
Test																	
FC	10	16	5	391	92*	35.54	-	3	-	-	1545	991	23	43.08	5-117	1	-
ODI																	
List A	13	8	3	74	27	14.80	-	-	4	-	474	458	15	30.53	5-31	1	
20/20 Int																	
20/20	10	3	2	19	9*	19.00	-	-	2	-	175	225	7	32.14	3-19	-	

Career Performances

	M	Inn	NO	Runs	HS	Avg	100	50	Ct	St	Balls	Runs	Wkts	Avg	BB	5I	10M
Test																	
FC	33	45	9	753	92*	20.91	-	3	10	-	4315	2998	78	38.43	5-58	2	-
ODI																	
List A	72	43	12	391	33	12.61	-	-	23	-	2407	2469	75	32.92	5-31	1	
20/20 Int																	
20/20	49	22	8	112	14	8.00	-	-	13	-	890	1257	43	29.23	4-22	-	

ANEESH KAPIL   Worcestershire

Name: Aneesh Kapil
Role: Right-hand bat, right-arm fast-medium bowler
Born: 3 August 1993, Wolverhampton
Height: 5ft 8in **Weight:** 11st 5lbs
Nickname: Simba
County debut: No first-team appearances
Education: Tettenhall College. Wolverhampton
Career highlights to date: 'Playing at Lord's'
Other sports followed: Badminton, hockey, rugby, tennis, football (Manchester United)
Relaxations: 'Socialising and music'
Extras: Represented Staffordshire at U13 and U15 levels. Played for Wolverhampton CC (Birmingham Premier League) 2008. Played for Worcestershire U17s and Worcestershire 2nd XI 2008, 2009. Awarded a summer contract for 2010

ANYON, J. E.   Sussex

Name: <u>James</u> Edward Anyon
Role: Left-hand bat, right-arm fast-medium bowler
Born: 5 May 1983, Lancaster
Height: 6ft 2in **Weight:** 13st
Nickname: Jimmy, Cheese'n'
County debut: 2005 (Warwickshire)
Place in bowling averages: (2008 89th av. 32.46)
Parents: Peter and Christine
Marital status: Single
Family links with cricket: 'Dad used to play
village cricket for Calder Vale CC'
Education: Garstang High School; Preston College;
Loughborough University
Qualifications: GCSEs, 3 A-levels, BSc Sports
Science with Management, Level 1 coaching
Overseas teams played for: Claremont-Nedlands, Perth 2004-05
Career highlights to date: 'Bowling at Brian Lara, Twenty20 hat-trick in 2005'
Cricket moments to forget: 'A few run-outs, getting relegated'
Cricketers particularly admired: Glenn McGrath, Michael Atherton
Other sports played: Football, darts
Other sports followed: Football (Preston North End, AC Roma), Moto GP
Favourite band: Muse
Relaxations: 'Music, films'
Extras: Young Player of the Year awards at Preston CC. Bowler of the Year award at
Farsley CC (Bradford League) 2004. Played for Loughborough UCCE 2003, 2004.
Took Twenty20 hat-trick for Warwickshire (Durston, Andrew, Caddick) v Somerset
at Edgbaston 2005. Spent a month on loan to Surrey in August 2009 but signed a new
two-year contract with Sussex in November 2009
Best batting: 37* Warwickshire v Durham, Riverside 2007
Best bowling: 6-82 Warwickshire v Glamorgan, Swalec Stadium (Cardiff) 2008

2009 Season

	M	Inn	NO	Runs	HS	Avg	100	50	Ct	St	Balls	Runs	Wkts	Avg	BB	5I	10M
Test																	
FC	4	5	4	39	15*	39.00	-	-	-	-	434	311	4	77.75	2-38	-	-
ODI																	
List A	1	0	0	0	0		-	-	-	-	30	28	0		-	-	
20/20 Int																	
20/20	2	0	0	0	0		-	-	-	-	24	48	1	48.00	1-32	-	

Career Performances

	M	Inn	NO	Runs	HS	Avg	100	50	Ct	St	Balls	Runs	Wkts	Avg	BB	5I	10M
Test																	
FC	47	59	25	364	37*	10.70	-	-	15	-	7363	4509	112	40.25	6-82	2	-
ODI																	
List A	37	10	5	22	12	4.40	-	-	8	-	1333	1225	38	32.23	3-6	-	
20/20 Int																	
20/20	21	3	3	16	8*		-	-	3	-	333	481	25	19.24	3-6	-	

ASHLING, C. P.   Glamorgan

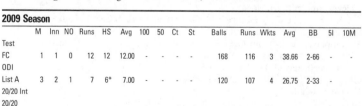

Name: Christopher (<u>Chris</u>) Paul Ashling
Role: Right-arm fast-medium opening bowler, lower-order right-hand bat
Born: 26 November 1988, Manchester
Nickname: Bruce
County debut: 2009
Marital status: Single
Education: Millfield School, UWIC
Overseas tours: England U16 to South Africa 2005
Cricket moments to forget: 'Being on a hat-trick twice when younger, and bowling a wide on each occasion!'
Cricketers particularly admired: Brett Lee, Darren Gough
Other sports followed: Football (Manchester City)
Extras: Played for England U15, U16, U17 and Select XI. Played for Lancashire 2nd XI 2004-07. Signed a development contract with Glamorgan in 2008; signed a new two-year contract with the county in September 2009
Best batting: 12 Glamorgan v Leicestershire, Leicester 2009
Best bowling: 2-66 Glamorgan v Leicestershire, Leicester 2009

2009 Season

	M	Inn	NO	Runs	HS	Avg	100	50	Ct	St	Balls	Runs	Wkts	Avg	BB	5I	10M
Test																	
FC	1	1	0	12	12	12.00	-	-	-	-	168	116	3	38.66	2-66	-	-
ODI																	
List A	3	2	1	7	6*	7.00	-	-	-	-	120	107	4	26.75	2-33	-	
20/20 Int																	
20/20																	

	M	Inn	NO	Runs	HS	Avg	100	50	Ct	St	Balls	Runs	Wkts	Avg	BB	5I	10M
Test																	
FC	1	1	0	12	12	12.00	-	-	-	-	168	116	3	38.66	2-66	-	-
ODI																	
List A	3	2	1	7	6*	7.00	-	-	-	-	120	107	4	26.75	2-33	-	
20/20 Int																	
20/20																	

AZEEM RAFIQ Yorkshire

Name: Azeem Rafiq
Role: Right-hand bat, right-arm off-spin bowler;
all-rounder
Born: 27 February 1991, Karachi, Pakistan
Nickname: Raffa, Az
County debut: 2008 (Twenty20), 2009 (first-class)
Parents: Muhammad Rafiq and Rehana Rafiq
Education: Holgate School Sports College;
Barnsley College
Qualifications: 8 GCSEs, BTEC National Diploma
in Sport Development, Coaching and Fitness
Off-season: 'Playing cricket, relaxing with my family'
Overseas tours: Yorkshire Academy to Abu

Dhabi 2008; Yorkshire to Dubai 2009; England U18
to Malaysia 2009; England U19 to South Africa 2009,
to Bangladesh 2009, to New Zealand (ICC U19 World Cup) (c) 2010
Career highlights to date: 'First-class century in my second game. A 7-wicket
haul and a 5-wicket haul in my debut Test series for England U19'
Cricket moments to forget: 'The Twenty20 incident' (*see Extras*)
Cricket superstitions: None
Cricketers particularly admired: Muttiah Muralitharan, Sachin Tendulkar,
Michael Vaughan, Saqlain Mushtaq
Young players to look out for: Nathan Buck (Leicestershire), James Vince
(Hampshire), Ajmal Shahzad (Yorkshire)
Other sports played: Football, squash
Other sports followed: Football (Barnsley)
Favourite band: Akon
Relaxations: 'Going out, chilling with family and friends'

Extras: Captained England U15, North U15 and Yorkshire U15 in 2006. BBC Young Sports Personality of the Year for Yorkshire 2006. Yorkshire CC Academy Junior Performer of the Year 2007. Captained England U17 2007. Yorkshire CC Academy Player of the Year 2008. After making his first-team debut in the Twenty20 Cup, it was found that he was ineligible to play for the county. The situation was resolved in August 2008, and in October he signed a three-year contract. Took 5-77 as England U19 narrowly failed to beat Bangladesh U19 in second Test at Derby 2009. This followed his seven-wicket haul from the first Test.

Best batting: 100 Yorkshire v Worcestershire, Worcester 2009
Best bowling: 3-34 Yorkshire v Sussex, Headingley 2009

2009 Season

	M	Inn	NO	Runs	HS	Avg	100	50	Ct	St	Balls	Runs	Wkts	Avg	BB	5I	10M
Test																	
FC	4	5	0	117	100	23.40	1	-	1	-	747	487	10	48.70	3-34	-	-
ODI																	
List A	2	0	0	0	0		-	-	1	-	30	36	1	36.00	1-36	-	
20/20 Int																	
20/20	4	3	2	18	11*	18.00	-	-	2	-	90	99	4	24.75	2-21	-	

Career Performances

	M	Inn	NO	Runs	HS	Avg	100	50	Ct	St	Balls	Runs	Wkts	Avg	BB	5I	10M
Test																	
FC	4	5	0	117	100	23.40	1	-	1	-	747	487	10	48.70	3-34	-	-
ODI																	
List A	2	0	0	0	0		-	-	1	-	30	36	1	36.00	1-36	-	
20/20 Int																	
20/20	5	3	2	18	11*	18.00	-	-	2	-	102	117	4	29.25	2-21	-	

6. In which year did Bangladesh first play a short Test series in England?

AZHAR MAHMOOD   Kent

Name: Azhar Mahmood Sagar
Role: Right-hand bat, right-arm
fast-medium bowler; all-rounder
Born: 28 February 1975, Rawalpindi, Pakistan
Height: 6ft **Weight:** 13st 5lbs
Nickname: Aju
County debut: 2002 (Surrey), 2008 (Kent)
County cap: 2004 (Surrey), 2008 (Kent)
Test debut: 1997-98
ODI debut: 1996
1st-Class 200s: 1
Place in batting averages: 259th av. 13.00
(2008 22nd av. 51.00)
Place in bowling averages: 2nd av. 18.19
(2008 9th av. 19.23)
Parents: Mohammed Aslam Sagar and Nusrat Perveen
Wife and date of marriage: Ebba Azhar, 13 April 2003
Education: FG No. 1 High School, Islamabad
Qualifications: 'A-level equivalent'
Overseas tours: Pakistan Youth to New Zealand 1994-95; Pakistan A to Bangladesh
1996, to England 1997; Pakistan to India (Pepsi Independence Cup) 1997, to South
Africa and Zimbabwe 1997-98, to Bangladesh (Wills International Cup) 1998-99,
to India 1998-99, to UK, Ireland and Netherlands (World Cup) 1999, to Australia
1999-2000, to Sri Lanka 2000, to Kenya (ICC Knockout Trophy) 2000-01, to New
Zealand 2000-01, to England 2001, to Bangladesh 2001-02, to Zimbabwe 2002-03, to
Africa (World Cup) 2002-03, to New Zealand 2003-04, to England (ICC Champions
Trophy) 2004, to South Africa 2006-07 (one-day series), to West Indies (World Cup)
2006-07, plus other one-day tournaments in Toronto, Kenya, Sharjah, Bangladesh,
Singapore, Australia, Morocco and England
Overseas teams played for: Islamabad; United Bank; Rawalpindi; Pakistan
International Airlines; Habib Bank; Hyderabad Heroes (ICL); Lahore Badshahs (ICL)
Career highlights to date: 'First Test match (debut) against South Africa in 1997
in Pakistan (Rawalpindi). I scored 128* in the first innings and 50* in the second,
plus two wickets – Man of the Match'
Cricket moments to forget: 'World Cup 1999 – the final against Australia (which
we lost)'
Cricket superstitions: None
Other sports played: Snooker, basketball, kite-flying
Other sports followed: Football (Manchester United)
Relaxations: 'Listening to music, training, spending time with my family'

Extras: Scored 128* and 50* on Test debut in the first Test v South Africa at Rawalpindi 1997-98; during first innings shared with Mushtaq Ahmed (59) in a stand of 151, equalling the world tenth-wicket record in Tests. Scored century (136) in the first Test v South Africa at Johannesburg 1997-98, becoming the first Pakistan player to score a Test century in South Africa and achieving feat of scoring a century on Test debuts home and away. Took 6-18 v West Indies in the Coca-Cola Champions Trophy in Sharjah 1999-2000 and 5-28 v Sri Lanka in the final of the same competition, winning the Man of the Match award on both occasions. An overseas player with Surrey at the start of the 2002 season and 2003-07. Signed a two-year deal with Kent (as a non-overseas player) in late 2007 having moved from Surrey

Best batting: 204* Surrey v Middlesex, The Oval 2005
Best bowling: 8-61 Surrey v Lancashire, The Oval 2002

2009 Season

	M	Inn	NO	Runs	HS	Avg	100	50	Ct	St	Balls	Runs	Wkts	Avg	BB	5I	10M
Test																	
FC	4	6	0	78	35	13.00	-	-	-	-	783	382	21	18.19	5-39	1	-
ODI																	
List A	13	11	1	190	51	19.00	-	1	3	-	585	532	15	35.46	4-41	-	
20/20 Int																	
20/20	12	5	1	45	15	11.25	-	-	2	-	271	328	16	20.50	3-16	-	

Career Performances

	M	Inn	NO	Runs	HS	Avg	100	50	Ct	St	Balls	Runs	Wkts	Avg	BB	5I	10M
Test	21	34	4	900	136	30.00	3	1	14	-	3015	1402	39	35.94	4-50	-	-
FC	155	240	29	6635	204*	31.44	9	33	126	-	25882	13430	536	25.05	8-61	22	3
ODI	143	110	26	1521	67	18.10	-	3	37	-	6242	4813	123	39.13	6-18	3	
List A	281	225	45	3789	101*	21.05	2	15	83	-	12473	9597	304	31.56	6-18	5	
20/20 Int																	
20/20	60	52	17	1023	65*	29.22	-	3	10	-	1208	1497	68	22.01	4-20	-	

BAIRSTOW, J. M.   Yorkshire

Name: <u>Jonathan</u> Mark Bairstow
Role: Right-hand bat, right-arm bowler,
wicket-keeper
Born: 26 September 1989, Bradford, Yorkshire
County debut: 2009
Parents: David (deceased) and Janet
Family links with cricket: Father, David Bairstow
kept wicket for Yorkshire and England
Education: St Peter's School, York
Other sports played: Rugby (Yorkshire Schools
U16), Football (Leeds Utd U15)
Extras: Represented Yorkshire Schools from U11
through to U15. Member of Yorkshire's ECB U15
Championship and Cup double side 2005. Selected
for North of England at various levels. Selected for

England U17. *Young Wisden* Schools Cricketer of the Year 2008, the first winner of
this award. Signed a two-year contract in September 2008 after averaging over 60 in
the season's 2nd XI championship. NBC Denis Compton Award for most promising
young Yorkshire player 2009. Member of England Performance Programme squad
2009-10.
Best batting: 84* Yorkshire v Nottinghamshire, Scarborough 2009

2009 Season

	M	Inn	NO	Runs	HS	Avg	100	50	Ct	St	Balls	Runs	Wkts	Avg	BB	5I	10M
Test																	
FC	12	19	6	592	84*	45.53	-	6	21	-	0	0	0		-	-	-
ODI																	
List A	8	5	0	26	20	5.20	-	-	4	-	0	0	0		-	-	
20/20 Int																	
20/20																	

Career Performances

	M	Inn	NO	Runs	HS	Avg	100	50	Ct	St	Balls	Runs	Wkts	Avg	BB	5I	10M
Test																	
FC	12	19	6	592	84*	45.53	-	6	21	-	0	0	0		-	-	-
ODI																	
List A	8	5	0	26	20	5.20	-	-	4	-	0	0	0		-	-	
20/20 Int																	
20/20																	

BALCOMBE, D. J.   Hampshire

Name: <u>David</u> John Balcombe
Role: Right-hand bat, right-arm fast-medium bowler
Born: 24 December 1984, City of London
Height: 6ft 4in
Nickname: Balcs, Spalko
County debut: 2006 (one-day), 2007 (first-class)
Place in batting averages: (2008 248th av. 12.14)
Parents: Peter and Elizabeth
Marital status: Single
Education: St John's School, Leatherhead; Durham
University
Qualifications: 9 GCSEs, 3 A-levels, BA (Hons) 2.1,
Level 1 coaching
Overseas tours: Surrey Academy to Perth 2004;
MCC A to Canada 2005; Hampshire to Cape
Town 2007
Overseas teams played for: Midland-Guildford CC, Western Australia 2003-04;
Mount Lawley CC, Western Australia 2005-06
Career highlights to date: 'Taking maiden first-class five-wicket return against
Durham. Making my Championship and Pro40 debuts for Hampshire'
Cricket moments to forget: 'Bowling two overs for 35 in a one-day game'
Cricket superstitions: 'Left equipment on first – i.e. left shoe, left pad'
Cricketers particularly admired: Shane Warne
Other sports followed: Rugby (London Wasps), football (Arsenal)
Favourite band: Five for Fighting, Kings of Leon
Relaxations: 'Sleeping, films'
Extras: Played for Durham UCCE 2005-07 (awarded cap for performances in 2005).
Represented British Universities 2006. Recorded best match figures by a Hampshire
bowler in a 2nd XI game – 14-88 (8-40/6-48) v Gloucestershire 2nd XI at The Rose
Bowl 2007. Has also played extensively in the Surrey leagues.
Best batting: 73 DUCCE v Leicestershire, Leicester 2005
Best bowling: 5-112 DUCCE v Durham, Durham 2005

2009 Season

	M	Inn	NO	Runs	HS	Avg	100	50	Ct	St	Balls	Runs	Wkts	Avg	BB	5I	10M
Test																	
FC	3	3	0	10	10	3.33	-	-	-	-	468	288	9	32.00	3-76	-	-
ODI																	
List A	4	1	0	2	2	2.00	-	-	1	-	216	249	6	41.50	2-56	-	
20/20 Int																	
20/20																	

	M	Inn	NO	Runs	HS	Avg	100	50	Ct	St	Balls	Runs	Wkts	Avg	BB	5I	10M
Test																	
FC	21	30	6	366	73	15.25	-	1	6	-	3081	2020	45	44.88	5-112	1	-
ODI																	
List A	9	3	0	4	2	1.33	-	-	3	-	384	378	10	37.80	2-39	-	
20/20 Int																	
20/20	1	1	0	3	3	3.00	-	-	-	-	12	15	0		-	-	
20/20	1	1	0	3	3	3.00	-	-	-	-	12	15	0		-	-	

BALL, J. T. Nottinghamshire

Name: Jacob (<u>Jake</u>) Timothy Ball
Role: Right-hand bat, right-arm medium-fast bowler
Born: 14 March 1991, Mansfield, Nottinghamshire
County debut: 2009 (one-day)
Family links with cricket: Brother Jonathan played for Lincolnshire and Nottinghamshire U15, U17 and 2nd XI.
Overseas tours: ECB U18 Scholarship Tour to Malaysia 2009
Extras: Former Nottinghamshire Academy player who has played in the county's U15, U17 and 2nd XI sides. Was also selected for an ECB Elite Player Development XI in 2008

2009 Season

	M	Inn	NO	Runs	HS	Avg	100	50	Ct	St	Balls	Runs	Wkts	Avg	BB	5I	10M
Test																	
FC																	
ODI																	
List A	1	1	0	0	0	0.00	-	-	-	-	36	33	1	33.00	1-33	-	
20/20 Int																	
20/20																	

Career Performances

	M	Inn	NO	Runs	HS	Avg	100	50	Ct	St	Balls	Runs	Wkts	Avg	BB	5I	10M
Test																	
FC																	
ODI																	
List A	1	1	0	0	0	0.00	-	-	-	-	36	33	1	33.00	1-33	-	
20/20 Int																	
20/20																	

BALLANCE, G. S. Yorkshire

Name: <u>Gary</u> Simon Ballance
Role: Left-hand top-order bat, occasional right-arm leg-spin bowler
Born: 22 November 1989, Harare, Zimbabwe
Nickname: Gazza
County debut: 2006 (one-day, Derbyshire) 2008 (first-class, Yorkshire)
Parents: Simon and Gail
Marital status: Single
Family links with cricket: 'Father – Zimbabwe Country Districts.' Is nephew of David Houghton, former captain of Zimbabwe
Education: Peterhouse, Zimbabwe; Harrow School
Overseas tours: Zimbabwe U19 to Sri Lanka (U19 World Cup) 2005-06

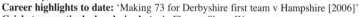

Career highlights to date: 'Making 73 for Derbyshire first team v Hampshire [2006]'
Cricketers particularly admired: Andy Flower, Shane Warne
Other sports played: Golf, tennis, rugby
Other sports followed: Football (Liverpool)
Extras: Man of the Match v England U19 at Colombo in the U19 World Cup 2005-06 (3-21/47). Made Derbyshire one-day debut aged 16 v West Indies A in a 50-over match at Derby 2006, scoring 48. Made Pro40 debut v Hampshire at The Rose Bowl 2006, scoring 73. Left Derbyshire at the end of the 2007 season and joined Yorkshire
Best batting: 5 Yorkshire v Kent, Canterbury 2008

2009 Season

	M	Inn	NO	Runs	HS	Avg	100	50	Ct	St	Balls	Runs	Wkts	Avg	BB	5I	10M
Test																	
FC																	
ODI																	
List A	1	1	0	33	33	33.00	-	-	-	-	0	0	0		-	-	
20/20 Int																	
20/20																	

Career Performances

	M	Inn	NO	Runs	HS	Avg	100	50	Ct	St	Balls	Runs	Wkts	Avg	BB	5I	10M
Test																	
FC	1	2	0	6	5	3.00	-	-	-	-	0	0	0		-	-	-
ODI																	
List A	5	5	0	162	73	32.40	-	1	1	-	0	0	0		-	-	
20/20 Int																	
20/20																	

BANDARA, C. M. Kent

Name: Charitha <u>Malinga</u> Bandara
Role: Right-hand bat, right arm leg-break bowler
Born: 31 December 1979, Kulatara, Sri Lanka
Nickname: Billy
County debut: 2005 (Gloucestershire)
County cap: 2005 (Gloucestershire)
Test debut: 1998
ODI debut: 2005-06
Twenty20 Int debut: 06
Overseas tours: Sri Lanka U19 to India 1997, to
South Africa (U19 World Cup) 1998; Sri Lanka A
to England 1999, to West Indies 2006-07, to South
Africa 2008-09; Sri Lanka to New Zealand 1998,
to India and Bangladesh 2005-06, to South Africa
2005-06, to New Zealand (one-day series) 2005-06,

to Australia (VB Series) 2005-06, to the Netherlands (one-day series) 2005-06, to
England 2006 (one-day series), to India (one-day series) 2006-07, to West Indies (ICC
World Cup) 2006-07, to Bangladesh (Idea Cup) 2009-10
Overseas teams played for: Kulatara 1996-97; Nondescripts 1998-99 – 2002-03;
Tamil Union 2003-04; Galle 2004-05; Ragama 2006 – ; Basnahira South 2008 –
Extras: Made his Test debut v New Zealand at Colombo at the age of 18. Has played
for Sri Lanka A against various touring sides – took 11-126 (8-49/3-77) v England A at
Colombo 2005. Played for Normandy CC (Surrey Championship) 2003, 2004.
Overseas player with Gloucestershire 2005, replacing Upul Chandana for the second
half of the season; took 39 wickets in seven matches (av. 25.15) to win Gloucestershire
Player of the Season. Signed for Kent in January 2010 as an overseas player for the
second half of the 2010 season, when he will replace Stuart Clark
Best batting: 79 Sri Lanka A v Pakistan A, Dambulla 2004-05
Best bowling: 8-49 Sri Lanka A v England A, Colombo 2004-05

2009 Season (Did not make any first-class or one-day appearances)

Career Performances

	M	Inn	NO	Runs	HS	Avg	100	50	Ct	St	Balls	Runs	Wkts	Avg	BB	5I	10M
Test	8	11	3	124	43	15.50			4		1152	633	16	39.56	3-84	-	-
FC	133	190	41	3047	79	20.44	-	14	88	-	18304	9411	365	25.78	8-49	11	2
ODI	30	17	4	160	31	12.30			8		1410	1188	36	33.00	4-31	-	
List A	115	79	24	854	64	15.52	-	1	37	-	4863	3802	159	23.91	5-22	3	
20/20 Int	4	3	1	12	7	6.00			1		84	96	4	24.00	3-32	-	
20/20	14	9	4	61	31*	12.20	-	-	2	-	288	324	16	20.25	3-18	-	

BANERJEE, V.   Gloucestershire

Name: Vikram Banerjee
Role: Left-hand bat, left-arm orthodox spin bowler
Born: 20 March 1984, Bradford
Height: 6ft **Weight:** 11st
Nickname: Banners
County debut: 2006
County cap: 2006
Place in bowling averages: 58th av. 31.76
Parents: Biren and Shyamli
Marital status: Single
Education: King Edward's School, Birmingham;
Cambridge University
Qualifications: 12 GCSEs, 4 A-levels, BA (Econ),
Level 2 coaching
Overseas tours: ECB Emerging Players to Mumbai
(World Cricket Academy) 2006-07
Overseas teams played for: Shivaji Park Gymkhana, Mumbai 2003
Career highlights to date: 'Winning at Lord's in 2005 Varsity Match. First wicket
for Gloucestershire (Mark Butcher)'
Cricket moments to forget: 'Innings defeat to Somerset on debut'
Cricket superstitions: 'Right pad on first'
Cricketers particularly admired: Viv Richards, Sachin Tendulkar, Bishan Bedi
Other sports followed: Football (Aston Villa)
Favourite band: U2, Status Quo, Sting, Jack Johnson, Coldplay
Relaxations: 'Movies, reading, spending time with mates'
Extras: Cambridge Blue 2004-06. Played for Cambridge UCCE 2006. ECB National
Skills Set. NBC Denis Compton Award for the most promising young Gloucestershire
player 2006. Member of England Performance Programme squad 2009-10
Best batting: 29 Cambridge University v Oxford University, Fenner's 2005
Best bowling: 4-38 Gloucestershire v Northamptonshire, Gloucester 2007

2009 Season

	M	Inn	NO	Runs	HS	Avg	100	50	Ct	St	Balls	Runs	Wkts	Avg	BB	5I	10M
Test																	
FC	7	12	3	71	16	7.88	-	-	2	-	1203	667	21	31.76	4-58	-	-
ODI																	
List A	10	6	3	11	6	3.66	-	-	4	-	492	386	14	27.57	3-47	-	
20/20 Int																	
20/20	6	2	2	5	5*		-	-	2	-	138	175	6	29.16	2-30	-	

Careeer Performances

	M	Inn	NO	Runs	HS	Avg	100	50	Ct	St	Balls	Runs	Wkts	Avg	BB	5I	10M
Test																	
FC	33	48	17	278	29	8.96	-	-	8	-	5979	3391	70	48.44	4-38	-	-
ODI																	
List A	10	6	3	11	6	3.66	-	-	4	-	492	386	14	27.57	3-47	-	
20/20 Int																	
20/20	6	2	2	5	5*		-	-	2	-	138	175	6	29.16	2-30	-	

BANKS, O. A. C. Somerset

Name: <u>Omari</u> Ahmed Clemente Banks
Role: Right-hand bat, right-arm off-spin bowler;
all-rounder
Born: 17 July 1982, Anguilla, Leeward Islands
County debut: 2001 (Leicestershire),
2008 (one-day, Somerset)
Test debut: 2002-03
ODI debut: 2002-03
Overseas tours: West Indies U19 to England 2001;
West Indies A to England 2006; West Indies to
Zimbabwe and South Africa 2003-04, to England
2004, to Sri Lanka 2005, to Pakistan 2006-07
Overseas teams played for: Leeward Islands
2000-01 – ; Anguilla (Stanford Twenty20) 2007-08
Extras: Played for Leicestershire 2nd XI in 2000 and
2001, making one first-class appearance for the county against the Pakistani tourists at
Leicester. First cricketer from the island of Anguilla to play Test cricket for West
Indies. In only his second Test, scored 47* as West Indies chased down a Test record
fourth innings target of 418 in the fourth Test v Australia in St John's 2002-03. His
awards include Man of the Match v Jamaica in the Busta Cup 2000-01 (7-70/3-78 plus
43) and v Jamaica in the Carib Beer Cup 2006-07 (2-88/1-3 plus 100), both at grounds
on St Kitts. Man of the Match v Jamaica (62/2-46) and v West Indies U19 (2-18/55*),
both in Guyana in the KFC Cup 2007-08. Released by Somerset at the end of the 2009
season. Is not considered an overseas player
Best batting: 108 Leeward Islands v Jamaica, Basseterre 2008-09
Best bowling: 7-70 Leeward Islands v Jamaica, Molyneux 2000-01

2009 Season

	M	Inn	NO	Runs	HS	Avg	100	50	Ct	St	Balls	Runs	Wkts	Avg	BB	5I	10M
Test																	
FC	6	7	2	156	53	31.20	-	1	1	-	667	456	7	65.14	4-120	-	-
ODI																	
List A	11	5	1	38	21	9.50	-	-	2	-	306	302	6	50.33	3-40	-	
20/20 Int																	
20/20	2	0	0	0	0		-	-	1	-	42	40	2	20.00	1-14	-	

Career Performances

	M	Inn	NO	Runs	HS	Avg	100	50	Ct	St	Balls	Runs	Wkts	Avg	BB	5I	10M
Test	10	16	4	318	50*	26.50	-	1	6	-	2401	1367	28	48.82	4-87	-	-
FC	72	111	18	2398	108	25.78	2	14	40	-	13395	6977	179	38.97	7-70	6	1
ODI	5	5	0	83	33	16.60	-	-	-	-	270	189	7	27.00	2-24	-	
List A	71	58	17	1187	77*	28.95	-	9	16	-	3043	2241	81	27.66	4-23	-	
20/20 Int																	
20/20	8	6	2	150	50*	37.50	-	1	1	-	138	198	6	33.00	1-14	-	

BARKER, K. H. D.   Warwickshire

Name: <u>Keith</u> Hubert Douglas Barker
Role: Left-hand bat, left-arm medium-pace bowler
Born: 21 October 1986, Manchester
County debut: 2009
Family links with cricket: Son of Keith Henderson Barker (British Guiana and Natal). Half-brother of Andrew Barker (Enfield and Accrington) and Gary Barker (Enfield and Lancashire 2nd XI). Former West Indies captain Clive Lloyd is his godfather.
Other sports played: Football (with Blackburn Rovers, Rochdale and Northwich Victoria)
Extras: Clive Lloyd is his godfather. Former England U20 footballer. Turned down a contract with Lancashire aged 16 because Blackburn Rovers had offered terms the previous week. Released by Blackburn Rovers in 2008 – made debut for Warwickshire 2nd XI v Hampshire, Sutton Coldfield, June 2008 and scored 118 in the team's second innings. Signed a two-year contract with Warwickshire in August 2008. Member of England Performance Programme squad 2009-10
Best batting: 23 Warwickshire v DUCCE, Durham 2009
Best bowling: 1-51 Warwickshire v England XI, Birmingham 2009

2009 Season

	M	Inn	NO	Runs	HS	Avg	100	50	Ct	St	Balls	Runs	Wkts	Avg	BB	5I	10M
Test																	
FC	3	4	0	28	23	7.00	-	-	-	-	318	175	1	175.00	1-51	-	-
ODI																	
List A	12	6	4	85	30*	42.50	-	-	2	-	402	354	12	29.50	3-23	-	
20/20 Int																	
20/20	11	3	1	20	9	10.00	-	-	1	-	210	283	16	17.68	4-19	-	

Career Performances

	M	Inn	NO	Runs	HS	Avg	100	50	Ct	St	Balls	Runs	Wkts	Avg	BB	5I	10M
Test																	
FC	3	4	0	28	23	7.00	-	-	-	-	318	175	1	175.00	1-51	-	-
ODI																	
List A	12	6	4	85	30*	42.50	-	-	2	-	402	354	12	29.50	3-23	-	
20/20 Int																	
20/20	11	3	1	20	9	10.00	-	-	1	-	210	283	16	17.68	4-19	-	

BATES, A. M.   Hampshire

Name: Alexander <u>Michael</u> Bates
Role: Right-hand bat, wicket-keeper
Born: 10 October 1990, Portsmouth, Hampshire
County debut: No first-team appearance
Overseas tours: England U18 to Malaysia 2009; England U19 to Bangladesh 2009, to New Zealand (ICC U19 World Cup) 2010
Extras: First played for Hampshire at U10 level, working his way through the age groups until joining Hampshire Academy in 2007. Has represented England at U15, U17 and U18 level. Awarded a 12-month development contract with Hampshire for 2010

BATTY, G. J.   Surrey

Name: <u>Gareth</u> Jon Batty
Role: Right-hand bat, off-spin bowler, county
vice-captain; all-rounder
Born: 13 October 1977, Bradford, Yorkshire
Height: 5ft 11in **Weight:** 12st 8lbs
Nickname: Batts, Boris, Red, Terry, Stuta
County debut: 1997 (Yorkshire), 1998 (one-day,
Surrey), 1999 (first-class, Surrey), 2002
(Worcestershire)
County colours: 2002 (Worcestershire)
Test debut: 2003-04
ODI debut: 2002-03
50 wickets in a season: 2
Place in batting averages: 267th av. 10.93
(2008 124th av. 30.14)
Place in bowling averages: 141st av. 72.40 (2008 76th av. 30.64)
Parents: David and Rosemary
Marital status: Single
Family links with cricket: Father was Yorkshire Academy coach. Brother played for
Yorkshire and Somerset
Education: Bingley Grammar; Worcester College
Qualifications: 9 GCSEs, BTEC Art and Design, Level 2 coaching
Career outside cricket: Property development and coaching
Off-season: 'Training and working on my game'
Overseas tours: England U15 to South Africa 1993; England U19 to Zimbabwe
1995-96, to Pakistan 1996-97; ECB National Academy to Australia and Sri Lanka
2002-03; England to Bangladesh and Sri Lanka 2003-04, to West Indies 2003-04,
to Zimbabwe (one-day series) 2004-05, to South Africa 2004-05, to India 2005-06
(one-day series), to West Indies 2009; England A to West Indies 2005-06; England
Lions to New Zealand 2009
Overseas teams played for: Marist Newman, Australia 1999
Career highlights to date: 'Every time I've pulled on an England shirt'
Cricket moments to forget: 'Every time I'm on the losing team'
Cricket superstitions: None
Cricketers particularly admired: Adam Hollioake, Alec Stewart, Graeme Hick,
Vik Solanki
Young players to look out for: Daryl Mitchell and Richard Jones (both
Worcestershire)
Other sports played: Golf, rugby
Other sports followed: Rugby league (Leeds Rhinos), 'all sports'
Favourite band: Rick Astley

Relaxations: 'Food and fine wines'
Extras: *Daily Telegraph* Young Player of the Year 1993. Surrey Supporters' Club Most Improved Player Award 2001. Surrey CCC Young Player of the Year Award 2001. ECB 2nd XI Player of the Year 2001. Leading all-rounder in the inaugural Twenty20 Cup 2003. Made Test debut in the first Test v Bangladesh at Dhaka 2003-04, taking a wicket (Alok Kapali) with his third ball. Vice-captain of Worcestershire since 2005. ECB National Academy 2005-06. Selected for England Lions in 2009. Moved from Worcestershire back to Surrey for 2010
Opinions on cricket: 'Wickets in general are batter-friendly. Would be good to see it evened out. Keep the kids interested at all costs.'
Best batting: 133 Worcestershire v Surrey, The Oval 2004
Best bowling: 7-52 Worcestershire v Northamptonshire, Northampton 2004

2009 Season

	M	Inn	NO	Runs	HS	Avg	100	50	Ct	St	Balls	Runs	Wkts	Avg	BB	5I	10M
Test																	
FC	11	16	0	175	46	10.93	-	-	9	-	1363	724	10	72.40	2-71	-	-
ODI																	
List A	16	11	0	127	31	11.54	-	-	6	-	744	522	16	32.62	5-35	1	
20/20 Int																	
20/20	10	6	3	21	5*	7.00	-	-	9	-	216	234	11	21.27	3-21	-	

Career Performances

	M	Inn	NO	Runs	HS	Avg	100	50	Ct	St	Balls	Runs	Wkts	Avg	BB	5I	10M
Test	7	8	1	144	38	20.57	-	-	3	-	1394	733	11	66.63	3-55	-	-
FC	135	204	36	4302	133	25.60	2	22	91	-	25501	12380	368	33.64	7-52	15	1
ODI	10	8	2	30	17	5.00	-	-	4	-	440	366	5	73.20	2-40	-	
List A	185	147	31	1969	83*	16.97	-	5	66	-	7265	5452	160	34.07	5-35	1	
20/20 Int	1	1	0	4	4	4.00	-	-	-	-	18	17	0		-	-	
20/20	50	43	11	441	87	13.78	-	1	21	-	912	1173	41	28.60	3-21	-	

7. Name the Pakistan cricketer who took a wicket with his first ball in Test cricket at the tender age of 17.

BATTY, J. N.   Gloucestershire

Name: <u>Jonathan</u> Neil Batty
Role: Right-hand bat, wicket-keeper
Born: 18 April 1974, Chesterfield
Height: 5ft 10in **Weight:** 11st 6lbs
Nickname: JB
County debut: 1997 (Surrey)
County cap: 2001 (Surrey)
1000 runs in a season: 1
Place in batting averages: 104th av. 36.03
(2008 130th av. 29.33)
Parents: Roger and Jill
Marital status: Single
Family links with cricket: Father played club
cricket to a high standard
Education: Wheatley Park; Repton; Durham
University (St Chad's); Keble College, Oxford
Qualifications: 10 GCSEs, 4 A-levels, BSc (Hons) in Natural Sciences, Diploma
in Social Studies (Oxon)
Overseas tours: Repton School to Netherlands 1991; MCC to Bangladesh 1996;
Surrey to South Africa 1997, 2001
Overseas teams played for: Mount Lawley CC, Perth 1997-2002
Career highlights to date: 'Winning three County Championships'
Cricket moments to forget: 'None!'
Cricketers particularly admired: David Gower, Alec Stewart, Jack Russell
Other sports played: Golf, squash
Other sports followed: Football (Nottingham Forest)
Relaxations: Reading, listening to music, movies
Extras: Represented Combined Universities 1994, 1995. Oxford Blue 1996.
Surrey Supporters' Club Most Improved Player 2002, 2003. BBC Radio London
Listeners' Cricketer of the Year 2003. Became second wicket-keeper (after Kent's
Steve Marsh in 1991) to take eight catches in an innings (a new Surrey record)
and score a century (129) in the same match, v Kent at The Oval 2004. Captain of
Surrey 2004. Achieved double of 1000 (1025) runs and 50 (53) dismissals in
first-class cricket 2006. Left Surrey to join Gloucestershire in October 2009
Best batting: 168* Surrey v Essex, Chelmsford 2003
Best bowling: 1-21 Surrey v Lancashire, Old Trafford 2000

2009 Season

	M	Inn	NO	Runs	HS	Avg	100	50	Ct	St	Balls	Runs	Wkts	Avg	BB	5I	10M
Test																	
FC	16	26	0	937	120	36.03	2	1	46	4	0	0	0	-	-	-	
ODI																	
List A	3	3	0	17	9	5.66	-	-	6	-	0	0	0	-	-		
20/20 Int																	
20/20	1	1	1	4	4*	-	-	-	-	-	0	0	0	-	-		

Career Performances

	M	Inn	NO	Runs	HS	Avg	100	50	Ct	St	Balls	Runs	Wkts	Avg	BB	5I	10M
Test																	
FC	191	294	34	8788	168*	33.80	20	38	500	64	78	61	1	61.00	1-21	-	-
ODI																	
List A	181	148	26	2743	158*	22.48	1	13	191	33	0	0	0	-	-		
20/20 Int																	
20/20	51	44	15	593	59	20.44	-	2	31	18	0	0	0	-	-		

BEER, W. A. T.   Sussex

Name: William (Will) Andrew Thomas Beer
Role: Right-hand bat, leg-spin bowler
Born: 8 October 1988, Crawley
Height: 5ft 9in **Weight:** 12st
Nickname: Ferret, Beero
County debut: 2008
Parents: Andrew and Sarah
Marital status: Single
Family links with cricket: 'Dad and Uncle Robin both played for Horsham 1st XI for many years'
Education: Reigate Grammar School
Qualifications: 3 A-levels
Overseas teams played for: Western Province, Cape Town 2007-08, Lindisfarne CC, Hobart 2008-09
Career highlights to date: 'Five wickets v Hants in 2nd XI Championship 2007. Playing for England U17. Figures of 6-53 for England U19 v New Zealand 2008.'
Cricket moments to forget: 'Getting out first ball in first ever county game, for Sussex U10'
Cricket superstitions: None
Cricketers particularly admired: Shane Warne

Young players to look out for: Ben Brown, Matt Machan and Michael Thornely (all Sussex)
Other sports played: Golf, squash (Sussex U15)
Other sports followed: Football (Manchester United), rugby, golf
Favourite band: Maroon 5
Relaxations: 'Listening to music'
Extras: Sussex Academy Player of the Year 2006. Part of ECB's elite spin-bowling programme 2009. Member of England Performance Programme squad 2009-10
Best batting: 6* Sussex v MCC, Lord's 2008
Best bowling: 1-18 Sussex v MCC, Lord's 2008

2009 Season

	M	Inn	NO	Runs	HS	Avg	100	50	Ct	St	Balls	Runs	Wkts	Avg	BB	5I	10M
Test																	
FC																	
ODI																	
List A	14	4	0	34	14	8.50	-	-	4	-	540	420	8	52.50	2-17	-	
20/20 Int																	
20/20	11	3	1	20	16*	10.00	-	-	1	-	192	234	7	33.42	2-27	-	

Career Performances

	M	Inn	NO	Runs	HS	Avg	100	50	Ct	St	Balls	Runs	Wkts	Avg	BB	5I	10M
Test																	
FC	2	2	1	6	6*	6.00	-	-	-	-	96	81	1	81.00	1-18	-	-
ODI																	
List A	14	4	0	34	14	8.50	-	-	4	-	540	420	8	52.50	2-17	-	
20/20 Int																	
20/20	15	7	3	42	17*	10.50	-	-	1	-	276	339	10	33.90	2-27	-	

8. Majid Khan made his first Test match appearance in 1964.
Which year saw his last Test appearance?

BELL, I. R.   Warwickshire

Name: Ian Ronald Bell
Role: Right-hand bat, right-arm
medium bowler
Born: 11 April 1982, Coventry
Height: 5ft 10in **Weight:** 11st
Nickname: Belly
County debut: 1999
County cap: 2001
Test debut: 2004
ODI debut: 2004-05
Twenty20 Int debut: 2006
1000 runs in a season: 3
1st-Class 200s: 3
Place in batting averages: 53rd av. 43.88
(2008 23rd av. 50.81)
Parents: Terry and Barbara
Marital status: Single
Family links with cricket: Brother Keith played for England U18, Staffordshire
and Warwickshire 2nd XI
Education: Princethorpe College, Rugby
Career highlights to date: 'The Ashes 2005'
Overseas tours: Warwickshire U19 to Cape Town 1998-99; England U19 to
New Zealand 1998-99, to Malaysia and (U19 World Cup) Sri Lanka 1999-2000,
to India 2000-01 (c); England A to West Indies 2000-01, to Sri Lanka 2004-05 (c);
ECB National Academy to Australia 2001-02, to Sri Lanka 2002-03; England to
Zimbabwe (one-day series) 2004-05, to South Africa 2004-05, to Pakistan 2005-06,
to India 2005-06, to India (ICC Champions Trophy) 2006-07, to Australia 2006-07,
to West Indies (World Cup) 2006-07, to Sri Lanka 2007-08, to New Zealand
2007-08, to India 2008-09, to West Indies 2008-09, to South Africa 2009-10
Overseas teams played for: University of Western Australia, Perth 2003-04
Cricketers particularly admired: Dominic Ostler, Alec Stewart, Robin Smith
Other sports played: Football (was at Coventry City School of Excellence),
rugby, golf
Other sports followed: Football (Aston Villa), rugby union (Northampton Saints)
Relaxations: Golf, listening to music
Extras: Played for England U14, U15, U16, U17; captained England U19. NBC
Denis Compton Award for the most promising young Warwickshire player 1999,
2000, 2001. Gray-Nicolls Trophy for Best Young Schools Cricketer 2000. Cricket
Society's Most Promising Young Cricketer of the Year Award 2001. Recorded
maiden one-day century (125) and maiden one-day five-wicket return (5-41) v
Essex at Chelmsford in the NCL 2003. Scored maiden first-class double century

(262*) v Sussex at Horsham 2004, in the process setting with Tony Frost (135*) a new Warwickshire record partnership for the seventh wicket (289*). Cricket Writers' Club Young Cricketer of the Year 2004. PCA Young Player of the Year award 2004. ECB National Academy 2004-05. Made ODI debut in the first ODI v Zimbabwe at Harare 2004-05, scoring 75 and winning Man of the Match award. His other match and series awards include Man of the Match in the fourth ODI v Pakistan at Trent Bridge 2006 (86*) and Player of the [ODI] Series v India 2007. Appointed MBE in 2006 New Year Honours as part of 2005 Ashes-winning England team. Recalled to the Test side for series v Pakistan 2006, scoring three hundreds (100*, 106*, 119) in successive Tests. ICC Emerging Player of the Year award 2006. Named as one of *Wisden*'s Five Cricketers of the Year 2008. Part of the England team which regained the Ashes 2009. Scored a century in second Test against South Africa December 2009, England 12-month central contract 2009-10

Best batting: 262* Warwickshire v Sussex, Horsham 2004
Best bowling: 4-4 Warwickshire v Middlesex, Lord's 2004

2009 Season

	M	Inn	NO	Runs	HS	Avg	100	50	Ct	St	Balls	Runs	Wkts	Avg	BB	5I	10M
Test	3	5	0	140	72	28.00	-	2	1	-	0	0	0	-	-	-	-
FC	19	30	3	1185	172	43.88	4	6	15	-	60	43	0	-	-	-	-
ODI																	
List A	13	11	3	570	108	71.25	2	4	6	-	0	0	0	-	-		
20/20 Int																	
20/20	7	7	0	132	42	18.85	-	-	3	-	0	0	0	-	-		

Career Performances

	M	Inn	NO	Runs	HS	Avg	100	50	Ct	St	Balls	Runs	Wkts	Avg	BB	5I	10M
Test	49	88	9	3144	199	39.79	8	21	45	-	108	76	1	76.00	1-33	-	-
FC	157	267	25	10475	262*	43.28	27	56	111	-	2809	1564	47	33.27	4-4	-	-
ODI	79	76	6	2483	126*	35.47	1	15	23	-	88	88	6	14.66	3-9	-	
List A	185	175	17	5808	137	36.75	5	42	62	-	1290	1138	33	34.48	5-41	1	
20/20 Int	5	5	1	109	60*	27.25	-	1	4	-	0	0	0	-	-		
20/20	34	33	5	596	66*	21.28	-	2	15	-	132	186	3	62.00	1-12	-	

BENHAM, C. C.   Hampshire

Name: Christopher (<u>Chris</u>) Charles Benham
Role: Right-hand bat, right-arm off-spin bowler
Born: 24 March 1983, Frimley, Surrey
Height: 6ft 2in   **Weight:** 'It varies'
Nickname: Cut-snake, Togo, Benoit, Benny
County debut: 2004
Place in batting averages: 48th av. 45.14
(2008 135th av. 28.76)
Parents: Frank and Sandie
Marital status: Single
Family links with cricket: 'Both older brothers,
Nick and Andy, played local club cricket'
Education: Yateley Comprehensive School; Yateley
Sixth Form College; Loughborough University
Qualifications: 10 GCSEs, 3 A-levels,
BSc (Hons) 2.1 Sport and Exercise Science
Overseas tours: West of England U15 to West Indies 1998
Overseas teams played for: Perth CC 2004-05; Casey-South Melbourne 2007-08
Career highlights to date: '158 (off 130 balls) in Pro40 play-off match v Glamorgan
at The Rose Bowl, September 2006, which we won to gain promotion to first division'
Cricket moments to forget: 'Getting a king pair in a pre-season friendly match
against Essex in 2005'
Cricket superstitions: 'There's a few!'
Cricketers particularly admired: Ricky Ponting, Sachin Tendulkar, Shane Warne,
John Crawley, Darren Lehmann, Mark Ramprakash
Young players to look out for: Benny Howell and Liam Dawson (both Hampshire)
Other sports played: Football (school, district and county sides, and trials with
Swindon and Crystal Palace), tennis, golf
Other sports followed: Football (Reading FC), 'follow all sports'
Favourite band: Newton Faulkner
Relaxations: 'Reading, music, PlayStation, "Champ Man"'
Extras: Played for ESCA U15 and England U16. Played for Loughborough UCCE
2002, 2004. Represented British Universities 2004. Scored 74 on Championship
debut v Derbyshire at Derby 2004. NBC Denis Compton Award for the most
promising young Hampshire player 2006. Scored 130-ball 158 v Glamorgan at
The Rose Bowl in Pro40 play-off 2006, winning Man of the Match award.
Best batting: 111 Hampshire v LUCCE, Rose Bowl 2009

2009 Season

	M	Inn	NO	Runs	HS	Avg	100	50	Ct	St	Balls	Runs	Wkts	Avg	BB	5I	10M
Test																	
FC	6	9	2	316	111	45.14	2	1	7	-	0	0	0		-	-	-
ODI																	
List A	18	15	3	420	108*	35.00	1	1	11	-	0	0	0		-	-	
20/20 Int																	
20/20	11	8	1	129	39	18.42	-	-	8	-	0	0	0		-	-	

Career Performances

	M	Inn	NO	Runs	HS	Avg	100	50	Ct	St	Balls	Runs	Wkts	Avg	BB	5I	10M
Test																	
FC	41	67	3	1825	111	28.51	2	10	40	-	30	37	0		-	-	-
ODI																	
List A	55	50	6	1564	158	35.54	4	7	25	-	0	0	0		-	-	
20/20 Int																	
20/20	34	29	3	421	59	16.19	-	1	19	-	0	0	0		-	-	

BENKENSTEIN, D. M.   Durham

Name: <u>Dale</u> Martin Benkenstein
Role: Right-hand bat, right-arm off-break
or medium bowler
Born: 9 June 1974, Harare, Zimbabwe
County debut: 2005
County cap: 2005
ODI debut: 1998-99
1000 runs in a season: 4
1st-Class 200s: 2
Place in batting averages: 41st av. 48.66
(2008 49th av. 43.00)
Family links with cricket: Father, Martin, and two
brothers, Brett and Boyd, played first-class cricket
Education: Michaelhouse, KwaZulu-Natal
Overseas tours: KwaZulu-Natal to Australia
(Champions Cup) 2000-01; South Africa U24 to Sri Lanka 1995; South Africa A to
Sri Lanka 1998, to West Indies 2000; South Africa to Malaysia (Commonwealth
Games) 1998-99, to Bangladesh (Wills International Cup) 1998-99, to New Zealand
1998-99, to Sri Lanka (ICC Champions Trophy) 2002-03, plus one-day series and
tournaments in Kenya, India and Sharjah
Overseas teams played for: Natal/KwaZulu-Natal 1992-93 – 2003-04; Dolphins
2003-04 – 2006-07; Delhi Giants (ICL) 2007-08 –

Extras: Captained Natal Schools and South Africa Schools and has played ODI cricket for South Africa. One of *South African Cricket Annual*'s Five Cricketers of the Year 1997. Was captain of KwaZulu-Natal, leading the side to the double (SuperSport Series and Standard Bank Cup) in 1996-97 and 2001-02. Has won numerous domestic awards, including Man of the Match in the final of the Standard Bank Cup 2001-02 at Durban (77*) and in the final of the SuperSport Series 2005-06 at Durban (151). Scored century (125) v Middlesex at Lord's 2006, in the process sharing with Gareth Breese (110) in a new record fifth-wicket partnership for Durham (222). Scored century (151) v Yorkshire at Headingley 2006, in the process sharing with Ottis Gibson (155) in a new record seventh-wicket partnership for Durham (315). Captain of Durham 2006, but stood down as captain at the end of 2008 season in favour of Will Smith. Named as one of *Wisden*'s Five Cricketers of the Year 2009. Contracted to Durham until 2011. Is not considered an overseas player

Best batting: 259 KwaZulu-Natal v Northerns, Durban 2001-02

2009 Season

	M	Inn	NO	Runs	HS	Avg	100	50	Ct	St	Balls	Runs	Wkts	Avg	BB	5I	10M
Test																	
FC	18	24	0	1168	181	48.66	5	4	10	-	300	173	8	21.62	3-20	-	-
ODI																	
List A	11	11	3	330	77*	41.25	-	3	5	-	66	76	0		-	-	
20/20 Int																	
20/20	10	10	2	276	53	34.50	-	1	4	-	18	13	0		-	-	

Career Performances

	M	Inn	NO	Runs	HS	Avg	100	50	Ct	St	Balls	Runs	Wkts	Avg	BB	5I	10M
Test																	
FC	209	315	37	12901	259	46.40	33	67	139	-	6551	3232	93	34.75	4-16	-	-
ODI	23	20	3	305	69	17.94	-	1	3	-	65	44	4	11.00	3-5	-	
List A	267	240	58	6471	107*	35.55	1	39	99	-	3029	2541	83	30.61	4-16	-	
20/20 Int																	
20/20	54	52	11	1136	56*	27.70	-	3	19	-	282	352	14	25.14	3-10	-	

9. Name the player who appeared in all of Pakistan's first 39 Test matches between 1952 and 1962.

BENNING, J. G. E.   Leicestershire

Name: <u>James</u> Graham Edward Benning
Role: Right-hand bat, right-arm medium bowler; batting all-rounder
Born: 4 May 1983, Mill Hill, London
Height: 5ft 11in **Weight:** 13st
Nickname: Benno
County debut: 2002 (one-day, Surrey), 2003 (first-class. Surrey)
Place in batting averages: 158th av. 28.20 (2008 205th av. 19.87)
Parents: Sandy and David
Marital status: Single
Family links with cricket: 'Dad played for Middlesex'

Education: Caterham School
Qualifications: 12 GCSEs, 3 AS-levels
Overseas tours: Surrey YC to Barbados 1999-2000, to Sri Lanka 2002
Overseas teams played for: North Dandenong, Australia 2001-02
Cricket moments to forget: 'Dropping two catches in front of a lively crowd at Canterbury, live on Sky'
Cricket superstitions: 'Order in which I put my kit on'
Cricketers particularly admired: Alec Stewart, Adam Hollioake
Other sports played: Rugby, football
Other sports followed: Football (Watford)
Favourite band: 'Listen to almost all music apart from thrash metal'
Relaxations: 'Going to the gym, music, spending time around friends'
Extras: Played for England U15-U19. First recipient of Ben Hollioake Scholarship. NBC Denis Compton Award for the most promising young Surrey player 2003. Scored maiden Championship century from 100 balls (finishing with 112) v Gloucestershire at The Oval 2006 on his 23rd birthday. Carried bat for 146-ball 189* as Surrey fell two short of Gloucestershire's 339-8 at Bristol in the C&G 2006. Scored 134-ball 152 v Gloucestershire at The Oval in the Friends Provident 2007, in the process sharing with Alistair Brown (176) in a Surrey record one-day partnership (294) as the county posted a world record List A total of 496-4. Loaned to Leicestershire by Surrey in August 2009, a move that became permanent at the end of the season
Best batting: 128 Surrey v OUCCE, The Parks 2004
Best bowling: 3-43 Leicestershire v Glamorgan, Leicester 2009

2009 Season

	M	Inn	NO	Runs	HS	Avg	100	50	Ct	St	Balls	Runs	Wkts	Avg	BB	5I	10M
Test																	
FC	7	12	2	282	72	28.20	-	1	2	-	762	436	9	48.44	3-43	-	-
ODI																	
List A	7	7	0	212	89	30.28	-	2	-	-	206	183	4	45.75	1-24	-	
20/20 Int																	
20/20	8	7	1	79	38	13.16	-	-	4	-	12	14	0		-	-	

Career Performances

	M	Inn	NO	Runs	HS	Avg	100	50	Ct	St	Balls	Runs	Wkts	Avg	BB	5I	10M
Test																	
FC	41	65	6	1883	128	31.91	4	8	16	-	1959	1374	21	65.42	3-43	-	-
ODI																	
List A	83	82	3	2670	189*	33.79	3	17	27	-	1174	1270	35	36.28	4-43	-	
20/20 Int																	
20/20	50	49	3	1032	88	22.43	-	7	15	-	42	57	2	28.50	1-7	-	

BERG, G. K. Middlesex

Name: <u>Gareth</u> Kyle Berg
Role: Right-hand bat, right-arm
fast-medium bowler; all-rounder
Born: 18 January 1981, Cape Town,
South Africa
Height: 6ft **Weight:** 13st 7lbs
Nickname: Weirdo, Bergy
County debut: 2008
Place in batting averages: 133rd av. 31.80
Place in bowling averages: 97th av. 38.52
Parents: Gina and Richard
Wife and date of marriage: Kelly,
1 April 2004
Children: Roman, 17 July 2007
Family links with cricket: 'Grandfather put
cricket bat and ball in my hand at early age of three years old'
Education: South African College School (SACS)
Qualifications: Level 2 coaching,
Level 1 hockey coach, Level 1 rugby coach, Level 1 athletics coach
Career outside cricket: Professional sports coach in schools
Off-season: 'Working on my fitness and improving my game'
Career highlights to date: 'Playing alongside Hansie Cronje and Shaun Pollock in a
friend's benefit game. Scoring 65 in my first game at Lord's'

Cricket moments to forget: 'Being left out of South Africa U15 World Cup squad one week before the World Cup in England. Missing out on the Champions League'
Cricket superstitions: 'Always put my right boot and pad on first. Always look at the sun when stepping on to the field'
Cricketers particularly admired: Steve Waugh, Herschelle Gibbs, Brian McMillan
Young players to look out for: Adam London and Sam Robson (both Middlesex)
Other sports played: Football (Western Province), rugby
Other sports followed: Football (Manchester United 'since three years old')
Favourite band: Red Hot Chili Peppers, Oasis, Beatles, Dean Martin
Relaxations: 'Surfing, sleeping, spending quality time with my family'
Extras: Played for Western Province Academy and Western Province B. Has played for Northamptonshire 2nd XI and Middlesex 2nd XI in the 2nd XI Championship. In his first one-day game for the county in April 2008, he took four wickets (against Surrey)
Opinions on cricket: 'Love all the new formats that are coming out, which allow more specialist players to shine! I'm enjoying all the formats these days…'
Best batting: 98 Middlesex v Kent, Canterbury 2009
Best bowling: 5-55 Middlesex v Gloucestershire, Lord's 2009

2009 Season

	M	Inn	NO	Runs	HS	Avg	100	50	Ct	St	Balls	Runs	Wkts	Avg	BB	5I	10M
Test																	
FC	13	23	2	668	98	31.80	-	7	9	-	1495	886	23	38.52	5-55	2	-
ODI																	
List A	15	11	1	136	33	13.60	-	-	3	-	438	376	15	25.06	3-18	-	
20/20 Int																	
20/20	7	7	3	137	33	34.25	-	-	1	-	105	151	3	50.33	2-31	-	

Career Performances

	M	Inn	NO	Runs	HS	Avg	100	50	Ct	St	Balls	Runs	Wkts	Avg	BB	5I	10M
Test																	
FC	16	28	2	786	98	30.23	-	7	10	-	1807	1057	28	37.75	5-55	2	-
ODI																	
List A	21	16	2	228	65	16.28	-	1	4	-	624	583	22	26.50	4-50	-	
20/20 Int																	
20/20	7	7	3	137	33	34.25	-	-	1	-	105	151	3	50.33	2-31	-	

BLACKWELL, I. D.   Durham

Name: <u>Ian</u> David Blackwell
Role: Left-hand bat, slow left-arm bowler;
all-rounder/'team ball shiner'
Born: 10 June 1978, Chesterfield
Height: 6ft 2in
Nickname: Black Dog, Donk, Ying, Goatage
County debut: 1997 (Derbyshire), 2000 (Somerset),
2009 (Durham)
County cap: 2001 (Somerset)
Test debut: 2005-06
ODI debut: 2002-03
1000 runs in a season: 3
1st-Class 200s: 1
Place in batting averages: 47th av. 45.19
(2008 39th av. 46.45)

Place in bowling averages: 9th av. 22.63 (2008 136th av. 44.45)
Parents: John and Marilyn
Wife and date of marriage: Elizabeth Rachel, 30 September 2006
Family links with cricket: 'Dad played for Derbyshire Over 50s.'
Education: Old Hall Primary; Manor School; Brookfield Community School
Qualifications: 9 GCSEs, 2 A-levels, Level 3 coaching
Career outside cricket: 'None as yet'
Overseas tours: Somerset to Cape Town 2000, 2001; England VI to Hong Kong
2001; England to Sri Lanka (ICC Champions Trophy) 2002-03, to Australia 2002-03
(VB Series), to Africa (World Cup) 2002-03, to Bangladesh and Sri Lanka 2003-04
(one-day series), to West Indies 2003-04 (one-day series), to Pakistan 2005-06 (one-
day series), to India 2005-06; ECB National Academy to Australia 2002-03
Overseas teams played for: Delacombe Park CC, Melbourne 1997, 1999; Spotswood
CC, Melbourne
Career highlights to date: 'Playing for England. Winning the C&G Trophy 2001.
Winning the Twenty20 2005. Being promoted as champions of division two 2007'
Cricket moments to forget: 'All my noughts for England'
Cricket superstitions: 'Left pad first – always chew gum'
Cricketers particularly admired: Ricky Ponting, Graeme Smith, Jamie Cox, Marcus
Trescothick, Andrew Caddick, Viv Richards, Ian Botham, Peter Trego
Young players to look out for: Liam Dawson (Hampshire), Dawid Malan
(Middlesex), Adil Rashid (Yorkshire)
Other sports played: Golf (6 handicap), football (winter 5-a-side)
Other sports followed: Football (Chesterfield FC – 'Up the Spireites!')
Relaxations: 'PS3 and King.com'
Extras: Became first batsman in Championship history to score two centuries
(103/122) in a match batting at No. 7, v Northants at Northampton 2001. Scored

134-ball double century (finishing with 247*) v Derbyshire at Taunton 2003, the fastest double century on record by an Englishman in terms of balls received. Won the Walter Lawrence Trophy 2005 (fastest first-class century of the season) for his 67-ball hundred (finishing with 107) v Derbyshire at Taunton. Captain of Somerset July 2005-2006, although absent injured for most of the 2006 season. Joined Durham for 2009
Best batting: 247* Somerset v Derbyshire, Taunton 2003
Best bowling: 7-85 Durham v Lancashire, Old Trafford 2009

2009 Season

	M	Inn	NO	Runs	HS	Avg	100	50	Ct	St	Balls	Runs	Wkts	Avg	BB	5I	10M
Test																	
FC	18	24	3	949	158	45.19	2	6	4	-	2741	1064	47	22.63	7-85	3	-
ODI																	
List A	15	15	0	386	64	25.73	-	3	5	-	656	510	22	23.18	4-36	-	
20/20 Int																	
20/20	10	10	1	127	59	14.11	-	1	1	-	162	183	4	45.75	2-18	-	

Career Performances

	M	Inn	NO	Runs	HS	Avg	100	50	Ct	St	Balls	Runs	Wkts	Avg	BB	5I	10M
Test	1	1	0	4	4	4.00	-	-	-	-	114	71	0				
FC	165	245	19	9103	247*	40.27	23	47	59	-	24423	11140	286	38.95	7-85	10	-
ODI	34	29	2	403	82	14.92	-	1	8	-	1230	877	24	36.54	3-26	-	
List A	231	212	18	5337	134*	27.51	3	33	60	-	8055	6422	184	34.90	5-26	1	
20/20 Int																	
20/20	40	39	6	625	82	18.93	-	2	11	-	739	877	27	32.48	4-26	-	

BLAIN, J. A. R.   Yorkshire

Name: <u>John</u> Angus Rae Blain
Role: Right-hand bat, right-arm fast-medium bowler
Born: 4 January 1979, Edinburgh, Scotland
Height: 6ft 2in **Weight:** 13st 7lbs
Nickname: Blainy, Haggis, William, JB
County debut: 1997 (Northamptonshire), 2004 (Yorkshire)
Parents: John and Elma
Marital status: Single
Education: Pencuik High School; Jewel and Esk Valley College
Qualifications: 8 GCSEs, 1 A-level, HNC Leisure and Recreation, Level 1 coaching

Overseas tours: Northants CCC to Zimbabwe 1997, to Grenada 2001, 2002; Scotland U19 to Netherlands (International Youth Tournament) 1994-95, to Bermuda (International Youth Tournament) 1997, to South Africa (U19 World Cup) 1997-98 (captain); Scotland to Denmark (European Championships) 1996, to Malaysia (ICC Trophy) 1996-97, to Malaysia (Commonwealth Games) 1998-99, to Sharjah (World Cup warm-up) 1999, to Canada (ICC Trophy) 2001, to UAE (ICC Six Nations Challenge) 2003-04, to UAE (ICC Inter-Continental Cup) 2004, to Bangladesh (one-day series) 2006-07, to Kenya (including ICC World Cricket League) 2006-07, to Sharjah 2006-07, to West Indies (World Cup) 2006-07, to South Africa 2007-08 (one-day series), 2008-09 (ICC World Cup Qualifying tournament)
Overseas teams played for: New Plymouth Old Boys, New Zealand 1998-99; Taranaki Cricket Association, New Zealand 1998-99
Career highlights to date: 'World Cup 1999, England. Signing for Yorkshire CCC'
Cricket moments to forget: 'Not qualifying for the 2003 World Cup – failing to qualify by losing the last match by six runs in Canada 2001. Not qualifying for the Champions Trophy in England 2004, losing the last game to the USA in Dubai 2004' [*USA qualified for the Champions Trophy ahead of Scotland by virtue of a net run-rate that was superior by just 0.028 runs*]
Cricket superstitions: 'Keeping a tidy kitbag'
Cricketers particularly admired: Devon Malcolm, Darren Lehmann
Other sports played: Football (schoolboy forms with Hibernian FC and Falkirk FC, making youth and reserve team appearances)
Other sports followed: Rugby
Relaxations: 'Music, going out for a beer. Spending time with my girlfriend and going home to Scotland to see family. Watching football, going to the gym, and sleeping!'
Extras: Has played for Scotland in first-class cricket and in the B&H and NatWest competitions. Also played for Scottish Saltires in NCL. Took 5-24 on Sunday League debut for Northamptonshire v Derbyshire at Derby 1997. Represented Scotland in the 1999 World Cup, taking 10 wickets and finishing top of the strike rate chart for the tournament. Man of the Match in the final of the ICC Inter-Continental Cup v Canada in the UAE 2004, returning match figures of 7-55 (3-27/4-28). Released by Yorkshire at the end of the 2006 season. Returned to Yorkshire in 2009
Best batting: 93 Scotland v Ireland, Belfast 2007
Best bowling: 6-42 Northamptonshire v Kent, Canterbury 2001

2009 Season (Did not make any first-class or one-day appearances for his county)

Career Performances

	M	Inn	NO	Runs	HS	Avg	100	50	Ct	St	Balls	Runs	Wkts	Avg	BB	5I	10M
Test																	
FC	42	47	16	495	93	15.96	-	2	12	-	5945	4266	120	35.55	6-42	4	-
ODI	33	25	6	284	41	14.94	-	-	8	-	1329	1173	41	28.60	5-22	1	
List A	102	66	25	635	41	15.48	-	-	27	-	4388	3679	143	25.72	5-22	4	
20/20 Int	6	3	1	4	3*	2.00	-	-	1	-	120	108	6	18.00	2-23	-	
20/20	6	3	1	4	3*	2.00	-	-	1	-	120	108	6	18.00	2-23	-	

BLAKE, A, J.   Kent

Name: Alexander (<u>Alex</u>) James Blake
Role: Left-hand bat, right-arm fast-medium bowler;
all-rounder
Born: 25 January 1989, Bromley, Kent
Height: 6ft 1in **Weight:** 13st 7lbs
Nickname: Blakey, Butler, Brakey
County debut: 2007 (one-day), 2008 (first-class)
Parents: Andrew and Michelle
Marital status: Single
Education: Hayes Secondary School; Leeds
Metropolitan University
Qualifications: 8 GCSEs, 3 A-levels, Level 1 cricket
coaching, Level 1 hockey coach
Overseas tours: England U19 to Malaysia 2006-07
Overseas teams played for: Balcatta CC, Perth
2007-08
Career highlights to date: 'Making my debut for Kent against Surrey in a Pro40
floodlit game on Sky Sports. Taking my first Pro40 wicket v Glamorgan in 2007'
Cricket moments to forget: 'Being hit for three consecutive sixes by Inzamam-ul-
Haq [Pro40 Kent v Yorkshire 2007]'
Cricket superstitions: 'Turn left at top of bowling mark'
Cricketers particularly admired: Brian Lara, Steve Waugh
Young players to look out for: James Goodman and Adam Ball (both Kent)
Other sports played: Hockey (HSBC 1st XI; Leeds Metropolitan University 1st XI)
Other sports followed: Football (Tottenham Hotspur)
Favourite band: Kings of Leon
Relaxations: 'FIFA, poker, Facebook'
Extras: Kent Academy Scholar of the Year 2005, 2006. Kent League Young Player
of the Year 2007. Borough of Bromley Sports Personality of the Year 2007. Member
of England Performance Programme squad 2009-10
Best batting: 47 Kent v Gloucestershire, Bristol 2009

2009 Season

	M	Inn	NO	Runs	HS	Avg	100	50	Ct	St	Balls	Runs	Wkts	Avg	BB	5I	10M
Test																	
FC	4	5	0	125	47	25.00	-	-	1	-	24	15	0		-	-	-
ODI																	
List A	7	6	0	142	80	23.66	-	1	6	-	0	0	0		-	-	
20/20 Int																	
20/20																	

Career Performances

	M	Inn	NO	Runs	HS	Avg	100	50	Ct	St	Balls	Runs	Wkts	Avg	BB	5I	10M
Test																	
FC	5	5	0	125	47	25.00	-	-	1	-	48	32	0		-	-	-
ODI																	
List A	10	8	2	157	80	26.16	-	1	6	-	72	61	1	61.00	1-25	-	
20/20 Int																	
20/20																	

BOJE, N. Northamptonshire

Name: Nico (<u>Nicky</u>) Boje
Role: Left-hand bat, slow left-arm bowler;
all-rounder, county captain
Born: 20 March 1973, Bloemfontein,
South Africa
Nickname: Bodge
Height: 5ft 10in
County debut: 2002 (Nottinghamshire),
2007 (Northamptonshire)
Test debut: 1999-2000
ODI debut: 1995-96
Twenty20 Int debut: 2005-06
1st-Class 200s: 1
Place in batting averages: 81st av. 40.05
(2008 63rd av. 40.25)
Place in bowling averages: 42nd av. 29.70 (2008 108th av. 36.18)
Family links with cricket: Older brother Eduard (E.H.L.) Boje played for Orange
Free State 1989-90 – 1990-91
Education: Grey College, Bloemfontein
Overseas tours: South Africa A to Zimbabwe 1994-95, to England 1996, to Sri Lanka
1998-99 (vc), to Australia 2002-03; South Africa U24 to Sri Lanka 1995-96; South
Africa to Zimbabwe 1995-96 (one-day series), to India 1996-97, to Bangladesh (Wills
International Cup) 1998-99, to New Zealand 1998-99, to UK, Ireland and Netherlands
(World Cup) 1999, to India 1999-2000, to Sri Lanka 2000, to Kenya (ICC Knockout
Trophy) 2000-01, to West Indies 2000-01, to Australia 2001-02, to Sri Lanka (ICC
Champions Trophy) 2002-03, to New Zealand 2003-04, to Sri Lanka 2004, to England
(ICC Champions Trophy) 2004, to West Indies 2004-05, to Australia 2005-06, to Sri
Lanka 2006, plus other one-day series and tournaments in Sharjah, Australia,
Singapore, Morocco and England; South Africa VI to Hong Kong 2006 (c)
Overseas teams played for: Orange Free State/Free State 1990-91 – 2002-03; Eagles
2003-04 – 2006-07; Hyderabad Heroes (ICL) 2007-08 – 2008-09; Warriors 2009-10

Other sports played: Rugby, tennis

Extras: Represented South Africa Schools 1989-91. Attended South Africa Academy. One of *South African Cricket Annual*'s five Cricketers of the Year 2001. Represented South Africa in the 2002-03 World Cup. Represented African XI in the Afro-Asia Cup 2005-06. His series and match awards include Man of the [ODI] Series v New Zealand 2000-01 (had scores of 105*, 64 and 129 in the first three ODIs), Man of the Match in the second Test v India at Bangalore 1999-2000 (85 as nightwatchman plus 5-83 in India's second innings) and Man of the Match in the seventh ODI v Australia at Cape Town 2001-02 (49/5-21). Man of the Match in the final of the 2006 Hong Kong Sixes. Was Nottinghamshire's overseas player in 2002. Retired from international cricket in December 2006. Was a temporary overseas player with Northamptonshire during the 2007 season as a replacement for Johannes van der Wath; returned for 2008 as a non-overseas player. Scored a century (125), then followed up with second innings figures of 6-110 v Leicestershire at Leicester 2007

Best batting: 226* Northamptonshire v Worcestershire, Wantage Road 2008
Best bowling: 8-93 Eagles v Dolphins, Durban 2005-06

2009 Season

	M	Inn	NO	Runs	HS	Avg	100	50	Ct	St	Balls	Runs	Wkts	Avg	BB	5I	10M
Test																	
FC	15	25	5	801	98	40.05	-	8	7	-	1890	891	30	29.70	4-59	-	-
ODI																	
List A	13	11	1	289	56	28.90	-	2	6	-	455	364	15	24.26	3-49	-	
20/20 Int																	
20/20	9	6	1	134	45	26.80	-	-	5	-	162	159	12	13.25	3-14	-	

Career Performances

	M	Inn	NO	Runs	HS	Avg	100	50	Ct	St	Balls	Runs	Wkts	Avg	BB	5I	10M
Test	43	62	10	1312	85	25.23	-	4	18	-	8620	4265	100	42.65	5-62	3	-
FC	203	303	54	8504	226*	34.15	8	51	120	-	40966	17960	562	31.95	8-93	22	2
ODI	115	71	18	1414	129	26.67	2	4	33	-	4541	3415	96	35.57	5-21	1	
List A	271	193	47	3815	129	26.13	2	16	84	-	11441	8222	262	31.38	5-21	1	
20/20 Int	1	0	0	0	0		-	-	-	-	24	27	1	27.00	1-27	-	
20/20	39	26	8	516	58*	28.66	-	2	13	-	706	819	36	22.75	3-14	-	

10. In the First Test against Bangladesh at Lord's in May 2005, what was England's winning margin?

BOPARA, R. S.　　　　　　　　　Essex

Name: Ravinder (<u>Ravi</u>) Singh Bopara
Role: Right-hand bat, right-arm medium bowler; batting all-rounder
Born: 4 May 1985, Forest Gate, London
Height: 5ft 10in　**Weight:** 12st 7lbs
Nickname: Puppy, Bops
County debut: 2002
County cap: 2005
Test debut: 2007-08
ODI debut: 2006-07
Twenty20 Int debut: 2008
1000 runs in a season: 1
1st-Class 200s: 2
Place in batting averages: 17th av. 59.38
(2008 16th av. 54.60)
Place in bowling averages: (2008 101st av. 34.25)
Parents: Baldish and Charanjit
Marital status: Single
Education: Brampton Manor School

Overseas tours: England U19 to Australia 2002-03, to Bangladesh (U19 World Cup) 2003-04; England A to West Indies 2005-06, to Bangladesh 2006-07; England to Australia (Commonwealth Bank Series) 2006-07, to West Indies (World Cup) 2006-07, to Sri Lanka 2007-08, to New Zealand 2007-08 (one-day series): to India (one-day series) 2008; to West Indies 2008-09, to South Africa (ICC Champions Trophy) 2009-10; England Lions to New Zealand 2009
Overseas teams played for: Rockingham-Mandurah CC, Perth 2004; Auckland 2009-10
Career highlights to date: 'Winning Sri Lanka [ODI] series away from home [2007-08]. The 2008 season'
Cricket moments to forget: 'My first Test tour'
Cricketers particularly admired: Sachin Tendulkar, Jacques Kallis, Viv Richards
Favourite band: Usher, Ne-Yo
Relaxations: 'Music, pets'
Player website: www.ravinderbopara.com
Extras: Played for Development of Excellence XI (South) v West Indies U19 2001. Represented England U19 2003 and 2004. C&G Man of the Match award v Devon at Exmouth 2005 (65*). Scored 135 v Australians in a two-day game at Chelmsford 2005. Represented England A v Sri Lankans and v Pakistanis 2006. ECB National Academy 2005-06, 2006-07. Man of the Match v Sri Lanka in Antigua in the World Cup 2006-07 (52). NBC Denis Compton Award for the most promising young Essex player 2007. Cricket Writers' Club Young Cricketer of the Year 2008. Bought by

Kings XI Punjab for $450,000 in IPL Auction 2009. Member of England's Ashes winning side in 2009. Signed for Auckland in November 2009 to play in New Zealand's domestic season. England increment contract 2009-10
Opinions on cricket: 'Make franchise teams'
Best batting: 229 Essex v Northamptonshire, Chelmsford 2007
Best bowling: 5-75 Essex v Surrey, Colchester 2006

2009 Season

	M	Inn	NO	Runs	HS	Avg	100	50	Ct	St	Balls	Runs	Wkts	Avg	BB	5I	10M
Test	6	9	0	356	143	39.55	2	-	4	-	62	52	0		-	-	-
FC	9	15	2	772	201	59.38	4	1	7	-	110	82	0		-	-	-
ODI	9	9	0	259	49	28.77	-	-	4	-	54	51	1	51.00	1-12	-	
List A	11	11	0	269	49	24.45	-	-	6	-	132	115	3	38.33	1-12	-	
20/20 Int	6	6	0	146	55	24.33	-	1	2	-	0	0	0		-	-	
20/20	10	10	0	253	55	25.30	-	2	4	-	84	113	4	28.25	1-17	-	

Career Performances

	M	Inn	NO	Runs	HS	Avg	100	50	Ct	St	Balls	Runs	Wkts	Avg	BB	5I	10M
Test	10	15	0	502	143	33.46	3	-	5	-	296	199	1	199.00	1-39	-	-
FC	89	146	20	5448	229	43.23	15	20	60	-	6188	4094	90	45.48	5-75	1	-
ODI	50	46	8	1037	60	27.28	-	4	17	-	331	293	6	48.83	2-43	-	
List A	140	131	28	3437	201*	33.36	4	18	42	-	2568	2346	81	28.96	4-52	-	
20/20 Int	8	7	0	159	55	22.71	-	1	2	-	0	0	0		-	-	
20/20	51	43	4	917	84	23.51	-	5	13	-	514	656	27	24.29	3-18	-	

BORRINGTON, P. M.   Derbyshire

Name: <u>Paul</u> Michael Borrington
Role: Right-hand opening bat, right-arm off-spin bowler, occasional wicket-keeper
Born: 24 May 1988, Nottingham
Height: 5ft 11in **Weight:** 11st 2lbs
Nickname: Boz, Bozza, Borrers
County debut: 2005
Place in batting averages: (2008 99th av. 33.56)
Parents: Tony and Sharron
Marital status: Single
Family links with cricket: Father played for Derbyshire 1970-82
Education: Chellaston School; Repton School (sixth form); Loughborough University
Qualifications: 10 GCSEs, 3 A-levels, degree in Sports Science

Overseas tours: Derbyshire U15 to South Africa 2003; England U16 to South Africa 2004; Repton School to Sri Lanka 2005; Derbyshire Academy to South Africa 2007
Off-season: 'Cricket Academy, Perth, Australia'
Overseas tours: England U16 to South Africa 2004; Derbyshire to Grenada 2008
Career highlights to date: 'Captaining the Midlands to victory in the 2003 Bunbury Festival. First-class debut v Leicestershire at the age of 17. Getting my first half-century. Maiden first-class century [102* for LUCCE v Worcestershire at Kidderminster, May 2008]'
Cricket moments to forget: 'Leaving a straight ball on my first-class debut'
Cricket superstitions: 'Left pad on first'
Cricketers particularly admired: Michael Vaughan
Young players to look out for: Chris Paget (Durham UCCE), Dan Redfern (Derbyshire)
Other sports played: Football, occasional golf
Other sports followed: Football (Crewe Alexandra)
Favourite band: Razorlight, The Killers
Relaxations: 'Spending time with my friends'
Extras: NBC Denis Compton Award for the most promising young Derbyshire player 2005, 2007. Derbyshire Academy Player of the Year 2006. Scored maiden first-class century for Loughborough University v Worcester in 2008
Opinions on cricket: 'There's too much Twenty20 – should be more five-day first-class games so players like me have time to get in.'
Best batting: 105 LUCCE v Hampshire, Southampton 2009

2009 Season

	M	Inn	NO	Runs	HS	Avg	100	50	Ct	St	Balls	Runs	Wkts	Avg	BB	5I	10M
Test																	
FC	3	3	0	174	105	58.00	1	-	-	-	0	0	0		-	-	-
ODI																	
List A	1	1	0	25	25	25.00	-	-	-	-	0	0	0		-	-	
20/20 Int																	
20/20																	

Career Performances

	M	Inn	NO	Runs	HS	Avg	100	50	Ct	St	Balls	Runs	Wkts	Avg	BB	5I	10M
Test																	
FC	19	29	4	863	105	34.52	2	4	12	-	6	5	0		-	-	-
ODI																	
List A	1	1	0	25	25	25.00	-	-	-	-	0	0	0		-	-	
20/20 Int																	
20/20																	

BORTHWICK, S. G.   Durham

Name: <u>Scott</u> George Borthwick
Role: Left-hand bat, leg-break bowler
Born: 19 April 1990, Sunderland, County Durham
County debut: 2008 (one-day), 2009 (first-class)
Family links with cricket: Uncle, David, played
for Northumberland
Overseas tours: England U19 to South Africa 2009
Extras: Durham 2nd XI 2006-09. Durham Academy
2006-08. North of Enmgland U17, 2007. Selected
for the ECB Elite Player Development XI, 2008. In
his debut game at Old Trafford in June 2008, he
claimed three wickets in four impressive overs
including that of Lancashire opener Mal Loye. NBC
Denis Compton Award for most promising young
Durham player 2009

Best batting: 26* Durham v Hampshire, Rose Bowl 2009
Best bowling: 3-95 Durham v Hampshire, Rose Bowl 2009

2009 Season

	M	Inn	NO	Runs	HS	Avg	100	50	Ct	St	Balls	Runs	Wkts	Avg	BB	5I	10M
Test																	
FC	1	1	1	26	26*		-	-	-	-	162	95	3	31.66	3-95	-	-
ODI																	
List A	6	2	2	5	3*		-	-	4	-	120	178	4	44.50	2-11	-	
20/20 Int																	
20/20																	

Career Performances

	M	Inn	NO	Runs	HS	Avg	100	50	Ct	St	Balls	Runs	Wkts	Avg	BB	5I	10M
Test																		
FC	1	1	1	26	26*		-	-	-	-	162	95	3	31.66	3-95	-	-
ODI																	
List A	6	2	2	5	3*		-	-	4	-	120	178	4	44.50	2-11	-	
20/20 Int																	
20/20	3	0	0	0	0		-	-	1	-	36	55	3	18.33	3-23	-	

BOTHA, A. G. Warwickshire

Name: Anthony (<u>Ant</u>) Greyvensteyn Botha
Role: Left-hand bat, slow left-arm spin bowler
Born: 17 November 1976, Pretoria,
South Africa
Height: 6ft **Weight:** 12st 7lbs
Nickname: Boats
County debut: 2004 (Derbyshire),
2007 (Warwickshire)
County cap: 2004 (Derbyshire)
50 wickets in a season: 1
Place in batting averages: 176th av. 26.11
(2008 184th av. 21.76)
Place in bowling averages: 105th av. 40.91
(2008 138th av. 45.13)

Parents: Elise and Ian
Wife and date of marriage: Katie, 12 December 2009
Children: Jesse, 13 November 2008
Education: Maritzburg College; Natal Tech
Qualifications: Marketing Manager Diploma, Level 2 coaching
Career outside cricket: 'Own business'
Off-season: 'In Australia as Katie is from there'
Overseas tours: South Africa U19 to India 1995-96
Overseas teams played for: Natal/KwaZulu-Natal 1995-96 – 1998-99; Easterns
1999-2000 – 2002-03; Joondalup CC, Perth 2005-06
Career highlights to date: 'Winning the four-day championship with Easterns 2002'
Cricket moments to forget: 'Getting badly injured in 2004 against Yorkshire. Steve
Stubbings's fielding!'
Cricketers particularly admired: Steve Waugh
Young players to look out for: Chris Woakes (Warwickshire)
Other sports played: Hockey, tennis
Other sports followed: Football (Liverpool), Super 14 rugby (Natal Sharks)
Favourite band: Live
Relaxations: 'Watersports, beach, fishing, trading'
Extras: Represented South African Schools 1995. Played for South Africa Academy
1997. Scored maiden first-class century (103) v DUCCE at Derby 2004, then took
5-55 in the DUCCE second innings to become the first Derbyshire player since 1937
to score a century and record a five-wicket innings return in the same first-class match.
C&G Man of the Match award v Durham at Riverside 2005 (4-44/34*). Derbyshire
Twenty20 player of the year 2005, 2006. Left Derbyshire towards the end of the 2007
season and joined Warwickshire. Is England-qualified

Opinions on cricket: 'I think we play far too much cricket which is diluting the intensity and quality, especially in one-day cricket. One-day cricket is all about intensity and it's impossible to get that right with the amount of cricket we play.'
Best batting: 156* Derbyshire v Yorkshire, Derby 2005
Best bowling: 8-53 Natal B v Northerns B, Centurion 1997-98

2009 Season

	M	Inn	NO	Runs	HS	Avg	100	50	Ct	St	Balls	Runs	Wkts	Avg	BB	5I	10M
Test																	
FC	14	19	2	444	64	26.11	-	2	5	-	1899	941	23	40.91	5-51	1	-
ODI																	
List A	15	9	5	141	37*	35.25	-	-	8	-	557	436	18	24.22	3-27	-	
20/20 Int																	
20/20	11	7	4	81	35*	27.00	-	-	7	-	216	268	7	38.28	3-31	-	

Career Performances

	M	Inn	NO	Runs	HS	Avg	100	50	Ct	St	Balls	Runs	Wkts	Avg	BB	5I	10M
Test																	
FC	127	195	27	4063	156*	24.18	4	19	95	-	21292	10321	298	34.63	8-53	9	1
ODI																	
List A	137	103	32	1608	60*	22.64	-	4	61	-	4936	3995	137	29.16	5-43	2	
20/20 Int																	
20/20	47	32	11	372	35*	17.71	-	-	21	-	879	997	48	20.77	4-14	-	

BOYCE, M. A. G. Leicestershire

Name: Matthew (<u>Matt</u>) Andrew Golding Boyce
Role: Left-hand opening bat, right-arm medium bowler
Born: 13 August 1985, Cheltenham
Height: 5ft 10in **Weight:** 11st 4lbs
Nickname: Boycey, Ferret
County debut: 2006
Place in batting averages: 163rd av. 27.33 (2008 150th av. 26.96)
Parents: Anne and Andrew
Marital status: Single
Family links with cricket: 'My father played recreational cricket for more than twenty years and coached youth cricket for ten years. My aunt played

for Cambridge University and my brother for Oakham School 1st XI for three years.'

Education: Oakham School; Nottingham University
Qualifications: 2.1 in Management and Economics
Overseas teams played for: Hoppers Crossing, Melbourne 2003-04
Career highlights to date: 'First-class debut and one-day debut. Scoring a double century [150-ball 225 for Rutland Championship side v Peterborough 2004]'
Cricket moments to forget: 'Going out to bat against Northants without a box on!'
Cricket superstitions: None
Cricketers particularly admired: Graham Thorpe, Mark Ramprakash, Paul Nixon
Young players to look out for: Tom New and Josh Cobb (both Leicestershire)
Other sports played: Rugby (Oakham School *Daily Mail* Cup winner), hockey (Midlands U14 and U16)
Favourite band: The Fray, The Wallflowers
Relaxations: 'Poker, socialising, relaxing in general!'
Extras: County Council Special Award for Youth Cricket. *Rutland Times* Young Cricketer of the Year. Sporting Moment of the Year 2004 (225 – *see above*). Rutland League Teenage Cricketer of the Year. Leading batsman in Leicestershire League 2007
Opinions on cricket: 'In a game where so much is said about Kolpak players, I believe the best young English players will still come through. Chances are for taking, not giving.'
Best batting: 106 Leicestershire v Warwickshire, Edgbaston 2008

2009 Season

	M	Inn	NO	Runs	HS	Avg	100	50	Ct	St	Balls	Runs	Wkts	Avg	BB	5I	10M
Test																	
FC	15	29	2	738	98	27.33	-	5	5	-	0	0	0	-	-	-	-
ODI																	
List A	11	11	0	269	80	24.45	-	1	2	-	0	0	0	-	-		
20/20 Int																	
20/20	10	7	0	145	34	20.71	-	-	2	-	0	0	0	-	-		

Career Performances

	M	Inn	NO	Runs	HS	Avg	100	50	Ct	St	Balls	Runs	Wkts	Avg	BB	5I	10M
Test																	
FC	34	58	3	1427	106	25.94	1	9	7	-	36	61	0	-	-	-	-
ODI																	
List A	24	22	3	544	80	28.63	-	3	4	-	0	0	0	-	-		
20/20 Int																	
20/20	16	12	1	228	34	20.72	-	-	3	-	0	0	0	-	-		

BRAGG, W. D. — Glamorgan

Name: William (<u>Will</u>) David Bragg
Role: Left-hand bat, wicket-keeper
Born: 24 October 1986, Newport, Gwent, South Wales
Height: 5ft 10in **Weight:** 12st 6lbs
Nickname: Braggy, Milf, Braggpot, Pottsy
County debut: 2007
Place in batting averages: 141st av. 30.58
Parents: Susan and Steven
Marital status: Single
Family links with cricket: 'Father and brother have both played for local sides (Malpas CC)'
Education: Rougemont Independent School; Cardiff University

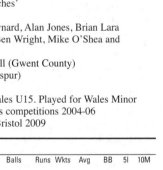

Qualifications: 11 GCSEs, 4 A-levels
Career highlights to date: 'Playing for Glamorgan'
Cricket moments to forget: 'Dropping easy catches'
Cricket superstitions: 'Put box on last'
Cricketers particularly admired: Matthew Maynard, Alan Jones, Brian Lara
Young players to look out for: Tom Maynard, Ben Wright, Mike O'Shea and James Harris (all Glamorgan)
Other sports played: Rugby (for school), football (Gwent County)
Other sports followed: Football (Tottenham Hotspur)
Favourite band: Razorlight
Extras: Scored most runs by any batsman for Wales U15. Played for Wales Minor Counties in the C&G 2005 and in Minor Counties competitions 2004-06
Best batting: 92 Glamorgan v Gloucestershire, Bristol 2009

2009 Season

	M	Inn	NO	Runs	HS	Avg	100	50	Ct	St	Balls	Runs	Wkts	Avg	BB	5I	10M
Test																	
FC	9	12	0	367	92	30.58	-	2	4	-	30	23	0		-	-	-
ODI																	
List A	6	6	0	190	78	31.66	-	1	-	-	0	0	0		-	-	
20/20 Int																	
20/20																	

Career Performances

	M	Inn	NO	Runs	HS	Avg	100	50	Ct	St	Balls	Runs	Wkts	Avg	BB	5I	10M
Test																	
FC	11	16	0	418	92	26.12	-	2	4	-	30	23	0		-	-	-
ODI																	
List A	7	7	1	231	78	38.50	-	1	1	-	0	0	0		-	-	
20/20 Int																	
20/20																	

BREESE, G. R. Durham

Name: <u>Gareth</u> Rohan Breese
Role: Right-hand bat, right-arm
off-spin bowler; all-rounder
Born: 9 January 1976, Montego Bay, Jamaica
Height: 5ft 8in **Weight:** 13st 2lbs
Nickname: Briggy
County debut: 2004
Test debut: 2002-03
Parents: Brian and Jean
Wife and date of marriage: Celia, 13 October 2007
Children: Savannah
Family links with cricket: 'Father played league
cricket in Somerset and Wales – he also played
representative cricket for two parishes in Jamaica
as wicket-keeper/batsman. He has worked in cricket
as far back as I can remember'

Education: Wolmer's Boys School, Kingston; University of Technology, Kingston
Qualifications: 7 CXCs, 2 A-Levels, Diploma in Hotel and Resort Management,
Level 2 coaching
Off-season: 'Training and possibly some coaching courses'
Overseas tours: West Indies U19 to Pakistan and Bangladesh 1995-96; Jamaica to
Malaysia (Commonwealth Games) 1998-99; West Indies A to England 2002; West
Indies to India 2002-03
Overseas teams played for: Jamaica 1995-96 – 2005-06
Career highlights to date: 'Playing in my only Test match and being part of
Durham's success'
Cricket moments to forget: 'My two Test innings'
Cricket superstitions: None
Cricketers particularly admired: Jimmy Adams, Courtney Walsh, Delroy Morgan
(Jamaica), Dale Benkenstein, Gordon Muchall
Young players to look out for: Scott Borthwick (Durham)

Other sports played: 'Rugby and football for the Durham Oldies!!'
Favourite band: Black-Eyed Peas
Relaxations: 'Playing with Celia and Savannah. Gadgets and going to the movies'
Extras: Represented West Indies U19 1994-95. Second-highest wicket-taker in the Busta Cup 2000-01 with 36 (av. 15.11) and in 2001-02 with 44 (av. 20.18). Captain of Jamaica in first-class cricket 2003-04 and in one-day cricket 2004-05. Scored 165* as Durham made 453-9 to beat Somerset at Taunton 2004. Scored century (110) v Middlesex at Lord's 2006, in the process sharing with Dale Benkenstein (125) in a new record fifth-wicket partnership for Durham (222). Scored 121* in Durham's only innings as they defeated Kent to clinch the County title in September 2008. Is a British passport-holder and is not considered an overseas player
Opinions on cricket: 'Not enough is played in schools in the UK.'
Best batting: 165* Durham v Somerset, Taunton 2004
Best bowling: 7-60 Jamaica v Barbados, Bridgetown 2000-01

2009 Season

	M	Inn	NO	Runs	HS	Avg	100	50	Ct	St	Balls	Runs	Wkts	Avg	BB	5I	10M
Test																	
FC	2	2	0	62	48	31.00	-	-	3	-	223	76	6	12.66	4-10	-	-
ODI																	
List A	16	14	4	235	47	23.50	-	-	4	-	624	492	16	30.75	3-34	-	
20/20 Int																	
20/20	10	7	0	78	37	11.14	-	-	4	-	192	235	6	39.16	2-22	-	

Career Performances

	M	Inn	NO	Runs	HS	Avg	100	50	Ct	St	Balls	Runs	Wkts	Avg	BB	5I	10M
Test	1	2	0	5	5	2.50	-	-	1	-	188	135	2	67.50	2-108	-	-
FC	114	182	20	4332	165*	26.74	4	27	95	-	18075	8364	280	29.87	7-60	12	3
ODI																	
List A	138	106	27	1569	68*	19.86	-	3	55	-	5340	4087	146	27.99	5-41	2	
20/20 Int																	
20/20	46	32	6	283	37	10.88	-	-	17	-	817	914	43	21.25	4-14	-	

11. Which Pakistan fast bowler made his Test debut in 1989,
just one day before his 18th birthday?

BRESNAN, T. T. Yorkshire

Name: Timothy (Tim) Thomas Bresnan
Role: Right-hand bat, right-arm fast bowler; all-rounder
Born: 28 February 1985, Pontefract
Height: 6ft 1in **Weight:** 14st 7lbs
Nickname: Brez, Brezzie, Tikka
County debut: 2001 (one-day), 2003 (first-class)
County cap: 2006
ODI debut: 2006
Twenty20 Int debut: 2006
Place in batting averages: 178th av. 25.73
(2008 98th av. 33.73)
Place in bowling averages: 88th av. 36.50
(2008 63rd av. 28.40)
Parents: Julie and Ray
Marital status: Single
Family links with cricket: 'Dad played local league cricket'
Education: Castleford High School; Pontefract New College
Qualifications: 11 GCSEs, UKCC 2 cricket coaching, Advanced Scuba Diver Level 2
Overseas tours: England U17 to Australia 2000-01; Yorkshire U16 to Cape Town 2001; England U19 to Australia and (U19 World Cup) New Zealand 2001-02, to Australia 2002-03, to Bangladesh (U19 World Cup) 2003-04; England VI to Hong Kong 2006; England A to Bangladesh 2006-07; England Performance Programme to India 2007-08; England to South Africa (one-day series) 2009-10. Selected for England Performance Programme squad to India 2008
Overseas teams played for: Sutherland CC, Sydney 2005-06
Career highlights to date: 'Making England debut, Lord's 2006'
Cricket moments to forget: 'First big injury, June 2006'
Cricket superstitions: None
Cricketers particularly admired: Ian Botham
Young players to look out for: Jack Hughes (Yorkshire Academy)
Other sports played: Golf
Other sports followed: Football (Sheffield United)
Favourite band: Razorlight, Snow Patrol
Relaxations: 'PlayStation, cinema'
Extras: Bunbury Festival Best All-rounder and Most Outstanding Player 2000. One-day debut v Kent at Headingley 2001 aged 16 years 102 days, the youngest player to represent Yorkshire since Paul Jarvis in 1981. NBC Denis Compton Award for the most promising young Yorkshire player 2002, 2003. England U19 2002 and 2003. Scored maiden first-class century (116) v Surrey at The Oval 2007, while sharing with Jason Gillespie (123*) in a new record ninth-wicket partnership for Yorkshire (246). Only Rashid took more first-class wickets for the county in 2008.

Called into the England ODI squad in August 2008 as cover for the injured Ryan Sidebottom.Member of the successful England Hong Kong Sixes team in November 2008. England increment contract 2009-10

Best batting: 126* England A v Indians, Chelmsford 2007
Best bowling: 5-42 Yorkshire v Worcestershire, Worcester 2005

2009 Season

	M	Inn	NO	Runs	HS	Avg	100	50	Ct	St	Balls	Runs	Wkts	Avg	BB	5I	10M
Test	2	1	0	9	9	9.00	-	-	2	-	186	97	3	32.33	3-45	-	-
FC	14	17	2	386	97	25.73	-	1	7	-	2662	1168	32	36.50	4-116	-	-
ODI	8	7	4	101	31*	33.66	-	-	-	-	389	329	8	41.12	2-41	-	
List A	14	13	5	132	31*	16.50	-	-	2	-	665	568	18	31.55	4-35	-	
20/20 Int																	
20/20	6	4	1	38	19*	12.66	-	-	1	-	138	157	7	22.42	3-26	-	

Career Performances

	M	Inn	NO	Runs	HS	Avg	100	50	Ct	St	Balls	Runs	Wkts	Avg	BB	5I	10M
Test	2	1	0	9	9	9.00	-	-	2	-	186	97	3	32.33	3-45	-	-
FC	87	116	21	2563	126*	26.97	3	11	38	-	13793	7176	222	32.32	5-42	3	-
ODI	15	13	6	246	80	35.14	-	1	2	-	647	593	14	42.35	2-10	-	
List A	142	98	29	1331	80	19.28	-	3	36	-	5845	4869	141	34.53	4-25	-	
20/20 Int	1	1	1	6	6*		-	-	-	-	12	20	0		-		
20/20	45	33	12	369	42	17.57	-	-	15	-	878	1081	46	23.50	3-21	-	

BRIGGS, D. R.   Hampshire

Name: Daniel (<u>Danny</u>) Richard Briggs
Role: Right-hand bat, slow left-arm orthodox bowler
Born: 30 April 1991, Newport, Isle of Wight
Nickname: Briggsy
County debut: 2009
Overseas tours: England U19 to Bangladesh 2009, to New Zealand (ICC U19 World Cup) 2010
Cricketers particularly admired: Daniel Vettori
Extras: Represented Hampshire in youth cricket from the age of nine. Has also played for Berkshire, Hampshire Academy and Hampshire 2nd XI. Selected for the ECB National Skill Set Programme, Loughborough, 2007. Took 8-96 (3-46 and 5-50) in his England U19 Test debut v Bangladesh in Chittagong, October 2009. Awarded a development contract for 2010

Best batting: 36 Hampshire v Somerset, Rose Bowl 2009
Best bowling: 3-62 Hampshire v Somerset, Rose Bowl 2009

2009 Season

	M	Inn	NO	Runs	HS	Avg	100	50	Ct	St	Balls	Runs	Wkts	Avg	BB	5I	10M
Test																	
FC	3	3	0	37	36	12.33	-	-	1	-	514	295	8	36.87	3-62	-	-
ODI																	
List A	4	1	0	4	4	4.00	-	-	1	-	198	156	2	78.00	2-36	-	
20/20 Int																	
20/20																	

Career Performances

	M	Inn	NO	Runs	HS	Avg	100	50	Ct	St	Balls	Runs	Wkts	Avg	BB	5I	10M
Test																	
FC	3	3	0	37	36	12.33	-	-	1	-	514	295	8	36.87	3-62	-	-
ODI																	
List A	4	1	0	4	4	4.00	-	-	1	-	198	156	2	78.00	2-36	-	
20/20 Int																	
20/20																	

BROAD, S. C. J.   Nottinghamshire

Name: <u>Stuart</u> Christopher John Broad
Role: Left-hand bat, right-arm
fast-medium bowler
Born: 24 June 1986, Nottingham
Height: 6ft 6in **Weight:** 13st
Nickname: Broady
County debut: 2005 (Leicestershire),
2008 (Nottinghamshire)
County cap: 2007 (Leicestershire)
Test debut: 2007
Test debut: 2007-08
ODI debut: 2006
Twenty20 Int debut: 2006
Place in batting averages: 89th av. 38.20
(2008 91st av. 35.70)
Place in bowling averages: 22nd av. 26.08 (2008 100th av. 34.09)
Parents: Carole and Chris
Marital status: Single
Family links with cricket: 'Dad played for Gloucestershire, Nottinghamshire
and England'

Education: Oakham School
Qualifications: 10 GCSEs, 3 A-levels
Overseas tours: Oakham School to South Africa 2000-01; England A to West Indies 2005-06, to Bangladesh 2006-07; England to Australia 2006-07 (Commonwealth Bank Series), to West Indies (World Cup) 2006-07, to South Africa (World 20/20) 2007-08, to Sri Lanka 2007-08, to New Zealand 2007-08, to India (Test and one-day series) 2008, to West Indies (Test and one-day series) 2009, to South Africa (ICC Champions Trophy) 2009, to South Africa 2009-10
Overseas teams played for: Hoppers Crossing CC, Melbourne 2004-05
Career highlights to date: 'England ODI debut v Pakistan 2006. Winning Twenty20 Cup 2006 with Leicestershire'
Cricket superstitions: 'Three warm-up balls before I bowl a new spell'
Cricketers particularly admired: Glenn McGrath, Shaun Pollock
Other sports played: Hockey (Midlands age groups), golf
Other sports followed: Football (Nottingham Forest), rugby (Leicester Tigers)
Relaxations: 'PSP, playing golf, films'
Extras: Leicestershire Young Cricketers' Batsman of the Year 2003. Represented England U19 2005. Cricket Writers' Club Young Cricketer of the Year 2006. Cricket Society Most Promising Young Cricketer of the Year 2006. ECB National Academy 2005-06, 2006-07. NBC Denis Compton Award for most promising young Leicestershire player 2005, 2006, 2007. Man of the Match in the fourth ODI v India at Old Trafford 2007 (4-51/45*). Made Test debut in the second Test v Sri Lanka in Colombo 2007-08. Only Mitchell Johnson and Graeme Swann took more Test wickets in 2009. Claimed four second-innings wickets as England beat South Africa in Durban, December 2009. England 12-month central contract 2009-10
Best batting: 91* Leicestershire v Derbyshire, Leicester 2007
Best bowling: 6-91 England v Australia, Leeds 2009

2009 Season

	M	Inn	NO	Runs	HS	Avg	100	50	Ct	St	Balls	Runs	Wkts	Avg	BB	5I	10M
Test	7	11	2	300	61	33.33	-	2	1	-	1233	747	26	28.73	6-91	2	-
FC	9	13	3	382	61	38.20	-	3	3	-	1611	887	34	26.08	6-91	3	-
ODI	5	4	1	32	22	10.66	-	-	-	-	273	261	8	32.62	4-46	-	
List A	5	4	1	32	22	10.66	-	-	-	-	273	261	8	32.62	4-46	-	
20/20 Int	6	3	2	22	10*	22.00	-	-	3	-	120	137	8	17.12	3-17	-	
20/20	6	3	2	22	10*	22.00	-	-	3	-	120	137	8	17.12	3-17	-	

Career Performances

	M	Inn	NO	Runs	HS	Avg	100	50	Ct	St	Balls	Runs	Wkts	Avg	BB	5I	10M
Test	22	31	6	767	76	30.68	-	5	5	-	4187	2290	64	35.78	6-91	3	-
FC	61	77	18	1569	91*	26.59	-	11	17	-	10534	6005	201	29.87	6-91	10	-
ODI	55	36	14	328	45*	14.90	-	-	13	-	2733	2340	88	26.59	5-23	1	
List A	71	41	15	363	45*	13.96	-	-	15	-	3491	3000	111	27.02	5-23	1	
20/20 Int	18	10	4	36	10*	6.00	-	-	6	-	390	518	22	23.54	3-17	-	
20/20	29	11	5	45	10*	7.50	-	-	7	-	642	727	37	19.64	3-13	-	

BROOKS, J. A.   Northamptonshire

Name: Jack Alexander Brooks
Role: Right-hand bat, right-arm
fast-medium bowler
Born: 4 June 1984, Tiddington, Oxfordshire
Height: 6ft 2in   **Weight:** 13st 2lbs
Nickname: Brooksy, Ferret, Susan Boyle, SuBo,
Boyley, Willis, Gianluigi Von Burgernips, Colin
Milburn, Old School Cricketer, Headband Warrior,
DK Lillee, Caravan, Cousin Slayer, Garth, The Trio,
Therapist, The Animal, JB, Yorath
County debut: 2009
Parents: Donny B and Sue
Marital status: Single

Family links with cricket: 'Brother, Nathan,
represented Oxfordshire Development XI and now
plays for local village sides Dinton and Tiddington. Father, Don, played and captained
Tiddington for 100 years!'
Education: Wheatley Park Secondary School
Qualifications: Level 2 coaching, farmer. 'Honours degree in Life'
Career outside cricket: 'Worked as a sales rep for three years prior to cricket'
Off-season: 'Will be spending 12 weeks in Perth, Australia, playing club cricket'
Overseas teams played for: Willetton Dragons CC, Perth 2004-05
Career highlights to date: 'Signing a pro contract with Northants after playing
village cricket until I was 20. Playing Australia on my first-class debut and picking
up the wickets of Andrew McDonald and Mitchell Johnson...cue bizarre celebrations'
Cricket moments to forget: 'Dropping two catches on my TV debut in Pro40 v
Warwickshire. Whenever I bowl badly or drop a catch'
Cricket superstitions: 'Wear a headband when bowling'
Favourite sledging line: '"Bowl him a single mum and see if he can pull that" –
aimed at a friend who was a compulsive hooker and puller, and was, at the time,
dating a single mother'
Cricketers particularly admired: Colin Milburn, Alan Donald, Curtly Ambrose,
Dennis Lillee. 'Any old-school cricketer'
Young players to look out for: Rupert Evans (Oxfordshire), Graeme White
(Nottinghamshire), David Sales (Northamptonshire)
Other sports played: Football ('In my youth I was billed as the new Geoff Horsfield
before I chose cricket'), rugby, squash, pool
Other sports followed: Football (Oxford United)
Favourite band: DJ Hyper, Not My Day, Juliet The Sun, Foo Fighters, Oasis, Red
Hot Chili Peppers, Bob Dylan
Relaxations: 'Surfing, travelling, sleeping'

Extras: Oxfordshire Sportsman of the Year nominee 2008. Was on trial at Surrey and Northamptonshire, and played for Oxfordshire, during the 2008 season before signing a contract with Northamptonshire

Opinions on cricket: 'There's always room for an old-school cricketer in the modern game.'

Best batting: 10* Northamptonshire v Australia, Northampton 2009
10* Northamptonshire v Glamorgan, Northampton 2009

Best bowling: 4-76 Northamptonshire v Derbyshire, Chesterfield 2009

2009 Season

	M	Inn	NO	Runs	HS	Avg	100	50	Ct	St	Balls	Runs	Wkts	Avg	BB	5I	10M
Test																	
FC	3	3	3	20	10*		-	-	1	-	486	325	9	36.11	4-76	-	-
ODI																	
List A	3	1	0	10	10	10.00	-	-	-	-	108	99	0		-	-	
20/20 Int																	
20/20																	

Career Performances

	M	Inn	NO	Runs	HS	Avg	100	50	Ct	St	Balls	Runs	Wkts	Avg	BB	5I	10M
Test																	
FC	3	3	3	20	10*		-	-	1	-	486	325	9	36.11	4-76	-	-
ODI																	
List A	3	1	0	10	10	10.00	-	-	-	-	108	99	0		-	-	
20/20 Int																	
20/20																	

12. Ian Botham passed 5,000 Test match runs at the Oval in 1987. Which Pakistan batsman collected his 6,000th run during the same match?

BROPHY, G. L.   Yorkshire

Name: <u>Gerard</u> Louis Brophy
Role: Right-hand bat, wicket-keeper
Born: 26 November 1975, Welkom,
South Africa
Height: 5ft 11in   **Weight:** 12st
Nickname: Scuba, Broph
County debut: 2002 (Northamptonshire), 2006
(Yorkshire)
County cap: 2009 (Yorkshire)
Place in batting averages: 52nd av. 44.00 (2008
169th av. 23.73)
Parents: Gerard and Trish
Wife and date of marriage: Alison,
3 January 2004

Children: Georgia Beau, 22 December 2006
Education: Christian Brothers College, Boksburg; Wits Technikon, Gauteng
(both South Africa)
Qualifications: Marketing Diploma, Level 2 coach
Overseas tours: South Africa U17 to England 1993; South Africa Academy to
Zimbabwe 1998-99
Overseas teams played for: Gauteng 1996-97 – 1998-99; Free State 1999-2000 –
2000-01
Career highlights to date: 'Captaincy of Free State 2000-01. First dismissal [in
collaboration] with Allan Donald'
Cricket moments to forget: 'Messing up a live TV interview'
Cricket superstitions: 'Right pad on first and right glove on first'
Cricketers particularly admired: Ray Jennings, Ian Healy, Allan Donald,
Hansie Cronje
Other sports played: Golf, rugby
Other sports followed: Golf, rugby
Favourite band: Coldplay
Relaxations: 'Fishing, travelling, braais, scuba diving'
Extras: Captained South Africa U17. Played for Ireland in the NatWest 2000.
Played hockey for East Transvaal in 1991. Holds a British passport and is not
considered an overseas player.
Opinions on cricket: 'The introduction of IPL and ICL is fantastic, the exposure
for cricketers and potential for wealth is fantastic (as long as you can crack the
Twenty20 version)'
Best batting: 185 South Africa Academy v ZCU President's XI, Harare (S) 1998-99

2009 Season

	M	Inn	NO	Runs	HS	Avg	100	50	Ct	St	Balls	Runs	Wkts	Avg	BB	5I	10M
Test																	
FC	14	22	5	748	99	44.00	-	6	37	2	6	0	0		-	-	-
ODI																	
List A	6	5	2	201	68*	67.00	-	2	12	1	0	0	0		-	-	
20/20 Int																	
20/20	4	3	1	42	26	21.00	-	-	-	1	0	0	0		-	-	

Career Performances

	M	Inn	NO	Runs	HS	Avg	100	50	Ct	St	Balls	Runs	Wkts	Avg	BB	5I	10M
Test																	
FC	106	167	21	4646	185	31.82	6	25	266	21	12	1	0		-	-	-
ODI																	
List A	101	82	17	1677	68*	25.80	-	10	102	19	0	0	0		-	-	
20/20 Int																	
20/20	36	32	8	581	57*	24.20	-	2	14	5	0	0	0		-	-	

BROWN, A. D. Nottinghamshire

Name: Alistair Duncan Brown
Role: Right-hand bat, right-arm off-spin bowler, occasional wicket-keeper
Born: 11 February 1970, Beckenham
Height: 5ft 10in **Weight:** 12st 7lbs
Nickname: The Lord
County debut: 1990 (one-day, Surrey), 1992 (first-class, Surrey)
County cap: 1994 (Surrey)
Benefit: 2002 (Surrey)
ODI debut: 1996
1000 runs in a season: 8
1st-Class 200s: 3
List A 200s: 2
Place in batting averages: 79th av. 40.42 (2008 87th av. 36.00)
Parents: Robert and Ann
Wife and date of marriage: Sarah, 10 October 1998
Children: Max Charles, 9 March 2001; Joe Robert, 11 March 2003
Family links with cricket: Father played for Surrey Young Amateurs in the 1950s

Education: Caterham School
Qualifications: 5 O-levels, Level 2 coaching
Overseas tours: England VI to Singapore 1993, 1994, 1995, to Hong Kong 1997; England to Sharjah (Champions Trophy) 1997-98, to Bangladesh (Wills International Cup) 1998-99
Overseas teams played for: North Perth, Western Australia 1989-90
Career highlights to date: '118 v India at Old Trafford 1996; 203 v Hampshire at Guildford 1997; 268 v Glamorgan at The Oval 2002'
Cricket moments to forget: 'A great couple of days in Ireland!'
Cricket superstitions: 'Always get to the ground before 11 a.m.'
Cricketers particularly admired: Ian Botham, Viv Richards
Other sports played: Football, golf
Other sports followed: Football (West Ham United), rugby union (London Wasps)
Favourite band: Roachford, Snow Patrol
Relaxations: 'Golf and sleep'
Extras: Man of the Match for his 118 against India in the third ODI at Old Trafford 1996. Recorded the highest-ever score in the Sunday League with 203 off 119 balls against Hampshire at Guildford in 1997 and received an individual award at the PCA dinner for that achievement. Joint winner (with Carl Hooper) of the EDS Walter Lawrence Trophy for the fastest first-class 100 of the 1998 season (72 balls v Northants at The Oval). Surrey CCC Batsman of the Season 2001. Scored 160-ball 268 out of 438-5 v Glamorgan at The Oval in the C&G 2002 – it set a new record for the highest individual score in professional one-day cricket worldwide and Brown also became the first batsman to have scored two double centuries in one-day cricket. Scored 154 v Lancashire at Old Trafford 2004 to complete full set of first-class hundreds against all 17 other counties. Scored 97-ball 176 v Gloucestershire at The Oval in the Friends Provident 2007, in the process sharing with James Benning (152) in a Surrey record one-day partnership (294) as the county posted a world record List A total of 496-4. Signed a two-year contract with Nottinghamshire in January 2009
Best batting: 295* Surrey v Leicestershire, Oakham School 2000
Best bowling: 3-25 Surrey v Somerset, Guildford 2006

2009 Season

	M	Inn	NO	Runs	HS	Avg	100	50	Ct	St	Balls	Runs	Wkts	Avg	BB	5I	10M
Test																	
FC	16	24	3	849	148	40.42	1	6	18	-	139	83	1	83.00	1-16	-	-
ODI																	
List A	14	13	0	214	89	16.46	-	1	2	-	0	0	0		-	-	
20/20 Int																	
20/20	10	10	0	251	72	25.10	-	3	2	-	0	0	0		-	-	

Career Performances

	M	Inn	NO	Runs	HS	Avg	100	50	Ct	St	Balls	Runs	Wkts	Avg	BB	5I	10M
Test																	
FC	263	412	46	15806	295*	43.18	45	68	264	1	1363	718	6	119.66	3-25	-	-
ODI	16	16	0	354	118	22.12	1	1	6	-	6	5	0		-	-	
List A	390	373	19	11052	268	31.22	19	50	128	-	520	561	14	40.07	3-39	-	
20/20 Int																	
20/20	61	61	1	1421	83	23.68	-	10	35	-	2	2	0			-	-

BROWN, B. C. Sussex

Name: <u>Ben</u> Christopher Brown
Role: Right-hand bat, wicket-keeper
Born: 23 November 1988, Crawley
Height: 5ft 8in **Weight:** 11st 10lbs
County debut: 2007
Parents: Diana and Chris
Marital status: Single
Education: Ardingly College
Qualifications: 9 GCSEs, 2 A-levels, Level 2 coaching, NVQ in Cricket
Overseas tours: Sussex Academy to Cape Town 2005; England U19 to Malaysia 2006-07, to Malaysia (U19 World Cup) 2007-08
Career highlights to date: 'Getting my first contract at Sussex'
Cricket moments to forget: 'Running into Billy Godleman and subsequently being run out for 0 on TV debut!'
Cricket superstitions: None
Cricketers particularly admired: Alec Stewart, Adam Gilchrist
Young players to look out for: Matt Machan, Will Beer and Michael Thornely (all Sussex),
Other sports played: Football
Other sports followed: Football (Chelsea FC)
Extras: Represented England U19 2007. Played for England U19 against New Zealand during the 2008 tour. Signed a new two-year contract in October 2008
Opinions on cricket: 'I would prefer to see fewer Kolpak players in county cricket and still have two overseas players for young players to learn from and compete against.'
Best batting: 46 Sussex v Sri Lanka A, Hove 2007

2009 Season

	M	Inn	NO	Runs	HS	Avg	100	50	Ct	St	Balls	Runs	Wkts	Avg	BB	5I	10M
Test																	
FC																	
ODI																	
List A	7	3	2	27	18*	27.00	-	-	5	1	0	0	0		-	-	
20/20 Int																	
20/20	8	4	1	13	7	4.33	-	-	3	-	0	0	0		-	-	

Career Performances

	M	Inn	NO	Runs	HS	Avg	100	50	Ct	St	Balls	Runs	Wkts	Avg	BB	5I	10M
Test																	
FC	1	1	0	46	46	46.00	-	-	-	-	0	0	0		-	-	-
ODI																	
List A	9	5	2	31	18*	10.33	-	-	5	1	0	0	0		-	-	
20/20 Int																	
20/20	9	5	1	19	7	4.75	-	-	3	-	0	0	0		-	-	

BROWN, D. O. Glamorgan

Name: <u>David</u> Owen Brown
Role: Right-hand bat, right-arm
fast-medium bowler; all-rounder
Born: 8 December 1982, Burnley, Lancashire
Height: 6ft **Weight:** 13st 7lbs
Nickname: Wally, Bomber, Dangerous Dave
County debut: 2006 (Gloucestershire)
County cap: 2006 (Gloucestershire)
Place in batting averages: (2008 93rd av. 35.00)
Place in bowling averages: (2008 49th av. 27.00)
Parents: Peter and Valerie
Marital status: Single
Family links with cricket: 'Brother Michael played
at Hampshire and Middlesex, now with Surrey. Dad
played league cricket for many years, mum made
'cracking' teas.'
Education: Queen Elizabeth's Grammar School, Blackburn; Collingwood College,
Durham University 2002-2005
Qualifications: 10 GCSEs, 4 A-levels, BA (Hons) Sport in the Community
Career outside cricket: 'Open to offers – haven't decided'
Overseas tours: MCC B to Nepal 2003; MCC A to Canada 2005; Gloucestershire
CCC to Pretoria 2006 and 2007

Overseas teams played for: Claremont-Nedlands, Perth 2001-02; Perth CC 2005-06, 2006-07; Northcote CC, Melbourne, 2007-08
Career highlights to date: 'C&G debut for Gloucestershire v Surrey' (*see Extras*). Championship debut for Gloucestershire. Any win'
Cricket moments to forget: 'Any dropped catch. Any time I self-destruct. Any loss'
Cricketers particularly admired: Dale Benkenstein, Michael Brown, Craig Spearman, Marcus North, Ian Harvey
Young players to look out for: Jonathan Clare, Steve Snell, Josh Cobb, Bharat Tripathi
Other sports played: Golf – 'great driver, terrible putter'. Football – 'ex-centre forward, now play Owen Hargreaves role just in front of the back four'
Other sports followed: Football (Burnley FC)
Favourite band: Dire Straits, The Carpenters, Leona Lewis, Bon Jovi
Relaxations: 'Championship Manager, golf, going out.'
Extras: Part of the Burnley CC 2000 side that produced four current professional players (D. Brown, M. Brown, S. Anderson and J. Clare). Played for Durham UCCE 2003-05. Represented British Universities 2005. Struck 26-ball 63* on one-day debut v Surrey at Bristol in the C&G 2006. Released by Gloucestershire in October 2009, joined Glamorgan the following month
Best batting: 83 Gloucestershire v Worcestershire, Cheltenham 2008
Best bowling: 5-38 Gloucestershire v Derbyshire, Derby 2008

2009 Season

	M	Inn	NO	Runs	HS	Avg	100	50	Ct	St	Balls	Runs	Wkts	Avg	BB	5I	10M
Test																	
FC																	
ODI																	
List A	8	5	1	52	19*	13.00	-	-	5	-	66	92	1	92.00	1-36	-	
20/20 Int																	
20/20	4	4	0	101	56	25.25	-	1	3	-	24	36	1	36.00	1-25	-	

Career Performances

	M	Inn	NO	Runs	HS	Avg	100	50	Ct	St	Balls	Runs	Wkts	Avg	BB	5I	10M
Test																	
FC	23	39	4	975	83	27.85	-	7	12	-	1755	1251	28	44.67	5-38	1	-
ODI																	
List A	28	22	6	361	63*	22.56	-	1	10	-	504	521	12	43.41	3-29	-	
20/20 Int																	
20/20	18	15	1	263	56	18.78	-	1	6	-	60	71	4	17.75	1-11	-	

BROWN, J. F.   Nottinghamshire

Name: <u>Jason</u> Fred Brown
Role: Right-hand bat, off-spin bowler
Born: 10 October 1974,
Newcastle-under-Lyme
Height: 6ft **Weight:** 13st
Nickname: Cheese, Fish, Brownie
County debut: 1996 (Northamptonshire)
County cap: 2000 (Northamptonshire)
Benefit: 2008 (Northamptonshire)
50 wickets in a season: 3
Place in bowling averages: (2008 149th av. 82.50)
Parents: Peter and Cynthia
Wife and date of marriage: Sam,
26 September 1998
Children: Millie

Education: St Margaret Ward RC School, Stoke-on-Trent
Qualifications: 9 GCSEs, Level 1 coaching
Overseas tours: Kidsgrove League U18 to Australia 1990; Northants CCC to
Zimbabwe 1998, to Grenada 2000; England A to West Indies 2000-01; England to Sri
Lanka 2000-01
Overseas teams played for: North East Valley, Dunedin, New Zealand 1996-97
Cricketers particularly admired: John Emburey, Carl Hooper
Other sports played: Golf
Other sports followed: Football (Port Vale)
Relaxations: 'Reading, listening to music'
Extras: Represented Staffordshire at all junior levels, in Minor Counties, and in the
NatWest 1995. Once took 10-16 in a Kidsgrove League game against Haslington U18
playing for Sandyford U18. Took 100th first-class wicket in 23rd match, v Sussex at
Northampton 2000, going on to take his 50th wicket of the season in the same game,
only his seventh of the summer. Took 5-27 v Somerset at Northampton 2003, the best
return by a Northants bowler in the Twenty20 Cup. C&G Man of the Match award for
his 5-19 v Cambridgeshire at Northampton 2004. Joined Nottinghamshire for 2009.
Released by Nottinghamshire at the end of the 2009 season
Best batting: 38 Northamptonshire v Hampshire, Northampton 2003
Best bowling: 7-69 Northamptonshire v Durham, Riverside 2003

2009 Season

	M	Inn	NO	Runs	HS	Avg	100	50	Ct	St	Balls	Runs	Wkts	Avg	BB	5I	10M
Test																	
FC	1	0	0	0	0	-	-	-	-	6	4	0		-	-	-	
ODI																	
List A	7	5	4	10	5	10.00	-	-	-	-	294	257	3	85.66	2-36	-	
20/20 Int																	
20/20	2	0	0	0	0		-	-	2	-	30	49	0		-	-	

Career Performances

	M	Inn	NO	Runs	HS	Avg	100	50	Ct	St	Balls	Runs	Wkts	Avg	BB	5I	10M
Test																	
FC	130	147	59	655	38	7.44	-	-	26	-	31146	14039	414	33.91	7-69	22	5
ODI																	
List A	160	61	38	146	16	6.34	-	-	29	-	7526	5517	140	39.40	5-19	1	
20/20 Int																	
20/20	44	4	3	23	13*	23.00	-	-	11	-	863	1057	41	25.78	5-27	1	

BROWN, K. R. — Lancashire

Name: Karl Robert Brown
Role: Right-hand bat, right-arm medium bowler
Born: 17 May 1988, Bolton
Height: 5ft 11in **Weight:** 11st 7lbs
Nickname: Brownie, Charlie
County debut: 2006
Parents: Paul and Lorraine
Marital status: Single
Family links with cricket: Father a club cricketer with Atherton CC for over 30 years and had two seasons as club professional at Clifton CC in the Bolton Association
Education: Hesketh Fletcher CE, Atherton, Lancashire
Qualifications: 8 GCSEs
Overseas tours: England U16 to South Africa 2003-04; England U19 to Bangladesh 2005-06, to Malaysia 2006-07
Overseas teams played for: Noble Park, Victoria, 2007-08
Career highlights: 'Walking out to bat in my first County Championship game in 2008'
Cricket moments to forget: 'Walking back about three minutes later after getting a duck!'

Cricket superstitions: None
Cricketers particularly admired: Andrew Flintoff, Stuart Law
Other sports played: Golf. 'Used to play football'
Other sports followed: Football (Bolton Wanderers), golf
Favourite band/music: The Courteeners
Relaxations: 'My computer, music, Facebook, etc.'
Extras: Lancashire Junior Player of the Year 2004. Represented England U19 2007. Appeared in both first-class and one-day games in 2008. NBC Denis Compton Award for most promising young Lancashire player 2008
Opinions on cricket: 'The game seems to be getting bigger and bigger – probably because of Twenty20, but that must be a good thing for all forms of cricket.'
Best batting: 40 Lancashire v Kent, Liverpool 2008
Best bowling: 2-30 Lancashire v Nottinghamshire, Trent Bridge 2009

2009 Season

	M	Inn	NO	Runs	HS	Avg	100	50	Ct	St	Balls	Runs	Wkts	Avg	BB	5I	10M
Test																	
FC	2	4	0	40	19	10.00	-	-	5	-	48	37	2	18.50	2-30	-	-
ODI																	
List A																		
20/20 Int																		
20/20																		

Career Performances

	M	Inn	NO	Runs	HS	Avg	100	50	Ct	St	Balls	Runs	Wkts	Avg	BB	5I	10M
Test																		
FC	7	12	1	156	40	14.18	-	-	7	-	66	44	2	22.00	2-30	-	-
ODI																		
List A	5	5	0	72	41	14.40	-	-	1	-	0	0	0		-	-	
20/20 Int																		
20/20																		

13. What was the Bangladesh first-innings total in the First Test in England in May 2005?

BROWN, M. J.   Surrey

Name: <u>Michael</u> James Brown
Role: Right-hand bat, wicket-keeper
Born: 9 February 1980, Burnley
Height: 6ft **Weight:** 12st
Nickname: Fagmo, Weasel, Stone, Dawson
County debut: 1999 (Middlesex),
2004 (Hampshire), 2009 (Surrey)
County cap: 2007 (Hampshire)
1000 runs in a season: 1
Place in batting averages: 103rd av. 36.74
(2008 61st av. 40.86)
Parents: Peter and Valerie
Marital status: Single
Family links with cricket: 'Father played league
cricket for 30 years. Mum makes great tuna
sandwiches.' Younger brother David played for DUCCE and Gloucestershire and now
plays for Glamorgan
Education: Queen Elizabeth's Grammar School, Blackburn; Durham University
Qualifications: 10 GCSEs, 4 A-levels, 2.1 Economics/Politics
Career outside cricket: 'Stockbroking'
Overseas teams played for: Western Province CC, Cape Town 1998-99; Fremantle
CC 2002-05; South Perth CC 2005-06
Career highlights to date: 'Durham 2007 – 56* and 126* gained a draw for
Hampshire'
Cricket moments to forget: 'Leaving straight balls'
Cricket superstitions: 'Always tap non-striker's end four times at end of over when
at that end'
Cricketers particularly admired: Dale Benkenstein, Nic Pothas, Michael Yardy
Young players to look out for: Liam Dawson, Ben Howell
Other sports played: Football ('badly'), golf ('occasional bandit')
Other sports followed: Football (Burnley FC)
Favourite band: Goo Goo Dolls, Razorlight, The Killers, Oasis
Relaxations: 'Golf, shares'
Extras: Represented ECB U19 A v Pakistan U19 1998. Played for Durham UCCE and
represented British Universities 2001, 2002. 'Was at non-striker's end as five wickets
fell in one over, Middlesex 2nd XI v Glamorgan 2nd XI, July 2001.' Carried bat for
56* v Durham at Riverside 2007 (as Ottis Gibson took all ten Hampshire wickets),
following up with 126* in the second innings (out of 262-9) to save the game. Joined
Surrey for 2009
Best batting: 133 Hampshire v LUCCE, Rose Bowl 2006

2009 Season

	M	Inn	NO	Runs	HS	Avg	100	50	Ct	St	Balls	Runs	Wkts	Avg	BB	5I	10M
Test																	
FC	16	28	1	992	120	36.74	2	4	7	-	18	20	0		-	-	-
ODI																	
List A	15	15	0	557	87	37.13	-	5	2	-	0	0	0		-	-	
20/20 Int																	
20/20	2	2	0	100	77	50.00	-	1	-	-	0	0	0		-	-	

Career Performances

	M	Inn	NO	Runs	HS	Avg	100	50	Ct	St	Balls	Runs	Wkts	Avg	BB	5I	10M
Test																	
FC	92	164	16	5131	133	34.66	9	28	71	-	18	20	0		-	-	-
ODI																	
List A	30	29	2	922	96*	34.14	-	7	9	-	0	0	0		-	-	
20/20 Int																	
20/20	12	12	1	284	77	25.81	-	1	4	-	0	0	0		-	-	

BUCK, N. L.   Leicestershire

Name: <u>Nathan</u> Liam Buck
Role: Right-hand bat, right-arm fast-medium bowler
Born: 26 April 1991, Leicester
Height: 6ft 2in **Weight:** 12st 3lbs
Nickname: Bucky, Rogers
County debut: 2009
Parents: Julie and John
Marital status: Single
Education: Ashby School, Ashby-de-la-Zouch, Leicestershire
Qualifications: 11 GCSEs, 3A-Levels
Overseas tours: England U19 to South Africa 2009, to New Zealand (ICC U19 World Cup) 2009-10
Career highlights to date: 'My first first-class wicket – Mark Ramprakash, on my debut'
Cricket moments to forget: 'None as yet!'
Cricketers particularly admired: Dale Steyn, James Anderson
Other sports followed: Football (Leicester City)
Favourite band: Dizzee Rascal, Calvin Harris
Relaxations: 'Socialising and eating out'
Extras: Trained with Stuart Broad, Simon Jones and Graham Onions at the National Performance Centre in 2006, aged 15. Has represented England at U16 and U17 level.

Plays club cricket for Loughborough Town CC. Took 28 wickets at an average of 20.46 in all competitions in 2007. Leicestershire 2nd XI 2007-08. Signed a three-year contract with Leicestershire in June 2009
Best batting: 24* Leicestershire v Derbyshire, Leicester 2009
Best bowling: 1-35 Leicestershire v LUCCE, Leicester 2009

2009 Season

	M	Inn	NO	Runs	HS	Avg	100	50	Ct	St	Balls	Runs	Wkts	Avg	BB	5I	10M
Test																	
FC	4	5	2	29	24*	9.66	-	-	1	-	528	276	3	92.00	1-35	-	-
ODI																	
List A	4	1	0	21	21	21.00	-	-	1	-	150	151	4	37.75	2-38	-	
20/20 Int																	
20/20																	

Career Performances

	M	Inn	NO	Runs	HS	Avg	100	50	Ct	St	Balls	Runs	Wkts	Avg	BB	5I	10M
Test																	
FC	4	5	2	29	24*	9.66	-	-	1	-	528	276	3	92.00	1-35	-	-
ODI																	
List A	4	1	0	21	21	21.00	-	-	1	-	150	151	4	37.75	2-38	-	
20/20 Int																	
20/20																	

BURKE, J. E.   Somerset

Name: James Edward Burke
Role: Right-hand bat, right-arm medium-fast bowler; all-rounder
Born: 25 January 1991, Plymouth, Devon
County debut: No first-team appearances
Education: Plymouth College
Overseas tours: England U17 to New Zealand 2008. England U19 to South Africa 2009, to India 2009
Extras: Was the first Plymouth College pupil in over 20 years to score two centuries in a season at U12 level in 2003. Devon Cricket Board Youth Awards Cricketer of the Year 2005. ECB U18 Scholarship Programme 2008. Has played for Sidmouth CC (2007), Exmouth CC (2008), Devon CCC, Somerset Academy, Somerset Second XI and West of England

BURROWS, T. G.   Hampshire

Name: Thomas (<u>Tom</u>) George Burrows
Role: Right-hand bat, wicket-keeper
Born: 5 May 1985, Reading, Berkshire
Height: 5ft 8in **Weight:** 10st 10lbs
Nickname: TB
County debut: 2005 (*see Extras*)
Place in batting averages: 258th av. 13.00
Parents: Tony and Victoria
Marital status: Single
Family links with cricket: 'My father was briefly
on Gloucestershire groundstaff and played club
cricket'
Education: Reading School; Solent University
Qualifications: 12 GCSEs, 4 AS-levels,
3 A-levels, Level 1 cricket coach

Overseas tours: MCC to Namibia and Uganda 2004-05
Overseas teams played for: Melville CC, Perth 2003-04
Career highlights to date: 'First-class debut v Kent, scoring 42 and putting on 131
with Shane Warne when we were 130-7'
Cricket moments to forget: 'Any dropped catch'
Cricket superstitions: 'Left pad on first'
Cricketers particularly admired: Adi Aymes, Jack Russell, Steve Waugh,
John Crawley
Other sports played: Rugby, football
Other sports followed: Football (Chelsea), rugby (London Irish)
Favourite band: Gavin DeGraw
Relaxations: 'Watching films'
Extras: Appeared as substitute wicket-keeper for Hampshire v Yorkshire at The Rose
Bowl 2002 but did not make full debut until 2005. Played for Berkshire in the C&G
2003. Released by Hampshire at the end of the 2009 season
Best batting: 42 Hampshire v Kent, Canterbury 2005

2009 Season

	M	Inn	NO	Runs	HS	Avg	100	50	Ct	St	Balls	Runs	Wkts	Avg	BB	5I	10M
Test																	
FC	6	7	1	78	32	13.00	-	-	14	1	0	0	0		-	-	-
ODI																	
List A	7	3	0	33	25	11.00	-	-	6	-	0	0	0		-	-	
20/20 Int																	
20/20	1	1	0	0	0	0.00	-	-	2	-	0	0	0		-	-	

Career Performances

	M	Inn	NO	Runs	HS	Avg	100	50	Ct	St	Balls	Runs	Wkts	Avg	BB	5I	10M
Test																	
FC	12	16	3	247	42	19.00	-	-	36	1	0	0	0		-	-	-
ODI																	
List A	10	6	1	51	25	10.20	-	-	9	2	0	0	0		-	-	
20/20 Int																	
20/20	2	1	0	0	0	0.00	-	-	2	-	0	0	0		-	-	

BURTON, D. A. Middlesex

Name: <u>David</u> Alexander Burton
Role: Right-hand bat, right-arm
fast-medium bowler
Born: 23 August 1985, Dulwich, London
Height: 5ft 11in **Weight:** 11st 3lbs
Nickname: Burts, Burtna, DB
County debut: 2006 (Gloucestershire), 2008
(Middlesex)
County cap: 2006 (Gloucestershire)
Parents: Denise Careless and
Cuthbert Burton
Education: Sacred Heart RC Secondary School,
Camberwell; Lambeth College, Vauxhall
Qualifications: 2 GCSEs, First Diploma in
Electronic Engineering, Diploma in Electronics
and PC Systems, Levels 1 and 2 coaching
Career outside cricket: 'Coaching, modelling'
Off-season: 'Coaching to continue earning a living, developing my game, and
furthering my career outside cricket.'
Career highlights to date: '52* for Gloucestershire v Glamorgan [2006]; 5-68 for
Middlesex v Gloucestershire [2009]'
Cricket moments to forget: 'Getting hit for 24 runs off three overs in my first
televised game for Middlesex.'
Cricketers particularly admired: Darren Gough, Curtly Ambrose, Mark Butcher,
Allan Donald, Angus Fraser
Young players to look out for: Chris Thompson (Leicestershire), Gemaal Hussain
(Gloucestershire)
Other sports played: Mountain biking, BMX
Other sports followed: Mountain biking, BMX, basketball, athletics (Jamaica)
Favourite band: Ginuwine
Relaxations: 'Driving, walking, riding, relaxing with my girlfriend, computers'

Extras: Played for South London Schools Hobbs Trophy runners-up side 2000.
Dulwich CC Player of the Year 2006. Scored 52* on first-class debut at Cardiff 2006,
in the process sharing with Mark Hardinges (101) in a record ninth-wicket partnership
for Gloucestershire in matches v Glamorgan (128). Released by Middlesex at the end
of the 2009 season.

Opinions on cricket: 'Every ball and run represents you, and only you can write your
own article.'

Best batting: 52* Gloucestershire v Glamorgan, Cardiff 2006
Best bowling: 5-68 Middlesex v Gloucestershire, Bristol 2009

2009 Season

	M	Inn	NO	Runs	HS	Avg	100	50	Ct	St	Balls	Runs	Wkts	Avg	BB	5I	10M
Test																	
FC	2	4	2	3	2*	1.50	-	-	-	-	320	249	8	31.12	5-68	1	-
ODI																	
List A	3	1	0	2	2	2.00	-	-	1	-	90	94	2	47.00	1-26	-	
20/20 Int																	
20/20	1	0	0	0	0		-	-	-	-	24	13	2	6.50	2-13	-	

Career Performances

	M	Inn	NO	Runs	HS	Avg	100	50	Ct	St	Balls	Runs	Wkts	Avg	BB	5I	10M
Test																	
FC	4	6	3	56	52*	18.66	-	1	-	-	578	475	9	52.77	5-68	1	-
ODI																	
List A	3	1	0	2	2	2.00	-	-	1	-	90	94	2	47.00	1-26	-	
20/20 Int																	
20/20	3	0	0	0	0		-	-	1	-	54	51	4	12.75	2-13	-	

BUTCHER, M. A.   Surrey

Name: <u>Mark</u> Alan Butcher
Role: Left-hand bat, right-arm medium bowler,
Born: 23 August 1972, Croydon, Surrey
Height: 5ft 11in **Weight:** 13st
Nickname: Butch, Baz
County debut: 1991 (one-day),
1992 (first-class)
County cap: 1996
Benefit: 2005
Test debut: 1997
1000 runs in a season: 8
1st-Class 200s: 3
Place in batting averages: 67th av. 41.83
(2008 10th av. 57.88)
Parents: Alan and Elaine
Children: Alita, 1999

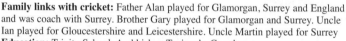

Family links with cricket: Father Alan played for Glamorgan, Surrey and England and was coach with Surrey. Brother Gary played for Glamorgan and Surrey. Uncle Ian played for Gloucestershire and Leicestershire. Uncle Martin played for Surrey
Education: Trinity School; Archbishop Tenison's, Croydon
Qualifications: 5 O-levels, senior coaching award
Career outside cricket: Singer, guitar player
Overseas tours: England YC to New Zealand 1990-91; Surrey to Dubai 1990, 1993, to Perth 1995; England A to Australia 1996-97; England to West Indies 1997-98, to Australia 1998-99, to South Africa 1999-2000, to India and New Zealand 2001-02, to Australia 2002-03, to Bangladesh and Sri Lanka 2003-04, to West Indies 2003-04, to South Africa 2004-05
Overseas teams played for: South Melbourne, Australia 1993-94; North Perth, Australia 1994-95
Cricketers particularly admired: Ian Botham, David Gower, Viv Richards, Larry Gomes, Graham Thorpe, Alec Stewart, Michael Holding, Andrew Flintoff
Other sports followed: Football (Crystal Palace)
Relaxations: 'Music, playing the guitar, novels, wine'
Extras: Played his first game for Surrey in 1991 against his father's Glamorgan in the Refuge Assurance League at The Oval, the first-ever match of any sort between first-class counties in which a father and son have been in opposition. Captained England in the third Test v New Zealand at Old Trafford 1999, deputising for the injured Nasser Hussain. Scored match-winning 173* in the fourth Test v Australia at Headingley in 2001, winning Man of the Match award, and was England's Man of the Series with 456 runs (more than any other batsman on either side) at an average of 50.66. His other Test awards include England's Man of the Series v Sri Lanka 2002 and v

Zimbabwe 2003. Slazenger Sheer Instinct Award 2001 for the cricketer who has impressed the most in the recent season. Scored century in each innings (151/108) v Glamorgan at The Oval 2006, emulating achievement of his father, Alan (117*/114), in the corresponding fixture in 1984. Reached the final of BBC celebrity singing show *Just the Two of Us* in January 2007 with Sarah Brightman. Scored 179 at Hove 2007, in the process sharing with Mark Ramprakash (266*) in the highest partnership ever recorded against Sussex in the County Championship (403). Captain of Surrey 2005-09. (Stewart Walters was appointed stand-in captain in Butcher's absence for the latter part of the 2009 season). Struggled to regain fitness after a knee operation in November 2008, and announced his retirement at the end of the 2009 season after playing only a handful of games

Best batting: 259 Surrey v Leicestershire, Leicester 1999
Best bowling: 5-86 Surrey v Lancashire, Old Trafford 2000

2009 Season

	M	Inn	NO	Runs	HS	Avg	100	50	Ct	St	Balls	Runs	Wkts	Avg	BB	5I	10M
Test																	
FC	5	8	2	251	65	41.83	-	2	10	-	0	0	0		-	-	-
ODI																	
List A																	
20/20 Int																	
20/20																	

Career Performances

	M	Inn	NO	Runs	HS	Avg	100	50	Ct	St	Balls	Runs	Wkts	Avg	BB	5I	10M
Test	71	131	7	4288	173*	34.58	8	23	61	-	901	541	15	36.06	4-42	-	-
FC	280	478	39	17870	259	40.70	38	95	263	-	7703	4237	125	33.89	5-86	1	-
ODI																	
List A	191	171	31	4460	139	31.85	2	28	63	-	2527	2210	49	45.10	3-23	-	
20/20 Int																	
20/20	13	12	0	210	60	17.50	-	2	4	-	0	0	0		-	-	

14. Who was sometimes described as 'the Alec Bedser of Pakistan'?

BUTTLER, J. C. Somerset

Name: Joseph (<u>Jos</u>) Charles Buttler
Role: Right-handed batsman, wicket-keeper
Born: 8 September 1990, Taunton, Somerset
County debut: 2009
Education: King's College, Taunton
Overseas tours: Somerset to India (ICC Champions League) 2009; England U19 to Bangladesh 2009, to New Zealand (ICC U19 World Cup) 2010

Extras: Somerset Academy, Somerset 2nd XI. Played for Glastonbury CC 2008. Scored 71 in the second innings of his first game for Somerset 2nd XI in 2006 to help his county beat Nottinghamshire by 51 runs. In that same match Buttler claimed five catches. Scored a rapid 77 off 49 balls for England U17 v New Zealand U19, and 140 for Somerset 2nd XI v Hampshire, both in 2008
Best batting: 30 Somerset v Lancashire, Taunton 2009

2009 Season

	M	Inn	NO	Runs	HS	Avg	100	50	Ct	St	Balls	Runs	Wkts	Avg	BB	5I	10M
Test																	
FC	1	1	0	30	30	30.00	-	-	-	-	0	0	0		-	-	-
ODI																	
List A	1	0	0	0	0		-	-	1	-	0	0	0		-	-	
20/20 Int																	
20/20																	

Career Performances

	M	Inn	NO	Runs	HS	Avg	100	50	Ct	St	Balls	Runs	Wkts	Avg	BB	5I	10M
Test																	
FC	1	1	0	30	30	30.00	-	-	-	-	0	0	0		-	-	-
ODI																	
List A	1	0	0	0	0		-	-	1	-	0	0	0		-	-	
20/20 Int																	
20/20	1	1	1	6	6*		-	-	1	-	0	0	0		-	-	

CADDICK, A. R.   Somerset

Name: <u>Andrew</u> Richard Caddick
Role: Right-hand bat, right-arm
fast-medium bowler, county vice-captain
Born: 21 November 1968, Christchurch,
New Zealand
Height: 6ft 5in **Weight:** 14st 13lbs
Nickname: Des, Shack
County debut: 1990 (one-day),
1991 (first-class)
County cap: 1992
Benefit: 1999
Testimonial: 2009
Test debut: 1993
ODI debut: 1993
50 wickets in a season: 11
100 wickets in a season: 1
Place in batting averages: (2008 217th av. 17.50)
Place in bowling averages: 131st av. 52.50 (2008 130th av. 41.88)
Parents: Christopher and Audrey
Wife and date of marriage: Sarah, 27 January 1995
Children: Ashton Faye, 24 August 1998; Fraser Michael, 12 October 2001
Education: Papanui High School, Christchurch, New Zealand
Qualifications: Qualified plasterer and tiler. Qualified helicopter pilot
Overseas tours: New Zealand YC to Australia (U19 World Cup) 1987-88, to England
1988; England A to Australia 1992-93; England to West Indies 1993-94, to Zimbabwe
and New Zealand 1996-97, to West Indies 1997-98, to South Africa and Zimbabwe
1999-2000, to Kenya (ICC Knockout Trophy) 2000-01, to Pakistan and Sri Lanka
2000-01, to India (one-day series) and New Zealand 2001-02, to Sri Lanka (ICC
Champions Trophy) 2002-03, to Australia 2002-03, to Africa (World Cup) 2002-03
Career highlights to date: 'Bowling West Indies out at Lord's [2000] and thus getting
my name up on the board'
Cricketers particularly admired: Dennis Lillee, Richard Hadlee, Robin Smith,
Jimmy Cook
Other sports followed: 'Mostly all'
Relaxations: Golf
Extras: Whyte and Mackay Bowler of the Year 1997. Took 105 first-class wickets
(av. 19.82) in 1998 season. Leading wicket-taker in the single-division four-day era of
the County Championship with 422 wickets (av. 22.48) 1993-99. Cornhill England
Player of the Year 1999-2000. Took 5-16 from 13 overs as West Indies were bowled
out for 54 in their second innings in the second Test at Lord's 2000. Took 5-14 in the
fourth Test v West Indies at Headingley 2000, including four wickets (Jacobs,

McLean, Ambrose, King) in an over. One of *Wisden*'s Five Cricketers of the Year 2001. Took 200th Test wicket (Craig McMillan) in the third Test v New Zealand at Auckland 2001-02. His international awards include England's Man of the [Test] Series v New Zealand 1999 and joint Man of the Match (with Gary Kirsten) in the third Test v South Africa at Durban 1999-2000 (7-46). Retired from ODI cricket in March 2003. Took 1000th first-class wicket (Joe Sayers) v Yorkshire at Taunton 2005. Returned career-best match figures of 12-71 (7-30/5-41) v Gloucestershire at Bristol 2007. Appointed vice-captain of Somerset for 2008. Announced his retirement at the end of the 2009 season, during which he had his second benefit match

Best batting: 92 Somerset v Worcestershire, Worcester 1995
Best bowling: 9-32 Somerset v Lancashire, Taunton 1993

2009 Season

	M	Inn	NO	Runs	HS	Avg	100	50	Ct	St	Balls	Runs	Wkts	Avg	BB	5I	10M
Test																	
FC	5	3	1	15	11*	7.50	-	-	1	-	787	525	10	52.50	3-53	-	-
ODI																	
List A																		
20/20 Int																		
20/20																		

Career Performances

	M	Inn	NO	Runs	HS	Avg	100	50	Ct	St	Balls	Runs	Wkts	Avg	BB	5I	10M
Test	62	95	12	861	49*	10.37	-	-	21	-	13558	6999	234	29.91	7-46	13	1
FC	275	356	70	4259	92	14.89	-	9	88	-	59663	31387	1180	26.59	9-32	78	17
ODI	54	38	18	249	36	12.45	-	-	9	-	2937	1965	69	28.47	4-19	-	
List A	262	135	59	810	39	10.65	-	-	44	-	12827	9085	341	26.64	6-30	5	
20/20 Int																	
20/20	16	1	0	0	0	0.00	-	-	1	-	306	468	15	31.20	2-12	-	

CARBERRY, M. A. Hampshire

Name: <u>Michael</u> Alexander Carberry
Role: Left-hand bat, right-arm
medium bowler
Born: 29 September 1980, Croydon, Surrey
Height: 5ft 11in **Weight:** 14st 7lbs
Nickname: Carbs
County debut: 2001 (Surrey), 2003 (Kent),
2006 (Hampshire)
County cap: 2006 (Hampshire)
1st-Class 200s: 1
1000 runs in a season: 2
Place in batting averages: 10th av. 69.50
(2008 114th av. 31.34)
Parents: Maria and Neville
Marital status: Single
Family links with cricket: 'My dad played club cricket'
Education: St John Rigby College
Qualifications: 10 GCSEs
Overseas tours: Surrey U17 to South Africa 1997; England U19 to New Zealand
1998-99, to Malaysia and (U19 World Cup) Sri Lanka 1999-2000; England A to
Bangladesh 2006-07; England Lions to India 2007-08; England Performance
Programme to South Africa 2009
Overseas teams played for: Portland CC, Melbourne; University CC, Perth 2005
Career highlights to date: 'Every day is a highlight'
Cricket moments to forget: None
Cricketers particularly admired: Ricky Ponting, Brian Lara
Relaxations: 'Sleeping'
Extras: Scored century (126*) for ECB U18 v Pakistan U19 at Abergavenny 1998.
Represented England U19 1999, 2000. NBC Denis Compton Award for the most
promising young Surrey player 1999, 2000. Scored century (137) on Kent debut v
Cambridge UCCE at Fenner's 2003. Scored 112 as Kent scored a then county record
fourth innings 429-5 to beat Worcestershire at Canterbury 2004. Scored career-best
192* as Hampshire scored 331-5 to beat Warwickshire with three balls to spare at
The Rose Bowl 2007. Scored century in each innings (127/120) v Worcestershire at
Kidderminster 2007. Scored a century (113*) v Yorkshire at Headingley 2007, in the
process passing 1000 first-class runs in a season for the first time. Member of the
England Performance Programme squad 2009-10; scored 100 for EPP side against
Gauteng in Pretoria December 2009. Called into England squad as cover for injured
Paul Collingwood South Africa 2009
Best batting: 204 Hampshire v Warwickshire, Rose Bowl 2009
Best bowling: 2-85 Hampshire v Durham, Riverside 2006

2009 Season

	M	Inn	NO	Runs	HS	Avg	100	50	Ct	St	Balls	Runs	Wkts	Avg	BB	5I	10M
Test																	
FC	12	21	3	1251	204	69.50	4	8	6	-	259	242	2	121.00	1-64	-	-
ODI																	
List A	12	11	3	431	121*	53.87	1	1	7	-	84	60	2	30.00	2-11	-	
20/20 Int																	
20/20	11	10	0	307	62	30.70	-	2	7	-	12	16	1	16.00	1-16	-	

Career Performances

	M	Inn	NO	Runs	HS	Avg	100	50	Ct	St	Balls	Runs	Wkts	Avg	BB	5I	10M
Test																	
FC	95	168	17	6383	204	42.27	17	32	40	-	949	763	9	84.77	2-85	-	-
ODI																	
List A	105	99	10	2555	121*	28.70	1	20	41	-	126	101	3	33.66	2-11	-	
20/20 Int																	
20/20	53	49	8	1228	90	29.95	-	10	24	-	12	16	1	16.00	1-16	-	

CARTER, A.   Nottinghamshire

Name: Andrew (<u>Andy</u>) Carter
Role: Right-hand bat, right-arm medium bowler
Born: 27 August 1988, Lincoln
County debut: 2009
Overseas tours: Nottinghamshire to South Africa 2008 (pre-season)
Extras: Has played for Lincolnshire U17 and Lincolnshire. Played extensively in the Lincolnshire Premier League 2004-08. His match figures of 13-99 (6-43, 7-56) v Warwickshire in July 2009 set a new record for a Nottinghamshire bowler in the 2nd XI Championship. Nottinghamshire 2nd XI Player of the Year 2009. Signed a new two-year contract at the end of the 2009 season Member of England Performance Programme squad 2009-10.
Best batting: 4 Nottinghamshire v Worcestershire, Worcester 2009
Best bowling: 1-27 Nottinghamshire v OUCCE, The Parks 2009

2009 Season

	M	Inn	NO	Runs	HS	Avg	100	50	Ct	St	Balls	Runs	Wkts	Avg	BB	5I	10M
Test																	
FC	2	1	0	4	4	4.00	-	-	-	-	318	164	3	54.66	1-27	-	-
ODI																	
List A	6	5	0	20	12	4.00	-	-	2	-	186	169	7	24.14	3-32	-	
20/20 Int																	
20/20																	

Career Performances

	M	Inn	NO	Runs	HS	Avg	100	50	Ct	St	Balls	Runs	Wkts	Avg	BB	5I	10M
Test																	
FC	2	1	0	4	4	4.00	-	-	-	-	318	164	3	54.66	1-27	-	-
ODI																	
List A	6	5	0	20	12	4.00	-	-	2	-	186	169	7	24.14	3-32	-	
20/20 Int																	
20/20																	

CARTER, N. M.　　　　　　　Warwickshire

Name: Neil Miller Carter
Role: Left-hand bat, left-arm fast-medium bowler
Born: 29 January 1975, Mowbray, Cape Town, South Africa
Height: 6ft 2in **Weight:** 14st 8lbs
Nickname: Carts
County debut: 2001
County cap: 2005
Place in batting averages: 189th av. 24.46 (2008 118th av. 30.71)
Place in bowling averages: 115th av. 44.00 (2008 78th av. 31.17)
Parents: John and Heather
Marital status: Single
Education: Hottentots Holland High School; Cape Technikon; ITI; stock market training
Qualifications: Certified Novell Engineer, Level 2 coaching
Career outside cricket: Investing and sports marketing
Overseas tours: SA Country Schools U15 to England 1992; Warwickshire to Cape Town 2001-03, to Grenada 2007
Overseas teams played for: Boland 1998-99 – 2003-04; Cape Cobras 2009-10

Career highlights to date: 'Lord's finals and Championship win plus 2005 season'
Cricket moments to forget: 'Losing C&G final 2005'
Cricketers particularly admired: Allan Donald, Shaun Pollock
Other sports played: Swimming, golf, hockey, squash
Other sports followed: Rugby union (Stormers in Super 14, Springboks), football (Sheffield Wednesday), baseball (LA Angels), ice hockey (Anaheim Ducks)
Favourite band: Mike and the Mechanics
Relaxations: Gricing (steam train photography)
Extras: Won Man of the Match award in first one-day match for Warwickshire v Essex at Edgbaston in the C&G 2001 (4-21/43-ball 40). Warwickshire Player of the Year 2005 (1088 runs and 94 wickets in all cricket and, including Twenty20, equalled Allan Donald's club season record of 53 one-day wickets). Is England-qualified. Was on loan to Middlesex for 2008 Stanford Series
Best batting: 103 Warwickshire v Sussex, Hove 2002
Best bowling: 6-63 Boland v Griqualand West, Kimberley 2000-01

2009 Season

	M	Inn	NO	Runs	HS	Avg	100	50	Ct	St	Balls	Runs	Wkts	Avg	BB	5I	10M
Test																	
FC	9	13	0	318	67	24.46	-	2	-	-	1140	704	16	44.00	5-37	1	-
ODI																	
List A	13	11	1	438	103*	43.80	1	4	-	-	495	361	15	24.06	3-18	-	
20/20 Int																	
20/20	11	11	0	180	45	16.36	-	-	1	-	240	289	9	32.11	3-16	-	

Career Performances

	M	Inn	NO	Runs	HS	Avg	100	50	Ct	St	Balls	Runs	Wkts	Avg	BB	5I	10M
Test																	
FC	96	128	21	2255	103	21.07	1	9	24	-	15587	9129	246	37.10	6-63	9	-
ODI																	
List A	149	126	14	2388	135	21.32	2	10	14	-	6428	5097	204	24.98	5-31	2	
20/20 Int																	
20/20	62	59	2	986	58	17.29	-	2	9	-	1246	1486	61	24.36	5-19	1	

CHAMBERS, M. A.   Essex

Name: <u>Maurice</u> Anthony Chambers
Role: Right-hand bat, right-arm fast bowler
Born: 14 September 1987, Portland, Jamaica
Height: 6ft 4in **Weight:** 14st
Nickname: Mozza
County debut: 2005
Place in bowling averages: 81st av. 35.06
Parents: Elaine Lewis
Marital status: Single
Education: Homerton College of Technology; Sir
George Monoux College
Qualifications: BTEC National Diploma in
Business Studies
Career outside cricket: 'College and playing
basketball with my mates'

Off-season: 'Going to Brisbane, Australia in
January for two and a half months, then straight to
Barbados for pre-season with Essex'
Overseas tours: Essex Academy to India 2006-07; England U19 to Malaysia
2006-07; Essex pre-season tours to Dubai 2008, to Barbados 2010
Overseas teams played for: University of Queensland 2009-10
Career highlights to date: 'Playing for Essex 2nd XI v Middlesex [2006] and
bowling 16 overs, 7 maidens, and taking 3 wickets for 25 runs. Playing Twenty20 v
Northants, it felt really good getting Matt Prior and Murray Goodwin out. Essex v
West Indies at Chelmsford 2009 – 4-62'
Cricket moments to forget: 'Playing for England U19 v India, we were 8 wickets
down with 2 balls to go and I was the last batsman. I told myself I was not going to
pad up, and then my mate was out and I went in to bat with no abdo guard or gloves.'
Cricket superstitions: 'No sexy time before cricket'
Cricketers particularly admired: Courtney Walsh, Curtly Ambrose, Stuart Broad,
Brian Lara, Kevin Pietersen, Brett Lee
Young players to look out for: Mervyn Westfield (Essex), Steve Finn (Middlesex),
Chris Jordan and Jade Dernbach (Surrey), Jonathan Clare (Derbyshire), Chris Woakes
(Warwickshire), Mark Turner (Somerset)
Other sports played: 'Basketball – I just train with my cousin for the fitness. Play
badminton with a few of my friends.'
Other sports followed: Football (Manchester United)
Injuries: 'Bone spur in my ankle – lost a month of cricket'
Favourite band: 50 Cent, Vybz Kartel
Relaxations: 'Shopping, playing Xbox, listening to music and partying real hard'
Extras: London Schools Cricket Association Bowler of the Year 2004. Jack Petchey
Award 2004. Played for MCC Young Cricketers 2004. Wanstead CC Bowler of the

Year. Acquired British citizenship in 2007. Out for the whole of the 2007 season with a stress fracture in the lower back. Signed fresh two-year contract in November 2008. Attended Loughborough ECB fast bowling training camp in 2008 that included a December trip to Florida

Opinions on cricket: 'It's the best game in the world...'

Best batting: 8* Essex v Middlesex, Chelmsford 2009

Best bowling: 4-62 Essex v West Indies, Chelmsford 2009

2009 Season

	M	Inn	NO	Runs	HS	Avg	100	50	Ct	St	Balls	Runs	Wkts	Avg	BB	5I	10M
Test																	
FC	7	8	7	19	8*	19.00	-	-	1	-	850	526	15	35.06	4-62	-	-
ODI																	
List A	1	0	0	0	0		-	-	-	-	36	39	1	39.00	1-39	-	
20/20 Int																	
20/20	1	1	0	0	0	0.00	-	-	-	-	24	32	1	32.00	1-32	-	

Career Performances

	M	Inn	NO	Runs	HS	Avg	100	50	Ct	St	Balls	Runs	Wkts	Avg	BB	5I	10M
Test																	
FC	11	14	11	30	8*	10.00	-	-	2	-	1342	861	24	35.87	4-62	-	-
ODI																	
List A	3	1	1	1	1*		-	-	1	-	90	93	3	31.00	1-26	-	
20/20 Int																	
20/20	12	7	4	19	10*	6.33	-	-	5	-	186	253	11	23.00	3-31	-	

15. Name the Pakistani brothers who played against England in 1983-84.

CHANDERPAUL, S.   Durham

Name: Shivnarine Chanderpaul
Role: Left-hand bat, leg-break bowler
Born: 16 August 1974, Demerara, Guyana
Nickname: Shiv
County debut: 2007
Test debut: 1993-94
ODI debut: 1994-95
Twenty20 Int debut: 2005-06
1000 runs in a season: 1
1st-Class 200s: 5
1st-Class 300s: 1
Place in batting averages: 2nd av. 85.37
(2008 77th av. 37.36)
Wife: Amy

Overseas tours: West Indies U19 to England 1993;
West Indies to India 1994-95, to New Zealand 1994-95, to England 1995, to Australia
(B&H World Series) 1995-96, to India, Pakistan and Sri Lanka (World Cup) 1995-96,
to Australia 1996-97, to Pakistan 1997-98, to Bangladesh (Wills International Cup)
1998-99, to South Africa 1998-99, to UK, Ireland and Netherlands (World Cup) 1999,
to Bangladesh 1999-2000, to New Zealand 1999-2000, to England 2000, to Australia
2000-01, to Zimbabwe and Kenya 2001, to Sharjah (v Pakistan) 2001-02, to Sri Lanka
(ICC Champions Trophy) 2002-03, to India and Bangladesh 2002-03, to Africa (World
Cup) 2002-03, to Zimbabwe and South Africa 2003-04, to England 2004, to England
(ICC Champions Trophy) 2004, to Sri Lanka 2005 (c), to Australia 2005-06 (c), to
New Zealand 2005-06 (c), to India (ICC Champions Trophy) 2006-07, to Pakistan
2006-07, to England 2007, to South Africa (World 20/20) 2007-08, to Zimbabwe and
South Africa 2007-08, to New Zealand 2008-09, to England 2009, to Australia 2009-
10 plus other one-day tournaments and series in Sharjah, Singapore, Toronto,
Bangladesh, Australia, Malaysia, India and Ireland
Overseas teams played for: Guyana 1991-92 – 2007-08; Bangalore Royal
Challengers (IPL) 2007-08
Extras: Scored century (104) as West Indies made a Test record 418 in the fourth
innings to beat Australia in Antigua 2002-03, winning Man of the Match award. His
other series and match awards include Man of the [Test] Series v India 2001-02 (562
runs – av. 140.50), West Indies Man of the [Test] Series v England 2004 (437 runs –
av. 72.83) and 2007 (446 runs – av 148.66) and overall Man of the [ODI] Series v
England 2007 (202 runs – av. 202.00). Represented West Indies in the 2006-07 World
Cup. Captain of West Indies from March 2005 to April 2006, scoring a double century
(203*) in his first Test in charge, v South Africa 2004-05 in his home country of
Guyana. In 2007 he scored 446 runs against England in three Tests. Named as one of
Wisden's Five Cricketers of the Year 2008. ICC Player of the Year 2008. Durham's

overseas player for 2009. Scored 201* in Durham's final championship match of the 2009 season, the third highest score in the county's first-class history.
Best batting: 303* Guyana v Jamaica, Kingston 1995-96
Best bowling: 4-48 Guyana v Leeward Islands, Basseterre 1992-93

2009 Season

	M	Inn	NO	Runs	HS	Avg	100	50	Ct	St	Balls	Runs	Wkts	Avg	BB	5I	10M
Test	2	4	0	74	47	18.50	-	-	-	-	0	0	0		-	-	-
FC	9	13	5	683	201*	85.37	3	2	3	-	0	0	0		-	-	-
ODI	2	2	0	95	68	47.50	-	1	-	-	0	0	0		-	-	
List A	5	5	0	177	68	35.40	-	2	1	-	0	0	0		-	-	
20/20 Int	6	6	3	51	18*	17.00	-	-	1	-	0	0	0		-	-	
20/20	6	6	3	51	18*	17.00	-	-	1	-	0	0	0		-	-	

Career Performances

	M	Inn	NO	Runs	HS	Avg	100	50	Ct	St	Balls	Runs	Wkts	Avg	BB	5I	10M
Test	121	206	32	8576	203*	49.28	21	52	50	-	1680	845	8	105.62	1-2	-	-
FC	245	395	71	17569	303*	54.22	51	88	141	-	4634	2453	56	43.80	4-48	-	-
ODI	252	236	38	8250	150	41.66	10	55	69	-	740	636	14	45.42	3-18	-	
List A	361	335	58	11602	150	41.88	11	83	103	-	1681	1388	56	24.78	4-22	-	
20/20 Int	15	15	4	207	41	18.81	-	-	6	-	0	0	0		-	-	
20/20	24	23	4	323	48	17.00	-	-	10	-	0	0	0		-	-	

CHAPPLE, G.   Lancashire

Name: Glen Chapple
Role: Right-hand bat, right-arm fast-medium bowler; all-rounder; county captain
Born: 23 January 1974, Skipton, Yorkshire
Height: 6ft 1in **Weight:** 13st
Nickname: Chappy
County debut: 1992
County cap: 1994
Benefit: 2004
ODI debut: 2006
50 wickets in a season: 4
Place in batting averages: 129th av. 32.50 (2008 153rd av. 26.18)
Place in bowling averages: 19th av. 25.25 (2008 15th av. 20.50)
Parents: Mike and Eileen
Wife and date of marriage: Kerry, 31 January 2004
Children: Annie, 6 August 2003; Joe, 16 January 2006

Family links with cricket: Father played in Lancashire League for Nelson and was a professional for Darwen and Earby
Education: West Craven High School; Nelson and Colne College
Qualifications: 8 GCSEs, 2 A-levels
Overseas tours: England U18 to Canada (International Youth Tournament) 1991; England YC to New Zealand 1990-91; England U19 to Pakistan 1991-92, to India 1992-93; England A to India 1994-95, to Australia 1996-97; England VI to Hong Kong 2002, 2003, 2004, 2006
Cricket superstitions: None
Cricketers particularly admired: Dennis Lillee, Robin Smith
Other sports followed: Football (Liverpool), golf
Favourite band: U2, Oasis, Stone Roses
Relaxations: 'Golf'
Extras: Set record for fastest century in first-class cricket (21 minutes, against declaration bowling) v Glamorgan at Old Trafford 1993. Man of the Match in the 1996 NatWest final against Essex at Lord's (6-18). Lancashire Player of the Year 2002. Returned match figures of 10-86 (7-53/3-33) v Durham at Blackpool 2007. Topped the Lancashire wicket-takers for the 2008 first-class season with 42. Appointed county captain prior to the 2009 season
Best batting: 155 Lancashire v Somerset, Old Trafford 2001
Best bowling: 7-53 Lancashire v Durham, Blackpool 2007

2009 Season

	M	Inn	NO	Runs	HS	Avg	100	50	Ct	St	Balls	Runs	Wkts	Avg	BB	5I	10M
Test																	
FC	11	14	2	390	89	32.50	-	3	3	-	2014	884	35	25.25	6-19	2	-
ODI																	
List A	8	5	2	36	18*	12.00	-	-	5	-	412	285	13	21.92	3-46	-	
20/20 Int																	
20/20	8	4	2	27	12	13.50	-	-	2	-	180	186	11	16.90	2-11	-	

Carer Performances

	M	Inn	NO	Runs	HS	Avg	100	50	Ct	St	Balls	Runs	Wkts	Avg	BB	5I	10M
Test																	
FC	238	324	59	6701	155	25.28	6	31	79	-	40532	20097	728	27.60	7-53	29	2
ODI	1	1	0	14	14	14.00	-	-	-	-	24	14	0		-	-	
List A	267	153	41	1987	81*	17.74	-	9	60	-	11451	8580	299	28.69	6-18	4	
20/20 Int																	
20/20	36	21	7	203	55*	14.50	-	1	12	-	660	800	37	21.62	2-11	-	

CHAWLA, P. P. Surrey

Name: Piyush Pramod Chawla
Role: Left-hand bat, right-arm leg-break
bowler; all-rounder
Born: 24 December 1988, Aligarh,
Uttar Pradesh, India
Height: 5ft 7in
County debut: 2009 (Sussex)
County cap: 2009 (Sussex)
Test debut: 2006
ODI debut: 2007
Place in batting averages: 151st av. 29.42
Place in bowling averages: 28th av. 27.25
Overseas tours: India to Bangladesh 2007 (one-day
series), to England, Scotland and Ireland 2007 (one-
day series), to Australia (CB Series) 2007-08, to
Pakistan (Asia Cup) 2008

Overseas teams played for: Air India; India Green; Uttar Pradesh 2005-06 – ;
Kings XI Punjab (IPL) 2008 –
Extras: Played for India U19 when only 15. Signed for Sussex as an overseas player
in June 2009, covering for Yasir Arafat. Overseas player with Surrey for 2010
Best batting: 102* Sussex v Worcestershire, Worcester 2009
Best bowling: 6-46 India A v Zimbabwe Select XI, Bulawayo 2007-08

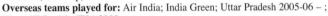

2009 Season

	M	Inn	NO	Runs	HS	Avg	100	50	Ct	St	Balls	Runs	Wkts	Avg	BB	5I	10M
Test																	
FC	6	10	3	206	102*	29.42	1	-	2	-	2051	981	36	27.25	6-52	4	1
ODI																	
List A	2	2	0	32	32	16.00	-	-	1	-	57	45	3	15.00	2-10	-	
20/20 Int																	
20/20	1	0	0	0	0		-	-	-	-	24	17	2	8.50	2-17	-	

Career Performances

	M	Inn	NO	Runs	HS	Avg	100	50	Ct	St	Balls	Runs	Wkts	Avg	BB	5I	10M
Test	2	2	0	5	4	2.50	-	-	-	-	205	137	3	45.66	2-66	-	-
FC	52	75	7	1764	102*	25.94	1	12	23	-	11567	5683	211	26.93	6-46	14	2
ODI	21	10	5	28	13*	5.60	-	-	9	-	1102	911	28	32.53	4-23	-	
List A	66	42	13	637	93	21.96	-	4	21	-	3193	2657	98	27.11	4-23	-	
20/20 Int																	
20/20	38	24	9	222	33	14.80	-	-	12	-	747	915	43	21.27	3-22	-	

CHEETHAM, S. P.   Lancashire

Name: <u>Steven</u> Philip Cheetham
Role: Right-hand bat, right-arm fast
opening bowler
Born: 5 September 1987, Oldham
Height: 6ft 5in **Weight:** 14st 6lbs
Nickname: Cheets
County debut: 2007
Parents: Philip and Joan
Marital status: Single
Education: Bury Grammar School; Holy
Cross College
Qualifications: 10 GCSEs, 4 A-levels
Off-season: 'Doing rehab after my bone spur
operation'
Overseas tours: Lancashire to Sharjah (Pro Arch
Trophy) 2009

Overseas teams played for: Cheltenham CC, Melbourne 2007-08, 2008-09
Career highlights to date: 'First-team debut for Lancashire v Durham UCCE.
Representing England U17. Taking a hat-trick in the VTCA Cup semi-final v Old
Mentonians in Melbourne, March 2008. 7-30 for the 2nd XI v Leicester and 5-11
in Dubai'
Cricket moments to forget: 'Two seasons of injuries – stress fracture of back and
double hernia. Having my hat-trick ball and five-wicket haul dropped at Derby, first
game of the 2008 season. Breaking my finger in the pre-match warm-up at the first
game of the 2009 season'
Cricket superstitions: 'Too many to mention'
Cricketers particularly admired: Marcus Trescothick, Chris Gayle, Brett Lee,
Andrew Flintoff
Young players to look out for: Tom Smith and Simon Kerrigan (Lancashire)
Other sports played: Football (Bury GS Old Boys, Oldham Athletic Academy)
Other sports followed: Football (Oldham Athletic), AFL (Collingwood)
Injuries: 'Broken finger – out for 6 weeks. Bone spur operation – out for 6 months'
Favourite band: Arctic Monkeys, The Courteeners, Pendulum
Relaxations: 'Football, the internet, socialising with friends'
Extras: Best figures of 5-11 for Radcliffe v Ramsbottom in the Inter League Club
Challenge Trophy as a 17-year-old. Attended Dennis Lillee's MRF Pace Foundation,
India 2007. Is a Lancashire Scholarship player and appeared in one first-class match
for the county in 2007. Helped Cheltenham CC (Melbourne) to their first league win
for 102 years in 2007-08. Did not play any first-class games for Lancashire in 2009
Opinions on cricket: 'Enjoy it and keep it simple…'
Best bowling: 1-44 Lancashire v DUCCE, Durham 2007

Career Performances

	M	Inn	NO	Runs	HS	Avg	100	50	Ct	St	Balls	Runs	Wkts	Avg	BB	5I	10M
Test																	
FC	1	0	0	0	0		-	-	1	-	144	127	1	127.00	1-44	-	-
ODI																	
List A	4	2	2	3	3*		-	-	-	-	168	126	7	18.00	3-25	-	
20/20 Int																	
20/20																	

CHILTON, M. J.   Lancashire

Name: <u>Mark</u> James Chilton
Role: Right-hand bat, right-arm
medium bowler
Born: 2 October 1976, Sheffield
Height: 6ft 2in **Weight:** 13st 6lbs
Nickname: Chill, Chilly, Peter, Roger, Dougie
County debut: 1997
County cap: 2002
1000 runs in a season: 1
Place in batting averages: 28th av. 52.41
(2008 143rd av. 27.54)
Parents: Jim and Sue
Wife and date of marriage: Hayley,
29 December 2006
Children: Bethan, 31 October 2007
Family links with cricket: 'Dad played
local leagues'
Education: Manchester Grammar School; Durham University
Qualifications: BA (Hons) Business Economics, Level 3 coaching
Overseas tours: Manchester Grammar School to Barbados 1993-94, to South Africa
1995-96; Durham University to Zimbabwe 1997-98
Overseas teams played for: East Torrens, Adelaide 2000-01; North Sydney CC,
Sydney 2002-03
Career highlights to date: 'Playing for and captaining Lancashire'
Cricket moments to forget: 'Losing C&G final 2006'
Cricket superstitions: None
Cricketers particularly admired: John Crawley, David Gower
Young players to look out for: Karl Brown (Lancashire), Steve Mullaney
(Nottinghamshire)

Other sports played: Golf
Other sports followed: Football (Manchester United)
Favourite band: The Charlatans
Relaxations: 'Guitar'
Extras: Represented England U14, U15, U17. England U15 Batsman of the Year award 1992. Played for North of England v New Zealand U19 1996. Played for British Universities in 1997 Benson and Hedges Cup, winning the Gold Award against Sussex at Fenner's (34/5-26). Captain of Lancashire from 2005 until October 2007, when he stood down
Opinions on cricket: 'It's important to maintain a balance between the four-day game and Twenty20. These are exciting times, but let's not lose sight of all forms of the game.'
Best batting: 131 Lancashire v Kent, Old Trafford 2006
Best bowling: 2-3 Lancashire v DUCCE, Durham 2009

2009 Season

	M	Inn	NO	Runs	HS	Avg	100	50	Ct	St	Balls	Runs	Wkts	Avg	BB	5I	10M
Test																	
FC	16	23	6	891	114	52.41	2	6	15	-	32	3	2	1.50	2-3	-	-
ODI																	
List A	17	14	4	471	101*	47.10	1	1	4	-	0	0	0		-	-	
20/20 Int																	
20/20	9	6	2	58	34	14.50	-	-	3	-	0	0	0		-	-	

Career Performances

	M	Inn	NO	Runs	HS	Avg	100	50	Ct	St	Balls	Runs	Wkts	Avg	BB	5I	10M
Test																		
FC	166	268	23	8159	131	33.30	20	32	126	-	1343	667	12	55.58	2-3	-	-
ODI																	
List A	176	165	24	4356	115	30.89	5	20	53	-	1082	992	41	24.19	5-26	1	
20/20 Int																	
20/20	41	28	10	294	38	16.33	-	-	16	-	0	0	0		-	-	

16. Pakistan's two lowest Test match innings totals against England came in the 1954 series. What were those totals?

CHOPRA, V.　　　　　　　　　Warwickshire

Name: Varun Chopra
Role: Right-hand opening bat, right-arm
swing/leg-spin bowler
Born: 21 June 1987, Barking, Essex
Height: 6ft 1in　**Weight:** 12st 7lbs
Nickname: Chops, Chopper, Tiddles, Tidz
County debut: 2006 (Essex)
Place in batting averages: 180th av. 25.57
(2008 132nd av. 29.23)
Parents: Chander and Surinder
Marital status: Single
Education: Ilford County HS
Qualifications: 11 GCSEs, 4 A-levels
Overseas tours: England U19 to Bangladesh

2005-06 (c), to Sri Lanka (U19 World Cup) 2005-06;
Essex to South Africa 2006, to Dubai 2007 and 2008
Overseas teams played for: Willetton CC, Perth 2006-07, 2007-08
Career highlights to date: 'Captaining England U19. Man of Series v India U19
2006. Century [106 plus 50* in second innings] on Championship debut v
Gloucestershire [at Chelmsford 2006]. Winning the Friends Provident trophy, 2008'
Cricket moments to forget: 'Any dropped catch. England U19 [World Cup] semi-
final v India 2005-06' [*England lost by 234 runs, having been bowled out for 58*]
Cricketers particularly admired: Sachin Tendulkar, Shane Warne, Kevin Pietersen
Young players to look out for: Jaik Mickleburgh (Essex)
Other sports played: 'Football – Spot!'
Other sports followed: Football (Manchester United)
Favourite band: Musiq Soulchild, Ginuwine, T.I., Lil Wayne, Kanye
Relaxations: 'Jamming with mates, poker, Pro Evo'
Extras: Lord's Taverners Player of the Year U13, U15, U19. Sony Sports Personality
of the Year runner-up. Captained England U19 2005 and 2006 – Man of the Match v
Bangladesh U19 at Colombo in the quarter-finals of the U19 World Cup 2005-06
and Man of the Series v India U19 2006, scoring a century in each innings (123/164)
in the second 'Test' at Taunton. Scored century (106) on Championship debut v
Gloucestershire at Chelmsford 2006, in the process becoming the youngest player
to score a Championship hundred for Essex. Scored his career best 155 in the final
2008 Championship game. In October 2009 left Essex to sign for Warwickshire
Best batting: 155 Essex v Gloucestershire, Bristol 2008

	M	Inn	NO	Runs	HS	Avg	100	50	Ct	St	Balls	Runs	Wkts	Avg	BB	5I	10M
Test																	
FC	12	21	0	537	88	25.57	-	5	6	-	91	39	0		-	-	-
ODI																	
List A	14	13	1	691	101*	57.58	1	7	5	-	18	18	0		-	-	
20/20 Int																	
20/20	5	5	1	78	51	19.50	-	1	1	-	0	0	0		-	-	

Career Performances

	M	Inn	NO	Runs	HS	Avg	100	50	Ct	St	Balls	Runs	Wkts	Avg	BB	5I	10M
Test																	
FC	48	81	5	2252	155	29.63	2	16	40	-	131	78	0		-	-	
ODI																	
List A	34	32	1	1179	102	38.03	2	10	10	-	18	18	0		-	-	
20/20 Int																	
20/20	12	12	3	136	51	15.11	-	1	2	-	0	0	0		-	-	

CHOUDHRY, S. H.　　　　　　　Warwickshire

Name: Shaaiq Hussain Choudhry
Role: Right-hand bat, slow left-arm bowler
Born: 3 November 1985, Sheffield, Yorkshire
Height: 5ft 10in **Weight:** 11st 7lbs
Nickname: Shak, Chouds
County debut: 2009
Parents: Sabir and Badar-u-Nasa
Marital status: Single
Education: Fir Vale School; Rotherham College of Arts and Technology; University of Bradford
Qualifications: 9 GCSEs, BTEC National Diploma, BSc (Hons) degree
Overseas tours: MCC Universities to Ireland 2006; Bradford/Leeds UCCE to India 2007; British Universities to South Africa 2008

Career highlights to date: '54* against West Indians for MCC in 2007. Six wickets against Surrey CCC at The Oval [for Bradford/Leeds UCCE 2007]. As a cricket fan, I have grown up watching cricketers like Mark Ramprakash and Vikram Solanki, and having the opportunity to play against them and get their wickets was a huge personal achievement for me.'

Cricket moments to forget: 'Getting hit out of the ground by Rikki Clarke at The Oval'

Cricketers particularly admired: Shane Warne, Muttiah Muralitharan, Michael Vaughan, Sachin Tendulkar
Other sports followed: 'Follow a little of most sports'
Favourite band: Kanye West, Usher, Timbaland
Relaxations: 'Going to the gym, socialising with friends and family and listening to music'
Extras: Played for Bradford/Leeds UCCE 2006, 2007. Made first-class debut for MCC v West Indians at Durham 2007, scoring 54*
Opinions on cricket: 'I believe the game today is a faster-moving game as it is played in a more aggressive manner. I also think the standard of the game has developed and improved a great deal since I've been following it due to the help of the advanced technology that's around in this day and age.'
Best batting: 75 Warwickshire v DUCCE, Durham 2009

2009 Season

	M	Inn	NO	Runs	HS	Avg	100	50	Ct	St	Balls	Runs	Wkts	Avg	BB	5I	10M
Test																	
FC	1	1	0	75	75	75.00	-	1	-	-	6	11	0		-	-	-
ODI																	
List A																	
20/20 Int																	
20/20																	

Career Performances

	M	Inn	NO	Runs	HS	Avg	100	50	Ct	St	Balls	Runs	Wkts	Avg	BB	5I	10M
Test																	
FC	2	3	2	136	75	136.00	-	2	-	-	78	54	0		-	-	-
ODI																	
List A																	
20/20 Int																	
20/20																	

CLARE, J. L. Derbyshire

Name: <u>Jonathan</u> Luke Clare
Role: Right-hand bat, right-arm fast-medium bowler; all-rounder
Born: 14 June 1986, Burnley, Lancashire
Height: 6ft 3in **Weight:** 15st
Nickname: JC, Unit, Beefy
County debut: 2007
Place in batting averages: (2008 50th av. 42.69)
Place in bowling averages: 103rd av. 40.70 (2008 61st av. 28.09)
Parents: John and Elaine
Marital status: Single
Family links with cricket: Grandfather and father played club cricket for Burnley CC
Education: St Theodore's RC High School and Sixth Form
Qualifications: 10 GCSEs, 3 A-levels
Overseas tours: Derbyshire to Grenada, 2008
Overseas teams played for: Northern Districts, New Zealand; Hamilton Old Boys, New Zealand
Career highlights to date: 'Taking 5-90 on first-class debut v Notts. Scoring my maiden first-class century (129*) and taking 7-79 in game v Northamptonshire in 2008'
Cricket superstitions: None
Cricketers particularly admired: Dale Benkenstein, Andrew Flintoff, Carl Hooper
Young players to look out for: Dan Redfern (Derbyshire)
Other sports played: Football, golf ('handicap 14') 'any sports'
Other sports followed: Football (Burnley FC season-ticket holder)
Favourite band: Glasvegas, Arctic Monkeys, 'any Manchester music'
Relaxations: 'Pub games – darts, pool and cribbage.'
Extras: Was member of Burnley U15 with three other players currently playing county/international cricket – David Brown (Gloucestershire), Michael Brown (Hampshire), James Anderson (Lancashire/England). Recorded maiden first-class five-wicket return (5-90) on debut v Nottinghamshire at Chesterfield 2007. Was selected with six other fast bowlers for the 2008 ECB Skills Set trip to Florida which included tuition from Dennis Lillee in India. NBC Denis Compton Award for most promising young Derbyshire player 2008
Opinions on cricket: 'Too many Championship games – not enough time to recover between games'
Best batting: 129* Derbyshire v Northamptonshire, Northampton 2008
Best bowling: 7-74 Derbyshire v Northamptonshire, Northampton 2008

2009 Season

	M	Inn	NO	Runs	HS	Avg	100	50	Ct	St	Balls	Runs	Wkts	Avg	BB	5I	10M
Test																	
FC	5	5	0	13	6	2.60	-	-	1	-	714	407	10	40.70	3-64	-	-
ODI																	
List A	4	3	1	56	34	28.00	-	-	1	-	133	104	1	104.00	1-24	-	
20/20 Int																	
20/20																	

Career Performances

	M	Inn	NO	Runs	HS	Avg	100	50	Ct	St	Balls	Runs	Wkts	Avg	BB	5I	10M
Test																	
FC	20	26	5	610	129*	29.04	1	5	6	-	2556	1481	51	29.03	7-74	2	-
ODI																	
List A	19	14	1	143	34	11.00	-	-	5	-	715	664	15	44.26	3-39	-	
20/20 Int																	
20/20	6	3	1	10	4*	5.00	-	-	1	-	53	72	2	36.00	2-20	-	

CLARK, S. R. Kent

Name: <u>Stuart</u> Rupert Clark
Role: Right-hand bat, right-arm fast-medium bowler
Born: 28 September 1975, Sutherland, Sydney, Australia
Height: 6ft 5½in
Nickname: Sarfraz
County debut: 2004 (Middlesex), 2007 (Hampshire)
County cap: 2007 (Hampshire)
Test debut: 2005-06
ODI debut: 2005-06
Twenty20 Int debut: 2005-06
Parents: Bruce and Mary
Wife: Michelle
Children: Lachlan and Sophie
Education: Christ Church Anglo-Indian High School, Chennai; University of Sydney
Qualifications: Bachelor of Commerce
Career outside cricket: Was a real estate agent before becoming a professional cricketer
Overseas tours: Australia A to South Africa 2002-03, to Pakistan 2005-06; Australia to England 2005, to New Zealand (one-day series) 2005-06, to South Africa 2005-06, to Bangladesh 2005-06, to Malaysia (DLF Cup) 2006-07, to

West Indies (World Cup) 2006-07, to South Africa (World Twenty20) 2007-08, to India (one-day series) 2007-08, to West Indies 2008, to India 2008-09, to UAE (one-day series) 2008-09, to England 2009

Overseas teams played for: New South Wales 1997-98 –

Extras: Took 45 Pura Cup wickets (av. 23.27) 2001-02 and was New South Wales Player of the Year. Returned third best match figures by an Australian Test debutant (9-89 – 5-55/4-34) in the first Test v South Africa at Cape Town 2005-06, winning Man of the Match award and going on to win Man of the [Test] Series award (20 wickets – av. 15.85). Was leading wicket-taker in the 2006-07 Ashes series (26 wickets – av. 17.03). His domestic match awards include Man of the Match v Western Australia at Perth in the ING Cup final 2002-03 (3-34) and v Western Australia at Perth in the Pura Cup 2006-07 (8-58/2-36, including first innings hat-trick – North, Voges, Magoffin). Was a temporary overseas player with Middlesex during the 2004 and 2005 seasons, an overseas player with Hampshire during the 2007 season and has signed as an overseas player with Kent for 2010

Best batting: 62 New South Wales v South Australia, Adelaide 2006-07

Best bowling: 8-58 New South Wales v Western Australia, Perth 2006-07

2009 Season

	M	Inn	NO	Runs	HS	Avg	100	50	Ct	St	Balls	Runs	Wkts	Avg	BB	5I	10M
Test	2	3	0	38	32	12.66	-	-	-	-	282	176	4	44.00	3-18	-	-
FC	4	4	1	48	32	16.00	-	-	-	-	564	301	10	30.10	3-18	-	-
ODI																	
List A																	
20/20 Int																	
20/20																	

Career Performances

	M	Inn	NO	Runs	HS	Avg	100	50	Ct	St	Balls	Runs	Wkts	Avg	BB	5I	10M
Test	24	26	7	248	39	13.05	-	-	4	-	5146	2243	94	23.86	5-32	2	-
FC	102	130	37	1314	62	14.12	-	1	27	-	20906	10047	369	27.22	8-58	13	1
ODI	39	12	7	69	16*	13.80	-	-	10	-	1829	1477	53	27.86	4-54	-	
List A	134	40	16	196	26*	8.16	-	-	29	-	6789	4868	182	26.74	6-27	1	
20/20 Int	9	0	0	0	0		-	-	4	-	216	237	13	18.23	4-20	-	
20/20	15	1	1	0	0*		-	-	5	-	353	349	22	15.86	4-20	-	

CLARKE, R.   Warwickshire

Name: Rikki Clarke
Role: Right-hand bat, right-arm fast-medium
bowler; all-rounder
Born: 29 September 1981, Orsett, Essex
Height: 6ft 4½in **Weight:** 14st 13lbs
Nickname: Clarkey, Crouchy, Rock
County debut: 2001 (one-day, Surrey),
2002 (first-class, Surrey), 2008 (Derbyshire),
2008 (Warwickshire)
County cap: 2005 (Surrey)
Test debut: 2003-04
ODI debut: 2003

1000 runs in a season: 1
1st-Class 200s: 1
Place in batting averages: 96th av. 37.11
(2008 155th av. 25.90)
Place in bowling averages: 136th av. 58.18 (2008 131st av. 42.00)
Parents: Bob and Janet
Marital status: Engaged to Harriett
Children: Ella-May 26 June 2008
Family links with cricket: 'Dad tried to play but then realised he was rubbish'
Education: Broadwater; Godalming College
Qualifications: 5 GCSEs, GNVQ Leisure and Tourism
Career outside cricket: 'Poker player'
Off-season: 'A little rest, then back into training around November time'
Overseas tours: Surrey U19 to Barbados; MCC Young Cricketers to Cape Town;
England to Sri Lanka (ICC Champions Trophy) 2002-03, to Bangladesh and Sri
Lanka 2003-04, to West Indies 2003-04, to India (ICC Champions Trophy) 2006-07;
ECB National Academy to Australia and Sri Lanka 2002-03; England A to Sri Lanka
2004-05, to West Indies 2005-06
Career highlights to date: 'Playing for England in Test and one-day cricket'
Cricket moments to forget: 'Too many to mention'
Cricket superstitions: 'Nope, none – managed to get rid of them all, thank God'
Favourite sledging line: 'From Shane Warne when he was at Hampshire. I have a
very upright stance and, as he was walking in to bowl, he stopped and shouted down
the pitch – "Sorry mate, I thought you were waiting for a throw down!" Made me
laugh even though I was trying hard to be serious'
Cricketers particularly admired: Andrew Flintoff, Darren Gough, Mark Ramprakash
Young players to look out for: Jade Dernbach (Surrey), Chris Woakes and Ateeq
Javid (Warwickshire)
Other sports played: Football, golf, snooker, poker – 'all sports really'

Other sports followed: Football (Tottenham Hotspur)
Favourite band: Akon, Ne-Yo, Tinchy Stryder
Relaxations: 'Being a dad, watching TV and films, playing poker'
Extras: Named after former Tottenham Hotspur and Argentina footballer Ricky Villa. Represented England U17. Scored maiden first-class century (107*) on first-class debut v CUCCE at Fenner's 2002. NBC Denis Compton Award for the most promising young Surrey player 2002. Cricket Writers' Club Young Player of the Year 2002. Surrey Supporters' Young Player of the Year 2002. Surrey Sponsors' Young Player of the Year 2002. Made ODI debut v Pakistan at Old Trafford in the NatWest Challenge 2003, taking the wicket of Imran Nazir with his first ball in international cricket. ECB National Academy 2004-05, 2005-06, 2006-07. Vice-captain of Surrey 2006 to June 2007. Scored 28-ball 82* v Gloucestershire at The Oval in the Friends Provident 2007 as Surrey posted a world record List A total of 496-4. Left Surrey at the end of the 2007 season and joined Derbyshire for 2008 as captain. Left Derbyshire in August 2008 and joined Warwickshire. Scored a 78-ball century against Hampshire, April 2009
Opinions on cricket: 'The county cricket format should emulate international cricket. Umpires in county cricket should be able to use light meters, and in Championship four-day cricket the last day should be called off a lot sooner than 5pm if both captains agree that the game is heading for a draw'
Best batting: 214 Surrey v Somerset, Guildford 2006
Best bowling: 4-21 Surrey v Leicestershire, Leicester 2003

2009 Season

	M	Inn	NO	Runs	HS	Avg	100	50	Ct	St	Balls	Runs	Wkts	Avg	BB	5I	10M
Test																	
FC	14	18	1	631	112	37.11	1	5	25	-	985	640	11	58.18	2-15	-	-
ODI																	
List A	14	7	3	121	33*	30.25	-	-	9	-	282	233	4	58.25	2-24	-	
20/20 Int																	
20/20	5	5	4	95	51*	95.00	-	1	3	-	102	166	10	16.60	3-20	-	

Career Performances

	M	Inn	NO	Runs	HS	Avg	100	50	Ct	St	Balls	Runs	Wkts	Avg	BB	5I	10M
Test	2	3	0	96	55	32.00	-	1	1	-	174	60	4	15.00	2-7	-	
FC	103	160	14	5350	214	36.64	11	25	138	-	8575	5855	136	43.05	4-21	-	
ODI	20	13	0	144	39	11.07	-	-	11	-	469	415	11	37.72	2-28	-	
List A	138	116	17	2525	98*	25.50	-	12	63	-	3323	3105	80	38.81	4-49	-	
20/20 Int																	
20/20	47	45	13	726	79*	22.68	-	3	21	-	666	870	41	21.21	3-11	-	

CLAYDON, M. E. Durham

Name: <u>Mitchell</u> Eric Claydon
Role: Left-hand bat, right-arm fast bowler
Born: 25 November 1982, Fairfield, Australia
Height: 6ft 4in **Weight:** 15st 9lbs
Nickname: Lips
County debut: 2005 (Yorkshire), 2007 (Durham)
Place in batting averages: 270th av. 10.00
Place in bowling averages: 52nd av. 31.08
Parents: Robert (Tosh) and Sue
Marital status: Single
Children: Lachlan Robert Bickhoff-Claydon,
25 February 2004
Family links with cricket: Father played for
Markington CC in the Nidderdale League

Education: Westfields Sports High School, Sydney
Qualifications: Level 1 coaching
Career outside cricket: 'Real estate agent'
Overseas teams played for: Campbelltown-Camden Ghosts 1999 –
Career highlights to date: 'Being a part of Durham 2007, even though I only played one game'
Cricket moments to forget: 'While participating in a fielding drill consisting of high catches, I misjudged the height of the ball – the next thing I knew I was lying on the physio table with an ice pack on my forehead.'
Cricket superstitions: 'Must wear my gold chain that has a photo of my sister who died in 2003.'
Cricketers particularly admired: Steve Waugh
Young players to look out for: Ben Harmison and Mark Stoneman (both Durham)
Other sports played: Rugby league, rugby union
Other sports followed: Rugby league (West Tigers), football (Leeds United)
Favourite band: Denham Reagh
Relaxations: 'Surfing whilst home in Australia. Golf'
Extras: Only player in history of Campbelltown-Camden Ghosts to have taken two first grade hat-tricks. Played in all forms of the game for the first team during 2008 season. Holds a British passport and is not considered an overseas player
Best batting: 40 Durham v Lancashire, Old Trafford 2008
Best bowling: 4-90 Durham v Sussex, Hove 2009

2009 Season

	M	Inn	NO	Runs	HS	Avg	100	50	Ct	St	Balls	Runs	Wkts	Avg	BB	5I	10M
Test																	
FC	12	12	1	110	38	10.00	-	-	3	-	1404	777	25	31.08	4-90	-	-
ODI																	
List A	13	7	0	49	19	7.00	-	-	-	-	530	441	10	44.10	2-34	-	
20/20 Int																	
20/20	10	5	2	22	9*	7.33	-	-	4	-	227	254	17	14.94	5-26	1	

Career Performances

	M	Inn	NO	Runs	HS	Avg	100	50	Ct	St	Balls	Runs	Wkts	Avg	BB	5I	10M
Test																	
FC	18	17	2	206	40	13.73	-	-	3	-	2292	1353	35	38.65	4-90	-	-
ODI																	
List A	22	10	0	66	19	6.60	-	-	-	-	986	784	22	35.63	3-31	-	
20/20 Int																	
20/20	19	8	5	40	12*	13.33	-	-	6	-	402	502	22	22.81	5-26	1	

CLIFF, S. J. Leicestershire

Name: Samuel (<u>Sam</u>) James Cliff
Role: Right-hand bat, right-arm
fast-medium bowler
Born: 3 October 1987, Nottingham
Height: 6ft 2in **Weight:** 11st 8lbs
Nickname: Cliffy, Jacko
County debut: 2007
Parents: Colin Cliff and Julie Silverwood
Marital status: Single
Family links with cricket: 'Father plays village
cricket "very well" and has scored over 60 centuries
(he keeps reminding me)'
Education: Colonel Frank Seely Comprehensive,
Calverton, Nottingham
Qualifications: 10 GCSEs
Career outside cricket: Painter and decorator
Overseas tours: Leicestershire Young Cricketers to India 2005-06
Career highlights to date: 'Getting a contract. Playing Twenty20 and in the
Championship! Taking 4-26 v Derbyshire in Pro40, August 2008'
Cricket moments to forget: 'None yet!'
Cricket superstitions: 'A few little ones but nothing specific'
Cricketers particularly admired: David Masters, HD Ackerman

Young players to look out for: Josh Cobb (Leicestershire)
Other sports played: Golf, football
Other sports followed: Ice hockey (Nottingham Panthers), football (Notts County), rugby (Nottingham)
Relaxations: 'Going out, chilling'
Extras: Played for Leicestershire Academy v England U19 2007. Played in Loughborough Town's Leicestershire County Cup winning side 2007, taking 2-13 from eight overs in the final v Market Harborough at Leicester. Appearances in 2009 were limited by injury.
Opinions on cricket: 'Keep politics out of the changing room'
Best batting: 26 Leicestershire v Northamptonshire, Grace Road 2009
Best bowling: 4-42 Leicestershire v Derbyshire, Grace Road 2008

2009 Season

	M	Inn	NO	Runs	HS	Avg	100	50	Ct	St	Balls	Runs	Wkts	Avg	BB	5I	10M
Test																	
FC	1	1	0	26	26	26.00	-	-	-	-	138	92	2	46.00	2-92	-	-
ODI																	
List A	3	2	0	10	9	5.00	-	-	-	-	150	157	1	157.00	1-69	-	
20/20 Int																	
20/20	2	1	0	4	4	4.00	-	-	1	-	24	33	0		-	-	

Career Performances

	M	Inn	NO	Runs	HS	Avg	100	50	Ct	St	Balls	Runs	Wkts	Avg	BB	5I	10M
Test																	
FC	6	7	2	71	26	14.20	-	-	1	-	752	459	13	35.30	4-42	-	-
ODI																	
List A	7	3	1	10	9	5.00	-	-	1	-	318	308	6	51.33	4-26	-	
20/20 Int																	
20/20	5	1	0	4	4	4.00	-	-	2	-	90	111	1	111.00	1-24	-	

17. This Pakistan batsman took more than nine hours to complete a Test century against England in 1977. Name him.

COBB, J. J.   Leicestershire

Name: Joshua (<u>Josh</u>) James Cobb
Role: Right-hand bat, leg-spin bowler;
'batter that bowls'
Born: 17 August 1990, Leicester
Height: 6ft 1in   **Weight:** 12st 6lbs
Nickname: Cobby
County debut: 2007
Place in batting averages: 219th av. 19.61
Parents: Russell and Sharon
Family links with cricket: 'Father
ex-Leicestershire player'
Education: Bosworth College; Oakham School
Qualifications: GCSEs

Overseas tours: Leicestershire U14 to South
Africa 2003; Leicestershire U19 to India 2006;
England U19 to South Africa 2008-09.
Career highlights to date: 'Making first-class debut v Northamptonshire [2007]
having just turned 17'
Cricket superstitions: 'Putting on left pad before right pad'
Cricketers particularly admired: Shane Warne, Darren Stevens, Paul Nixon
Young players to look out for: Shiv Thakor (Leicestershire)
Other sports played: Badminton (Leicestershire U13-15), football ('played in
goal for Leicester District at U16')
Other sports followed: Football (Manchester United), rugby (Leicester Tigers)
Favourite band: D12
Relaxations: 'Listening to music, socialising with friends, playing sports and
reading and writing books!'
Extras: Made 2nd XI Championship debut 2006. Scored 102* for Leicestershire
Academy v Victoria Emerging Players at Grace Road 2007. Scored maiden century
(148*) v Middlesex in August 2008. NBC Denis Compton Award for most promising
young Leicestershire player 2008. Scored 220 for England U19 v Bangladesh U19,
Scarborough 2009.
Opinions on cricket: 'Should use more technology where possible, trying not to slow
the game down in the process.'
Best batting: 148* Leicestershire v Middlesex 2008
Best bowling: 2-11 Leicestershire v Gloucestershire, Grace Road 2008

2009 Season

	M	Inn	NO	Runs	HS	Avg	100	50	Ct	St	Balls	Runs	Wkts	Avg	BB	5I	10M
Test																	
FC	14	26	0	510	95	19.61	-	4	4	-	114	71	1	71.00	1-8	-	-
ODI																	
List A	7	5	0	86	43	17.20	-	-	1	-	6	12	1	12.00	1-12	-	
20/20 Int																	
20/20																	

Career Performances

	M	Inn	NO	Runs	HS	Avg	100	50	Ct	St	Balls	Runs	Wkts	Avg	BB	5I	10M
Test																	
FC	23	38	3	952	148*	27.20	1	6	9	-	288	205	5	41.00	2-11	-	-
ODI																	
List A	10	8	1	117	43	16.71	-	-	2	-	6	12	1	12.00	1-12	-	
20/20 Int																	
20/20	1	1	1	2	2*		-	-	-	-	0	0	0		-	-	

COETZER, K. J. Durham

Name: <u>Kyle</u> James Coetzer
Role: Right-hand bat, right-arm medium bowler
Born: 14 April 1984, Aberdeen
Height: 5ft 11in
Nickname: Costa, Meerkat
County debut: 2004
ODI debut: 2008
Twenty20 Int debut: 2008
Place in batting averages: 109th av. 35.50
Parents: Peter and Megan
Marital status: Single
Family links with cricket: 'Uncle and grandfather played provincial cricket, brothers played senior levels for Scotland and father set us our standards in club cricket like they usually do.'
Education: Aberdeen Grammar School
Qualifications: Standard grades, 4 Intermediate 2s
Career outside cricket: 'Coaching and property improvement'
Off-season: 'Two months in Cape Town for a long holiday with a few games of cricket'
Overseas tours: Scotland U19 to New Zealand (U19 World Cup) 2001-02, to Bangladesh (U19 World Cup) 2003-04 (c), plus other Scotland age-group and A tours;

Scotland to UAE (ICC Inter-Continental Cup) 2004, to Ireland (ICC Trophy) 2005, to Barbados 2005-06, to Johannesburg (ICC World Cup qualifiers) 2008-09; Durham to Dubai 2005, 2006, to Mumbai 2006, to Cape Town 2007, to Pretoria 2008

Overseas teams played for: Cape Town CC 2002-03 – 2005-06; Gosnells CC 2005; Western Province Academy, Cape Town; Delhi Daredevils (IPL) 2009

Career highlights to date: 'Playing a part in winning the County Championship in 2009, and scoring a century in the title-winning game v Nottinghamshire in a record opening partnership with Michael DiVenuto. A good personal performance in World Twenty20 in 2009, and taking a diving catch on the boundary off Boucher in the match against South Africa'

Cricket moments to forget: 'The Twenty20 quarter-final v Kent 2009'

Cricket superstitions: 'Touch bat in crease after "over" is called'

Cricketers particularly admired: Jacques Kallis, Brian McMillan, Dale Benkenstein, Alan Donald, Robin Smith, Michael DiVenuto, Shivnarine Chanderpaul

Young players to look out for: Scott Borthwick and Ben Stokes (Durham), Mark Wood (Northumberland)

Other sports played: Golf, football

Other sports followed: Football (Aberdeen, Arsenal)

Favourite band: Red Hot Chili Peppers, U2, Matchbox 20

Relaxations: 'Listening to music'

Extras: Man of the Match v Italy in the ECC U19 Championships at Deventer 2003 (146*). Has played for Scotland in first-class and one-day cricket, including NCL 2003 and C&G 2003, 2004, 2006. Scored 67 on first-class debut, for Durham v Glamorgan at Cardiff 2004. Chosen by Scotland to face Pakistan in 2007, he opted to play for Durham instead. Played for Scotland in ICC World Twenty20 tournament 2009

Opinions on cricket: 'It's becoming a Twenty20 overload'

Best batting: 153* Durham v DUCCE, Durham 2007

2009 Season

	M	Inn	NO	Runs	HS	Avg	100	50	Ct	St	Balls	Runs	Wkts	Avg	BB	5I	10M
Test																	
FC	6	9	1	284	107	35.50	1	-	7	-	0	0	0		-	-	-
ODI																	
List A	12	12	3	351	63	39.00	-	2	3	-	24	26	0		-	-	
20/20 Int	2	2	0	75	42	37.50	-	-	2	-	0	0	0		-	-	
20/20	10	10	1	223	42	24.77	-	-	5	-	0	0	0		-	-	

Career Performances

	M	Inn	NO	Runs	HS	Avg	100	50	Ct	St	Balls	Runs	Wkts	Avg	BB	5I	10M
Test																	
FC	33	57	7	1676	153*	33.52	4	4	23	-	54	22	0		-	-	-
ODI	4	4	0	81	44	20.25	-	-	2	-	0	0	0		-	-	
List A	55	53	6	1385	127	29.46	1	8	20	-	84	73	0		-	-	
20/20 Int	5	5	1	174	48*	43.50	-	-	2	-	0	0	0		-	-	
20/20	16	15	2	333	48*	25.61	-	-	5	-	0	0	0		-	-	

COLES, M. T.

Name: Matthew (<u>Matt</u>) Thomas Coles
Role: Left-hand bat, right-arm medium bowler; all-rounder
Born: 26 May 1990, Maidstone, Kent
County debut: 2009
Extras: Represented Kent at U13, U15 and U17 level, and played for Kent 2nd XI. Kent Academy 2007-09. Plays club cricket for Hartley CC (Kent Cricket League). Made his first-class debut for Kent in 2009. Took 3-50 on his Pro40 debut v Middlesex 2009. Signed a new one-year contract in October 2009. Selected by the ECB to attend MRF Pace Foundation with Dennis Lillee in Chennai in February 2010
Best batting: 16 Kent v Gloucestershire, Bristol 2009
Best bowling: 2-130 Kent v Gloucestershire, Bristol 2009

2009 Season

	M	Inn	NO	Runs	HS	Avg	100	50	Ct	St	Balls	Runs	Wkts	Avg	BB	5I	10M
Test																	
FC	2	2	0	30	16	15.00	-	-	-	-	106	130	2	65.00	2-130	-	-
ODI																	
List A	4	2	0	10	5	5.00	-	-	-	-	102	127	4	31.75	3-50	-	
20/20 Int																	
20/20																	

Career Performances

	M	Inn	NO	Runs	HS	Avg	100	50	Ct	St	Balls	Runs	Wkts	Avg	BB	5I	10M
Test																	
FC	2	2	0	30	16	15.00	-	-	-	-	106	130	2	65.00	2-130	-	-
ODI																	
List A	4	2	0	10	5	5.00	-	-	-	-	102	127	4	31.75	3-50	-	
20/20 Int																	
20/20																	

COLLINGWOOD, P. D. Durham

Name: <u>Paul</u> David Collingwood
Role: Right-hand bat, right-arm medium bowler
Born: 26 May 1976, Shotley Bridge, Tyneside
Height: 5ft 11in **Weight:** 12st
Nickname: Colly
County debut: 1995 (one-day), 1996 (first-class)
County Cap: 1998
Benefit: 2007
Test debut: 2003-04
ODI debut: 2001
Twenty20 Int debut: 2005
1000 runs in a season: 2
1st-Class 200s: 1
Place in batting averages: 94th av. 37.54
(2008 111th av. 31.70)

Parents: David and Janet
Wife: Vicki
Children: Shannon, 2006
Family links with cricket: Father and brother play in the Tyneside Senior League for Shotley Bridge CC
Education: Blackfyne Comprehensive School; Derwentside College
Qualifications: 9 GCSEs, 2 A-levels
Overseas tours: Durham Cricket Academy to Sri Lanka 1996 (c); England VI to Hong Kong 2001, 2002; England to Zimbabwe (one-day series) 2001-02, to India and New Zealand 2001-02 (one-day series), to Australia (VB Series) 2002-03, to Africa (World Cup) 2002-03, to Bangladesh and Sri Lanka 2003-04, to West Indies 2003-04, to Zimbabwe (one-day series) 2004-05, to South Africa 2004-05, to Pakistan 2005-06, to India 2005-06, to India (ICC Champions Trophy) 2006-07, to Australia 2006-07, to West Indies (World Cup) 2006-07, to South Africa (World Twenty20) 2007-08 (c), to Sri Lanka 2007-08 (ODI, c), to New Zealand 2007-08 (ODI, c), to India (Test and one-day series) 2008-09, to West Indies 2008-09, to South Africa 2009-10 (vc)
Overseas teams played for: Bulleen CC, Melbourne 1995-96, 1996-97 ('won flag on both occasions'); Cornwall CC, Auckland 1997-98; Alberton CC, Johannesburg 1998-99; Richmond CC, Melbourne 2000-01; Delhi Daredevils (IPL) 2009
Cricket moments to forget: 'Being Matthew Walker's (Kent) first first-class wicket'
Cricket superstitions: 'Left pad on first, and wearing them on the wrong legs'
Cricketers particularly admired: Steve Waugh, Jacques Kallis, Glenn McGrath, Shane Warne
Other sports played: Golf (9 handicap)
Other sports followed: Football ('The Red and Whites' – Sunderland)

Extras: Took wicket (David Capel) with first ball on first-class debut against Northants, then scored 91 in Durham's first innings. Durham Player of the Year 2000. Joint (and first English) winner of the Jack Ryder Medal, awarded by the umpires, for his performances in Victorian Premier Cricket 2000-01. Scored 112* and took England ODI record 6-31 v Bangladesh at Trent Bridge in the NatWest Series 2005, winning Man of the Match award. His other match awards include Man of the Match v Sri Lanka at Perth in the VB Series 2002-03 (100) and in three consecutive matches (including the two finals) in the Commonwealth Bank Series 2006-07, and Man of the Match in the first Twenty20 International v West Indies at The Oval 2007 (79). Vice-captain of Durham 2005-06. Slazenger Sheer Instinct Award 2005. Appointed MBE in 2006 New Year Honours as part of 2005 Ashes-winning England team. Scored 206 in the second Test at Adelaide 2006-07, becoming the first England batsman to score a Test double century in Australia since Wally Hammond in 1936-37 and sharing with Kevin Pietersen (158) in a record fourth-wicket stand for England v Australia (310). One of *Wisden*'s Five Cricketers of the Year 2007. England 12-month central contract 2007-08, 2009-10. England one-day captain from June 2007 until relinquishing the position in 2008. Delhi Daredevils (IPL) paid $275,000 for his services in January 2009 auction

Best batting: 206 England v Australia, Adelaide 2006-07

Best bowling: 5-52 Durham v Somerset, Stockton-on-Tees 2005

2009 Season

	M	Inn	NO	Runs	HS	Avg	100	50	Ct	St	Balls	Runs	Wkts	Avg	BB	5I	10M
Test	7	11	1	318	74	31.80	-	4	7	-	108	76	1	76.00	1-38	-	-
FC	8	13	2	413	79*	37.54	-	5	7	-	108	76	1	76.00	1-38	-	-
ODI	6	6	2	190	56	47.50	-	1	2	-	228	186	6	31.00	3-16	-	
List A	6	6	2	190	56	47.50	-	1	2	-	228	186	6	31.00	3-16	-	
20/20 Int	6	5	0	63	19	12.60	-	-	3	-	36	37	3	12.33	2-20	-	
20/20	7	6	0	72	19	12.00	-	-	3	-	60	75	5	15.00	2-20	-	

Career Performances

	M	Inn	NO	Runs	HS	Avg	100	50	Ct	St	Balls	Runs	Wkts	Avg	BB	5I	10M
Test	53	93	9	3565	206	42.44	9	16	67	-	1527	846	15	56.40	3-23	-	-
FC	177	308	25	10354	206	36.58	23	52	194	-	9431	4818	120	40.15	5-52	1	-
ODI	170	154	32	4285	120*	35.12	4	23	97	-	4466	3742	97	38.57	6-31	1	
List A	338	316	56	8659	120*	33.30	6	51	174	-	8972	7278	210	34.65	6-31	1	
20/20 Int	21	19	0	407	79	21.42	-	2	6	-	192	282	16	17.62	4-22	-	
20/20	28	26	1	479	79	19.16	-	2	6	-	294	381	27	14.11	5-14	1	

COLLINS, P. T. Surrey

Name: <u>Pedro</u> Tyrone Collins
Role: Right-hand bat, left-arm
fast-medium bowler
Born: 12 August 1976, Boscobelle, Barbados
County debut: 2008
Test debut: 1998-99
ODI debut: 1999-2000
Place in bowling averages: 55th av. 31.50
Family links with cricket: Half-brother Fidel
Edwards plays for Barbados and
West Indies
Overseas tours: West Indies A to South Africa
1997-98, to Bangladesh and India 1998-99; West
Indies to Bangladesh 1999-2000, to New Zealand
1999-2000, to Zimbabwe and Kenya 2001, to Sri

Lanka 2001-02, to Sharjah (v Pakistan) 2001-02, to Sri Lanka (ICC Champions
Trophy) 2002-03, to India and Bangladesh 2002-03, to Africa (World Cup) 2002-03,
to England 2004, to Australia (VB Series) 2004-05, to South Africa (World 20/20)
2007-08, to South Africa 2007-08, plus one-day tournament in Sharjah
Overseas teams played for: Barbados 1996-97 –
Extras: Man of the Match v Windward Islands in Dominica in the Carib Beer Cup
2006-07 (6-24/1-15). Played for Benwell Hill in the North East Premier League 2007.
Took 7-11 v West Indies U19 at Berbice in the KFC Cup 2007-08, winning Man of
the Match award. Signed as a Surrey player just before the start of the 2008 season.
he withdrew from the West Indies squad to play Sri Lanka in favour of his county.
Only Saqlain Mushtaq took more first-class wickets for Surrey during 2008. Is not
considered an overseas player. Released by Surrey at the end of the 2009 season
Best batting: 25 Barbados v Trinidad and Tobago, Pointe-a-Pierre 2003-04
Best bowling: 6-24 Barbados v Windward Islands, Portsmouth (BP) 2006-07

2009 Season

	M	Inn	NO	Runs	HS	Avg	100	50	Ct	St	Balls	Runs	Wkts	Avg	BB	5I	10M
Test																	
FC	5	8	3	49	23	9.80	-	-	1	-	824	504	16	31.50	5-75	1	-
ODI																	
List A	8	2	0	4	2	2.00	-	-	1	-	258	215	5	43.00	3-56	-	
20/20 Int																	
20/20	3	1	1	0	0*	-	-	-	-	-	72	108	3	36.00	2-45	-	

Career Performances

	M	Inn	NO	Runs	HS	Avg	100	50	Ct	St	Balls	Runs	Wkts	Avg	BB	5I	10M
Test	32	47	7	235	24	5.87	-	-	7	-	6964	3671	106	34.63	6-53	3	-
FC	125	158	43	767	25	6.66	-	-	29	-	21436	11068	416	26.60	6-24	11	-
ODI	30	12	5	30	10*	4.28	-	-	8	-	1577	1212	39	31.07	5-43	1	
List A	91	36	10	153	55*	5.88	-	1	14	-	4443	3200	136	23.52	7-11	2	
20/20 Int																	
20/20	13	3	2	2	1*	2.00	-	-	1	-	274	355	10	35.50	3-13	-	

COLLYMORE, C. D. — Sussex

Name: Corey Dalanelo Collymore
Role: Right-hand bat, right-arm fast bowler
Born: 21 December 1977, Boscobelle,
St Peter, Barbados
Height: 6ft **Weight:** 13st 9lbs
Nickname: Screw, CC
County debut: 2003 (Warwickshire), 2008 (Sussex)
Test debut: 1998-99
ODI debut: 1999
Place in batting averages: 279th av. 7.41
Place in bowling averages: 69th av. 33.45
Parents: Maytred Collymore, Gordon Maxwell
Marital status: 'Married'
Children: 'Dionne, 24 December 2005; Dicoreya,
25 October 2006; Dicyrah, 5 March 2008'
Education: Alexandra Secondary School
Qualifications: 4 CXCs
Overseas tours: West Indies to Toronto (DMC Cup) 1999, to England 2000, to Zimbabwe 2001, to Kenya 2001, to Sri Lanka (LG Abans Triangular Series) 2001-02, to Sharjah (v Pakistan) 2001-02, to Sri Lanka (ICC Champions Trophy) 2002-03, to India 2002-03 (one-day series), to Bangladesh 2002-03, to Africa (World Cup) 2002-03, to Zimbabwe 2003-04, to South Africa 2003-04, to Australia 2005, to Malaysia, India and Pakistan 2006; to England 2007; to South Africa (World Cup) 2003; West Indies (World Cup) 2007
Overseas teams played for: Barbados 1998-99 –
Career highlights to date: 'Taking 11-134 v Pakistan, June 2005'
Cricket moments to forget: 'None!'
Cricket superstitions: None
Cricketers particularly admired: Courtney Walsh, Vasbert Drakes, Steve Waugh
Young players to look out for: Oliver Rayner, Will Beer (both Sussex)
Other sports followed: Football (Arsenal, Brazil)

Relaxations: 'Listening to music, spending time with family and friends'
Extras: Represented West Indies U19 in home series v Pakistan U19 1996-97. Took 4-49 in the final of the Coca-Cola Cup v India at Harare 2001, winning the Man of the Match award. Took 5-51 v Sri Lanka at Colombo in the LG Abans Triangular Series 2001-02, winning the Man of the Match award. Player of the [Test] Series v Sri Lanka 2002-03, performances including 7-57 in the second Test at Kingston. Was an overseas player with Warwickshire in August and September 2003, replacing the injured Collins Obuya. Signed as a Kolpak player in May 2008.
Opinions on cricket: 'Need better wickets so as to keep fast bowlers in the game'
Best batting: 23 Sussex v Nottinghamshire, Horsham 2009
Best bowling: 7-57 West Indies v Sri Lanka, Kingston 2003

2009 Season

	M	Inn	NO	Runs	HS	Avg	100	50	Ct	St	Balls	Runs	Wkts	Avg	BB	5I	10M
Test																	
FC	14	17	5	89	23	7.41	-	-	2	-	2376	1104	33	33.45	4-66	-	-
ODI																	
List A	1	1	1	4	4*		-	-	1	-	48	47	1	47.00	1-47	-	
20/20 Int																	
20/20																	

Career Performances

	M	Inn	NO	Runs	HS	Avg	100	50	Ct	St	Balls	Runs	Wkts	Avg	BB	5I	10M
Test	30	52	27	197	16*	7.88	-	-	6	-	6337	3004	93	32.30	7-57	4	1
FC	120	170	77	741	23	7.96	-	-	42	-	20486	9584	349	27.46	7-57	10	2
ODI	84	35	17	104	13*	5.77	-	-	12	-	4074	2924	83	35.22	5-51	1	
List A	131	50	25	151	13*	6.04	-	-	20	-	6139	4374	139	31.46	5-27	2	
20/20 Int																	
20/20	6	2	1	5	4	5.00	-	-	4	-	95	133	3	44.33	1-21	-	

COMBER, M. A.   Essex

Name: <u>Michael</u> Andrew Comber
Role: Right-hand bat, right-arm fast-medium bowler
Born: 26 October 1989, Colchester, Essex
County debut: No first-team appearance
Family links with cricket: Brother Nicholas played in the East Anglian Premier league
Overseas teams played for: Newtown & Chilwell CC, Geelong, Victoria 2008-09
Extras: Essex Academy 2003-09. Essex 2nd XI 2007-09. Clacton-on-Sea CC (East Anglian Premier Legaue) 2005-09. Awarded a one-year Academy-Professional contract for 2010

COMPTON, N. R. D.   Somerset

Name: Nicholas (<u>Nick</u>) Richard Denis Compton
Role: Right-hand bat, right-arm off-spin bowler
Born: 26 June 1983, Durban, South Africa
Height: 6ft 2in **Weight:** 13st 7lb
Nickname: Compo, Compdog, Ledge
County debut: 2001 (one-day, Middlesex), 2004 (first-class, Middlesex)
County cap: 2006
1000 runs in a season: 1
Place in batting averages: 126th av. 33.07
Parents: Richard and Glynis
Marital status: Single
Family links with cricket: Grandfather Denis Compton played football and cricket for England
Education: Harrow School; Durham University
Qualifications: 3 A-levels, ECB coach Level 1
Career outside cricket: 'Media, TV, journalism'
Off-season: 'Working on media-related skills. Training and working on my fitness. Taking a holiday and spending time with my family'
Overseas tours: England U19 World Cup 2001-02; England Lions to Bangladesh 2006-07
Overseas teams played for: University of Western Australia, Perth 2001; Western Suburbs (Sydney); Berea Rovers, Durban; Western Province (Cape Town); University of Cape Town

Career highlights to date: 'England A tour to Bangladesh, 2002. Reaching 100 at Lord's with a six v Kent to score my first Championship century [2006] – champagne moment! Scoring six centuries and making 1300 runs in the 2006 season'

Cricket moments to forget: 'Relegation to second division [2006]. Being left out of the Twenty20 campaign in 2008'

Cricketers particularly admired: Rahul Dravid, Jacques Kallis, Steve Waugh, Ed Joyce, Fanie De Villiers

Young players to look out for: Phil Hughes, Sam Robson, Adam London, James Kuiper

Other sports played: Golf (6 handicap), waterskiing, represented Natal at junior level at tennis

Other sports followed: Football ('Arsenal – big fan!'), Super 14 rugby union (Sharks)

Favourite band: Empire of the Sun, REM

Relaxations: 'Chilling with mates on the beach, golf, travelling to faraway places.'

Extras: Played for Natal U13 and U15. Natal Academy award 1997. Middlesex U17 Batsman of the Season 1999. Middlesex U19 Player of the Season 2000. NBC Denis Compton Award for the most promising young Middlesex player 2001, 2002, 2006. Represented England U19 2002. Scored maiden first-class century (101) v OUCCE at The Parks 2006 and maiden Championship century (124) in the following match v Kent at Lord's 2006. Carried bat for 105* v Nottinghamshire at Lord's 2006, in the process passing 1000 first-class runs for the season in his first full season of county cricket. Released by Middlesex at the end of the 2009 season. Signed for Somerset in October 2009. Is England-qualified

Opinions on cricket: 'Let's not lose sight of the fact that Test cricket still remains the pinnacle for any professional cricketer.'

Best batting: 190 Middlesex v Durham, Lord's 2006

Best bowling: 1-94 Middlesex v Sussex, Southgate 2006

2009 Season

	M	Inn	NO	Runs	HS	Avg	100	50	Ct	St	Balls	Runs	Wkts	Avg	BB	5I	10M
Test																	
FC	14	28	2	860	178	33.07	2	3	8	-	12	5	0		-	-	-
ODI																	
List A	13	13	4	694	131	77.11	3	2	7	-	7	8	1	8.00	1-0	-	
20/20 Int																	
20/20	7	6	0	65	24	10.83	-	-	-	-	0	0	0		-	-	

Career Performances

	M	Inn	NO	Runs	HS	Avg	100	50	Ct	St	Balls	Runs	Wkts	Avg	BB	5I	10M
Test																	
FC	54	97	9	2988	190	33.95	8	12	28	-	78	128	1	128.00	1-94	-	-
ODI																	
List A	56	50	12	1525	131	40.13	4	6	29	-	61	53	1	53.00	1-0	-	
20/20 Int																	
20/20	29	23	1	252	50*	11.45	-	1	13	-	0	0	0		-	-	

COOK, A. N. Essex

Name: <u>Alastair</u> Nathan Cook
Role: Left-hand opening bat, right-arm
off-spin bowler
Born: 25 December 1984, Gloucester
Height: 6ft 2in **Weight:** 12st 10lbs
Nickname: Ali, Cooky, Chef
County debut: 2003
County cap: 2005
Test debut: 2005-06
ODI debut: 2006
Twenty20 Int debut: 2007
1000 runs in a season: 4
Place in batting averages: 58th av. 43.25
(2008 73rd av. 38.52)
Parents: Graham and Elizabeth
Marital status: Single
Family links with cricket: 'Dad played for village side, brothers play for Maldon CC'
Education: Bedford School
Qualifications: 9 GCSEs, 3 A-levels
Overseas tours: Bedford School to Barbados 2001; England U19 to Bangladesh
(U19 World Cup) 2003-04 (c); England A to Sri Lanka 2004-05, to West Indies 2005-
06; England to India 2005-06, to Australia 2006-07, to Sri Lanka 2007-08, to New
Zealand 2007-08, to India 2008-09, to West Indies 2008-09, to South Africa 2009-10
Cricket moments to forget: 'Running myself out first ball in U15 World Cup game
against India'
Cricket superstitions: 'A few!'
Cricketers particularly admired: Graham Thorpe, Andy Flower, Graham Gooch
Other sports played: Squash, golf
Other sports followed: 'All sports'
Relaxations: 'Spending time with friends'
Extras: Played for England U15 in U15 World Cup 2000. Represented England U19
2003 and (as captain) 2004. Scored 69* on first-class debut v Nottinghamshire at
Chelmsford 2003 and a further two half-centuries in his next two Championship
matches. Had consecutive scores of 108*, 108* and 87 in the U19 World Cup 2003-04
in Bangladesh. NBC Denis Compton Award for the most promising young Essex
player 2003, 2004, 2005 and 2006. ECB National Academy 2004-05 (part-time), 2005-
06. Scored 214 v Australians at Chelmsford in a two-day game 2005. Cricket Writers'
Club Young Player of the Year 2005. PCA Young Player of the Year 2005, 2006.
Called up as a replacement to the England tour of India 2005-06, scoring century
(104*) on Test debut in the first Test at Nagpur (following 60 in first innings). Scored
maiden Ashes century (116) in the third Test at Perth 2006-07, becoming the first
England player to score four Test hundreds before his 22nd birthday. Man of the

Match in the first Test v West Indies at Lord's 2007 (105/65). England 12-month central contract 2007-08, 2009-10. Man of the Match in the fourth ODI v Sri Lanka in Colombo 2007-08 (80). Became the youngest England player to achieve 2000 Test runs whilst in New Zealand 2008. Scored a century in England's victory over South Africa in Durban, December 2009. Appointed captain form England's tour to Bangladesh February-March 2010

Best batting: 195 Essex v Northamptonshire, Northampton 2005
Best bowling: 3-13 Essex v Northamptonshire, Chelmsford 2005

2009 Season

	M	Inn	NO	Runs	HS	Avg	100	50	Ct	St	Balls	Runs	Wkts	Avg	BB	5I	10M
Test	7	12	1	431	160	39.18	1	1	9	-	0	0	0		-	-	-
FC	17	30	3	1168	160	43.25	2	6	20	-	60	51	2	25.50	1-3	-	-
ODI																	
List A	6	6	1	312	104*	62.40	2	1	2	-	0	0	0		-	-	
20/20 Int																	
20/20	8	8	1	337	100*	48.14	1	2	1	-	0	0	0		-	-	

Career Performances

	M	Inn	NO	Runs	HS	Avg	100	50	Ct	St	Balls	Runs	Wkts	Avg	BB	5I	10M
Test	48	87	5	3509	160	42.79	9	20	44	-	6	1	0		-	-	-
FC	113	202	16	8298	195	44.61	21	47	111	-	222	169	5	33.80	3-13	-	-
ODI	23	23	0	702	102	30.52	1	3	7	-	0	0	0		-	-	
List A	62	61	5	1980	125	35.35	4	9	26	-	18	10	0		-	-	
20/20 Int	2	2	0	24	15	12.00	-	-	1	-	0	0	0		-	-	
20/20	14	13	1	387	100*	32.25	1	2	3	-	0	0	0		-	-	

COOK, S. J.   Kent

Name: <u>Simon</u> James Cook
Role: Right-hand bat, right-arm fast-medium bowler
Born: 15 January 1977, Oxford
Height: 6ft 4in   **Weight:** 13st
Nickname: Cookie, Donk, Chef
County debut: 1997 (one-day, Middlesex), 1999 (first-class, Middlesex), 2005 (Kent)
County cap: 2003 (Middlesex), 2007 (Kent)
Place in batting averages: 190th av. 24.44
Place in bowling averages: 48th av. 30.79
Parents: Phil and Sue
Marital status: Single

Family links with cricket: Brothers played for Oxfordshire
Education: Matthew Arnold School
Qualifications: GCSEs, NVQ Business Administration II, Level 3 ECB coach
Career outside cricket: Coaching and property development
Overseas tours: Middlesex to South Africa 2000
Overseas teams played for: Rockingham, Perth 2001, 2002
Career highlights to date: 'Beating Australia in one-day game at Lord's. Winning division two of NCL and equalling league record for wickets in a season (39). Winning Twenty20 cup in 2007'
Cricket moments to forget: 'Being outside the circle in a one-day game when I was supposed to be in it. Danny Law was bowled, the ball went for four [off the stumps, making six no-balls in total] and he went on to win the game for Durham'
Cricket superstitions: None
Cricketers particularly admired: Angus Fraser, Glenn McGrath
Young players to look out for: Billy Godleman, Eoin Morgan, Joe Denly
Other sports followed: Football (Liverpool), 'any other ball sport'
Player website: www.vcamcricket.co.uk
Extras: Scored career best 93* v Nottinghamshire at Lord's 2001, helping Middlesex to avoid the follow-on, then took a wicket with the first ball of his opening spell. Equalled Adam Hollioake's record for the most wickets in a one-day league season (39) 2004.
Best batting: 93* Middlesex v Nottinghamshire, Lord's 2001
Best bowling: 8-63 Middlesex v Northamptonshire, Northampton 2002

2009 Season

	M	Inn	NO	Runs	HS	Avg	100	50	Ct	St	Balls	Runs	Wkts	Avg	BB	5I	10M
Test																	
FC	13	13	4	220	60*	24.44	-	1	-	-	2245	1047	34	30.79	5-22	3	-
ODI																	
List A	6	4	1	41	21	13.66	-	-	2	-	276	200	9	22.22	4-37	-	
20/20 Int																	
20/20	12	2	2	9	8*		-	-	2	-	252	279	10	27.90	2-29	-	

Career Performances

	M	Inn	NO	Runs	HS	Avg	100	50	Ct	St	Balls	Runs	Wkts	Avg	BB	5I	10M
Test																	
FC	117	146	22	2107	93*	16.99	-	6	31	-	18104	9394	293	32.06	8-63	12	-
ODI																	
List A	170	105	32	1234	67*	16.90	-	2	28	-	7567	5944	214	27.77	6-37	2	
20/20 Int																	
20/20	51	15	8	115	25*	16.42	-	-	9	-	1087	1348	60	22.46	3-14	-	

CORK, D. G. Hampshire

Name: <u>Dominic</u> Gerald Cork
Role: Right-hand bat, right-arm
fast-medium bowler
Born: 7 August 1971, Newcastle-under-Lyme,
Staffordshire
Height: 6ft 2½in **Weight:** 14st
Nickname: Corky
County debut: 1990 (Derbyshire),
2004 (Lancashire)
County cap: 1993 (Derbyshire),
2004 (Lancashire), 2009 (Hampshire)
Benefit: 2001 (Derbyshire)
Test debut: 1995
ODI debut: 1992
50 wickets in a season: 7

1st-Class 200s: 1
Place in batting averages: 205th av. 22.30 (2008 227th av. 16.20)
Place in bowling averages: 35th av. 28.40 (2008 56th av. 27.60)
Parents: Gerald and Mary
Wife and date of marriage: Donna, 28 August 2000
Children: Ashleigh, 28 April 1990; Gregory, 29 September 1994
Family links with cricket: 'Father and two brothers played in the same side at Betley
CC in Staffordshire'
Education: St Joseph's College, Trent Vale, Stoke-on-Trent; Newcastle College
Qualifications: 2 O-levels, Level 2 coach
Overseas tours: England YC to Australia 1989-90; England A to Bermuda and West
Indies 1991-92, to Australia 1992-93, to South Africa 1993-94, to India 1994-95;
England to South Africa 1995-96, to India and Pakistan (World Cup) 1995-96,
to New Zealand 1996-97, to Australia 1998-99, to Pakistan and Sri Lanka 2000-01,
to Sri Lanka (ICC Champions Trophy) 2002-03; England VI to Hong Kong 2005,
2006 (c)
Overseas teams played for: East Shirley, Christchurch, New Zealand 1990-91
Career highlights to date: 'Making my debut for England'
Cricket moments to forget: 'Every time the team loses'
Cricket superstitions: None
Cricketers particularly admired: Kim Barnett, Mike Atherton, Ian Botham,
Malcolm Marshall
Other sports played: Golf, football
Other sports followed: Football (Stoke City)
Favourite band: 'Anything R&B'
Relaxations: 'Listening to music'

Extras: Scored century (110) as nightwatchman for England Young Cricketers v Pakistan Young Cricketers at Taunton 1990. Took 8-53 before lunch on his 20th birthday, v Essex at Derby 1991. Selected for England A in 1991 – his first full season of first-class cricket. PCA Young Player of the Year 1991. Took 7-43 on Test debut against West Indies at Lord's 1995, the best innings figures ever by an England debutant. Took hat-trick (Richardson, Murray, Hooper) against the West Indies at Old Trafford in the fourth Test 1995. PCA Player of the Year 1995. Finished top of the Whyte and Mackay bowling ratings 1995. Cornhill England Player of the Year 1995-96. One of *Wisden*'s Five Cricketers of the Year 1996. Man of the Match in the second Test v West Indies at Lord's 2000 – on his recall to the Test side he had match figures of 7-52 followed by a match-winning 33* in England's second innings. Derbyshire captain 1998-2003. Took Twenty20 hat-trick (Pietersen, Ealham, Patel) v Nottinghamshire at Old Trafford 2004. Joined Hampshire for 2009. His 4-41 earned him the Man of the Match award in the Friends Provident Trophy final at Lord's in 2009

Best batting: 200* Derbyshire v Durham, Derby 2000
Best bowling: 9-43 Derbyshire v Northamptonshire, Derby 1995

2009 Season

	M	Inn	NO	Runs	HS	Avg	100	50	Ct	St	Balls	Runs	Wkts	Avg	BB	5I	10M
Test																	
FC	12	15	2	290	52	22.30	-	1	18	-	1722	767	27	28.40	5-14	1	-
ODI																	
List A	15	6	3	61	35*	20.33	-	-	5	-	693	509	24	21.20	4-18	-	
20/20 Int																	
20/20	9	5	4	41	18*	41.00	-	-	-	-	192	237	11	21.54	3-30	-	

Career Performances

	M	Inn	NO	Runs	HS	Avg	100	50	Ct	St	Balls	Runs	Wkts	Avg	BB	5I	10M
Test	37	56	8	864	59	18.00	-	3	18	-	7678	3906	131	29.81	7-43	5	-
FC	299	433	57	9417	200*	25.04	8	51	223	-	50205	24595	922	26.67	9-43	33	5
ODI	32	21	3	180	31*	10.00	-	-	6	-	1772	1368	41	33.36	3-27	-	
List A	297	225	35	4056	93	21.34	-	19	110	-	14051	9961	367	27.14	6-21	4	
20/20 Int																	
20/20	46	35	10	345	28	13.80	-	-	8	-	774	935	41	22.80	4-16	-	

18. Which Pakistan batsman sadly made a pair on his Test match debut in 1990?

COSGROVE, M. J.   *Glamorgan*

Name: <u>Mark</u> James Cosgrove
Role: Left-hand bat, right-arm
medium bowler
Born: 14 June 1984, Adelaide,
South Australia
Height: 5ft 9in
Nickname: Cozzie, Baby Boof
County debut: 2006
County cap: 2006
ODI debut: 2005-06
1st-Class 200s: 1
Place in batting averages: 16th av. 60.00
(2008 42nd av. 50.35)
Overseas tours: Australia U19 to New Zealand
(U19 World Cup) 2001-02; Australia to Malaysia
(DLF Cup) 2006-07

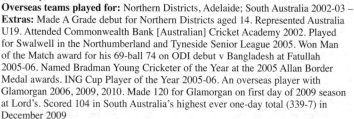

Overseas teams played for: Northern Districts, Adelaide; South Australia 2002-03 –
Extras: Made A Grade debut for Northern Districts aged 14. Represented Australia
U19. Attended Commonwealth Bank [Australian] Cricket Academy 2002. Played
for Swalwell in the Northumberland and Tyneside Senior League 2005. Won Man
of the Match award for his 69-ball 74 on ODI debut v Bangladesh at Fatullah
2005-06. Named Bradman Young Cricketer of the Year at the 2005 Allan Border
Medal awards. ING Cup Player of the Year 2005-06. An overseas player with
Glamorgan 2006, 2009, 2010. Made 120 for Glamorgan on first day of 2009 season
at Lord's. Scored 104 in South Australia's highest ever one-day total (339-7) in
December 2009
Best batting: 233 Glamorgan v Derbyshire, Derby 2006
Best bowling: 3-3 South Australia v Tasmania, Adelaide 2006-07

2009 Season

	M	Inn	NO	Runs	HS	Avg	100	50	Ct	St	Balls	Runs	Wkts	Avg	BB	5I	10M
Test																	
FC	10	15	2	780	175	60.00	3	5	4	-	348	202	6	33.66	3-30	-	-
ODI																	
List A	8	8	0	257	73	32.12	-	3	1	-	144	153	4	38.25	2-44	-	
20/20 Int																	
20/20	6	6	0	136	52	22.66	-	1	4	-	36	39	2	19.50	2-11	-	

	M	Inn	NO	Runs	HS	Avg	100	50	Ct	St	Balls	Runs	Wkts	Avg	BB	5I	10M
Test																	
FC	68	121	7	4804	233	42.14	12	32	46	-	2214	1222	31	39.41	3-3	-	-
ODI	3	3	0	112	74	37.33	-	1	-	-	30	13	1	13.00	1-1	-	
List A	83	82	4	2629	121	33.70	2	20	24	-	803	829	14	59.21	2-21	-	
20/20 Int																	
20/20	19	18	1	304	52	17.88	-	2	5	-	111	189	4	47.25	2-11	-	

COSKER, D. A. Glamorgan

Name: <u>Dean</u> Andrew Cosker
Role: Right-hand bat, left-arm
spin bowler
Born: 7 January 1978, Weymouth, Dorset
Height: 5ft 11in **Weight:** 12st 7lbs
Nickname: Lurks, The Lurker, Bryn
County debut: 1996
County cap: 2000
Benefit: 2010 (Glamorgan)
Place in batting averages: 256th av. 13.37 (2008
232nd av. 14.54)
Place in bowling averages: 40th av. 29.57 (2008
102nd av. 34.52)
Parents: Des and Carol
Wife and date of marriage: Katie,
24 November 2006
Children: Jak Ruben, 19 February 2008
Family links with cricket: 'Brother dabbles in Welsh League when his missus lets
him! Father still refuses to give his knees that much-wanted rest, and plays for
Thornford CC.'
Education: Millfield School; 'University of Roath'
Qualifications: 10 GCSEs, 4 A-levels
Overseas tours: West of England U15 to West Indies 1993-94; Millfield School to Sri
Lanka 1994-95; England U17 to Netherlands 1995; England U19 to Pakistan 1996-97;
England A to Kenya and Sri Lanka 1997-98, to Zimbabwe and South Africa 1998-99;
Glamorgan CCC to Cape Town and Jersey
Overseas teams played for: Gordon CC, Sydney 1996-97; Crusaders, Durban
2001-02
Career highlights to date: 'Debut at Glamorgan in 1997, Championship medal 1997,
England A caps, trophies with Glamorgan, and seeing the grimace on Gareth Rees's
face when he gets hit in short leg!'

Cricket moments to forget: 'Every time I bowl from the Taff End at the SWALEC Stadium in the Twenty20 with the wind with the batsmen...'

Cricketers particularly admired: Mike Kasprowicz, Matt Elliott, Matt Maynard, Robert Croft, Steven Watkin, Graham Thorpe

Other sports played: Golf

Other sports followed: Football ('Spurs and the Swans'), WWF wrestling ('The Undertaker')

Favourite band: 'Bananarama'

Relaxations: 'Time with my son, Jak. Long winter walks'

Extras: England U15, U17 and U19. Played for U19 TCCB Development of Excellence XI v South Africa U19 1995. NBC Denis Compton Award for most promising young Glamorgan player 1996. Leading wicket-taker on England A tour of Zimbabwe and South Africa 1998-99 (22 – av. 22.90). Third youngest Glamorgan player to receive county cap. Benefit in 2010

Opinions on cricket: 'Great to see more money coming into the game. Let's not see the young players at clubs not getting the opportunities because of Kolpaks...'

Best batting: 52 Glamorgan v Gloucestershire, Bristol 2005

Best bowling: 6-91 Glamorgan v Essex, Cardiff 2009

2009 Season

	M	Inn	NO	Runs	HS	Avg	100	50	Ct	St	Balls	Runs	Wkts	Avg	BB	5I	10M
Test																	
FC	8	11	3	107	46*	13.37	-	-	5	-	1873	769	26	29.57	6-91	2	1
ODI																	
List A	14	9	2	105	50*	15.00	-	1	6	-	575	472	15	31.46	3-26	-	
20/20 Int																	
20/20	10	8	6	29	16*	14.50	-	-	3	-	198	233	6	38.83	2-25	-	

Career Performances

	M	Inn	NO	Runs	HS	Avg	100	50	Ct	St	Balls	Runs	Wkts	Avg	BB	5I	10M
Test																	
FC	161	206	61	1891	52	13.04	-	1	103	-	30297	14666	392	37.41	6-91	6	1
ODI																	
List A	190	99	42	595	50*	10.43	-	1	76	-	8107	6407	194	33.02	5-54	1	
20/20 Int																	
20/20	51	17	14	59	16*	19.66	-	-	16	-	864	1181	40	29.52	3-18	-	

COX, O. B. Worcestershire

Name: Oliver Benjamin (<u>Ben</u>) Cox
Role: Right-hand bat, wicket-keeper
Born: 2 February 1992, Stourbridge, West Midlands
Height: 5ft 10in **Weight:** 11st 2lbs
Nickname: Coxy
County debut: 2009
Parents: Tim and Gail
Marital status: Single
Education: Bromsgrove School
Qualifications: 10 GCSEs, 2 AS-levels
Off-season: 'Finish studying at Bromsgrove, where I'm in my final year completing my A-levels.'
Career highlights to date: 'Getting 61 on my debut for Worcestershire and stumping Marcus Trescothick as my first victim.'
Cricket superstitions: 'Always put my right pad on first, whether batting or keeping'
Cricketers particularly admired: Steve Davies
Young players to look out for: Jonathan Webb (Warwickshire), Adam Rouse (Hampshire)
Other sports played: Rugby union (England U18 trial)
Other sports followed: Rugby union (Worcester Warriors)
Injuries: 'Dislocated left shoulder, leading to an operation that meant I missed the first four weeks of the season.'
Favourite band: John Mayer, Justin Nozuka
Relaxations: 'Music, films'
Extras: Worcestershire Academy Player of the Year 2009
Best batting: 61 Worcestershire v Somerset, Taunton 2009

2009 Season

	M	Inn	NO	Runs	HS	Avg	100	50	Ct	St	Balls	Runs	Wkts	Avg	BB	5I	10M
Test																	
FC	1	1	0	61	61	61.00	-	1	4	1	0	0	0		-	-	-
ODI																	
List A																	
20/20 Int																	
20/20																	

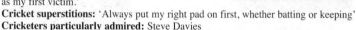

Career Performances

	M	Inn	NO	Runs	HS	Avg	100	50	Ct	St	Balls	Runs	Wkts	Avg	BB	5I	10M
Test																	
FC	1	1	0	61	61	61.00	-	1	4	1	0	0	0		-	-	-
ODI																	
List A																		
20/20 Int																		
20/20																		

CRAWLEY, J. P. Hampshire

Name: <u>John</u> Paul Crawley
Role: Right-hand bat, occasional wicket-keeper
Born: 21 September 1971, Maldon, Essex
Height: 6ft 2in **Weight:** 13st 7lbs
Nickname: Creepy, Jonty, JC
County debut: 1990 (Lancashire), 2002 (Hampshire)
County cap: 1994 (Lancashire), 2002 (Hampshire)
Benefit: 2008 (Hampshire)
Test debut: 1994
ODI debut: 1994-95
1000 runs in a season: 10
1st-Class 200s: 6
1st-Class 300s: 2
Place in batting averages: 160th av. 28.00
(2008 141st av. 27.73)
Parents: Frank and Jean (deceased)
Marital status: Married
Family links with cricket: Father played in Manchester Association. Brother Mark played for Lancashire and Nottinghamshire, brother Peter plays for Warrington CC and has played for Scottish Universities and Cambridge University. Uncle was excellent fast bowler. Godfather umpires in Manchester Association
Education: Manchester Grammar School; Trinity College, Cambridge; Open University Business School
Qualifications: 10 O-levels, 2 AO-Levels, 3 A-levels, 2 S-levels, BA in History, MA (Cantab), Professional Certificate in Management
Overseas tours: England YC to Australia 1989-90, to New Zealand 1990-91 (c); England A to South Africa 1993-94, to West Indies 2000-01; England to Australia 1994-95, to South Africa 1995-96, to Zimbabwe and New Zealand 1996-97, to West Indies 1997-98, to Australia 1998-99, 2002-03
Overseas teams played for: Midland-Guildford, Perth 1990

Cricketers particularly admired: Michael Atherton, Neil Fairbrother, Graham Gooch, Alec Stewart, David Gower, Allan Donald, Ian Salisbury
Other sports followed: Football (Manchester United), golf
Relaxations: 'Playing or trying to play the guitar'
Extras: Sir John Hobbs Silver Jubilee Memorial Prize 1987. Played for England YC 1989, 1990 and (as captain) 1991. First to score 1000 runs in U19 'Tests'. Lancashire vice-captain 1998. Topped English first-class batting averages for 1998 season (1851 runs – av. 74.04). Lancashire Player of the Year 1998. Lancashire captain 1999-2001. Scored 272 on debut for Hampshire v Kent at Canterbury 2002, a Hampshire debut record. Captain of Hampshire 2003. Hampshire Player of the Year 2006. Retired at the end of the 2009 season
Best batting: 311* Hampshire v Nottinghamshire, Rose Bowl 2005
Best bowling: 1-7 Hampshire v Surrey, The Oval 2005

2009 Season

	M	Inn	NO	Runs	HS	Avg	100	50	Ct	St	Balls	Runs	Wkts	Avg	BB	5I	10M
Test																	
FC	8	14	3	308	81*	28.00	-	2	8	-	0	0	0		-	-	-
ODI																	
List A	5	5	0	169	100	33.80	1	-	3	-	0	0	0		-	-	
20/20 Int																	
20/20																	

Career Performances

	M	Inn	NO	Runs	HS	Avg	100	50	Ct	St	Balls	Runs	Wkts	Avg	BB	5I	10M
Test	37	61	9	1800	156*	34.61	4	9	29	-	0	0	0		-	-	-
FC	351	584	60	24361	311*	46.49	54	133	222	1	215	283	2	141.50	1-7	-	-
ODI	13	12	1	235	73	21.36	-	2	1	1	0	0	0		-	-	
List A	309	295	23	8681	114	31.91	8	55	97	4	6	4	0		-	-	
20/20 Int																	
20/20	10	10	1	107	23	11.88	-	-	3	-	0	0	0		-	-	

19. Who to date has been the Bangladesh captain, in both Test and one-day internationals, the most times?

CROFT, R. D. B.   Glamorgan

Name: <u>Robert</u> Damien Bale Croft
Role: Right-hand bat, off-spin bowler
Born: 25 May 1970, Morriston, Swansea
Height: 5ft 11in   **Weight:** 13st 7lbs
Nickname: Crofty
County debut: 1989
County cap: 1992
Benefit: 2000
Test debut: 1996
ODI debut: 1996
50 wickets in a season: 10
Place in batting averages: 121st av. 33.76
(2008 128th av. 29.62)
Place in bowling averages: 43rd av. 29.77
(2008 60th av. 28.04)
Parents: Malcolm and Susan
Wife: Marie
Children: Callum James Bale Croft
Family links with cricket: Father and grandfather played league cricket
Education: St John Lloyd Catholic School, Llanelli; Neath Tertiary College;
West Glamorgan Institute of Higher Education
Qualifications: 6 O-levels, OND Business Studies, HND Business Studies,
NCA senior coaching certificate
Overseas tours: England A to Bermuda and West Indies 1991-92, to South Africa
1993-94; England to Zimbabwe and New Zealand 1996-97, to West Indies 1997-98,
to Australia 1998-99, to Sharjah (Coca-Cola Cup) 1998-99, to Sri Lanka 2000-01,
2003-04; England VI to Hong Kong 2003, 2005 (c)
Career highlights to date: 'Playing for England and winning the Championship
with Glamorgan in 1997'
Cricket moments to forget: 'None. This career is too short to forget any of it'
Cricketers particularly admired: Ian Botham, Viv Richards, Shane Warne
Other sports played: 'Give anything a go'
Other sports followed: Football (Liverpool FC), rugby (Llanelli and Wales)
Interests/relaxations: 'Everything'
Extras: Captained England South to victory in International Youth Tournament 1989
and was voted Player of the Tournament. Glamorgan Young Player of the Year 1992.
Scored Test best 37* in the third Test at Old Trafford 1998, resisting for 190 minutes
to deny South Africa victory. Represented England in the 1999 World Cup. Honorary
fellow of West Glamorgan Institute of Higher Education. Scored 69-ball 119 v Surrey
at The Oval in the C&G 2002 as Glamorgan made 429 in reply to Surrey's 438-5.
Glamorgan Player of the Year 2003 (jointly with Michael Kasprowicz) and 2004.

Glamorgan vice-captain 2002-03. Appointed captain during 2003, taking over from the injured Steve James. Stood down as captain in mid-September 2006. Man of the Match in England's victory v Pakistan in the final of the Hong Kong Sixes 2003. Retired from international cricket in January 2004. Cricket Society's Wetherell Award 2004 for the leading all-rounder in English first-class cricket. Took 1000th first-class wicket (Niall O'Brien) v Northamptonshire at Northampton 2007 to become the first Welshman to have scored 10,000 runs and taken 1000 wickets in first-class cricket. Finished top of the county's first-class bowling averages in 2008

Best batting: 143 Glamorgan v Somerset, Taunton 1995
Best bowling: 8-66 Glamorgan v Warwickshire, Swansea 1992

2009 Season

	M	Inn	NO	Runs	HS	Avg	100	50	Ct	St	Balls	Runs	Wkts	Avg	BB	5I	10M
Test																	
FC	17	21	4	574	121	33.76	1	1	4	-	4421	1727	58	29.77	5-65	1	-
ODI																	
List A	5	3	1	31	15	15.50	-	-	1	-	156	120	5	24.00	4-43	-	
20/20 Int																	
20/20	10	9	3	94	52*	15.66	-	1	-	-	186	240	4	60.00	1-19	-	

Career Performances

	M	Inn	NO	Runs	HS	Avg	100	50	Ct	St	Balls	Runs	Wkts	Avg	BB	5I	10M
Test	21	34	8	421	37*	16.19	-	-	10	-	4619	1825	49	37.24	5-95	1	-
FC	382	562	100	12365	143	26.76	8	52	175	-	84595	39190	1107	35.40	8-66	49	9
ODI	50	36	12	345	32	14.37	-	-	11	-	2466	1743	45	38.73	3-51	-	
List A	399	334	60	6400	143	23.35	4	31	94	-	18205	13138	408	32.20	6-20	1	
20/20 Int																	
20/20	52	38	8	633	62*	21.10	-	4	18	-	1024	1304	46	28.34	3-12	-	

CROFT, S. J. Lancashire

Name: <u>Steven</u> John Croft
Role: Right-hand bat, right-arm medium-fast
and off-spin bowler; all-rounder
Born: 11 October 1984, Blackpool
Height: 5ft 11in **Weight:** 13st
Nickname: Crofty
County debut: 2005
Place in batting averages: 148th av. 30.00
(2008 105th av. 32.50)
Place in bowling averages: (2008 112th av. 36.62)
Parents: Elizabeth and Lawrence
Marital status: Single
Family links with cricket: 'Father watched it
on TV! (And played for local team)'
Education: Highfield High, Blackpool;
Myerscough College
Qualifications: 10 GCSEs, First Diploma in Sports Studies, Level 2 coaching
Career outside cricket: Coaching
Off-season: Holidays and rest
Overseas teams played for: St Kilda, Melbourne 2005-06; Noble Park, Melbourne
2006-07; Auckland 2008-09
Career highlights to date: 'Signing for Lancashire CCC. Maiden first-class century'
Cricket moments to forget: 'Duck on 2nd XI debut. Going out on a bowl-out in the
quarter-final of Twenty20 in 2009 '
Cricket superstitions: 'Left pad on first'
Cricketers particularly admired: Andrew Flintoff, Stuart Law, Jacques Kallis,
VVS Laxman
Young players to look out for: Gareth Cross and Luke Proctor (Lancashire)
Other sports played: Football ('played for Blackpool town team and trialled at
Oldham FC and Wimbledon FC'), tennis
Other sports followed: Football (Blackpool)
Favourite band: Kings of Leon
Relaxations: 'Socialising with friends, music, movies, gigs'
Extras: Played for Lancashire Board XI in the C&G 2003. Only third amateur to
score over 1000 runs in a season in the Northern Premier League. Lancashire Young
Player of the Year 2007. Lancashire Player of the Year and One-Day Player of the Year
2008
Opinions on cricket: 'Twenty20 has been good for the game. County cricket is
getting stronger.'
Best batting: 122 Lancashire v Nottinghamshire, Old Trafford 2008
Best bowling: 4-51 Lancashire v Nottinghamshire, Trent Bridge 2008

2009 Season

	M	Inn	NO	Runs	HS	Avg	100	50	Ct	St	Balls	Runs	Wkts	Avg	BB	5I	10M
Test																	
FC	9	14	2	360	79	30.00	-	2	6	-	180	155	4	38.75	2-42	-	-
ODI																	
List A	17	13	3	265	70	26.50	-	2	10	-	145	153	3	51.00	1-4	-	
20/20 Int																	
20/20	9	9	2	259	83*	37.00	-	1	6	-	60	69	4	17.25	2-35	-	

Career Performances

	M	Inn	NO	Runs	HS	Avg	100	50	Ct	St	Balls	Runs	Wkts	Avg	BB	5I	10M
Test																	
FC	43	64	6	1626	122	8.03	1	9	35	-	2065	1324	30	44.13	4-51	-	-
ODI																	
List A	63	55	12	1227	70	28.53	-	7	22	-	1242	1065	36	29.58	4-24	-	
20/20 Int																	
20/20	41	37	7	780	83*	26.00	-	3	18	-	370	510	17	30.00	3-6	-	

CROOK, S. P.   Northamptonshire

Name: <u>Steven</u> Paul Crook
Role: Right-hand bat, right-arm
fast-medium bowler; all-rounder
Born: 28 May 1983, Adelaide, South Australia
Height: 5ft 11in **Weight:** 13st 3lbs
Nickname: Crooky, Crookster
County debut: 2003 (Lancashire),
2005 (Northamptonshire)
Place in batting averages: (2008 80th av. 37.16)
Parents: 'Dad Martyn, mum Sue and step-
father Doug'
Marital status: Single
Family links with sport: Brother Andrew played
for Lancashire and Northamptonshire, where he
now has a commercial role. Father, Martyn, played
professional football
Education: Rostrevor College
Qualifications: Matriculation
Overseas tours: Lancashire to Cape Town 2003, 2004
Overseas teams played for: Northern Districts, South Australia
Career highlights to date: 'Playing semi-final of Twenty20 2004'
Cricket moments to forget: 'Getting beaten in semi of Twenty20 2004'

Cricketers particularly admired: Andrew Flintoff, Stuart Law
Other sports followed: Football (Tottenham Hotspur FC)
Favourite band: The Doors, The Strokes
Relaxations: 'Hanging out with mates'
Extras: Attended South Australia Cricket Academy. Represented South Australia U13-U19. Selected for Australia U19 preliminary World Cup squad 2001-02. Released by Northamptonshire at the end of the 2009 season. Is not considered an overseas player
Best batting: 97 Northamptonshire v Yorkshire, Northampton 2005
Best bowling: 5-71 Northamptonshire v Essex, Northampton, 2009

2009 Season

	M	Inn	NO	Runs	HS	Avg	100	50	Ct	St	Balls	Runs	Wkts	Avg	BB	5I	10M
Test																	
FC	2	3	0	84	55	28.00	-	1	2	-	288	193	6	32.16	5-71	1	-
ODI																	
List A	3	3	0	128	72	42.66	-	1	-	-	90	93	1	93.00	1-31	-	
20/20 Int																	
20/20	6	4	0	15	9	3.75	-	-	1	-	6	16	0			-	-

Career Performances

	M	Inn	NO	Runs	HS	Avg	100	50	Ct	St	Balls	Runs	Wkts	Avg	BB	5I	10M
Test																	
FC	35	47	7	1261	97	31.52	-	9	12	-	4303	2842	59	48.16	5-71	1	-
ODI																	
List A	30	20	2	281	72	15.61	-	1	6	-	1050	1059	21	50.42	4-20	-	
20/20 Int																	
20/20	34	18	3	186	27	12.40	-	-	6	-	228	352	9	39.11	2-24	-	

20. Which Pakistan wicketkeeper made a pair in his first Test as captain in 1998?

CROSS, G. D. Lancashire

Name: <u>Gareth</u> David Cross
Role: Right-hand bat, wicket-keeper
Born: 20 June 1984, Bury
Height: 5ft 10in **Weight:** 11st 2lbs
Nickname: Crossy, Squirrel
County debut: 2005
Parents: Duncan and Margaret
Marital status: Single
Family links with cricket: 'Dad played for
Prestwich. Brother Matthew plays for Monton
and Weaste'
Education: Moorside High School; Eccles College
Qualifications: 9 GCSEs, GNVQ Science
Off-season: 'Rest, then back into training.'

Overseas teams played for: St Kilda, Melbourne
2002-03 – 2006-07
Career highlights to date: 'My debuts for Lancashire in each form of the game'
Cricket moments to forget: 'Tim Rees top-edging the ball into my head whilst I
was keeping for Salford against Bolton. The first ball of the Twenty20 quarter-final –
lbw to Steve Finn.'
Cricket superstitions: 'Just putting batting gear on in the same order'
Cricketers particularly admired: Adam Gilchrist, VVS Laxman, Andrew Symonds
Young players to look out for: Joe Root (Yorkshire), Chris Jordan (Surrey)
Other sports played: Football ('had a trial for Manchester United when I was 13')
Other sports followed: Football (Manchester United)
Favourite band: The Killers, Arctic Monkeys
Relaxations: 'Going out for food, drinks, films'
Extras: Manchester Association Young Player of the Year. Bolton Association Young
Player of the Year 2000. ECB Premier League Young Player of the Year. Liverpool
Competition Player of the Year 2004. Played for Lancashire Board XI in the C&G
2003. Made five dismissals in first innings of Championship debut v Leicestershire
at Old Trafford 2005
Opinions on cricket: 'We need to do something to improve as a one-day country…
not sure what, though!'
Best batting: 72 Lancashire v Kent, Canterbury 2006

	M	Inn	NO	Runs	HS	Avg	100	50	Ct	St	Balls	Runs	Wkts	Avg	BB	5I	10M
Test																	
FC																	
ODI																	
List A	7	4	1	87	34	29.00	-	-	3	3	0	0	0		-	-	
20/20 Int																	
20/20	9	5	2	42	19	14.00	-	-	7	-	0	0	0		-	-	

Career Performances

	M	Inn	NO	Runs	HS	Avg	100	50	Ct	St	Balls	Runs	Wkts	Avg	BB	5I	10M
Test																	
FC	8	13	1	309	72	25.75	-	3	27	8	0	0	0		-	-	-
ODI																	
List A	35	29	3	491	76	18.88	-	1	21	9	36	26	2	13.00	2-26	-	
20/20 Int																	
20/20	34	25	6	313	62	16.47	-	1	25	10	0	0	0		-	-	

CROWE, C. D.   Leicestershire

Name: <u>Carl</u> Daniel Crowe
Role: Right-hand bat, right-arm off-spinner
Born: 25 November 1975, Leicester
Height: 6ft **Weight:** 12st 7lbs
Nickname: 'Crowey!'
County debut: 1995
Parents: Jeannette and Eddie (deceased)
Wife and date of marriage: Helen, 14 October 2000
Family links with cricket: Brother Craig
has played for Leicestershire 2nd XI
Education: Lutterworth High School;
Lutterworth Grammar School
Qualifications: 11 GCSEs, 2 A-levels,
NCA Senior Coach
Career outside cricket: 'Business world'
Overseas tours: Leicestershire U19 to South Africa 1993-94; Leicestershire to
Holland 1996, 1998, to Barbados 1998, to Sri Lanka 1999, to Anguilla 2000, to
South Africa 2001
Overseas teams played for: Old Mentonians, Melbourne 1997-99
Cricketers particularly admired: The Waughs
Other sports played: 'Try all sports. Had a hole in one'
Other sports followed: 'Support Leicester at everything and follow Spurs'

Extras: Played for Leicestershire U12–U19 and Midlands Schools U14–U19. One of the Cricketers of the Festival at Cambridge U19 Festival 1994. Won Leicestershire 2nd XI batting award 1998. Played in Leicestershire's victory in the AON Trophy final 2000. B&H Gold Award for his 1-7 from four overs (in a game shortened to 22 overs per side) v Nottinghamshire at Leicester 2002. Released by Leicestershire at the end of the 2002 season, after which he played regularly for Berkshire and moved into coaching. Played for Leicester Ivanhoe (Everards League). Returned to first-class cricket in 2009, playing in early season games for Leicestershire

Best batting: 44* Leicestershire v Northamptonshire, Northampton 1999
Best bowling: 4-47 Leicestershire v Surrey, The Oval 2001

2009 Season

	M	Inn	NO	Runs	HS	Avg	100	50	Ct	St	Balls	Runs	Wkts	Avg	BB	5I	10M
Test																	
FC	4	7	2	114	41*	22.80	-	-	-	-	618	346	3	115.33	3-84	-	-
ODI																	
List A	5	2	1	33	20	33.00	-	-	3	-	192	137	3	45.66	2-36	-	
20/20 Int																	
20/20	1	1	0	9	9	9.00	-	-	-	-	0	0	0			-	-

Career Performances

	M	Inn	NO	Runs	HS	Avg	100	50	Ct	St	Balls	Runs	Wkts	Avg	BB	5I	10M
Test																	
FC	42	56	12	695	44*	15.79	-	-	18	-	4534	2271	60	37.85	4-47	-	-
ODI																	
List A	40	24	12	187	23*	15.58	-	-	10	-	1334	1071	33	32.45	4-30	-	
20/20 Int																	
20/20	1	1	0	9	9	9.00	-	-	-	-	0	0	0			-	-

CUMMINS, R. A. G.　　　Northamptonshire

Name: Ryan Anthony Gilbert Cummins
Role: Right-hand bat, right-arm
fast-medium bowler
Born: 14 April 1984, Sutton, Surrey
Height: 6ft 4in　**Weight:** 13st 4lbs
Nickname: Rhino, Yummins
County debut: 2005 (Leicestershire), 2009
(Northamptonshire, one-day)
Parents: Tony and Sheila
Marital status: Single
Family links with cricket: 'Great-grandfather,
Gilly Reay, played for Surrey. Father played
county 2nd XI and sister plays county cricket
for Northamptonshire'
Education: Wallington County Grammar School
for Boys; Loughborough University
Qualifications: 11 GCSEs, 4 A-levels, BSc (Hons) Geography (2.2), Level 2 cricket
coach, Level 1 hockey coach
Overseas tours: Club Cricket Conference to Australia 2008; PCA Benevolent Fund
Everest Trek 2007 – 'the highest game of cricket ever!'
Career highlights to date: 'Playing in the winning Twenty20 side of 2006'
Cricket moments to forget: 'Bowling in the Twenty20 final 2006'
Cricketers particularly admired: Phil DeFreitas, Brian Lara, Adam Hollioake
Other sports played: Hockey, golf
Other sports followed: Rugby (Leicester Tigers), golf
Favourite band: Counting Crows
Extras: Played for LUCCE 2003-05. Represented British Universities 2005. Signed
for Northamptonshire from Leicestershire in October 2008. Released at the end of the
2009 season
Opinions on cricket: 'Level of professionalism in the game must continue to
improve, so as to improve both individuals and the standard of English cricket.'
Best batting: 34* Leicestershire v OUCCE, The Parks 2007
Best bowling: 5-60 Leicestershire v Northamptonshire, Leicester 2007

2009 Season

	M	Inn	NO	Runs	HS	Avg	100	50	Ct	St	Balls	Runs	Wkts	Avg	BB	5I	10M
Test																	
FC																	
ODI																	
List A	2	2	1	13	12*	13.00	-	-	-	-	84	70	1	70.00	1-28	-	
20/20 Int																	
20/20																	

Career Performances

	M	Inn	NO	Runs	HS	Avg	100	50	Ct	St	Balls	Runs	Wkts	Avg	BB	5I	10M
Test																	
FC	22	27	11	221	34*	13.81	-	-	7	-	3526	2184	49	44.57	5-60	1	-
ODI																	
List A	24	8	4	36	12*	9.00	-	-	6	-	941	776	30	25.86	3-21	-	
20/20 Int																	
20/20	1	0	0	0	0			-	1	-	18	40	0		-	-	

DAGGETT, L. M.   Northamptonshire

Name: <u>Lee</u> Martin Daggett
Role: Right-hand bat, right-arm
fast-medium bowler
Born: 1 October 1982, Bury, Lancashire
Height: 6ft **Weight:** 13st 6lbs
Nickname: Terry, Dags, Dagsy, Daggers,
Len Dugout
County debut: 2006 (Warwickshire), 2009
(Northamptonshire)
Place in bowling averages: (2008 79th av. 31.21)
Parents: Peter and Kathleen
Marital status: Single
Family links with cricket: 'Father was captain
of Ramsbottom CC in the Lancashire League. Also
coached Ramsbottom CC and me'
Education: Woodhey High School, Bury; Holy Cross College, Bury;
Durham University; Salford University
Qualifications: 10 GCSEs, 4 A-levels, BSc (Hons) Sport, Health and Exercise,
Level 2 coaching, first aid
Career outside cricket: 'Studying physiotherapy at Salford Uni'
Overseas tours: BUSA to South Africa 2004; Warwickshire to Grenada 2007
Overseas teams played for: Joondalup CC, Perth 2001, 2006, 2007
Career highlights to date: '8-94 v Durham for DUCCE in 2004; 6-30 v Durham for
Warwickshire in 2006'
Cricket moments to forget: 'First game on Sky – getting swept out of the ground
three times by Mal Loye'
Cricket superstitions: 'To run inside my mark'
Cricketers particularly admired: Allan Donald, Graeme Fowler, Brett Lee
Young players to look out for: Chris Woakes (Warwickshire)
Other sports played: Football ('played for Bury School of Excellence and North-
West'), squash, tennis, golf
Other sports followed: Football (Manchester United) – 'I watch Bury's progress'

Favourite band: Oasis, Ocean Colour Scene, Arctic Monkeys
Relaxations: 'Cinema/movies'
Extras: Played for DUCCE 2003-05. Durham University Sportsman of the Year 2004.
Represented British Universities 2004-05. On loan with Leicestershire in 2008
Opinions on cricket: 'Young English cricketers trying to make their way in the game
are suffering due to the amount of overseas-based cricketers who are playing county
cricket. I feel there are fewer young cricketers going to University because of
academies. Although academies are great for cricketers' development, in the bigger
scheme of things, young cricketers will suffer when careers end.'
Best batting: 33 Warwickshire v Durham, Riverside 2007
Best bowling: 8-94 DUCCE v Durham, Riverside 2004

2009 Season

	M	Inn	NO	Runs	HS	Avg	100	50	Ct	St	Balls	Runs	Wkts	Avg	BB	5I	10M
Test																	
FC	5	4	0	3	2	.75	-	-	1	-	528	311	8	38.87	3-39	-	-
ODI																	
List A	13	6	5	53	14*	53.00	-	-	2	-	492	436	16	27.25	4-51	-	
20/20 Int																	
20/20	11	3	1	4	3*	2.00	-	-	3	-	132	168	5	33.60	2-19	-	

Career Performances

	M	Inn	NO	Runs	HS	Avg	100	50	Ct	St	Balls	Runs	Wkts	Avg	BB	5I	10M
Test																	
FC	27	33	13	135	33	6.75	-	-	2	-	3743	2270	61	37.21	8-94	2	-
ODI																	
List A	31	11	9	69	14*	34.50	-	-	4	-	1298	1089	34	32.02	4-51	-	
20/20 Int																	
20/20	14	3	1	4	3*	2.00	-	-	5	-	168	230	6	38.33	2-19	-	

21. It tends to rain a bit at Headingley. Due to frequent interruptions,
how many times did Sadiq Mohammad have to go to the wicket
in order to complete an innings of 97 in 1978?

DAGNALL, C. E. Leicestershire

Name: Charles (<u>Charlie</u>) Edward Dagnall
Role: Right-hand bat, right-arm medium-fast bowler
Born: 10 July 1976, Bury, Lancashire
County debut: 1999 (Warwickshire), 2002
(Leicestershire)
Career outside cricket: Sports reporter, radio
presenter (BBC Radio Leicester) and 'part-time
soul singer'
Extras: Played for a number of county 2nd XI sides
(including Lancashire, Nottinghamshire, Hampshire,
Middlesex, Kent and Worcestershire) 1994-96.
Appearances restricted to Minor Counties cricket in
1997. Made first-class debut for Warwickshire 1999.
Moved to Leicestershire in 2002. Abandoned first-
class cricket in 2004 and established himself as a

sports reporter and radio presenter with the BBC while continuing to play local
league cricket in Nottinghamshire and Leicestershire. Made an unexpected return
to county cricket in August 2009, playing a single Pro40 game for an injury-hit
Leicestershire side
Best batting: 23* Leicestershire v Surrey, The Oval 2003
Best bowling: 6-50 Warwickshire v Derbyshire, Derby 2001

2009 Season

	M	Inn	NO	Runs	HS	Avg	100	50	Ct	St	Balls	Runs	Wkts	Avg	BB	5I	10M
Test																	
FC																	
ODI																	
List A	1	1	1	1	1*		-	-	-	-	30	34	0		-	-	
20/20 Int																	
20/20																	

Career Performances

	M	Inn	NO	Runs	HS	Avg	100	50	Ct	St	Balls	Runs	Wkts	Avg	BB	5I	10M
Test																	
FC	31	32	10	223	23*	10.13	-	-	5	-	4848	2746	87	31.56	6-50	2	-
ODI																	
List A	57	28	11	197	28	11.58	-	-	6	-	2490	1726	71	24.30	4-34	-	
20/20 Int																	
20/20	6	1	0	2	2	2.00	-	-	1	-	120	161	6	26.83	4-22	-	

DALRYMPLE, J. W. M.   Glamorgan

Name: James (Jamie) William Murray Dalrymple
Role: Right-hand bat, off-spin bowler;
county captain
Born: 21 January 1981, Nairobi, Kenya
Height: 6ft **Weight:** 13st 7lbs
Nickname: JD, Pest
County debut: 2000 (one-day, Middlesex),
2001 (first-class, Middlesex), 2008 (Glamorgan)
County cap: 2004 (Middlesex)
ODI debut: 2006
Twenty20 Int debut: 2006
1000 runs in a season: 1
1st-Class 200s: 2
Place in batting averages: 35th av. 50.45
(2008 125th av. 30.12)

Place in bowling averages: 68th av. 33.00
Parents: Douglas and Patricia
Marital status: Single
Family links with cricket: 'Dad played lots of club cricket.' Brother Simon played
for Oxford University in 2002 and 2004
Education: Radley College, Abingdon; St Peter's College, Oxford University
Qualifications: 10 GCSEs, 5 A-levels, degree in History
Overseas tours: Middlesex to South Africa 2000; England A to West Indies 2005-06;
England to India (ICC Champions Trophy) 2006-07, to Australia 2006-07, to West
Indies (World Cup) 2006-07; MCC to Uganda 2008 (captain)
Cricket moments to forget: 'Middlesex v Warwickshire at Edgbaston 2003 – being
part of the loss of eight wickets in a session, and the match'
Cricketers particularly admired: David Gower, Carl Hooper, Ian Botham,
Mark Waugh
Other sports played: Rugby (college), hockey (university)
Other sports followed: Rugby (Northampton RUFC)
Favourite band: 'Don't have a favourite'
Relaxations: Reading, golf
Extras: Represented England U19 2000. Played for OUCCE 2001 and 2002 (c).
Represented British Universities 2001 and 2002 (c). Oxford Blue 2001, 2002 (c) and
2003 (c). Scored double century (236*) in the Varsity Match at Fenner's 2003 and took
5-49 in the Cambridge first innings. C&G Man of the Match awards v Wales Minor
Counties at Lamphey (104* – second fifty in 14 balls) and v Glamorgan at Lord's
(107) 2004. ECB National Academy 2005-06, 2006-07. Left Middlesex at the end of
the 2007 season and joined Glamorgan for 2008. Glamorgan Player of the Year 2009.
Appointed club captain for 2009, a role he will keep for 2010

Best batting: 244 Middlesex v Surrey, The Oval 2004
Best bowling: 5-49 Oxford University v Cambridge University, Fenner's 2003

2009 Season

	M	Inn	NO	Runs	HS	Avg	100	50	Ct	St	Balls	Runs	Wkts	Avg	BB	5I	10M
Test																	
FC	17	23	3	1009	128	50.45	3	5	17	-	1395	726	22	33.00	3-11	-	-
ODI																	
List A	12	11	3	277	78*	34.62	-	2	5	-	346	284	6	47.33	2-27		
20/20 Int																	
20/20	10	10	0	318	63	31.80	-	3	3	-	115	164	11	14.90	2-17	-	

Career Performances

	M	Inn	NO	Runs	HS	Avg	100	50	Ct	St	Balls	Runs	Wkts	Avg	BB	5I	10M
Test																	
FC	108	170	16	5459	244	35.44	9	30	63	-	11727	6502	149	43.63	5-49	1	-
ODI	27	26	1	487	67	19.48	-	2	12	-	840	666	14	47.57	2-5	-	
List A	154	142	28	3110	107	27.28	2	18	60	-	4715	3973	110	36.11	4-14	-	
20/20 Int	3	3	0	60	32	20.00	-	-	1	-	30	39	2	19.50	1-10	-	
20/20	44	40	6	890	63	26.17	-	4	12	-	493	683	31	22.03	2-8	-	

DANISH KANERIA   Essex

Name: Danish Prabha Shanker Kaneria
Role: Right-hand bat, right-arm
leg-spin and googly bowler
Born: 16 December 1980, Karachi, Pakistan
Height: 6ft 1in
Nickname: Danny Boy, Dani
County debut: 2004
County cap: 2004
Test debut: 2000-01
ODI debut: 2001-02
50 wickets in a season: 3
Place in batting averages: 263rd av. 12.15
(2008 254th av. 11.18)
Place in bowling averages: 14th av. 23.69
(2008 18th av. 21.30)
Parents: Prabha Shanker Kaneria and Babita P. Kaneria
Wife and date of marriage: Dharmeta Danish Kaneria, 15 February 2004
Family links with cricket: Cousin, wicket-keeper Anil Dalpat, played nine Tests
for Pakistan 1983-84
Education: St Patrick's High School, Karachi

Overseas tours: Pakistan U19 to Sri Lanka (U19 World Cup) 1999-2000; Pakistan A to Kenya 2000, to Sri Lanka 2001; Pakistan to Bangladesh 2001-02, to Sharjah (v West Indies) 2001-02, to Sharjah (v Australia) 2002-03, to New Zealand 2003-04, to Australia 2004-05, to India 2004-05, to West Indies 2004-05, to Sri Lanka 2005-06, to Scotland and England 2006, to South Africa 2006-07, to West Indies (World Cup) 2006-07, to India 2007-08, to Sri Lanka 2009, to Australia & New Zealand 2009-10, plus other one-day tournaments in Sharjah, Sri Lanka and England
Overseas teams played for: Several in Pakistan, including Karachi Whites 1998-99 – 2001-02; Habib Bank 1999-2000; Baluchistan Bears 2007-08 –
Career highlights to date: 'Playing for Pakistan. English county cricket'
Cricket superstitions: 'I kiss the ground when taking the field'
Cricketers particularly admired: Abdul Qadir, Viv Richards, Joel Garner
Other sports played: Football, table tennis
Other sports followed: Football (Brazil)
Favourite band: 'I like Indian music'
Relaxations: 'Listening to music and being with family'
Extras: Represented Pakistan U19 1998-99. The second Hindu to play in Tests for Pakistan, after his cousin Anil Dalpat. Had match figures of 12-94 (6-42/6-52) v Bangladesh at Multan in the first match of the Asian Test Championship 2001-02, winning Man of the Match award. His other international awards include Man of the [Test] Series v Bangladesh 2001-02 and Man of the Match in the second Test v Sri Lanka at Karachi 2004-05 (3-72/7-118). Became sixth Pakistan bowler to take 200 Test wickets when he dismissed Ashwell Prince in the first Test v South Africa in Karachi 2007-08. An overseas player with Essex 2004-05 and 2007-08. Signed central contract for Pakistan 2009. Essex's overseas player for 2009, 2010
Best batting: 65 Essex v Nottinghamshire, Trent Bridge 2007
Best bowling: 8-59 Habib Bank v Sui Southern Gas Corporation, Karachi 2008-09

2009 Season

	M	Inn	NO	Runs	HS	Avg	100	50	Ct	St	Balls	Runs	Wkts	Avg	BB	5I	10M
Test																	
FC	11	15	2	158	37	12.15	-	-	5	-	3587	1777	75	23.69	8-116	6	2
ODI																	
List A	14	3	1	43	23	21.50	-	-	3	-	683	556	22	25.27	5-32	1	
20/20 Int																	
20/20	9	5	1	34	12	8.50	-	-	3	-	172	237	11	21.54	3-21	-	

Career Performances

	M	Inn	NO	Runs	HS	Avg	100	50	Ct	St	Balls	Runs	Wkts	Avg	BB	5I	10M
Test	54	71	31	266	29	6.65	-	-	16	-	15947	8022	232	34.57	7-77	13	2
FC	166	206	78	1374	65	10.73	-	1	57	-	44415	21520	827	26.02	8-59	59	10
ODI	18	10	8	12	6*	6.00	-	-	2	-	854	682	15	45.46	3-31	-	
List A	138	64	31	274	33*	8.30	-	-	27	-	6790	4831	211	22.89	5-21	6	
20/20 Int																	
20/20	43	19	7	73	12	6.08	-	-	9	-	862	1034	55	18.80	4-22	-	

DAVEY, J. H. — Middlesex

Name: Joshua (<u>Josh</u>) Henry Davey
Role: Right-hand bat, right-arm medium bowler
Born: 3 August 1990, Aberdeen, Scotland.
County debut: No first-team appearance
Education: Culford School, Bury St Edmunds, Suffolk; Oxford Brookes University
Overseas teams played for: Port Adelaide, South Australia 2008-09
Extras: Played for Bury St Edmunds CC (Suffolk Premier League) 2006-09, Suffolk U15 2005, Suffolk U17 2005-07, Middlesex 2nd XI 2008-09, Suffolk (Minor Counties Trophy) 2009. Played for Culford School – holds the record for the most runs scored in a season by a Culford player. Attended Darren Lehmann Cricket Academy 2009. Signed a three-year contract with Middlesex in September 2009

DAVIES, M. A. — Durham

Name: <u>Mark</u> Anthony Davies
Role: Right-hand bat, right-arm fast-medium bowler
Born: 4 October 1980, Stockton-on-Tees
Height: 6ft 3in **Weight:** 13st
Nickname: Davo
County debut: 1998 (one-day), 2002 (first-class)
County cap: 2005
50 wickets in a season: 1
Place in bowling averages: 41st av. 29.57 (2008 1st av. 14.63)
Parents: Howard and Mandy
Marital status: Single
Education: Northfield School, Billingham; Stockton Sixth Form College
Qualifications: 5 GCSEs, NVQ Level 3 Sport and Recreation
Overseas tours: Durham to South Africa 2002; England Performance Programme Squad to India 2008; England Lions to New Zealand 2008-09
Overseas teams played for: North Kalgoorlie CC, Western Australia

Cricketers particularly admired: Glenn McGrath
Other sports played: Football, golf, boxing
Other sports followed: Football (Middlesbrough)
Relaxations: Socialising, golf
Extras: Represented England U19 2000. Attended Durham Academy. Was the
first bowler to reach 50 first-class wickets in 2004. Played one first-class match
for Nottinghamshire on loan 2007, returning then career-best innings figures of
7-59 v Northamptonshire at Trent Bridge. Top of bowling averages 2008
Member of England Performance Programme squad 2009-10
Best batting: 62 Durham v Somerset, Stockton 2005
Best bowling: 8-24 Durham v Hampshire, Basingstoke 2008

2009 Season

	M	Inn	NO	Runs	HS	Avg	100	50	Ct	St	Balls	Runs	Wkts	Avg	BB	5I	10M
Test																	
FC	9	8	4	37	16*	9.25	-	-	2	-	1303	562	19	29.57	4-87	-	-
ODI																	
List A																	
20/20 Int																	
20/20																	

Career Performances

	M	Inn	NO	Runs	HS	Avg	100	50	Ct	St	Balls	Runs	Wkts	Avg	BB	5I	10M
Test																	
FC	77	102	39	701	62	11.12	-	1	17	-	11754	5444	251	21.68	8-24	12	2
ODI																	
List A	72	36	14	166	31*	7.54	-	-	10	-	2934	2036	68	29.94	4-13	-	
20/20 Int																	
20/20	9	4	3	11	6	11.00	-	-	2	-	204	241	8	30.12	2-14	-	

---

22. Which Pakistan batsman on two occasions took over seven
hours to score a Test century?

DAVIES, S. M. Surrey

Name: Steven (<u>Steve</u>) Michael Davies
Role: Left-hand bat, wicket-keeper
Born: 17 June 1986, Bromsgrove
Height: 5ft 11in **Weight:** 11st 8lbs
Nickname: Davo
County debut: 2004 (one-day, Worcestershire),
2005 (first-class, Worcestershire)
County colours: 2005 (Worcestershire)
1000 runs in a season: 2
Place in batting averages: 75th av. 40.92
(2008 57th av. 41.55)
Parents: Lin and Michael
Marital status: Single
Education: King Charles I School, Kidderminster
Qualifications: 9 GCSEs, 1 A-level, 2 AS-levels
Overseas tours: England U17 to Netherlands 2003; England U19 to Bangladesh
U19 World Cup) 2003-04, to India 2004-05 (c); England A to West Indies 2005-06,
to Bangladesh 2006-07; England Performance Programme to India 2007-08; England
Lions to India 2007-08, to New Zealand 2008-09. England to West Indies (one-day
series) 2009, to South Africa (ICC Champions Trophy) 2009-10.
Career highlights to date: 'Maiden first-class century against Somerset 2005. Pro40
champions 2007'
Cricket superstitions: None
Cricketers particularly admired: Adam Gilchrist, Michael Hussey,
Matthew Hayden
Other sports played: Basketball (trials for England), tennis, golf
Other sports followed: Football (Arsenal)
Favourite band: Chris Brown
Relaxations: 'Playing golf and basketball, socialising with friends, listening to music'
Extras: Represented England U19 2004, 2005. NBC Denis Compton Award for most
promising young Worcestershire player 2004, 2005, 2006, 2007, 2008. Took six
catches in Leicestershire's first innings at Worcester 2006, equalling Worcestershire
record for wicket-keeping catches in a first-class innings. Achieved double of 1000
(1052) runs and 50 (68) dismissals in first-class cricket 2006. ECB National Academy
2004-05 (part-time), 2005-06 (including visit to World Cricket Academy, India), 2006-
07. Forced to withdraw from England Lions tour to India 2007-08 with a knee injury.
Called up to join England tour party in West Indies 2009 when Matt Prior was given
permission to return home. Moved from Worcestershire to Surrey at the end of the
2009 season
Best batting: 192 Worcestershire v Gloucestershire, Bristol 2006

2009 Season

	M	Inn	NO	Runs	HS	Avg	100	50	Ct	St	Balls	Runs	Wkts	Avg	BB	5I	10M
Test																	
FC	15	28	3	1023	126	40.92	2	5	40	2	0	0	0	-	-	-	-
ODI																	
List A	16	15	1	705	106	50.35	2	4	8	7	0	0	0	-	-		
20/20 Int																	
20/20	10	10	0	259	73	25.90	-	2	3	2	0	0	0	-	-		

Career Performances

	M	Inn	NO	Runs	HS	Avg	100	50	Ct	St	Balls	Runs	Wkts	Avg	BB	5I	10M
Test																	
FC	77	130	15	4281	192	37.22	6	19	237	14	0	0	0	-	-	-	-
ODI	1	1	0	5	5	5.00	-	-	1	-	0	0	0	-	-		
List A	85	75	11	2262	119	35.34	4	12	70	24	0	0	0	-	-		
20/20 Int	1	1	0	27	27	27.00	-	-	-	-	0	0	0	-	-		
20/20	35	30	5	510	73	20.40	-	2	13	4	0	0	0	-	-		

DAWSON, L. A. Hampshire

Name: Liam Andrew Dawson
Role: Right-hand bat, slow left-arm bowler;
all-rounder
Born: 1 March 1990, Swindon
Height: 5ft 8in **Weight:** 11st
Nickname: Daws, Lemmy, Kimya, Chav
County debut: 2007
Place in batting averages: 147th av. 30.05
(2008 142nd av. 27.57)
Place in bowling averages: 110th av. 42.10
Parents: Andy and Bev
Marital status: Single
Family links with cricket: 'Dad played club
cricket for Goatacre and Cheltenham. Brother
also plays, for Wiltshire U14/U15 and Goatacre'
Education: The John Bentley School, Calne
Qualifications: GCSEs
Overseas tours: West of England U15 to West Indies 2005; England U16 to South
Africa 2006; England U19 to Malaysia 2006-07, to Malaysia (U19 World Cup)
2007-08, to South Africa 2008-09
Overseas teams played for: Melville, Perth 2006-07, 2007-08

Career highlights to date: 'Making my one-day and first-class debuts. Being Man of the Match at Lord's in the Pro40 v Middlesex'
Cricket moments to forget: 'Being hit for 20-odd in an over'
Cricket superstitions: None
Cricketers particularly admired: Shane Warne, Dan Vettori
Other sports played: Football (Calne Town Youth)
Other sports followed: Football (Bury)
Favourite band: The Wombats, Coldplay
Relaxations: 'Rugby League'
Extras: Hampshire Academy Player of the Year 2005. Bunbury Festival All-rounder of the Tournament 2005. Represented England U19 2007. Made List A debut v Northamptonshire at Northampton in the Pro40 2007 aged 17, scoring a 31-ball 32. NBC Denis Compton Award for the most promising young Hampshire player 2007, 2008. Man of the Series for England U19 v New Zealand 2008. Made 100* in the final Championship fixture against Nottingham in September 2008. Member of England Performance Programme squad 2009-10
Best batting: 100* Hampshire v Nottinghamshire, Trent Bridge 2008
Best bowling: 2-3 Hampshire v Sussex, Rose Bowl 2009

2009 Season

	M	Inn	NO	Runs	HS	Avg	100	50	Ct	St	Balls	Runs	Wkts	Avg	BB	5I	10M
Test																	
FC	15	23	4	571	69	30.05	-	4	13	-	582	421	10	42.10	2-3	-	-
ODI																	
List A	18	14	4	272	69*	27.20	-	2	10	-	567	488	13	37.53	4-48	-	
20/20 Int																	
20/20	11	8	1	59	23	8.42	-	-	8	-	114	146	5	29.20	3-25	-	

Career Performances

	M	Inn	NO	Runs	HS	Avg	100	50	Ct	St	Balls	Runs	Wkts	Avg	BB	5I	10M
Test																	
FC	21	31	5	764	100*	29.38	1	4	13	-	925	634	16	39.62	2-3	-	-
ODI																	
List A	28	23	5	470	69*	26.11	-	2	16	-	825	730	24	30.41	4-45	-	
20/20 Int																	
20/20	16	12	4	76	23	9.50	-	-	9	-	150	199	8	24.87	3-25	-	

DAWSON, R. K. J.　　　　Gloucestershire

Name: <u>Richard</u> Kevin James Dawson
Role: Right-hand bat, right-arm
off-spin bowler
Born: 4 August 1980, Doncaster
Height: 6ft 4in　**Weight:** 11st 4lbs
Nickname: Billy Dog
County debut: 2001 (Yorkshire),
2007 (Northamptonshire), 2008 (Gloucestershire)
County cap: 2004 (Yorkshire)
Test debut: 2001-02
Place in batting averages: 181st av. 25.40
(2008 182nd av. 22.00)
Place in bowling averages: 128th av. 50.83
Parents: Kevin and Pat
Marital status: Single

Family links with cricket: Brother Gareth plays for Doncaster Town CC
Education: Batley GS; Exeter University
Qualifications: 10 GCSEs, 4 A-levels, degree in Exercise and Sports Science
Overseas tours: England U18 to Bermuda 1997; England U19 to New Zealand
1998-99; England to India and New Zealand 2001-02, to Australia 2002-03; ECB
National Academy to Sri Lanka 2002-03; England A to Sri Lanka 2004-05
Cricketers particularly admired: Steve Waugh, Graeme Swann
Other sports played: Football
Other sports followed: Football (Doncaster Rovers FC)
Relaxations: Sleeping, listening to music
Extras: Captained England U15. Sir John Hobbs Silver Jubilee Memorial Prize 1995.
Represented England U19 1999. Captained British Universities 2000. NBC Denis
Compton Award for the most promising young Yorkshire player 2001. Made Test
debut in the first Test v India at Mohali 2001-02, taking 4-134 in India's first innings.
Released by Northamptonshire at the end of the 2007 season. Signed for
Gloucestershire towards the end of the 2008 season
Best batting: 87 Yorkshire v Kent, Canterbury 2002
Best bowling: 6-82 Yorkshire v Glamorgan, Scarborough 2001

2009 Season

	M	Inn	NO	Runs	HS	Avg	100	50	Ct	St	Balls	Runs	Wkts	Avg	BB	5I	10M
Test																	
FC	7	10	0	254	50	25.40	-	1	12	-	952	610	12	50.83	4-76	-	-
ODI																	
List A	9	6	0	71	31	11.83	-	-	2	-	226	198	7	28.28	2-39	-	
20/20 Int																	
20/20	9	9	1	69	27*	8.62	-	-	4	-	192	224	5	44.80	2-30	-	

Career Performances

	M	Inn	NO	Runs	HS	Avg	100	50	Ct	St	Balls	Runs	Wkts	Avg	BB	5I	10M
Test	7	13	3	114	19*	11.40	-	-	3	-	1116	677	11	61.54	4-134	-	-
FC	103	153	17	2927	87	21.52	-	12	63	-	15467	8770	199	44.07	6-82	5	-
ODI																	
List A	119	74	15	594	41	10.06	-	-	39	-	4475	3647	118	30.90	4-13	-	
20/20 Int																	
20/20	34	17	4	140	27*	10.76	-	-	11	-	653	828	29	28.55	3-24	-	

DE BRUYN, Z.   Somerset

Name: Zander de Bruyn
Role: Right-hand bat, right-arm fast-medium
bowler; all-rounder
Born: 5 July 1975, Johannesburg, South Africa
Height: 6ft 2in **Weight:** 12st 8lbs
Nickname: 'Z'
County debut: 2005 (Worcestershire),
2008 (Somerset)
County colours: 2005 (Worcestershire)
Place in batting averages: 139th av. 31.18
(2008 45th av. 45.31)
Test debut: 2004-05
1st-Class 200s: 1
Parents: Hans and Ronel

Wife and date of marriage: Bronwyn, 13 April 2003
Children: Tyler James, 23 November 2007
Education: Hoerskool Helpmekaar; Hoerskool Randburg: University of
Johannesburg (RAU)
Off-season: 'Playing in South Africa for Highveld Lions.'
Overseas tours: South Africa A to Zimbabwe 2004, to Sri Lanka 2005-06; South
Africa to India 2004-05
Overseas teams played for: Transvaal/Gauteng 1995-96 – 2000-01; Easterns
2002-03, 2003-04; Nashua Titans 2004-05; Chevrolet Warriors 2006-07 – 2008-09;
Highveld Lions 2009-10
Career highlights to date: 'Playing for South Africa'
Cricket moments to forget: 'Scoring my first pair'
Cricket superstitions: None
Cricketers particularly admired: Steve Waugh
Other sports played: Rugby – played at provincial level up to U19
Other sports followed: Rugby (Lions and South Africa)
Favourite band: Live
Relaxations: 'Golf, gadgets, barbecues'

Extras: Represented South Africa Schools. Played for Surrey Board XI in the NatWest 2000 and C&G 2001. Scored 1015 runs (av. 72.50) in the SuperSport Series 2003-04, becoming only the second player (after Barry Richards) to record 1000 runs in a season in the South African domestic first-class competition. Has won numerous awards, including Man of the Match v Western Province in the semi-finals of the Standard Bank Cup at Cape Town 2003-04 (5-44/29) and v Yorkshire at Headingley in the C&G 2005 (3-24/82). An overseas player with Worcestershire 2005, and with Somerset since 2008
Best batting: 266* Easterns v Griqualand West, Kimberley 2003-04
Best bowling: 7-67 Chevrolet Warriors v Nashua Titans, Port Elizabeth 2007-08

2009 Season

	M	Inn	NO	Runs	HS	Avg	100	50	Ct	St	Balls	Runs	Wkts	Avg	BB	5I	10M
Test																	
FC	16	25	3	686	106	31.18	1	6	3	-	816	541	7	77.28	3-47	-	-
ODI																	
List A	17	14	5	712	109*	79.11	1	7	3	-	454	360	15	24.00	4-20	-	
20/20 Int																	
20/20	12	10	3	391	83*	55.85	-	3	4	-	60	91	4	22.75	2-2	-	

Career Performances

	M	Inn	NO	Runs	HS	Avg	100	50	Ct	St	Balls	Runs	Wkts	Avg	BB	5I	10M
Test	3	5	1	195	83	38.75	-	1	-	-	216	92	3	30.66	2-32	-	-
FC	146	247	27	8732	266*	39.69	20	46	91	-	11680	6724	168	40.02	7-67	3	-
ODI																	
List A	158	142	28	4062	113*	35.63	3	26	36	-	3914	3402	107	31.79	5-44	1	
20/20 Int																	
20/20	52	46	10	1103	83*	30.63	-	5	6	-	426	589	26	22.65	4-18	-	

23. Which two England batsmen made centuries in the
First Test v Bangladesh in May 2005?

DENLY, J. L. Kent

Name: Joseph (<u>Joe</u>) Liam Denly
Role: Right-hand bat, leg-spin bowler
Born: 16 March 1986, Canterbury
Height: 6ft **Weight:** 11st 9lbs
Nickname: No Pants
County debut: 2004
1000 runs in a season: 1
Place in batting averages: 61st av. 42.50
(2008 123rd av. 30.16)
Parents: Jayne and Nick
Marital status: Single
Family links with cricket: 'Dad and brother play
local cricket'
Education: Chaucer Technology School
Qualifications: 10 GCSEs, Level 1 coaching
Overseas tours: England U18 to Netherlands 2003; England U19 to India 2004-05;
England Performance Programme to India 2007-08, 2008-09; England Lions to India
2007-08, to New Zealand 2009; England to South Africa 2009-10 (one-day series)
Overseas teams played for: Hamersley Carine, Perth 2003; UTS Balmain Tigers,
Sydney 2005-07
Career highlights to date: 'First first-class hundred'
Cricket moments to forget: 'Golden duck on first-class debut'
Cricket superstitions: 'Left pad on first'
Cricketers particularly admired: Steve Waugh
Other sports played: Football (Charlton Athletic U14, U15)
Other sports followed: Football (Arsenal)
Favourite band: Westlife
Extras: Represented England U17, U18 and U19. Carried bat in scoring his first
Championship century (115*) v Hampshire at Canterbury 2007. Represented England
Lions 2007. In 2008, he scored over 1900 runs in all forms of cricket, including three
centuries and eleven fifties
Best batting: 149 Kent v Somerset, Tunbridge Wells 2008
Best bowling: 2-13 Kent v Surrey, Canterbury 2007

2009 Season

	M	Inn	NO	Runs	HS	Avg	100	50	Ct	St	Balls	Runs	Wkts	Avg	BB	5I	10M
Test																	
FC	11	17	1	680	123	42.50	3	2	7	-	174	93	0		-	-	-
ODI	4	4	0	134	53	33.50	-	1	3	-	0	0	0		-	-	
List A	13	13	1	563	115	46.91	1	3	6	-	0	0	0		-	-	
20/20 Int	1	1	0	0	0	0.00	-	-	-	-	0	0	0		-	-	
20/20	13	13	2	185	32*	16.81	-	-	2	-	0	0	0		-	-	

Career Performances

	M	Inn	NO	Runs	HS	Avg	100	50	Ct	St	Balls	Runs	Wkts	Avg	BB	5I	10M
Test																	
FC	52	88	5	3058	149	36.84	9	14	23	-	877	447	10	44.70	2-13	-	-
ODI	9	9	0	268	67	29.77	-	2	5	-	0	0	0		-	-	
List A	64	62	6	1803	115	32.19	3	9	21	-	12	15	0		-	-	
20/20 Int	1	1	0	0	0	0.00	-	-	-	-	0	0	0		-	-	
20/20	42	39	3	928	91	25.77	-	6	13	-	0	0	0		-	-	

DENT, C. D. J.   Gloucestershire

Name: Christopher (Chris) David James Dent
Role: Left-hand bat, left-arm spin bowler, wicket-keeper
Born: 20 January 1991, Bristol
County debut: 2009 (one-day)
Overseas tours: England U19 to Bangladesh 2009, to New Zealand (ICC U19 World Cup) 2010
Extras: Played for Gloucestershire age groups and 2nd XI before signing a two-year contract with the county in August 2009. Made his debut in a Pro40 match v Nottinghamshire at Trent Bridge the following month. Gloucestershire Academy Player of the Year 2009. Scored an unbeaten half-century (53*) for England U19 v Afghanistan U19 in the ICC U19 World Cup in New Zealand, January 2010

2009 Season

	M	Inn	NO	Runs	HS	Avg	100	50	Ct	St	Balls	Runs	Wkts	Avg	BB	5I	10M
Test																	
FC																	
ODI																	
List A	1	0	0	0	0		-	-	2		-	0	0	0	-	-	
20/20 Int																	
20/20																	

Career Performances

	M	Inn	NO	Runs	HS	Avg	100	50	Ct	St	Balls	Runs	Wkts	Avg	BB	5I	10M
Test																	
FC																	
ODI																	
List A	1	0	0	0	0		-	-	2	-	0	0	0		-	-	
20/20 Int																	
20/20																	

DERNBACH, J. W.   Surrey

Name: <u>Jade</u> Winston Dernbach
Role: Right-hand bat, right-arm fast bowler
Born: 3 March 1986, Johannesburg, South Africa
Height: 6ft 2in **Weight:** 13st
County debut: 2003
Place in batting averages: 268th av. 10.61
Place in bowling averages: 98th av. 38.81
Parents: Carmen and Graeme
Marital status: Single
Education: St John the Baptist
Overseas tours: La Manga tournament, Spain 2003
Cricketers particularly admired: Jacques Kallis,
Jonty Rhodes, James Anderson, Rikki Clarke
Other sports played: Rugby (Surrey U16)
Other sports followed: Football (Arsenal)
Relaxations: 'Going out with friends, swimming, playing football and rugby,
listening to music'
Extras: Sir Jack Hobbs Fair Play Award. Surrey U19 Player of the Year. Made first-
class debut v India A at The Oval 2003 aged 17, becoming the youngest player for 30
years to play first-class cricket for Surrey. Surrey Academy 2003, 2004. NBC Denis
Compton Award for the most promising young Surrey player 2003, 2009. Selected for
the England Performance Fast Bowlng programme squad 2009-10
Best batting: 19 Surrey v Northamptonshire, Northampton 2009
Best bowling: 6-47 Surrey v Leicestershire, Leicester 2009

2009 Season

	M	Inn	NO	Runs	HS	Avg	100	50	Ct	St	Balls	Runs	Wkts	Avg	BB	5I	10M
Test																	
FC	14	19	6	138	19	10.61	-	-	1	-	2372	1436	37	38.81	6-47	2	-
ODI																	
List A	10	3	2	22	8*	22.00	-	-	3	-	411	417	10	41.70	3-23	-	
20/20 Int																	
20/20	5	2	1	4	2*	4.00	-	-	-	-	95	147	4	36.75	2-31	-	

Career Performances

	M	Inn	NO	Runs	HS	Avg	100	50	Ct	St	Balls	Runs	Wkts	Avg	BB	5I	10M
Test																	
FC	34	42	14	250	19	8.92	-	-	3	-	4771	3115	78	39.93	6-47	3	-
ODI																	
List A	49	22	9	111	21	8.53	-	-	12	-	2000	2041	83	24.59	5-31	2	
20/20 Int																	
20/20	29	6	1	14	9	2.80	-	-	6	-	499	796	18	44.22	3-32	-	

DEXTER, N. J.   Middlesex

Name: <u>Neil</u> John Dexter
Role: Right-hand bat, right-arm medium bowler; all-rounder
Born: 21 August 1984, Johannesburg, South Africa
Height: 6ft **Weight:** 11st 4lbs
Nickname: Ted, Dex, Sexy Dexy
County debut: 2005 (Kent), 2009 (Middlesex)
Place in batting averages: 69th av. 41.70 (2008 133rd av. 29.16)
Parents: John and Susan
Marital status: Single
Education: Northwood School, Durban; UNISA (University of South Africa)
Qualifications: Matriculation
Overseas teams played for: Crusaders CC 2000-06
Career highlights to date: 'Scoring first ton, against Glamorgan 2006'
Cricket moments to forget: 'Being hit for 25 in one over against Worcester'
Cricketers particularly admired: Steve Waugh, Brett Lee
Young players to look out for: Alex Blake, Sam Northeast, Joe Denly
Other sports played: Golf, tennis, 'most sports'
Other sports followed: Football (Manchester United)
Favourite band: Simple Plan, Goo Goo Dolls
Relaxations: 'Lying around doing nothing'
Extras: Played for Natal U13-19, Natal Academy and Natal A. Loaned to Essex in 2008. Signed for Middlesex in September 2008. Played for Middlesex in Stanford Twenty20 series 2009. Is not considered an overseas player
Best batting: 146 Middlesex v Kent, Uxbridge 2009
Best bowling: 2-37 Middlesex v Glamorgan, Lord's 2009

2009 Season

	M	Inn	NO	Runs	HS	Avg	100	50	Ct	St	Balls	Runs	Wkts	Avg	BB	5I	10M
Test																	
FC	10	19	2	709	146	41.70	2	2	15	-	528	266	6	44.33	2-37	-	-
ODI																	
List A	13	13	3	353	79	35.30	-	3	5	-	286	246	3	82.00	2-28	-	
20/20 Int																	
20/20	10	10	0	186	73	18.60	-	1	4	-	30	39	1	39.00	1-5	-	

Career Performances

	M	Inn	NO	Runs	HS	Avg	100	50	Ct	St	Balls	Runs	Wkts	Avg	BB	5I	10M
Test																	
FC	39	60	10	2048	146	40.96	5	10	34	-	1344	789	15	52.60	2-37	-	-
ODI																	
List A	40	35	6	955	135*	32.93	2	4	9	-	730	632	17	37.17	3-17	-	
20/20 Int																	
20/20	37	31	3	521	73	18.60	-	1	16	-	144	238	5	47.60	3-27	-	

DIBBLE, A. J.   Somerset

Name: <u>Adam</u> John Dibble
Role: Right-hand bat, right-arm
fast-medium bowler
Born: 9 March 1991, Exeter, Devon
Height: 6ft 4in **Weight:** 14st
Nickname: Dibbs, Officer
County debut: No first-team appearance
Parents: Mike and Liz
Marital status: Single
Education: St John's School, Sidmouth;
Taunton School
Cricketers particularly admired: Brett Lee,
Andrew Flintoff
Other sports played: Rugby
Other sports followed: Rugby, football, tennis
Favourite band: Coldplay
Relaxations: 'Music, TV, computer, Starbuck's'
Extras: Elite Player Development 2008. Has played for Somerset Second XI and for
Devon at U15 and U17 level. Played club cricket for Sidmouth CC 2007-08. Joined
the county on a summer contract after completing A-level studies in June 2009

DIPPENAAR, H. H.   Leicestershire

Name: Hendrik Human (<u>Boeta</u>) Dippenaar
Role: Right-hand bat, right-arm
off-break bowler
Born: 14 June 1977, Kimberley, South Africa
Height: 5ft 11in **Weight:** 11st 13lbs
Nickname: Dipps
County debut: 2008
Test debut: 1999-2000
ODI debut: 1999-2000
Twenty20 Int debut: 2005-06
1000 runs in a season: 1
1st-Class 200s: 2
Place in batting averages: 59th av. 43.11
(2008 158th av.25.35)
Parents: Frank and Alet
Wife and date of marriage: Charleen, 16 April 2004
Education: Grey College, Bloemfontein
Career outside cricket: Commercial helicopter pilot
Off-season: Domestic cricket in South Africa
Overseas tours: South Africa U19 to England 1995, to India 1995-96; Free State to West Indies 1996-97; South Africa A to Zimbabwe 2004, to Zimbabwe 2007-08 (c), to India 2007-08 (c); South Africa to Kenya (LG Cup) 1999-2000, to Zimbabwe 1999-2000, to Kenya (ICC Knockout Trophy) 2000-01, to West Indies 2000-01, to Zimbabwe 2001-02, to Australia 2001-02, to Sri Lanka (ICC Champions Trophy) 2002-03, to Bangladesh 2003, to England 2003, to Pakistan 2003-04, to Sri Lanka 2004, to India 2004-05, to West Indies 2004-05, to Sri Lanka 2006, to India (ICC Champions Trophy) 2006-07, plus other one-day tournaments and series in Australia, Singapore, Morocco and New Zealand
Overseas teams played for: Free State 1995-96 – 2003-04; Eagles 2004-05 –
Career highlights to date: 'Test match at Lord's, 2003'
Cricket moments to forget: 'South Africa v Sri Lanka, World Cup 2003'
Cricketers particularly admired: Steve Waugh
Young players to look out for: Dean Elgar (Diamond Eagles, South Africa)
Other sports played: Golf, tennis, rugby
Other sports followed: Golf, rugby (Cheetahs)
Favourite band: Hillsong
Relaxations: 'Fly fishing and hunting'
Extras: Represented South Africa in the 2002-03 World Cup. Scored 177* in the first Test v Bangladesh in Chittagong 2003, in the process sharing with Jacques Rudolph (222*) in the highest partnership for any wicket for South Africa in Tests (429*). One of *South African Cricket Annual*'s five Cricketers of the Year 2005. Played for an

African XI in the Afro-Asian Cup 2005-06, 2007. His numerous match and series awards include Man of the [ODI] Series v Pakistan 2003-04 and v West Indies 2004-05 (317 runs; av. 105.66). Announced his retirement from international cricket in 2008. Joined Leicestershire as overseas player for 2009. Released by Leicestershire at the end of the 2009 season

Best batting: 250* Eagles v Warriors, Kimberley 2006-07
Best bowling: 1-6 Leicestershire v West Indians, Leicester 2009

2009 Season

	M	Inn	NO	Runs	HS	Avg	100	50	Ct	St	Balls	Runs	Wkts	Avg	BB	5I	10M
Test																	
FC	17	31	5	1121	143	43.11	2	8	6	-	59	44	1	44.00	1-6	-	-
ODI																	
List A	13	12	2	396	65	39.60	-	2	4	-	12	5	1	5.00	1-5	-	
20/20 Int																	
20/20	10	8	3	167	63	33.40	-	1	3	-	0	0	0		-	-	

Career Performances

	M	Inn	NO	Runs	HS	Avg	100	50	Ct	St	Balls	Runs	Wkts	Avg	BB	5I	10M
Test	38	62	5	1718	177*	30.14	3	7	27	-	12	1	0		-	-	-
FC	176	298	29	11318	250*	42.07	32	49	180	-	90	61	1	61.00	1-6	-	-
ODI	107	95	14	3421	125*	42.23	4	26	36	-	0	0	0		-	-	
List A	235	214	31	7380	125*	40.32	8	51	89	-	18	7	1	7.00	1-5	-	
20/20 Int	1	1	0	1	1	1.00	-	-	-	-	0	0	0		-	-	
20/20	54	47	7	795	63	19.87	-	2	22	-	0	0	0		-	-	

DI VENUTO, M. J.   Durham

Name: <u>Michael</u> James Di Venuto
Role: Left-hand bat, right-arm medium/leg-break bowler
Born: 12 December 1973, Hobart, Tasmania
Height: 5ft 11in **Weight:** 12st 12lbs
Nickname: Diva
County debut: 1999 (Sussex), 2000 (Derbyshire), 2007 (Durham)
County cap: 1999 (Sussex), 2000 (Derbyshire)
ODI debut: 1996-97
1000 runs in a season: 9
1st-Class 200s: 5
Place in batting averages: 3rd av. 78.76 (2008 40th av. 46.45)

Parents: Enrico and Elizabeth
Wife and date of marriage: Renae, 31 December 2003
Children: Sophia Lily, 21 March 2005; Luca Michael, 3 September 2007
Family links with cricket: 'Dad and older brother Peter both played grade cricket in Tasmania.' Brother Peter also played for Italy
Education: St Virgil's College, Hobart
Qualifications: HSC (5 x Level III subjects), Level 3 coaching
Career outside cricket: 'Own a cafe, "Say Cheese Salamanca", in Hobart'
Off-season: 'Assistant coach with the Tasmanian Tigers for 2009-10.'
Overseas tours: Australian Cricket Academy to India and Sri Lanka 1993, to South Africa 1996; Australia A to Malaysia (Super 8s) 1997 (c), to Scotland and Ireland 1998 (c), to Los Angeles 1999; Australia to South Africa 1996-97 (one-day series), to Hong Kong (Super 6s) 1997, to Malaysia (Super 8s) 1998; Tasmania to Zimbabwe 1995-96
Overseas teams played for: North Hobart CC, Tasmania; Kingborough, Tasmania; Tasmania 1991-92 –
Career highlights to date: 'Playing for Australia. Man of the Match award v South Africa at Johannesburg 1997. Dismissing Jamie Cox at Taunton in 1999, my first wicket in first-class cricket. Winning Tasmania's first Pura Cup 2006-07. Winning Durham's first trophy and being part of the awesome 2007 season with Durham. Back-to-back Championship titles with Durham'
Cricket moments to forget: 'Being dismissed by Jamie Cox at Taunton in 1999, *his* first wicket in first-class cricket'
Cricketers particularly admired: David Boon, Dean Jones, Kepler Wessels, Mark and Steve Waugh, Viv Richards, Ricky Ponting
Young players to look out for: Scott Borthwick, Mark Stoneman, Ben Harmison (all Durham)
Other sports played: Australian Rules (Tasmanian U15, U16 and Sandy Bay FC)
Other sports followed: Australian Rules football (Geelong Cats)
Injuries: Groin strain – out for 3 weeks
Favourite band: U2, Black-Eyed Peas
Relaxations: Golf, sleeping and eating
Extras: Man of the Match in the fifth ODI v South Africa at Johannesburg 1997 (89). Was Sussex overseas player 1999, an overseas player with Derbyshire 2000-06, an overseas player with Durham 2007. Scored 173* v Derbyshire Board XI at Derby in NatWest 2000, a record for Derbyshire in one-day cricket. Carried bat for 192* v Middlesex at Lord's 2002; also scored 113 in the second innings. Derbyshire Player of the Year 2002 (jointly with Kevin Dean). First batsman to 1000 Championship runs 2003. Vice-captain of Derbyshire 2002-06 (was appointed captain for 2004 but was unable to take up post due to back surgery). Tasmania Pura Cup Player of the Year (David Boon Medal) 2006-07. Carried bat for 155* on Durham first-class debut v Worcestershire at Worcester 2007 and again for 204* v Kent at Riverside 2007. Made an invaluable 90 runs in Durham's title-clinching victory over Kent in September 2008. Retired from Tasmanian international cricket at the end of the 2007-08 season, and is now part-time batting coach with Tasmanian Cricket Association. The champion

county's highest first-class runs scorer in 2009. Holds an Italian passport and is no longer considered an overseas player

Opinions on cricket: 'The domestic game should do its best to mirror international cricket. especially with regard to the one-day game. While 50-over cricket is still being played internationally, it should still be played domestically.'

Best batting: 254* Durham v Sussex, Riverside 2009
Best bowling: 1-0 Tasmania v Queensland, Brisbane (AB) 1999-2000

2009 Season

	M	Inn	NO	Runs	HS	Avg	100	50	Ct	St	Balls	Runs	Wkts	Avg	BB	5I	10M
Test																	
FC	17	27	6	1654	254*	78.76	6	6	23	-		0	0	0		-	-	-
ODI																	
List A	5	5	0	116	32	23.20	-	-	-	-		0	0	0		-	-	
20/20 Int																	
20/20	6	6	0	109	55	18.16	-	1	1	-		0	0	0		-	-	

Career Performances

	M	Inn	NO	Runs	HS	Avg	100	50	Ct	St	Balls	Runs	Wkts	Avg	BB	5I	10M
Test																		
FC	298	528	38	22751	254*	46.43	53	134	349	-	807	484	5	96.80	1-0	-	-
ODI	9	9	0	241	89	26.77	-	2	1	-	0	0	0		-	-	
List A	295	289	18	8948	173*	33.01	15	45	120	-	200	181	5	36.20	1-10	-	
20/20 Int																	
20/20	46	44	4	951	95*	23.77	-	7	10	-	78	88	5	17.60	3-19	-	

DIXEY, P. G. Kent

Name: Paul Garrod Dixey
Role: Right-hand bat, wicket-keeper
Born: 2 November 1987, Canterbury
Height: 5ft 8in **Weight:** 11st 11lbs
Nickname: Dix
County debut: 2005
Place in batting averages: 195th av. 23.66
(2008 275th av. 10.50)
Parents: James and Lindsay
Marital status: Single
Family links with cricket: 'Dad used to play club cricket for St Lawrence and Highland Court'
Education: King's School, Canterbury; Durham University (Hatfield College)
Qualifications: 8 GCSEs, 4 AS-levels, 3 A-levels

Overseas tours: England U16 to South Africa
Career highlights to date: 'First-class debut against Bangladesh A at Canterbury'
Cricket moments to forget: 'Losing to Western Province U17 at Fairbairn College off the last ball of a closely fought two-day game'
Cricket superstitions: 'None'
Cricketers particularly admired: Adam Gilchrist, Ian Healy, Alan Knott
Young players to look out for: Alex Blake, Sam Northeast and James Iles (all Kent)
Other sports played: Hockey, rugby
Other sports followed: Rugby ('follow the Premiership')
Favourite band: Ne-Yo
Relaxations: 'Skiing, fly fishing, listening to music'
Extras: Daily Telegraph Bunbury ESCA Wicket-keeping Scholarship Award 2003. Magic Moment Award (Bunbury 2003). Represented England U19 2006. Played for MCC 2007, and for DUCCE 2007-09
Best batting: 103 DUCCE v Lancashire, Durham 2009

2009 Season

	M	Inn	NO	Runs	HS	Avg	100	50	Ct	St	Balls	Runs	Wkts	Avg	BB	5I	10M
Test																	
FC	3	6	0	142	103	23.66	1	-	8	2	0	0	0	-	-	-	
ODI																	
List A	3	3	2	32	16	32.00	-	-	1	-	0	0	0	-	-		
20/20 Int																	
20/20																	

Career Performances

	M	Inn	NO	Runs	HS	Avg	100	50	Ct	St	Balls	Runs	Wkts	Avg	BB	5I	10M
Test																	
FC	12	21	1	312	103	15.60	1	-	27	3	0	0	0	-	-	-	
ODI																	
List A	4	3	2	32	16	32.00	-	-	4	-	0	0	0	-	-		
20/20 Int																	
20/20																	

---

24. At which venue was the England v Bangladesh Second Test played in June 2005?

Name: Francois du Plessis
Role: Right-hand bat, leg-break bowler
Born: 13 July 1984, Pretoria, South Africa
Nickname: Faf
County debut: 2008
Place in batting averages: 138th av. 31.23
(2008 159th av. 25.16)
Overseas tours: South Africa U19 to England 2003;
South Africa Academy to Pakistan 2004-05; South
Africa Emerging Players to Australia (Cricket
Australia Emerging Players Tournament) 2007;
South Africa VI to Hong Kong 2007
Overseas teams played for: Northerns 2003-04 –
2005-06; Titans 2005-06 –
Extras: Scored 177 v England U19 in the third 'Test'
at Chelmsford 2003. Played for Nottinghamshire 2nd XI 2006, scoring 138-ball 203*
v Minor Counties U25 at the Brian Wakefield Sports Ground, Nottingham, in the
2nd XI Trophy. Man of the Match v Warriors in East London in the MTN Domestic
Championship 2006-07 (80). Played for Todmorden in the Lancashire League 2007.
Is not considered an overseas player
Best batting: 176 Nashua Titans v Highveld Lions, Centurion 2008-09
Best bowling: 4-39 Northerns v Free State, Pretoria (LCD) 2004-05

2009 Season

	M	Inn	NO	Runs	HS	Avg	100	50	Ct	St	Balls	Runs	Wkts	Avg	BB	5I	10M
Test																	
FC	13	20	3	531	86*	31.23	-	5	8	-	325	199	4	49.75	2-14	-	-
ODI																	
List A	16	12	4	449	113*	56.12	2	2	7	-	161	151	1	151.00	1-45	-	
20/20 Int																	
20/20	8	8	1	153	78*	21.85	-	1	-	-	102	103	5	20.60	1-4	-	

Career Performances

	M	Inn	NO	Runs	HS	Avg	100	50	Ct	St	Balls	Runs	Wkts	Avg	BB	5I	10M
Test																	
FC	65	106	9	3471	176	35.78	4	26	56	-	1856	1051	30	35.03	4-39	-	-
ODI																	
List A	79	69	16	2240	114*	42.26	4	13	39	-	1333	1195	33	36.21	4-47	-	
20/20 Int																	
20/20	37	34	3	633	78*	20.41	-	3	12	-	462	554	30	18.46	3-24	-	

Name: Wesley (<u>Wes</u>) John Durston
Role: Right-hand bat, right-arm off-spin bowler, 'very occasional' wicket-keeper
Born: 6 October 1980, Taunton
Height: 5ft 10in **Weight:** 12st 7lbs
Nickname: Bestie
County debut: 2002
Parents: Gill and Steve
Wife and date of marriage: Christina, 4 October 2003
Children: Daisy, 4 July 2004; Joseph, 29 September 2006
Family links with cricket: 'Dad and my brothers, Dan and Greg, all play. On occasions all four of us played in same local team (Compton Dundon)'
Education: Millfield School; University College Worcester
Qualifications: 3 A-levels, BSc Sport & Exercise Science, Level 2 cricket coaching, Level 1 hockey coaching, Level 1 football coaching
Career outside cricket: 'Coaching at Millfield School'
Overseas tours: West of England to West Indies 1996; Somerset to Cape Town 2006, to India (Champions League) 2009
Career highlights to date: 'Winning the Twenty20 trophy with Somerset CCC in 2005. County Championship 2007' [*Somerset were division two champions*]
Cricket moments to forget: 'Being out lbw for first-ball duck on Sky Sports v Kent in 2006'
Cricket superstitions: 'Right foot on to and off field first. Saluting magpies'
Cricketers particularly admired: Ian Botham
Young players to look out for: Jos Buttler (Somerset), Joseph Durston
Other sports played: Hockey (Firebrands HC), golf (12 handicap)
Other sports followed: Football (Manchester United)
Favourite band: Barenaked Ladies
Relaxations: 'Spending time with family and children'
Extras: Captained winning Lord's Taverners team v Shrewsbury School at Trent Bridge 1996. Wetherell Schools All-rounder Award 1999; scored 956 runs and took 35 wickets. Has captained Somerset 2nd XI on occasion. Scored 44-ball 55 on first-class debut at Taunton 2002 as Somerset, chasing 454 to win, tied with West Indies A. Attended World Cricket Academy, Mumbai, 2005. Released by Somerset at the end of the 2009 season
Opinions on cricket: 'With the success of Twenty20 it may be very easy to lose sight of the importance of Championship cricket, which would be very detrimental to the game, as it provides English cricket with the only specific grooming for the Test arena.'

Best batting: 146* Somerset v Derbyshire, Derby 2005
Best bowling: 3-23 Somerset v Sri Lanka A, Taunton 2004WJ Durston

2009 Season

	M	Inn	NO	Runs	HS	Avg	100	50	Ct	St	Balls	Runs	Wkts	Avg	BB	5I	10M
Test																	
FC	1	2	1	54	54*	54.00	-	1	-	-	12	13	0		-	-	-
ODI																	
List A	3	0	0	0	0	-		-	2	-	6	11	0		-	-	
20/20 Int																	
20/20	1	1	1	10	10*		-	-	-	-	0	0	0		-	-	

Career Performances

	M	Inn	NO	Runs	HS	Avg	100	50	Ct	St	Balls	Runs	Wkts	Avg	BB	5I	10M
Test																	
FC	34	57	12	1726	146*	38.35	1	13	34	-	2157	1420	24	59.16	3-23	-	-
ODI																	
List A	56	46	15	952	62*	30.70	-	6	15	-	810	838	19	44.10	3-44	-	
20/20 Int																	
20/20	38	30	7	386	57	16.78	-	1	14	-	214	338	17	19.88	3-25	-	

DU TOIT, J.   Leicestershire

Name: Jacques du Toit
Role: Left-hand bat, left-arm medium bowler
Born: 2 January 1980, Port Elizabeth, South Africa
County debut: 2008
Place in batting averages: (2008 162nd av. 24.93)
Overseas teams played for: Western Province;
Boland; Impalas
Extras: Arrived in the Leicestershire First XI via
the East Anglian leagues and the Second XI. Played
in all competitions in 2008, scoring a couple of
centuries in the process. After his maiden first-class
century (103) against Northamptonshire, he went
on to score 144 off 119 balls in the Pro40 game
against Glamorgan in Colwyn Bay in August 2008,
but couldn't prevent a four-wicket defeat

Best batting: 103 Leicestershire v Northamptonshire, Grace Road 2008
Best bowling: 3-31 Leicestershire v Gloucestershire, Grace Road 2008

2009 Season

	M	Inn	NO	Runs	HS	Avg	100	50	Ct	St	Balls	Runs	Wkts	Avg	BB	5I	10M
Test																	
FC	2	3	1	142	100*	71.00	1	-	1	-	114	89	0		-	-	-
ODI																	
List A	8	8	0	79	31	9.87	-	-	4	-	0	0	0		-	-	
20/20 Int																	
20/20	8	7	3	90	39	22.50	-	-	7	-	6	9	0		-	-	

Career Performances

	M	Inn	NO	Runs	HS	Avg	100	50	Ct	St	Balls	Runs	Wkts	Avg	BB	5I	10M
Test																	
FC	15	23	2	700	103	33.33	2	3	8	-	462	335	5	67.00	3-31	-	-
ODI																	
List A	24	22	2	403	144	20.15	1	-	9	-	66	66	2	33.00	2-30	-	
20/20 Int																	
20/20	17	16	3	207	39	15.92	-	-	10	-	32	41	2	20.50	2-15	-	

EALHAM, M. A.   Nottinghamshire

Name: <u>Mark</u> Alan Ealham
Role: Right-hand bat, right-arm medium bowler; all-rounder
Born: 27 August 1969, Ashford, Kent
Height: 5ft 10in **Weight:** 14st
Nickname: Ealy, Border, Skater
County debut: 1989 (Kent), 2004 (Nottinghamshire)
County cap: 1992 (Kent), 2004 (Nottinghamshire)
Benefit: 2003 (Kent)
Test debut: 1996
ODI debut: 1996
1000 runs in a season: 1
50 wickets in a season: 1
Place in batting averages: 90th av. 37.92 (2008 194th av. 20.56)
Place in bowling averages: 82nd av. 35.10 (2008 67th av. 29.56)
Parents: Alan and Sue
Wife and date of marriage: Kirsty, 24 February 1996
Children: George, 8 March 2002
Family links with cricket: Father played for Kent
Education: Stour Valley Secondary School
Qualifications: 9 CSEs

Career outside cricket: Plumber
Overseas tours: England A to Australia 1996-97, to Kenya and Sri Lanka 1997-98; England VI to Hong Kong 1997, 2001; England to Sharjah (Champions Trophy) 1997-98, to Bangladesh (Wills International Cup) 1998-99, to Australia 1998-99 (CUB Series), to Sharjah (Coca-Cola Cup) 1998-99, to South Africa and Zimbabwe 1999-2000 (one-day series), to Kenya (ICC Knockout Trophy) 2000-01, to Pakistan and Sri Lanka 2000-01 (one-day series)
Overseas teams played for: South Perth, Australia 1992-93; University, Perth 1993-94
Cricketers particularly admired: Ian Botham, Viv Richards, Robin Smith, Steve Waugh, Paul Blackmore and Albert 'for his F and G'
Other sports followed: Football (Manchester United), 'and most other sports'
Relaxations: Playing golf and snooker, watching films
Extras: Set then record for fastest Sunday League century (44 balls), v Derbyshire at Maidstone 1995. Represented England in the 1999 World Cup. Returned a then England record ODI bowling analysis with his 5-15 v Zimbabwe at Kimberley in 1999-2000; all five were lbw. Vice-captain of Kent 2001. Won the Walter Lawrence Trophy 2006 (fastest first-class century of the season) for his 45-ball hundred (finishing with 112*) v MCC at Lord's. Retired from first-class cricket at the end of the 2009 season
Best batting: 153* Kent v Northamptonshire, Canterbury 2001
Best bowling: 8-36 Kent v Warwickshire, Edgbaston 1996

2009 Season

	M	Inn	NO	Runs	HS	Avg	100	50	Ct	St	Balls	Runs	Wkts	Avg	BB	5I	10M
Test																	
FC	14	20	7	493	70*	37.92	-	2	6	-	2322	983	28	35.10	5-31	1	-
ODI																	
List A	8	6	2	115	42*	28.75	-	-	1	-	285	207	7	29.57	4-40	-	
20/20 Int																	
20/20	10	6	3	49	21	16.33	-	-	1	-	186	256	7	36.57	3-20	-	

Career Performances

	M	Inn	NO	Runs	HS	Avg	100	50	Ct	St	Balls	Runs	Wkts	Avg	BB	5I	10M
Test	8	13	3	210	53*	21.00	-	2	4	-	1060	488	17	28.70	4-21	-	-
FC	281	422	67	11349	153*	31.96	13	67	158	-	38434	17962	643	27.93	8-36	24	2
ODI	64	45	4	716	45	17.46	-	-	9	-	3227	2197	67	32.79	5-15	2	
List A	417	341	77	6326	112	23.96	1	26	110	-	18506	12644	477	26.50	6-53	4	
20/20 Int																	
20/20	52	42	9	568	91	17.21	-	1	6	-	1109	1342	46	29.17	3-20	-	

EDWARDS, G. A.   Surrey

Name: <u>George</u> Alexander Edwards
Role: Right-hand bat, right-arm fast bowler
Born: 29 July 1992, Lambeth, London
Nickname: G
County debut: No first-team appearance
Education: St Joseph's College, West Dulwich
Career outside cricket: Student
Cricketers particularly admired: Sir Viv Richards
Other sports played: Football, table tennis,
badminton
Extras: Played club cricket with Spencer CC,
Wandsworth, 2008-09. Has played for Surrey U17,
England U18 and Surrey 2nd XI. Returned figures
of 5-25 in a friendly fixture v Durham 2nd XI in
2009. Awarded 12-month Emerging Player contract in

September 2009. One of six players attending the Pemberton Greenish Surrey
Academy 2010

EDWARDS, N. J.   Nottinghamshire

Name: <u>Neil</u> James Edwards
Role: Left-hand bat, occasional
right-arm medium bowler
Born: 14 October 1983, Truro, Cornwall
Height: 6ft 3in **Weight:** 14st 6lbs
Nickname: Toastie, Shanksy
County debut: 2002 (Somerset)
1000 runs in a season: 1
1st-Class 200s: 1
Place in batting averages: (2008 177th av.22.73)
Parents: Lynn and John
Marital status: Single
Family links with cricket: 'Cousin played first-class
cricket for Worcestershire'
Education: Cape Cornwall School; Richard Huish
College

Qualifications: 11 GCSEs, 3 A-levels, Level 1 coaching
Overseas tours: Cornwall U13 to South Africa 1997; West of England to West Indies
1999; Somerset Academy to Australia 2002; England U19 to Australia 2002-03

Overseas teams played for: Richmond CC (Melbourne) 2007-08
Career highlights to date: 'Division 2 title 2007'
Cricket moments to forget: 'Duck on debut for Cornwall'
Cricket superstitions: 'Never change batting gloves when batting'
Cricketers particularly admired: Marcus Trescothick, Matthew Hayden
Young players to look out for: Jordan Lee
Other sports played: Football
Other sports followed: Football (Stoke City FC)
Favourite band: 'I listen to any music'
Extras: Scored 213 for Cornwall U19 v Dorset U19 at 16 years old. Scored a second innings 97 in England U19 victory over Australia U19 in the first 'Test' at Adelaide 2002-03. Represented England U19 2003. Somerset Wyverns Award for Best Performance by an Uncapped Player 2003 (160 v Hampshire). Signed a three-year contract with Nottinghamshire in August 2009, after having played no first-team cricket for Somerset during the season
Best batting: 212 Somerset v LUCCE, Taunton 2007
Best bowling: 1-16 Somerset v Derbyshire, Taunton 2004

2009 Season (Did not make any first-class or one-day appearances for his county)

Career Performances

	M	Inn	NO	Runs	HS	Avg	100	50	Ct	St	Balls	Runs	Wkts	Avg	BB	5I	10M
Test																	
FC	49	82	0	2898	212	35.34	3	15	35	-	287	194	2	97.00	1-16	-	-
ODI																	
List A	5	5	0	113	65	22.60	-	1	1	-	0	0	0		-	-	
20/20 Int																	
20/20	1	1	0	1	1	1.00	-	-	-	-	0	0	0		-	-	

---

25. Danish Kaneria is a great bowler. But he has scored more Test match ducks than any other Pakistan player. How many?

EDWARDS, P. D. Kent

Name: Philip (<u>Phil</u>) Duncan Edwards
Role: Right-hand bat, right-arm fast-medium bowler
Born: 16 April 1984, Minster, Isle of Sheppey, Kent
Height: 6ft 4in **Weight:** 14st 3lbs
County debut: 2009
Extras: His first-class career stretches back to 2004-05, although he has played only ten first-class games in all. Played for Sussex Second XI 2006, and Kent Second XI 2008. Has also played for CUCCE 2004-05, and Suffolk 2007-08
Best batting: 43 CUCCE v Middlesex, Fenner's 2004
Best bowling: 3-721 Kent v Surrey, Canterbury 2009

2009 Season

	M	Inn	NO	Runs	HS	Avg	100	50	Ct	St	Balls	Runs	Wkts	Avg	BB	5I	10M
Test																	
FC	5	4	2	5	5	2.50	-	-	1	-	570	325	7	46.42	3-72	-	-
ODI																	
List A	7	3	2	3	2*	3.00	-	-	-	-	204	241	7	34.42	3-57	-	
20/20 Int																	
20/20																	

Career Performances

	M	Inn	NO	Runs	HS	Avg	100	50	Ct	St	Balls	Runs	Wkts	Avg	BB	5I	10M
Test																	
FC	10	12	7	101	43	20.20	-	-	2	-	1278	820	12	68.33	3-72	-	-
ODI																	
List A	7	3	2	3	2*	3.00	-	-	-	-	204	241	7	34.42	3-57	-	
20/20 Int																	
20/20																	

ELLIOTT, G. D.   *Surrey*

Name: <u>Grant</u> David Elliott
Role: Right-hand bat, right-arm fast-medium
bowler; all-rounder
Born: 21 March 1979, Johannesburg, South Africa
Nickname: Shunt, Magic
County debut: 2009
Test debut: 2008
ODI debut: 2008
Twenty20 Int debut: 2009
Education: St Stithian's College, Johannesburg
Overseas tours: New Zealand to England (one-day
series) 2008, to Australia (one-day series) 2008-09,
to Bangladesh 2008-09, to Australia 2008-09
Overseas teams played for: Griqualand West
1999-2000, 2000-01; Gauteng 2001-02, 2002-03;
Wellington CC 2005 –

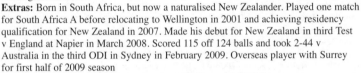

Extras: Born in South Africa, but now a naturalised New Zealander. Played one match
for South Africa A before relocating to Wellington in 2001 and achieving residency
qualification for New Zealand in 2007. Made his debut for New Zealand in third Test
v England at Napier in March 2008. Scored 115 off 124 balls and took 2-44 v
Australia in the third ODI in Sydney in February 2009. Overseas player with Surrey
for first half of 2009 season
Best batting: 196* Wellington v Auckland, Wellington 2007-08
Best bowling: 4-56 Gauteng v Easterns, Johannesburg 2002-03

2009 Season

	M	Inn	NO	Runs	HS	Avg	100	50	Ct	St	Balls	Runs	Wkts	Avg	BB	5I	10M
Test																	
FC	1	2	0	23	22	11.50	-	-	2	-	12	15	0		-	-	-
ODI																	
List A	8	8	1	105	30*	15.00	-	-	5	-	288	285	7	40.71	4-14	-	
20/20 Int																	
20/20	9	8	1	83	26	11.85	-	-	7	-	192	253	9	28.11	2-13	-	

Career Performances

	M	Inn	NO	Runs	HS	Avg	100	50	Ct	St	Balls	Runs	Wkts	Avg	BB	5I	10M
Test	3	5	1	27	9	6.75	-	-	2	-	240	129	2	64.50	1-15	-	-
FC	49	76	4	2193	196*	30.45	5	12	31	-	5265	2393	63	37.98	4-56	-	-
ODI	28	20	6	610	115	43.57	1	3	5	-	458	376	17	22.11	4-31	-	
List A	105	85	19	2103	115	31.86	2	11	32	-	2760	2374	79	30.05	5-34	1	
20/20 Int	1	1	1	23	23*		-	-	-	-	6	11	1	11.00	1-11	-	
20/20	22	20	6	339	57	24.21	-	2	10	-	309	430	16	26.87	2-13	-	

ERVINE, S. M.   Hampshire

Name: <u>Sean</u> Michael Ervine
Role: Left-hand bat, right-arm
fast-medium bowler; all-rounder
Born: 6 December 1982, Harare, Zimbabwe
Height: 6ft 2in **Weight:** 14st
Nickname: Slug
County debut: 2005
County cap: 2005
Test debut: 2003
ODI debut: 2001-02
Place in batting averages: 70th av. 41.60
(2008 139th av.27.95)
Place in bowling averages: 138th av. 61.00
Parents: Rory and Judy
Family links with cricket: 'Grandfather played
cricket for Rhodesia and father and uncle both played for Rhodesia'
Education: Lomagundi College, Zimbabwe
Qualifications: 5 O-levels, Levels 1 and 2 coaching
Overseas tours: Zimbabwe U19 to Sri Lanka (U19 World Cup) 1999-2000, to
New Zealand (U19 World Cup) 2001-02; Zimbabwe to Bangladesh 2001-02, to
Sri Lanka 2001-02 (one-day series), to Sri Lanka (ICC Champions Trophy) 2002-03,
to England 2003, to Australia 2003-04, plus one-day tournaments in Sharjah
Overseas teams played for: Midlands, Zimbabwe 2001-02 – 2003-04; Western
Australia 2006-07 –
Cricket moments to forget: 'Fielding the ball off my own bowling and rupturing
my knee, needing a total knee reconstruction'
Cricket superstitions: 'None'
Cricketers particularly admired: Andy Flower, Shane Warne
Young players to look out for: Shaun Marsh (Western Australia)
Other sports played: Golf, tennis, squash, fishing
Other sports followed: AFL (Kangaroos)
Favourite band: Snow Patrol
Relaxations: 'Music, art'
Extras: CFX [Zimbabwean] Academy 2000-01. Represented Zimbabwe in the World
Cup 2002-03. Struck 99-ball century (100) at Adelaide in the VB Series 2003-04 as
Zimbabwe fell just three runs short of India's 280-7. Man of the Match in the first
Test v Bangladesh at Harare 2003-04 (86/74). C&G Man of the Match awards in the
semi-final v Yorkshire at The Rose Bowl (100) and in the final v Warwickshire at
Lord's (104) 2005. Holds an Irish passport and is not considered an overseas player
Best batting: 126 Midlands v Manicaland, Mutare 2002-03
Best bowling: 6-82 Midlands v Mashonaland, Kwekwe 2002-03

2009 Season

	M	Inn	NO	Runs	HS	Avg	100	50	Ct	St	Balls	Runs	Wkts	Avg	BB	5I	10M
Test																	
FC	15	22	2	832	114	41.60	3	3	6	-	1401	793	13	61.00	3-22	-	-
ODI																	
List A	18	16	2	514	167*	36.71	1	1	4	-	558	513	14	36.64	3-23	-	
20/20 Int																	
20/20	11	11	3	230	53	28.75	-	1	7	-	174	220	13	16.92	4-16	-	

Career Performances

	M	Inn	NO	Runs	HS	Avg	100	50	Ct	St	Balls	Runs	Wkts	Avg	BB	5I	10M
Test	5	8	0	261	86	32.62	-	3	7	-	570	388	9	43.11	4-146	-	
FC	98	154	15	4494	126	32.33	8	25	88	-	10747	6563	157	41.80	6-82	5	-
ODI	42	34	7	698	100	25.85	1	2	5	-	1649	1561	41	38.07	3-29	-	
List A	159	141	24	3676	167*	31.41	6	15	44	-	5584	5159	152	33.94	5-50	2	
20/20 Int																	
20/20	42	39	8	718	56*	23.16	-	3	20	-	426	602	27	22.29	4-16	-	

EVANS, D. Middlesex

Name: Daniel (<u>Danny</u>) Evans
Role: Right-hand bat, right-arm
fast-medium bowler
Born: 24 July 1987, Hartlepool
Height: 6ft 6in **Weight:** 15st
Nickname: Hightower, Stella, Asbo
County debut: 2007
Place in bowling averages: (2008 85th av.31.80)
Parents: Richard and Barbara
Marital status: Single
Family links with cricket: 'Brother played for
Durham – he now plays for Newcastle. My dad
played a little bit, too… He said he was awesome'
Education: Brierton Comprehensive, Hartlepool
Qualifications: 9 GCSEs, GNVQ in IT

Overseas tours: England U17 to Netherlands 2003; MCC A to Papua New Guinea
and New Zealand 2007
Overseas teams played for: Tea Tree Gully, Adelaide 2006
Career highlights to date: 'Making debut at Lord's, getting a wicket maiden
first over'
Cricket moments to forget: 'Getting a run of ducks towards the end of the
season in 2007'

Cricketers particularly admired: Brett Lee, Steve Harmison
Young players to look out for: Billy Godleman (Essex), Steve Finn and Eoin Morgan (both Middlesex)
Other sports played: Five-a-side football, rugby (West Hartlepool RUFC)
Other sports followed: Football (Newcastle)
Favourite band: Bloc Party, The Verve, Oasis
Relaxations: 'Poker, pool, films'
Extras: Played for Durham U17, Durham Academy and Durham 2nd XI, 2004-06. Middlesex 2nd XI 2007-09. Attended Darren Lehmann Academy, Adelaide 2006. Made one appearance for England U19 2006. Dismissed Craig Spearman in wicket maiden first over on first-class debut v Gloucestershire at Lord's 2007
Opinions on cricket: 'Youngsters should be given more of a chance. I think we play too much as well, players not getting enough rest between games.'
Best batting: 12* Middlesex v Worcestershire, Lord's 2008
Best bowling: 6-35 Middlesex v Essex, Chelmsford 2008

2009 Season

	M	Inn	NO	Runs	HS	Avg	100	50	Ct	St	Balls	Runs	Wkts	Avg	BB	5I	10M
Test																	
FC	1	0	0	0	0	-	-	-	-	-	252	190	3	63.33	2-69	-	-
ODI																	
List A	4	1	1	1	1*	-	-	-	-	-	208	199	6	33.16	2-58	-	
20/20 Int																	
20/20	4	3	2	6	5*	6.00	-	-	1	-	60	102	0		-	-	

Career Performances

	M	Inn	NO	Runs	HS	Avg	100	50	Ct	St	Balls	Runs	Wkts	Avg	BB	5I	10M
Test																	
FC	15	18	4	52	12*	3.71	-	-	3	-	2022	1313	38	34.55	6-35	2	-
ODI																	
List A	6	1	1	1	1*	-	-	-	-	-	328	291	9	32.33	3-36	-	
20/20 Int																	
20/20	4	3	2	6	5*	6.00	-	-	1	-	60	102	0		-	-	

26. Name the first Pakistan wicketkeeper to do the Test double of
1,000 runs and 100 dismissals.

EVANS, L.   Durham

Name: Luke Evans
Role: Right-hand bat, right-arm fast bowler
Born: 26 April 1987, Sunderland
Height: 6ft 7in **Weight:** 14st 8lbs
Nickname: Daisy Duke, Longshanks,
Lukey, Evo, Cool Hand
County debut: 2007
Parents: Gayle and Stephen
Marital status: Single ('long-term girlfriend')
Family links with cricket: 'Dad played for
Farringdon School in the 1970s, anchoring the
middle order. No relation to Danny'
Education: St Aidan's Comprehensive RC School;
St Aidan's Sixth Form
Qualifications: 10 GCSEs, 2 A-levels. 'Also
working towards my pilot's licence'
Career outside cricket: 'Aviation and teaching guitar'
Off-season: 'A little rest, then fitness – I hope to go to Perth again in the New Year'
Overseas tours: Durham to Dubai 2006, to Cape Town 2007, to Potchefstroom 2009
Overseas teams played for: Doubleview Carine CC (WASTCA), Perth 2008-09
Career highlights to date: 'First-class debut against Sri Lanka A. Forty wickets in the
2nd XI Championship in 2007. Appearing in a televised Pro40 match against Notts
Outlaws in the 2009 season'
Cricket moments to forget: 'Any attempted slower balls that end up as beamers. My
first few balls at Taunton in the last game of the 2009 season'
Cricket superstitions: 'None'
Favourite sledging line: '"I hope it rains on your wedding day," – courtesy of Adam
Heather (South Northumberland) served up to Quentin Hughes (Chester-le-Street)'
Cricketers particularly admired: Curtly Ambrose, Jason Gillespie, Stephen
Harmison, Ottis Gibson, Dale Steyn, Morne Morkel
Young players to look out for: Andrew Smith, Scott Borthwick, Karl Turner, Ben
Stokes (all Durham), Paul Hindmarch (Cumberland), Mark Wood and Paul Muchall
(both Northumberland)
Other sports played: Recreational darts, and basketball 'for the school'
Other sports followed: Football (Sunderland AFC)
Favourite band: Pantera, Van Halen, Extreme, Soundgarden, RATM ('anything with
frightening guitar skill')
Relaxations: 'Flying, eating out, sketching, playing piano and guitars'
Extras: Represented ECB Development of Excellence XI v Bangladesh U19 2004.
Represented England U17 v MCC YC. City of Sunderland Young Achievers Award for
Sport 2004. Sue Wright Sporting Achievement Award (from school)

Opinions on cricket: 'An entirely floodlit competition would be interesting. Also the amount of time spent travelling on the M1 is often outrageous. Hopefully the roadworks near Nottingham will be gone by next season…'

Best batting: 1 Durham v Sri Lanka A, Riverside 2007
Best bowling: 2-39 Durham v Sri Lanka A, Riverside 2007

2009 Season

	M	Inn	NO	Runs	HS	Avg	100	50	Ct	St	Balls	Runs	Wkts	Avg	BB	5I	10M
Test																	
FC																	
ODI																	
List A	3	1	0	0	0	0.00	-	-	-	-	84	95	4	23.75	2-53	-	
20/20 Int																	
20/20																	

Career Performances

	M	Inn	NO	Runs	HS	Avg	100	50	Ct	St	Balls	Runs	Wkts	Avg	BB	5I	10M
Test																	
FC	1	2	1	1	1	1.00	-	-	-	-	121	115	4	28.75	2-39	-	-
ODI																	
List A	3	1	0	0	0	0.00	-	-	-	-	84	95	4	23.75	2-53	-	
20/20 Int																	
20/20																	

EVANS, L. J. — Surrey

Name: Laurie John Evans
Role: Right-hand bat, right-arm fast-medium bowler; all-rounder
Born: 12 October 1987, Lambeth, London
Height: 6ft **Weight:** 13st 7lbs
Nickname: Lau, Lozza, LJ
County debut: 2009
Parents: Sue and Marcus
Marital status: Single
Education: John Fisher, Purley; Whitgift School, South Croydon; Durham University
Qualifications: BTEC Sport, 3 A-levels
Career outside cricket: 'Coaching'
Off-season: 'Training'
Overseas tours: Surrey Academy to South Africa 2006

Career highlights to date: 'Captaining Surrey 2nd XI on their way to the Championship in 2009.'
Cricket moments to forget: 'I only dropped three catches all season in 2005 and they were all in the U17 national final v Yorkshire'
Cricket superstitions: 'None'
Cricketers particularly admired: Mark Ramprakash
Young players to look out for: Simon King (Surrey), Zafar Ansari (Surrey Academy)
Other sports played: Rugby (Harlequins Academy; won U15 *Daily Mail* National Schools Cup with Whitgift, v Millfield at Twickenham 2003)
Other sports followed: Football (Arsenal)
Favourite band: Lil Wayne
Relaxations: 'Guitar, piano, clothes, golf'
Extras: Represented ECB Development of Excellence XI v India U19 2006. Played for DUCCE 2007, scoring 133* v Lancashire at Durham. Played for MCC v West Indians at Durham 2007, scoring 51
Opinions on cricket: 'It's moving on… The game today is more exciting than ever. It's got quicker and more interesting to spectators. However, I think that it shouldn't be changed too much, otherwise it will lose its history and essence.'
Best batting: 133* DUCCE v Lancashire, Durham 2007

2009 Season

	M	Inn	NO	Runs	HS	Avg	100	50	Ct	St	Balls	Runs	Wkts	Avg	BB	5I	10M
Test																	
FC	2	4	0	23	9	5.75	-	-	-	-	0	0	0		-	-	-
ODI																	
List A	1	1	1	36	36*		-	-	1	-	0	0	0		-	-	
20/20 Int																	
20/20	1	1	0	7	7	7.00	-	-	-	-	0	0	0		-	-	

Career Performances

	M	Inn	NO	Runs	HS	Avg	100	50	Ct	St	Balls	Runs	Wkts	Avg	BB	5I	10M
Test																	
FC	6	12	1	388	133*	35.27	1	2	4	-	0	0	0		-	-	-
ODI																	
List A	1	1	1	36	36*		-	-	1	-	0	0	0		-	-	
20/20 Int																	
20/20	1	1	0	7	7	7.00	-	-	-	-	0	0	0		-	-	

FERLEY, R. S.   Kent

Name: <u>Robert</u> Steven Ferley
Role: Right-hand bat, left-arm spin bowler
Born: 4 February 1982, Norwich
Height: 5ft 8in **Weight:** 12st 4lbs
Nickname: Mr Shaky Shake, Billy Bob,
Bob Turkey
County debut: 2003 (Kent),
2007 (Nottinghamshire)
Parents: Pam and Tim (divorced)
Marital status: Single
Education: King Edward VII High School;
Sutton Valence School (A-levels); Grey College,
Durham University
Qualifications: 10 GCSEs, 3 A-levels
Overseas tours: England U19 to India 2000-01;
British Universities to South Africa 2002
Cricketers particularly admired:
Steve Waugh, Steve Marsh, Min Patel, Charles Clarke
Other sports played: Rugby, hockey, tennis, football
Other sports followed: Football (Liverpool)
Relaxations: 'Films, interior design, keeping fit'
Extras: Represented England U17 1999. Played for DUCCE 2001, 2002 and 2003.
Represented British Universities 2001, 2002 and 2003. Represented England U19
2001. Took 4-76 on Championship debut v Surrey at The Oval 2003. Rejoined Kent
from Nottinghamshire in November 2008
Best batting: 78* DUCCE v Durham, Durham 2003
Best bowling: 6-136 Kent v Middlesex, Canterbury 2006

2009 Season

	M	Inn	NO	Runs	HS	Avg	100	50	Ct	St	Balls	Runs	Wkts	Avg	BB	5I	10M
Test																	
FC	3	1	0	17	17	17.00	-	-	1	-	450	189	7	27.00	3-73	-	-
ODI																	
List A	12	6	1	29	9*	5.80	-	-	3	-	538	465	12	38.75	3-34	-	
20/20 Int																	
20/20	1	0	0	0	0	-	-	-	-	18	24	0		-	-		

Career Performances

	M	Inn	NO	Runs	HS	Avg	100	50	Ct	St	Balls	Runs	Wkts	Avg	BB	5I	10M
Test																	
FC	33	39	10	630	78*	21.72	-	2	10	-	4927	2876	64	44.93	6-136	1	-
ODI																	
List A	54	27	7	285	42	14.25	-	-	21	-	2417	1983	66	30.04	4-33	-	
20/20 Int																	
20/20	18	7	4	23	16*	7.66	-	-	4	-	339	415	14	29.64	3-17	-	

FINN, S. T.   Middlesex

Name: <u>Steven</u> Thomas Finn
Role: Right-hand bat, right-arm
fast-medium bowler
Born: 4 April 1989, Watford
Height: 6ft 7in **Weight:** 14st
Nickname: Finny, Lurch, Big Nose, Gonzo
County debut: 2005
County cap: 2009
50 wickets in a season: 1
Place in bowling averages: 47th av. 30.64
(2008 122nd av. 38.78)
Parents: Diana and Terry
Marital status: Single
Family links with cricket: 'Dad played top-level
club cricket and Minor Counties. Grandad played
club cricket'
Education: Parmiter's School, Watford, Herts
Qualifications: 11 GCSEs, 4 A-levels
Career outside cricket: Journalism
Off-season: 'Training'
Overseas tours: England U16 to South Africa 2004-05; England U19 to Malaysia
2006-07, to Malaysia (U19 World Cup) 2007-08, to Sri Lanka 2008; England
Performance Programme to India 2007-08; Middlesex to Antigua 2008-09 for
Stanford Super Series
Career highlights to date: 'First-class debut at 16. Debut at Lord's. Man of the Match
award in TV play-off against Northamptonshire in 2007. First five-wicket haul for
Middlesex [5-57] v Essex at Chelmsford [June 2009]'
Cricket moments to forget: 'Third man out in a hat-trick v India U19 2006 – on TV'
Cricket superstitions: 'Too many to mention'
Cricketers particularly admired: Glenn McGrath, Curtly Ambrose, Courtney Walsh,
Angus Fraser

Young players to look out for: Billy Godleman (Essex), Sam Robson and Adam London (Middlesex), Chris Woakes (Warwickshire)
Other sports played: Basketball (county), football (district)
Other sports followed: Football (Watford)
Injuries: Missed one County Championship game with a bruised ankle
Favourite band: Arctic Monkeys
Relaxations: 'Music, films'
Extras: Has represented England U15, U16, U17 and U19. Youngest person to play first-class cricket for Middlesex since Fred Titmus in 1949. Called up to the England Performance Programme in India 2007-08 as a replacement for the injured Luke Wright. NBC Denis Compton Award for the most promising young Middlesex player 2009. Part of England Performance Programme squad 2009-10
Opinions on cricket: 'Would like to see more rest time between games in order to maintain the intensity of cricket.'
Best batting: 26* Middlesex v Worcestershire, Kidderminster 2008
Best bowling: 5-57 Middlesex v Essex, Chelmsford 2009

2009 Season

	M	Inn	NO	Runs	HS	Avg	100	50	Ct	St	Balls	Runs	Wkts	Avg	BB	5I	10M
Test																	
FC	14	22	4	107	24*	5.94	-	-	4	-	2511	1624	53	30.64	5-57	1	-
ODI																	
List A	13	4	1	26	13	8.66	-	-	-	-	432	417	13	32.07	3-67	-	
20/20 Int																	
20/20	6	2	1	8	8	8.00	-	-	2	-	104	172	3	57.33	1-7	-	

Career Performances

	M	Inn	NO	Runs	HS	Avg	100	50	Ct	St	Balls	Runs	Wkts	Avg	BB	5I	10M
Test																	
FC	31	42	11	198	26*	6.38	-	-	9	-	4858	3002	94	31.93	5-57	1	-
ODI																	
List A	27	7	2	33	13	6.60	-	-	3	-	1020	929	28	33.17	3-23	-	
20/20 Int																	
20/20	13	3	2	14	8	14.00	-	-	4	-	248	351	12	29.25	3-22	-	

27. In which Asian city did Pakistan play their first ever Test match in 1952?

FISHER, I. D. Worcestershire

Name: <u>Ian</u> Douglas Fisher
Role: Left-hand bat, left-arm spin bowler
Born: 31 March 1976, Bradford
Height: 5ft 11in **Weight:** 13st 6lbs
Nickname: Fish, Flash, Fishy
County debut: 1995-96 (Yorkshire),
2002 (Gloucestershire), 2009 (Worcestershire)
County cap: 2004 (Gloucestershire)
Parents: Geoff and Linda
Marital status: Single
Family links with cricket: Father played club cricket
Education: Beckfoot Grammar School
Qualifications: 9 GCSEs, NCA coaching award,
sports leader's award, lifesaver (bronze), YMCA
gym instructor
Overseas tours: Yorkshire to Zimbabwe 1996, to South Africa 1998, 1999, 2001,
to Perth 2000; MCC to Sri Lanka 2001
Overseas teams played for: Somerset West, Cape Town 1994-95; Petone Riverside,
Wellington, New Zealand 1997-98
Career highlights to date: 'Winning the Championship with Yorkshire [2001]'
Cricket moments to forget: 'My pair'
Cricketers particularly admired: Darren Lehmann, Shane Warne
Other sports played: Football (Westbrook)
Other sports followed: Football (Leeds United)
Relaxations: Music, movies, catching up with friends, shopping, eating out
Extras: Played for England U17, Yorkshire Schools U15, U16 and Yorkshire U19.
Bowled the last first-class ball delivered at Northlands Road, Southampton, September
2000. Recorded three Championship five-wicket returns in successive innings 2003,
including his maiden ten-wicket match (5-30/5-93) v Durham at Bristol. After being
on loan from Gloucestershire, signed for Worcestershire in October 2008. Released
by Worcestershire at the end of the 2009 season
Best batting: 103* Gloucestershire v Essex, Gloucester 2002
Best bowling: 5-30 Gloucestershire v Durham, Bristol 2003

2009 Season

	M	Inn	NO	Runs	HS	Avg	100	50	Ct	St	Balls	Runs	Wkts	Avg	BB	5I	10M
Test																	
FC	1	0	0	0	0	-	-	-	-	18	15	0		-	-	-	
ODI																	
List A	13	7	3	65	31*	16.25	-	-	4	-	491	451	12	37.58	3-18	-	
20/20 Int																	
20/20	7	2	2	5	5*		-	-	7	-	102	117	6	19.50	3-16	-	

Career Performances

	M	Inn	NO	Runs	HS	Avg	100	50	Ct	St	Balls	Runs	Wkts	Avg	BB	5I	10M
Test																	
FC	80	119	19	2201	103*	22.01	1	7	27	-	12456	6728	157	42.85	5-30	7	1
ODI																	
List A	83	49	17	356	37*	11.12	-	-	25	-	3188	2601	81	32.11	3-18	-	
20/20 Int																	
20/20	39	16	6	84	14	8.40	-	-	21	-	569	724	33	21.93	4-22	-	

FLETCHER, L. J.　　　Nottinghamshire

Name: <u>Luke</u> Jack Fletcher
Role: Right-hand bat, right-arm fast-medium bowler
Born: 18 September 1988, Nottingham
Nickname: Fletch, Sloff
County debut: 2008
Place in bowling averages: 31st av. 27.58
Parents: Alan and Jane
Marital status: Single
Family links with cricket: 'None'
Education: Henry Mellish School
Career highlights to date: 'Making my debut for Nottinghamshire in the Friends' Provident. Playing for England U19'
Cricketers particularly admired: Andrew Flintoff
Young players to look out for: Alex Hales (Nottinghamshire), Ian Saxelby (Gloucestershire)
Other sports played: Football (played for Notts County for a season)
Other sports followed: Football (Nottingham Forest)
Favourite band: Basshunter
Relaxations: 'Spending time with friends. Eating. Sleeping'
Extras: Member of England Performance Programme squad 2009-10. Signed a new two-year contract with Nottinghamshire in December 2009

Best batting: 92 Nottinghamshire v Hampshire, Rose Bowl 2009
Best bowling: 1-70 Nottinghamshire v Somerset, Trent Bridge 2009

2009 Season

	M	Inn	NO	Runs	HS	Avg	100	50	Ct	St	Balls	Runs	Wkts	Avg	BB	5I	10M
Test																	
FC	8	8	3	121	92	24.20	-	1	-	-	1473	800	29	27.58	4-38	-	-
ODI																	
List A	11	7	3	61	40*	15.25	-	-	-	-	441	398	11	36.18	2-35	-	
20/20 Int																	
20/20	10	2	1	2	1*	2.00	-	-	2	-	222	298	8	37.25	2-23	-	

Career Performances

	M	Inn	NO	Runs	HS	Avg	100	50	Ct	St	Balls	Runs	Wkts	Avg	BB	5I	10M
Test																	
FC	9	8	3	121	92	24.20	-	1	-	-	1593	870	30	29.00	4-38	-	-
ODI																	
List A	15	9	4	63	40*	12.60	-	-	1	-	651	507	14	36.21	2-35	-	
20/20 Int																	
20/20	10	2	1	2	1*	2.00	-	-	2	-	222	298	8	37.25	2-23	-	

28. Name the Pakistani cricketer who played in his only Test match at the age of 14.

FLINTOFF, A.   Lancashire

Name: Andrew Flintoff
Role: Right-hand bat, right-arm fast-medium bowler; all-rounder
Born: 6 December 1977, Preston
Height: 6ft 4in
Nickname: Freddie
County debut: 1995
County cap: 1998
Benefit: 2006
Test debut: 1998
ODI debut: 1998-99
Twenty20 Int debut: 2005
Place in batting averages: 174th av. 26.18 (2008 165th av. 24.50)
Place in bowling averages: 49th av. 30.84 (2008 73rd av. 30.18)
Parents: Colin and Susan
Wife and date of marriage: Rachael, 5 March 2005
Children: Holly, 6 September 2004; Corey, 8 March 2006; Rocky, 7 April 2008
Family links with cricket: Brother Chris and father both local league cricketers
Education: Ribbleton Hall High School, Preston
Qualifications: 9 GCSEs
Overseas tours: England Schools U15 to South Africa 1993; England U19 to West Indies 1994-95, to Zimbabwe 1995-96, to Pakistan 1996-97 (c); England A to Kenya and Sri Lanka 1997-98, to Zimbabwe and South Africa 1998-99; England to Sharjah (Coca-Cola Cup) 1998-99, to South Africa and Zimbabwe 1999-2000, to Kenya (ICC Knockout Trophy) 2000-01, to Pakistan and (one-day series) Sri Lanka 2000-01, to Zimbabwe (one-day series) 2001-02, to India and New Zealand 2001-02, to Australia 2002-03, to Africa (World Cup) 2002-03, to Bangladesh and Sri Lanka 2003-04, to West Indies 2003-04, to South Africa 2004-05, to Pakistan 2005-06, to India 2005-06, to India (ICC Champions Trophy) 2006-07 (c), to Australia 2006-07 (Test c), to West Indies (World Cup) 2006-07, to South Africa (World 20/20) 2007-08, to India 2008-09, to West Indies 2008-09; ECB National Academy to Australia 2001-02; England VI to Hong Kong 2001; ICC World XI to Australia (Super Series) 2005-06
Other sports/games played: Represented Lancashire Schools at chess
Extras: Represented England U14 to U19. NBC Denis Compton Award for the most promising young Lancashire player 1997. Cricket Writers' Club Young Player of the Year and PCA Young Player of the Year 1998. Scored first century before lunch by a Lancashire batsman in a Roses match, v Yorkshire at Old Trafford 1999. Won the EDS Walter Lawrence Trophy 1999 (for the fastest first-class century of the season). Lancashire Player of the Year 2000. Vice-captain of Lancashire 2002. BBC North West

Sports Personality of the Year 2003. One of *Wisden*'s Five Cricketers of the Year 2004. Vodafone England Cricketer of the Year 2003-04 and 2005-06. Shared with Andrew Strauss in a record stand for any wicket for England in ODIs (226), v West Indies at Lord's in the NatWest Series 2004. His Test awards include England's Man of the Series v West Indies 2004 and v Australia 2005 (plus the inaugural Compton-Miller Medal 2005 for Ashes Player of the Series), and Man of the Series v India 2005-06. His ODI awards include Man of the NatWest Series 2003 and Man of the Series v Bangladesh 2003-04. Winner of inaugural ICC One-Day Player of the Year award 2003-04. PCA Player of the Year award 2004, 2005. ICC Player of the Year award (jointly with Jacques Kallis) 2005. BBC Sports Personality of the Year 2005. Appointed MBE in 2006 New Year Honours as part of 2005 Ashes-winning England team. Lancashire benefit season 2006. Out for much of the 2007 season with a recurrence of an ankle problem. Named Man of the Series after England had beaten South Africa 4-0 in the ODIs 2008. Chennai Super Kings paid $1.55m for his services in winter 2009 IPL auction. Secured his third Test match five-wicket haul in an innings at Lord's to set up an England victory 2009. In July 2009, announced his retirement from Test cricket, but will still play one-day cricket for both club and country. Signed a new three-year contract to play one-day cricket for Lancashire in 2009. England increment contract 2009-10. There are now week-long cricket courses under the Flintoff name available at various venues around the UK

Best batting: 167 England v West Indies, Edgbaston 2004
Best bowling: 5-24 Lancashire v Hampshire, Southampton 1999

2009 Season

	M	Inn	NO	Runs	HS	Avg	100	50	Ct	St	Balls	Runs	Wkts	Avg	BB	5I	10M
Test	4	7	1	200	74	33.33	-	1	1	-	773	417	8	52.12	5-92	1	-
FC	7	12	1	288	74	26.18	-	2	5	-	1160	586	19	30.84	5-92	1	-
ODI																	
List A																	
20/20 Int																	
20/20	2	2	0	98	93	49.00	-	1	-	-	48	61	2	30.50	2-32	-	

Career Performances

	M	Inn	NO	Runs	HS	Avg	100	50	Ct	St	Balls	Runs	Wkts	Avg	BB	5I	10M
Test	79	130	9	3845	167	31.77	5	26	52	-	14951	7410	226	32.78	5-58	3	-
FC	183	290	23	9027	167	33.80	15	53	185	-	22800	11059	350	31.59	5-24	4	-
ODI	141	122	16	3394	123	32.01	3	18	47	-	5624	4121	169	24.38	5-19	2	
List A	282	251	28	6641	143	29.78	6	34	106	-	9416	6536	289	22.61	5-19	2	
20/20 Int	7	7	1	76	31	12.66	-	-	5	-	150	161	5	32.20	2-23	-	
20/20	29	27	3	588	93	24.50	-	3	16	-	525	609	30	20.30	4-12	-	

FLOWER, G. W. Essex

Name: <u>Grant</u> William Flower
Role: Right-hand top-order bat, left-arm spin
bowler; all-rounder
Born: 20 December 1970, Harare, Zimbabwe
Height: 5ft 10in **Weight:** 11st
Nickname: Gobby
County debut: 2002 (Leicestershire), 2005 (Essex)
County cap: 2005 (Essex)
Test debut: 1992-93
ODI debut: 1992-93
1st-Class 200s: 4
Place in batting averages: (2008 246th av.12.42)
Parents: Bill and Jean
Marital status: Single
Family links with cricket: Younger brother of Andy
Flower (formerly of Zimbabwe and Essex and now England coach)
Education: St George's College, Harare
Qualifications: 8 O-levels, 1 A-level, Level 3 coaching
Career outside cricket: Coaching
Overseas tours: Zimbabwe to India 1992-93, to Pakistan 1993-94, to Australia
(one-day series) 1994-95, to New Zealand 1995-96, to India and Pakistan (World
Cup) 1995-96, to Sri Lanka and Pakistan 1996-97, to Sri Lanka and New Zealand
1997-98, to Bangladesh (Wills International Cup) 1998-99, to Pakistan 1998-99, to
UK, Ireland and Netherlands (World Cup) 1999, to West
Indies 1999-2000, to England 2000, to Kenya (ICC Knockout Trophy) 2000-01, to
India 2000-01, to New Zealand and Australia 2000-01, to Bangladesh, Sri Lanka
and India 2001-02, to Sri Lanka (ICC Champions Trophy) 2002-03, to England 2003,
to Australia 2003-04 (VB Series), plus other one-day tournaments in Sharjah, South
Africa, Kenya, India, Bangladesh and Singapore
Overseas teams played for: Mashonaland 1994-95 – 2003-04
Career highlights to date: 'Scoring 201* v Pakistan in 1994-95 in our first Test
match victory in Harare. Being named Man of the Match in the Friends Provident
Trophy final against Kent at Lord's [August 2008].'
Cricket moments to forget: 'Losing to Kenya in the 2002-03 World Cup for
Zimbabwe'
Cricket superstitions: 'None'
Cricketers particularly admired: Graeme Hick, Sachin Tendulkar
Young players to look out for: Jaik Mickleburgh (Essex)
Other sports played: Squash, tennis
Other sports followed: Squash, tennis, football, rugby, golf
Relaxations: 'Reading, TV, films, fishing and drinking'

Extras: Appeared in Zimbabwe's inaugural Test, v India at Harare 1992-93. Scored 201* v Pakistan at Harare 1994-95 in Zimbabwe's first Test win, in the process sharing with Andy Flower (156) in a record fourth-wicket stand for Zimbabwe in Tests (269). Became the first player to score a hundred in each innings of a Test for Zimbabwe (104/151) in the first Test v New Zealand at Harare 1997-98. His Test awards include Man of the Series v New Zealand 1997-98. His ODI awards include Zimbabwe's Man of the Series v Pakistan 1996-97, as well as Man of the Match v England at Trent Bridge in the NatWest Series 2003 (96*) and v Australia at Adelaide in the VB Series 2003-04 (94). Was Leicestershire's overseas player during June 2002. Announced his retirement from international cricket in 2004. Is no longer considered an overseas player

Best batting: 243* Mashonaland v Matabeleland, Harare (A) 1996-97
Best bowling: 7-31 Zimbabweans v Lahore City, Lahore 1998-99

2009 Season

	M	Inn	NO	Runs	HS	Avg	100	50	Ct	St	Balls	Runs	Wkts	Avg	BB	5I	10M
Test																	
FC	1	1	0	9	9	9.00	-	-	-	-	0	0	0		-	-	-
ODI																	
List A	14	12	5	301	54	43.00	-	1	4	-	246	193	6	32.16	2-9	-	
20/20 Int																	
20/20	10	8	1	157	61	22.42	-	1	4	-	120	139	9	15.44	3-25	-	

Career Performances

	M	Inn	NO	Runs	HS	Avg	100	50	Ct	St	Balls	Runs	Wkts	Avg	BB	5I	10M
Test	67	123	6	3457	201*	29.54	6	15	43	-	3378	1537	25	61.48	4-41	-	-
FC	185	313	23	10775	243*	37.15	23	58	171	-	12457	5573	165	33.77	7-31	3	-
ODI	219	212	18	6536	142*	33.69	6	40	86	-	5420	4187	104	40.25	4-32	-	
List A	351	331	34	10186	148*	34.29	11	68	134	-	8650	6427	183	35.12	4-32	-	
20/20 Int																	
20/20	38	28	5	507	61	22.04	-	1	11	-	274	354	22	16.09	3-20	-	

29. In 2006 a total of 1,553 runs were scored in an England v Pakistan Test. At which ground?

FOOTITT, M. H. A.   Derbyshire

Name: <u>Mark</u> Harold Alan Footitt
Role: Right-hand bat, left-arm fast bowler
Born: 25 November 1985, Nottingham
Height: 6ft 2in **Weight:** 12st 7lbs
Nickname: Footy
County debut: 2005 (Nottinghamshire)
Parents: Graham and Julie
Family links with cricket: 'Dad and grandad
played local cricket'
Education: Carlton le Willows School
Qualifications: 3 GCSEs, Level 1 coaching
Overseas tours: Nottinghamshire to South
Africa 2006
Career highlights to date: 'Playing my first
game for Notts. Being picked for the National
Academy 2006'
Cricket moments to forget: 'My first Twenty20 game'
Cricket superstitions: 'None'
Cricketers particularly admired: Brett Lee
Other sports played: Football
Other sports followed: Football (Manchester United)
Favourite band: The Killers
Relaxations: 'Playing on PS2 and PC, watching TV/DVDs'
Extras: Attended MRF Pace Foundation, India 2000, 2001, 2006. Played for
Nottinghamshire Board XI in the 2002 C&G. Represented England U19 2005.
ECB National Academy 2005-06. Due to back problems did not make any
appearances in 2008. Played only one first-class match for Nottinghamshire in 2009.
Released by Nottinghamshire at the end of the 2009 season. Signed for Derbyshire
November 2009
Best batting: 19* Nottinghamshire v Hampshire, Rose Bowl 2005
Best bowling: 5-45 Nottinghamshire v West Indies A, Trent Bridge 2006

2009 Season

	M	Inn	NO	Runs	HS	Avg	100	50	Ct	St	Balls	Runs	Wkts	Avg	BB	5I	10M
Test																	
FC	1	1	1	9	9*		-	-	-	-	96	58	3	19.33	3-58	-	-
ODI																	
List A																	
20/20 Int																	
20/20																	

Career Performances

	M	Inn	NO	Runs	HS	Avg	100	50	Ct	St	Balls	Runs	Wkts	Avg	BB	5I	10M
Test																	
FC	9	7	5	49	19*	24.50	-	-	1	-	931	729	23	31.69	5-45	2	-
ODI																	
List A	1	0	0	0	0		-	-	-	-	18	18	0		-	-	
20/20 Int																	
20/20	1	0	0	0	0		-	-	-	-	12	34	0		-	-	

FOSTER, J. S.   Essex

Name: <u>James</u> Savin Foster
Role: Right-hand bat, wicket-keeper;
county vice-captain
Born: 15 April 1980, Whipps Cross, London
Height: 6ft **Weight:** 12st
Nickname: Fozzy, Chief
County debut: 2000
County cap: 2001
Test debut: 2001-02
ODI debut: 2001-02
1000 runs in a season: 1
1st-Class 200s: 2
Place in batting averages: 85th av. 39.20
(2008 47th av.44.09)
Parents: Martin and Diana
Marital status: Single
Family links with cricket: 'Dad played for Essex Amateurs'
Education: Forest School; Durham University
Qualifications: 10 GCSEs, 3 A-levels, hockey and cricket Level 1 coaching awards
Overseas tours: BUSA to South Africa 1999; Durham University to South Africa 1999, to Vienna (European Indoor Championships) 1999; England A to West Indies 2000-01; England to Zimbabwe (one-day series) 2001-02, to India 2001-02, to New Zealand 2001-02, to Australia 2002-03; England Lions to India 2007-08
Overseas teams played for: Claremont-Nedlands, Perth 2006-07
Career highlights to date: 'Playing for my country'
Cricketers particularly admired: Nasser Hussain, Stuart Law, Robert Rollins, Ian Healy, Jack Russell, Alec Stewart, Adam Gilchrist
Other sports played: Hockey (Essex U21), tennis (played for GB U14 v Sweden U14; national training squad)
Other sports followed: Football
Relaxations: 'Socialising'

Extras: Essex U17 Player of the Year 1997. Represented ECB U19 1998 and England U19 1999. Represented BUSA 1999, 2000 and 2001. Voted Essex Cricket Society 2nd XI Player of the Year 2000. Played for Durham UCCE 2001. NBC Denis Compton Award for the most promising young Essex player 2001. Achieved double (1037 first-class runs plus 51 dismissals) 2004. Vice-captain of Essex since part-way through the 2007 season. Called up to squad for England Lions tour to India 2007-08 as a replacement for the injured Steve Davies. Finished the 2008 Championship season with a flourish, scoring 122 against Gloucestershire. Member of England's squad in the ICC World Twenty20 competition 2009. In Pro40 match against Durham in September 2009, he hit five sixes in consecutive balls from Scott Borthwick

Best batting: 212 Essex v Leicestershire, Chelmsford 2004
Best bowling: 1-122 Essex v Northamptonshire, Northampton 2008

2009 Season

	M	Inn	NO	Runs	HS	Avg	100	50	Ct	St	Balls	Runs	Wkts	Avg	BB	5I	10M
Test																	
FC	17	27	2	980	103*	39.20	1	6	61	4	0	0	0		-	-	-
ODI																	
List A	17	11	6	412	83*	82.40	-	4	19	12	0	0	0		-	-	
20/20 Int	5	5	2	37	14*	12.33	-	.	3	3	0	0	0		-	-	
20/20	12	10	3	106	23*	15.14	-	-	6	6	0	0	0		-	-	

Career Performances

	M	Inn	NO	Runs	HS	Avg	100	50	Ct	St	Balls	Runs	Wkts	Avg	BB	5I	10M
Test	7	12	3	226	48	25.11	-	-	17	1	0	0	0		-	-	-
FC	157	234	29	7342	212	35.81	13	37	435	38	84	128	1	128.00	1-122	-	-
ODI	11	6	3	41	13	13.66	-	-	13	7	0	0	0		-	-	
List A	151	115	32	2257	83*	27.19	-	10	183	49	0	0	0		-	-	
20/20 Int	5	5	2	37	14*	12.33	-	-	3	3	0	0	0		-	-	
20/20	58	48	11	775	62*	20.94	-	3	25	21	0	0	0		-	-	

FRANKLIN, J. E. C. Gloucestershire

Name: <u>James</u> Edward Charles Franklin
Role: Left-hand bat, left-arm fast-medium
bowler; all-rounder
Born: 7 November 1980, Wellington,
New Zealand
Height: 6ft 4in **Weight:** 15st
Nickname: Tank
County debut: 2004 (Gloucestershire),
2006 (Glamorgan)
County cap: 2004 (Gloucestershire),
2006 (Glamorgan)
Test debut: 2000-01
ODI debut: 2000-01
Twenty20 Int debut: 2005-06
1st-Class 200s: 2
Place in batting averages: 37th av. 50.22 (2008 178th av. 24.71)
Place in bowling averages: 37th av. 29.16 (2008 49th av. 30.64)
Parents: Monica and Russell
Wife: Kerry
Children: Charlie, November 2008
Family links with cricket: 'No family links, which means I am not related to Trevor
Franklin and Clive Franklin!'
Education: Wellington College, New Zealand
Off-season: 'Playing more cricket back home'
Overseas tours: New Zealand U19 to South Africa (U19 World Cup) 1997-98, to Sri
Lanka (U19 World Cup) 1999-2000; New Zealand A to South Africa 2004-05, to Sri
Lanka 2005-06; New Zealand to Australia 2001-02 (VB Series), to England 2004, to
Bangladesh 2004-05, to Australia 2004-05, to Zimbabwe 2005-06, to South Africa
2005-06, to India (ICC Champions Trophy) 2006-07, to Australia (Commonwealth
Bank Series) 2006-07, to West Indies (ICC World Cup) 2006-07, to Australia 2008-09,
to England 2009, to South Africa (ICC Champions Trophy) 2009-10, plus one-day
tournaments in Sharjah; New Zealand Emerging Players to Queensland 2008
Overseas teams played for: Wellington 1998-99 –
Career highlights to date: 'Winning Test matches'
Cricket moments to forget: 'Being hit for four consecutive sixes by Shaun Pollock!'
Cricket superstitions: 'None. Plenty of routines, though'
Cricketers particularly admired: Wasim Akram, Mark Waugh
Other sports played: Football ('College 1st XI – could have gone on, but chose
cricket!')
Other sports followed: Rugby (Hurricanes, All Blacks), football (Liverpool FC),
baseball (NY Yankees)

Extras: Represented New Zealand U19. New Zealand Academy 1999-2000. Man of the Match v England at Riverside in the NatWest Series 2004 (5-42). Was an overseas player with Gloucestershire for part of the 2004 season. Took 7-60 v Lancashire at Cheltenham 2004, the best figures by a bowler on Championship debut for Gloucestershire since 1900. Became the second New Zealand cricketer to take a Test hat-trick (Manjural Islam Rana, Mohammad Rafique, Tapash Baisya), in the first Test v Bangladesh at Dhaka 2004-05. Scored maiden Test century (122*) in the second Test v South Africa at Cape Town 2005-06, batting at No. 9. *New Zealand Cricket Almanack* Player of the Year 2006. An overseas player with Glamorgan 2006. Returned to Gloucestershire for 2009 season. Played in Test series against India 2009. Called into New Zealand's ICC Champions Trophy squad September 2009. Will continue with Gloucestershire in 2010

Best batting: 219 Wellington v Auckland, Auckland 2008-09
Best bowling: 7-30 Wellington v Central Districts, Wellington 2005-06

2009 Season

	M	Inn	NO	Runs	HS	Avg	100	50	Ct	St	Balls	Runs	Wkts	Avg	BB	5I	10M
Test																	
FC	14	22	4	904	109	50.22	3	4	6	-	1755	904	31	29.16	5-30	1	-
ODI																	
List A	13	12	1	447	85	40.63	-	4	3	-	405	375	13	28.84	3-18	-	
20/20 Int	3	2	1	14	7*	14.00	-	-	2	-	36	48	0		-	-	
20/20	7	6	1	82	44	16.40	-	-	3	-	120	148	5	29.60	2-21	-	

Career Performances

	M	Inn	NO	Runs	HS	Avg	100	50	Ct	St	Balls	Runs	Wkts	Avg	BB	5I	10M
Test	26	36	6	644	122*	21.46	1	2	11	-	4399	2612	80	32.65	6-119	3	-
FC	114	169	25	4875	219	33.85	9	22	41	-	18235	9573	359	26.66	7-30	12	1
ODI	69	47	17	571	45*	19.03	-	-	19	-	2996	2538	66	38.45	5-42	1	
List A	158	125	40	2346	87*	27.60	-	11	49	-	6755	5401	162	33.33	5-42	1	
20/20 Int	9	8	3	73	20	14.60	-	-	4	-	102	117	3	39.00	3-23	-	
20/20	30	27	8	570	69*	30.00	-	3	10	-	521	682	17	40.11	3-23	-	

FRANKS, P. J. Nottinghamshire

Name: Paul John Franks
Role: Left-hand bat, right-arm
fast-medium bowler; all-rounder
Born: 3 February 1979, Sutton-in-Ashfield
Height: 6ft 2in **Weight:** 14st
Nickname: Franksie, Pike
County debut: 1996
County cap: 1999
Benefit: 2007
ODI debut: 2000
50 wickets in a season: 2
Place in batting averages: 124th av. 33.50
(2008 147th av. 27.22)
Place in bowling averages: 100th av. 38.90
(2008 144th av. 52.66)

Parents: Patricia and John
Wife and date of marriage: Helen, 1 October 2005
Family links with cricket: 'Dad was a league legend for twenty-five years'
Education: Minster School, Southwell; West Notts College
Qualifications: 7 GCSEs, GNVQ (Advanced) Leisure Management, Level 1 coaching
Overseas tours: England U19 to Pakistan 1996-97, to South Africa (including U19
World Cup) 1997-98; England A to Zimbabwe and South Africa 1998-99, to
Bangladesh and New Zealand 1999-2000, to West Indies 2000-01, to Sri Lanka
2004-05; Notts CCC to South Africa 1998, 1999
Overseas teams played for: Bellville CC, Cape Town 2006
Career highlights to date: 'England debut. Notts Championship win 2005.
Twenty20 finals day 2006'
Cricket moments to forget: 'Being injured'
Cricketers particularly admired: Ian Botham, Andrew Flintoff, Chris Cairns,
Mark Ealham
Other sports played: Golf
Other sports followed: Football (Mansfield Town)
Favourite band: The Killers, Red Hot Chili Peppers
Extras: Took Championship hat-trick (Penney, Brown, Welch) v Warwickshire at
Trent Bridge 1997 (aged 18 years 163 days). NBC Denis Compton Award for most
promising young Nottinghamshire player 1997, 1998, 1999. Won U19 World Cup
winner's medal in Johannesburg 1998. Cricket Writers' Young Player of the Year 2000.
Vice-captain of Nottinghamshire 2003-04. ECB National Academy 2004-05 'Youngest
Notts player to be awarded a benefit year, aged 28'
Best batting: 123* Nottinghamshire v Leicestershire, Leicester 2003
Best bowling: 7-56 Nottinghamshire v Middlesex, Lord's 2000

2009 Season

	M	Inn	NO	Runs	HS	Avg	100	50	Ct	St	Balls	Runs	Wkts	Avg	BB	5I	10M
Test																	
FC	5	6	0	201	64	33.50	-	2	1	-	819	428	11	38.90	3-52	-	-
ODI																	
List A	11	7	3	153	50	38.25	-	1	2	-	273	256	2	128.00	1-30	-	
20/20 Int																	
20/20	5	2	0	1	1	.50	-	-	-	-	72	103	1	103.00	1-9	-	

Career Performances

	M	Inn	NO	Runs	HS	Avg	100	50	Ct	St	Balls	Runs	Wkts	Avg	BB	5I	10M
Test																	
FC	159	227	43	4878	123*	26.51	3	24	55	-	24108	13556	418	32.43	7-56	11	-
ODI	1	1	0	4	4	4.00	-	-	1	-	54	48	0		-	-	
List A	156	115	35	1757	84*	21.96	-	5	24	-	5846	4800	165	29.09	6-27	2	
20/20 Int																	
20/20	35	21	8	201	29*	15.46	-	-	4	-	237	333	12	27.75	2-12	-	

FROST, T. Warwickshire

Name: Tony Frost
Role: Right-hand bat, wicket-keeper
Born: 17 November 1975, Stoke-on-Trent
Height: 5ft 10in **Weight:** 10st 6lbs
County debut: 1997
County cap: 1999
Benefit: 2009
1000 runs in a season: 1
1st-Class 200s: 1
Place in batting averages: 165th av. 27.18
(2008 1st av. 83.58)
Parents: Ivan and Christine
Marital status: Single
Family links with cricket: Father played
for Staffordshire
Education: James Brinkley High School;
Stoke-on-Trent College
Qualifications: 5 GCSEs
Overseas tours: Kidsgrove U18 to Australia 1990-91
Other sports followed: Football, golf
Extras: Represented Staffordshire at all levels from U11 to U19. Won Texaco U16
competition with Staffordshire in 1992. Played for Development of Excellence XI

U17, U18, and U19. Scored century (135*) v Sussex at Horsham 2004, in the process setting with Ian Bell (262*) a new Warwickshire record partnership for the seventh wicket (289*). C&G Man of the Match award in the semi-final v Lancashire at Edgbaston 2005. Retired at the end of the 2006 season. Rejoined Warwickshire for 2008 and topped first-class batting averages. Retired at the end of the 2009 season
Best batting: 242* Warwickshire v Essex, Chelmsford 2008
Best bowling: 1-12 Warwickshire v Hampshire, Rose Bowl 2009

2009 Season

	M	Inn	NO	Runs	HS	Avg	100	50	Ct	St	Balls	Runs	Wkts	Avg	BB	5I	10M
Test																	
FC	15	23	1	598	105	27.18	1	2	8	-	31	12	1	12.00	1-12	-	-
ODI																	
List A	3	2	1	47	28	47.00	-	-	1	-	0	0	0		-	-	
20/20 Int																	
20/20	4	2	0	14	8	7.00	-	-	3	-	0	0	0		-	-	

Career Performances

	M	Inn	NO	Runs	HS	Avg	100	50	Ct	St	Balls	Runs	Wkts	Avg	BB	5I	10M
Test																	
FC	120	175	28	4779	242*	32.51	6	22	259	18	55	30	1	30.00	1-12	-	-
ODI																	
List A	88	50	18	652	56	20.37	-	2	79	19	0	0	0		-	-	
20/20 Int																	
20/20	27	17	3	289	53	20.64	-	1	15	11	0	0	0		-	-	

30. Two Pakistani batsmen have each made more than 8,800 Test match runs. Name them.

GALE, A. W. Yorkshire

Name: <u>Andrew</u> William Gale
Role: Left-hand bat, right-arm
off-spin bowler, county captain
Born: 28 November 1983, Dewsbury
Height: 6ft 1in **Weight:** 14st
Nickname: Galey
County debut: 2004
County cap: 2009
Place in batting averages: 101st av. 36.84
(2008 70th av. 39.08)
Parents: Denise and Alan
Wife and date of marriage: Kate, 10 October 2009
Family links with cricket: 'Grandfather – local
league legend'
Education: Whitcliffe Mount; Heckmondwike
Grammar

Qualifications: 10 GCSEs, 3 A-levels, Level 3 coaching
Career outside cricket: 'Cricket coaching' (see *Player Website*)
Off-season: 'ECB Performance Programme to South Africa'
Overseas tours: England U17 to Australia 2001; England U19 to Australia 2002-03;
Yorkshire to Grenada 2001, to India 2005
Overseas teams played for: Blacktown, Sydney 2004-05
Career highlights to date: 'Scoring maiden first-class hundred. Any hundred...'
Cricket moments to forget: 'Any ducks'
Cricket superstitions: 'No odd numbers on the radio volume'
Cricketers particularly admired: Marcus Trescothick, Michael Vaughan,
Darren Lehmann
Young players to look out for: Joe and Billy Root (both Yorkshire)
Other sports played: Football ('played for district')
Other sports followed: Football (Huddersfield Town)
Favourite band: Oasis, Simply Red
Relaxations: 'Watching the mighty Huddersfield Town'
Player website: www.procricketcoachingacademy.com
Extras: Played for England age groups from U15. Yorkshire League Young Batsman
of the Year 2002. Yorkshire Player of the Year 2006. Jointly responsible for the Pro
Cricket Coaching Academy, which operates in the North of England and the Midlands.
Only Jacques Rudolph scored more first-class runs for Yorkshire in 2008. Member of
England Performance Programme squad 2009-10. Became the youngest Yorkshire
captain for over 75 years when appointed in December 2009
Opinions on cricket: 'Glad to see overseas players back down to one.'
Best batting: 150 Yorkshire v Surrey, The Oval 2008
Best bowling: 1-33 Yorkshire v LUCCE, Headingley 2007

2009 Season

	M	Inn	NO	Runs	HS	Avg	100	50	Ct	St	Balls	Runs	Wkts	Avg	BB	5I	10M
Test																	
FC	17	26	1	921	121	36.84	2	5	6	-	6	11	0		-	-	-
ODI																	
List A	12	12	1	314	83	28.54	-	2	-	-	0	0	0		-	-	
20/20 Int																	
20/20	10	10	1	383	91	42.55	-	3	4	-	0	0	0		-	-	

Career Performances

	M	Inn	NO	Runs	HS	Avg	100	50	Ct	St	Balls	Runs	Wkts	Avg	BB	5I	10M
Test																	
FC	47	73	1	2340	150	32.50	6	10	24	-	24	47	1	47.00	1-33	-	-
ODI																	
List A	72	64	8	1650	89	29.46	-	10	10	-	0	0	0		-	-	
20/20 Int																	
20/20	38	34	5	748	91	25.79	-	5	17	-	0	0	0		-	-	

GALLIAN, J. E. R.　　　　　　　　　Essex

Name: Jason Edward Riche Gallian
Role: Right-hand bat, right-arm medium bowler
Born: 25 June 1971, Manly, NSW, Australia
Height: 6ft **Weight:** 14st 7lbs
Nickname: Gal
County debut: 1990 (Lancashire),
1998 (Nottinghamshire), 2008 (Essex)
County cap: 1994 (Lancashire),
1998 (Nottinghamshire)
Benefit: 2005 (Nottinghamshire)
Test debut: 1995
1000 runs in a season: 6
1st-Class 300s: 1
Place in batting averages: 212th av. 20.41
(2008 145th av. 27.35)
Parents: Ray and Marilyn
Wife and date of marriage: Charlotte, 2 October 1999
Children: Tom, 11 May 2001; Harry, 8 September 2003; Emily, 6 October 2006
Family links with cricket: Father played for Stockport. 'Tom and Harry are showing a keen eye for a ball!'
Education: The Pittwater House Schools, Australia; Keble College, Oxford
Qualifications: Higher School Certificate, Diploma in Social Studies (Oxford)

Career outside cricket: 'Working for Clydesdale Bank in London'
Overseas tours: Australia U20 to West Indies 1989-90; England A to India 1994-95, to Pakistan 1995-96, to Australia 1996-97; England to South Africa 1995-96; Nottinghamshire to Johannesburg 2000, to South Africa 2001; MCC to UAE and Oman 2004
Overseas teams played for: NSW U19 1988-89; NSW Colts and NSW 2nd XI 1990-91; Manly 1993-94
Career highlights to date: 'First Test match'
Cricket moments to forget: 'Breaking a finger in my first Test match'
Cricket superstitions: 'None'
Cricketers particularly admired: Desmond Haynes, Mike Gatting
Young players to look out for: Adam Wheater (Essex)
Other sports played: Golf, shooting, darts (known as 'see it off')
Other sports followed: Rugby league and union, football
Favourite band: Midnight Oil, INXS
Relaxations: 'Looking after the kids'
Extras: Represented Australia YC 1988-90 (captain v England YC 1989-90); also represented Australia U20 and U21 1991-92. Took wicket of D. A. Hagan of Oxford University with his first ball in first-class cricket 1990. Played for Oxford University and Combined Universities 1992; captained Oxford University 1993. Qualified to play for England 1994. Recorded highest individual score in history of Old Trafford with his 312 v Derbyshire in 1996. Captain of Nottinghamshire from part-way through the 1998 season to 2002 and in 2004; Nottinghamshire club captain and captain in first-class cricket 2003. Left Nottinghamshire at the end of the 2007 season and joined Essex for 2008. Announced his retirement in August 2009
Opinions on cricket: 'The changes to Championship cricket have been very positive in recreating Test cricket conditions to bring on up-and-coming players.'
Best batting: 312 Lancashire v Derbyshire, Old Trafford 1996
Best bowling: 6-115 Lancashire v Surrey, Southport 1996

2009 Season

	M	Inn	NO	Runs	HS	Avg	100	50	Ct	St	Balls	Runs	Wkts	Avg	BB	5I	10M
Test																	
FC	7	13	1	245	125	20.41	1	-	5	-	0	0	0	-	-	-
ODI																	
List A	3	3	0	70	38	23.33	-	-	-	-	0	0	0	-	-	
20/20 Int																	
20/20																	

Career Performances

	M	Inn	NO	Runs	HS	Avg	100	50	Ct	St	Balls	Runs	Wkts	Avg	BB	5I	10M
Test	3	6	0	74	28	12.33	-	-	1	-	84	62	0		-	-	-
FC	259	443	36	15266	312	37.50	38	72	231	-	7162	4164	96	43.37	6-115	1	-
ODI																	
List A	231	227	18	6754	134	32.31	11	40	77	-	2049	1808	55	32.87	5-15	1	
20/20 Int																	
20/20	16	16	0	315	62	19.68	-	2	5	-	0	0	0		-	-	

GATTING, J. S. Sussex

Name: <u>Joe</u> Stephen Gatting
Role: Right-hand bat, right-arm offbreak bowler
Born: 25 November 1987, Brighton, Sussex
Height: 6ft **Weight:** 14st
Nickname: Gatt
County debut: 2009
Place in batting averages: 32nd av. 51.66
Parents: Steve and Joy
Marital status: Single
Family links with cricket: Uncle is Mike Gatting, former England captain. Dad played for Middlesex 2nd XI
Education: St Andrews Primary School; Cardinal Newman; Brighton College
Career outside cricket: 'Football'
Off-season: 'Australia and Dubai'
Overseas tours: Sussex CCC Academy to South Africa 2004; Sussex to Dubai 2008-09, to Abu Dhabi 2009, to India (Twenty20 Champions League) 2009
Overseas teams played for: Tea Tree Gully DCC, South Australia 2009-10
Career highlights to date: 'Champions League in India. 99* v Yorkshire in Pro40'
Cricket superstitions: 'Left pad on first'
Cricketers particularly admired: Brian Lara, Ricky Ponting
Young players to look out for: Matt Machan (Sussex)
Other sports played: Football (see *Extras*)
Other sports followed: Football (Manchester United)
Favourite band: The Verve, The Kooks
Relaxations: 'Golf'
Extras: Had been on Brighton & Hove Albion's books for three years before turning his back on football and signing for Sussex in spring 2009. Once scored 200* off 90 balls for Preston Nomads in the Sussex League. Attended the Darren Lehmann Academy in Adelaide 2009-10
Best batting: 152 Sussex v CUCCE, Fenner's, 2009

2009 Season

	M	Inn	NO	Runs	HS	Avg	100	50	Ct	St	Balls	Runs	Wkts	Avg	BB	5I	10M
Test																	
FC	4	6	0	310	152	51.66	1	1	2	-	0	0	0		-	-	-
ODI																	
List A	13	12	1	325	99*	29.54	-	2	3	-	8	5	0		-	-	
20/20 Int																	
20/20	5	2	0	22	17	11.00	-	-	-	-	0	0	0		-	-	

Career Performances

	M	Inn	NO	Runs	HS	Avg	100	50	Ct	St	Balls	Runs	Wkts	Avg	BB	5I	10M
Test																	
FC	4	6	0	310	152	51.66	1	1	2	-	0	0	0		-	-	-
ODI																	
List A	13	12	1	325	99*	29.54	-	2	3	-	8	5	0		-	-	
20/20 Int																	
20/20	7	4	0	56	25	14.00	-	-	-	-	0	0	0		-	-	

GAZZARD, C. M. Somerset

Name: <u>Carl</u> Matthew Gazzard
Role: Right-hand bat, wicket-keeper
Born: 15 April 1982, Penzance
Height: 6ft **Weight:** 13st
Nickname: Gazza, Larry
County debut: 2002
Parents: Paul and Alison
Wife and date of marriage: Laura,
29 September 2006
Children: Ruby and Noah, 17 September 2007
Family links with cricket: Father and brother both
played for Cornwall Schools. Mother's a keen
follower of the game
Education: Mounts Bay Comprehensive;
Richard Huish College, Taunton
Qualifications: 10 GCSEs, 2 A-levels, Levels 1 and 2 coaching
Overseas tours: Cornwall Schools U13 to Johannesburg; West of England U15 to
West Indies; Somerset Academy to Durban 1999
Overseas teams played for: Subiaco-Floreat, Perth 2000-01; Scarborough, Perth
2002-03
Career highlights to date: '157 v Derby in Totesport game [2004]'
Cricket moments to forget: 'Dislocating my shoulder in Perth – kept me out for
2001 season'

Cricket superstitions: 'None'
Cricketers particularly admired: Marcus Trescothick, Graham Rose
Young players to look out for: James Hildreth (Somerset)
Other sports played: Football (played through the age groups for Cornwall)
Other sports followed: Football (West Ham United)
Favourite band: Red Hot Chili Peppers
Extras: Played for England U13, U14, U15, U19. Won the Graham Kersey Award for Best Wicket-keeper at Bunbury Festival. Played for Cornwall in Minor Counties aged 16. Scored 136-ball 157 (his maiden one-day century) v Derbyshire at Derby in the Totesport League 2004. Man of the Match in the Twenty20 Cup semi-final v Leicestershire at The Oval 2005, Retired at the end of the 2009 season
Best batting: 74 Somerset v Worcestershire, Worcester 2005

2009 Season

	M	Inn	NO	Runs	HS	Avg	100	50	Ct	St	Balls	Runs	Wkts	Avg	BB	5I	10M
Test																	
FC																	
ODI																	
List A	1	0	0	0	0	-		-	-	-	0	0	0		-	-	
20/20 Int																	
20/20																	

Career Performances

	M	Inn	NO	Runs	HS	Avg	100	50	Ct	St	Balls	Runs	Wkts	Avg	BB	5I	10M
Test																	
FC	28	43	6	738	74	19.94	-	1	58	1	0	0	0		-	-	-
ODI																	
List A	54	45	5	954	157	23.85	1	4	51	7	0	0	0		-	-	
20/20 Int																	
20/20	27	17	4	221	39	17.00	-	-	14	6	0	0	0		-	-	

31. Mohammad Yousuf scored 631 runs at an average of 90.14 in the 2006 Test series in England. What was his highest score?

GIBBS, H. H. Yorkshire

Name: <u>Herschelle</u> Herman Gibbs
Role: Right-hand bat, right-arm fast-medium
leg-break bowler
Born: 23 February 1974, Green Point,
Cape Town, South Africa
Height: 5ft 8in
Nickname: Scooter
County debut: 2008 (Glamorgan, one-day)
Test debut: 1997
ODI debut: 1996
Twenty20 Int debut: 2005
1st-Class 200s: 4
Place in batting averages: 99th av. 37.00
Parents: Herman and Barbara
Marital status: Divorced

Family links with cricket: Father Herman is a leading sports writer
Education: Diocesan College
Overseas tours: South Africa to India 1996-97, to Australia 1997-98, to England (ICC World Cup 1999), to New Zealand 1999, to India 2000, to West Indies 2001, to Zimbabwe 2001, to Australia 2001-02, to Morocco 2002 (Morocco Cup), to Bangladesh 2003, to England 2003, to Pakistan 2003, to New Zealand 2004, to England 2004 (ICC Champions Trophy), to Sri Lanka 2004, to West Indies 2005, to Australia 2005-06, to Sri Lanka 2006, to Pakistan 2007, to West Indies 2007 (ICC World Cup), to England 2008 (one-day series), to Australia 2008-09 (one-day series), to England 2009 (one-day series)
Overseas teams played for: Western Province 1994-95 – 2003-04; Western Province Boland 2004-05; Cape Cobras 2005-06 – ; Deccan Chargers (IPL) 2007-08
Career highlights to date: '1999 World Cup semi-final at Edgbaston. It ended in a tie but could have gone either way – the complete one-day match that had everything.'
Cricket moments to forget: 'The game before, when I dropped Steve Waugh and we lost the game.'
Cricketers particularly admired: Peter Kirsten, Viv Richards
Other sports played: Golf ('I play off five')
Other sports followed: Football (Manchester United)
Favourite band: Luther Vandross, George Benson and Frank Sinatra
Relaxations: Shopping
Extras: In a World Cup match against the Netherlands in 2007 he hit six sixes in an over from Dan van Bunge, an international record. Has featured in three 300-plus opening partnerships with Graeme Smith in Test matches. Scored 175 off 111 balls to give South Africa victory over Australia in Johannesburg 2006. Signed with Glamorgan in 2008, finishing top of the county's batting averages. Glamorgan's

overseas player again in 2009, from July until end of season. Recalled to South Africa one-day squad November 2009. Signed Twenty20 for Yorkshire February 2010

Best batting: 228 South Africa v Pakistan, Cape Town 2003
Best bowling: 2-14 South Africa A v Somerset, Taunton 1996

2009 Season

	M	Inn	NO	Runs	HS	Avg	100	50	Ct	St	Balls	Runs	Wkts	Avg	BB	5I	10M
Test																	
FC	5	7	0	259	96	37.00	-	2	7	-	0	0	0		-	-	-
ODI																	
List A	2	2	1	54	47*	54.00	-	-	1	-	0	0	0		-	-	
20/20 Int	6	6	0	114	55	19.00	-	1	-	-	0	0	0		-	-	
20/20	6	6	0	114	55	19.00	-	1	-	-	0	0	0		-	-	

Career Performances

	M	Inn	NO	Runs	HS	Avg	100	50	Ct	St	Balls	Runs	Wkts	Avg	BB	5I	10M
Test	90	154	7	6167	228	41.95	14	26	94	-	6	4	0		-	-	-
FC	193	331	13	13425	228	42.21	31	60	176	-	138	78	3	26.00	2-14	-	-
ODI	245	238	16	8060	175	36.30	21	37	106	-	0	0	0		-	-	
List A	368	353	29	11306	175	34.89	25	59	164	-	66	57	2	28.50	1-16	-	
20/20 Int	20	20	1	359	90*	18.89	-	3	3	-	0	0	0		-	-	
20/20	69	67	6	1526	98	25.01	-	12	34	-	0	0	0		-	-	

GIDMAN, A. P. R. Gloucestershire

Name: Alexander (<u>Alex</u>) Peter Richard Gidman
Role: Right-hand bat, right-arm medium bowler, county captain
Born: 22 June 1981, High Wycombe
Height: 6ft 2in **Weight:** 15st 7lbs
Nickname: G, Giddo
County debut: 2001 (one-day), 2002 (first-class)
County cap: 2004
1000 runs in a season: 4
Place in batting averages: 49th av. 44.69 (2008 166th av. 24.05)
Parents: Alistair and Jane
Marital status: Engaged
Family links with cricket: Younger brother Will is at Durham
Education: Wycliffe College, Stonehouse, Gloucestershire
Qualifications: 6 GCSEs, 1 A-level, GNVQ Level 2 in Leisure and Tourism

Off-season: 'Playing my guitar, learning piano'
Overseas tours: MCC Young Cricketers to Cape Town 1999; Gloucestershire to South Africa; England A to Malaysia and India 2003-04 (c), to Sri Lanka 2004-05, to Bangladesh 2006-07
Overseas teams played for: Albion CC, New Zealand 2001; Otago, New Zealand 2007-08
Career highlights to date: 'England A tours. Two C&G Trophy final victories. Academy captain'
Cricket moments to forget: '2008'
Cricketers particularly admired: Steve Waugh
Young players to look out for: Will Gidman (Durham)
Other sports played: Golf
Other sports followed: Football (Wolves), rugby (Gloucester)
Favourite band: Oasis, Pink Floyd
Relaxations: 'Just chilling out... Movies, golf, playing guitar'
Extras: Gloucestershire Young Player of the Year 2002, 2003. NBC Denis Compton Award for the most promising young Gloucestershire player 2002, 2003. ECB National Academy 2003-04, 2004-05. Included in England's preliminary squad for ICC Champions Trophy in 2004. Gloucestershire Players' Player of the Year 2006. Vice-captain of Gloucestershire 2006-08. Scored century in each innings (130/105*) v Northamptonshire at Gloucester 2007. Represented England Lions 2007. Gloucestershire county captain since January 2009
Opinions on cricket: 'None – just enjoy. Cricket is not the be-all and end-all...'
Best batting: 176 Gloucestershire v Surrey, Bristol 2009
Best bowling: 4-47 Gloucestershire v Glamorgan, Cardiff 2005

2009 Season

	M	Inn	NO	Runs	HS	Avg	100	50	Ct	St	Balls	Runs	Wkts	Avg	BB	5I	10M
Test																	
FC	15	23	0	1028	176	44.69	4	4	9	-	355	162	4	40.50	3-23	-	-
ODI																	
List A	16	16	1	291	116	19.40	1	-	1	-	396	321	6	53.50	2-29	-	
20/20 Int																	
20/20	7	7	0	140	64	20.00	-	1	2	-	18	34	1	34.00	1-20	-	

Career Performances

	M	Inn	NO	Runs	HS	Avg	100	50	Ct	St	Balls	Runs	Wkts	Avg	BB	5I	10M
Test																	
FC	113	196	20	6623	176	37.63	15	37	63	-	6449	3994	87	45.90	4-47	-	-
ODI																	
List A	142	133	14	2968	116	24.94	3	15	42	-	2758	2370	57	41.57	5-42	1	
20/20 Int																	
20/20	46	40	7	680	64	20.60	-	3	11	-	204	271	7	38.71	2-24	-	

GIDMAN, W. R. S.   Durham

Name: William (<u>Will</u>) Robert Simon Gidman
Role: Left-hand bat, right-arm medium bowler;
all-rounder
Born: 14 February 1985, High Wycombe
Height: 6ft 2in **Weight:** 12st 7lbs
Nickname: Gidders, Giddo, Rev, PT
County debut: 2007
Parents: Alistair and Jane
Marital status: Single
Family links with cricket: Brother of Alex
Gidman, captain of Gloucestershire
Education: Wycliffe College, Stonehouse,
Gloucestershire; Berkshire College of Agriculture

Qualifications: 7 GCSEs, Level 2 cricket coaching,
Level 1 rugby and football coaching
Career outside cricket: 'Part-time teacher'
Overseas tours: Wycliffe College to South Africa 2000; MCC YC to Sri Lanka 2004,
to India 2005, to Lanzarote 2006; Durham to Cape Town 2007
Overseas teams played for: Gold Coast Dolphins, Australia 2004-05
Career highlights to date: 'Signing for Durham CCC'
Cricket moments to forget: 'Giving away four overthrows off Freddie Flintoff's
bowling whilst doing 12th man duties for England against Bangladesh'
Cricket superstitions: 'None'
Cricketers particularly admired: Garfield Sobers, Graham Thorpe, Mike Hussey,
Alex Gidman
Other sports played: Football (Stroud and District), rugby, golf, table tennis
Other sports followed: Football (Wolves), rugby (Gloucester)
Favourite band: Embrace
Relaxations: 'Music, TV, walking the dog, Sudoku'
Extras: Was first Gloucestershire U10 to score a hundred. Played for Gloucestershire
Board XI in the 2003 C&G. MCC YC cap
Opinions on cricket: 'I love the traditions of our game and the prospect of things
like drop-in pitches and taking too many decisions away from the umpires in the
middle, I am not sure about.'
Best batting: 8 Durham v Sri Lanka A, Riverside 2007
Best bowling: 3-37 Durham v Sri Lanka A, Riverside 2007

2009 Season

	M	Inn	NO	Runs	HS	Avg	100	50	Ct	St	Balls	Runs	Wkts	Avg	BB	5I	10M
Test																	
FC																	
ODI																	
List A	13	7	2	72	18*	14.40	-	-	5	-	414	308	9	34.22	2-23	-	
20/20 Int																	
20/20																	

Career Performances

	M	Inn	NO	Runs	HS	Avg	100	50	Ct	St	Balls	Runs	Wkts	Avg	BB	5I	10M
Test																	
FC	1	2	0	8	8	4.00	-	-	-	-	138	86	4	21.50	3-37	-	-
ODI																	
List A	16	10	2	105	21	13.12	-	-	6	-	498	369	13	28.38	2-21	-	
20/20 Int																	
20/20																	

GILCHRIST, A.   Middlesex

Name: Adam Gilchrist
Role: Left-hand bat, right-arm off-break bowler, wicket-keeper
Born: 14 November 1971, Bellingen, New South Wales
Height: 6ft 1in
Nickname: Gilly, Churchy
Test debut: 1999
ODI debut: 1996
Twenty20 Int debut: 2005-06
1st-Class 200s: 2
Wife: Melinda
Children: Harrison, Archie
Education: Deniliquin South Public School; Kadina High School, Lismore,
Overseas tours: Australia Young Cricketers to England 1991; Australian Cricket Academy to South Africa 1992; Young Australia
to England 1995; Australia to India (one-day series)1996, to South Africa (one-day series) 1997, to England (Texaco Trophy) 1997, to New Zealand (one-day series) 1998, to West Indies (one-day series) 1999, to England (ICC World Cup) 1999, to New Zealand (one-day series) 2000, to South Africa 2000, to India 2001, to England 2001, to South Africa 2002, to Pakistan 2002-03, to West Indies 2002-03,

to Sri Lanka 2004, to Zimbabwe 2004, to India 2004-05 (captain), to England 2005, to South Africa 2005-06, to Bangladesh 2005-06, to India (ICC Champions Trophy) 2006-07, to India 2007-08 (one-day series), to South Africa 2007-08 (one-day series)
Overseas teams played for: New South Wales 1992-93, 1993-94; Western Australia 1994-95 – 2007-08; Deccan Chargers (IPL) 2008 –
Extras: Australian Cricket Academy 1991-92. Top wicket-taker in Australian domestic cricket 1994-95, 1995-96, 1996-97, 1997-98. Scored 189* off 187 balls in the Sheffield Shield final 1995. Selected for Australia A 1996. Man of the Match in two ODIs v New Zealand 2000. Scored 122 off 112 balls in a 197-run partnership with Matthew Hayden v India in Mumbai 2001 to extend Australia's run to 16 consecutive Test wins, winning the Man of the Match award. One of *Wisden*'s Five Cricketers of the Year 2002. One-day International Player of the Year 2003, 2004. Scored the second fastest-ever Test century in Perth against England December 2006, made off only 57 balls. His scoring rate in one-day internationals is 96 per 100 balls, in Test matches 81. Claimed 472 victims from behind the stumps for Australia. Made captain of Deccan Chargers, September 2008, and still holds that position. Signed for Middlesex in November 2009 and will play Twenty20 cricket for the county in 2010. Last played for Australia in 2008, the year he announced his retirement from all forms of cricket other than the IPL (Indian Premier League). Only Matthew Hayden scored more runs in the IPL in 2009
Best batting: 204* South Africa v Australia, Johannesburg 2002

2009 Season (Did not make any first-class or one-day appearances)

Career Performances

	M	Inn	NO	Runs	HS	Avg	100	50	Ct	St	Balls	Runs	Wkts	Avg	BB	5I	10M
Test	96	137	20	5570	204*	47.60	17	26	379	37	0	0	0		-	-	-
FC	190	280	46	10334	204*	44.16	30	43	756	55	0	0	0		-	-	-
ODI	287	279	11	9619	172	35.89	16	55	417	55	0	0	0		-	-	
List A	355	342	19	11288	172	34.94	18	63	526	65	12	10	0		-	-	
20/20 Int	13	13	1	272	48	22.66	-	-	17	-	0	0	0		-	-	
20/20	45	45	2	1272	109*	29.58	1	7	35	10	0	0	0		-	-	

32. Which Pakistan bowler was banned from bowling by the umpires during a Test match in 1976, after he bowled too many bouncers?

GLOVER, J. C.   Glamorgan

Name: <u>John</u> Charles Glover
Role: Right-hand bat, right-arm fast-medium bowler
Born: 29 August 1989, Cardiff
Height: 6ft 4in **Weight:** 12st 8lbs
Nickname: Gloves
County debut: No first-team appearance
Parents: Ian and Julie
Marital status: Single
Education: Llantarnam Comprehensive School;
Durham University
Qualifications: GCSEs, A-levels and a degree
Career outside cricket: 'Student'
Off-season: 'At Durham University finishing my
final year, and training with the Centre of Excellence'
Overseas tours: DUCCE to South Africa 2008
Career highlights to date: 'Taking five wickets for DUCCE v Durham'
Cricket moments to forget: 'Batsman hitting me on the back of the head during a net
session the day before my first-class debut for Durham University'
Cricketers particularly admired: Courtney Walsh
Young players to look out for: Tom Westley (Essex)
Other sports played: 'Try and play most sports, but mainly football'
Other sports followed: Football (Cardiff City FC)
Favourite band: Metallica
Relaxations: 'Cinema, playing guitar, watching all sports'
Extras: Has played for Wales Minor Counties. Awarded a development contract with
Glamorgan for 2010
Best batting: 14 DUCCE v Durham, Durham 2009
Best bowling: 5-38 DUCCE v Durham, Durham 2009

2009 Season

	M	Inn	NO	Runs	HS	Avg	100	50	Ct	St	Balls	Runs	Wkts	Avg	BB	5I	10M
Test																	
FC	3	6	0	27	14	4.50	-	-	-	-	456	233	7	33.28	5-38	1	-
ODI																	
List A																	
20/20 Int																	
20/20																	

Career Performances

	M	Inn	NO	Runs	HS	Avg	100	50	Ct	St	Balls	Runs	Wkts	Avg	BB	5I	10M
Test																	
FC	6	9	1	37	14	4.62	-	-	-	-	754	421	13	32.38	5-38	1	-
ODI																	
List A																	
20/20 Int																	
20/20																	

GODDARD, L. J. Derbyshire

Name: <u>Lee</u> James Goddard
Role: Right-hand bat, wicket-keeper
Born: 22 October 1982, Dewsbury
Height: 5ft 10in **Weight:** 11st 6lbs
Nickname: Godders, Goddy
County debut: 2004 (Derbyshire),
2007 (Durham)
Parents: Steve and Lynda
Wife and date of marriage: Kelly, 25 October 2008
Family links with cricket: 'Dad played a little'
Education: Batley Grammar School; Loughborough
University
Qualifications: GCSEs, Foundation degree in Sports
Science, ECB Level 1 coaching
Career outside cricket: 'Estate agents, property'
Off-season: 'Working hard on fitness and cricket skills'
Overseas tours: Durham to South Africa (Pretoria) 2008, to South Africa
(Potchefstroom) 2009
Overseas teams played for: Parramatta DCC, Sydney 2001-02
Career highlights to date: 'My first-class debut. Five catches in first innings on
Championship debut for Derbyshire [v Hampshire 2004]. Fifty off 31 balls (fastest
first-class fifty in Durham history) on first-class debut for Durham [v Sri Lanka A
2007]. Friends Provident win [2007] (Durham's first trophy). Being part of Durham's
back-to-back Championship-winning squad'
Cricket moments to forget: 'Any dropped catch'
Cricket superstitions: 'Left pad on first'
Favourite sledging line: 'Mark Boucher "having words" with Tatenda Taibu – it's on
YouTube! Any Luke Evans comment on his follow-through – priceless!'
Cricketers particularly admired: Adam Gilchrist, Damien Martyn, Paul Nixon, Jack
Russell, Michael Di Venuto

Young players to look out for: Scott Borthwick and Ben Stokes (both Durham), Dan Redfern (Derbyshire)
Other sports played: Squash, golf, football (Huddersfield Town aged 9-15)
Other sports followed: Football (Leeds United), rugby league (Leeds Rhinos)
Favourite band: Matchbox Twenty
Relaxations: 'Spending time with my wife!'
Extras: Played in Yorkshire's U17 County Championship winning side. Played for Yorkshire Board XI in the 2003 C&G. Played for Loughborough UCCE in 2003. Was in British Universities squad for match v Zimbabweans 2003. Derbyshire CCC 2nd XI Player of the Year 2004. Shared with Graham Wagg in a new record seventh-wicket partnership for Derbyshire in matches v Surrey (181) at Derby 2006. Scored 31-ball fifty on first-class debut for Durham v Sri Lanka A at Riverside 2007, breaking record (jointly held by Ian Botham, Martin Speight and Phil Mustard) for fastest first-class fifty for the county. Returned to Derbyshire for 2010 after three seasons with Durham
Best batting: 91 Derbyshire v Surrey, Derby 2006

2009 Season

	M	Inn	NO	Runs	HS	Avg	100	50	Ct	St	Balls	Runs	Wkts	Avg	BB	5I	10M
Test																	
FC																	
ODI																	
List A	1	0	0	0	0		-	-	3	-	0	0	0		-	-	
20/20 Int																	
20/20																	

Career Performances

	M	Inn	NO	Runs	HS	Avg	100	50	Ct	St	Balls	Runs	Wkts	Avg	BB	5I	10M
Test																	
FC	10	14	4	324	91	32.40	-	2	22	-	0	0	0		-	-	-
ODI																	
List A	9	7	3	100	36	25.00	-	-	16	-	0	0	0		-	-	
20/20 Int																	
20/20	1	0	0	0	0		-	-	-	-	0	0	0		-	-	

---

33. England made 447-3 dec in their first and only innings v Bangladesh
in the Second Test of the 2005 two-match series.
Which two batsmen scored centuries?

GODLEMAN, B-A.   Essex

Name: Billy-Ashley (<u>Billy</u>) Godleman
Role: Left-hand opening bat, right-arm
leg-spin bowler
Born: 11 February 1989, Islington, London
Height: 6ft 2in **Weight:** 13st
Nickname: G
County debut: 2005 (Middlesex)
Place in batting averages: 231st av. 17.77
(2008 129th av. 29.44)
Parents: Ashley Fitzgerald and John Godleman
Marital status: Single
Family links with cricket: 'Dad played club
cricket for Hampstead'
Education: Central Foundation School; Islington
Green School
Qualifications: 7 GCSEs
Overseas tours: England U16 to South Africa 2004-05; England U19 to Malaysia
2006-07, to Malaysia (U19 World Cup) 2007-08; England Performance Programme
to India 2007-08
Career highlights to date: 'Maiden first-class century – 113* v Somerset [2007]'
Cricketers particularly admired: Graeme Smith, Andy Flower, Matthew Hayden
Young players to look out for: Steven Finn and Eoin Morgan (both Middlesex),
Tom Westley (Essex), Ben Brown (Sussex), Alex Wakely (Northamptonshire)
Other sports played: Football
Other sports followed: Football (Liverpool FC), cricket (Brondesbury)
Favourite band: Pink Floyd, Led Zeppelin, Fleetwood Mac
Relaxations: 'Spending time with my little brother Johnny and family, reading,
watching Liverpool FC'
Extras: Named best player in country U13, U14 and U15 at regional tournaments.
Scored a 168-ball 143 for South v West at Bunbury U15 Festival at Nottingham 2004.
Made 2nd XI Trophy debut for Middlesex 2003. Scored 69* on first-class debut v
CUCCE at Fenner's 2005. NBC Denis Compton Award for the most promising young
Middlesex player 2005, 2007. Represented England U19 2006, 2007, 2008. Scored
maiden first-class century (113*) on Championship debut v Somerset at Taunton 2007.
Made over 1000 runs in all forms of cricket in 2008. Signed a three-year deal with
Essex in August 2009 after spending the season there on loan from Middlesex.
Member of England Performance Programme squad 2009-10
Opinions on cricket: 'You get out what you put in.'
Best batting: 113* Middlesex v Somerset, Taunton 2007

2009 Season

	M	Inn	NO	Runs	HS	Avg	100	50	Ct	St	Balls	Runs	Wkts	Avg	BB	5I	10M
Test																	
FC	5	9	0	160	48	17.77	-	-	3	-	0	0	0		-	-	-
ODI																	
List A	6	6	0	137	82	22.83	-	1	1	-	0	0	0		-	-	
20/20 Int																	
20/20	9	9	0	147	57	16.33	-	1	4	-	0	0	0		-	-	

Career Performances

	M	Inn	NO	Runs	HS	Avg	100	50	Ct	St	Balls	Runs	Wkts	Avg	BB	5I	10M
Test																	
FC	36	59	3	1807	113*	32.26	2	10	30	-	30	35	0		-	-	-
ODI																	
List A	14	14	1	321	82	24.69	-	1	4	-	0	0	0		-	-	
20/20 Int																	
20/20	24	23	0	419	69	18.21	-	3	11	-	0	0	0		-	-	

GOODMAN, J. E.   Kent

Name: <u>James</u> Elliott Goodman
Role: Right-hand bat, right-arm medium bowler; all-rounder
Born: 19 November 1990, Farnborough, Kent
Height: 5ft 10in **Weight:** 10st 12lbs
Nickname: Goody
County debut: 2007 (one-day)
Parents: Elizabeth and Trevor
Marital status: Single
Education: St Olave's Grammar School, Orpington
Career outside cricket: 'Student'
Off-season: 'At school; net sessions at Canterbury'
Overseas tours: England U19 to Malaysia (U19 World Cup) 2007-08, to Bangladesh 2009-10 (see *Extras*)
Career highlights to date: 'Being picked for England U19 World Cup squad'
Cricket moments to forget: 'Having Marvan Atapattu hit 24 off one of my overs in a game against Lashings'
Cricketers particularly admired: Sachin Tendulkar, Michael Bevan
Other sports followed: Football (Chelsea)
Favourite band: Kanye West
Relaxations: 'Watching sport'

Extras: Youngest player to captain Kent 2nd XI, aged 16. Kent Academy Player of the Year 2007. England U16 captain 2007. Ill-health forced his early return home from the England U19 tour to Bangladesh in October 2009

2009 Season

	M	Inn	NO	Runs	HS	Avg	100	50	Ct	St	Balls	Runs	Wkts	Avg	BB	5I	10M
Test																	
FC																	
ODI																	
List A	2	2	1	38	26*	38.00	-	-	1	-	0	0	0		-	-	
20/20 Int																	
20/20																	

Career Performances

	M	Inn	NO	Runs	HS	Avg	100	50	Ct	St	Balls	Runs	Wkts	Avg	BB	5I	10M
Test																	
FC																	
ODI																	
List A	3	2	1	38	26*	38.00	-	-	2	-	0	0	0		-	-	
20/20 Int																	
20/20																	

GOODWIN, M. W.   Sussex

Name: <u>Murray</u> William Goodwin
Role: Right-hand bat, right-arm medium/
leg-spin bowler, county vice-captain
Born: 11 December 1972, Harare, Zimbabwe
Height: 5ft 9in **Weight:** 11st 2lbs
Nickname: Muzza, Fuzz, Goodie
County debut: 2001
County cap: 2001
Test debut: 1997-98
ODI debut: 1997-98
1000 runs in a season: 7
1st-Class 200s: 6
1st-Class 300s: 2
Place in batting averages: 125th av. 33.33
(2008 10th av. 58.39)
Parents: Penny and George
Wife and date of marriage: Tarsha, 13 December 1997
Children: Jayden William; Ashton George, 19 November 2006
Family links with cricket: 'Dad is a coach. Eldest brother played for Zimbabwe'

Education: St John's, Harare, Zimbabwe; Newtonmoore Senior High, Bunbury, Western Australia
Qualifications: Level 2 coaching
Overseas tours: Australian Cricket Academy to South Africa 1992, to Sri Lanka and India 1993; Zimbabwe to Sri Lanka and New Zealand 1997-98, to Bangladesh (Wills International Cup) 1998-99, to Pakistan 1998-99, to UK, Ireland and Netherlands (World Cup) 1999, to South Africa 1999-2000, to West Indies 1999-2000, to England 2000
Overseas teams played for: Excelsior, Netherlands 1997; Mashonaland 1997-98 – 1998-99; Western Australia 1994-95 – 1996-97, 2000-01 – 2005-06; Warriors 2006-07; Ahmedabad Rockets (ICL) 2007-08 –
Career highlights to date: 'Becoming the highest individual scorer in Sussex's history – 335* v Leicestershire, September 2003 at Hove. Broke Duleepsinhji's record of 333 from 1930'
Cricketers particularly admired: Allan Border, Steve Waugh, Curtly Ambrose, Sachin Tendulkar
Other sports played: Hockey (WA Country), golf, tennis
Other sports followed: 'All'
Favourite band: 'No real favourites – I have a very eclectic collection'
Relaxations: 'Socialising with friends'
Extras: Attended Australian Cricket Academy. Scored 166* v Pakistan at Bulawayo 1997-98, in the process sharing with Andy Flower (100*) in the highest partnership for Zimbabwe for any wicket in Tests (277*). His international awards include Man of the Match in the second ODI v Sri Lanka at Colombo 1997-98 (111) and in the second Test v England at Trent Bridge 2000 (148*). Retired from international cricket in 2000. Scored double century (203*) and century (115) v Nottinghamshire at Trent Bridge 2001 and again (119/205*) v Surrey at Hove 2007. Joint Sussex Player of the Year (with Richard Montgomerie) 2001. Scored 335* v Leicestershire at Hove 2003, surpassing K. S. Duleepsinhji's 333 in 1930 to set a new record for the highest individual score for Sussex (and winning the Sussex Outstanding Performance of the Year Award 2003); set a new club record in August 2009, scoring 344* as Sussex amassed 742-5 dec in a County Championship match v Somerset at Taunton. Scored 214* v Warwickshire at Hove 2006, in the process sharing with Michael Yardy (159*) in a new Sussex record partnership for the third wicket (385*). Overseas player with Sussex 2001-04. His 87* against Nottinghamshire in the final Pro40 Division 1 game of 2008 helped Sussex secure the trophy. Finished top of the Sussex first-class batting averages 2008. County vice-captain for 2010. Is no longer considered an overseas player
Best batting: 344* Sussex v Somerset, Taunton 2009
Best bowling: 2-23 Zimbabweans v Lahore City, Lahore 1998-99

2009 Season

	M	Inn	NO	Runs	HS	Avg	100	50	Ct	St	Balls	Runs	Wkts	Avg	BB	5I	10M
Test																	
FC	16	27	3	800	344*	33.33	1	2	6	-	12	13	0		-	-	-
ODI																	
List A	18	16	1	673	144	44.86	1	3	5	-	0	0	0		-	-	
20/20 Int																	
20/20	10	10	2	273	80*	34.12	-	2	4	-	0	0	0		-	-	

Career Performances

	M	Inn	NO	Runs	HS	Avg	100	50	Ct	St	Balls	Runs	Wkts	Avg	BB	5I	10M
Test	19	37	4	1414	166*	42.84	3	8	10	-	119	69	0		-	-	-
FC	250	435	35	19180	344*	47.95	59	79	139	-	713	376	7	53.71	2-23	-	-
ODI	71	70	3	1818	112*	27.13	2	8	20	-	248	210	4	52.50	1-12	-	
List A	329	315	37	9982	167	35.90	13	62	102	-	351	306	7	43.71	1-9	-	
20/20 Int																	
20/20	56	51	7	1266	102*	28.77	1	7	11	-	0	0	0		-	-	

GRIFFITHS, D. A. Hampshire

Name: David Andrew Griffiths
Role: Left-hand bat, right-arm fast-medium bowler
Born: 10 September 1985, Newport, Isle of Wight
Height: 6ft **Weight:** 12st 12lbs
Nickname: Sog, Griff, Griffta, Chozza
County debut: 2006
Place in bowling averages: 64th av. 32.46
(2008 93rd av. 34.25)
Parents: Adrian Griffiths and Lizbeth Porter; Dave Porter (stepfather); Sharon Griffiths (stepmother)
Marital status: Single ('girlfriend Sophia')
Family links with cricket: 'Father captained Wales. Stepfather captained Isle of Wight. Uncles play league cricket'
Education: Sandown High School, Isle of Wight
Qualifications: Levels 1, 2 and 3 coaching
Career outside cricket: 'Coaching'

Off-season: 'In America with fast bowlers' development squad, then India in January'
Overseas tours: West of England U15 to West Indies 2001; England U19 to India 2004-05
Overseas teams played for: Melville, Perth 2007

Career highlights to date: 'Making Championship debut against Durham [2007]'
Cricket moments to forget: 'The first ball in Championship cricket – Ottis Gibson hitting me on the head'
Cricket superstitions: 'Always turn right at end of run-up'
Cricketers particularly admired: Darren Gough, Brett Lee, Brian Lara
Young players to look out for: Michael Bates and Daniel Briggs (both Hampshire)
Other sports played: Football (Isle of Wight U11-U18), rugby (IOW), 5-a-side (Hawks)
Other sports followed: Football (Manchester United), rugby league (St Helens)
Injuries: Left arm triceps – out for two weeks
Favourite band: 'Any R&B music'
Relaxations: 'Golf. Spending time with Sophia and family'
Extras: Represented England U19 2004. Southern League Young Player of the Year 2004. Took 3-13 on Twenty20 debut v Essex at The Rose Bowl 2007. Selected for the England Performance Fast Bowlng programme 2009-10
Best batting: 31* Hampshire v Surrey, Rose Bowl 2007
Best bowling: 4-46 Hampshire v Durham, Riverside 2007

2009 Season

	M	Inn	NO	Runs	HS	Avg	100	50	Ct	St	Balls	Runs	Wkts	Avg	BB	5I	10M
Test																	
FC	10	13	4	45	20*	5.00	-	-	-	-	1700	1039	32	32.46	4-48	-	-
ODI																	
List A	1	0	0	0	0	-	-	-	-	48	29	4	7.25	4-29	-		
20/20 Int																	
20/20																	

Career Performances

	M	Inn	NO	Runs	HS	Avg	100	50	Ct	St	Balls	Runs	Wkts	Avg	BB	5I	10M
Test																	
FC	17	23	8	107	31*	7.13	-	-	1	-	2591	1657	46	36.02	4-46	-	-
ODI																	
List A	4	1	1	3	3*		-	-	1	-	174	171	5	34.20	4-29	-	
20/20 Int																	
20/20	3	1	1	4	4*		-	-	-	-	42	55	3	18.33	3-13	-	

34. Geoff Boycott scored his hundredth first class century during a Test match. Which Pakistan batsman also did this?

GROENEWALD, T. D. Derbyshire

Name: Timothy (Tim) Duncan Groenewald
Role: Right-hand bat, right-arm fast-medium bowler; bowling all-rounder
Born: 10 January 1984, Pietermaritzburg, South Africa
Height: 6ft 3in **Weight:** 13st
Nickname: Groeners
County debut: 2006 (Warwickshire), 2009 (Derbyshire)
Place in batting averages: 220th av. 19.40
Place in bowling averages: 26th av. 27.08 (2008 55th av. 27.54)
Parents: Neil and Tessa
Wife and date of marriage: Michelle, 5 January 2008
Education: Maritzburg College, Natal; University of South Africa (UNISA)
Qualifications: Matric, degree (B.Comm) in Marketing
Career outside cricket: Part-time student
Off-season: 'Coaching with Maritzburg College until Christmas, playing club cricket in Durban after Christmas'
Overseas tours: Natal U15 to UK 1999; Warwickshire to Grenada 2007
Overseas teams played for: Zingari CC, Natal 1999-2005; Natal Dolphins 2002-03; KwaZulu-Natal Inland 2004-05; Rovers CC 2006
Career highlights to date: 'Getting Kevin Pietersen out in the Friends Provident semi-final [2007]. Playing Twenty20 against Gloucestershire in 2008, putting on 95 with Tony Frost in six overs to tie the game – I was 39 not out off 18 balls. Getting a career-best 6-50 for Derbyshire v Surrey, then 6-60 v Northamptonshire two weeks later'
Cricket moments to forget: 'Double relegation in 2007. Every six I've ever been hit for. First day of the 2008 season, fielding at Edgbaston – it was about -2°C. Losing to Kent in the Twenty20 quarter-final in 2008.'
Favourite sledging line: 'Steffan Jones (Derbyshire) to Garry Park (Derbyshire) as he was about to bowl to James Taylor (Leicestershire) – "Can we please shorten the pitch for the gnomes?"' [Park and Taylor each stand just 5ft 7in]
Cricketers particularly admired: Allan Donald, Steve Waugh, Hansie Cronje, Brett Lee, Andrew Flintoff
Young players to look out for: James Taylor (Leicestershire)
Other sports played: Hockey (Midlands U21 A 2003), tennis and golf ('socially')
Other sports followed: Super 14 rugby (Natal Sharks)
Injuries: 'Double stress fracture in the lower back – out for five months from October 2008 to February 2009'

Favourite band: Kings of Leon, The Killers
Relaxations: 'Golf, and fishing on the Natal south coast with the family in December.'
Extras: Leading wicket-taker at National U19 Week and represented South African Schools Colts U19. Seventh in the Sky Sports Sixes League 2007 with 20. Left Warwickshire to join Derbyshire in October 2008
Opinions on cricket: 'The one-day game is too much in favour of batsmen'
Best batting: 78 Warwickshire v Bangladesh A, Edgbaston 2008
Best bowling: 6-50 Surrey v Derbyshire, Croydon 2009

2009 Season

	M	Inn	NO	Runs	HS	Avg	100	50	Ct	St	Balls	Runs	Wkts	Avg	BB	5I	10M
Test																	
FC	9	11	1	194	50	19.40	-	1	2	-	1640	921	34	27.08	6-50	2	-
ODI																	
List A	10	8	2	68	31*	11.33	-	-	-	-	459	367	12	30.58	3-33	-	
20/20 Int																	
20/20	9	3	2	8	5*	8.00	-	-	-	-	169	219	7	31.28	2-19	-	

Career Performances

	M	Inn	NO	Runs	HS	Avg	100	50	Ct	St	Balls	Runs	Wkts	Avg	BB	5I	10M
Test																	
FC	26	32	5	562	78	20.81	-	3	13	-	3689	2050	60	34.16	6-50	3	-
ODI																	
List A	37	27	5	285	36	12.95	-	-	6	-	1213	1138	31	36.70	3-25	-	
20/20 Int																	
20/20	30	16	8	235	41	29.37	-	-	10	-	457	645	23	28.04	3-40	-	

GURNEY, H. F. Leicestershire

Name: <u>Harry</u> Frederick Gurney
Role: Right-hand bat, left-arm seam bowler
Born: 25 October 1986, Nottingham
Height: 6ft 2in **Weight:** 12st
Nickname: Gurns
County debut: 2007
Place in bowling averages: 130th av. 51.81
Parents: Jane and John
Marital status: Single
Education: Garendon High School; Loughborough Grammar School; University of Leeds
Qualifications: 9 GCSEs, 4 A-levels BA Economics
Off-season: 'Gym and indoor training, then a month in Potchefstroom, South Africa'

Overseas tours: Loughborough GS to Cape Town 2004; Leicestershire Academy/U19 to India 2005-06; Leicestershire to Sri Lanka 2007

Career highlights to date: 'First-class debut. Maiden 5-wicket haul v Surrey'

Cricket moments to forget: 'My performance in first game against first-class opposition – Yorkshire at Headingley. Bagging my first pair v Northamptonshire!'

Cricket superstitions: 'None'

Cricketers particularly admired: Glenn McGrath, Courtney Walsh, Ryan Sidebottom

Young players to look out for: Joe Root (Yorkshire)

Other sports played: 'Recreational football'

Other sports followed: Football (West Ham United)

Favourite band: Kings of Leon

Relaxations: 'Poker, reading, golf, Xbox'

Extras: Played for Bradford/Leeds UCCE 2006, 2007

Opinions on cricket: 'Feels like Twenty20 cricket may eventually replace 50-over cricket as the sole form of limited-overs cricket.'

Best batting: 24* Leicestershire v Middlesex, Leicester, 2009

Best bowling: 5-82 Leicestershire v Surrey, Leicester, 2009

2009 Season

	M	Inn	NO	Runs	HS	Avg	100	50	Ct	St	Balls	Runs	Wkts	Avg	BB	5I	10M
Test																	
FC	10	11	6	54	24*	10.80	-	-	2	-	1373	829	16	51.81	5-82	1	-
ODI																	
List A	10	1	0	0	0	0.00	-	-	-	-	345	327	3	109.00	1-16	-	
20/20 Int																	
20/20	9	0	0	0	0		-	-	2	-	162	184	8	23.00	3-21	-	

Career Performances

	M	Inn	NO	Runs	HS	Avg	100	50	Ct	St	Balls	Runs	Wkts	Avg	BB	5I	10M
Test																	
FC	11	13	7	55	24*	9.16	-	-	2	-	1589	1002	18	55.66	5-82	1	-
ODI																	
List A	10	1	0	0	0	0.00	-	-	-	-	345	327	3	109.00	1-16	-	
20/20 Int																	
20/20	9	0	0	0	0		-	-	2	-	162	184	8	23.00	3-21	-	

GUY, S. M. Yorkshire

Name: <u>Simon</u> Mark Guy
Role: Right-hand bat, wicket-keeper
Born: 17 November 1978, Rotherham
Height: 5ft 7in **Weight:** 10st 7lbs
Nickname: Rat
County debut: 2000
Parents: Darrell and Denise
Wife and date of marriage: Suzanne,
13 October 2001
Children: Isaac Simon, 15 January 2004;
Rowan Joseph, 25 March 2007

Family links with cricket: 'Father played for
Nottinghamshire and Worcestershire 2nd XI and
for Rotherham Town CC. Brothers play local
cricket for Treeton CC'
Education: Wickersley Comprehensive School
Qualifications: GNVQ in Leisure and Recreation, Level 3 coaching
Overseas tours: Yorkshire to South Africa 1999, 2001, to Grenada 2002
Overseas teams played for: Orange CYMS, NSW 1999-2000
Career highlights to date: 'Playing the last ever County Championship game at
Southampton [Northlands Road in 2000] and winning off the last ball with 13
Yorkshire and past Yorkshire men on the pitch at the same time'
Cricket moments to forget: 'On my debut against the Zimbabweans, smashing
a door after getting out – but I still say it was an accident'
Cricket superstitions: 'Just a lot of routines'
Cricketers particularly admired: Jack Russell, Darren Lehmann
Young players to look out for: Joe Root
Other sports played: 'I like to play all sports', rugby (played for South Yorkshire
and Yorkshire)
Other sports followed: Rugby (Rotherham RUFC), 'Treeton Welfare CC, where all
my family play'
Favourite band: My Chemical Romance
Relaxations: 'Playing all sports, socialising with friends, watching cartoons,
and eating a lot'
Extras: Topped Yorkshire 2nd XI batting averages 1998 (106.00). Awarded 2nd XI
cap 2000. Took five catches in an innings for first time for Yorkshire 1st XI v Surrey
at Scarborough 2000. Released at the end of the 2009 season
Opinions on cricket: 'The division structure has improved the standard of
competitiveness of the county championship.'
Best batting: 52* Yorkshire v Durham, Headingley 2006

2009 Season

	M	Inn	NO	Runs	HS	Avg	100	50	Ct	St	Balls	Runs	Wkts	Avg	BB	5I	10M
Test																	
FC																	
ODI																	
List A	5	4	1	22	22	7.33	-	-	9	3	0	0	0			-	-
20/20 Int																	
20/20	6	4	1	33	13	11.00	-	-	1	-	0	0	0			-	-

Career Performances

	M	Inn	NO	Runs	HS	Avg	100	50	Ct	St	Balls	Runs	Wkts	Avg	BB	5I	10M
Test																	
FC	36	50	6	727	52*	16.52	-	1	97	12	24	8	0		-	-	-
ODI																	
List A	31	23	4	282	40	14.84	-	-	32	10	0	0	0			-	-
20/20 Int																	
20/20	10	6	1	44	13	8.80	-	-	2	-	0	0	0			-	-

HAGGETT, C. J.   Somerset

Name: Calum John Haggett
Role: Left-hand bat, right-arm medium bowler;
all-rounder
Born: 30 October 1990, Taunton, Somerset
Height: 6ft 5in
County debut: No first team appearance
Family links with cricket: Father and younger
brother both involved with Ashcott and Shapwick CC
(West of England Premier League)
Education: Millfield School
Overseas tours: England U19 to Bangladesh 2009
Extras: Somerset Academy 2004-09. Represented
Somerset in age-group sides from the age of 13. A
stress fracture of the lower back saw him out for the
whole of the 2007 season, and restricted his bowling
in 2008. Somerset 2nd XI 2009. Was selected for 2010 U19 World Cup in New
Zealand, but had to withdraw after taking medical advice. Signed for Somerset
until the end of the 2010 season in July 2009

HALES, A. D. — Nottinghamshire

Name: Alexander (<u>Alex</u>) Daniel Hales
Role: Right-hand bat, off-spin bowler, occasional wicket-keeper
Born: 3 January 1989, Hillingdon, Middlesex
Height: 6ft 5in **Weight:** 13st 6lbs
Nickname: Halesy, Trigg
County debut: 2008
Place in batting averages: 77th av. 40.63
Parents: Gary and Lisa
Marital status: Single
Education: Chesham High School, Chesham, Buckinghamshire
Qualifications: 10 GCSEs, 3 AS-levels
Overseas tours: London County CC to Cape Town 2006; MCC YC to St Kitts and Nevis 2007
Overseas teams played for: Pennant Hills District CC, Sydney 2007
Cricket moments to forget: 'Dropping a sitter against Kent 2nd XI for MCC Young Cricketers – if I had held the catch we would have won the game and qualified for the semi-finals!'
Cricket superstitions: 'Always put my left pad on before my right one'
Cricketers particularly admired: Ian Bell, Nick Lines, Vinnie Fazio
Other sports played: 'Play a bit of football in the winter for my local team. Used to play county tennis and table tennis'
Other sports followed: Football (Arsenal)
Favourite band: Oasis
Relaxations: 'Enjoy playing poker and socialising with mates'
Extras: Once scored 52 in one over on the Lord's Nursery ground – over included eight sixes and a four plus three no-balls for an overall total of 55. Played for Buckinghamshire in Minor Counties competitions 2006, 2007. Played for MCC YC 2006, 2007. NBC Denis Compton Award for the most promising young Nottinghamshire player 2008. Scored an 85-ball century against Ireland in Friends Provident Trophy match 2009. Member of England Performance Programme squad 2009-10. 'Grandfather once took Rod Laver to five sets at Wimbledon'
Best batting: 78 Nottinghamshire v Durham, Riverside 2009
Best bowling: 2-63 Nottinghamshire v Yorkshire, Trent Bridge 2009

2009 Season

	M	Inn	NO	Runs	HS	Avg	100	50	Ct	St	Balls	Runs	Wkts	Avg	BB	5I	10M
Test																	
FC	7	12	1	447	78	40.63	-	4	3	-	240	140	3	46.66	2-63	-	-
ODI																	
List A	13	13	1	427	150*	35.58	2	1	3	-	0	0	0		-	-	
20/20 Int																	
20/20	6	6	0	49	15	8.16	-	-	3	-	0	0	0		-	-	

Career Performances

	M	Inn	NO	Runs	HS	Avg	100	50	Ct	St	Balls	Runs	Wkts	Avg	BB	5I	10M
Test																	
FC	8	12	1	447	78	0.63	-	4	3	-	240	140	3	46.66	2-63	-	-
ODI																	
List A	14	13	1	427	150*	35.58	2	1	3	-	0	0	0		-	-	
20/20 Int																	
20/20	6	6	0	49	15	8.16	-	-	3	-	0	0	0		-	-	

HALL, A. J.   Northamptonshire

Name: <u>Andrew</u> James Hall
Role: Right-hand bat, right-arm
fast-medium bowler; all-rounder
Born: 31 July 1975, Johannesburg,
South Africa
Height: 6ft **Weight:** 14st
Nickname: Hally
County debut: 2003 (Worcestershire),
2005 (Kent), 2008 (Northamptonshire)
County cap: 2003 (Worcestershire colours),
2005 (Kent), 2009 (Northamptonshire)
Test debut: 2001-02
ODI debut: 1998-99
Twenty20 Int debut: 2005-06
1000 runs in a season: 1
Place in batting averages: 34th av. 50.47 (2008 106th av. 32.12)
Place in bowling averages: 11th av. 22.77 (2008 19th av. 22.29)
Parents: John and Frances
Wife and date of marriage: Leanie, 2 September 2000
Education: Hoërskool Alberton
Qualifications: Level 3 coaching

Overseas tours: South Africa to Sri Lanka (Singer Triangular Series) 2000, to Australia (Super Challenge) 2000, to Singapore (Godrej Singapore Challenge) 2000-01, to Kenya (ICC Knockout Trophy) 2000-01, to Bangladesh (TVS Cup) 2003, to England 2003, to Pakistan 2003-04, to India 2004-05, to West Indies 2004-05, to India (one-day series) 2005-06, to Australia 2005-06 (VB Series), to Sri Lanka 2006, to India (ICC Champions Trophy) 2006-07, to West Indies (World Cup) 2006-07, to Ireland (one-day series v India) 2007; South Africa A to Zimbabwe 2007-08

Overseas teams played for: Transvaal/Gauteng 1994-95 – 2000-01; Easterns 2001-02 – 2003-04; Lions 2004-05 – 2005-06; Dolphins 2006-07; Chandigarh Lions (ICL) 2007-08 –

Career highlights to date: 'Scoring 163 against India in Kanpur, and taking 5-18 against England in the 2007 World Cup'

Cricket moments to forget: 'Losing to Australia in the World Cup semi-final, 2007'

Cricketers particularly admired: Ray Jennings, Clive Rice, Jimmy Cook

Young players to look out for: Alex Wakely (Northamptonshire)

Other sports played: Golf (12 handicap)

Other sports followed: Formula One (Ferrari), rugby (Golden Lions)

Favourite band: Crowded House

Relaxations: 'Movies and shopping with Leanie'

Extras: Played for South Africa Academy 1997. Was shot in the hand and face by a mugger in Johannesburg in 1999 and was car-jacked in 2002. Man of the Match in the tied second indoor ODI v Australia at Melbourne 2000 (37/2-8). His other international awards include Man of the Match in the first Test v India at Kanpur 2004-05 (163), in the fifth ODI v New Zealand at Centurion 2005-06 (4-23) and v England at Bridgetown in the 2006-07 World Cup (5-18). One of *South African Cricket Annual*'s five Cricketers of the Year 2002. His South African domestic awards include Man of the SuperSport Series 2002-03 and Man of the Match in the final (6-77/5-22). An overseas player with Worcestershire 2003-04. Man of the Match v Lancashire in the C&G semi-final at Worcester 2003. An overseas player with Kent 2005-07. Retired from international cricket in late summer 2007. Left Kent at the end of the 2007 season and joined Northamptonshire for 2008. Took 20 wickets in Twenty20 matches at a fairly economical rate. Is no longer considered an overseas player

Best batting: 163 South Africa v India, Kanpur 2004-05

Best bowling: 6-77 Easterns v Western Province, Benoni 2002-03

2009 Season

	M	Inn	NO	Runs	HS	Avg	100	50	Ct	St	Balls	Runs	Wkts	Avg	BB	5I	10M
Test																	
FC	16	25	2	1161	159	50.47	2	6	16	-	1862	911	40	22.77	5-29	1	-
ODI																	
List A	11	10	2	256	104*	32.00	1	1	3	-	380	298	8	37.25	4-14	-	
20/20 Int																	
20/20	12	8	2	111	39*	18.50	-	-	5	-	247	267	14	19.07	4-19	-	

Career Performances

	M	Inn	NO	Runs	HS	Avg	100	50	Ct	St	Balls	Runs	Wkts	Avg	BB	5I	10M
Test	21	33	4	760	163	26.20	1	3	16	-	3001	1617	45	35.93	3-1	-	-
FC	155	223	29	6830	163	35.20	7	44	131	-	24549	11633	450	25.85	6-77	15	1
ODI	88	56	13	905	81	21.04	-	3	29	-	3341	2515	95	26.47	5-18	1	
List A	261	204	36	5035	129*	29.97	6	27	74	-	10562	8018	296	27.08	5-18	1	
20/20 Int	2	1	0	11	11	11.00	-	-	-	-	48	60	3	20.00	3-22	-	
20/20	52	45	5	940	66*	23.50	-	4	17	-	1076	1353	71	19.05	6-21	2	

HAMILTON-BROWN, R. J. Surrey

Name: Rory James Hamilton-Brown
Role: Right-hand bat, right-arm
off-spin bowler; county captain
Born: 3 September 1987, London
Height: 6ft **Weight:** 13st 7lbs
Nickname: Bear, Stewi, RHB
County debut: 2005 (Surrey), 2008 (Sussex)
Place in batting averages: 30th av. 51.83
Parents: Roger and Holly
Marital status: Single
Family links with cricket: 'Dad played for
Warwickshire'
Education: Millfield School
Qualifications: 9 GCSEs, 3 A-levels
Overseas tours: England U16 to South Africa;
England U19 to Bangladesh 2005-06, to Sri Lanka (U19 World Cup) 2005-06;
England Performance Programme squad to South Africa 2009
Career highlights to date: 'Facing Mushtaq Ahmed on debut against Sussex in the
Totesport League'
Cricket moments to forget: 'Dropping a very simple catch which single-handedly
meant Surrey U19 were knocked out of a national competition'
Cricket superstitions: 'None'
Cricketers particularly admired: Damien Martyn, Mark Ramprakash, Alec Stewart
Young players to look out for: Billy Godleman (Essex), Ben Wright (Glamorgan)
Other sports played: Rugby (England U16, England Junior National Academy)
Other sports followed: Football (Birmingham City)
Favourite band: Donell Jones, Trey Songz
Relaxations: 'Relaxing with friends'
Extras: Captained England U15. *Daily Telegraph* Bunbury Scholar (Batsman) 2003.
Broke Millfield batting record 2004 at 16. Made 2nd XI Championship debut 2004,
scoring 43 and 84 v Sussex 2nd XI at Hove. Represented England U19 2006 and (as

captain) 2007. Left Surrey at the end of the 2007 season and joined Sussex for 2008.
Released by Sussex in December 2009, he rejoined Surrey for 2010 where he will be
the county's youngest captain since 21-year-old George Strachan in 1872. Member of
the England Performance Programme squad 2009-10

Best batting: 171* Sussex v Yorkshire, Hove 2009
Best bowling: 2-49 Sussex v Yorkshire, Hove 2009

2009 Season

	M	Inn	NO	Runs	HS	Avg	100	50	Ct	St	Balls	Runs	Wkts	Avg	BB	5I	10M
Test																	
FC	5	8	2	311	171*	51.83	2	-	5	-		222	109	3	36.33	2-49	-	-
ODI																	
List A	19	17	1	381	49	23.81	-	-	6	-		467	460	11	41.81	3-37	-
20/20 Int																	
20/20	13	12	1	227	69*	20.63	-	1	9	-		96	108	9	12.00	4-15	-

Career Performances

	M	Inn	NO	Runs	HS	Avg	100	50	Ct	St	Balls	Runs	Wkts	Avg	BB	5I	10M
Test																	
FC	8	13	2	433	171*	39.36	2	1	6	-		359	194	6	32.33	2-49	-	-
ODI																	
List A	37	30	2	542	49	19.35	-	-	12	-		870	817	24	34.04	3-28	-
20/20 Int																	
20/20	25	22	1	314	69*	14.95	-	1	10	-		204	250	15	16.66	4-15	-

HANNON-DALBY, O. J.   Yorkshire

Name: <u>Oliver</u> James Hannon-Dalby
Role: Left-hand bat, right-arm
fast-medium bowler
Born: 20 June 1989, Halifax
Height: 6ft 7in **Weight:** 13st 8lbs
Nickname: Bunse, Dave, Shaggy
County debut: 2008
Parents: Sally Hannon and Stephen Dalby
Marital status: Single
Family links with cricket: 'Whole family on
both sides play and support cricket'
Education: The Brooksbank School Sports College
and Sixth Form; Leeds Metropolitan University
Qualifications: 13 GCSEs, 3 A-levels,
1 NVQ, Community Sports Leader Award and
Higher Sports Leader Award

Career outside cricket: 'Teacher, coach'
Off-season: 'Studying at Leeds Met'
Overseas tours: Yorkshire Schools Cricket Association to Cape Town 2007; Yorkshire to Abu Dhabi 2008
Overseas teams played for: St Andrews, Bloemfontein 2008; Old Andreans, Bloemfontein 2008
Career highlights to date: 'Taking 6-32 v Scotland for Yorkshire 2nd XI 2007. First-class debut, May 2008'
Cricket moments to forget: 'Jersey Cricket Festival final 2005'
Cricket superstitions: 'None'
Cricketers particularly admired: Fred Hemmingway, Peter Blake, Brett Lee
Young players to look out for: Gary Ballance and Johnny Bairstow (both Yorkshire)
Other sports played: Football (Hebden Bridge Saints, Copley United)
Other sports followed: Football (Leeds United), 'all England teams'
Favourite band: Stone Roses, Arctic Monkeys, Oasis, The Verve
Relaxations: 'Snooker, guitar playing, golf'
Extras: Ian Steen Memorial Award 2004 for Most Improved U15 Player. YCB Alec Holdsworth U17 Bowling Award 2006. YCCSA Young Player of the Year 2007. Did not make a first-team appearance in 2009. Attended Darren Lehmann Academy in Adelaide 2009
Best batting: 1 Yorkshire v Surrey, The Oval 2008
Best bowling: 1-58 Yorkshire v Surrey, The Oval 2008

2009 Season (Did not make any first-class or one-day appearances)

Career Performances

	M	Inn	NO	Runs	HS	Avg	100	50	Ct	St	Balls	Runs	Wkts	Avg	BB	5I	10M
Test																	
FC	1	1	0	1	1	1.00	-	-	-	-	174	114	1	114.00	1-58	-	-
ODI																	
List A																		
20/20 Int																		
20/20																		

---

35. In which year did Wasim Akram take his 300th Test wicket at the Oval?

HARDINGES, M. A.   Essex

Name: <u>Mark</u> Andrew Hardinges
Role: Right-hand bat, right-arm
fast-medium bowler
Born: 5 February 1978, Gloucester
Height: 6ft 1in **Weight:** 13st 7lbs
Nickname: Dinges
County debut: 1999 (Gloucestershire)
County cap: 2004 (Gloucestershire)
Place in batting averages: (2008 74th av. 38.28)
Place in bowling averages: (2008 111th av. 36.60)
Parents: David and Jean
Marital status: Single
Family links with cricket: 'Brother and father
played club cricket'
Education: Malvern College; Bath University
Qualifications: 10 GCSEs, 3 A-levels, BSc (Hons) Economics and Politics
Overseas tours: Malvern College to South Africa 1996; Gloucestershire to South
Africa 1999, 2000
Overseas teams played for: Newtown and Chilwell, Geelong, Australia 1997
Career highlights to date: 'Norwich Union debut v Notts 2001 – scored 65 and
set [then] domestic one-day seventh-wicket partnership record (164) with J. Snape.
Also Lord's final v Surrey'
Cricket moments to forget: 'Glos v Somerset [Norwich Union 2001] – bowled three
overs for 30 and was run out for 0 on Sky TV'
Cricketers particularly admired: Kim Barnett, Steve Waugh, Mark Alleyne
Other sports played: Golf, tennis (Gloucester U14), football (university first team)
Other sports followed: Football (Tottenham Hotspur)
Relaxations: Golf
Extras: Represented British Universities 2000. C&G Man of the Match award for his
4-19 v Shropshire at Shrewsbury School 2002. Scored maiden one-day century (111*)
v Lancashire at Old Trafford in the totesport League 2005, in the process sharing with
Ramnaresh Sarwan (118*) in a new competition record fifth-wicket partnership
(221*). Released by Gloucestershire at the end of September 2008, he signed for Essex
in May 2009 to play in the Twenty20 competition
Best batting: 172 Gloucestershire v OUCCE, The Parks 2002
Best bowling: 5-51 Gloucestershire v Kent, Maidstone 2005

2009 Season

	M	Inn	NO	Runs	HS	Avg	100	50	Ct	St	Balls	Runs	Wkts	Avg	BB	5I	10M
Test																	
FC																	
ODI																	
List A																	
20/20 Int																	
20/20	2	1	1	14	14*	-	-	-	-	-	30	43	2	21.50	2-12	-	

Career Performances

	M	Inn	NO	Runs	HS	Avg	100	50	Ct	St	Balls	Runs	Wkts	Avg	BB	5I	10M
Test																	
FC	50	76	9	1778	172	26.53	4	6	26	-	6396	3851	95	40.53	5-51	1	-
ODI																	
List A	85	74	14	1318	111*	21.96	1	7	32	-	2996	2744	77	35.63	4-19	-	
20/20 Int																	
20/20	45	32	7	543	94*	21.72	-	2	10	-	671	951	35	27.17	4-30	-	

HARINATH, A.   Surrey

Name: Arun Harinath
Role: Left-hand bat, off-spin bowler
Born: 26 March 1987, Carshalton, Surrey
Height: 5ft 11in **Weight:** 11st 10lbs
Nickname: The Baron
County debut: 2009
Place in batting averages: 191st av. 24.33
Parents: Mala and Suppiah
Marital status: Single
Family links with cricket: Younger brother
Muhunthan has been awarded an Emerging Player
contract with Surrey for 2010
Education: Tiffin Boys Grammar School;
Loughborough University
Overseas tours: Surrey U19 to Sri Lanka 2002, to
Cape Town 2005; Surrey Academy to Perth 2004; England U17 to Netherlands 2004
Overseas teams played for: Randwick Petersham, Sydney 2005-06
Cricket moments to forget: 'Dropping Samit Patel against Nottinghamshire
Seconds at Sutton'
Cricketers particularly admired: Steve Waugh, Michael Hussey, Justin Langer,
Brian Lara, Rahul Dravid, Mohammad Yousuf
Young players to look out for: Muhunthan Harinath (Surrey)

Other sports played: Rugby, badminton
Other sports followed: Rugby (Bath), NFL (Atlanta Falcons)
Relaxations: 'Films and music mainly'
Extras: Made 2nd XI Championship debut 2003. Played for LUCCE 2007
Opinions on cricket: 'The harder you work, the more you will get out of the game.'
Best batting: 69 LUCCE v Worcestershire, Worcester 2007

2009 Season

	M	Inn	NO	Runs	HS	Avg	100	50	Ct	St	Balls	Runs	Wkts	Avg	BB	5I	10M
Test																	
FC	6	9	0	219	57	24.33	-	1	-	-	24	18	0		-	-	-
ODI																	
List A	1	1	1	21	21*		-	-	-	-	0	0	0		-	-	
20/20 Int																	
20/20																	

Career Performances

	M	Inn	NO	Runs	HS	Avg	100	50	Ct	St	Balls	Runs	Wkts	Avg	BB	5I	10M
Test																		
FC	10	15	0	380	69	25.33	-	3	4	-	24	18	0		-	-	-
ODI																	
List A	1	1	1	21	21*		-	-	-	-	0	0	0		-	-	
20/20 Int																	
20/20																	

HARINATH, M.   Surrey

Name: Muhunthan Harinath
Role: Right-hand bat, right-arm leg-break bowler
Born: 31 May 1991, Carshalton, Surrey
Nickname: Muzza
County debut: No first-team appearance
Parents: Mala and Suppiah
Family links with cricket: Older brother Arun plays for Surrey
Cricketers particularly admired: Shivnarine Chanderpaul
Other sports played: Rugby
Relaxations: 'Socialising'
Extras: Played club cricket for Sutton CC. Surrey Academy 2009. Awarded a 12-month Emerging Player contract in October 2009

Name: <u>Ben</u> William Harmison
Role: Left-hand bat, right-arm fast-medium bowler; all-rounder
Born: 9 January 1986, Ashington, Northumberland
Height: 6ft 5in **Weight:** 14st
Nickname: Harmy
County debut: 2005 (one-day), 2006 (first-class)
Place in batting averages: (2008 225th av. 16.52)
Place in bowling averages: (2008 52nd av. 16.27)
Parents: Jimmy and Margaret
Marital status: Single
Family links with cricket: Brother Stephen plays for Durham and England. Father Jim and brother James play league cricket for Ashington CC
Education: Ashington High School
Overseas tours: England U19 to Bangladesh (U19 World Cup) 2003-04, to India 2004-05; Durham to India 2005
Career highlights to date: 'Two hundreds in my first two [first-class] games for Durham'
Cricket moments to forget: 'Getting a first-baller v Bangladesh A in a one-dayer'
Cricket superstitions: 'Left pad first'
Cricketers particularly admired: Andrew Flintoff
Young players to look out for: Moeen Ali (Worcestershire) 'and the Durham Academy lads'
Other sports played: Golf, fishing, football
Other sports followed: Football (Newcastle United)
Relaxations: 'Fishing, listening to music'
Extras: NBC Denis Compton Award for the most promising young Durham player 2004, 2006, 2008. Represented England U19 2005. Scored century (110) on first-class debut v OUCCE at The Parks 2006 and another (105) in his next first-class match v West Indies A at Riverside 2006
Best batting: 110 Durham v OUCCE, The Parks 2006
Best bowling: 4-27 Durham v Surrey, Guildford 2008

2009 Season

	M	Inn	NO	Runs	HS	Avg	100	50	Ct	St	Balls	Runs	Wkts	Avg	BB	5I	10M
Test																	
FC	1	1	0	0	0	0.00	-	-	1	-	36	19	0		-	-	-
ODI																	
List A	8	8	0	246	67	30.75	-	1	4	-	222	253	7	36.14	2-29	-	
20/20 Int																	
20/20	7	4	2	25	14*	12.50	-	-	1	-	144	180	14	12.85	3-20	-	

Career Performances

	M	Inn	NO	Runs	HS	Avg	100	50	Ct	St	Balls	Runs	Wkts	Avg	BB	5I	10M
Test																	
FC	31	52	5	1202	110	25.57	3	5	23	-	1037	742	19	39.05	4-27	-	-
ODI																	
List A	36	32	3	627	67	21.62	-	2	14	-	607	588	18	32.66	3-43	-	
20/20 Int																	
20/20	19	11	4	66	21	9.42	-	-	7	-	186	243	15	16.20	3-20	-	

HARMISON, S. J. Durham

Name: Stephen James Harmison
Role: Right-hand bat, right-arm
fast bowler
Born: 23 October 1978, Ashington, Northumberland
Height: 6ft 4in **Weight:** 14st
Nickname: Harmy
County debut: 1996
County cap: 1999
Test debut: 2002
ODI debut: 2002-03
Twenty20 Int debut: 2005
50 wickets in a season: 6
Place in batting averages: (2008 210th av. 19.11)
Place in bowling averages: 15th av. 23.85
(2008 23rd av. 22.86)
Parents: Jimmy and Margaret
Wife and date of marriage: Hayley, 8 October 1999
Children: Emily Alice, 1 June 1999; Abbie Meg; Isabel Grace, May 2006
Family links with cricket: Brother James has played for Northumberland. Brother Ben played for England U19 and is now at Durham. Father Jim plays league cricket for Ashington CC
Education: Ashington High School

Overseas tours: England U19 to Pakistan 1996-97; England A to Zimbabwe and South Africa 1998-99; ECB National Academy to Australia 2001-02; England to Australia 2002-03, to Africa (World Cup) 2002-03, to Bangladesh 2003-04, to West Indies 2003-04, to South Africa 2004-05, to Pakistan 2005-06, to India 2005-06, to India (ICC Champions Trophy) 2006-07, to Australia 2006-07, to Sri Lanka 2007-08, to New Zealand 2007-08, to India (Test and one-day series) 2008-09, to West Indies (Test and one-day series) 2008-09; ICC World XI to Australia (Super Series) 2005-06
Overseas teams played for: Highveld Lions, South Africa 2007-08
Cricketers particularly admired: David Boon, Courtney Walsh
Other sports played: Football (for Ashington in the Northern League), golf, snooker
Other sports followed: Football (Newcastle United)
Relaxations: Spending time with family
Extras: Man of the [Test] Series v West Indies 2003-04 (23 wickets at 14.86, including 7-12 at Kingston) and England's Man of the [Test] Series v New Zealand 2004 (21 wickets at 22.09). Had match figures of 9-121 (6-46/3-75) in the fourth Test v West Indies at The Oval 2004 to go to the top of the PricewaterhouseCoopers ratings for Test bowlers. His other international awards include Man of the Match in the second Test v Pakistan at Old Trafford 2006 (6-19/5-57). Became second England bowler (after James Anderson) to take an ODI hat-trick (Kaif, Balaji, Nehra), v India at Trent Bridge in the NatWest Challenge 2004. One of *Wisden*'s Five Cricketers of the Year 2005. Became first bowler to take a first-class hat-trick for Durham (Pipe, Mason, Wigley) v Worcestershire at Riverside 2005. Appointed MBE in 2006 New Year Honours as part of 2005 Ashes-winning England team. Retired from ODI cricket in December 2006 – was enticed back by (then England captain) Kevin Pietersen in 2008. Part of England squad which regained the Ashes 2009
Best batting: 49* England v South Africa, The Oval 2008
Best bowling: 7-12 England v West Indies, Kingston 2003-04

2009 Season

	M	Inn	NO	Runs	HS	Avg	100	50	Ct	St	Balls	Runs	Wkts	Avg	BB	5I	10M
Test	2	3	2	31	19*	31.00	-	-	-	-		258	167	5	33.40	3-54	-	-
FC	17	15	5	79	25*	7.90	-	-	2	-	3080	1503	63	23.85	6-20	4	-
ODI																	
List A	5	4	4	5	3*	-	-	-	1	-	246	254	4	63.50	1-44	-	
20/20 Int																	
20/20	1	1	0	0	0	0.00	-	-	-	-	24	31	0		-	-	

Career Performances

	M	Inn	NO	Runs	HS	Avg	100	50	Ct	St	Balls	Runs	Wkts	Avg	BB	5I	10M
Test	63	86	23	743	49*	11.79	-	-	7	-	13375	7192	226	31.82	7-12	8	1
FC	189	246	68	1776	49*	9.97	-	-	27	-	36485	19032	679	28.02	7-12	26	1
ODI	58	25	14	91	18*	8.27	-	-	10	-	2899	2481	76	32.64	5-33	1	
List A	140	66	34	259	25*	8.09	-	-	22	-	6760	5595	182	30.74	5-33	1	
20/20 Int	2	0	0	0	0	-	-	-	1	-	39	42	1	42.00	1-13	-	
20/20	16	4	0	11	6	2.75	-	-	3	-	307	385	15	25.66	4-38	-	

HARRIS, A. J. Leicestershire

Name: <u>Andrew</u> James Harris
Role: Right-hand bat, right-arm
fast-medium bowler
Born: 26 June 1973, Ashton-under-Lyne, Lancashire
Height: 6ft **Weight:** 11st 9lbs
Nickname: AJ, Honest
County debut: 1994 (Derbyshire),
2000 (Nottinghamshire), 2009 (Leicestershire)
County cap: 1996 (Derbyshire),
2000 (Nottinghamshire)
Benefit: 2008 (Nottinghamshire)
50 wickets in a season: 2
Place in bowling averages: 107th av. 41.11
Parents: Norman (deceased) and Joyce
Wife and date of marriage: Kate, 7 October 2000
Children: Jacob Alexander, 28 August 2002
Education: Hadfield Comprehensive School; Glossopdale Community College
Qualifications: 6 GCSEs, 1 A-level
Overseas tours: England A to Australia 1996-97
Overseas teams played for: Ginninderra West Belconnen, Australian Capital
Territory 1992-93; Victoria University of Wellington CC, New Zealand 1997-98
Cricket superstitions: 'None'
Cricketers particularly admired: Merv Hughes, Allan Donald
Other sports played: Golf, snooker, football
Other sports followed: Football (Man City)
Relaxations: 'Good food, good wine and the odd game of golf'
Extras: Nottinghamshire Player of the Year 2002. Had the misfortune to be 'timed
out' v Durham UCCE at Trent Bridge 2003 (was suffering from groin injury). On loan
at Worcestershire for part of the 2008 season. Released by Nottinghamshire September
2008. Signed for Leicestershire for the 2009 season, extending his contract by a further
year in October 2009
Best batting: 41* Nottinghamshire v Northamptonshire, Northampton 2002
Best bowling: 7-54 Nottinghamshire v Northamptonshire, Trent Bridge 2002

2009 Season

	M	Inn	NO	Runs	HS	Avg	100	50	Ct	St	Balls	Runs	Wkts	Avg	BB	5I	10M
Test																	
FC	16	19	3	143	22*	8.93	-	-	-	-	2371	1439	35	41.11	5-26	1	-
ODI																	
List A	4	2	1	7	5*	7.00	-	-	-	-	168	161	4	40.25	1-25	-	
20/20 Int																	
20/20	6	0	0	0	0		-	-	-	-	107	138	7	19.71	2-26	-	

Career Performances

	M	Inn	NO	Runs	HS	Avg	100	50	Ct	St	Balls	Runs	Wkts	Avg	BB	5I	10M
Test																	
FC	143	190	46	1226	41*	8.51	-	-	36	-	23874	14348	442	32.46	7-54	17	3
ODI																	
List A	149	57	25	224	34	7.00	-	-	28	-	6610	5582	194	28.77	5-35	1	
20/20 Int																	
20/20	29	7	4	12	6*	4.00	-	-	4	-	524	737	28	26.32	2-13	-	

HARRIS, J. A. R. Glamorgan

Name: James Alexander Russell Harris
Role: Right-hand bat, right-arm fast-medium bowler; all-rounder
Born: 16 May 1990, Morriston, Swansea
Height: 6ft 1in **Weight:** 12st
Nickname: Bones
County debut: 2007
Place in batting averages: 218th av. 19.69 (2008 168th av. 23.85)
Place in bowling averages: 80th av. 34.83 (2008 95th av. 32.90)
Parents: Helen and Russ
Marital status: Single
Family links with cricket: 'Dad played for British Universities'
Education: Pontarddulais Comprehensive; Gorseinon College
Qualifications: 9 GCSEs, 3 A-levels
Career outside cricket: 'Entrepreneur'
Off-season: 'On a month-long physical training camp with England's young seamers in Florida before Christmas, and 10 days at Dennis Lillee's bowling academy in Chennai in January'
Overseas tours: West of England U15 to West Indies 2004-05 (c); England U16 to South Africa 2005-06 (c); England Performance Programme to India 2007-08; England U19 to Malaysia (U19 World Cup) 2007-08, to South Africa 2009.
Career highlights to date: 'Taking 12 wickets in a match May 2007, becoming the youngest player in Championship history to do so' (see *Extras*)
Cricket moments to forget: 'Any weak half-volleys I reel off'
Cricket superstitions: 'Left before right – shoes, pads, gloves etc.'
Cricketers particularly admired: Glenn McGrath, Ricky Ponting, Jason Gillespie, Courtney Walsh, Jacques Kallis
Young players to look out for: Tom Maynard, Ben Wright and Will Bragg (all Glamorgan)

Other sports played: Golf 'off about 10-14 handicap, which will improve if I can learn how to putt', snooker, football
Other sports followed: Football (Manchester City), golf
Favourite band: The Killers, Daughtry
Relaxations: 'Music, playing golf '
Extras: ESCA Bunbury Scholarship 2005. Signed professional contract aged 16 years 9 days. Youngest Glamorgan player to take a Championship wicket, v Nottinghamshire at Trent Bridge 2007 aged 16 years 351 days. Youngest player in Championship history to take ten wickets in a match – 7-66/5-52 v Gloucestershire at Bristol 2007 on only his second first-class appearance, aged 17 years 3 days. Youngest Glamorgan player to score a Championship fifty – 87* v Nottinghamshire at Swansea 2007. Represented England U19 2007. Glamorgan Young Player of the Year 2007, BBC Wales Young Sports Personality of the Year 2007. NBC Denis Compton Award for the most promising young Glamorgan player 2007, 2008, 2009. Selected for the England Performance Fast Bowlng programme 2009-10
Opinions on cricket: 'The re-introduction of the Sunday League will be a good thing, and get the crowds back in. The new system of three competitions will make the domestic system easier to understand for the public.'
Best batting: 87* Glamorgan v Nottinghamshire, Swansea 2007
Best bowling: 7-66 Glamorgan v Gloucestershire, Bristol 2007

2009 Season

	M	Inn	NO	Runs	HS	Avg	100	50	Ct	St	Balls	Runs	Wkts	Avg	BB	5I	10M
Test																	
FC	14	16	3	256	76*	19.69	-	1	1	-	2636	1498	43	34.83	4-69	-	-
ODI																	
List A	9	6	0	54	21	9.00	-	-	1	-	413	340	7	48.57	2-44	-	
20/20 Int																	
20/20	5	4	2	21	11	10.50	-	-	1	-	96	105	6	17.50	4-23	-	

Career Performances

	M	Inn	NO	Runs	HS	Avg	100	50	Ct	St	Balls	Runs	Wkts	Avg	BB	5I	10M
Test																	
FC	28	39	7	619	87*	19.34	-	2	5	-	4779	2671	87	30.70	7-66	2	1
ODI																	
List A	18	13	1	97	21	8.08	-	-	4	-	761	629	23	27.34	4-48	-	
20/20 Int																	
20/20	9	5	2	29	11	9.66	-	-	2	-	156	194	10	19.40	4-23	-	

Name: <u>Ryan</u> James Harris
Role: Right-hand bat, right-arm fast-medium bowler
Born: 11 October 1979, Nowra, New South Wales, Australia
Height: 5ft 10in
Nickname: Ryano
County debut: 2009 (Surrey)
Overseas teams played for: South Australia (Southern Redbacks) 2001-02 – 2007-08; Queensland 2008-09; Deccan Chargers (IPL) 2008-09
Extras: Signed by Sussex in 2008 but played only one game after it was found he was not an England-qualified player. Appeared for Australia in one-day international January 2009. Spent short period with Surrey during the 2009 season. Signed for Deccan Chargers as an 'uncapped player' at the request of head coach Darren Lehmann. Joined Yorkshire as overseas player for 2010
Best batting: 94 Northamptonshire v Surrey, Northampton 2009
Best bowling: 7-108 South Australia v Tasmania, Adelaide 2008

2009 Season

	M	Inn	NO	Runs	HS	Avg	100	50	Ct	St	Balls	Runs	Wkts	Avg	BB	5I	10M
Test																	
FC	2	2	0	98	94	49.00	-	1	1	-	203	135	3	45.00	2-66	-	-
ODI																	
List A																	
20/20 Int																	
20/20																	

Career Performances

	M	Inn	NO	Runs	HS	Avg	100	50	Ct	St	Balls	Runs	Wkts	Avg	BB	5I	10M
Test																	
FC	37	63	7	1063	94	18.98	-	5	17	-	6716	3524	107	32.93	7-108	2	-
ODI	1	1	0	7	7	7.00	-	-	-	-	60	54	1	54.00	1-54	-	
List A	54	34	11	339	39	14.73	-	-	23	-	2565	2103	59	35.64	5-58	1	
20/20 Int																	
20/20	21	15	7	101	31	12.62	-	-	7	-	462	527	24	21.95	3-26	-	

HARRISON, D. S.   Glamorgan

Name: <u>David</u> Stuart Harrison
Role: Right-hand bat, right-arm
fast-medium bowler
Born: 31 July 1981, Newport, Gwent
Height: 6ft 4in **Weight:** 16st
Nickname: Harry, Hazza, Des, Moorehead, Butter,
Pass Me, Get Off My Train, Your Eyes, Gangster
County debut: 1999
County cap: 2006
50 wickets in a season: 1
Place in batting averages: (2008 200th av. 20.31)
Place in bowling averages: 95th av. 38.50
(2008 120th av. 38.33)
Parents: Stuart and Susan
Marital status: Single
Family links with cricket: Father played for Glamorgan in the 1970s. Brother Adam
also played for Glamorgan. 'Mum tea lady for local club'
Education: West Monmouth School; Pontypool College; UWIC
Qualifications: 8 GCSEs, 2 A-levels, Levels 1 and 2 cricket coaching, 'qualified
school caretaker'
Career outside cricket: 'Coaching/developing CV'
Overseas tours: Wales U15 to Ireland; Gwent YC to South Africa 1996; Wales U16
to Jersey 1997, 1998; England U19 to Malaysia and (U19 World Cup) Sri Lanka
1999-2000; Glamorgan to Cape Town 2002; England A to Sri Lanka 2004-05; MCC
to Bahrain 2005-06, to Papua New Guinea and New Zealand 2007, to Uganda 2008
Overseas teams played for: Claremont, Cape Town 2002 (one game during
Glamorgan tour)
Career highlights to date: 'Glamorgan debut 1999. Winning National League 2002
at Canterbury with friends and family present. England A selection'
Cricket superstitions: 'Always wear a cap so don't burn my head!'
Cricketers particularly admired: Matthew Maynard, Mike Kasprowicz
Other sports played: Squash (Wales junior squads), rugby (East Wales U11 caps),
boxing (Welsh champion at U14 – 'still have odd spar')
Other sports followed: 'All sports (i.e. Sky Sports)', rugby (Pontypool),
football (Manchester United), darts (Terry Jenkins)
Extras: Has played for Glamorgan from U12. Represented England at U17, U18 and
U19. Glamorgan Young Player of the Year 2003, 2004. ECB National Academy 2004-
05. NBC Denis Compton Award for the most promising young Glamorgan player
2004. Spent the whole of the 2007 season out of the game because of a serious back
injury
Best batting: 88 Glamorgan v Essex, Chelmsford 2004
Best bowling: 5-48 Glamorgan v Somerset, Swansea 2004

2009 Season

	M	Inn	NO	Runs	HS	Avg	100	50	Ct	St	Balls	Runs	Wkts	Avg	BB	5I	10M
Test																	
FC	8	7	2	98	51	19.60	-	1	2	-	1243	770	20	38.50	4-60	-	-
ODI																	
List A	12	8	3	46	17	9.20	-	-	3	-	516	487	17	28.64	3-31	-	
20/20 Int																	
20/20	6	2	1	6	4*	6.00	-	-	-	-	108	196	4	49.00	2-33	-	

Career Performances

	M	Inn	NO	Runs	HS	Avg	100	50	Ct	St	Balls	Runs	Wkts	Avg	BB	5I	10M
Test																	
FC	90	123	18	1764	88	16.80	-	7	28	-	14064	8120	220	36.90	5-48	6	-
ODI																	
List A	81	52	19	423	37*	12.81	-	-	9	-	3405	2750	95	28.94	5-26	2	
20/20 Int																	
20/20	25	7	2	12	4*	2.40	-	-	4	-	447	653	21	31.09	2-17	-	

HARRISON, P. W.   Northamptonshire

Name: Paul William Harrison
Role: Right-hand bat, wicket-keeper
Born: 22 May 1984, Cuckfield, West Sussex
Height: 6ft 2in **Weight:** 12st 12lbs
Nickname: Harry, Potter
County debut: 2005 (Warwickshire), 2005 (one-day, Leicestershire), 2006 (first-class, Leicestershire), 2009 (Northamptonshire)
Parents: Angela and Brian
Marital status: Single
Family links with cricket: 'Dad and uncle played league cricket in Sussex. Brother Leigh played YCs and 2nd XI at Sussex'
Education: The Forest School; College of Richard Collyer, Horsham; Loughborough University
Qualifications: 3 A-levels, Level 1 coaching
Overseas tours: Sussex Young Cricketers to Sri Lanka 2001, to South Africa 2003
Overseas teams played for: Tuart Hill, Perth 2002
Career highlights to date: 'Beating Worcestershire first team with LUCCE 2005'
Cricket moments to forget: 'Dropping a catch on the boundary for my club that would have got us promoted to the premier division'
Cricketers particularly admired: Mark Waugh, Alec Stewart, Adam Gilchrist

Young players to look out for: David Wainwright (Yorkshire), Ryan Cummins (Northamptonshire)
Other sports played: Football (county U18), golf (Mannings Heath – 7 handicap)
Other sports followed: Football (Arsenal, Brighton & Hove Albion)
Favourite band: Red Hot Chili Peppers
Extras: Sussex U19 Player of the Year. Played for Loughborough UCCE 2004-06. Played one first-class game for Warwickshire 2005 and played for Leicestershire in the International Twenty20 Club Championship 2005. Represented British Universities 2006. Released by Leicestershire at the end of the 2007 season. Joined Northamptonshire in 2009
Best batting: 54 LUCCE v Nottinghamshire, Trent Bridge 2005

2009 Season

	M	Inn	NO	Runs	HS	Avg	100	50	Ct	St	Balls	Runs	Wkts	Avg	BB	5I	10M
Test																	
FC	2	3	0	53	32	17.66	-	-	-	-	0	0	0		-	-	-
ODI																	
List A	2	1	0	26	26	26.00	-	-	-	-	0	0	0		-	-	
20/20 Int																	
20/20																	

Career Performances

	M	Inn	NO	Runs	HS	Avg	100	50	Ct	St	Balls	Runs	Wkts	Avg	BB	5I	10M
Test																	
FC	13	20	4	351	54	21.93	-	1	16	-	0	0	0		-	-	-
ODI																	
List A	9	8	0	165	61	20.62	-	1	5	-	0	0	0		-	-	
20/20 Int																	
20/20	12	11	1	119	26	11.90	-	-	2	-	0	0	0		-	-	

36. Which Pakistani made both a duck and a century on his Test debut in 1996? He was 19 at the time.

HARVEY, I. J.　　　　　　Northamptonshire

Name: <u>Ian</u> Joseph Harvey
Role: Right-hand bat, right-arm fast-medium bowler
Born: 10 April 1972, Wonthaggi,
Victoria, Australia
Height: 5ft 9in **Weight:** 12st 8lbs
Nickname: Freak
County debut: 1999 (Gloucestershire),
2004 (Yorkshire), 2007 (Derbyshire), 2008 (Twenty20,
Hampshire), 2009 (Twenty20, Northamptonshire)
County cap: 1999 (Gloucestershire),
2005 (Yorkshire)
ODI debut: 1997-98
1st-Class 200s: 1
Marital status: Married
Family links with cricket: Brothers club cricketers in
Australia
Education: Wonthaggi Technical College
Overseas tours: Australian Academy to New Zealand 1994-95; Australia to Sharjah
(Coca-Cola Cup) 1997-98, to New Zealand 1999-2000 (one-day series), to Kenya
(ICC Knockout Trophy) 2000-01, to India 2000-01 (one-day series), to England 2001
(one-day series), to South Africa 2001-02 (one-day series), to Africa (World Cup)
2002-03, to West Indies 2002-03 (one-day series), to India (TVS Cup) 2003-04, to Sri
Lanka 2003-04 (one-day series), to Zimbabwe (one-day series) 2004, to Netherlands
(Videocon Cup) 2004, to England (ICC Champions Trophy) 2004; Australia A to
South Africa 2002-03; FICA World XI to New Zealand 2004-05
Overseas teams played for: Victoria 1993-94 – 2004-05; Cape Cobras 2005-06 – ;
Chennai Superstars (ICL) 2007-08 –
Extras: The nickname 'Freak' is a reference to his brilliant fielding and was
reportedly coined by Shane Warne. Attended Commonwealth Bank [Australian]
Cricket Academy 1994. An overseas player with Gloucestershire 1999-2003 and in
2006, and with Yorkshire 2004-05. Man of the Match in the Carlton Series first final v
West Indies at Sydney 2000-01 (47*/2-5). Won the Walter Lawrence Trophy 2001 for
the season's fastest first-class hundred with his 61-ball century v Derbyshire at Bristol;
also took 5-89 in Derbyshire's second innings. Has won numerous Australian and
English domestic awards, including C&G Man of the Match in the final v
Worcestershire at Lord's 2003 (2-37/36-ball 61). Scored the first ever century in the
Twenty20 Cup (100* from 50 balls), v Warwickshire at Edgbaston 2003. One of
Wisden's Five Cricketers of the Year 2004. Appeared as an overseas player for
Derbyshire 2007. Joined Hampshire for 2008, playing only in Twenty20 games.
Signed to Northamptonshire for 2009, again specialising in Twenty20
Best batting: 209* Yorkshire v Somerset, Headingley 2005
Best bowling: 8-101 Australia A v South Africa A, Adelaide 2002-03

2009 Season

	M	Inn	NO	Runs	HS	Avg	100	50	Ct	St	Balls	Runs	Wkts	Avg	BB	5I	10M
Test																	
FC																	
ODI																	
List A																	
20/20 Int																	
20/20	10	10	1	279	64	31.00	-	1	7	-	132	138	12	11.50	4-18	-	

Career Performances

	M	Inn	NO	Runs	HS	Avg	100	50	Ct	St	Balls	Runs	Wkts	Avg	BB	5I	10M
Test																	
FC	165	272	29	8409	209*	34.60	15	46	114	-	24274	11693	425	27.51	8-101	15	2
ODI	73	51	11	715	48*	17.87	-	-	17	-	3279	2577	85	30.31	4-16	-	
List A	304	267	27	5973	112	24.88	2	28	83	-	13601	9949	445	22.35	5-19	9	
20/20 Int																	
20/20	51	50	4	1469	109	31.93	3	5	18	-	917	1171	52	22.51	4-18	-	

HAYMAN, J. T.   Somerset

Name: James Taylor Hayman
Role: Right-hand bat, right-arm fast bowler
Born: 22 November 1986, Musgrove, Taunton, Somerset
Height: 6ft 5in
Nickname: Blondie
County debut: No first-team appearance
Parents: Andrew and Elaine
Marital status: Single
Education: Huish Episcopi Secondary School
Qualifications: GCSEs
Off-season: 'Fitness training'
Career highlights to date: 'Signing for Somerset'
Cricket superstitions: None
Cricketers particularly admired: Michael Vaughan
Young players to look out for: James Haggett (Somerset)
Other sports played: Golf
Other sports followed: Football (Liverpool); MotoGP (Valentino Rossi)
Favourite band: Jet
Extras: Somerset snapped him up from local club Ashcott and Shapwick CC in September 2009
Opinions on cricket: 'It's batsman-friendly'

HAYWARD, M. Hampshire

Name: Mortnantau (<u>Nantie</u>) Hayward
Role: Right-hand bat, right arm fast bowler
Born: 6 March 1977, Uitenhage, Cape Province,
South Africa
Nickname: Nantie
County debut: 2003 (Worcestershire),
2004 (Middlesex), 2008 (Hampshire),
2009 (Derbyshire)
Test debut: 1999
ODI debut: 1998
50 wickets in a season: 1
Overseas teams played for: Eastern Province B
1995-96; Eastern Province 1996-97 – 2003-04;
Warriors 2004-05 – 2006-07; Dolphins 2005-06;
Kolkata Tigers (ICL) 2007-08 ; Chennai Superstars
(ICL) 2008-09; ICL World XI 2008-09
Overseas tours: South Africa to England 1998, to India 1999-2000, to Sri
Lanka 2000, to Australia 2001-02, to Sri Lanka 2004
Other sports played: Baseball (provincial level in South Africa)
Extras: *South African Cricket Annual* Cricketer of the Year 2000. Signed for
Worcestershire in 2003 season, then moved to Middlesex in 2004. Played as an
overseas player for Ireland in the Friends Provident Trophy 2007. Signed for
Hampshire as a Kolpak player in May 2008, but played in only one first-class match
for the county all season. Signed for Derbyshire June 2009
Best batting: 55* Eastern Province v Boland, Port Elizabeth 1997
Best bowling: 6-31 Eastern Province v Easterns, Port Elizabeth 1999

2009 Season

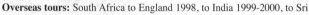

	M	Inn	NO	Runs	HS	Avg	100	50	Ct	St	Balls	Runs	Wkts	Avg	BB	5I	10M
Test																	
FC	5	5	2	14	6	4.66	-	-	1	-	740	472	11	42.90	4-99	-	-
ODI																	
List A	2	1	1	1	1*		-	-	-	-	96	84	2	42.00	1-34	-	
20/20 Int																	
20/20	4	0	0	0	0		-	-	-	-	96	133	3	44.33	1-22	-	

Career Performances

	M	Inn	NO	Runs	HS	Avg	100	50	Ct	St	Balls	Runs	Wkts	Avg	BB	5I	10M
Test	16	17	8	66	14	7.33	-	-	4	-	2821	1609	54	29.79	5-56	1	-
FC	133	150	55	1074	55*	11.30	-	1	36	-	23678	12735	442	28.81	6-31	9	2
ODI	21	5	1	12	4	3.00	-	-	4	-	993	858	21	40.85	4-31	-	
List A	151	46	24	207	19*	9.40	-	-	30	-	6624	5515	203	27.16	5-37	3	
20/20 Int																	
20/20	24	4	0	11	5	2.75	-	-	7	-	477	660	21	31.42	3-21	-	

HENDERSON, C. W.　　　　　Leicestershire

Name: Claude William Henderson
Role: Right-hand bat, left-arm spin bowler
Born: 14 June 1972, Worcester, South Africa
Height: 6ft 2in **Weight:** 14st 2lbs
Nickname: Hendy, Hendo
County debut: 2004
County cap: 2004
Test debut: 2001-02
ODI debut: 2001-02
Place in batting averages: 206th av. 21.90
(2008 195th av. 20.52)
Place in bowling averages: 120th av. 45.39
(2008 81st av. 31.56)
Parents: Henry and Susan
Wife and date of marriage: Nicci,
29 March 2003
Children: Mia, 2007
Family links with cricket: Brother James played first-class cricket
Education: Worcester High School
Qualifications: Level 2 coaching, basic computer skills, basic bookkeeping skills
Career outside cricket: 'Family business'
Overseas tours: South Africa A to Sri Lanka 1998; South Africa to Zimbabwe
2001-02, to Australia 2001-02
Overseas teams played for: Boland 1990-91 – 1997-98; Western Province
1998-99 – 2003-04; Highveld Lions 2006-07; Cape Cobras 2008-09
Career highlights to date: 'Playing for South Africa'
Cricket moments to forget: 'Losing to Devon in C&G 2004'
Cricket superstitions: 'None'
Cricketers particularly admired: Shane Warne, Jacques Kallis
Other sports played: Golf, tennis, fishing
Other sports followed: Rugby (Leicester Tigers)

Favourite band: U2
Relaxations: 'Cinema, travelling, spending time with family'
Extras: Has won several match awards in South African domestic cricket. Scored fifty (63) and recorded five-wicket innings return (5-28) on Championship debut for Leicestershire v Glamorgan at Leicester 2004; recorded a further five-wicket return (5-24) on one-day debut v Yorkshire at Headingley in the totesport League 2004. Appointed player/coach at Leicestershire for 2008 with responsibility for spin bowling. South Africa Player of the Year 2009. Granted British Citizenship in 2009.
Best batting: 81 Leicestershire v Gloucestershire, Leicester 2007
Best bowling: 7-57 Boland v Eastern Province, Paarl (PCC) 1994-95

2009 Season

	M	Inn	NO	Runs	HS	Avg	100	50	Ct	St	Balls	Runs	Wkts	Avg	BB	5I	10M
Test																	
FC	10	13	2	241	79*	21.90	-	1	1	-	2369	1044	23	45.39	6-152	1	-
ODI																	
List A	11	6	3	10	6	3.33	-	-	1	-	426	303	13	23.30	3-30	-	
20/20 Int																	
20/20	7	3	1	12	6	6.00	-	-	1	-	168	194	11	17.63	3-32	-	

Career Performances

	M	Inn	NO	Runs	HS	Avg	100	50	Ct	St	Balls	Runs	Wkts	Avg	BB	5I	10M
Test	7	7	0	65	30	9.28	-	-	2	-	1962	928	22	42.18	4-116	-	-
FC	223	305	69	4510	81	19.11	-	15	76	-	54296	23234	735	31.61	7-57	27	1
ODI	4	0	0	0	0		-	-	-	-	217	132	7	18.85	4-17	-	
List A	235	133	63	1093	45	15.61	-	-	52	-	10447	7455	292	25.53	6-29	2	
20/20 Int																	
20/20	55	22	6	84	16	5.25	-	-	14	-	1012	1144	50	22.88	3-23	-	

37. Which international side did Bangladesh surprisingly beat in the 2005 NatWest Series at Sophia Gardens?

HENDERSON, T.   Middlesex

Name: Tyron Henderson
Role: Right-hand bat, right-arm fast-medium
bowler; all-rounder
Born: 1 August 1974, Durban, South Africa
Nickname: The Blacksmith
County debut: 2006 (Kent),
2007 (one-day, Middlesex)
Twenty20 Int debut: 2006-07
Family links with cricket: Grandfather
(J. K. Henderson) and great-uncle (W. A. Henderson)
both played first-class cricket for North Eastern
Transvaal
Overseas tours: South Africa Academy to Ireland
and Scotland 1999; South Africa A to Sri Lanka
2005-06
Overseas teams played for: Border 1998-99 – 2003-04; Eastern Cape 2003-04;
Warriors 2004-05 – 2005-06; Lions 2006-07; Cape Cobras 2007-08 – ;
Boland 2007-08 –
Extras: Played for Berkshire in the 2003 C&G. Has represented South Africa A. His
awards include Man of the Match v Griqualand West at Kimberley in the Standard
Bank Cup 2003-04 (3-45/126*) and v Dolphins at Port Elizabeth in the Standard Bank
Pro20 Series 2004-05 (3-24/44). An overseas player with Kent from June to September
2006; was a temporary overseas player with Middlesex during the 2007 season as a
locum for Chaminda Vaas. One of the heroes of the Twenty20 Cup final win over Kent
in 2008, scoring 43 runs and running out Justin Kemp off the final ball of the game,
Signed by Rajasthan for IPL 2009 – leading Twenty20 wicket-taker. Released by
Middlesex at the end of the 2009 season
Best batting: 81 Border v Gauteng, Johannesburg 2000
Best bowling: 7-67 Boland v Western Province, Paarl 2007

2009 Season

	M	Inn	NO	Runs	HS	Avg	100	50	Ct	St	Balls	Runs	Wkts	Avg	BB	5I	10M
Test																	
FC																	
ODI																	
List A	8	5	2	108	55	36.00	-	1	2	-	226	176	6	29.33	2-19	-	
20/20 Int																	
20/20	11	11	2	171	32	19.00	-	-	-	-	224	321	9	35.66	3-34	-	

Career Performances

	M	Inn	NO	Runs	HS	Avg	100	50	Ct	St	Balls	Runs	Wkts	Avg	BB	5I	10M
Test																	
FC	86	137	17	1897	81	15.80	-	6	31	-	15744	7024	262	26.80	7-67	10	1
ODI																	
List A	114	92	18	1608	126*	21.72	1	9	27	-	4915	3567	130	27.43	5-5	3	
20/20 Int	1	1	0	0	0	0.00	-	-	-	-	24	31	0		-	-	
20/20	75	68	10	1245	85	21.46	-	7	10	-	1614	1937	84	23.05	4-29	-	

HERATH, H. M. R. K. B. Surrey

Name: Herath Mudiyanselage <u>Rangana</u> Keerthi Bandara Herath

Role: Left-hand bat, slow left-arm orthodox spin bowler

Born: 19 March 1978, Kurunegala, Sri Lanka

County debut: 2009

Test debut: 1999

ODI debut: 2004

Education: Maliyadeva College, Kurunegala

Overseas tours: Sri Lanka A to Zimbabwe 2007, to South Africa, 2008-09; Sri Lanka to Zimbabwe 2004 (one-day series), to Pakistan 2004-05, to New Zealand 2004-05, to West Indies 2007-08, to Bangladesh 2008-09, to India 2009-10

Overseas teams played for: Kurunegala Youth Cricket Club 1996-97, 1997-98; Moors Sports Club 1998-99 – 2009-10; Wayamba 2007-08 – 2009-10

Extras: Man of the Match in the first Test against Pakistan, Galle 2009, returning career-best figures of 4-15. Signed a short-term contract with Surrey for the final month of the 2009 season. His 34 wickets from 7 Test matches made him Sri Lanka's most prolific wicket-taker in 2009

Best batting: 71* Moors Sports Club v Galle CC, Colombo 2002-03

Best bowling: 8-43 Moors Sports Club v Police Sports Club, Colombo 2003-04

2009 Season

	M	Inn	NO	Runs	HS	Avg	100	50	Ct	St	Balls	Runs	Wkts	Avg	BB	5I	10M
Test																	
FC	3	5	1	80	52*	20.00	-	1	-	-	650	431	8	53.87	4-151	-	-
ODI																	
List A	2	2	0	47	39	23.50	-	-	-	-	30	37	0		-	-	
20/20 Int																	
20/20																	

Career Performances

	M	Inn	NO	Runs	HS	Avg	100	50	Ct	St	Balls	Runs	Wkts	Avg	BB	5I	10M
Test	18	23	4	179	33*	9.42	-	-	4	-	4222	2031	59	34.42	5-99	3	-
FC	172	244	56	3035	71*	16.14	-	10	80	-	33324	14977	623	24.04	8-43	35	5
ODI	6	1	1	0	0*		-	-	3	-	234	149	5	29.80	3-28	-	
List A	98	65	29	775	88*	21.52	-	1	24	-	4057	2693	126	21.37	4-19	-	
20/20 Int																	
20/20	18	12	4	44	9	5.50	-	-	4	-	355	329	24	13.70	3-14	-	

HILDRETH, J. C. Somerset

Name: James Charles Hildreth
Role: Right-hand bat, right-arm medium bowler; all-rounder
Born: 9 September 1984, Milton Keynes
Height: 5ft 10in **Weight:** 12st
Nickname: Hildy, Hildz
County debut: 2003
County cap: 2007
1000 runs in a season: 1
1st-Class 200s: 1
1st-Class 300s: 1
Place in batting averages: 50th av. 44.47
(2008 108th av. 32.06)
Parents: David and Judy
Marital status: Single

Family links with cricket: 'Dad played county league cricket in Kent and Northants'
Education: Millfield School
Qualifications: 10 GCSEs, 3 A-levels, Level 1 coaching
Overseas tours: 'West' to West Indies 1999, 2000; Millfield to Sri Lanka 2001; England U19 to Bangladesh (U19 World Cup) 2003-04; England Performance Programme to India 2007-08; England Lions to India 2007-08; Somerset to India (Champions League) 2009-10

Cricket moments to forget: 'Being bowled first ball by Shoaib Akhtar'
Cricket superstitions: 'Left pad before right when getting padded up'
Other sports played: Hockey (West of England), squash (South of England),
tennis (South of England), football (England Independent Schools, Luton Town),
rugby (Millfield)
Other sports followed: Football (Charlton Athletic)
Favourite band: Jack Johnson
Relaxations: Travelling, snowboarding, music
Extras: NBC Denis Compton Award for the most promising young Somerset player
2003, 2004, 2005. Scored maiden first-class century (101) plus 72 in the second
innings v Durham at Taunton 2004 in his second Championship match. Represented
England U19 v Bangladesh U19 2004, scoring 210 in second 'Test' at Taunton. Cricket
Society's Most Promising Young Cricketer of the Year 2004. Scored maiden first-class
double century (227*) at Taunton 2006, setting a new record for the highest score by a
Somerset batsman v Northamptonshire. ECB National Academy 2004-05 (part-time).
Scored almost 1000 first-class runs in both 2008 and 2009. His triple-century scored
against Warwickshire in April 2009 was the earliest ever in an English season
Best batting: 303* Somerset v Warwickshire, Taunton 2009
Best bowling: 2-39 Somerset v Hampshire, Taunton 2004

2009 Season

	M	Inn	NO	Runs	HS	Avg	100	50	Ct	St	Balls	Runs	Wkts	Avg	BB	5I	10M
Test																	
FC	15	23	2	934	303*	44.47	2	4	10	-	0	0	0		-	-	-
ODI																	
List A	17	17	1	526	151	32.87	1	2	6	-	0	0	0		-	-	
20/20 Int																	
20/20	12	10	1	183	48*	20.33	-	-	4	-	0	0	0		-	-	

Career Performances

	M	Inn	NO	Runs	HS	Avg	100	50	Ct	St	Balls	Runs	Wkts	Avg	BB	5I	10M
Test																	
FC	94	156	13	5670	303*	39.65	12	30	71	-	396	316	4	79.00	2-39	-	-
ODI																	
List A	109	105	14	2674	151	29.38	3	9	30	-	150	185	6	30.83	2-26	-	
20/20 Int																	
20/20	54	51	5	813	71	17.67	-	3	21	-	169	247	10	24.70	3-24	-	

HINDS, W. W. Derbyshire

Name: <u>Wavell</u> Wayne Hinds
Role: Left-hand bat, right-arm medium bowler
Born: 7 September 1976, Kingston, Jamaica
County debut: 2008
Test debut: 1999-2000
ODI debut: 1999
Twenty20 Int debut: 2005-06
1st-Class 200s: 1
Place in batting averages: 114th av. 35.04 (2008 115th av. 31.30)
Place in bowling averages: (2008 41st av. 26.10)
Overseas tours: West Indies U19 to Pakistan 1995-96; West Indies A to South Africa 1997-98, to Bangladesh and India 1998-99; West Indies to Singapore (Coca-Cola Singapore Challenge) 1999,

to Bangladesh 1999-2000, to New Zealand 1999-2000, to England 2000, to Kenya (ICC Knockout Trophy) 2000-01, to Australia 2000-01, to Zimbabwe and Kenya 2001, to Sharjah (v Pakistan) 2001-02, to Sri Lanka (ICC Champions Trophy) 2002-03, to India and Bangladesh 2002-03, to Africa (World Cup) 2002-03, to Zimbabwe and South Africa 2003-04, to England (ICC Champions Trophy) 2004, to Australia 2005-06, to India (ICC Champions Trophy) 2006-07, plus other one-day tournaments and series in Toronto, Sharjah, Australia, New Zealand and Malaysia
Overseas teams played for: Jamaica 1995-96 – ; Ahmedabad Rockets (ICL) 2007-08
Extras: Scored 213 in the first Test at Georgetown 2004-05, in the process sharing with Shivnarine Chanderpaul (203*) in a record fourth-wicket partnership for West Indies in Tests against South Africa (284). His match and series awards include Man of the [Test] Series v Pakistan 1999-2000 and of the [ODI] Series v Australia 2002-03. Released by Derbyshire at the end of the 2009 season. Is not considered an overseas player
Best batting: 213 West Indies v South Africa, Georgetown 2004-05
Best bowling: 3-9 Jamaica v West Indies B, Montego Bay 2000-01

2009 Season

	M	Inn	NO	Runs	HS	Avg	100	50	Ct	St	Balls	Runs	Wkts	Avg	BB	5I	10M
Test																	
FC	16	26	2	841	148	35.04	2	2	7	-	360	181	4	45.25	2-19	-	-
ODI																	
List A	10	10	0	278	95	27.80	-	3	1	-	18	14	0		-	-	
20/20 Int																	
20/20	10	10	3	299	66	42.71	-	1	1	-	18	26	0		-	-	

Career Performances

	M	Inn	NO	Runs	HS	Avg	100	50	Ct	St	Balls	Runs	Wkts	Avg	BB	5I	10M
Test	45	80	1	2608	213	33.01	5	14	32	-	1123	590	16	36.87	3-79	-	-
FC	163	277	13	9146	213	34.64	20	46	74	-	3664	1736	48	36.16	3-9	-	-
ODI	114	107	9	2835	127*	28.92	5	14	28	-	945	837	28	29.89	3-24	-	
List A	204	193	14	5047	127*	28.19	6	29	46	-	1508	1353	49	27.61	4-35	-	
20/20 Int	1	1	0	14	14	4.00	-	-	-	-	0	0	0		-	-	
20/20	27	25	6	673	72*	35.42	-	3	3	-	138	163	4	40.75	2-14	-	

HOCKLEY, J. B. Kent

Name: <u>James</u> Bernard Hockley
Role: Right-hand bat, right-arm offbreak bowler;
all-rounder
Born: 16 April 1979, Beckenham
Height: 6ft 2in **Weight:** 13st
Nickname: Hickers, Ice
County debut: 1998 (Kent)
Place in batting averages: 82nd av. 40.00
Parents: Bernard and Joan
Education: Churchfields Primary School,
Beckenham; Kelsey Park Secondary School,
Beckenham
Qualifications: 7 GCSEs, NCA Level 1
coaching award

Career outside cricket: Teaching
Overseas tours: Kent to Jamaica 1999, to South Africa 2001
Overseas teams played for: North City, Wellington, New Zealand 1999-2000
Career highlights to date: 'Winning the Norwich Union League Trophy with
Kent in 2001'
Cricket moments to forget: 'Playing at Lord's for the first time – out for a duck
and dropped a catch.'
Other sports played: Football, golf, snooker
Other sports followed: Football (Arsenal)
Extras: ACKL Player of the Year Award 1995. Equalled Trevor Ward's Kent U15
batting record with a total of 1000 runs in the season. Kent Schools Player of the Year
1996. Played for Kent 2nd XI 1996-98, Kent 1998-2002. Represented Kent Cricket
Board in the Minor Counties Trophy 1998-2000. Scored a 102-ball 90 in the title-
clinching Norwich Union League victory v Warwickshire at Edgbaston 2001. B&H
Gold Award for his 32-ball 33* v Middlesex at Canterbury 2002. C&G Man of the
Match Award for his 107-ball 121 (his maiden one-day century) v Warwickshire at
Canterbury 2002. After being released by Kent in 2002, combined a career in teaching

with a return to club cricket, playing for Kent Cricket League sides Bexley CC (2003-05) and Hartley Country Club (2006-08). His performances as a member of Hartley's 2008 Kent Premier League championship side prompted Kent to re-sign him for 2009

Best batting: 74 Kent v Zimbabweans, Canterbury 2000
Best batting: 1-21 Kent v Glamorgan, Hove 2001

2009 Season

	M	Inn	NO	Runs	HS	Avg	100	50	Ct	St	Balls	Runs	Wkts	Avg	BB	5I	10M
Test																	
FC	5	8	2	240	72	40.00	-	2	5	-	0	0	0		-	-	-
ODI																	
List A	12	12	1	257	55	23.36	-	2	4	-	48	32	2	16.00	2-32	-	
20/20 Int																	
20/20	4	2	0	14	14	7.00	-	-	1	-	0	0	0		-	-	

Career Performances

	M	Inn	NO	Runs	HS	Avg	100	50	Ct	St	Balls	Runs	Wkts	Avg	BB	5I	10M
Test																	
FC	24	38	4	663	74	19.50	-	3	14	-	366	233	3	77.66	1-21	-	-
ODI																	
List A	69	67	6	1586	121	26.00	1	8	24	-	72	67	3	22.33	2-32	-	
20/20 Int																	
20/20	4	2	0	14	14	7.00	-	-	1	-	0	0	0		-	-	

HODD, A. J. Sussex

Name: <u>Andrew</u> John Hodd
Role: Right-hand bat, wicket-keeper
Born: 12 January 1984, Chichester
Height: 5ft 9½in **Weight:** 11st 8lbs
Nickname: Hoddy
County debut: 2002 (one-day, Sussex), 2003 (first-class, Sussex), 2005 (Surrey)
Place in batting averages: 185th av. 24.95
Parents: Karen and Adrian
Marital status: Single
Family links with cricket: 'Long line of enthusiastic club cricketers'
Education: Bexhill High School; Bexhill College; 'short stint at Loughborough Uni'
Qualifications: 9 GCSEs, 4 A-levels, Level 1 coaching
Career outside cricket: Coaching

Overseas tours: South of England U14 to West Indies 1998; Sussex Academy to Cape Town 1999, to Sri Lanka 2001; England U17 to Australia 2000-01; England U19 to Australia 2002-03; Sussex to India (Champions League) 2009
Cricket superstitions: 'Too many! Must drink coffee the morning of a game'
Cricketers particularly admired: David Hussey, Matt Prior
Other sports played: Golf, football, boxing
Other sports followed: Football (Brighton & Hove Albion)
Favourite band: Hard-Fi
Relaxations: 'Cinema, DVDs, gym, going out'
Extras: Played for England U14, U15, U17 and U19. Graham Kersey Trophy, Bunbury 1999. Several junior Player of the Year awards at Sussex. Sussex County League Young Player of the Year 2002. Sussex 2nd XI Player of the Year 2003. Joined Surrey for 2004, leaving at the end of the 2005 season to rejoin Sussex for 2006
Best batting: 123 Sussex v Yorkshire, Hove 2007

2009 Season

	M	Inn	NO	Runs	HS	Avg	100	50	Ct	St	Balls	Runs	Wkts	Avg	BB	5I	10M
Test																	
FC	16	23	3	499	101	24.95	1	2	25	3	10	7	0		-	-	-
ODI																	
List A	10	8	4	99	22	24.75	-	-	13	2	0	0	0		-	-	
20/20 Int																	
20/20	4	1	0	6	6	6.00	-	-	-	2	0	0	0		-	-	

Career Performances

	M	Inn	NO	Runs	HS	Avg	100	50	Ct	St	Balls	Runs	Wkts	Avg	BB	5I	10M
Test																	
FC	38	54	10	1367	123	31.06	3	7	64	10	10	7	0		-	-	-
ODI																	
List A	27	22	6	327	42	20.43	-	-	22	2	0	0	0		-	-	
20/20 Int																	
20/20	21	8	0	68	16	8.50	-	-	10	6	0	0	0		-	-	

38. Which Bangladesh batsman made a century at Sophia Gardens in the famous NatWest victory in June 2005?

HODGE, B. J.   Leicestershire

Name: Bradley (Brad) John Hodge
Role: Right-hand bat, right-arm off-spin bowler
Born: 29 December 1974, Sandringham, Melbourne, Australia
Height: 5ft 7½in **Weight:** 12st 8lbs
Nickname: Bunk
County debut: 2002 (Durham),
2003 (Leicestershire), 2005 (Lancashire)
County cap: 2003 (Leicestershire), 2006 (Lancashire)
Test debut: 2005-06
ODI debut: 2005-06
Twenty20 Int debut: 2007-08
1000 runs in a season: 2
1st-Class 200s: 9
1st-Class 300s: 1
Parents: John and Val
Wife: Megan
Children: Jesse
Education: St Bede's College, Mentone; Deakin University
Overseas tours: Australia U19 to New Zealand 1992-93; Commonwealth Bank [Australian] Cricket Academy to Zimbabwe 1998-99; Australia A to Los Angeles (Moov America Challenge) 1999, to Pakistan 2005-06; Australia to India 2004-05, to New Zealand 2004-05, to England 2005, to New Zealand (one-day series) 2005-06, 2006-07, to West Indies (World Cup) 2006-07, to South Africa (World 20/20) 2007-08, to India (one-day series) 2007-08, to West Indies 2008
Overseas teams played for: Victoria 1993-94 –
Cricketers particularly admired: Allan Border, Dennis Lillee, Dean Jones, Sachin Tendulkar
Other sports played/followed: Australian Rules football (Melbourne), golf, tennis, soccer, skiing
Extras: Attended Commonwealth Bank [Australian] Cricket Academy 1993. Leading run-scorer for Victoria in the Sheffield Shield in his first season (1993-94) with 903 runs (av. 50.16). Victoria's Pura Cup Player of the Year 2000-01 and 2001-02; winner of the national Pura Cup Player of the Season Award 2001-02 (jointly with Jimmy Maher of Queensland). Was Durham's overseas player 2002 from late July; an overseas player with Leicestershire 2003, 2004 (appointed vice-captain for 2004; assumed the captaincy in July on the resignation of Phillip DeFreitas). Scored 202* v LUCCE at Leicester 2003, in the process sharing with Darren Maddy (229*) in a record partnership for any wicket for Leicestershire (436*). His 302* v Nottinghamshire at Trent Bridge 2003 was the then highest individual first-class score by a Leicestershire player. ING Cup Player of the Year 2003-04. Has won numerous

Australian and English domestic awards, including Man of the Match in the Twenty20 Cup final at Edgbaston 2004 for his 53-ball 77*. Man of the Match in the first Test v South Africa at Perth 2005-06 (41/203*) and v Netherlands in St Kitts in the 2006-07 World Cup (123). First player to score a century (106 off 54 balls) in Australian domestic Twenty20 for Victoria v New South Wales in Sydney in 2006. An overseas player with Lancashire 2005-08. Announced his retirement from first-class cricket to concentrate on one-day and Twenty20 in December 2009; has signed as overseas player with Leicestershire for 2010

Best batting: 302* Leicestershire v Nottinghamshire, Trent Bridge 2003
Best bowling: 4-17 Australia A v West Indians, Hobart 2000-01

2009 Season (Did not make any first-class or one-day appearances)

Career Performances

	M	Inn	NO	Runs	HS	Avg	100	50	Ct	St	Balls	Runs	Wkts	Avg	BB	5I	10M
Test	6	11	2	503	203*	55.88	1	2	9	-	12	8	0		-	-	-
FC	220	384	38	16808	302*	48.57	50	63	125	-	5481	3038	74	41.05	4-17	-	-
ODI	25	21	2	575	123	30.26	1	3	16	-	66	51	1	51.00	1-17	-	
List A	223	213	26	7633	164	40.81	21	35	89	-	1524	1344	38	35.36	5-28	1	
20/20 Int	8	5	2	94	36	31.33	-	-	3	-	12	20	0		-	-	
20/20	73	70	11	2366	106	40.10	1	17	28	-	540	689	31	22.22	4-17	-	

HODGSON, L. J.   Yorkshire

Name: <u>Lee</u> John Hodgson
Role: Right-hand bat, right-arm fast-medium bowler; all-rounder
Born: 29 June 1986, Middlesbrough
County debut: 2008 (Surrey), 2009 (Yorkshire)
Extras: Played for Saltburn CC in North Yorkshire and South Durham League. MCC Young Cricketer 2006. On first-class debut scored 63, including 13 fours, v Nottinghamshire. Signed a two-year contract with Yorkshire in November 2008, and an extension (committing him to the county until the end of the 2011 season) in November 2009
Best batting: 63 Surrey v Nottinghamshire, The Oval 2008

2009 Season

	M	Inn	NO	Runs	HS	Avg	100	50	Ct	St	Balls	Runs	Wkts	Avg	BB	5I	10M
Test																	
FC	1	1	0	32	32	32.00	-	-	-	-	60	30	0		-	-	-
ODI																	
List A	4	1	0	9	9	9.00	-	-	1	-	108	108	2	54.00	2-44	-	
20/20 Int																	
20/20																	

Career Performances

	M	Inn	NO	Runs	HS	Avg	100	50	Ct	St	Balls	Runs	Wkts	Avg	BB	5I	10M
Test																	
FC	2	3	0	98	63	32.66	-	1	2	-	114	88	0		-	-	-
ODI																	
List A	6	1	0	9	9	9.00	-	-	3	-	156	160	2	80.00	2-44	-	
20/20 Int																	
20/20																	

HODNETT, G. P. Gloucestershire

Name: <u>Grant</u> Phillip Hodnett
Role: Right-hand top-order bat, right-arm
leg-spin bowler, occasional wicket-keeper
Born: 17 August 1982, Johannesburg,
South Africa
Height: 6ft 4in **Weight:** 14st
Nickname: Hodders, Hoddy
County debut: 2005
County cap: 2005
Parents: Phillip and Julia
Marital status: Single
Family links with cricket: Brother Kyle is an
MCC Young Cricketer
Education: Northwood High School, Durban
Qualifications: Matriculation, Level 1 coaching,
GFA Fitness Instructor
Overseas tours: Gloucestershire to South Africa 2006
Overseas teams played for: Durban Collegians 2005-06
Cricket superstitions: 'None'
Cricketers particularly admired: Hansie Cronje, Jonty Rhodes, Steve Waugh,
Andrew Flintoff, Michael Atherton
Other sports played: Golf, squash, bodyboarding, football, rugby
Other sports followed: Rugby union (England), football (Newcastle United)

Favourite band: Blink-182
Relaxations: 'Going to gym; swimming; reading sports magazines'
Extras: Represented KwaZulu-Natal Schools. West of England Premier League Batsman of the Year 2004. Limited appearances in 2008. Released by Gloucestershire at the end of the 2009 season. Is not considered an overseas player
Best batting: 168 Gloucestershire v Derbyshire, Bristol 2007
Best bowling: 2-91 Gloucestershire v LUCCE, Bristol 2008

2009 Season

	M	Inn	NO	Runs	HS	Avg	100	50	Ct	St	Balls	Runs	Wkts	Avg	BB	5I	10M
Test																	
FC	1	1	0	31	31	31.00	-	-	-	-	36	41	1	41.00	1-41	-	-
ODI																	
List A																	
20/20 Int																	
20/20	4	4	0	133	60	33.25	-	1	2	-	0	0	0		-	-	

Career Performances

	M	Inn	NO	Runs	HS	Avg	100	50	Ct	St	Balls	Runs	Wkts	Avg	BB	5I	10M
Test																	
FC	20	33	1	1051	168	32.84	2	7	14	-	165	183	3	61.00	2-91	-	-
ODI																	
List A	4	4	0	114	50	28.50	-	1	2	-	0	0	0		-	-	
20/20 Int																	
20/20	4	4	0	133	60	3.25	-	1	2	-	0	0	0		-	-	

---

39. Which Pakistan batsman scored centuries in both his first Test and in his 100th?

HOGG, K. W.   Lancashire

Name: Kyle William Hogg
Role: Left-hand bat, right-arm fast-medium
bowler; all-rounder
Born: 2 July 1983, Birmingham
Height: 6ft 3in **Weight:** 14st 7lbs
Nickname: Boss, Hoggy
County debut: 2001
Place in batting averages: 179th av. 25.61
Place in bowling averages: 38th av. 29.41
Parents: Sharon and William
Marital status: Engaged
Family links with cricket: Father played for
Lancashire and Warwickshire; grandfather Sonny
Ramadhin played for Lancashire and West Indies
Education: Saddleworth High School, Oldham
Qualifications: GCSEs, Level 2 coaching
Career outside cricket: 'Coaching'
Off-season: 'Resting'
Overseas tours: England U19 to India 2000-01, to Australia and (U19 World Cup)
New Zealand 2001-02; Lancashire to South Africa, to Grenada; ECB National
Academy to Australia and Sri Lanka 2002-03
Overseas teams played for: Otago 2006-07
Career highlights to date: 'Lord's [C&G] final 2006'
Cricket moments to forget: '[B&H 2002] semi-final v Warwickshire. Lord's [C&G]
final 2006'
Cricket superstitions: 'None'
Cricketers particularly admired: Andrew Flintoff, David Byas, Stuart Law,
Carl Hooper
Other sports played: Football
Other sports followed: Football (Manchester United), darts, rugby league
Favourite band: The Stone Roses, The Libertines, The Courteeners
Relaxations: 'Music, guitar, relaxing with friends'
Extras: Represented England U19 2001, 2002. NBC Denis Compton Award for the
most promising young Lancashire player 2001. Recorded maiden first-class five-
wicket return (5-48) on Championship debut v Leicestershire at Old Trafford 2002.
Included in provisional England squad of 30 for the 2002-03 World Cup. Played two
first-class and four List A matches for Worcestershire on loan 2007 and two first-class
and three List A matches for Nottinghamshire on loan in 2007. Enjoyed a successful
2009 season after several years blighted by a series of injuries
Opinions on cricket: 'Too many Kolpaks!'
Best batting: 71 Otago v Central Districts, Napier 2006-07
Best bowling: 5-48 Lancashire v Leicestershire, Old Trafford 2002

2009 Season

	M	Inn	NO	Runs	HS	Avg	100	50	Ct	St	Balls	Runs	Wkts	Avg	BB	5I	10M
Test																	
FC	14	15	2	333	69	25.61	-	2	2	-	2030	1000	34	29.41	4-22	-	-
ODI																	
List A	17	9	1	74	28*	9.25	-	-	4	-	786	545	17	32.05	3-18	-	
20/20 Int																	
20/20	1	0	0	0	0		-	-	-	-	12	29	0		-	-	

Career Performances

	M	Inn	NO	Runs	HS	Avg	100	50	Ct	St	Balls	Runs	Wkts	Avg	BB	5I	10M
Test																	
FC	55	65	7	1348	71	23.24	-	9	13	-	7252	3756	104	36.11	5-48	1	-
ODI																	
List A	115	71	18	835	66*	15.75	-	1	20	-	4360	3362	113	29.75	4-20	-	
20/20 Int																	
20/20	21	15	2	209	44	16.07	-	-	3	-	271	388	12	32.33	2-10	-	

HOGGARD, M. J.   Leicestershire

Name: <u>Matthew</u> James Hoggard
Role: Right-hand bat, right-arm
fast-medium bowler, county captain
Born: 31 December 1976, Leeds
Height: 6ft 2in **Weight:** 14st
Nickname: Oggie
County debut: 1996 (Yorkshire)
County cap: 2000 (Yorkshire)
Benefit: 2008 (Yorkshire)
Test debut: 2000
ODI debut: 2001-02
50 wickets in a season: 2
Place in batting averages: 247th av. 15.00
(2008 245th av. 12.83)
Place in bowling averages: 63rd av. 32.30
(2008 32nd av. 24.35)
Parents: Margaret and John
Wife and date of marriage: Sarah, 2 October 2004
Children: Ernie, May 2007
Family links with cricket: 'Dad is a cricket badger'
Education: Pudsey Grangefield School, West Yorkshire
Qualifications: GCSEs and A-levels

Overseas tours: Yorkshire CCC to South Africa; England U19 to Zimbabwe 1995-96; England to Kenya (ICC Knockout Trophy) 2000-01, to Pakistan and Sri Lanka 2000-01, to Zimbabwe (one-day series) 2001-02, to India and New Zealand 2001-02, to Sri Lanka (ICC Champions Trophy) 2002-03, to Australia 2002-03, to Africa (World Cup) 2002-03, to Bangladesh and Sri Lanka 2003-04, to West Indies 2003-04, to South Africa 2004-05, to Pakistan 2005-06, to India 2005-06, to Australia 2006-07, to Sri Lanka 2007-08, to New Zealand 2007-08

Overseas teams played for: Pirates, Johannesburg 1995-97; Free State 1998-2000

Cricketers particularly admired: Allan Donald, Courtney Walsh

Other sports played: Rugby

Other sports followed: Rugby league (Leeds Rhinos)

Relaxations: 'Dog walking'

Extras: NBC Denis Compton Award for most promising young Yorkshire player 1998. Was top wicket-taker in the 2000 National League competition with 37 wickets at 12.37. PCA Young Player of the Year 2000. Took 7-63 v New Zealand in the first Test at Christchurch 2001-02, the best innings return by an England pace bowler in Tests v New Zealand. Took hat-trick (Sarwan, Chanderpaul, Ryan Hinds) in the third Test v West Indies at Bridgetown 2003-04. His international awards include Man of the [Test] Series v Bangladesh 2003-04 and Man of the Match in the fourth Test v South Africa at Johannesburg 2004-05 (5-144/7-61) and in the first Test v India at Nagpur 2005-06 (6-57). Appointed MBE in 2006 New Year Honours as part of 2005 Ashes-winning England team. One of *Wisden*'s Five Cricketers of the Year 2006. Took 200th Test wicket (Farveez Maharoof) in the first Test v Sri Lanka at Lord's 2006. Took 237th Test wicket (Dwayne Bravo) in the fourth Test v West Indies at Riverside 2007 to move into sixth place in the England list of Test wicket-takers. England 12-month central contract 2007-08. Briefly returned to the England squad in 2008. Having had his Yorkshire contract terminated in October 2009, he joined Leicestershire the following month as their new captain for 2010

Best batting: 89* Yorkshire v Glamorgan, Headingley 2004
Best bowling: 7-49 Yorkshire v Somerset, Headingley 2003

2009 Season

	M	Inn	NO	Runs	HS	Avg	100	50	Ct	St	Balls	Runs	Wkts	Avg	BB	5I	10M
Test																	
FC	16	17	4	195	56*	15.00	-	1	5	-	2875	1486	46	32.30	5-56	2	-
ODI																	
List A	3	1	1	0	0*		-	-	-	-	126	83	2	41.50	1-25	-	
20/20 Int																	
20/20																	

Career Performances

	M	Inn	NO	Runs	HS	Avg	100	50	Ct	St	Balls	Runs	Wkts	Avg	BB	5I	10M
Test	67	92	27	473	38	7.27	-	-	24	-	13903	7564	248	30.50	7-61	7	1
FC	195	246	71	1653	89*	9.44	-	4	55	-	35554	18288	668	27.37	7-49	22	1
ODI	26	6	2	17	7	4.25	-	-	5	-	1306	1152	32	36.00	5-49	1	
List A	130	40	22	67	7*	3.72	-	-	14	-	6127	4535	179	25.33	5-28	4	
20/20 Int																	
20/20	15	2	1	19	18	19.00	-	-	4	-	324	472	13	36.30	3-23	-	

HOPKINSON, C. D. Sussex

Name: Carl Daniel Hopkinson
Role: Right-hand bat, right-arm fast-medium
bowler; 'batter that bowls'
Born: 14 September 1981, Brighton
Height: 5ft 11in
Nickname: Hoppo
County debut: 2001 (one-day), 2002 (first-class)
Place in batting averages: 100th av. 36.91
(2008 102nd av. 32.87)
Parents: Jane and Jerry
Marital status: Single
Family links with cricket: 'Dad played in the
local team, which got me interested, and coached
me from a young age'
Education: Chailey; Brighton College
Qualifications: 7 GCSEs, 3 A-levels, Level 1 coaching
Overseas tours: Tours to India 1997-98, to South Africa 1999
Overseas teams played for: Rockingham-Mandurah, Western Australia 2000-01
Cricketers particularly admired: Dennis Lillee, Ian Botham, Viv Richards,
Graham Thorpe
Other sports played: Rugby ('won Rosslyn Park National Sevens'), squash, football
Other sports followed: Football (West Ham)
Favourite band: 50 Cent
Extras: South of England and England squads until U17. Sussex Young Player of the
Year 2000. Sussex 2nd XI Fielder of the Year 2001, 2003. Took wicket (John Wood)
with his third ball on county debut, in the Norwich Union League v Lancashire at
Hove 2001. C&G Man of the Match award v Nottinghamshire at Hove 2005 (51 plus
run-out of Stephen Fleming). Retired as a player at the end of the 2009 season to join
the Sussex coaching staff
Best batting: 139 Sussex v Somerset, Taunton 2009
Best bowling: 1-20 Sussex v LUCCE, Hove 2004

2009 Season

	M	Inn	NO	Runs	HS	Avg	100	50	Ct	St	Balls	Runs	Wkts	Avg	BB	5I	10M
Test																	
FC	9	13	1	443	139	36.91	2	-	2	-	0	0	0		-	-	-
ODI																	
List A	1	1	0	10	10	10.00	-	-	-	-	0	0	0		-	-	
20/20 Int																	
20/20																	

Career Performances

	M	Inn	NO	Runs	HS	Avg	100	50	Ct	St	Balls	Runs	Wkts	Avg	BB	5I	10M
Test																	
FC	64	103	5	2705	139	27.60	3	15	39	-	340	262	2	131.00	1-20	-	-
ODI																	
List A	92	72	11	1400	123*	22.95	1	6	39	-	566	560	15	37.33	3-19	-	
20/20 Int																	
20/20	28	18	5	165	26*	12.69	-	-	11	-	0	0	0		-	-	

HORTON, P. J.   Lancashire

Name: <u>Paul</u> James Horton
Role: Right-hand bat, right-arm medium/off-spin bowler
Born: 20 September 1982, Sydney, Australia
Height: 5ft 10in   **Weight:** 11st 3lbs
Nickname: Horts, Ozzy
County debut: 2003
County cap: 2007
1000 runs in a season: 2
Place in batting averages: 136th av. 31.46 (2008 33rd av. 47.26)
Parents: Donald William and Norma
Marital status: Single
Education: Colo High School, Sydney; Broadgreen Comprehensive, Liverpool; St Margaret's High School, Liverpool
Qualifications: 11 GCSEs, 3 A-levels, Level 2 coaching
Overseas tours: Hawkesbury U15 to New Zealand 1997; Lancashire to Cape Town 2002-03, to Grenada 2003
Overseas teams played for: Hawkesbury, Sydney 1992-93 – 1997-98; Penrith, NSW 2002-03

Cricket moments to forget: 'First 2nd XI game for Lancashire at Old Trafford – out for 0'
Cricket superstitions: 'None'
Cricketers particularly admired: Dean Jones, Sachin Tendulkar, Mark Waugh
Other sports played: Football, golf, squash, tennis, badminton
Other sports followed: Football (Liverpool)
Favourite band: Red Hot Chili Peppers
Relaxations: 'Golf, socialising with friends, watching sport'
Extras: Captained Lancashire U17 and U19. Captained Lancashire Board XI in the C&G 2003. Lancashire Young Player of the Year Award 2001, 2002. Leading run-scorer for Lancashire 2nd XI in the 2nd XI Championship 2003 (861 runs – av. 50.65). Lancashire Player of the Year 2007. Scored over 1000 runs in 2008
Best batting: 173 Lancashire v Somerset, Taunton 2009

2009 Season

	M	Inn	NO	Runs	HS	Avg	100	50	Ct	St	Balls	Runs	Wkts	Avg	BB	5I	10M
Test																	
FC	17	30	2	881	173	31.46	2	4	16	-	12	10	0		-	-	-
ODI																	
List A	16	15	1	569	111*	40.64	2	2	8	-	0	0	0		-	-	
20/20 Int																	
20/20	9	9	0	166	41	18.44	-	-	5	-	0	0	0		-	-	

Career Performances

	M	Inn	NO	Runs	HS	Avg	100	50	Ct	St	Balls	Runs	Wkts	Avg	BB	5I	10M
Test																	
FC	59	99	10	3685	173	41.40	8	20	49	1	12	10	0		-	-	-
ODI																	
List A	42	38	1	993	111*	26.83	2	3	12	-	0	0	0		-	-	
20/20 Int																	
20/20	14	13	1	194	41	16.16	-	-	7	-	0	0	0		-	-	

40. These two Pakistanis recorded a ninth wicket partnership of 190 against England in 1967, then a Test match record. Name them.

HOUSEGO, D. M. Middlesex

Name: Daniel (<u>Dan</u>) Mark Housego
Role: Right-hand top-order bat, right-arm
off-spin bowler
Born: 12 October 1988, Windsor, Berkshire
Height: 5ft 10in **Weight:** 11st 2lbs
Nickname: Harry Housego, Housey
County debut: 2008
Place in batting averages: 252nd av. 14.33
Parents: Beryl and Jim
Marital status: In a relationship
Education: The Oratory School, Reading
Qualifications: 8 GCSEs, 3 A-levels,
Level 1 coaching
Career outside cricket: 'Personal training'

Off-season: 'Playing Grade cricket in Adelaide'
Overseas tours: England U15 to South Africa; England U16 to South Africa and
Barbados
Overseas teams played for: Adelaide 2007-08; Prospect, North Adelaide, 2008-09
Career highlights to date: 'Making my first-class debut against Derbyshire'
Cricket moments to forget: 'Two low scores at Lord's'
Cricket superstitions: 'None'
Cricketers particularly admired: Ian Bell, Michael Clarke, Callum Ferguson
Young players to look out for: Sam Northeast (Kent)
Other sports played: Football (Oxford United Academy 1998-2003), athletics (U12
200m national champion 2002), golf, fishing
Other sports followed: Football (Chelsea), golf (Tiger Woods)
Injuries: Slap lesion tear of the left shoulder – out for three months
Favourite band: Lil Wayne
Relaxations: 'Fishing, golf, reading'
Extras: Neil Lloyd Trophy (for best batting) at the Bunbury Festival 2004.
Represented England U15, U16, U17. Played for Berkshire in the Minor Counties
Championship 2006, making a personal best 170* against Shropshire
Opinions on cricket: 'Loving the changes that are being made, but still favour the
longer version of the game.'
Best batting: 36 Middlesex v Derbyshire, Derby 2008

2009 Season

	M	Inn	NO	Runs	HS	Avg	100	50	Ct	St	Balls	Runs	Wkts	Avg	BB	5I	10M
Test																	
FC	3	6	0	86	34	14.33	-	-	2	-	7	17	0		-	-	-
ODI																	
List A																	
20/20 Int																	
20/20	1	1	0	1	1	1.00	-	-	-	-	0	0	0		-	-	

Career Performances

	M	Inn	NO	Runs	HS	Avg	100	50	Ct	St	Balls	Runs	Wkts	Avg	BB	5I	10M
Test																	
FC	5	10	0	152	36	15.20	-	-	2	-	7	17	0		-	-	-
ODI																	
List A																	
20/20 Int																	
20/20	5	4	0	37	18	9.25	-	-	-	-	0	0	0		-	-	

HOWELL, B. A. C. — Hampshire

Name: Benjamin (<u>Benny</u>) Alexander Cameron Howell
Role: Right-hand opening bat, right-arm medium-fast bowler
Born: 5 October 1988, Bordeaux, France
Height: 5ft 11in **Weight:** 12st
Nickname: Growler, Howly, Schofield
County debut: No first-team appearance
Parents: Jonathan and Julie
Marital status: Single
Family links with cricket: 'Dad played one game for Warwickshire first team; made a half-century. Brother Nick played county age-group cricket for Berkshire'
Education: The Oratory School, Reading
Qualifications: 9 GCSEs, 3 A-levels
Overseas tours: Oratory School to Barbados 2003, 2004
Overseas teams played for: Melville, Perth 2007-08
Career highlights to date: '172 not out in a 50-over game for Hampshire Cricket Academy, August 2007'
Cricket moments to forget: 'Every time I bowl!'
Cricketers particularly admired: Shane Warne, Nic Pothas, Brett Lee, Steve Waugh, Sachin Tendulkar, Brian Lara

Other sports played: Football, rugby, golf, tennis, squash, basketball, real tennis, snooker, darts
Other sports followed: Football (Everton FC), AFL (Melbourne Demons)
Favourite band: Justin Timberlake, 50 Cent, Timbaland, Chris Brown, Akon, Eminem, Kanye West
Relaxations: 'Movies, music, sports (playing and watching), sleeping'
Extras: Hampshire Academy Player of the Year 2006. Southern Electric Premier League Player of the Month, August 2007. Awarded a development contract for 2009 and again for 2010
Opinions on cricket: 'At the end of the day, cricket is all about enjoying playing and entertaining the spectators. Twenty20 does that; it is exciting, explosive and highly skilful. This brings in the crowds and money to develop the game. It has to be played more often.'

HOWGEGO, B. H. N. Northamptonshire

Name: Benjamin (<u>Ben</u>) Harry Nicholas Howgego
Role: Left-hand opening bat, right-arm medium bowler
Born: 3 March 1988, King's Lynn, Norfolk
Height: 5ft 11in **Weight:** 12st 5lbs
Nickname: Benny
County debut: 2008
Place in batting averages: 207th av. 21.90
Parents: Peter and Julia
Marital status: Single
Education: The King's School, Ely; Stowe School; Exeter University
Qualifications: 10 GCSEs, 3 A-levels (2 A's, 1 B)
Career outside cricket: 'Student – studying for a BSc'

Off-season: Studying and training with the university team
Overseas tours: Stowe 1st XI to India 2005
Overseas teams played for: Claremeont CC, South Africa
Career highlights to date: 'Opening the batting for Northamptonshire v Australia in 2009'
Cricket moments to forget: 'Scoring a duck'
Cricketers particularly admired: Graham Thorpe
Young players to look out for: David Willey (Northamptonshire)
Other sports played: Tennis, rugby
Other sports followed: Rugby, football ('I follow Tottenham Hotspur sometimes')
Injuries: 'Back and knee injuries towards the end of the season – these inhibited my batting and stopped my fielding for 3-4 weeks'

Favourite band: Eminem
Relaxations: 'Watching films and listening to music'
Extras: Made 2nd XI Championship debut 2005. Represented both ECB Development of Excellence XI and ECB Schools v India U19 2006. Coached with Gary Kirsten in South Africa 2007. A student, he and Richard Browning were offered 2008 summer contracts to tie in with their studies. Howgego made his first-class debut for Northamptonshire as an opening batsman against Gloucestershire in August 2008, having played in the Second XI Championship just once up to that point in the season
Best batting: 47 Northamptonshire v Middlesex, Lord's 2009

2009 Season

	M	Inn	NO	Runs	HS	Avg	100	50	Ct	St	Balls	Runs	Wkts	Avg	BB	5I	10M
Test																	
FC	6	11	1	219	47	21.90	-	-	3	-	0	0	0		-	-	-
ODI																	
List A	1	1	0	7	7	7.00	-	-	-	-	0	0	0		-	-	
20/20 Int																	
20/20																	

Career Performances

	M	Inn	NO	Runs	HS	Avg	100	50	Ct	St	Balls	Runs	Wkts	Avg	BB	5I	10M
Test																		
FC	7	13	2	235	47	21.36	-	-	3	-	0	0	0		-	-	-
ODI																	
List A	1	1	0	7	7	7.00	-	-	-	-	0	0	0		-	-	
20/20 Int																	
20/20																	

41. Against whom did Pakistan record 13 wides during a
Test match innings in 1982?

HUGHES, C. F. Derbyshire

Name: <u>Chesney</u> Francis Hughes
Role: Left-hand bat, slow left-arm
orthodox spinner
Born: 20 January 1991, Anguilla
County debut: 2009 (one-day)
Extras: Made his Twenty20 debut for Anguilla aged
only 14. Played club cricket with Fleetwood CC
(Northern Premier League). Derbyshire 2nd XI 2009.
Signed a two-year contract with Derbyshire in June
2009. Holds a British passport and is not considered
an overseas player

2009 Season

	M	Inn	NO	Runs	HS	Avg	100	50	Ct	St	Balls	Runs	Wkts	Avg	BB	5I	10M
Test																	
FC																	
ODI																	
List A	4	3	0	34	27	11.33	-	-	1	-	126	119	1	119.00	1-34	-	
20/20 Int																	
20/20																	

Career Performances

	M	Inn	NO	Runs	HS	Avg	100	50	Ct	St	Balls	Runs	Wkts	Avg	BB	5I	10M
Test																	
FC																	
ODI																	
List A	6	5	0	65	31	13.00	-	-	1	-	156	136	2	68.00	1-17	-	
20/20 Int																	
20/20	2	2	0	28	20	14.00	-	-	-	-	12	19	0		-	-	

HUGHES, P. J.　　　　　　　　　　　Middlesex

Name: <u>Phillip</u> Joel Hughes
Role: Left-hand bat, off-break bowler
Born: 30 November 1988, Macksville,
New South Wales, Australia
Height: 5ft 7in
Nickname: Boofa
County debut: 2009
Test debut: 2009
Place in batting averages: 14th av. 65.81
Parents: Greg and Virginia
Education: Homebush Boys High School, Sydney
Overseas tours: Australia to South Africa 2008-09,
to England 2009

Overseas teams played for: Western Suburbs
2005-06 – 2006-07; New South Wales 2007-08 –
Other sports played: Rugby league
Extras: Represented Australia at the U19 World Cup in 2007. Aged 19 he became
the youngest player to score a century in a Pura Cup Final. Bradman Young Cricketer
of the Year 2009, Sheffield Shield Player of the Year 2008-9. Played for Middlesex
during the early part of the 2009 season, scoring a century in each of his three
County Championship games prior to the Australian Ashes tour
Best batting: 198 South Australia v New South Wales, Adelaide Oval, 2008-09

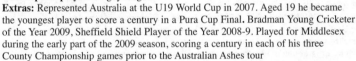

2009 Season

	M	Inn	NO	Runs	HS	Avg	100	50	Ct	St	Balls	Runs	Wkts	Avg	BB	5I	10M
Test	2	3	0	57	36	19.00	-	-	1	-	0	0	0	-	-	-	-
FC	7	12	1	724	195	65.81	3	3	6	-	18	9	0	-	-	-	-
ODI																	
List A	8	8	0	308	119	38.50	1	2	1	-	0	0	0	-	-		
20/20 Int																	
20/20																	

Career Performances

	M	Inn	NO	Runs	HS	Avg	100	50	Ct	St	Balls	Runs	Wkts	Avg	BB	5I	10M
Test	5	9	0	472	160	52.44	2	1	3	-	0	0	0	-	-	-	-
FC	28	50	5	2786	198	61.91	10	15	22	-	18	9	0	-	-	-	-
ODI																	
List A	26	26	3	863	119	37.52	1	6	8	-	0	0	0	-	-		
20/20 Int																	
20/20	10	10	2	390	83	48.75	-	3	6	-	0	0	0	-	-		

HUNTER, I. D. Derbyshire

Name: Ian David Hunter
Role: Right-hand bat, right-arm fast-medium bowler
Born: 11 September 1979, Durham City
Height: 6ft 2in **Weight:** 13st
Nickname: Sticks, Hunts, Kingsley
County debut: 1999 (one-day, Durham),
2000 (first-class, Durham), 2004 (Derbyshire)
Place in bowling averages: 34th av. 28.23
Parents: Ken and Linda
Marital status: Single
Family links with cricket: Brother is a local
village cricketer
Education: Fyndoune Community College,
Sacriston; New College, Durham

Qualifications: 9 GCSEs, 1 A-level (PE),
BTEC National Diploma in Sports Science, Level 1 and 2 coaching
Overseas tours: Durham U21 to Sri Lanka 1996; Durham to Cape Town 2002
Career highlights to date: 'Taking 5-63 against Durham at Riverside [2005]'
Cricket moments to forget: 'All of 2007 season – out through knee injuries'
Cricket superstitions: 'Always put my left pad on first'
Cricketers particularly admired: Allan Donald, Graeme Welch, Steve Waugh
Young players to look out for: Dan Redfern (Derbyshire), Gary Ballance (Yorkshire)
Other sports played: Football, golf
Other sports followed: Football (Newcastle United), rugby league (St Helens)
Favourite band: Arctic Monkeys
Relaxations: 'Golf, gym, socialising with friends'
Extras: Set a then Durham best analysis for the 2nd XI Championship with his 11-155
v Lancashire 2nd XI at Great Crosby 1999. Represented England U19 1999. Out for
most of the 2007 season with torn cartilage and patellar tendonopathy of the right
knee. Signed a new one-year contract in October 2009
Best batting: 65 Durham v Northamptonshire, Northampton 2002
Best bowling: 5-46 Derbyshire v Essex, Chelmsford 2009

2009 Season

	M	Inn	NO	Runs	HS	Avg	100	50	Ct	St	Balls	Runs	Wkts	Avg	BB	5I	10M
Test																	
FC	7	7	3	129	47	32.25	-	-	2	-	1090	593	21	28.23	5-46	2	-
ODI																	
List A	5	3	1	15	15	7.50	-	-	1	-	224	204	5	40.80	2-36	-	
20/20 Int																	
20/20	3	0	0	0	0	-	-	-	-	-	60	89	2	44.50	2-37	-	

Career Performances

	M	Inn	NO	Runs	HS	Avg	100	50	Ct	St	Balls	Runs	Wkts	Avg	BB	5I	10M
Test																	
FC	63	81	21	1064	65	17.73	-	2	18	-	9805	5835	150	38.90	5-46	3	-
ODI																	
List A	87	52	13	325	39	8.33	-	-	17	-	3769	3113	96	32.42	4-29	-	
20/20 Int																	
20/20	18	6	2	41	25*	10.25	-	-	3	-	378	542	19	28.52	3-26	-	

HUSSAIN, G. M. Gloucestershire

Name: <u>Gemaal</u> Maqsood Hussain
Role: Right-hand bat, right-arm medium-fast bowler
Born: 10 October 1983, Waltham Forest, London
County debut: 2009
County cap: 2009
Education: Leeds University (Sports Science)
Extras: Played club cricket in both the Bradford and
Birmingham Leagues. Had played in the 2nd XI
Championship for Sussex, Essex, Nottinghamshire and
Worcestershire in the three years prior to his signing a
two-year contract with Gloucestershire in May 2009
Best batting: 8 Gloucestershire v Kent,
Beckenham, 2009
Best bowling: 2-73 Gloucestershire v Kent,
Beckenham, 2009

2009 Season

	M	Inn	NO	Runs	HS	Avg	100	50	Ct	St	Balls	Runs	Wkts	Avg	BB	5I	10M
Test																	
FC	1	2	0	16	8	8.00	-	-	1	-	132	107	2	53.50	2-73	-	-
ODI																	
List A	1	0	0	0	0		-	-	-	-	30	17	2	8.50	2-17	-	
20/20 Int																	
20/20	7	7	4	23	8	7.66	-	-	2	-	150	193	10	19.30	3-22	-	

Career Performances

	M	Inn	NO	Runs	HS	Avg	100	50	Ct	St	Balls	Runs	Wkts	Avg	BB	5I	10M
Test																	
FC	1	2	0	16	8	8.00	-	-	1	-	132	107	2	53.50	2-73	-	-
ODI																	
List A	1	0	0	0	0		-	-	-	-	30	17	2	8.50	2-17	-	
20/20 Int																	
20/20	7	7	4	23	8	7.66	-	-	2	-	150	193	10	19.30	3-22	-	

HUSSEY, D. J.   Nottinghamshire

Name: David (<u>Dave</u>) John Hussey
Role: Right-hand bat, right-arm
off-spin bowler, occasional wicket-keeper
Born: 15 July 1977, Perth, Western Australia
Height: 5ft 11in   **Weight:** 13st 3lbs
Nickname: Huss, Hussa, Husscat
County debut: 2004
County cap: 2004
ODI debut: 2008
Twenty20 Int debut: 2008
1000 runs in a season: 4
1st-Class 200s: 3
Place in batting averages: (2008 2nd av. 83.93)
Parents: Helen and Ted
Marital status: Single

Family links with cricket: Brother Mike plays for Australia and Western Australia and has played for Northamptonshire, Gloucestershire and Durham
Education: Prendiville Catholic College; Edith Cowan University
Qualifications: Bachelor of Business (Sports Management and Sports Science)
Overseas tours: Commonwealth Bank [Australian] Cricket Academy to Sri Lanka 1997-98; Australia A to Pakistan 2007-08; Australia to West Indies 2008 (one-day series), to South Africa 2008-09 (one-day series), to UAE (one-day series) 2008-09
Overseas teams played for: Wanneroo DCC, Perth 1992-2001;
Prahran CC, Victoria; Victoria 2002-03 –
Career highlights to date: 'Winning Pura Cup with Victoria 2004. Winning Championship with Nottinghamshire 2005'
Cricket moments to forget: 'Debut for Victoria – dropped Steve Waugh on 4; he went on to make 211'
Cricket superstitions: 'Left shoe on first'
Cricketers particularly admired: Brendon Julian, Mark Waugh, Damien Martyn
Other sports played: Australian Rules football, squash, tennis, football
Other sports followed: AFL (St Kilda FC), football (Brighton & Hove Albion)
Favourite band: Keane, Foo Fighters
Relaxations: 'Reading'
Extras: Played for Western Australia U19 and 2nd XI. Represented Australia U19 1995-96. Has represented Australia A. Scored 212* and won Man of the Match award as Victoria scored 455-7 to beat New South Wales at Newcastle in the Pura Cup 2003-04. His other awards include Man of the Match v New South Wales at Melbourne in the Pura Cup 2003-04 (120/50), v South Australia at Adelaide in the ING Cup 2003-04 (113) and v South Australia at Adelaide (104/74*) and v Tasmania at Hobart (103/31*), both in the Pura Cup 2007-08; also won three match awards in five days in

the KFC Twenty20 Big Bash 2007-08. Scored 275 v Essex at Trent Bridge 2007, in the process sharing with Chris Read (165*) in a new record fifth-wicket partnership for Nottinghamshire (359). First season in county cricket as overseas player with Nottinghamshire in 2004. Had a truncated season with Nottinghamshire in 2008, returned in June 2009 and will be part of the county side in 2010. Scored his first ODI century against Scotland in Edinburgh 2009

Best batting: 275 Nottinghamshire v Essex, Trent Bridge 2007
Best bowling: 4-105 Nottinghamshire v Hampshire, Trent Bridge 2005

2009 Season

	M	Inn	NO	Runs	HS	Avg	100	50	Ct	St	Balls	Runs	Wkts	Avg	BB	5I	10M
Test																	
FC	3	5	0	407	189	81.40	2	1	5	-	30	18	0		-	-	-
ODI																	
List A	1	1	1	120	120*			1	-	-	0	0	0		-	-	
20/20 Int	3	3	0	55	28	18.33	-	-	1	-	6	16	0		-	-	
20/20	5	5	1	118	55	29.50	-	1	2	-	30	49	1	49.00	1-25	-	

Career Performances

	M	Inn	NO	Runs	HS	Avg	100	50	Ct	St	Balls	Runs	Wkts	Avg	BB	5I	10M
Test																	
FC	132	203	21	10048	275	55.20	35	44	159	-	2025	1281	20	64.05	4-105	-	-
ODI	23	21	0	598	111	28.47	1	4	12	-	257	230	3	76.66	1-6	-	
List A	162	151	22	5224	130	40.49	8	34	77	-	1360	1207	28	43.10	3-26	-	
20/20 Int	11	10	1	236	88*	26.22	-	1	4	-	132	140	7	20.00	3-25	-	
20/20	83	80	13	2113	100*	31.53	1	11	43	-	556	696	27	25.77	3-25	-	

42. Which Pakistan bowler was hit in the mouth by a bouncer from Bob Willis at Edgbaston in 1978?

IMRAN ARIF Worcestershire

Name: Imran Arif
Role: Right-hand bat, right-arm
fast-medium bowler
Born: 15 January 1984, Kotli, Pakistan
Height: 5ft 11in **Weight:** 11st 2lbs
Nickname: Immy, Ice Man
County debut: 2008
Place in batting averages: 254th av. 13.50
Place in bowling averages: 132nd av. 52.88
(2008 42nd av. 26.13)
Education: Government High School, Saidpur,
Kotli (AK); Bradford College
Qualifications: 5 GCSEs
Career highlights to date: 'Making my
first-class debut v Glamorgan (see *Best bowling*)'
Other sports followed: Football (Liverpool), tennis, snooker
Relaxations: 'Watching football, listening to music, computer games, movies,
spending time with friends and family.'
Extras: Has played for Sussex Second XI (in 2006), Hampshire Second XI and in the
Bradford League. After two years of Second XI cricket at Worcestershire, he signed a
two-year professional contract as an overseas player in July 2008
Best batting: 35 Worcestershire v Sussex, Hove, 2009
Best bowling: 5-50 Worcestershire v Glamorgan, New Road 2008

2009 Season

	M	Inn	NO	Runs	HS	Avg	100	50	Ct	St	Balls	Runs	Wkts	Avg	BB	5I	10M
Test																	
FC	9	13	7	81	35	13.50	-	-	4	-	1109	899	17	52.88	5-93	1	-
ODI																	
List A	5	0	0	0	0		-	-	2	-	174	177	3	59.00	2-51	-	
20/20 Int																	
20/20																	

Career Performances

	M	Inn	NO	Runs	HS	Avg	100	50	Ct	St	Balls	Runs	Wkts	Avg	BB	5I	10M
Test																	
FC	15	16	8	94	35	11.75	-	-	5	-	2062	1474	39	37.79	5-50	2	-
ODI																	
List A	10	2	2	17	16*		-	-	2	-	356	375	8	46.87	2-51	-	
20/20 Int																	
20/20																	

IMRAN TAHIR Warwickshire

Name: Mohammad Imran Tahir
Role: Right-hand bat, right-arm leg-spin bowler
Born: 27 March 1979, Lahore, Pakistan
County debut: 2003 (Middlesex),
2007 (Yorkshire), 2008 (Hampshire)
County cap: 2009 (Hampshire)
50 wickets in a season: 1
Place in batting averages: 224th av. 18.72
Place in bowling averages: 66th av. 32.90
(2008 2nd av. 16.68)
Overseas tours: Pakistan U19 to South Africa 1996-
97, to Australia 1997-98, to South Africa (U19 World
Cup) 1997-98; Pakistan A to Sri Lanka 2004-05
Overseas teams played for: Lahore City 1996-97 –

1997-98, Pakistan International Airlines 2004-05 –
2006-07 (and others in Pakistan); Titans 2007-08 – 2008-09; Easterns 2009-10
Extras: Played for Staffordshire in the C&G 2004 and 2005, winning Man of the
Match award v Lancashire at Stone 2004 (3-31/18-ball 41*). Represented both
Pakistan A and a PCB Patron's XI v England XI 2005-06. Was a temporary overseas
player with Middlesex in 2003, and with Yorkshire in 2007. Played for Hampshire
in both 2008 and 2009. Joined Warwickshire in October 2009
Best batting: 77* Hampshire v Somerset, Rose Bowl 2009
Best bowling: 8-76 REDCO v Karachi Blues, Lahore (C) 1999-2000

2009 Season

	M	Inn	NO	Runs	HS	Avg	100	50	Ct	St	Balls	Runs	Wkts	Avg	BB	5I	10M
Test																	
FC	12	15	4	206	77*	18.72	-	1	4	-	2926	1711	52	32.90	7-140	4	-
ODI																	
List A	11	1	0	5	5	5.00	-	-	2	-	574	429	18	23.83	3-30	-	
20/20 Int																	
20/20	11	3	1	3	2	1.50	-	-	3	-	264	286	8	35.75	2-32	-	

Career Performances

	M	Inn	NO	Runs	HS	Avg	100	50	Ct	St	Balls	Runs	Wkts	Avg	BB	5I	10M
Test																	
FC	95	115	26	1177	77*	13.22	-	1	44	-	18641	9891	382	25.89	8-76	24	5
ODI																	
List A	64	21	7	185	41*	13.21	-	-	14	-	2993	2170	95	22.84	5-27	2	
20/20 Int																	
20/20	20	8	3	28	13	5.60	-	-	7	-	456	467	20	23.35	3-13	-	

IRELAND, A. J.   Gloucestershire

Name: <u>Anthony</u> John Ireland
Role: Right-hand bat, right-arm
medium bowler
Born: 30 August 1984, Masvingo, Zimbabwe
County debut: 2007
County cap: 2007
ODI debut: 2005-06
Twenty20 Int debut: 2006-07
Place in bowling averages: 56th av. 31.61
(2008 114th av. 36.78)
Overseas tours: ZCU President's XI to India (Duleep
Trophy) 2005-06; Zimbabwe A to Bangladesh 2006-
07; Zimbabwe to West Indies (one-day series) 2006,
to South Africa (one-day series) 2006-07, to India
(ICC Champions Trophy) 2006-07, to Bangladesh
(one-day series) 2006-07, to West Indies (World Cup) 2006-07
Overseas teams played for: Midlands 2002-03 – 2005-06
Extras: Retired from international cricket in April 2007. Is not considered
an overseas player
Best batting: 16* Gloucestershire v Middlesex, Bristol 2008
Best bowling: 7-36 Zimbabwe A v Bangladesh A, Mirpur 2006-07

2009 Season

	M	Inn	NO	Runs	HS	Avg	100	50	Ct	St	Balls	Runs	Wkts	Avg	BB	5I	10M
Test																	
FC	7	7	2	21	16	4.20	-	-	3	-	1002	664	21	31.61	6-31	1	-
ODI																	
List A	8	3	1	5	5*	2.50	-	-	1	-	288	237	9	26.33	3-10	-	
20/20 Int																	
20/20	3	1	0	1	1	1.00	-	-	2	-	60	74	4	18.50	2-38	-	

Career Performances

	M	Inn	NO	Runs	HS	Avg	100	50	Ct	St	Balls	Runs	Wkts	Avg	BB	5I	10M
Test																	
FC	28	41	14	114	16*	4.22	-	-	10	-	3976	2487	77	32.29	7-36	2	1
ODI	26	13	5	30	8*	3.75	-	-	2	-	1326	1115	38	29.34	3-41	-	
List A	57	27	14	82	17	6.30	-	-	9	-	2523	2163	76	28.46	4-16	-	
20/20 Int	1	1	1	2	2*		-	-	-	-	18	33	1	33.00	1-33	-	
20/20	13	5	2	21	8*	7.00	-	-	5	-	225	321	18	17.83	3-10	-	

JAMES, N. A.   Glamorgan

Name: Nicholas (<u>Nick</u>) Alexander James
Role: Left-hand bat, slow left-arm
bowler; all-rounder
Born: 17 September 1986, Sandwell, West Midlands
Height: 5ft 10in **Weight:** 12st 2lbs
Nickname: Jaymo
County debut: 2006 (Warwickshire, one-day),
2008 (Warwickshire, first-class), 2009 (Glamorgan,
one-day)
Parents: Ann and Mike
Marital status: Single
Family links with cricket: 'Dad and brother
Chris play at Aldridge CC. Dad also coaches'
Education: King Edward VI Aston School,
Birmingham
Qualifications: 10 GCSEs, 3 A-levels
Overseas tours: England U19 to Bangladesh 2005-06, to Sri Lanka (U19 World Cup)
2005-06; CCC to Australia 2007-08
Overseas teams played for: Tea Tree Gully (Adelaide) 2008-09
Career highlights to date: 'Representing England U19. Reaching semi-final of 2006
U19 World Cup. Playing for Warwickshire first team in C&G, Pro40 and Twenty20'
Cricket moments to forget: 'Fracturing hand diving to stop ball (against Lancashire)
in 2006 – unavailable for six weeks. Watching ball I had just hit for six bounce and
smash through rear window of my car (while bringing my 150 up) v Hampshire
2nd XI at Basingstoke 2007.'
Cricketers particularly admired: Kevin Pietersen, Kumar Sangakkara
Young players to look out for: Andrew Miller, Chris Woakes and Richard Johnson
(all Warwickshire)
Other sports played: 'Recreational football, golf'
Other sports followed: Football (Aston Villa and Nottingham Forest)
Favourite band: Coldplay
Relaxations: 'Relaxing with friends'
Extras: Captain of Warwickshire U17 County Championship winning side 2004.
Member of ECB U18 Development Squad 2004. Represented England U19 and
captained ECB Development of Excellence XI v Sri Lanka U19 2005. Has won eight
Warwickshire youth awards, including Tiger Smith Memorial Award for the most
promising young player 2005. Acted as 12th man (one day only) for England A v Sri
Lankans at Worcester 2006. Attended ECB Elite Skills Set Spin Programme at
Loughborough 2006-07. Birmingham Premier League Young Player of the Year 2007.
ECB Scholarship for Club Cricket Conference tour to Australia 2007-08. Released by
Warwickshire in September 2008. Signed with Glamorgan for 2010 after a trial period
with the county at the end of the 2009 season

Opinions on cricket: 'It's faster and more exciting now...'
Best batting: 34 Warwickshire v CUCCE, Fenner's 2008
Best bowling: 1-6 Warwickshire v CUCCE, Fenner's 2008

2009 Season

	M	Inn	NO	Runs	HS	Avg	100	50	Ct	St	Balls	Runs	Wkts	Avg	BB	5I	10M
Test																	
FC																	
ODI																	
List A	2	2	0	10	6	5.00	-	-	-	-	36	35	1	35.00	1-35	-	
20/20 Int																	
20/20																	

Career Performances

	M	Inn	NO	Runs	HS	Avg	100	50	Ct	St	Balls	Runs	Wkts	Avg	BB	5I	10M
Test																	
FC	1	1	0	34	34	34.00	-	-	1	-	18	6	1	6.00	1-6	-	-
ODI																	
List A	11	8	2	112	30	18.66	-	-	2	-	246	176	7	25.14	2-34	-	
20/20 Int																	
20/20	2	2	1	13	12*	13.00	-	-	2	-	0	0	0		-	-	

JAQUES, P. A. Worcestershire

Name: Philip (Phil) Anthony Jaques
Role: Left-hand bat
Born: 3 May 1979, Wollongong, Australia
Height: 6ft 1in **Weight:** 14st 11lbs
Nickname: Pro, PJ
County debut: 2003 (Northamptonshire),
2004 (Yorkshire), 2006 (Worcestershire)
County cap: 2003 (Northamptonshire),
2005 (Yorkshire), 2006 (Worcestershire colours)
Test debut: 2005-06
ODI debut: 2005-06
1000 runs in a season: 4
1st-Class 200s: 8
Parents: Mary and Stuart
Wife and date of marriage: Danielle, 5 May 2006
Family links with cricket: 'Dad played league cricket in Sheffield, England'
Education: Figtree High School, Wollongong; Australian College of
Physical Education
Qualifications: Fitness certificate, Level 2 coaching

Overseas tours: New South Wales to New Zealand 2000-01; Australia A to Pakistan 2005-06, 2007-08; Australia to South Africa 2005-06 (one-day series), to Bangladesh 2005-06, to New Zealand (one-day series) 2006-07, to West Indies 2008, plus one-day tournament in Malaysia
Overseas teams played for: Sutherland DCC, Sydney; New South Wales Blues 2000-01 – 2001-02, 2003-04 –
Career highlights to date: 'Playing cricket for Australia'
Cricket moments to forget: 'Dropping an outfield catch on my first-class one-day debut.'
Cricket superstitions: 'Always put gear on same way in same order every time I bat'
Cricketers particularly admired: Steve Waugh, Mark Taylor
Other sports played: Tennis, rugby league, golf, basketball
Other sports followed: Rugby league (St George Illawarra), football (Liverpool)
Favourite band: Coldplay, Bon Jovi
Relaxations: 'Golf, beach, watching movies'
Extras: Attended Australian Cricket Academy 2000. Scored maiden first-class century (149*) v Worcestershire at Worcester 2003 and maiden first-class double century (222) in his next Championship innings v Yorkshire at Northampton 2003. Scored 1409 first-class runs in his first season of county cricket 2003. Holds a British passport and was not considered an overseas player with Northamptonshire in 2003. An overseas player with Yorkshire 2004 (having played for New South Wales 2003-04), deputising for Ian Harvey and Darren Lehmann, and in 2005. Named Australia's State Player of the Year at the 2006 Allan Border Medal awards; also won the Steve Waugh Medal (NSW Player of the Year) 2005-06. His match awards include Man of the Match v Tasmania at Sydney in the Pura Cup 2006-07 (192). His wife, Danielle Small, is an Australia soccer international. Was an overseas player with Worcestershire 2006-07. Scored century (107) on first-class debut for Worcestershire v Surrey at The Oval 2006 and another (112) on one-day debut for the county v Northamptonshire at Worcester in the C&G 2006. Has re-signed as an overseas player with Worcestershire for 2010
Best batting: 244 Worcestershire v Essex, Chelmsford 2006

2009 Season (Did not make any first-class or one-day appearances)

Career Performances

	M	Inn	NO	Runs	HS	Avg	100	50	Ct	St	Balls	Runs	Wkts	Avg	BB	5I	10M
Test	11	19	0	902	150	47.47	3	6	7	-	0	0	0		-	-	-
FC	129	229	9	11707	244	53.21	35	54	97	-	68	87	0		-	-	-
ODI	6	6	0	125	94	20.83	-	1	3	-	0	0	0		-	-	
List A	122	119	8	4738	158*	42.68	12	26	31	-	18	19	0		-	-	
20/20 Int																	
20/20	30	30	1	903	92	31.13	-	6	8	-	6	15	0		-	-	

JAVID, A.   Warwickshire

Name: Ateeq Javid
Role: Right-hand bat, right-arm seam and occasional leg-spin bowler
Born: 15 October 1991, Birmingham
County debut: 2009
Overseas tours: England U19 to Bangladesh 2009, to New Zealand (ICC U19 World Cup) 2010
Extras: Played for Aston Manor CC in the Birmingham League 2008. Represented Warwickshire Academy and Warwickshire 2nd XI 2008. Played for England U16 Elite Player Development side at the Bunbury Festival, August 2008, scoring 45 from 29 balls. Has made a century for Warwickshire U17, and three half-centuries for Warwickshire U19. Called up to England U18 squad October 2008. Signed a two-year contract for the county in September 2008. Part of the ECB Development Group 2008. Scored 63 runs as England U19 beat Bangladesh U19 in the sixth game of seven match series played in Bangladesh 2009
Best batting: 21 Warwickshire v Durham, Riverside, 2009

2009 Season

	M	Inn	NO	Runs	HS	Avg	100	50	Ct	St	Balls	Runs	Wkts	Avg	BB	5I	10M
Test																	
FC	3	6	0	55	21	9.16	-	-	3	-	78	78	0		-	-	-
ODI																	
List A																		
20/20 Int																		
20/20																		

Career Performances

	M	Inn	NO	Runs	HS	Avg	100	50	Ct	St	Balls	Runs	Wkts	Avg	BB	5I	10M
Test																		
FC	3	6	0	55	21	9.16	-	-	3	-	78	78	0		-	-	-
ODI																		
List A																		
20/20 Int																		
20/20																		

JEFFERSON, W. I. Leicestershire

Name: William (<u>Will</u>) Ingleby Jefferson
Role: Right-hand opening bat
Born: 25 October 1979, Derby
('but native of Norfolk')
Height: 6ft 10½in **Weight:** 15st 2lbs
Nickname: Santa, Lemar, Jeffo
County debut: 2000 (Essex),
2007 (Nottinghamshire)
County cap: 2002 (Essex)
1000 runs in a season: 1
1st-Class 200s: 1
Place in batting averages: 146th av. 30.16
(2008 181st av. 22.10)
Parents: Richard
Marital status: Single

Family links with cricket: Grandfather played for the Army and Combined
Services in the 1920s. Father, R. I. Jefferson, played for Cambridge University
1961 and Surrey 1961-66
Education: Oundle School, Northamptonshire; Durham University
Qualifications: 9 GCSEs, 3 A-levels, BA (Hons) Sport in the Community,
Level 3 coaching
Overseas tours: Oundle School to South Africa 1995; England A to
Bangladesh 2006-07
Overseas teams played for: Young People's Club, Paarl, South Africa 1998-99;
South Perth, Western Australia 2002-03
Career highlights to date: 'Being awarded [Essex] county cap on final day of the
2002 season. Scoring 165* to help beat Nottinghamshire and secure 2002 second
division Championship. Scoring 222 v Hampshire at Rose Bowl [2004]'
Cricket moments to forget: 'Any dropped catch; any time bowled playing
across the line'
Cricket superstitions: 'Put batting gear on in the same order'
Cricketers particularly admired: Andy Flower, Nasser Hussain
Young players to look out for: Jaik Mickleburgh (Essex)
Other sports played: Golf (12 handicap), tennis ('occasionally')
Other sports followed: Rugby (British & Irish Lions, England), golf (Ryder Cup)
Favourite band: Coldplay, U2, The Verve
Relaxations: 'Reading, pilates, listening to music, spending time with family'
Extras: Holmwoods School Cricketer of the Year 1998. Represented British
Universities 2000, 2001 and 2002. Played for DUCCE 2001 and 2002. NBC Denis
Compton Award for the most promising young Essex player 2002. Scored century
before lunch on the opening day for Essex v CUCCE at Fenner's 2003. C&G Man of

the Match awards for his 97 v Scotland at Edinburgh 2004 and for his 126 v
Nottinghamshire at Trent Bridge in the next round. Essex Player of the Year 2004.
Essex Boundary Club Trophy for scoring most runs for Essex 1st XI 2004.
Represented England Lions 2007. Released by Nottinghamshire in September 2009.
Signed a one-year deal with Leicestershire in October 2009
Opinions on cricket: 'Standard of cricket is getting nearer first-class played in
Australia, which is where we want to be. Last step is still to reduce number of days
during the summer to improve quality further. System in good health – Twenty20
skills converted into Pro40, which will convert more into 50-over cricket in the
future.'
Best batting: 222 Essex v Hampshire, Rose Bowl 2004
Best bowling: 1-16 Essex v Yorkshire, Headingley 2005

2009 Season

	M	Inn	NO	Runs	HS	Avg	100	50	Ct	St	Balls	Runs	Wkts	Avg	BB	5I	10M
Test																	
FC	4	6	0	181	133	30.16	1	-	7	-	0	0	0		-	-	-
ODI																	
List A	8	7	1	202	93	33.66	-	2	1	-	0	0	0		-	-	
20/20 Int																	
20/20	10	9	2	216	75	30.85	-	1	2	-	0	0	0		-	-	

Career Performances

	M	Inn	NO	Runs	HS	Avg	100	50	Ct	St	Balls	Runs	Wkts	Avg	BB	5I	10M
Test																	
FC	91	159	12	5292	222	36.00	12	20	88	-	120	60	1	60.00	1-16	-	-
ODI																	
List A	93	91	6	2969	132	34.92	4	17	41	-	24	9	2	4.50	2-9	-	
20/20 Int																	
20/20	35	34	4	633	75	21.10	-	2	12	-	0	0	0		-	-	

43. Name the Pakistan opening batsman who scored a double hundred
at Lord's in 1982.

Name: <u>Tom</u> Melvin Jewell
Role: Right-hand bat, right-arm
fast-medium bowler; all-rounder
Born: 13 January 1991, Reading, Berkshire
Height: 6ft 4in   **Weight:** 13st 6lbs
Nickname: TJ
County debut: 2008
Parents: Melvin and Caroline
Marital status: Single
Education: Bradfield College, Reading
Qualifications: 8 GCSEs, 3 A-levels
Career outside cricket: Student
Career highlights: 'Making my first-class debut
against Loughborough'
Cricketers particularly admired: Steve Waugh
Young players to look out for: Matthew Dunn (Surrey)
Other sports followed: Football (Reading)
Favourite band: Kings of Leon
Relaxations: 'Spending time with my girlfriend. The odd episode of *Friends*'
Extras: Won the Sir Jack Hobbs Award (for the best U15 cricketer in England) 2007.
Features in the book *Training for Success – Cricket*. Awarded an Emerging Player
contract for 12 months from October 2009
Opinions on cricket: 'Twenty20 cricket has reduced the number of County
Championship hundreds'
Best bowling: 1-16 Surrey v LUCCE, The Oval 2008

2009 Season

	M	Inn	NO	Runs	HS	Avg	100	50	Ct	St	Balls	Runs	Wkts	Avg	BB	5I	10M
Test																	
FC																	
ODI																	
List A	2	2	1	1	1	1.00	-	-	-	-	36	56	0		-	-	
20/20 Int																	
20/20																	

Career Performances

	M	Inn	NO	Runs	HS	Avg	100	50	Ct	St	Balls	Runs	Wkts	Avg	BB	5I	10M
Test																	
FC	1	0	0	0	0	-	-	-	-	-	42	16	1	16.00	1-16	-	-
ODI																	
List A	2	2	1	1	1	1.00	-	-	-	-	36	56	0		-	-	
20/20 Int																	
20/20																	

JOHNSON, R. M. Warwickshire

Name: <u>Richard</u> Matthew Johnson
Role: Right-hand bat, wicket-keeper
Born: 1 September 1988, Solihull
Height: 5ft 10in **Weight:** 11st
Nickname: Johnno
County debut: 2008 (*see below*)
Parents: Barry and Lorraine
Marital status: Single
Family links with cricket: 'Dad played
Saturday League club cricket'
Education: Solihull Secondary School;
Solihull School Sixth Form
Qualifications: 10 GCSEs, 3 A-levels,
Level 2 coaching

Career outside cricket: Cricket coach
Off-season: 'Here in England training hard with Warwickshire and ECB
Performance squads, and a three-week tour to South Africa in January with the
England Performance squads'
Overseas tours: England U16 to Cape Town 2005; Warwickshire Academy to
Cape Town 2007; Solihull School to Barbados 2007; Warwickshire to
Bloemfontein (South Africa) 2009
Overseas teams played for: Adelaide University CC 2009
Career highlights to date: 'Warwickshire first-team debut – top-scored with 71'
(*Note: this three-day match was against Bradford/Leeds UCCE in 2007 and was not
considered first-class*); List A debut against Northamptonshire, and scoring 72 on my
first-class debut against CUCCE, both in May 2008.'
Cricket moments to forget: 'Breaking a bone in my thumb before playing for
England U15'
Cricket superstitions: 'Consistent pre-match and match routines'
Favourite sledging line: 'Received during a 2nd XI county game – "You'll never
get signed as a professional player!"'
Cricketers particularly admired: Keith Piper, Sachin Tendulkar, Tony Frost
Young players to look out for: Ateeq Javid (Warwickshire)
Other sports played: Football (Wolverhampton Wanderers U10, U11, U12), rugby
(Solihull School 1st XV)
Other sports followed: Football (Aston Villa), darts, boxing
Favourite band: Take That, The Twang, The Skyline
Relaxations: 'Music, TV, computer, friends, watching Aston Villa'
Extras: Best Wicket-keeper Award at Bunbury Festival 2005. Warwickshire Second
XI most improved player 2008. Attended Darren Lehmann Academy, Adelaide, 2008.
Member of England Performance Programme squad 2009-10

Opinions on cricket: 'Keep a balance between the four-day game and the one-day game.'
Best batting: 72 Warwickshire v CUCCE, Fenners 2008

2009 Season

	M	Inn	NO	Runs	HS	Avg	100	50	Ct	St	Balls	Runs	Wkts	Avg	BB	5I	10M
Test																	
FC	1	2	0	33	22	16.50	-	-	7	-	0	0	0		-	-	-
ODI																	
List A																	
20/20 Int																	
20/20	2	1	0	0	0	0.00	-	-	-	-	0	0	0		-	-	

Career Performances

	M	Inn	NO	Runs	HS	Avg	100	50	Ct	St	Balls	Runs	Wkts	Avg	BB	5I	10M
Test																	
FC	2	3	0	105	72	35.00	-	1	8	-	0	0	0		-	-	-
ODI																	
List A	2	2	0	26	20	13.00	-	-	2	-	0	0	0		-	-	
20/20 Int																	
20/20	2	1	0	0	0	0.00	-	-	-	-	0	0	0		-	-	

JONES, A. J.   Glamorgan

Name: Alexander (<u>Alex</u>) John Jones
Role: Right-hand bat, left-arm seam bowler
Born: 10 November 1988, Bridgend, Glamorgan
Nickname: AJ
County debut: No first-team appearance
Education: Cowbridge Comprehensive School;
UWIC (degree course in Sport and Physical
Education)
Cricket moments to forget: 'Getting hit in the box!'
Cricketers particularly admired: Kevin Pietersen,
Chris Gayle
Young players to look out for: Chris Ashling,
Will Owen, Kyle Tudge (all Glamorgan)
Other sports followed: Rugby

Extras: Glamorgan and Wales Academy U17 2005,
Glamorgan U17 2006, Glamorgan U19 2008, Glamorgan and Wales Academy 2005-08, Glamorgan Second XI 2006-08, Wales Minor Counties 2007-08. Cardiff UCCE 2009. Awarded a development contract for 2010
Opinions on cricket: 'Under-rated... great game, great game!'

JONES, C. R.   Somerset

Name: Christopher (<u>Chris</u>) Robert Jones
Role: Right-hand bat
Born: 5 November 1990, Harold Wood, Essex
County debut: No first-team appearances
Education: Richard Huish College, Taunton
Overseas teams played for: Sydney University
2009-10
Extras: Ex-Somerset Academy. Has played for Poole
CC and Bashley CC (Southern League). Represented
Somerset at U17 level in 2008, finishing with an
average of 162.5. Played for England U17 v New
Zealand U19 in August 2008. Leading run scorer for
Somerset 2nd XI in 2009 with a total of 704. Signed
a Summer Development contract with the county after
completing his A-level studies in June 2009

JONES, E. P.   Derbyshire

Name: Edward (<u>Ed</u>) Peter Jones
Role: Right-hand bat, right-arm
slow-medium bowler
Born: 23 October 1989, Stoke-on-Trent
County debut: No first-team appearance
Extras: Played for Staffordshire in the Minor
Counties Championship 2007. Became the first
Derbyshire player to take up the Donald Carr
Scholarship (instituted by the county and the
University of Derby), offering a free university
degree course in business and sports management,
September 2008

JONES, G. O.   Kent

Name: <u>Geraint</u> Owen Jones
Role: Right-hand bat, wicket-keeper
Born: 14 July 1976, Kundiawa, Papua New Guinea
Height: 5ft 10in **Weight:** 12st
Nickname: Joner, Jonesy, 'G'
County debut: 2001
County cap: 2003
Test debut: 2003-04
ODI debut: 2004
Twenty20 Int debut: 2005
1000 runs in a season: 1
Place in batting averages: 31st av. 51.73
(2008 121st av. 30.36)
Parents: Emrys, Carol (deceased), Maureen
(stepmother)
Wife and date of marriage: 'Jennifer, 30 September 2006'
Family links with cricket: 'Father was star off-spinner in local school side'
Education: Harristown State High School, Toowoomba, Queensland;
MacGregor State High School, Brisbane
Qualifications: Level 1 coaching; pharmacy technician
Career outside cricket: Hobby farming
Off-season: 'Making sure the pigs, lambs and chickens fatten up nicely!'
Overseas tours: Beenleigh-Logan U19 to New Zealand 1995; Kent to Port Elizabeth
2001-02; England to Bangladesh and Sri Lanka 2003-04, to West Indies 2003-04, to
Zimbabwe (one-day series) 2004-05, to South Africa 2004-05, to Pakistan 2005-06,
to India 2005-06, to Australia 2006-07
Overseas teams played for: Beenleigh-Logan, Brisbane 1995-98, 2006-07;
Valleys, Brisbane 2001-02
Career highlights to date: 'Ashes 2005, Twenty20 final 2007'
Cricket moments to forget: 'Last Test played, finals of 2008'
Cricket superstitions: 'Left pad first'
Cricketers particularly admired: Adam Gilchrist
Young players to look out for: Joe Denly and Robbie Joseph (both Kent),
Neil Dexter (Middlesex)
Other sports played: Golf
Other sports followed: Football (Liverpool), Rugby (Crickhowell RFC)
Favourite band: Newton Faulkner
Relaxations: 'Rearing my own animals for meat and sausage production'
Extras: Set new competition record for a season's tally of wicket-keeping dismissals
in the one-day league (33; 27/6) 2003; also equalled record for number of wicket-
keeping catches in one match, six v Leicestershire at Canterbury 2003. Made 59 first-
class dismissals plus 985 first-class runs in his first full season of county cricket 2003.

Man of the Match in the second Test v New Zealand at Headingley 2004, in which he scored his maiden Test century (100). His other international awards include Man of the Match v Australia in the tied final of the NatWest Series 2005 (71 plus five catches). Appointed MBE in 2006 New Year Honours as part of 2005 Ashes-winning England team. Made 100th Test dismissal (Mahela Jayawardene, caught) in the first Test v Sri Lanka at Lord's 2006, becoming the fastest England wicket-keeper to the milestone (27 matches)

Opinions on cricket: 'The authorities need to sort out the worldwide Twenty20 situation, as it seems that the only ones missing out are the English players. Also, don't overkill the concept.'

Best batting: 156 Kent v Surrey, Canterbury 2009

2009 Season

	M	Inn	NO	Runs	HS	Avg	100	50	Ct	St	Balls	Runs	Wkts	Avg	BB	5I	10M
Test																	
FC	17	26	0	1345	156	51.73	5	6	41	3	0	0	0		-	-	-
ODI																	
List A	12	12	2	342	73	34.20	-	3	9	1	0	0	0		-	-	
20/20 Int																	
20/20	12	10	2	216	56	27.00	-	1	7	5	0	0	0		-	-	

Career Performances

	M	Inn	NO	Runs	HS	Avg	100	50	Ct	St	Balls	Runs	Wkts	Avg	BB	5I	10M
Test	34	53	4	1172	100	23.91	1	6	128	5	0	0	0		-	-	-
FC	126	187	20	5696	156	34.10	12	30	382	25	18	18	0		-	-	-
ODI	49	41	8	815	80	24.69	-	4	68	4	0	0	0		-	-	
List A	149	127	22	2569	86	24.46	-	11	171	27	0	0	0		-	-	
20/20 Int	2	2	1	33	19	33.00	-	-	2	-	0	0	0		-	-	
20/20	45	36	9	441	56	16.33	-	1	25	12	0	0	0		-	-	

44. Although Bangladesh lost the first Test in India in November 2000 by nine wickets, they achieved a highly respectable first-innings total. How many runs did they make?

JONES, P. S. Derbyshire

Name: Philip Steffan Jones
Role: Right-hand bat, right-arm fast-medium bowler
Born: 9 February 1974, Llanelli
Height: 6ft 1in **Weight:** 15st 2lbs
Nickname: Jona
County debut: 1997 (Somerset), 2004
(Northamptonshire), 2006 (Derbyshire)
50 wickets in a season: 2
Place in batting averages: 202nd av. 22.50
(2008 204th av. 19.90)
Place in bowling averages: 84th av. 35.58
(2008 80th av. 31.40)
Parents: Lyndon and Ann
Wife and date of marriage: Alex, 12 October 2002
Children: Seren, 2006
Family links with cricket: 'Father played locally in South Wales'
Education: Ysgol Gyfun y Strade, Llanelli; Loughborough University; Homerton
College, Cambridge University
Qualifications: BSc Sports Science, PGCE in Physical Education
Career outside cricket: 'Sports conditioner'
Overseas tours: Wales Minor Counties to Barbados 1996; Somerset CCC to South
Africa 1999, 2000, 2001
Overseas teams played for: Clarence CC, Tasmania 2005
Career highlights to date: 'C&G final 2001 with Somerset. 6-25 v Glamorgan for
Derbyshire [at Cardiff 2006]' (*His full second innings figures were 20-14-25-6*)
Cricket moments to forget: '2003-04'
Cricket superstitions: 'Getting early to the ground'
Cricketers particularly admired: 'Pop' Welch, Brett Lee
Other sports played: Rugby union ('professionally for Bristol and Moseley 1997-99')
Other sports followed: Rugby union
Favourite band: Pussycat Dolls, Black Eyed Peas
Relaxations: 'Going to the cinema'
Extras: Took nine wickets (6-67/3-81) in the Varsity Match at Lord's 1997.
Derbyshire's Championship Player of the Year 2006. Left Derbyshire at the end of the
2006 season and rejoined Somerset for 2007. Took over 40 wickets in championship
and one-day games in 2008. Signed two-year contract with Derbyshire in November
2009 after a period on loan there from Somerset at the end of the 2009 season. He will
also take on coaching duties
Best batting: 114 Somerset v Leicestershire, Leicester 2007
Best bowling: 6-25 Derbyshire v Glamorgan, Cardiff 2006

2009 Season

	M	Inn	NO	Runs	HS	Avg	100	50	Ct	St	Balls	Runs	Wkts	Avg	BB	5I	10M
Test																	
FC	12	13	3	225	54*	22.50	-	2	5	-	2388	1210	34	35.58	5-35	1	-
ODI																	
List A	4	2	1	11	11*	11.00	-	-	1	-	138	108	4	27.00	2-37	-	
20/20 Int																	
20/20																	

Career Performances

	M	Inn	NO	Runs	HS	Avg	100	50	Ct	St	Balls	Runs	Wkts	Avg	BB	5I	10M
Test																	
FC	134	157	39	2228	114	18.88	2	7	29	-	22281	13163	353	37.28	6-25	10	1
ODI																	
List A	180	96	45	639	42	12.52	-	-	31	-	8115	7114	241	29.51	6-56	3	
20/20 Int																	
20/20	26	12	6	62	24*	10.33	-	-	5	-	532	776	27	28.74	3-26	-	

JONES, R. A.   Worcestershire

Name: <u>Richard</u> Alan Jones
Role: Right-hand bat, right-arm fast-medium bowler
Born: 6 November 1986, Wordsley, West Midlands
Height: 6ft 2in **Weight:** 13st
Nickname: Jonesy, Jonah
County debut: 2007
County colours: 2007
Place in batting averages: 198th av. 23.22
Place in bowling averages: 71st av. 33.86
Parents: Bob and Julie
Marital status: Single
Education: The Grange School, Stourbridge; King Edward VI College, Stourbridge
Qualifications: 13 GCSEs, 3 A-levels
Overseas tours: England U19 to Bangladesh 2005-06
Overseas teams played for: Subiaco Floreat (Perth) 2007-08
Career highlights to date: 'Making first-class debut for Worcestershire against Warwickshire 2007'
Cricket moments to forget: 'Opening over against Sussex in last game of 2007 season – it went for plenty!'

Cricket superstitions: 'None'
Cricketers particularly admired: Ian Botham, Andrew Flintoff, Brett Lee
Other sports played: Football (district schools), golf
Other sports followed: Football (West Bromwich Albion)
Favourite band: Arctic Monkeys
Relaxations: 'Football, listening to music, staying fit, chatting with friends'
Extras: Scored first league hundred aged 17 for local side Old Hill (Birmingham & District Premier League). Member of England Performance Programme squad 2009-10
Opinions on cricket: 'Going back to one overseas per team will give more younger players a chance to shine in county cricket, which can only be a good thing. The emergence and success of Twenty20 cricket at international level will eventually see it becoming the leading form of cricket in the future.'
Best batting: 53* Worcestershire v Durham, Worcester 2009
Best bowling: 6-100 Worcestershire v Warwickshire, Edgbaston 2009

2009 Season

	M	Inn	NO	Runs	HS	Avg	100	50	Ct	St	Balls	Runs	Wkts	Avg	BB	5I	10M
Test																	
FC	7	11	2	209	53*	23.22	-	1	3	-	1044	745	22	33.86	6-100	1	-
ODI																	
List A	2	1	0	2	2	2.00	-	-	-	-	66	97	0		-	-	
20/20 Int																	
20/20																	

Career Performances

	M	Inn	NO	Runs	HS	Avg	100	50	Ct	St	Balls	Runs	Wkts	Avg	BB	5I	10M
Test																	
FC	12	17	3	249	53*	17.78	-	1	4	-	1640	1180	30	39.33	6-100	1	-
ODI																	
List A	4	2	0	8	6	4.00	-	-	1	-	102	140	0		-	-	
20/20 Int																	
20/20																	

45. Who made a century for Bangladesh in the first Test in India in November 2000?

JONES, S. P.   Hampshire

Name: <u>Simon</u> Philip Jones
Role: Left-hand bat, right-arm fast bowler
Born: 25 December 1978, Morriston, Swansea
Height: 6ft 3in **Weight:** 15st
Nickname: Horse
County debut: 1998 (Glamorgan),
2008 (Worcestershire)
County cap: 2002 (Glamorgan)
Test debut: 2002
ODI debut: 2004-05
Place in batting averages: (2008 236th av. 13.85)
Place in bowling averages: (2008 3rd av. 18.02)
Parents: Irene and Jeff
Marital status: Single
Family links with cricket: 'Father played for
England [1963-64 – 1967-68]'

Education: Coedcae Comprehensive School; Millfield School
Qualifications: 12 GCSEs, 1 A-level, basic and senior coaching awards
Overseas tours: Dyfed Schools to Zimbabwe 1994; Glamorgan to South Africa 1998;
ECB National Academy to Australia 2001-02; England to Australia 2002-03, to West
Indies 2003-04, to Zimbabwe (one-day series) 2004-05, to South Africa 2004-05, to
India 2005-06; England A to Malaysia and India 2003-04
Career highlights to date: 'Winning Ashes series 2005'
Cricket moments to forget: 'Every injury'
Cricket superstitions: 'Right boot on first'
Cricketers particularly admired: Allan Donald
Other sports played: Football (trials with Leeds United)
Favourite band: Eminem
Extras: NBC Denis Compton Award for the most promising young Glamorgan player
2001. Made Test debut in the first Test v India at Lord's 2002, striking a 43-ball 44
(more runs than his father scored in his 15-Test career); the Joneses are the eleventh
father and son to have played in Tests for England. ECB National Academy 2003-04.
Recorded maiden Test five-wicket return (5-57) in the second Test v West Indies at
Port-of-Spain 2003-04; the Joneses thus became the first father and son to have taken
five-wicket hauls for England. Had best strike rate among Test bowlers taking 20 or
more wickets in the calendar year 2005 (38.50 balls/wicket). Appointed MBE in 2006
New Year Honours as part of 2005 Ashes-winning England team. One of *Wisden*'s
Five Cricketers of the Year 2006. Left Glamorgan at the end of the 2007 season and
joined Worcestershire for 2008. Selected for England Lions against South Africa in
August 2008, but had to withdraw due to a knee injury that curtailed his season. Out
for the whole of the 2009 season after surgery. Released by Worcestershire in July
2009. Signed for Hampshire in September 2009

Best batting: 46 Glamorgan v Yorkshire, Scarborough 2001
Best bowling: 6-45 Glamorgan v Derbyshire, Cardiff 2002

2009 Season (Did not make any first-class or one-day appearances)

Career Performances

	M	Inn	NO	Runs	HS	Avg	100	50	Ct	St	Balls	Runs	Wkts	Avg	BB	5I	10M
Test	18	18	5	205	44	15.76	-	-	4	-	2821	1666	59	28.23	6-53	3	-
FC	88	108	35	899	46	12.31	-	-	17	-	12999	7947	260	30.56	6-45	15	1
ODI	8	1	0	1	1	1.00	-	-	-	-	348	275	7	39.28	2-43	-	
List A	34	13	8	76	26	15.20	-	-	2	-	1454	1239	31	39.96	5-32	1	
20/20 Int																	
20/20	4	2	1	22	11*	22.00	-	-	-	-	92	150	2	75.00	1-36	-	

JORDAN, C. J. Surrey

Name: Christopher (Chris) James Jordan
Role: Right-hand bat, right-arm
fast bowler; all-rounder
Born: 4 October 1988, Barbados
Height: 6ft 2in
Nickname: CJ
County debut: 2007
Place in batting averages: 142nd av. 30.42
(2008 216th av. 17.57)
Place in bowling averages: 137th av. 58.76
(2008 141st av. 47.50)
Parents: Robert and Rosie
Marital status: Single
Education: Dulwich College
Qualifications: 2 A-levels
Overseas tours: Barbados U15 to St Vincent 2004
Cricket superstitions: 'Have to touch my box, my thigh pad and my pads before
I settle down to bat'
Cricketers particularly admired: Dwayne Bravo, Brian Lara, Brett Lee
Other sports played: Football (Dulwich College 1st XI)
Other sports followed: Football (Manchester United)
Extras: Scored 208 in a semi-final for school. Surrey 2nd XI 2006. NBC Denis
Compton Award for most promising young Surrey player 2007. A series of injuries
blighted his 2008 season. Member of England Performance Programme squad 2009-10
Opinions on cricket: 'It has become more exciting since Twenty20 has been
introduced.'

Best batting: 57 Surrey v Nottinghamshire, Trent Bridge 2008
Best bowling: 4-84 Surrey v Essex, Guildford 2008

2009 Season

	M	Inn	NO	Runs	HS	Avg	100	50	Ct	St	Balls	Runs	Wkts	Avg	BB	5I	10M
Test																	
FC	8	10	3	213	42	30.42	-	-	4	-	1250	764	13	58.76	4-84	-	-
ODI																	
List A	4	3	1	13	7	6.50	-	-	1	-	78	94	0		-	-	
20/20 Int																	
20/20	4	4	0	54	28	13.50	-	-	1	-	72	112	4	28.00	2-34	-	

Career Performances

	M	Inn	NO	Runs	HS	Avg	100	50	Ct	St	Balls	Runs	Wkts	Avg	BB	5I	10M
Test																	
FC	21	25	7	433	57	24.05	-	1	7	-	3039	1824	45	40.53	4-84	-	-
ODI																	
List A	18	11	1	74	38	7.40	-	-	5	-	703	655	22	29.77	3-28	-	
20/20 Int																	
20/20	11	10	2	111	31	13.87	-	-	4	-	174	259	5	51.80	2-34	-	

JOSEPH, R. H. Kent

Name: <u>Robert</u> Hartman Joseph Jnr
Role: Right-hand bat, right-arm fast-medium bowler
Born: 20 January 1982, Antigua
Height: 6ft 1in **Weight:** 13st 7lbs
Nickname: RJ, Blueie
County debut: 2004
Place in bowling averages: 53rd av. 31.08
(2008 40th av. 26.05)
Education: Sutton Valence School; St Mary's
University College
Overseas tours: Antigua Young Lions to England
1997; Antigua and Leeward Islands U15 to Trinidad
and St Lucia. England Performance Programme to
India, 2008-09
Cricket moments to forget: 'Local school final –
getting out on 47 needing one to win with four wickets in hand and losing'
Cricketers particularly admired: Sir Vivian Richards, Andy Roberts
Other sports played: Golf
Other sports followed: Football (Arsenal)
Favourite band: Maroon 5

Relaxations: Listening to music
Extras: Made first-class debut for First-Class Counties XI v New Zealand A at Milton Keynes 2000. Took 55 first-class wickets in 2008 to top the county's bowling averages
Best batting: 36* Kent v Sussex, Hove 2007
Best bowling: 6-32 Kent v Durham, Riverside 2008

2009 Season

	M	Inn	NO	Runs	HS	Avg	100	50	Ct	St	Balls	Runs	Wkts	Avg	BB	5I	10M
Test																	
FC	4	5	2	11	9*	3.66	-	-	-	-	584	373	12	31.08	6-55	1	-
ODI																	
List A	5	3	3	12	7*		-	-	1	-	180	166	3	55.33	3-55	-	
20/20 Int																	
20/20	7	0	0	0	0		-	-	3	-	132	164	8	20.50	2-14	-	

Career Performances

	M	Inn	NO	Runs	HS	Avg	100	50	Ct	St	Balls	Runs	Wkts	Avg	BB	5I	10M
Test																	
FC	44	56	20	384	36*	10.66	-	-	9	-	6670	4073	128	31.82	6-32	5	-
ODI																	
List A	33	14	12	43	15	21.50	-	-	4	-	1307	1114	39	28.56	5-13	1	
20/20 Int																	
20/20	8	1	1	1	1*		-	-	3	-	156	188	10	18.80	2-14	-	

---

46. Which Pakistan batsman was only 17 when he became the youngest player to score a century in a Test match?

JOYCE, E. C.   Sussex

Name: Edmund (<u>Ed</u>) Christopher Joyce
Role: Left-hand bat, occasional right-arm
medium bowler
Born: 22 September 1978, Dublin
Height: 5ft 10in **Weight:** 12st 7lbs
Nickname: Joycey, Spud, Piece
County debut: 1999 (Middlesex), 2009 (Sussex)
County cap: 2002 (Middlesex)
ODI debut: 2006
Twenty20 Int debut: 2006
1st-Class 200s: 1
1000 runs in a season: 5
Place in batting averages: 74th av. 41.08
(2008 89th av. 35.77)
Parents: Maureen and Jimmy

Marital status: Single
Family links with cricket: Two brothers and two sisters have represented Ireland
Education: Presentation College, Bray, County Wicklow; Trinity College, Dublin
Qualifications: Irish Leaving Certificate, BA (Hons) Economics and Geography,
Level 2 coaching
Overseas tours: Ireland U19 to Bermuda (International Youth Tournament) 1997,
to South Africa (U19 World Cup) 1997-98; Ireland to Zimbabwe (ICC Emerging
Nations Tournament) 1999-2000, to Canada (ICC Trophy) 2001; MCC to Namibia
and Uganda 2004-05; England A to West Indies 2005-06; England to India (ICC
Champions Trophy) 2006-07, to Australia 2006-07, to West Indies (World Cup)
2006-07; England Lions to India 2007-08; Sussex to India (Champions League) 2009
Overseas teams played for: Coburg CC, Melbourne 1996-97; University CC,
Perth 2001-02
Cricket superstitions: 'None'
Cricketers particularly admired: Larry Gomes, Brian Lara
Other sports played: Golf, rugby, soccer, snooker
Other sports followed: Rugby (Leinster), football (Manchester United)
Favourite band: The Mars Volta
Relaxations: Cinema, eating out, listening to music
Extras: NBC Denis Compton Award for the most promising young Middlesex player
2000. Became the first Irish-born-and-bred player to record a century in the County
Championship with his 104 v Warwickshire at Lord's 2001. C&G Man of the Match
award for his 72 v Northamptonshire at Northampton 2003. Vice-captain of Middlesex
June 2004 to end of 2004 season (captaining the county in the absence of Andrew
Strauss on international duty) and from 2007 to end 2008. First batsman to 1000 first-
class runs in 2005 (18 June). Has represented Ireland in first-class and one-day cricket.

Made England ODI debut in Belfast 2006 v Ireland, for whom his brother Dominick was also making his ODI debut. Has also represented England in Twenty20 International cricket. ECB National Academy 2005-06. Scored maiden ODI century (107) v Australia at Sydney in the Commonwealth Bank Series 2006-07, winning Man of the Match award. Man of the Match v Kenya in St Lucia in the World Cup 2006-07 (75). Captained Middlesex to Twenty20 Cup Final win in 2008. Signed for Sussex November 2008

Best batting: 211 Middlesex v Warwickshire, Edgbaston 2006
Best bowling: 2-34 Middlesex v CUCCE, Fenner's 2004

2009 Season

	M	Inn	NO	Runs	HS	Avg	100	50	Ct	St	Balls	Runs	Wkts	Avg	BB	5I	10M
Test																	
FC	15	24	1	945	183	41.08	3	3	12	-	12	9	1	9.00	1-9	-	-
ODI																	
List A	19	18	2	941	146	58.81	3	4	2	-	0	0	0		-	-	
20/20 Int																	
20/20	13	11	4	169	41*	24.14	-	-	3	-	0	0	0		-	-	

Career Performances

	M	Inn	NO	Runs	HS	Avg	100	50	Ct	St	Balls	Runs	Wkts	Avg	BB	5I	10M
Test																	
FC	142	234	18	9606	211	44.47	22	53	109	-	1287	1025	11	93.18	2-34	-	-
ODI	17	17	0	471	107	27.70	1	3	6	-	0	0	0		-	-	
List A	184	174	19	5698	146	36.76	7	37	64	-	264	309	6	51.50	2-10	-	
20/20 Int	2	1	0	1	1	1.00	-	-	-	-	0	0	0		-	-	
20/20	49	45	9	635	47	17.63	-	-	14	-	6	12	0		-	-	

47. What was particularly unusual about Nasim-ul-Ghani's maiden first-class century, which he scored at Lord's in 1962?

KARTIK, M. Somerset

Name: Murali <u>Kartik</u>
Role: Left-hand bat, orthodox left-arm
spin bowler
Born: 11 September 1976, Chennai
(Madras), India
Height: 6ft **Weight:** 12st 12lbs
Nickname: Pirate, Gary, Karts, King, Kat,
Special K
County debut: 2005 (Lancashire),
2007 (Middlesex)
County cap: 2007 (Middlesex)
Test debut: 1999-2000
ODI debut: 2001-02
Twenty20 Int debut: 2007
50 wickets in a season: 1

Place in batting averages: 193rd av. 24.00 (2008 202nd av. 20.12)
Place in bowling averages: 12th av. 22.87 (2008 99th av. 34.06)
Parents: Mr R. Murali and the late Mrs Shanta Murali
Wife and date of marriage: Shweta Kartik, 11 September 2002
Education: Sardar Patel Vidyalaya, New Delhi; Hindu College, Delhi University
Qualifications: BCom (Hons); Masters in Computer Application
Career outside cricket: Broadcasting
Off-season: 'Playing the domestic season back home in India'
Overseas tours: India A to Pakistan 1997-98, to West Indies 1999-2000, to South
Africa 2001-02, to Sri Lanka 2002, to England 2003; India to Bangladesh 2000-01,
to Australia 2003-04, to Pakistan 2003-04, to Bangladesh 2004-05, to Zimbabwe
2005-06 (Videocon Tri-Series), to Pakistan 2005-06 (one-day series)
Overseas teams played for: Railways, India 1996-97 – ; Kolkata Knight Riders
(IPL) 2007-08
Career highlights to date: 'My Test debut in 1999 v South Africa. Our Test victories
in Australia and Pakistan in 2003-04. 9-70 v Bombay in the Irani Trophy. 6-27 v
Australia in 2007 ODIs, a world record for a left-arm spinner.'
Cricket moments to forget: 'Being dropped by India the day after being named as
Man of the Match against Australia in 2004'
Cricket superstitions: 'Lots of them!'
Cricketers particularly admired: Sir Garfield Sobers, Steve Waugh, Matthew
Hayden, Anil Kumble, VVS Laxman
Young players to look out for: Steve Finn and John Simpson (both Middlesex),
Craig Kieswetter (Somerset), Andrew Hales (Nottinghamshire), Ian Saxelby
(Gloucestershire)
Other sports played: Golf; table-tennis – 'represented my state'

Other sports followed: Formula One, tennis, golf, football (Chelsea)
Favourite band: Simon & Garfunkel
Relaxations: 'Photography, travelling, sleeping'
Extras: Represented India U19. Broke Ravi Shastri's 20-year-old record when taking 9-70 for Rest of India v Mumbai in October 2000. Spinner of the Year award in India 2001. Man of the Match in the fourth Test v Australia at Mumbai (Bombay) 2004-05 (4-44/3-32). Was a temporary overseas player with Lancashire during the 2005 and 2006 seasons, taking 10-168 (5-93/5-75) on Championship debut v Essex at Chelmsford 2005; an overseas player with Middlesex since 2007. Took 6-27 (world record figures for a left-arm spinner) and Man of the Match award in the seventh ODI v Australia in 2007. Played in both the Stanford Series and IPL in 2008. Released by Middlesex at the end of the 2009 season. Signed for Somerset as their overseas player for 2010
Opinions on cricket: 'Too much Twenty20 emphasis – looks like we might kill the goose that lays the golden eggs. Not happy that the 50-over competition has been done away with. Also too much cricket here in England without any rest.'
Best batting: 96 Railways v Rest of India, Delhi (KS) 2005-06
Best bowling: 9-70 Rest of India v Mumbai, Mumbai (Bombay) 2000-01

2009 Season

	M	Inn	NO	Runs	HS	Avg	100	50	Ct	St	Balls	Runs	Wkts	Avg	BB	5I	10M
Test																	
FC	10	19	5	336	62*	24.00	-	2	11	-	1903	755	33	22.87	5-65	1	-
ODI																	
List A	1	1	0	13	13	13.00	-	-	1	-	48	19	2	9.50	2-19	-	
20/20 Int																	
20/20	8	3	0	6	4	2.00	-	-	-	-	180	206	4	51.50	1-18	-	

Career Performances

	M	Inn	NO	Runs	HS	Avg	100	50	Ct	St	Balls	Runs	Wkts	Avg	BB	5I	10M
Test	8	10	1	88	43	9.77	-	-	2	-	1932	820	24	34.16	4-44	-	-
FC	142	179	28	2953	96	19.55	-	14	102	-	30741	12430	475	26.16	9-70	25	3
ODI	37	14	5	126	32*	14.00	-	-	10	-	1907	1612	37	43.56	6-27	1	
List A	166	81	26	612	44	11.12	-	-	50	-	8521	6163	208	29.62	6-27	2	
20/20 Int	1	0	0	0	0	-	-	-	-	-	24	27	0	-	-	-	
20/20	46	10	3	58	17	8.28	-	-	14	-	940	1045	37	28.24	5-13	1	

KEEDY, G. Lancashire

Name: Gary Keedy
Role: Left-hand bat, left-arm spin bowler
Born: 27 November 1974, Wakefield
Height: 5ft 11in **Weight:** 13st
Nickname: Keeds, Phil Mitchell, Minty
County debut: 1994 (Yorkshire),
1995 (Lancashire)
County cap: 2000 (Lancashire)
50 wickets in a season: 3
Place in batting averages: (2008 218th av. 17.35)
Place in bowling averages: 73rd av. 34.22
(2008 127th av. 41.32)
Parents: Roy and Pat
Wife and date of marriage: Andrea,
12 October 2002
Children: Erin Grace, 8 September 2006
Education: Garforth Comprehensive; Open University
Qualifications: 8 GCSEs, Level 2 coaching, Certificate in Natural Sciences
Overseas tours: England U18 to South Africa 1992-93, to Denmark 1993;
England U19 to Sri Lanka 1993-94; Lancashire to Portugal 1995, to Jamaica 1996,
to South Africa 1997; MCC to UAE and Oman 2004
Overseas teams played for: Frankston, Melbourne 1995-96
Career highlights to date: 'County cap. Playing for Lancashire. Fourteen wickets in
match v Gloucestershire at Old Trafford 2004. Five wickets v Yorkshire at Headingley'
Cricket superstitions: 'None'
Cricketers particularly admired: Graham Gooch, Shane Warne
Other sports followed: Rugby league (Leeds Rhinos), football (Leeds United)
Relaxations: 'Wine tasting. Looking after the family'
Extras: Player of the Series for England U19 v West Indies U19 1993; also played v
India U19 1994. Had match figures of 14-227 (7-95/7-132) v Gloucestershire at Old
Trafford 2004, the best return by an English spinner since Martyn Ball's 14-169 in
1993. Leading English wicket-taker (second overall) in the Championship 2004 (72 at
25.68). Lancashire Player of the Year 2004. Voted 'best county player never to have
played for England' in *All Out Cricket*'s October 2006 edition. Took more than 70
wickets in all competitions in 2009, moving more than 50 places up the bowling
averages from 2008
Best batting: 64 Lancashire v Sussex, Hove 2008
Best bowling: 7-95 Lancashire v Gloucestershire, Old Trafford 2004

2009 Season

	M	Inn	NO	Runs	HS	Avg	100	50	Ct	St	Balls	Runs	Wkts	Avg	BB	5I	10M
Test																	
FC	17	16	7	63	18	7.00	-	-	-	-	3263	1540	45	34.22	6-50	3	-
ODI																	
List A	17	5	2	8	4	2.66	-	-	4	-	780	583	24	24.29	4-43	-	
20/20 Int																	
20/20	9	1	1	0	0*		-	-	1	-	174	190	6	31.66	2-23	-	

Career Performances

	M	Inn	NO	Runs	HS	Avg	100	50	Ct	St	Balls	Runs	Wkts	Avg	BB	5I	10M
Test																	
FC	187	210	104	1201	64	11.33	-	2	46	-	37937	17810	554	32.14	7-95	27	5
ODI																	
List A	68	23	10	129	33	9.92	-	-	9	-	2770	2126	78	27.25	5-30	1	
20/20 Int																	
20/20	43	7	4	19	9*	6.33	-	-	4	-	837	890	39	22.82	4-15	-	

KEEGAN, C. B.   Sussex

Name: <u>Chad</u> Blake Keegan
Role: Right-hand bat, right-arm fast bowler
Born: 30 July 1979, Sandton, Johannesburg, South Africa
Height: 6ft 1in **Weight:** 12st
Nickname: Wick
County debut: 2001 (Middlesex)
County cap: 2003 (Middlesex)
50 wickets in a season: 1
Parents: Sharon and Blake
Marital status: Single
Education: Durban High School
Qualifications: YMCA fitness instructor
Overseas tours: MCC to Argentina and Chile 2001; Sussex to India (Champions League) 2009
Overseas teams played for: Durban High School Old Boys 1994-97; Crusaders, Durban 1998-99
Career highlights to date: 'Being awarded Player of the Year for Middlesex 2003'
Cricket moments to forget: 'Losing my pants diving for a ball at Lord's'
Cricket superstitions: 'Tapping the bat either side of the crease three times'
Cricketers particularly admired: Malcolm Marshall, Neil Johnson

Other sports played: 'Any extreme sports, golf'
Other sports followed: Football (Liverpool)
Favourite band: Jack Johnson
Relaxations: 'Making and listening to music (guitar); sketching'
Extras: Represented KwaZulu-Natal U13, KwaZulu-Natal Schools, KwaZulu-Natal U19, KwaZulu-Natal Academy. MCC Young Cricketer. Middlesex Player of the Year 2003. Is not considered an overseas player. Released by Middlesex November 2007. Given an extended non-contract trial in 2009 by Sussex
Best batting: 44 Middlesex v Surrey, The Oval 2004
Best bowling: 6-114 Middlesex v Leicestershire, Southgate 2003

2009 Season

	M	Inn	NO	Runs	HS	Avg	100	50	Ct	St	Balls	Runs	Wkts	Avg	BB	5I	10M
Test																	
FC																	
ODI																	
List A	2	2	0	39	38	19.50	-	-	1	-	66	79	3	26.33	2-53	-	
20/20 Int																	
20/20	2	0	0	0	0		-	-	-	-	18	23	1	23.00	1-13	-	

Career Performances

	M	Inn	NO	Runs	HS	Avg	100	50	Ct	St	Balls	Runs	Wkts	Avg	BB	5I	10M
Test																	
FC	47	57	6	607	44	11.90	-	-	14	-	8395	4887	140	34.90	6-114	6	-
ODI																	
List A	89	58	19	649	50	16.64	-	1	21	-	4073	3253	136	23.91	6-33	3	
20/20 Int																	
20/20	21	17	5	238	42	19.83	-	-	5	-	396	521	13	40.07	3-14	-	

KEMP, J. M. Kent

Name: <u>Justin</u> Miles Kemp
Role: Right-hand bat, right-arm fast medium bowler
Born: 2 October 1977, Queenstown, Cape Province, South Africa
Height: 6ft 4in **Weight:** 15st 2lbs
Nickname: Kempy
County debut: 2003 (Worcestershire), 2005 (Kent)
County cap: 2003 (Worcestershire colours), 2006 (Kent)
Test debut: 2000-01
ODI debut: 2000-01
Twenty20 Int debut: 2005-06
Place in batting averages: 57th av. 43.33 (2008 157th av. 25.75)

Family links with cricket: 'Grandfather (J. M. Kemp) played for Border 1947-48; father (J. W. Kemp) played for Border 1975-76 – 1976-77; cousin of former South Africa ODI player Dave Callaghan'
Education: Queens College; University of Port Elizabeth
Overseas tours: South Africa U19 to India 1995-96; South African Academy to Zimbabwe 1998-99; South Africa A to West Indies 2000, to Australia 2002-03, to Zimbabwe 2004; South Africa to West Indies 2000-01, to Zimbabwe 2001-02, to Australia 2001-02 (VB Series), to West Indies 2004-05 (one-day series), to India (one-day series) 2005-06, to Australia 2005-06, to India (ICC Champions Trophy) 2006-07

Overseas teams played for: Eastern Province 1996-97 – 2002-03; Northerns 2003-04 – 2004-05; Titans 2004-05 – 2006-07; Hyderabad Heroes (ICL) 2007-08 – ; Cape Cobras 2007-08, 2009-10
Extras: An overseas player with Worcestershire during the 2003 season as a locum for Andrew Hall. An overseas player with Kent 2005-06. Played for African XI v Asian Cricket Council XI in ODI series 2005-06. Has won numerous awards in domestic and international cricket, including Player of the [ODI] Series v New Zealand 2005-06 and Man of the Match v England in the fifth ODI at East London 2004-05 (50-ball 80). South Africa Player of the Year 2007
Best batting: 188 Eastern Province v North West, Port Elizabeth 2000-01
Best bowling: 6-56 Eastern Province v Border, Port Elizabeth 2000-01

2009 Season

	M	Inn	NO	Runs	HS	Avg	100	50	Ct	St	Balls	Runs	Wkts	Avg	BB	5I	10M
Test																	
FC	14	21	3	780	183	43.33	2	2	30	-	995	568	8	71.00	3-12	-	-
ODI																	
List A	12	12	3	284	69	31.55	-	1	6	-	78	120	1	120.00	1-11	-	
20/20 Int																	
20/20	12	8	3	89	20	17.80	-	-	7	-	78	102	3	34.00	2-38	-	

Career Performances

	M	Inn	NO	Runs	HS	Avg	100	50	Ct	St	Balls	Runs	Wkts	Avg	BB	5I	10M
Test	4	6	0	80	55	13.33	-	1	3	-	479	222	9	24.66	3-33	-	-
FC	123	198	24	6225	188	35.77	14	29	170	-	11632	5564	194	28.68	6-56	5	-
ODI	85	66	18	1512	100*	31.50	1	10	33	-	1303	1015	32	31.71	3-20	-	
List A	255	217	58	5649	107*	35.52	3	40	108	-	6623	5325	180	29.58	6-20	3	
20/20 Int	8	7	3	203	89*	50.75	-	1	3	-	6	5	0	-	-		
20/20	52	44	12	860	89*	26.87	-	2	23	-	402	521	26	20.03	3-19	-	

KERRIGAN, S. C. Lancashire

Name: <u>Simon</u> Christopher Kerrigan
Role: Left-hand bat, slow left-arm orthodox bowler
Born: 10 May 1989, Preston, Lancashire
Height: 5ft 10in **Weight:** 11st
Nickname: Keggsy
County debut: No first-team appearance
Parents: Catherine
Marital status: Single
Education: Corpus Christi Sports College;
Preston College
Qualifications: 10 GCSEs, BTEC National Diploma
in Sports and Exercise Science (Distinction)
Overseas teams played for: Spent the winter of
2009-10 playing in Australian grade cricket
Career highlights to date: 'Getting my contract with
Lancashire'

Cricket moments to forget: 'At the age of 15, playing for Fulwood and Broughton,
dropping a catch off my own bowling for a guy who had 30 runs on the board. He
went on to make 140, and later in the same game I got a golden duck when we needed
two runs to win with nine wickets down!'
Cricketers particularly admired: Mal Loye, Andrew Flintoff, Graeme Swann
Young players to look out for: Luke Procter and Karl Brown (Lancashire)
Other sports played: Golf
Other sports followed: Football (Blackburn Rovers)
Favourite band: The Courteeners
Extras: Former Lancashire Academy player. Played for Fulwood & Broughton CC
2005-07 and for Ormskirk CC in 2008, taking 69 wickets in their Liverpool
Competition Premier League title-winning campaign. Has represented Lancashire at
U15 and U17 level. Lancashire Second XI 2007-08. Signed a two-year contract in
September 2008
Opinions on cricket: 'Less powerplays!'

> 48. How many matches were drawn in the five-match series when
> Pakistan visited England in 1987?

KERVEZEE, A. N. Worcestershire

Name: <u>Alexei</u> Nicolaas Kervezee
Role: Right-hand bat, off-spin bowler
Born: 11 September 1989, Walvis Bay, Namibia
Nickname: Rowdy
County debut: 2008
ODI debut: 2006
Twenty20 Int debut: 2009
Place in batting averages: 164th av. 27.21
Overseas tours: Netherlands to UAE (EurAsia Series) 2006, to Scotland (European Championship) 2006, to South Africa (ICC Associates Tri-Series) 2006-07, to Kenya (ICC World Cricket League) 2006-07, to West Indies (World Cup) 2006-07, to Canada 2007, to Ireland (Quadrangular Series) 2007, to South Africa (ICC World Cup Qualifiers) 2008-09, to England (one-day series) 2009, plus various Netherlands age-group tours
Overseas teams played for: HBS, Netherlands
Extras: Made first-class debut for Netherlands v Scotland at Utrecht in the ICC Inter-Continental Cup 2005, aged 15. Made ODI debut for Netherlands v Sri Lanka at Amstelveen 2006, aged 16, scoring 47. Was still only 17 when playing in the World Cup in 2007. Played for the Netherlands in ICC World Twenty20 competition 2009. Scored 121* against Denmark in World Cup qualifying competition 2009
Best batting: 98 Netherlands v Canada, Toronto (MSE) 2007
Best bowling: 1-14 Netherlands v Namibia, Windhoek 2008

2009 Season

	M	Inn	NO	Runs	HS	Avg	100	50	Ct	St	Balls	Runs	Wkts	Avg	BB	5I	10M
Test																	
FC	8	14	0	381	66	27.21	-	2	2	-	0	0	0		-	-	-
ODI																	
List A	1	1	0	0	0	0.00	-	-	1	-	0	0	0		-	-	
20/20 Int	2	2	0	22	21	11.00	-	-	1	-	0	0	0		-	-	
20/20	2	2	0	22	21	11.00	-	-	1	-	0	0	0		-	-	

Career Performances

	M	Inn	NO	Runs	HS	Avg	100	50	Ct	St	Balls	Runs	Wkts	Avg	BB	5I	10M
Test																	
FC	19	30	2	805	98	28.75	-	4	6	-	120	59	2	29.50	1-14	-	-
ODI	24	21	2	505	75	26.57	-	2	9	-	6	8	0		-	-	
List A	34	31	3	946	121*	33.78	1	5	14	-	30	47	0		-	-	
20/20 Int	2	2	0	22	21	11.00	-	-	1	-	0	0	0		-	-	
20/20	2	2	0	22	21	11.00	-	-	1	-	0	0	0		-	-	

KEY, R. W. T. Kent

Name: <u>Robert</u> William Trevor Key
Role: Right-hand bat, off-spin bowler, county captain
Born: 12 May 1979, Dulwich, London
Height: 6ft 1in **Weight:** 12st 7lbs
Nickname: Keysy
County debut: 1998
County cap: 2001
Test debut: 2002
ODI debut: 2003
Twenty20 Int debut: 2009
1000 runs in a season: 6
1st-Class 200s: 2
Place in batting averages: 36th av. 50.37
(2008 75th av. 38.25)
Parents: Trevor and Lynn
Wife and date of marriage: Fleur, 2006
Children: Aaliyah, September 2006
Family links with cricket: Mother played for Kent Ladies. Father played club cricket in Derby. Sister Elizabeth played for her junior school side
Education: Langley Park Boys' School
Qualifications: 10 GCSEs, NCA coaching award, GNVQ Business Studies
Overseas tours: Kent U13 to Netherlands; England U17 to Bermuda (International Youth Tournament) 1997 (c); England U19 to South Africa (including U19 World Cup) 1997-98; England A to Zimbabwe and South Africa 1998-99; ECB National Academy to Australia 2001-02, to Sri Lanka 2002-03; England to Australia 2002-03, to South Africa 2004-05. England Performance Programme to India 2008-09; England Lions to New Zealand 2009 (c)
Overseas teams played for: Greenpoint CC, Cape Town 1996-97
Cricketers particularly admired: Min Patel, Neil Taylor, Alan Wells, Mark Ealham
Other sports played: Hockey, football, snooker, tennis (played for county)
Other sports followed: Football (Chelsea), basketball (Chicago Bulls)
Extras: Represented England U19 1997 and was England U19 Man of the Series v Pakistan U19 1998 (award shared with Graeme Swann). NBC Denis Compton Award for the most promising young Kent player 2001. Scored 221 in the first Test v West Indies 2004, in the process sharing with Andrew Strauss (137) in a record second-wicket stand for Test cricket at Lord's (291). Leading run-scorer in English first-class cricket 2004 with 1896 runs at 79.00, including nine centuries. One of *Wisden's* Five Cricketers of the Year 2005. Scored twin centuries (112/189) v Surrey at Tunbridge Wells 2005, in the second innings sharing with Martin van Jaarsveld (168) in a new Kent record third-wicket partnership (323). Carried bat for 75* v Surrey at Canterbury 2007. ECB National Academy 2005-06, 2006-07. Scored more than

1750 runs in all competitions during the 2008 season, including three hundreds and eight fifties. Enjoyed a very successful 2009 season, during which he made his Twenty20 International debut v Netherlands at Lord's in June, and hit a career-best 270* v Glamorgan at Cardiff in July. Captain of Kent since 2006
Best batting: 270* Kent v Glamorgan, Cardiff 2009
Best bowling: 1-14 Kent v Northamptonshire, Canterbury 2009

2009 Season

	M	Inn	NO	Runs	HS	Avg	100	50	Ct	St	Balls	Runs	Wkts	Avg	BB	5I	10M
Test																	
FC	17	28	4	1209	270*	50.37	4	3	15	-	132	59	1	59.00	1-14	-	-
ODI																	
List A	9	9	0	123	27	13.66	-	-	4	-	0	0	0		-	-	
20/20 Int	1	1	1	10	10*		-	-	1	-	0	0	0		-	-	
20/20	10	10	3	212	58*	30.28	-	1	2	-	0	0	0		-	-	

Career Performances

	M	Inn	NO	Runs	HS	Avg	100	50	Ct	St	Balls	Runs	Wkts	Avg	BB	5I	10M
Test	15	26	1	775	221	31.00	1	3	11	-	0	0	0		-	-	-
FC	210	362	26	14225	270*	42.33	41	55	126	-	296	153	1	153.00	1-14	-	-
ODI	5	5	0	54	19	10.80	-	-	-	-	0	0	0		-	-	
List A	184	177	12	5115	120*	31.00	5	32	38	-	0	0	0		-	-	
20/20 Int	1	1	1	10	10*		-	-	1	-	0	0	0		-	-	
20/20	46	46	8	1113	68*	29.28	-	7	11	-	0	0	0		-	-	

KHAN, A.   Kent

Name: Amjad Khan
Role: Right-hand bat, right-arm fast bowler
Born: 14 October 1980, Copenhagen, Denmark
Height: 6ft **Weight:** 11st 6lbs
Nickname: Ammy
County debut: 2001
County cap: 2005
50 wickets in a season: 2
Place in batting averages: 235th av. 17.00
Place in bowling averages: 59th av. 31.83
(2008 16th av. 20.61)
Parents: Aslam and Raisa
Marital status: Single
Education: Skolen på Duevej, Denmark;
Falkonёrgårdens Gymnasium

Overseas tours: Denmark U19 to Canada 1996, to Bermuda 1997, to South Africa (U19 World Cup) 1997-98, to Wales 1998, to Ireland 1999; Denmark to Netherlands 1998, to Zimbabwe (ICC Emerging Nations Tournament) 1999-2000, to Canada (ICC Trophy) 2001; England A to Bangladesh 2006-07; England Performance Programme to India 2008-09; England Lions to New Zealand 2009; England to West Indies 2009
Overseas teams played for: Kjøbenhavns Boldklub, Denmark
Cricket moments to forget: 'I try to forget most of the games where I didn't perform as well as I would like'
Cricketers particularly admired: Wasim Akram, Dennis Lillee
Other sports followed: Football (Denmark)
Favourite band: Marvin Gaye, George Michael, Nerd (Neptunes)
Relaxations: 'Music, sleeping, reading'
Extras: Made debut for Denmark at the age of 17. Took over 50 (63) first-class wickets in his first full season 2002. NBC Denis Compton Award for the most promising young Kent player 2002. Out for the whole of the 2007 season with a knee injury. Member of England Performance Programme squad 2009-10
Best batting: 78 Kent v Middlesex, Lord's 2003
Best bowling: 6-52 Kent v Yorkshire, Canterbury 2002

2009 Season

	M	Inn	NO	Runs	HS	Avg	100	50	Ct	St	Balls	Runs	Wkts	Avg	BB	5I	10M
Test																	
FC	11	12	3	153	62*	17.00	-	1	2	-	2035	1146	36	31.83	5-113	1	-
ODI																	
List A	2	1	1	7	7*		-	-	-	-	72	74	1	74.00	1-47	-	
20/20 Int																	
20/20	4	0	0	0	0	-	-	-	2	-	54	80	2	40.00	1-16	-	

Career Performances

	M	Inn	NO	Runs	HS	Avg	100	50	Ct	St	Balls	Runs	Wkts	Avg	BB	5I	10M
Test	1	0	0	0	0		-	-	-	-	174	122	1	122.00	1-111	-	-
FC	75	84	27	1023	78	17.94	-	4	12	-	12418	7893	248	31.82	6-52	7	-
ODI																	
List A	56	30	7	276	65*	12.00	-	1	13	-	2273	1973	61	32.34	4-26	-	
20/20 Int	1	1	0	2	2	2.00	-	-	-	-	24	34	2	17.00	2-34	-	
20/20	22	8	2	32	15	5.33	-	-	3	-	391	580	26	22.30	3-11	-	

49. In which year did Pakistan win their first Test series against England?

KIESWETTER, C.   Somerset

Name: Craig Kieswetter
Role: Right-hand bat, wicket-keeper
Born: 28 November 1987, Johannesburg,
South Africa
Height: 5ft 11in   **Weight:** 13st 5lbs
Nickname: Bangle, Hobnob, Shnitz,
Kitchen Utensil
County debut: 2007
1000 runs in a season: 1
Place in batting averages: 18th av. 59.14
(2008 134th av. 28.86)
Parents: Wayne and Belinda
Marital status: Single
Education: Diocesan College (Bishops),
Cape Town; Millfield School

Overseas tours: South Africa U19 to Sri Lanka (U19 World Cup) 2005-06
Overseas teams played for: Alma Marist CC, Cape Town 2005-06
Career highlights to date: 'Making first-class and List A debuts in first year,
aged 19'
Cricket superstitions: 'Routine to put gear on; mark guard after every ball;
certain amount of taps when bowler running in'
Cricketers particularly admired: Marcus Trescothick, Andrew Caddick, Ian
Blackwell, Justin Langer, Neil McKenzie, Damien Martyn, Adam Gilchrist
Other sports played: Hockey (provincial)
Other sports followed: Football (Aston Villa)
Favourite band: Justin Timberlake, Ne-Yo, R&B, NDubz, Plan B
Relaxations: 'PlayStation B, Pro Evolution Soccer, music, girlfriend'
Extras: Represented South Africa Schools 2005. Man of the Match v USA U19
at Colombo in the U19 World Cup 2005-06 (80). Struck 58-ball 69* on List A
debut v Glamorgan at Taunton in the Friends Provident 2007. Magic Moment v
Warwickshire at Edgbaston in the Twenty20 2007. NBC Denis Compton Award
for the most promising young Somerset player 2007, 2008, 2009. Claimed more
than 70 victims from behind the stumps in all competitions in 2008. Although
he has played for South Africa at U19 level, he has committed himself to an
England future.
Best batting: 153 Somerset v Lancashire, Taunton 2009
Stop press: Called up to England's one-day squad for the tour of Bangladesh,
February 2010, following impressive performances for the England Lions.

2009 Season

	M	Inn	NO	Runs	HS	Avg	100	50	Ct	St	Balls	Runs	Wkts	Avg	BB	5I	10M
Test																	
FC	16	24	3	1242	153	59.14	4	7	48	-		0	0	0		-	-	-
ODI																	
List A	16	16	3	634	138*	48.76	2	1	11	6		0	0	0		-	-	
20/20 Int																	
20/20	12	11	3	248	84	31.00	-	2	8	5		0	0	0		-	-	

Career Performances

	M	Inn	NO	Runs	HS	Avg	100	50	Ct	St	Balls	Runs	Wkts	Avg	BB	5I	10M
Test																	
FC	47	66	10	2254	153	40.25	4	12	142	2		0	0	0		-	-	-
ODI																	
List A	45	44	6	1500	138*	39.47	3	6	45	11		0	0	0		-	-	
20/20 Int																	
20/20	30	29	6	524	84	22.78	-	2	13	6		0	0	0		-	-	

KILLEEN, N.   Durham

Name: Neil Killeen
Role: Right-hand bat, right-arm fast-medium bowler
Born: 17 October 1975, Shotley Bridge
Height: 6ft 1in **Weight:** 15st
Nickname: Killer, Bully, Quinny, Squeaky, Bull
County debut: 1995
County cap: 1999
Benefit: 2006
50 wickets in a season: 1
Parents: Glen and Thora
Wife and date of marriage: Clare Louise,
5 February 2000
Children: Jonathan David
Family links with cricket: 'Dad's the best armchair
player in the game'
Education: Greencroft Comprehensive School; Derwentside College,
University of Teesside
Qualifications: 8 GCSEs, 2 A-levels, first year Sports Science, Level 3 coaching,
Level 1 staff coach
Career outside cricket: Cricket coaching
Overseas tours: Durham CCC to Zimbabwe 1992; England U19 to West Indies
1994-95; MCC to Bangladesh 1999-2000

Career highlights to date: 'My county cap and first-class debut'
Cricket moments to forget: 'Injury causing me to miss most of 2001 season'
Cricketers particularly admired: Ian Botham, Curtly Ambrose, Courtney Walsh, David Boon
Other sports played: Athletics (English Schools javelin)
Sports followed: Football (Sunderland AFC), cricket (Anfield Plain CC)
Relaxations: 'Good food, good wine; golf; spending time with wife and family'
Extras: Was first Durham bowler to take five wickets in a Sunday League game (5-26 v Northamptonshire at Northampton 1995). Scored 35 batting at No. 10 as Durham made 453-9 to beat Somerset at Taunton 2004. Had figures of 8.3-7-5-2 v Derbyshire at Riverside in the Totesport League 2004
Best batting: 48 Durham v Somerset, Riverside 1995
Best bowling: 7-70 Durham v Hampshire, Riverside 2003

2009 Season

	M	Inn	NO	Runs	HS	Avg	100	50	Ct	St	Balls	Runs	Wkts	Avg	BB	5I	10M
Test																	
FC																	
ODI																	
List A	3	2	1	11	11*	11.00	-	-	1	-	138	132	6	22.00	5-48	1	
20/20 Int																	
20/20	10	3	2	3	3	3.00	-	-	3	-	240	254	11	23.09	3-21	-	

Career Performances

	M	Inn	NO	Runs	HS	Avg	100	50	Ct	St	Balls	Runs	Wkts	Avg	BB	5I	10M
Test																	
FC	102	145	31	1302	48	11.42	-	-	26	-	16499	8215	262	31.35	7-70	9	-
ODI																	
List A	224	119	46	694	32	9.50	-	-	39	-	10559	7309	301	24.28	6-31	5	
20/20 Int																	
20/20	43	17	12	88	17*	17.60	-	-	9	-	897	1087	46	23.63	4-7	-	

---

50. Pakistan made their highest Test match total against England at The Oval in 1987. How many runs did they make?

KING, S. J. Surrey

Name: <u>Simon</u> James King
Role: Right-hand bat, right-arm
off-spin bowler
Born: 4 September 1987, Lambeth, London
Height: 6ft 1in **Weight:** 11st
Nickname: Kingy
County debut: 2009
Parents: Angela Pocock and David King
Marital status: Single
Family links with cricket: 'Brother plays'
Education: Warlingham Secondary School; John
Fisher Sixth Form College
Qualifications: GCSEs, BTEC National Diploma in
Sport, Level 2 coaching
Overseas tours: Surrey Academy to South Africa
2005; Surrey CCC to India 2006
Overseas teams played for: Mildura West CC, Victoria; Millewa CC, Victoria
Career highlights to date: 'Receiving first contract at the end of the 2006 season.
First five-wicket haul, v Sussex 2nd XI 2005, when I was 17'
Cricket moments to forget: 'Dropping a skyer into my face in an England
regional match'
Cricketers particularly admired: Alec Stewart, Shane Warne, Mark Ramprakash,
Phil Matthews
Other sports played: Football (Warlingham FC, Hamsey Rangers FC)
Other sports followed: Football (Fulham)
Favourite band: Goo Goo Dolls, Oasis, U2, Lifehouse
Relaxations: 'Sleeping'
Extras: Surrey U15 Player of the Year 2003. Surrey Academy Player of the Year 2006
Best batting: 8 Surrey v Derbyshire, Croydon 2009
Best bowling: 3-61 Surrey v Middlesex, Lord's 2009

2009 Season

	M	Inn	NO	Runs	HS	Avg	100	50	Ct	St	Balls	Runs	Wkts	Avg	BB	5I	10M
Test																	
FC	2	2	0	8	8	4.00	-	-	-	-	237	156	4	39.00	3-61	-	-
ODI																	
List A																	
20/20 Int																	
20/20	1	1	1	5	5*		-	-	-	-	18	28	0		-	-	

	M	Inn	NO	Runs	HS	Avg	100	50	Ct	St	Balls	Runs	Wkts	Avg	BB	5I	10M
Test																	
FC	2	2	0	8	8	4.00	-	-	-	-	237	156	4	39.00	3-61	-	-
ODI																	
List A																	
20/20 Int																	
20/20	1	1	1	5	5*	-	-	-	-	-	18	28	0		-	-	

KIRBY, S. P. Gloucestershire

Name: <u>Steven</u> Paul Kirby
Role: Right-hand bat, right-arm fast bowler
Born: 4 October 1977, Bury, Lancashire
Height: 6ft 3in **Weight:** 13st 5lbs
Nickname: Tango
County debut: 2001 (Yorkshire),
2005 (Gloucestershire)
County cap: 2003 (Yorkshire),
2005 (Gloucestershire)
50 wickets in a season: 2
Place in batting averages: 265th av. 11.21
Place in bowling averages: 7th av. 22.18
(2008 64th av. 28.72)
Parents: Paul and Alison
Wife and date of marriage: Sasha, 11 October 2003
Children: Joel, 2005; Aleisha, 2007
Education: Elton High School, Walshaw, Bury, Lancashire; Bury College
Qualifications: 10 GCSEs, BTEC/GNVQ Advanced Leisure and Tourism
Overseas tours: Yorkshire to Grenada 2001; ECB National Academy to Australia 2001-02; England A to India 2003-04; England Lions to India 2007-08
Overseas teams played for: Egmont Plains, New Zealand 1997-98
Cricket moments to forget: 'Being knocked out by Nixon McLean trying to take a return catch'
Cricketers particularly admired: Steve Waugh, Richard Hadlee, Glenn McGrath, Michael Atherton, Curtly Ambrose, Sachin Tendulkar
Other sports played: Basketball, table tennis, squash, golf – 'anything sporty and competitive'
Other sports followed: Football (Manchester United), rugby (Leicester Tigers)
Extras: Formerly with Leicestershire but did not appear for first team. Took 14 wickets (41-18-47-14) in one day for Egmont Plains v Hawera in a New Zealand club match 1997-98. Took 7-50 in Kent's second innings at Headingley 2001, the best bowling figures by a Yorkshire player on first-class debut; Kirby had replaced

Matthew Hoggard (called up by England) halfway through the match. Took 13-154 (5-74/8-80) v Somerset at Taunton 2003, the best match return by a Yorkshire bowler for 36 years. Took over 90 wickets in all forms of cricket in 2009

Best batting: 57 Yorkshire v Hampshire, Headingley 2002
Best bowling: 8-80 Yorkshire v Somerset, Taunton 2003

2009 Season

	M	Inn	NO	Runs	HS	Avg	100	50	Ct	St	Balls	Runs	Wkts	Avg	BB	5I	10M
Test																	
FC	16	22	8	157	27	11.21	-	-	2	-	2836	1420	64	22.18	5-44	1	-
ODI																	
List A	10	6	3	4	3	1.33	-	-	1	-	392	342	13	26.30	4-32	-	
20/20 Int																	
20/20	8	5	0	40	25	8.00	-	-	3	-	175	214	14	15.28	3-29	-	

Career Performances

	M	Inn	NO	Runs	HS	Avg	100	50	Ct	St	Balls	Runs	Wkts	Avg	BB	5I	10M
Test																	
FC	118	161	52	932	57	8.55	-	1	22	-	21155	12038	428	28.12	8-80	15	4
ODI																	
List A	66	30	12	76	15	4.22	-	-	12	-	2763	2571	80	32.13	5-36	1	
20/20 Int																	
20/20	24	11	2	45	25	5.00	-	-	5	-	505	648	31	20.90	3-29	-	

KIRTLEY, R. J. Sussex

Name: Robert James Kirtley
Role: Right-hand bat, right-arm fast-medium bowler
Born: 10 January 1975, Eastbourne
Height: 6ft **Weight:** 12st
Nickname: Ambi
County debut: 1995
County cap: 1998
Benefit: 2006
Test debut: 2003
ODI debut: 2001-02
Twenty20 Int debut: 2007-08
50 wickets in a season: 7
Parents: Bob and Pip
Wife and date of marriage: Jenny, 26 October 2002
Children: Robert Oliver (known as Oliver), 12 June 2008
Family links with cricket: Brother plays league cricket

Education: St Andrew's School, Eastbourne; Clifton College, Bristol
Qualifications: 9 GCSEs, 2 A-levels, NCA coaching first level
Overseas tours: Sussex YC to Barbados 1993, to Sri Lanka 1995; Sussex to Grenada 2001, to India (Champions League) 2009; England A to Bangladesh and New Zealand 1999-2000, to Bangladesh 2006-07; England to Zimbabwe (one-day series) 2001-02, to Sri Lanka (ICC Champions Trophy) 2002-03, to Australia 2002-03 (VB Series), to Bangladesh and Sri Lanka 2003-04, to West Indies 2003-04 (one-day series), to South Africa (World 20/20) 2007-08
Overseas teams played for: Mashonaland, Zimbabwe 1996-97; Namibian Cricket Board/Wanderers, Windhoek, Namibia 1998-99
Career highlights to date: 'My Test debut at Trent Bridge, the County Championship 2003, the C&G Final 2006'
Cricket moments to forget: 'The three times I've bagged a pair'
Cricket superstitions: 'Put my left boot on first!'
Cricketers particularly admired: Curtly Ambrose, Jim Andrew, Darren Gough
Other sports followed: Rugby (England), football (Brighton & Hove Albion)
Relaxations: 'Inviting friends round for a braai and enjoying a cold beer with them'
Extras: Played in the Mashonaland side which defeated England on their 1996-97 tour of Zimbabwe, taking seven wickets in the match. NBC Denis Compton Award for the most promising young Sussex player 1997. Leading wicket-taker in English first-class cricket 2001 with 75 wickets (av. 23.32). Sussex Player of the Year 2002. Made Test debut in the third Test v South Africa at Trent Bridge 2003, taking 6-34 in South Africa's second innings and winning Man of the Match award. Vice-captain of Sussex 2001-05. C&G Man of the Match award for his 5-27 in the final v Lancashire at Lord's 2006. Took 600th first-class wicket (Yuvraj Singh) v Indians at Hove 2007
Best batting: 59 Sussex v Durham, Eastbourne 1998
Best bowling: 7-21 Sussex v Hampshire, Southampton 1999

2009 Season

	M	Inn	NO	Runs	HS	Avg	100	50	Ct	St	Balls	Runs	Wkts	Avg	BB	5I	10M
Test																	
FC	3	3	1	45	33	22.50	-	-	2	-	341	185	6	30.83	2-59	-	-
ODI																	
List A	18	7	6	21	7*	21.00	-	-	5	-	743	737	27	27.29	6-50	2	
20/20 Int																	
20/20	12	3	3	2	2*		-	-	6	-	162	185	17	10.88	3-9	-	

Career Performances

	M	Inn	NO	Runs	HS	Avg	100	50	Ct	St	Balls	Runs	Wkts	Avg	BB	5I	10M
Test	4	7	1	32	12	5.33	-	-	3	-	1079	561	19	29.52	6-34	1	-
FC	170	231	76	2040	59	13.16	-	4	60	-	31916	16607	614	27.04	7-21	29	4
ODI	11	2	0	2	1	1.00	-	-	5	-	549	481	9	53.44	2-33	-	
List A	249	92	48	440	30*	10.00	-	-	69	-	10931	8659	371	23.33	6-50	9	
20/20 Int	1	1	1	2	2*		-	-	-	-	6	17	0		-	-	
20/20	54	16	8	12	2*	1.50	-	-	16	-	939	1251	51	24.52	4-22	-	

KLOKKER, F. A.   Derbyshire

Name: <u>Frederik</u> Andreas Klokker
Role: Left-hand bat, wicket-keeper
Born: 13 March 1983, Odense, Denmark
Height: 5ft 11in   **Weight:** 14st 2lbs
Nickname: Kloks, J-Lo, The Great Dane
County debut: 2006 (Warwickshire),
2007 (Derbyshire)
Parents: Peter Palle and Ingermarie
Marital status: Single
Family links with cricket: 'Dad played for
Denmark for many years and is now head coach
of Danish cricket. My two sisters played a bit
when they were younger'

Education: Hindsholmskolen, Denmark
Qualifications: Levels 1 and 2 coaching. Levels 1
and 2 fitness instructor
Career outside cricket: Philatelist
Overseas tours: Denmark U19 to South Africa (U19 World Cup) 1997-98;
Denmark to Zimbabwe (ICC Emerging Nations Tournament) 1999-2000, to Canada
(ICC Trophy) 2001, to Ireland (ICC Trophy) 2005, to Kenya 2007, to Namibia (ICC
World Cricket League) 2007-08, to South Africa (ICC World Cup) (c) 2009,
plus various other tours and tournaments with Denmark and Denmark age groups;
MCC YC to Sri Lanka 2003-04
Overseas teams played for: Kerteminde CC, Denmark 1989-99; Skanderborg CC,
Denmark 2000-01; South Perth CC 2001-02 – 2003-04; Prospect CC, Adelaide
2006-07
Career highlights to date: 'Playing in the 1997 U19 World Cup in South Africa.
Debut for Denmark. Debut for Warwickshire. Breaking record for most runs by an
MCC Young Cricketer. Hundred for Derbyshire on my first-class debut for them.'
Cricket moments to forget: 'The game against the West Indies in the 1997 U19
World Cup'
Cricket superstitions: 'Not really'
Cricketers particularly admired: Waugh twins, Dominic Ostler
Other sports played: 'Played handball in the winter before I started going
to Australia'
Other sports followed: Handball (GOG)
Favourite band: Live
Relaxations: 'Can't beat a good movie'
Extras: MCC Young Cricketer 2002-05, acting as substitute fielder for England in the
first Test v New Zealand at Lord's 2004. Has represented Denmark in one-day cricket,
including NatWest/C&G. Man of the Match v USA at Armagh in the ICC Trophy 2005

(149-ball 138*). Played for European XI v MCC at Rotterdam 2006. Played one first-class match and one C&G match for Warwickshire 2006 as injury cover in the wicket-keeping department, scoring 40 as nightwatchman v Sussex at Hove. Played two first-class matches for Derbyshire 2007, scoring century (100*) on debut for the county v CUCCE at Fenner's. Played four first-class games for Derbyshire in 2008, scoring a century in one of them. Captained Denmark in their unsuccessful World Cup qualifying campaign in South Africa 2009

Best batting: 103* Derbyshire v Warwickshire, Derby 2008

2009 Season

	M	Inn	NO	Runs	HS	Avg	100	50	Ct	St	Balls	Runs	Wkts	Avg	BB	5I	10M
Test																	
FC	2	4	1	53	32*	17.66	-	-	3	-	0	0	0		-	-	-
ODI																	
List A																		
20/20 Int																		
20/20																		

Career Performances

	M	Inn	NO	Runs	HS	Avg	100	50	Ct	St	Balls	Runs	Wkts	Avg	BB	5I	10M
Test																		
FC	9	16	3	424	103*	32.61	2	-	19	-	60	99	0		-	-	-
ODI																		
List A	28	24	2	708	138*	32.18	1	5	27	6	0	0	0		-	-	
20/20 Int																		
20/20																		

KNAPPETT, J. P. T. Worcestershire

Name: Joshua (<u>Josh</u>) Philip
Thomas Knappett
Role: Right-hand bat, wicket-keeper
Born: 15 April 1985, Westminster, London
Height: 6ft **Weight:** 12st 4lbs
Nickname: Badger, Edwin (van der Sar)
County debut: 2007
County colours: 2007
Parents: Phil and Janie
Marital status: Single
Family links with cricket: Father is Youth and Coaching Manager at Middlesex and has played club cricket. 'Brother, Jon, plays socially'
Education: East Barnet School; Oxford Brookes University

Qualifications: 10 GCSEs, 3 A-levels, Level 3 ECB, tutor-trained and assessor-trained cricket coach to level 2, swimming, football and rugby Level 1 coaching qualifications
Off-season: 'Touring, and training in Worcester.'
Career outside cricket: Coaching and coach education
Overseas tours: MCC A to Canada 2005; MCC B to Botswana and Zambia 2006, to Fiji and Samoa 2008
Career highlights to date: 'My championship debut v Sussex in 2007'
Cricket moments to forget: 'Being hit on the head by Jimmy Ormond on first-class debut for OUCCE. Getting out to Mushtaq twice in a day for 7 and 4.'
Cricketers particularly admired: Jack Russell, Adam Gilchrist
Young players to look out for: Phil Mellish, Keith Bradley, Jack Manual
Other sports played: Squash, trampolining
Other sports followed: Football (Tottenham Hotspur)
Favourite band: 'Architecture In Helsinki, Cold War Kids, The New Pornographers, Bernard Fanning, Bob Dylan, Daft Punk, Elbow, The Whitlams'
Relaxations: 'Listening to music, films, eating'
Extras: Played for OUCCE 2004-06. Represented British Universities 2005, 2006. Attended training camp in Mumbai, India 2005 (World Cricket Academy). Despite having made his first-class debut in 2007, he did not make an appearance in 2008. Released by Worcestershire at the end of the 2009 season
Opinions on cricket: 'Test match cricket is the pinnacle of the game.'
Best batting: 100* OUCCE v Durham, The Parks 2006

2009 Season

	M	Inn	NO	Runs	HS	Avg	100	50	Ct	St	Balls	Runs	Wkts	Avg	BB	5I	10M
Test																	
FC	2	2	1	5	4*	5.00	-	-	5	-	0	0	0		-	-	-
ODI																	
List A																	
20/20 Int																	
20/20																	

Career Performances

	M	Inn	NO	Runs	HS	Avg	100	50	Ct	St	Balls	Runs	Wkts	Avg	BB	5I	10M
Test																	
FC	13	20	3	523	100*	30.76	1	3	26	3	0	0	0		-	-	-
ODI																	
List A																	
20/20 Int																	
20/20																	

KRUGER, G. J-P.   Glamorgan

Name: <u>Garnett</u> John-Peter Kruger
Role: Right-hand bat, right-arm
fast-medium bowler
Born: 5 January 1977, Port Elizabeth,
South Africa
Height: 6ft 3in
County debut: 2007 (Leicestershire),
2009 (Glamorgan)
ODI debut: 2005-06
Twenty20 Int debut: 2005-06
Place in batting averages: 246th av. 15.16
Place in bowling averages: 99th av. 38.87
(2008 74th av. 30.31)
Family links with cricket: Father played cricket
in Eastern Province

Education: Gelvan High School; Russell Road College
Qualifications: Fitting and machinery; architecture
Overseas tours: South Africa A to West Indies 2000-01, to Zimbabwe 2004, to Sri
Lanka 2005-06; South Africa VI to Hong Kong 2003; South Africa to Australia
2005-06; South Africa Emerging Players to Australia (Cricket Australia Emerging
Players Tournament) 2006
Overseas teams played for: Eastern Province 1997-98 – 2002-03; Gauteng 2003-04;
Lions 2003-04 – 2008-09; Warriors 2009-10
Cricketers particularly admired: Glenn McGrath
Other sports played: Basketball
Extras: Has represented South Africa A against various touring teams. His match
awards include Man of the Match v North West at Port Elizabeth in the Standard
Bank Cup 1999-2000 (6-23), v Dolphins at Durban in the SuperSport Series
2005-06 (8-112) and v Warriors at Johannesburg in the SuperSport Series 2005-06
(7-44/4-46). Was due to join Leicestershire as an overseas player in 2004 but was
forced to pull out through injury. Is no longer considered an overseas player. Man of
the Match v Dolphins at Durban in the SuperSport Series 2007-08 (6-49). Took over
50 wickets for Leicestershire in all competitions in 2008. Signed for Glamorgan in
December 2008. Released at the end of the 2009 season
Best batting: 58 South Africa A v Windward Islands, Arnos Vale 2000-01
Best bowling: 8-112 Lions v Dolphins, Durban 2005-06

2009 Season

	M	Inn	NO	Runs	HS	Avg	100	50	Ct	St	Balls	Runs	Wkts	Avg	BB	5I	10M
Test																	
FC	13	13	7	91	28*	15.16	-	-	2	-	2122	1283	33	38.87	6-93	1	-
ODI																	
List A	8	3	1	2	1	1.00	-	-	1	-	252	263	6	43.83	2-54	-	
20/20 Int																	
20/20	7	2	2	10	6*		-	-	1	-	124	177	4	44.25	2-18	-	

Career Performances

	M	Inn	NO	Runs	HS	Avg	100	50	Ct	St	Balls	Runs	Wkts	Avg	BB	5I	10M
Test																	
FC	111	135	40	1075	58	11.31	-	2	25	-	19571	11042	356	31.01	8-112	14	2
ODI	3	2	1	0	0*	0.00	-	-	1	-	138	139	2	69.50	1-43	-	
List A	126	39	18	142	20*	6.76	-	-	20	-	5497	4473	169	26.46	6-23	4	
20/20 Int	1	1	0	3	3	3.00	-	-	-	-	24	29	0		-	-	
20/20	36	10	9	47	19*	47.00	-	-	5	-	722	963	34	28.32	4-10	-	

KRUIS, G. J.   Yorkshire

Name: Gideon (<u>Deon</u>) Jacobus Kruis
Role: Right-hand bat, right-arm
fast-medium bowler
Born: 9 May 1974, Pretoria, South Africa
Height: 6ft 3in   **Weight:** 14st 7lbs
Nickname: Kruisie, Chicken Head
County debut: 2005
County cap: 2006
50 wickets in a season: 1
Place in batting averages: 225th av. 18.71
(2008 120th av. 30.50)
Place in bowling averages: 89th av. 37.09
(2008 126th av. 41.04)
Parents: Fanie and Hester
Wife and date of marriage: Marna, 29 June 2002
Children: Elé, 5 October 2006
Family links with cricket: Brother-in-law P. J. Koortzen plays first-class cricket in
South Africa
Education: St Alban's College, Pretoria; University of Pretoria
Qualifications: BCom (Hotel and Catering Management)
Overseas tours: MCC to Bermuda, to Denmark; South African Invitation XI
to Malawi

Overseas teams played for: Northern Transvaal 1993-97; Griqualand West 1997-2004; Goodyear Eagles 2004-05
Career highlights to date: 'Playing for Yorkshire and being Player of the Year in 2005'
Cricket moments to forget: 'The 2007 season – too many injuries!'
Cricket superstitions: 'Left boot on first; four knots when batting, five when bowling on left boot'
Cricketers particularly admired: Allan Donald, Clive Rice, Richard Hadlee, Dennis Lillee, Glenn McGrath, Steve Waugh
Young players to look out for: Chris Woakes (Warwickshire), Joe Denly (Kent)
Other sports played: Golf, squash
Other sports followed: Golf, football (Liverpool)
Favourite band: The Killers
Relaxations: Golf, falconry
Extras: Yorkshire Player of the Year 2005. Retired at the end of the 2009 season
Opinions on cricket: 'I feel that first-division cricket is very strong and competitive. We have to guard against Twenty20 overkill, but it has brought some money into the game. I think the proposed changes to the 2010 season will benefit all players, as it will better prepare them for international cricket. From a bowling point of view, I'd like to see better balls for four-day cricket.'
Best batting: 59 Griqualand West v Bangladeshis, Kimberley 2000-01
Best bowling: 7-58 Griqualand West v Northerns, Centurion 1997-98

2009 Season

	M	Inn	NO	Runs	HS	Avg	100	50	Ct	St	Balls	Runs	Wkts	Avg	BB	5I	10M
Test																	
FC	9	9	2	131	37	18.71	-	-	1	-	1513	816	22	37.09	3-51	-	-
ODI																	
List A	12	6	1	23	11	4.60	-	-	2	-	573	419	17	24.64	3-24	-	
20/20 Int																	
20/20	10	3	2	35	22	35.00	-	-	4	-	237	241	10	24.10	2-16	-	

Career Performances

	M	Inn	NO	Runs	HS	Avg	100	50	Ct	St	Balls	Runs	Wkts	Avg	BB	5I	10M
Test																	
FC	130	180	58	1849	59	15.15	-	3	45	-	25664	12804	406	31.53	7-58	19	1
ODI																	
List A	131	58	20	430	31*	11.31	-	-	29	-	6062	4654	161	28.90	4-17	-	
20/20 Int																	
20/20	24	5	3	41	22	20.50	-	-	7	-	526	558	23	24.26	2-15	-	

LANCEFIELD, T. J.   Surrey

Name: Thomas (<u>Tom</u>) John Lancefield
Role: Left-hand bat, left-arm fast bowler
Born: 8 October 1990, Epsom, Surrey
Nickname: Lancey
County debut: 2009 (one-day)
Education: Whitgift School, Croydon, Surrey
Career highlights to date: '82* against Boland
at Paarl chasing 324'
Cricketers particularly admired: Mark Ramprakash
Other sports played: Rugby
Relaxations: 'Sudoku'
Extras: Plays club cricket with Banstead CC.
Awarded an Emerging Player contract for 12 months
from October 2009

2009 Season

	M	Inn	NO	Runs	HS	Avg	100	50	Ct	St	Balls	Runs	Wkts	Avg	BB	5I	10M
Test																	
FC																	
ODI																	
List A	1	1	0	20	20	20.00	-	-	1	-	0	0	0		-	-	
20/20 Int																	
20/20																	

Career Performances

	M	Inn	NO	Runs	HS	Avg	100	50	Ct	St	Balls	Runs	Wkts	Avg	BB	5I	10M
Test																	
FC																	
ODI																	
List A	1	1	0	20	20	20.00	-	-	1	-	0	0	0		-	-	
20/20 Int																	
20/20																	

51. Which Pakistan batsman made 260 before being caught
and bowled by Graham Dilley during the Test at The Oval in 1987?

LANGER, J. L.   Somerset

Name: <u>Justin</u> Lee Langer
Role: Left-hand top order bat, right-arm
medium bowler; county captain (2009 - *see Extras*)
Born: 21 November 1970, Subiaco,
Western Australia
Height: 5ft 8in **Weight:** 12st 4lbs
Nickname: JL, Alfie
County debut: 1998 (Middlesex), 2006 (Somerset)
County cap: 1998 (Middlesex), 2007 (Somerset)
Test debut: 1992-93
ODI debut: 1993-94
1000 runs in a season: 5
1st-Class 200s: 10
1st-Class 300s: 2
Place in batting averages: 56th av. 43.73
(2008 48th av. 43.32)

Parents: Colin and Joy-Anne
Wife and date of marriage: Sue, 13 April 1996
Children: Jessica, 28 March 1997; Ali-Rose, November 1998; Sophie, April 2001;
Grace, November 2005
Family links with cricket: Uncle, Robbie Langer, played Sheffield Shield cricket for
Western Australia and World Series for Australia; father played A Grade cricket in
Western Australia
Education: Liwara Catholic School; Aquinas College, Perth; University of
Western Australia
Career outside cricket: Journalism, writing and public speaking
Overseas tours: Young Australia to England 1995; Australia A to South Africa
2002-03 (c); Australia to New Zealand 1992-93, to Pakistan 1994-95, to West Indies
1994-95, to South Africa 1996-97, to England 1997, to Pakistan 1998-99, to West
Indies 1998-99, to Sri Lanka and Zimbabwe 1999-2000, to New Zealand 1999-2000,
to India 2000-01, to England 2001, to South Africa 2001-02, to Sri Lanka and Sharjah
(v Pakistan) 2002-03, to West Indies 2002-03, to Sri Lanka 2003-04, to India 2004-05,
to New Zealand 2004-05, to England 2005, to South Africa 2005-06, plus other one-
day tournaments in Sharjah, Sri Lanka and Pakistan; Somerset to India (Champions
League) 2009
Overseas teams played for: Scarborough CC, Perth; Western Australia 1991-92 –
Career highlights to date: 'Winning back the Ashes 2006-07. Being paid to
play cricket and keep fit for the past 20 years – I'm the luckiest man in the world!'
Cricket moments to forget: 'Losing the Ashes in 2005, although it was the best
series I played in.'
Cricket superstitions: 'Right pad on first – two chewies when I bat'

Cricketers particularly admired: 'Too many to single them out...'

Young players to look out for: James Hildreth, Craig Kieswetter, Jos Buttler, Arul Suppiah (all Somerset), Neil Edwards (Nottinghamshire), Luke Pomersbach (Western Warriors)

Other sports played: Tennis, golf, Australian Rules, martial arts (has black belt in zen do kai). 'Football and touch rugby in warm-ups.'

Other sports followed: Australian Rules (West Coast Eagles), football (Manchester United, Subiaco), the Australian cricket team

Favourite band: U2

Relaxations: Family, writing, fishing, crabbing, gardening

Extras: Scored 54 (Australia's only fifty of the match) in the second innings of his debut Test v West Indies at Adelaide 1992-93. Overseas player with Middlesex 1998-2000; county vice-captain 1999 and captain 2000. Scored 166 for Middlesex v Essex at Southgate 1998, in the process sharing with Mike Gatting (241) in a new Middlesex record partnership for the first wicket (372). Put on 238 for the sixth wicket with Adam Gilchrist as Australia successfully chased 369 to beat Pakistan in the second Test at Hobart 1999-2000; his 127 (coupled with 59 in the first innings) won him the Man of the Match award. His numerous other awards include Man of the [Test] Series v New Zealand 2001-02, and Man of the Match in the fourth Test v England at Melbourne 2002-03 (250) and in the first Test v West Indies at Georgetown 2002-03 (146/78*). One of *Wisden*'s Five Cricketers of the Year 2001. Became first Western Australian to make 100 Test appearances, in the third Test v South Africa at Johannesburg 2005-06. A temporary overseas player with Somerset during the 2006 season and an overseas player with the county and captain between 2007 and his retirement in 2009. Scored 342 v Surrey at Guildford 2006, setting a new record for the highest individual first-class score by a Somerset player. Retired from international cricket after the fifth Test v England at Sydney 2006-07. Has written three books, *From Outback To Outfield*, *The Power of Passion*, and *Seeing the Sunrise*, the most recent, published in February 2008. Member of the Order of Australia 2008. In the 2008 season he again scored over 1000 first-class runs. Announced in November 2008 that he intended to continue playing until he reached 40. Retired at the end of the 2009 season. Took up position as Assistant Coach with the Australian Test team in November 2009

Opinions on cricket: 'English cricket has worked hard to boast a world-class domestic system. Now the first division provides this, so I don't see any reason to change it. The only thing I would change is the competitiveness of the pitches being played on. As a general rule, I believe they are too flat to produce consistent outright results.'

Best batting: 342 Somerset v Surrey, Guildford 2006

Best bowling: 2-17 Australia A v South Africans, Brisbane 1997-98

2009 Season

	M	Inn	NO	Runs	HS	Avg	100	50	Ct	St	Balls	Runs	Wkts	Avg	BB	5I	10M
Test																	
FC	15	21	2	831	122*	43.73	2	4	17	-	0	0	0		-	-	-
ODI																	
List A	14	9	1	272	78*	34.00	-	2	7	-	0	0	0		-	-	
20/20 Int																	
20/20	13	10	1	180	44	20.00	-	-	2	-	0	0	0		-	-	

Career Performances

	M	Inn	NO	Runs	HS	Avg	100	50	Ct	St	Balls	Runs	Wkts	Avg	BB	5I	10M
Test	105	182	12	7696	250	45.27	23	30	73	-	6	3	0		-	-	-
FC	360	622	57	28382	342	50.23	86	110	323	-	386	210	5	42.00	2-17	-	-
ODI	8	7	2	160	36	32.00	-	-	2	1	0	0	0		-	-	
List A	239	226	22	7875	146	38.60	14	53	113	2	193	215	7	30.71	3-51	-	
20/20 Int																	
20/20	41	38	2	1015	97	28.19	-	5	8	-	0	0	0		-	-	

LAW, S. G.   Derbyshire

Name: Stuart Grant Law
Role: Right-hand bat, right-arm leg-break bowler
Born: 18 October 1968, Brisbane, Australia
Height: 6ft 1in **Weight:** 13st 7lbs
Nickname: Lawman, Judge
County debut: 1996 (Essex),
2002 (Lancashire), 2009 (Derbyshire)
County cap: 1996 (Essex), 2002 (Lancashire)
Benefit: 2007 (Lancashire)
Test debut: 1995-96
ODI debut: 1994-95
1000 runs in a season: 9
1st-Class 200s: 6
Place in batting averages: (2008 81st av. 37.05)
Parents: Grant and Pam
Wife and date of marriage: Debbie-Lee, 31 December 1998
Children: Max, 9 January 2002
Family links with cricket: 'Dad, grandad and uncles played'
Education: Craiglea State High School, Brisbane
Qualifications: Level 2 cricket coach
Overseas tours: Australia B to Zimbabwe 1991-92; Young Australia (Australia A) to
England and Netherlands 1995 (c); Australia to India and Pakistan (World Cup)
1995-96, to Sri Lanka (Singer World Series) 1996, to India (Titan World Series)

1996-97, to South Africa 1996-97 (one-day series), to New Zealand (one-day series) 1997-98

Overseas teams played for: Queensland Bulls 1988-89 – 2003-04

Career highlights to date: 'Playing for Australia. Winning first ever Sheffield Shield trophy with Queensland as captain [1994-95]'

Cricket superstitions: 'None'

Cricketers particularly admired: Greg Chappell, Viv Richards

Other sports played: Golf ('very socially')

Other sports followed: Rugby league

Favourite band: Red Hot Chili Peppers, Foo Fighters

Relaxations: 'Beach'

Extras: Sheffield Shield Player of the Year 1990-91. Captain of Queensland 1994-95 – 1996-97 and 1999-2000 – 2001-02. Is the most successful captain in modern-day Australian domestic cricket, having captained his state to five Sheffield Shield/Pura Cup titles and three one-day titles. Has a stand named after him at Queensland's Allan Border Field in Brisbane. One of *Wisden*'s Five Cricketers of the Year 1998. PCA Player of the Year 1999. Scored century (168) v Warwickshire at Edgbaston 2003, sharing with Carl Hooper (177) in a Lancashire record fifth-wicket partnership of 360 as the county scored 781. Lancashire Player of the Year 2003. Retired from Australian cricket at the end of 2003-04. Lancashire vice-captain 2005-07, and captain in 2008. Awarded Medal of the Order of Australia (OAM) in 2007 for service to cricket as a state, national and international player. Is a UK citizen and not considered an overseas player. Released by Lancashire at the end of the 2008 season. Signed for Derbyshire March 2009. Appointed assistant coach to Sri Lanka October 2009

Opinions on cricket: 'Very lucky to do what I do.'

Best batting: 263 Essex v Somerset, Chelmsford 1999

Best bowling: 5-39 Queensland v Tasmania, Brisbane 1995-96

2009 Season

	M	Inn	NO	Runs	HS	Avg	100	50	Ct	St	Balls	Runs	Wkts	Avg	BB	5I	10M
Test																	
FC	2	4	0	39	29	9.75	-	-	2	-	0	0	0		-	-	-
ODI																	
List A	6	6	1	222	95	44.40	-	2	1	-	0	0	0				
20/20 Int																	
20/20	10	9	1	184	59	23.00	-	1	1	-	5	6	2	3.00	2-6	-	

Career Performances

	M	Inn	NO	Runs	HS	Avg	100	50	Ct	St	Balls	Runs	Wkts	Avg	BB	5I	10M
Test	1	1	1	54	54*		-	1	1	-	18	9	0		-	-	-
FC	367	601	65	27080	263	50.52	79	128	408	-	8433	4236	83	51.03	5-39	1	-
ODI	54	51	5	1237	110	26.89	1	7	12	-	807	635	12	52.91	2-22	-	
List A	392	371	28	11812	163	34.43	20	64	154	-	3855	3166	90	35.17	5-26	1	
20/20 Int																	
20/20	51	49	4	1197	101	26.60	1	7	16	-	11	16	2	8.00	2-6	-	

LAWSON, M. A. K.   Derbyshire

Name: <u>Mark</u> Anthony Kenneth Lawson
Role: Right-hand bat, right-arm leg-spin bowler
Born: 24 November 1985, Leeds
Height: 5ft 8in   **Weight:** 12st ('approx')
Nickname: Sauce
County debut: 2004 (Yorkshire), 2008 (Derbyshire)
Parents: Anthony and Dawn
Marital status: Single
Family links with cricket: 'Father played local
league cricket and encouraged me to take up the game'
Education: Castle Hall Language College, Mirfield,
West Yorkshire
Qualifications: 11 GCSEs
Overseas tours: England U19 to Australia 2002-03,
to Bangladesh (U19 World Cup) 2003-04, to India
2004-05
Cricketers particularly admired: Shane Warne, Gareth Batty
Other sports played: Football (school), rugby union (school, Cleckheaton 'in early
teens'), rugby league (Dewsbury Moor ARLFC 'in early teens')
Other sports followed: Rugby league (Bradford Bulls)
Relaxations: Music, dining out, cinema
Extras: Played for Yorkshire Schools U11-U16 (captain U13-U15); ESCA North of
England U14 and U15; North of England Development of Excellence U17 and U19.
Represented England U15, U17 and U19. Awarded Brian Johnston Scholarship. Voted
Yorkshire Supporters' Young Player of the Year 2003. 2nd XI cap 2006. Spent 2007 in
the shadow of rising star Adil Rashid, making only two appearances. On loan at
Middlesex in 2008. Released by Yorkshire in August 2008. Agreed a short-term deal
with Derbyshire in time to appear in their final championship game of 2008 and
played for the county in 2009. Released at the end of the 2009 season
Best batting: 44 Yorkshire v Hampshire, Rose Bowl 2006
Best bowling: 6-88 Yorkshire v Middlesex, Scarborough 2006

2009 Season

	M	Inn	NO	Runs	HS	Avg	100	50	Ct	St	Balls	Runs	Wkts	Avg	BB	5I	10M
Test																	
FC	6	5	2	75	24*	25.00	-	-	3	-	630	333	4	83.25	2-20	-	-
ODI																	
List A	8	2	2	7	6*		-	-	3	-	351	311	6	51.83	2-36	-	
20/20 Int																	
20/20	8	1	1	1	1*		-	-	1	-	126	165	6	27.50	2-20	-	

Career Performances

	M	Inn	NO	Runs	HS	Avg	100	50	Ct	St	Balls	Runs	Wkts	Avg	BB	5I	10M
Test																	
FC	23	28	8	280	44	14.00	-	-	10	-	3057	2115	46	45.97	6-88	4	-
ODI																	
List A	12	6	2	37	20	9.25	-	-	4	-	469	452	9	50.22	2-36	-	
20/20 Int																	
20/20	10	2	2	5	4*		-	-	2	-	174	252	9	28.00	2-20	-	

LAXMAN, V. V. S.   Lancashire

Name: Vangipurappu Venkata Sai
(VVS) Laxman
Role: Right-hand bat, right-arm
off-break bowler
Born: 1 November 1974, Hyderabad, India
County debut: 2007
Test debut: 1996-97
ODI debut: 1997-98
1st-Class 200s: 6
1st-Class 300s: 2
Place in batting averages: 13th av. 65.92
(2008 49th av. 44.56)
Overseas tours: India U19 to England 1994; India
to South Africa 1996-97, to West Indies 1996-97, to
New Zealand 1998-99; to Australia 1999-2000, to

Zimbabwe 2001, to South Africa 2001-02, to West Indies 2001-02, to England 2002,
to Sri Lanka (ICC Champions Trophy) 2002-03, to New Zealand 2002-03, to Australia
2003-04, to Pakistan 2003-04, to England (ICC Champions Trophy) 2004, to
Bangladesh 2004-05, to Zimbabwe 2005-06, to Pakistan 2005-06, to West Indies 2006,
to South Africa 2006-07, to England 2007, to Australia 2007-08, to New Zealand
2008-09, to Bangladesh 2009-10 plus other one-day tournaments in Sharjah, Malaysia,
Sri Lanka, Netherlands and England
Overseas teams played for: Hyderabad, India 1992-93 – 2007-08; Deccan Chargers
(IPL) 2008, 2009
Extras: Popularly nicknamed 'Very Very Special'. One of *Wisden*'s Five Cricketers of
the Year 2002. Scored 281 in the second Test v Australia in Kolkata 2000-01
(following a first-innings 59), in the process sharing with Rahul Dravid (180) in a
record fifth-wicket partnership for India in Tests (376) and winning Man of the Match
award. Scored 178 in the fourth Test v Australia in Sydney 2003-04, in the process
sharing with Sachin Tendulkar (241) in a record fourth-wicket partnership for India in
Tests (353). His other series and match awards include Man of the [Test] Series v New

Zealand 2003-04 and Man of the Match v Australia in Brisbane in the VB Series 2003-04 (103*) and v Pakistan in the fifth ODI in Lahore 2003-04 (107). Was a temporary overseas player with Lancashire during the 2007 season as a replacement for Brad Hodge. Scored a double century in the third Test against Australia in October 2008 on the way to becoming only the second batsman to score more than 2000 runs against Australia. Returned to Lancashire June 2009 to play rest of the season and finished top of the county's batting averages

Best batting: 353 Hyderabad v Karnataka, Bangalore 1999-2000
Best bowling: 3-11 Hyderabad v Railways, Delhi (KS) 1999-2000

2009 Season

	M	Inn	NO	Runs	HS	Avg	100	50	Ct	St	Balls	Runs	Wkts	Avg	BB	5I	10M
Test																	
FC	11	16	3	857	135	65.92	4	4	15	-	78	26	1	26.00	1-13	-	-
ODI																	
List A	6	5	1	134	54	33.50	-	1	1	-	0	0	0			-	-
20/20 Int																	
20/20	3	3	1	159	78*	79.50	-	2	-	-	0	0	0			-	-

Career Performances

	M	Inn	NO	Runs	HS	Avg	100	50	Ct	St	Balls	Runs	Wkts	Avg	BB	5I	10M
Test	105	174	25	6741	281	45.24	14	39	111	-	324	126	2	63.00	1-2	-	-
FC	233	378	45	17384	353	52.20	51	79	249	-	1832	754	22	34.27	3-11	-	-
ODI	86	83	7	2338	131	30.76	6	10	39	-	42	40	0		-	-	
List A	173	166	19	5078	131	34.54	9	28	74	-	698	548	8	68.50	2-42	-	
20/20 Int																	
20/20	16	16	2	383	78*	27.35	-	3	2	-	0	0	0			-	-

52. Which England batsman made 150 not out against Pakistan in England's second innings at the Oval in 1987 to help his side gain a face-saving draw?

LEACH, J. Worcestershire

Name: Joseph (Joe) Leach
Role: Right-hand bat, right-arm
medium-fast bowler
Born: 30 October 1990, Stafford
Height: 6ft 1in **Weight:** 14st
Nickname: Leachie
County debut: No first-team appearance
Parents: Deborah
Marital status: Single
Family links with cricket: Younger brother
Stephen is with Worcestershire Academy and
plays for Shropshire
Education: Yarlet Secondary School; Shrewsbury
School

Qualifications: 10 GCSE's and 3 A-levels
Career outside cricket: Student
Off-season: 'Playing in Auckland, New Zealand'
Overseas teams played for: Howick Pakuranga (Auckland) 2009-10
Career highlights to date: 'Playing for Worcestershire 2nd XI. Being given a
contract with Worcestershire'
Cricket moments to forget: 'Being given out caught behind (the ball hit the
top edge of my pad) in final U17 Midland trials'
Cricket superstitions: None
Cricketers particularly admired: Justin Langer
Young players to look out for: Stephen Leach (Shropshire and
Worcestershire Academy)
Other sports played: Football and fives
Other sports followed: Football (Wolverhampton Wanderers)
Relaxations: Socialising and playing/watching football
Extras: Represented Staffordshire at all levels from U13 to U17. Captained
Shrewsbury 1st XI. Captained Midlands at Bunbury Festival
Opinions on cricket: 'Excellent – but there's always room for improvement.'

LEE, J. E.   Yorkshire

Name: <u>James</u> Edward Lee
Role: Left-hand bat, right-arm
fast-medium bowler
Born: 23 December 1988, Sheffield
Height: 6ft 1in **Weight:** 12st 8lbs
Nickname: Binga
County debut: 2006
Parents: Diane and Steven
Marital status: Single
Family links with cricket: Father played Yorkshire
Colts and England U19
Education: Immanuel Community College, Bradford
Qualifications: 8 GCSEs, 2 AS-levels,
Level 2 coaching
Off-season: 'Working hard at Headingley'
Overseas tours: England U19 to Malaysia (U19 World Cup) and Sri Lanka 2007-08
Career highlights to date: 'First-class debut v Lancashire in Roses match 2006.
Being given the opportunity to open the bowling for the 1st XI'
Cricket superstitions: 'I try hard not to get superstitious... Although I tend to
always put my left boot on first'
Cricketers particularly admired: Brett Lee, Andrew Flintoff, James Anderson
Young players to look out for: Joe Root (Yorkshire)
Other sports followed: Football (Arsenal and Bradford City)
Favourite band: The Editors
Relaxations: 'TV – *Family Guy*, *Two And A Half Men*, *Top Gear*'
Extras: JCT600 Bradford League Player of the Year 2009.
Opinions on cricket: 'The rapid increase in demand for Twenty20 cricket needs to
be monitored. And the best team should always be recognised by winning the County
Championship.'
Best batting: 21* Yorkshire v Lancashire, Old Trafford 2006
Best bowling: 2-63 Yorkshire v Somerset, Taunton 2009

2009 Season

	M	Inn	NO	Runs	HS	Avg	100	50	Ct	St	Balls	Runs	Wkts	Avg	BB	5I	10M
Test																	
FC	1	1	0	2	2	2.00	-	-	1	-	114	113	2	56.50	2-63	-	-
ODI																	
List A	4	0	0	0	0		-	-	-	-	106	116	7	16.57	3-43	-	
20/20 Int																	
20/20																	

Career Performances

	M	Inn	NO	Runs	HS	Avg	100	50	Ct	St	Balls	Runs	Wkts	Avg	BB	5I	10M
Test																	
FC	2	3	1	24	21*	12.00	-	-	1	-	168	149	2	74.50	2-63	-	-
ODI																	
List A	4	0	0	0	0		-	-	-	-	106	116	7	16.57	3-43	-	
20/20 Int																	
20/20																	

LEE, W. W. Kent

Name: <u>Warren</u> Wain Lee
Role: Right-hand bat, right-arm
fast-medium bowler
Born: 27th August 1987, Delhi, India
County debut: 2009 (one-day)
Education: Eaglesfield School, Shooters Hill
Extras: Blackheath CC 2002-08. Key member of
the Blackheath side that reached the Evening Standard
Challenge Trophy final in 2007. Has played for Kent
2nd XI (2005), Middlesex 2nd XI and Surrey 2nd XI
(2008). Attended MRF Pace Foundation in Chennai,
February 2009. Made his debut for Kent v Somerset
in April 2009

2009 Season

	M	Inn	NO	Runs	HS	Avg	100	50	Ct	St	Balls	Runs	Wkts	Avg	BB	5I	10M
Test																	
FC																	
ODI																	
List A	2	1	0	0	0	0.00	-	-	2	-	81	110	4	27.50	3-39	-	
20/20 Int																	
20/20																	

Career Performances

	M	Inn	NO	Runs	HS	Avg	100	50	Ct	St	Balls	Runs	Wkts	Avg	BB	5I	10M
Test																	
FC																	
ODI																	
List A	2	1	0	0	0	0.00	-	-	2	-	81	110	4	27.50	3-39	-	
20/20 Int																	
20/20																	

LETT, R. J. H.   Somerset

Name: <u>Robin</u> Jonathan Hugh Lett
Role: Right-hand bat, right-arm
fast-medium bowler
Born: 23 December 1986, London
County debut: 2006
Family links with cricket: Grandfather is
PH Jaques, who played for Leicestershire, 1949
Education: Millfield School; Oxford
Brookes University
Extras: Scored 50 on his first-class debut for
Somerset v Glamorgan in August 2006. Appeared
three times for Somerset in 2006, but has made no
further appearances for the county. Plays club cricket
for Bath CC (West of England Premier League).
Played for OUCCE 2007-09. Has also played
extensively for Somerset 2nd XI. Made three appearances for MCC Universities
in the 2009 2nd XI Championship
Best batting: 76* OUCCE v Nottinghamshire, The Parks 2009
Best bowling: 1-39 OUCCE v Nottinghamshire, The Parks 2009

2009 Season

	M	Inn	NO	Runs	HS	Avg	100	50	Ct	St	Balls	Runs	Wkts	Avg	BB	5I	10M
Test																	
FC	3	4	1	138	76*	46.00	-	1	1	-	102	67	1	67.00	1-39	-	-
ODI																	
List A																	
20/20 Int																	
20/20																	

Career Performances

	M	Inn	NO	Runs	HS	Avg	100	50	Ct	St	Balls	Runs	Wkts	Avg	BB	5I	10M
Test																	
FC	12	17	2	401	76*	26.73	-	5	4	-	102	67	1	67.00	1-39	-	-
ODI																	
List A																	
20/20 Int																	
20/20																	

LEWIS, J.   Gloucestershire

Name: Jonathan (Jon) Lewis
Role: Right-hand bat, right-arm
fast-medium bowler
Born: 26 August 1975, Aylesbury
Height: 6ft 3in **Weight:** 14st
Nickname: Lewy, JJ
County debut: 1995
County cap: 1998
Benefit: 2007
Test debut: 2006
ODI debut: 2005
Twenty20 Int debut: 2005
50 wickets in a season: 7
Place in batting averages: 204th av. 22.37
(2008 222nd av. 16.86)

Place in bowling averages: 4th av. 20.10 (2008 65th av. 28.82)
Parents: John and Jane
Wife and date of marriage: Kate, 16 October 2004
Children: Jacob, 28 April 2007
Education: Churchfields Comprehensive School, Swindon; Swindon College
Qualifications: 9 GCSEs, BTEC in Leisure and Hospitality, ECB Level 3 coach
Career outside cricket: Coaching
Off-season: 'Daddy Day Care!'
Overseas tours: Bath Schools to New South Wales 1993; England A to West Indies
2000-01, to Sri Lanka 2004-05; England to South Africa 2004-05, to India (ICC
Champions Trophy) 2006-07, to Australia 2006-07 (Commonwealth Bank Series), to
West Indies (World Cup) 2006-07
Overseas teams played for: Marist, Christchurch, New Zealand 1994-95; Richmond
City, Melbourne 1995-96; Wanderers, Johannesburg 1996-98; Techs CC, Cape Town
1998-99; Randwick-Petersham, Sydney 2003-04
Career highlights to date: 'Every time I've pulled on an England shirt'
Cricket moments to forget: 'Any injury'
Cricket superstitions: 'I always get a haircut if I go for a gallon'
Cricketers particularly admired: Courtney Walsh, Jack Russell, Jonty Rhodes
Other sports played: Golf (7 handicap), football (Bristol North West FC)
Other sports followed: Football (Swindon Town FC)
Favourite band: Brand New Heavies
Relaxations: Movies
Extras: Was on Northamptonshire staff in 1994 but made no first-team appearance.
Took Championship hat-trick (Gallian, Afzaal, Morris) v Nottinghamshire at Trent
Bridge 2000. Leading first-class wicket-taker among English bowlers in 2000 with 72

wickets (av. 20.91). Gloucestershire Player of the Year 2000. C&G Man of the Match award for his 4-39 v Hampshire at Bristol 2004. ECB National Academy 2004-05, 2006-07. Took 4-24 v Australia at The Rose Bowl in Twenty20 International 2005. Captain of Gloucestershire from 2006 until relinquishing the captaincy in November 2008

Best batting: 62 Gloucestershire v Worcestershire, Cheltenham 1999
Best bowling: 8-95 Gloucestershire v Zimbabweans, Gloucester 2000

2009 Season

	M	Inn	NO	Runs	HS	Avg	100	50	Ct	St	Balls	Runs	Wkts	Avg	BB	5I	10M
Test																	
FC	15	22	6	358	61*	22.37	-	2	5	-	2559	1146	57	20.10	5-73	1	-
ODI																	
List A	16	12	2	165	54	16.50	-	1	6	-	627	501	22	22.77	4-34	-	
20/20 Int																	
20/20	8	8	3	103	30*	20.60	-	-	2	-	185	265	8	33.12	4-37	-	

Career Performances

	M	Inn	NO	Runs	HS	Avg	100	50	Ct	St	Balls	Runs	Wkts	Avg	BB	5I	10M
Test	1	2	0	27	20	13.50	-	-	-	-	246	122	3	40.66	3-68	-	-
FC	195	272	59	3215	62	15.09	-	8	46	-	35584	17827	678	26.29	8-95	33	5
ODI	13	8	2	50	17	8.33	-	-	-	-	716	500	18	27.77	4-36	-	
List A	199	116	42	822	54	11.10	-	1	37	-	9226	6937	261	26.57	5-19	2	
20/20 Int	2	2	1	1	1	1.00	-	-	1	-	42	55	4	13.75	4-24	-	
20/20	35	21	7	247	43 1	7.64	-	-	7	-	744	1029	41	25.09	4-24	-	

53. When Pakistan played England at Lahore in 2005, the home side won by an innings – and how many runs?

LEWRY, J. D.   Sussex

Name: <u>Jason</u> David Lewry
Role: Left-hand bat, left-arm
fast-medium bowler
Born: 2 April 1971, Worthing
Height: 6ft 3in   **Weight:** 'Going up'
Nickname: Lew, Lewie
County debut: 1994
County cap: 1996
Benefit: 2002
50 wickets in a season: 5
Place in bowling averages: 133rd av. 53.50
(2008 71st av. 30.09)
Parents: David and Veronica
Wife and date of marriage: Naomi Madeleine,
18 August 1997
Children: William, 14 February 1998; Louis, 20 November 2000; Ruby and Poppy
(identical twins!), 8 March 2007
Family links with cricket: Father coaches
Education: Durrington High School, Worthing; Worthing Sixth Form College
Qualifications: 6 O-levels, 3 GCSEs, City and Guilds, NCA Award
Career outside cricket: 'Still looking, but with more urgency with each
passing year!'
Overseas tours: Goring CC to Isle of Wight 1992, 1993; England A to Zimbabwe
and South Africa 1998-99
Cricket moments to forget: 'King pair, Eastbourne 1995'
Cricketers particularly admired: David Gower, Martin Andrews, Darren Lehmann
Other sports played: Golf, squash; darts, pool ('anything you can do in a pub')
Other sports followed: Football (West Ham United)
Favourite band: REM
Relaxations: Golf, pub games, films
Extras: Took seven wickets in 14 balls v Hampshire at Hove 2001, the second most
(most by a seamer) outstanding spell of wicket-taking in first-class cricket (after Pat
Pocock's seven in 11 for Surrey v Sussex at Eastbourne in 1972). His 5-75 v
Lancashire at Liverpool 2006 included his 500th first-class wicket (Glen Chapple).
Leading wicket-taker for the county in first-class matches in 2008 with 41. Retired
at the end of the 2009 season
Opinions on cricket: 'More points should be awarded for a four-day win – 14 not
enough.'
Best batting: 72 Sussex v Surrey, The Oval 2004
Best bowling: 8-106 Sussex v Leicestershire, Hove 2003

2009 Season

	M	Inn	NO	Runs	HS	Avg	100	50	Ct	St	Balls	Runs	Wkts	Avg	BB	5I	10M
Test																	
FC	6	10	4	51	25	8.50	-	-	-	-	955	535	10	53.50	2-53	-	-
ODI																	
List A																	
20/20 Int																	
20/20																	

Career Performances

	M	Inn	NO	Runs	HS	Avg	100	50	Ct	St	Balls	Runs	Wkts	Avg	BB	5I	10M
Test																	
FC	187	247	66	1834	72	10.13	-	2	52	-	31895	16834	621	27.10	8-106	31	4
ODI																	
List A	79	44	15	217	16*	7.48	-	-	13	-	3579	2768	100	27.68	4-29	-	
20/20 Int																	
20/20	11	4	1	10	8*	3.33	-	-	4	-	197	239	14	17.07	3-34	-	

LIDDLE, C. J.   Sussex

Name: Christopher (<u>Chris</u>) John Liddle
Role: Right-hand bat,
left-arm fast-medium bowler
Born: 1 February 1984, Middlesbrough
Height: 6ft 4in   **Weight:** 13st
Nickname: Lids, Chuck, Ice Man, Dolce
County debut: 2005 (Leicestershire),
2007 (Sussex)
Parents: Pat and John
Marital status: Single
Family links with cricket: 'Brother plays cricket'
Education: Nunthorpe Comprehensive School,
Middlesbrough; TTE Modern Apprenticeship
Qualifications: 9 GCSEs, fully qualified instrument
artificer, Level 1 coaching
Overseas teams played for: Balcatta CC, Perth; Berea Rovers (South Africa) 2008-09
Cricket superstitions: 'Too many to list'
Cricketers particularly admired: Mushtaq Ahmed, Naved-ul-Hasan, Jason Lewry
Young players to look out for: Luke Wells and Tim Jarvis (both Sussex)
Other sports played: Football
Other sports followed: Football (Middlesbrough)
Favourite band: The Killers

Extras: Yorkshire Area Bowler of the Year 2001-02. Has attended Paul Terry Academy, Perth. Missed the whole of the 2009 season due to a fractured ankle
Best batting: 53 Sussex v Worcestershire, Hove 2007
Best bowling: 3-42 Leicestershire v Somerset, Grace Road 2006

2009 Season (Did not make any first-class or one-day appearances)

Career Performances

	M	Inn	NO	Runs	HS	Avg	100	50	Ct	St	Balls	Runs	Wkts	Avg	BB	5I	10M
Test																	
FC	14	14	5	113	53	12.55	-	1	5	-	1706	962	17	56.58	3-42	-	-
ODI																	
List A	14	3	0	13	11	4.33	-	-	6	-	504	532	10	53.20	3-60	-	
20/20 Int																	
20/20	5	2	1	10	10*	10.00	-	-	2	-	116	165	10	16.50	4-15	-	

LINLEY, T. E.   Surrey

Name: Timothy (Tim) Edward Linley
Role: Right-hand lower-order bat,
right-arm medium-fast bowler
Born: 23 March 1982, Leeds
Height: 6ft 2in **Weight:** 12st
Nickname: Joe Club, Sheephead,
Sloth, Bambi
County debut: 2006 (Sussex), 2009 (Surrey)
Parents: Francis and Jane
Education: St Mary's RC Comprehensive; Notre
Dame Sixth Form College; Oxford Brookes University
Qualifications: 10 GCSEs, 4 A-levels, BSc (Hons)
Geography/Theology
Career highlights to date: 'Playing for British
Universities v New Zealand in 2004. Signing my first
professional contract in 2005 for Sussex'
Cricket moments to forget: 'Being hit for six by my mate Pete "The Lumberjack" Lawrence in a friendly held at Horsforth CC in 2005. I've never lived it down'
Cricketers particularly admired: Glenn McGrath, Shaun Pollock, Andrew Flintoff, Jonty Rhodes
Other sports played: Pool, hockey (Leeds VIth team), badminton
Other sports followed: Football (Halifax Town FC)
Relaxations: 'Playing most other sports; historical fiction books, especially Conn Iggulden, Bernard Cornwell, Christian Jacq; also Paulo Coelho books; watching films or *Lost* or *Orange County* on TV'

Extras: Played for OUCCE 2003-05. Represented British Universities 2004. Won London County CC 'Search 4 A Star' bowling competition 2005. Released by Sussex at the end of the 2006 season. Rejoined Surrey in 2008 having previously played for the Second X1 in 2004

Opinions on cricket: 'Lunch and tea breaks are not long enough. By the time I've taken my size 13s off, it's time to go out again.'

Best batting: 42 OUCCE v Derbyshire, The Parks 2005

Best bowling: 4-77 Surrey v Essex, Guildford 2009

2009 Season

	M	Inn	NO	Runs	HS	Avg	100	50	Ct	St	Balls	Runs	Wkts	Avg	BB	5I	10M
Test																	
FC	5	6	1	98	36	19.60	-	-	1	-	786	442	8	55.25	4-77	-	-
ODI																	
List A	8	2	2	37	20*		-	-	-	-	288	253	4	63.25	2-38	-	
20/20 Int																	
20/20	2	1	0	8	8	8.00	-	-	1	-	32	42	0			-	-

Career Performances

	M	Inn	NO	Runs	HS	Avg	100	50	Ct	St	Balls	Runs	Wkts	Avg	BB	5I	10M
Test																	
FC	13	14	1	173	42	13.30	-	-	2	-	1656	978	22	44.45	4-77	-	-
ODI																	
List A	8	2	2	37	20*		-	-	-	-	288	253	4	63.25	2-38	-	
20/20 Int																	
20/20	2	1	0	8	8	8.00	-	-	1	-	32	42	0			-	-

---

54. Bangladesh won their first Test match in 35 attempts early in 2005 at Chittagong. Who did they beat?

LOGAN, R. J. Surrey

Name: <u>Richard</u> James Logan
Role: Right-hand bat, right-arm fast bowler
Born: 28 January 1980, Cannock, Staffordshire
Height: 6ft 1in **Weight:** 14st
Nickname: Bungle
County debut: 1999 (Northants),
2001 (Notts), 2005 (Hants), 2009 (Surrey)
Parents: Margaret and Robert
Marital status: Single
Family links with cricket: 'Dad played local
cricket for Cannock'
Education: Wolverhampton Grammar School
Qualifications: 11 GCSEs, 1 A-level
Overseas tours: England U17 to Bermuda (International Youth Tournament) 1997; England U19 to
South Africa (including U19 World Cup) 1997-98, to New Zealand 1998-99
Overseas teams played for: St George, Sydney 1999-2000; Lancaster Park,
New Zealand; Rovers, Durban; Northerns Goodwood, Cape Town
Career highlights to date: 'Winning junior World Cup'
Cricketers particularly admired: Malcolm Marshall, Dennis Lillee
Other sports played: Hockey
Other sports followed: Football (Wolverhampton Wanderers)
Relaxations: 'Spending time with my mates. Training'
Extras: Played for Staffordshire U11-U19 (captain U13-U17); Midlands U14 and U15
(both as captain); HMC Schools U15. 1995 *Daily Telegraph*/Lombard U15 Midlands
Bowler and Batsman of the Year. Played for Northamptonshire U17 and U19 national
champions 1997. Played for England U15, U17 and U19. C&G Man of the Match
award for his 5-24 v Suffolk at Mildenhall 2001. Took 5-26 v Lancashire at Trent
Bridge 2003, the best return by a Nottinghamshire bowler in the Twenty20 Cup.
Returned to Northamptonshire for 2007 season. Released September 2008. Played in
one first-class match for Surrey in 2009
Best batting: 37* Nottinghamshire v Hampshire, Trent Bridge 2001
Best bowling: 6-93 Nottinghamshire v Derbyshire, Trent Bridge 2001

2009 Season

	M	Inn	NO	Runs	HS	Avg	100	50	Ct	St	Balls	Runs	Wkts	Avg	BB	5I	10M
Test																	
FC	1	2	0	6	6	3.00	-	-	-	-	180	101	2	50.50	2-101	-	-
ODI																	
List A	2	1	0	5	5	5.00	-	-	-	-	72	74	0			-	-
20/20 Int																	
20/20																	

Career Performances

	M	Inn	NO	Runs	HS	Avg	100	50	Ct	St	Balls	Runs	Wkts	Avg	BB	5I	10M
Test																	
FC	55	75	16	533	37*	9.03	-	-	16	-	8116	5347	135	39.60	6-93	4	-
ODI																	
List A	67	31	11	220	28*	11.00	-	-	21	-	2620	2538	70	36.25	5-24	1	
20/20 Int																	
20/20	17	8	4	39	11*	9.75	-	-	-	-	244	315	17	18.52	5-26	1	

LONDON, A. B.   Middlesex

Name: <u>Adam</u> Brian London
Role: Left-hand bat, right-arm
off-spin bowler, occasional wicket-keeper
Born: 12 October 1988, Surrey
Height: 5ft 8in   **Weight:** 11st
Nickname: Londers
County debut: 2009
Place in batting averages: 166th av. 27.14
Parents: John and Terri
Marital status: Single
Family links with cricket: 'Dad played club cricket. Brother plays with me at Middlesex and at Sunbury CC.'
Education: Bishop Wand C of E school and sixth form college
Qualifications: 8 GCSEs, Level 1 coaching
Off-season: 'Going to Australia for the third season in a row'
Overseas teams played for: Melville CC (Perth) 2007-08; East Torrens (Adelaide) 2008-09
Career highlights to date: 'Scoring 68 at Lord's on my Middlesex debut'
Cricket moments to forget: 'All the dropped catches and getting ducks!'
Cricket superstitions: 'Right pad first'

Cricketers particularly admired: Mike Hussey, Andrew Strauss
Young players to look out for: Brad Erasmus (Middlesex), Joel Pope (Leicestershire)
Other sports played: Football ('used to play for Chelsea youth')
Other sports followed: Football (Manchester United)
Favourite band: The Script
Relaxations: 'Chilling with mates, fishing'
Extras: Former Sunbury CC and Middlesex Second XI player. Former Middlesex Youth Player of the Year and Batsman of the Year. Signed first summer contract with Middlesex June 2008. Signed a new two-year contract with the county October 2009
Opinions on cricket: 'Too congested sometimes – not enough time to recover.'
Best batting: 68 Middlesex v Gloucestershire, Lord's 2009

2009 Season

	M	Inn	NO	Runs	HS	Avg	100	50	Ct	St	Balls	Runs	Wkts	Avg	BB	5I	10M
Test																	
FC	4	8	1	190	68	27.14	-	2	1	-	48	39	0		-	-	-
ODI																	
List A	2	0	0	0	0		-	-	-	-	6	5	0		-	-	
20/20 Int																	
20/20																	

Career Performances

	M	Inn	NO	Runs	HS	Avg	100	50	Ct	St	Balls	Runs	Wkts	Avg	BB	5I	10M
Test																	
FC	4	8	1	190	68	27.14	-	2	1	-	48	39	0		-	-	-
ODI																	
List A	2	0	0	0	0		-	-	-	-	6	5	0		-	-	
20/20 Int																	
20/20																	

---

55. Most Bangladesh Tests have been part of two-match series.
They have, however, played two three-match series. Against whom?

LOYE, M. B.   Northamptonshire

Name: Malachy (<u>Mal</u>) Bernard Loye
Role: Right-hand bat, occasional
wicket-keeper
Born: 27 September 1972, Northampton
Height: 6ft 2in   **Weight:** 13st 12lbs
Nickname: Malcolm
County debut: 1991 (Northamptonshire),
2003 (Lancashire)
County cap: 1994 (Northamptonshire),
2003 (Lancashire)
Benefit: 2008 (Lancashire)
ODI debut: 2006-07
1000 runs in a season: 6
1st-Class 200s: 2
1st-Class 300s: 1
Place in batting averages: 25th av. 55.33 (2008 238th av. 13.53)
Parents: Patrick and Anne
Marital status: Single
Family links with cricket: 'Brother and Dad played for Cogenhoe CC
in Northampton'
Education: Moulton Comprehensive, Northampton
Qualifications: GCSEs, Levels 1 – 3 coaching
Overseas tours: England U18 to Canada (International Youth Tournament) 1991;
England U19 to Pakistan 1991-92; England A to South Africa 1993-94, to Zimbabwe
and South Africa 1998-99; Northamptonshire to Cape Town 1993, to Zimbabwe 1995,
1998, to Johannesburg 1996, to Grenada 2001, 2002; England VI to Hong Kong 2006;
England to Australia 2006-07 (Commonwealth Bank Series)
Overseas teams played for: Riccarton, Christchurch 1992-93 – 1994-95;
Canterbury B 1993; Onslow, Wellington 1995-96; North Perth 1997-98, 1999-2000;
Claremont, Western Australia 2000-01; Auckland 2006-07
Career highlights to date: 'PCA Player of the Year 1998'
Cricket moments to forget: '[C&G] semi-final against Worcester 2003'
Cricketers particularly admired: Gordon Greenidge, Wayne Larkins,
Peter Carlstein, Graeme Hick, John Crawley
Young players to look out for: Gareth Cross, Steven Croft
Other sports played: 'Muck about at anything'
Other sports followed: Football (Northampton Town, Liverpool), rugby union
Favourite band: U2
Extras: Played for England YC and for England U19. PCA Young Player of the Year
and Whittingdale Young Player of the Year 1993. Scored 322* v Glamorgan at
Northampton 1998 (the then highest individual first-class score for the county), in the

process sharing with David Ripley in a new record partnership for any wicket for Northamptonshire (401). PCA Player of the Year 1998. Scored century (126) on Championship debut for Lancashire v Surrey at The Oval 2003 and another (113) in the next match v Nottinghamshire at Old Trafford to become the first batsman to score centuries in his first two matches for the county. Finished top of Lancashire's Twenty20 averages for 2008. Returned to Northamptonshire from Lancashire September 2009

Best batting: 322* Northamptonshire v Glamorgan, Northampton 1998
Best bowling: 1-8 Lancashire v Kent, Blackpool 2003

2009 Season

	M	Inn	NO	Runs	HS	Avg	100	50	Ct	St	Balls	Runs	Wkts	Avg	BB	5I	10M
Test																	
FC	14	22	4	996	151*	55.33	2	6	4	-	0	0	0		-	-	-
ODI																	
List A	4	3	1	75	31	37.50	-	-	1	-	0	0	0		-	-	
20/20 Int																	
20/20	1	0	0	0	0		-	-	-	-	0	0	0		-	-	

Career Performances

	M	Inn	NO	Runs	HS	Avg	100	50	Ct	St	Balls	Runs	Wkts	Avg	BB	5I	10M
Test																	
FC	246	392	37	14516	322*	40.89	41	60	119	-	55	61	1	61.00	1-8	-	-
ODI	7	7	0	142	45	20.28	-	-	-	-	0	0	0		-	-	
List A	291	284	32	8661	127	34.36	10	56	64	-	0	0	0		-	-	
20/20 Int																	
20/20	39	38	4	1131	100	33.26	1	7	14	-	0	0	0		-	-	

LUCAS, D. S.   Northamptonshire

Name: <u>David</u> Scott Lucas
Role: Right-hand bat, left-arm fast-medium bowler
Born: 19 August 1978, Nottingham
Height: 6ft 3in **Weight:** 13st
Nickname: Muke, Lukey, Cesc
County debut: 1999 (Nottinghamshire),
2005 (Yorkshire), 2007 (Northamptonshire)
Place in batting averages: 228th av. 18.35
Place in bowling averages: 5th av. 21.65
(2008 132nd av. 42.58)
Parents: Mary and Terry
Wife and date of marriage: Donna-Marie,
22 November 2004
Children: 'Gizmo and Missy'
Education: Horsendale Primary School, Djanogly
City Technology College, Nottingham
Qualifications: 6 GCSEs, pass in Computer-Aided Design, Level 2 coaching
Career outside cricket: 'Running my own specialist cleaning company,
Pristine Clean'
Off-season: 'Back in the gym, expanding our business and also holidays'
Overseas tours: England (Indoor) to Australia (Indoor Cricket World Cup) 1998
Overseas teams played for: Bankstown-Canterbury Bulldogs, Sydney 1996-97;
Wanneroo, Perth 2001-02
Career highlights to date: 'The crack in the dressing-room; lunches at Lord's.
Taking 12 wickets against Gloucestershire at Cheltenham in 2008'
Cricket superstitions: 'Always walk back to the left of my mark when bowling.
Always put left pad on first. Can't bowl without my watch!'
Cricketers particularly admired: Chaminda Vaas, Brett Lee, Darren Gough,
Craig White, Robin Smith
Young players to look out for: David Willey (Northamptonshire),
Alex Hales (Nottinghamshire)
Other sports played: 'Football, FIFA 09.'
Other sports followed: Football (Arsenal)
Favourite band: Oasis, Red Hot Chili Peppers, Kings of Leon
Relaxations: 'Cooking, tidying, gaming'
Extras: Won Yorkshire League with Rotherham in 1996. NBC Denis Compton Award
for the most promising young Nottinghamshire player 2000. Only J. J. van der Wath
took more first-class wickets for the county in 2008
Opinions on cricket: 'If the game is going nowhere in 4-day cricket and both
captains agree, the game can be declared a draw at tea on the last day.'
Best batting: 55* Northamptonshire v Essex, Chelmsford 2009
Best bowling: 7-24 Northamptonshire v Gloucestershire, Cheltenham 2009

2009 Season

	M	Inn	NO	Runs	HS	Avg	100	50	Ct	St	Balls	Runs	Wkts	Avg	BB	5I	10M
Test																	
FC	16	24	7	312	55*	18.35	-	1	5	-	2487	1299	60	21.65	7-24	3	1
ODI																	
List A	9	5	2	35	32*	11.66	-	-	1	-	309	247	13	19.00	4-28	-	
20/20 Int																	
20/20	6	2	1	5	3*	5.00	-	-	-	-	84	132	3	44.00	1-20	-	

Career Performances

	M	Inn	NO	Runs	HS	Avg	100	50	Ct	St	Balls	Runs	Wkts	Avg	BB	5I	10M
Test																	
FC	64	81	23	1075	55*	18.53	-	1	13	-	9555	5576	175	31.86	7-24	7	1
ODI																	
List A	60	26	8	185	32*	10.27	-	-	11	-	2295	2141	72	29.73	4-27	-	
20/20 Int																	
20/20	15	5	4	15	5*	15.00	-	-	1	-	192	305	8	38.12	2-37	-	

LUMB, M. J.   Hampshire

Name: <u>Michael</u> John Lumb
Role: Left-hand bat, right-arm
medium bowler
Born: 12 February 1980, Johannesburg,
South Africa
Height: 6ft **Weight:** 13st
Nickname: China, Joe
County debut: 2000 (Yorkshire),
2007 (Hampshire)
County cap: 2003 (Yorkshire), 2008 (Hampshire)
1st-class 200s: 1
1000 runs in a season: 2
Place in batting averages: 55th av. 43.73
(2008 104th av. 32.72)
Parents: Richard and Sue
Marital status: Single
Family links with cricket: Father played for Yorkshire. Uncle played for Natal
Education: St Stithians College
Qualifications: Matriculation
Overseas tours: Transvaal U19 to Barbados; Yorkshire to Cape Town 2001, to
Grenada 2002; England A to Malaysia and India 2003-04
Overseas teams played for: Pirates CC, Johannesburg; Wanderers CC, Johannesburg

Cricket moments to forget: 'Relegation in 2002 [with Yorkshire]'
Cricket superstitions: 'None'
Cricketers particularly admired: Graham Thorpe, Darren Lehmann,
Craig White, Stephen Fleming
Other sports played: Golf
Other sports followed: Rugby union (Sharks in Super 14, Leeds Carnegie)
Favourite band: Oasis
Relaxations: 'Golf, socialising with friends'
Extras: Scored maiden first-class century (122) v Leicestershire at Headingley 2001;
the Lumbs thus became only the fourth father and son to have scored centuries for
Yorkshire. Yorkshire Young Player of the Year 2002, 2003. ECB National Academy
2003-04. C&G Man of the Match award in the quarter-final v Northamptonshire at
Headingley 2005 (89). Scored 98 v Durham at Headingley 2006, in the process
sharing with Darren Lehmann (339) in a new record fourth-wicket partnership
for Yorkshire (358)
Best batting: 219 Nottinghamshire v Hampshire, Trent Bridge 2009
Best bowling: 2-10 Yorkshire v Kent, Canterbury 2001

2009 Season

	M	Inn	NO	Runs	HS	Avg	100	50	Ct	St	Balls	Runs	Wkts	Avg	BB	5I	10M
Test																	
FC	16	24	1	1006	219	43.73	2	5	10	-	0	0	0		-	-	-
ODI																	
List A	18	18	2	676	100	42.25	1	7	8	-	0	0	0		-	-	
20/20 Int																	
20/20	11	11	1	442	124*	44.20	1	3	4	-	0	0	0		-	-	

Career Performances

	M	Inn	NO	Runs	HS	Avg	100	50	Ct	St	Balls	Runs	Wkts	Avg	BB	5I	10M
Test																	
FC	129	217	15	6885	219	34.08	11	44	88	-	318	242	6	40.33	2-10	-	-
ODI																	
List A	157	151	11	4477	108	31.97	2	35	52	-	12	28	0		-	-	
20/20 Int																	
20/20	54	54	4	1270	124*	25.40	1	9	15	-	36	65	3	21.66	3-32	-	

LUNGLEY, T. Derbyshire

Name: Tom Lungley
Role: Left-hand bat, right-arm medium bowler
Born: 25 July 1979, Derby
Height: 6ft 2in **Weight:** 13st
Nickname: Lungfish, Monkfish, Sweaty, Full Moon,
Half Moon, Lungo
County debut: 2000
County cap: 2007
50 wickets in a season: 1
Place in bowling averages: 104th av. 40.84
Parents: Richard and Christina
Marital status: 'Taken'
Family links with cricket: 'Dad was captain of Derby
Road CC. Grandad was bat maker in younger days'

Education: Saint John Houghton School, Kirk
Hallam; South East Derbyshire College
Qualifications: 9 GCSEs, Sport and Recreation Levels 1 and 2, pool lifeguard
qualification, coaching qualifications in cricket, tennis, basketball, football
and volleyball
Career outside cricket: Painter and decorator
Overseas teams played for: Delacombe Park, Melbourne 1999-2000
Cricket moments to forget: 'Unable to speak when interviewed by Sybil Ruscoe on
Channel 4 Cricket Roadshow (live)'
Cricketers particularly admired: Ian Botham, Dennis Lillee, Courtney Walsh,
Curtly Ambrose, Brian Lara, Richard Hadlee, Glenn McGrath
Other sports played: 'Enjoy playing most sports, mainly football and basketball'
Other sports followed: Football (Derby County), basketball
Extras: First home-grown cricketer to become professional from Ockbrook and
Borrowash CC (for whom he struck the Derbyshire Premier League 2006 season's
best, 213 v Marehay). NBC Denis Compton Award for the most promising young
Derbyshire player 2003. Spent four weeks on loan to Lancashire during 2009
Best batting: 50 Derbyshire v Warwickshire, Derby 2008
Best bowling: 5-20 Derbyshire v Leicestershire, Derby 2007

2009 Season

	M	Inn	NO	Runs	HS	Avg	100	50	Ct	St	Balls	Runs	Wkts	Avg	BB	5I	10M
Test																	
FC	6	6	2	99	33	24.75	-	-	4	-	797	531	13	40.84	3-56	-	-
ODI																	
List A	3	3	0	13	10	4.33	-	-	1	-	108	136	0			-	-
20/20 Int																	
20/20	6	1	1	2	2*		-	-	2	-	75	122	8	15.25	5-27	1	

Career Performances

	M	Inn	NO	Runs	HS	Avg	100	50	Ct	St	Balls	Runs	Wkts	Avg	BB	5I	10M
Test																	
FC	48	67	15	800	50	15.38	-	1	19	-	6431	4154	130	31.95	5-20	3	-
ODI																	
List A	76	45	11	384	45	11.29	-	-	19	-	2902	2522	82	30.75	4-28	-	
20/20 Int																	
20/20	29	13	5	107	25	13.37	-	-	8	-	457	610	29	21.03	5-27	1	

LYTH, A.   Yorkshire

Name: Adam Lyth
Role: Left-hand bat, right-arm off-spin bowler
Born: 25 September 1987, Whitby,
North Yorkshire
Height: 5ft 10in **Weight:** 10st 7lbs
Nickname: Lythie
County debut: 2006 (one-day), 2007 (first-class)
Place in batting averages: 149th av. 30.00
(2008 117th av. 30.71)
Parents: Alistair and Christine
Marital status: 'Engaged to Lily'
Family links with cricket: 'Grandfather was a
wicket-keeper; father and brother played cricket'
Education: Caedmon School; Whitby
Community College
Off-season: 'Training at the ECB headquarters in Loughborough with the England
Development squad, and then playing in South Africa in January'
Qualifications: GCSEs
Overseas tours: England U16 to South Africa 2004; England U19 to Malaysia
2006-07. England Development squad to South Africa 2010
Overseas teams played for: Stingrays (Adelaide) 2008-09

Career highlights to date: 'Getting hundred [122] for England U19 on home ground at Scarborough in the first "Test" against Pakistan [2007]. Scoring my first first-class century at Trent Bridge in 2008, and my first List A century on my home ground at Scarborough in 2009'

Cricket moments to forget: 'Getting caught by my brother when we played against each other'

Cricket superstitions: 'None'

Cricketers particularly admired: Craig White, Darren Lehmann, Graham Thorpe, Andrew Flintoff

Young players to look out for: Adil Rashid (Yorkshire), 'Archie Vaughan!'

Other sports played: Football (represented district and North Yorkshire; had trials with Man City and Sunderland); golf

Other sports followed: Football (Arsenal), 'follow all sports – sports mad'

Favourite band: Kings of Leon

Relaxations: 'Socialising'

Extras: North Player of Tournament at Taunton at U13. Played in Bunbury Festival 2003. Led Yorkshire to U17 County Championship 2005. Represented England at U15, U16, U17 and U19 levels, scoring 64 and 113 on U19 "Test" debut v India U19 at Canterbury 2006. Scarborough and District Best Male Achiever award. Promising Yorkshire Young Cricketer award. Yorkshire Player of the Year 2008. Attended Darren Lehmann Academy in Adelaide, 2009. Scored 112 for Yorkshire as they beat the UAE by eight wickets in tour match Sharjah, March 2009. Yorkshire's second-highest run scorer in one-day cricket 2009. Member of England Performance Programme squad 2009-10

Best batting: 132 Yorkshire v Nottinghamshire, Trent Bridge 2008
Best bowling: 1-12 Yorkshire v LUCCE, Headingley 2007

2009 Season

	M	Inn	NO	Runs	HS	Avg	100	50	Ct	St	Balls	Runs	Wkts	Avg	BB	5I	10M
Test																	
FC	5	8	0	240	71	30.00	-	2	1	-	114	38	1	38.00	1-38	-	-
ODI																	
List A	11	11	1	339	109*	33.90	1	1	1	-	12	11	0			-	-
20/20 Int																	
20/20	8	6	0	17	10	2.83	-	-	2	-	0	0	0			-	-

Career Performances

	M	Inn	NO	Runs	HS	Avg	100	50	Ct	St	Balls	Runs	Wkts	Avg	BB	5I	10M
Test																	
FC	20	30	0	916	132	30.53	1	7	12	-	301	155	3	51.66	1-12	-	-
ODI																	
List A	29	24	3	535	109*	25.47	1	1	9	-	18	14	0			-	-
20/20 Int																	
20/20	9	7	0	17	10	2.42	-	-	2	-	0	0	0			-	-

MacLEOD, C. S.
Warwickshire

Name: <u>Calum</u> Scott MacLeod
Role: Right-hand bat, right-arm
fast-medium bowler
Born: 15 November 1988, Rutherglen, Glasgow
Height: 6ft 2in **Weight:** 13st 5lbs
Nickname: Cloudy, Highlander, Scot
County debut: 2007
ODI debut: 2008
Twenty20 Int debut: 2009
Parents: Donald and Morag
Marital status: Single

Family links with cricket: 'Two brothers playing at
Uddingston CC – Allan also represented West District
U15 and U18 and Niall represented West District U13
and U15 and Scotland U12 and U13. Our mother
Morag managed Scotland U12 for four years'
Education: Hillpark Secondary School, Glasgow
Qualifications: 8 Standard Grades, 2 Higher Grades
Off-season: 'Preparing for next season at home in Scotland, and in Birmingham'
Overseas tours: West District to Australia 2004-05; Warwickshire Academy to South
Africa 2005-06; Scotland U19 to Sri Lanka (U19 World Cup) 2005-06, plus other
Scotland age-group tours to Holland, Ireland and Denmark; Scotland to South Africa
(ICC World Cup Qualifiers) 2009
Overseas teams played for: Penrith CC, Sydney 2007-08
Career highlights to date: 'Making first-class Scotland debut against UAE
on 27 June 2007 at Ayr as youngest ever player for Scotland at full international
level. Signing a two-year contract with Warwickshire. Scotland v England ODI,
August 2008'
Cricket moments to forget: 'Love them all!'
Cricket superstitions: 'Scratch my guard mark on the crease nine times
before batting'
Cricketers particularly admired: Glenn McGrath
Young players to look out for: Chris Woakes (Warwickshire)
Other sports played: Hockey (Stepps HC Glasgow; represented West District and
Scotland Select, and Scotland U16s)
Other sports followed: Football (Celtic FC)
Favourite band: Kings of Leon
Relaxations: 'Like to go shopping, spend time with friends and listen to music'
Extras: City of Glasgow Young Sportsperson of the Year 2005 and North Lanarkshire
Male Youth Sportsperson of the Year 2005. Has twice been European U19
Championship Player of the Year. Cricket Scotland National Young Player of the Year
2006, 2007. Warwickshire Most Improved 2nd XI Player 2007. Made first-class debut

for Scotland v UAE in the ICC Inter-Continental Cup 2007 at Ayr

Opinions on cricket: 'Cricket is in a pretty good state, with growing interest through Twenty20 and IPL in particular, leading to what looks like an exciting future for fans and players alike. In domestic cricket, make it easier for U16s to watch or be involved, especially if they bring an adult!'

Best batting: 10* Scotland v England, Edinburgh 2009

Best bowling: 4-66 Scotland v Canada, Aberdeen 2009

2009 Season

	M	Inn	NO	Runs	HS	Avg	100	50	Ct	St	Balls	Runs	Wkts	Avg	BB	5I	10M
Test																	
FC	1	1	0	26	26	26.00	-	-	3	-	60	26	1	26.00	1-10	-	-
ODI																	
List A																	
20/20 Int	2	1	0	0	0	0.00	-	-	1	-	30	56	0		-	-	
20/20	2	1	0	0	0	0.00	-	-	1	-	30	56	0		-	-	

Career Performances

	M	Inn	NO	Runs	HS	Avg	100	50	Ct	St	Balls	Runs	Wkts	Avg	BB	5I	10M
Test																	
FC	4	3	1	38	26	19.00	-	-	4	-	413	214	11	19.45	4-66	-	-
ODI	4	3	1	12	10*	6.00	-	-	-	-	138	139	3	46.33	2-46	-	
List A	11	7	2	22	10*	4.40	-	-	3	-	360	338	8	42.25	2-38	-	
20/20 Int	2	1	0	0	0	0.00	-	-	1	-	30	56	0		-	-	
20/20	2	1	0	0	0	0.00	-	-	1	-	30	56	0		-	-	

56. Who replaced Waqar Younis as captain of the Pakistan Test and one-day teams, following the 2003 World Cup?

MADDY, D. L.   Warwickshire

Name: <u>Darren</u> Lee Maddy
Role: Right-hand bat, right-arm medium bowler
Born: 23 May 1974, Leicester
Height: 5ft 9in   **Weight:** 12st 7lbs
Nickname: Madds
County debut: 1993 (one-day, Leicestershire),
1994 (first-class, Leicestershire),
2007 (Warwickshire)
County cap: 1996 (Leicestershire),
2007 (Warwickshire)
Benefit: 2006 (Leicestershire)
Test debut: 1999
ODI debut: 1998

Twenty20 Int debut: 2007-08
1000 runs in a season: 4
1st-Class 200s: 2
Place in batting averages: (2008 60th av. 40.94)
Place in bowling averages: (2008 39th av. 26.00)
Parents: William Arthur and Hilary Jean
Wife and date of marriage: Justine Marie, 7 October 2000
Children: George William, 13 October 2005; Isaac James, 12 July 2008
Family links with cricket: Father and younger brother, Greg, play club cricket
Education: Roundhill, Thurmaston; Wreake Valley, Syston
Qualifications: 8 GCSEs, Level 3 coach, CPT Reps 3, CES
Career outside cricket: Fitness advisor. Organising cricket tours to South East Asia
Off-season: 'Recovering from an ACL reconstruction in the gym'
Overseas tours: Leicestershire to Bloemfontein 1995, to Western Transvaal 1996, to Durban 1997, to Barbados 1998, to Anguilla 2000, to Potchefstroom 2001; England A to Kenya and Sri Lanka 1997-98, to Zimbabwe and South Africa 1998-99; England to South Africa and Zimbabwe 1999-2000, to South Africa (World 20/20) 2007-08; England VI to Hong Kong 2003, 2004, 2005, 2006, 2007, 2008; Lord's Taverners to Dubai 2006, 2007, 2008; Warwickshire to Grenada 2007, Bloemfontein 2008
Overseas teams played for: Wanderers, Johannesburg 1992-93; Northern Free State, South Africa 1993-95; Rhodes University, South Africa 1995-97; Sunshine CC, Grenada 2002; Perth CC, 2002-03, 2003-04
Career highlights to date: 'Winning two Championship medals. Playing for England. Winning Twenty20 final 2004 and 2006. Being awarded the Warwickshire captaincy 2007'
Cricket moments to forget: 'Being relegated in two competitions in 2007. Rupturing my ACL during a warm-up game'
Cricket superstitions: 'Always put my left pad on first'
Cricketers particularly admired: 'Anyone who has made a success of their career'

Young players to look out for: Ateq Javid (Warwickshire)
Other sports played: Touch rugby, golf, squash, 5-a-side football, soccer volley ball
Other sports followed: Rugby (Leicester Tigers), football (Leicester City), baseball, golf, boxing – 'most sports really except for horse racing and motor racing'
Injuries: 'ACL – out for 9 months'
Favourite band: Kings of Leon
Relaxations: 'Watching movies, listening to music, reading books, playing the drums and of course spending good time with the family'
Player website: www.darrenmaddy.com
Extras: Rapid Cricketline 2nd XI Championship Player of the Year 1994. Was leading run-scorer on England A's 1997-98 tour (687 – av. 68.7). NBC Denis Compton Award for most promising young Leicestershire player 1997. In 1998, broke the season record for runs scored in the B&H (629 – av. 125.80), winning five Gold Awards. Scored 229* v LUCCE at Leicester 2003, in the process sharing with Brad Hodge (202*) in a record partnership for any wicket for Leicestershire (436*). Struck 60-ball 111 v Yorkshire at Headingley in the Twenty20 2004, in the process sharing with Brad Hodge (78) in a then competition record partnership for any wicket (167). Scored 86* (also took a wicket and two catches) in the final of the Twenty20 Cup at Trent Bridge 2006, becoming the first player to pass 1000 career runs in the competition and winning the Man of the Match award. President of the Leicestershire School Sports Federation. Vice-captain of Leicestershire July 2004–2005. Made captain of Warwickshire in 2007, he relinquished the post towards the end of 2008
Opinions on cricket: 'Twenty20 overkill and the season starts far too early to help accommodate it.'
Best batting: 229* Leicestershire v LUCCE, Grace Road 2003
Best bowling: 5-37 Leicestershire v Hampshire, Rose Bowl 2002

2009 Season

	M	Inn	NO	Runs	HS	Avg	100	50	Ct	St	Balls	Runs	Wkts	Avg	BB	5I	10M
Test																	
FC	2	3	0	61	36	20.33	-	-	2	-	187	100	1	100.00	1-48	-	-
ODI																	
List A	1	1	0	0	0	0.00	-	-	-	-	30	21	0		-	-	
20/20 Int																	
20/20																	

Career Performances

	M	Inn	NO	Runs	HS	Avg	100	50	Ct	St	Balls	Runs	Wkts	Avg	BB	5I	10M
Test	3	4	0	46	24	11.50	-	-	4	-	84	40	0		-	-	-
FC	244	395	27	12308	229*	33.44	26	58	253	-	12559	6685	206	32.45	5-37	5	-
ODI	8	6	0	113	53	18.83	-	1	1	-	0	0	0		-	-	
List A	323	298	29	8263	167*	30.71	11	50	126	-	6494	5491	188	29.20	4-16	-	
20/20 Int	4	4	0	113	50	28.25	-	1	1	-	18	26	3	8.66	2-6	-	
20/20	48	48	5	1418	111	32.97	1	11	28	-	563	735	26	28.26	2-6	-	

MADSEN, W. L.   Derbyshire

Name: <u>Wayne</u> Lee Madsen
Role: Right-hand opening bat, right-arm off-spin bowler
Born: 2 January 1984, Durban, South Africa
Height: 5ft 11in **Weight:** 11st 8lbs
Nickname: Madders
County debut: 2009
Place in batting averages: 20th av. 57.78
Parents: Paddy and Adele
Wife and date of marriage: Kyla, 6 December 2008
Family links with cricket: Uncles Trevor Madsen (played for Natal 1976-90), Mike Madsen (played for Natal 1967-79) and Henry Fotheringham (played for Natal and Transvaal 1971-90). Cousin Greg Fotheringham (KwaZulu Natal and Durham 2nd XI)
Education: Kearsney College, Botha's Hill; University of South Africa
Qualifications: B.Com degree in Financial Management, Level 2 coaching
Off-season: 'Four months playing club cricket and coaching in Durban, South Africa'
Overseas teams played for: Nashua Dolphins 2004-08; KwaZulu-Natal 2003-08; Durban North Crusaders 2001-04; Berea Rovers 2005-09
Career highlights to date: '170* v Gloucestershire on my debut for Derbyshire'
Cricket moments to forget: 'None!'
Cricket superstitions: 'I always put my left pad on first – but not for superstitious reasons, more out of habit'
Cricketers particularly admired: Jonty Rhodes, Shaun Pollock, Dale Benkenstein
Young players to look out for: Dan Redfern (Derbyshire), James Taylor (Leicestershire)
Other sports played: Field hockey ('for South Africa – 39 Tests, five goals, Commonwealth Games in Melbourne 2006, Hockey World Cup in Germany 2006'), golf ('handicap of 5')
Other sports followed: Rugby (Natal Sharks), football (Liverpool)
Relaxations: 'Going on safari to Phinda Game Reserve with my wife. Beach holidays with the family'
Extras: Is one of nine members of the Madsen family, across three generations, to have played international hockey for South Africa. Set a Derbyshire record for highest individual score in a debut innings (170* v Gloucestershire at Cheltenham, 2009). Signed a two-year deal with Derbyshire August 2009. Holds an EU passport and is not considered an overseas player
Best batting: 170* Derbyshire v Gloucestershire, Cheltenham 2009
Best bowling: 3-45 KwaZulu-Natal v Eastern Province, Port Elizabeth 2007-08

2009 Season

	M	Inn	NO	Runs	HS	Avg	100	50	Ct	St	Balls	Runs	Wkts	Avg	BB	5I	10M
Test																	
FC	9	16	2	809	170*	57.78	3	3	8	-	108	67	0		-	-	-
ODI																	
List A	2	2	0	42	42	21.00	-	-	1	-	24	18	2	9.00	2-18	-	
20/20 Int																	
20/20																	

Career Performances

	M	Inn	NO	Runs	HS	Avg	100	50	Ct	St	Balls	Runs	Wkts	Avg	BB	5I	10M
Test																	
FC	33	57	6	2117	170*	41.50	4	12	41	-	636	304	6	50.66	3-45	-	-
ODI																	
List A	14	13	3	223	55*	22.30	-	1	14	-	102	74	5	14.80	2-18	-	
20/20 Int																	
20/20																	

MAHMOOD, S. I. Lancashire

Name: Sajid Iqbal Mahmood
Role: Right-hand bat, right-arm
fast-medium bowler
Born: 21 December 1981, Bolton
Height: 6ft 4in **Weight:** 12st 7lbs
Nickname: Saj, King
County debut: 2002
County cap: 2007
Test debut: 2006
ODI debut: 2004
Twenty20 Int debut: 2006
Place in batting averages: (2008 258th av. 10.27)
Place in bowling averages: 72nd av. 34.00
(2008 91st av. 32.77)
Parents: Shahid and Femida
Marital status: Single
Family links with cricket: Father played in Bolton League. Younger brother plays
in Bolton League
Education: Smithills School; North College, Bolton (sixth form)
Qualifications: 9 GCSEs, 3 A-levels
Overseas tours: Lancashire to South Africa 2003; England A to Malaysia and India
2003-04, to Sri Lanka 2004-05, to West Indies 2005-06; England to India 2005-06

(one-day series), to India (ICC Champions Trophy) 2006-07, to Australia 2006-07, to West Indies (World Cup) 2006-07, to India (one-day series) 2008, to South Africa 2009-10 (one-day series). England Performance Programme to India, 2008-09. England Lions to New Zealand 2009

Overseas teams played for: Napier, New Zealand 2002-03
Cricket moments to forget: 'None'
Cricket superstitions: 'None'
Cricketers particularly admired: Brett Lee, Shoaib Akhtar
Favourite band: Nelly, Eminem
Relaxations: 'Music and chillin' with mates'
Extras: NBC Denis Compton Award for the most promising young Lancashire player 2003. Man of the Match in the fifth ODI v Pakistan at Edgbaston 2006 (10-2-24-2) and v Bangladesh in Bridgetown in the World Cup 2006-07 (3-27). ECB National Academy 2003-04, 2004-05, 2005-06. Played in the winning England Lions team against the visiting South Africans in 2008. Is cousin of boxer Amir Khan
Best batting: 94 Lancashire v Sussex, Old Trafford 2004
Best bowling: 6-30 Lancashire v Durham, Riverside 2009

2009 Season

	M	Inn	NO	Runs	HS	Avg	100	50	Ct	St	Balls	Runs	Wkts	Avg	BB	5I	10M
Test																	
FC	14	14	1	100	30*	7.69	-	-	6	-	2277	1394	41	34.00	6-30	2	1
ODI																	
List A	16	6	1	40	15	8.00	-	-	4	-	734	560	24	23.33	3-17	-	
20/20 Int																	
20/20	9	2	1	11	9	11.00	-	-	4	-	204	242	11	22.00	4-29	-	

Career Performances

	M	Inn	NO	Runs	HS	Avg	100	50	Ct	St	Balls	Runs	Wkts	Avg	BB	5I	10M
Test	8	11	1	81	34	8.10	-	-	-	-	1130	762	20	38.10	4-22	-	-
FC	81	102	16	1134	94	13.18	-	3	20	-	12143	7491	231	32.42	6-30	6	1
ODI	25	15	4	85	22*	7.72	-	-	1	-	1155	1128	29	38.89	4-50	-	
List A	121	67	19	409	29	8.52	-	-	15	-	5282	4500	170	26.47	5-16	1	
20/20 Int	2	1	1	0	0*		-	-	-	-	42	63	1	63.00	1-34	-	
20/20	31	11	4	50	21	7.14	-	-	5	-	666	810	30	27.00	4-29	-	

MALAN, D. J.   Middlesex

Name: <u>Dawid</u> Johannes Malan
Role: Left-hand bat, right-arm
leg-spin bowler
Born: 3 September 1987, Roehampton, London
Height: 6ft **Weight:** 12st 12lbs
Nickname: AC ('as in AC Milan')
County debut: 2006 (one-day)
Place in batting averages: 95th av. 37.20
(2008 65th av. 39.71)
Parents: Dawid and Janet
Family links with cricket: Father played for the
University of Stellenbosch and for Western Province
B. Brother (Charl) an MCC Young Cricketer
Education: Paarl Boys' High, South Africa; UNISA
Overseas tours: England Performance Programe to
India, 2008-09

Overseas teams played for: Wellington CC 2005-06 – 2006-07; Boland 2005-06;
Western Province/Boland Cricket Academy 2006; Belville CC
Career highlights to date: 'Playing for Middlesex in a Twenty20 game against Surrey
at The Oval in front of a packed house'
Cricket moments to forget: 'Getting a first-ball in my school's yearly interschool
match in my final year at school'
Cricket superstitions: 'The way I pack my cricket bag'
Cricketers particularly admired: Gary Kirsten
Other sports played: Rugby, golf
Other sports followed: Rugby (Blue Bulls)
Favourite band: The Killers
Relaxations: 'Fishing'
Extras: Boland U19 Provincial Player of the Year 2005. Wellington CC Player of the
Year 2005-06. Western Province/Boland Academy Player of the Year 2006. NBC
Denis Compton Award for most promising young Middlesex player 2008. Is not
considered an overseas player
Opinions on cricket: 'In my opinion the game has changed dramatically in the past
few years. The introduction of Twenty20 has changed the mindset of batsmen and
caused them to become more attacking in all forms of the game, which in turn has
made cricket more exciting.'
Best batting: 132* Middlesex v Northamptonshire, Uxbridge 2008
Best bowling: 2-21 Middlesex v Leicestershire, Southgate 2009

	M	Inn	NO	Runs	HS	Avg	100	50	Ct	St	Balls	Runs	Wkts	Avg	BB	5I	10M
Test																	
FC	15	28	3	930	88	37.20	-	8	19	-	580	358	7	51.14	2-21	-	-
ODI																	
List A	16	16	2	281	60	20.07	-	2	4	-	305	294	9	32.66	2-4	-	
20/20 Int																	
20/20	11	11	2	178	38	19.77	-	-	2	-	132	122	9	13.55	2-10	-	

Career Performances

	M	Inn	NO	Runs	HS	Avg	100	50	Ct	St	Balls	Runs	Wkts	Avg	BB	5I	10M
Test																	
FC	29	51	5	1644	132*	35.73	1	13	24	-	1089	714	14	51.00	2-21	-	-
ODI																	
List A	29	29	3	477	60	18.34	-	2	8	-	353	344	10	34.40	2-4	-	
20/20 Int																	
20/20	27	25	8	552	103	32.47	1	1	6	-	204	213	12	17.75	2-10	-	

MALIK, M. N.   Leicestershire

Name: Muhammad <u>Nadeem</u> Malik
Role: Right-hand bat, right-arm
fast-medium bowler
Born: 6 October 1982, Nottingham
Height: 6ft 5in **Weight:** 14st 7lbs
Nickname: Nad, Busta, Nigel, Gerz
County debut: 2001 (Nottinghamshire), 2004
(Worcestershire), 2008 (Leicestershire)
County colours: 2004 (Worcestershire)
Place in batting averages: (2008 250th av. 11.86)
Place in bowling averages: (2008 105th av. 35.11)
Parents: Abdul and Arshad
Marital status: Married
Family links with cricket: Brother plays club
cricket for Carrington
Education: Wilford Meadows Secondary School; Bilborough College
Qualifications: 9 GCSEs
Career outside cricket: Personal trainer
Off-season: 'Training and fitness'
Overseas tours: ZRK to Pakistan 2000; Nottinghamshire to South Africa 2001;
England U19 to India 2000-01, to Australia and (U19 World Cup) New Zealand
2001-02

Career highlights to date: '5-57 against Derbyshire 2001. Pro40 winners 2007 [Worcestershire]'
Cricket moments to forget: 'Norwich Union match v Yorkshire at Scarborough 2001 – Lehmann 191'
Cricketers particularly admired: Glenn McGrath, Wasim Akram, Curtly Ambrose
Young players to look out for: Joe Root (Yorkshire)
Other sports played: Football
Other sports followed: 'Most major sports'
Injuries: 'Back and groin – missed more than 5 months'
Relaxations: Music, games consoles
Extras: Made Nottinghamshire 2nd XI debut in 1999, aged 16, and took 15 wickets at an average of 19.40 for the 2nd XI 2000. Represented England U19 2001 and 2002. Played one first-class and one List A match for Nottinghamshire on loan 2007. Left Worcestershire at the end of the 2007 season and joined Leicestershire for 2008. Finished top of the Leicestershire first-class bowling averages in 2008, subsequently winning the Frank S. Smith bowling award. Injuries prevented him from making any first-team appearances in 2009
Best batting: 41 Leicestershire v Essex, Grace Road 2008
Best bowling: 6-46 Leicestershire v Essex, Chelmsford 2008

2009 Season (Did not make any first-class or one-day appearances for his county)

Career Performances

	M	Inn	NO	Runs	HS	Avg	100	50	Ct	St	Balls	Runs	Wkts	Avg	BB	5I	10M
Test																	
FC	66	87	30	558	41	9.78	-	-	10	-	10570	6467	179	36.12	6-46	7	-
ODI																	
List A	69	28	18	97	11	9.70	-	-	10	-	2711	2371	66	35.92	4-42	-	
20/20 Int																	
20/20	24	6	3	6	3*	2.00	-	-	2	-	474	650	28	23.21	4-16	-	

57. Which Pakistani was the first to do the double of 1,000 Test match runs and 100 Test wickets?

MANUEL, J. K.   Worcestershire

Name: <u>Jack</u> Kenneth Manuel
Role: Left-hand opening bat, right-arm
off-break bowler
Born: 13 February 1991, Sutton Coldfield,
Warwickshire
Height: 6ft 1in **Weight:** 13st
Nickname: JK, Manwell, Jacko, Basil
County debut: No first-team appearance
Parents: John and Kay
Marital status: 'In a relationship'
Family links with cricket: Dad still plays club
cricket for Tamworth in the Birmingham League and
is a Level 3 coach who works on the Staffordshire
Elite Player Programme. Grandad played for Dorset
Young Cricketers.

Education: Wilnecote High School and sixth form college
Qualifications: 9 GCSEs, 4 AS Levels, 3 A Levels, Level 1 coaching
Career outside cricket: None
Off-season: 'Training with Worcestershire, and England U19s with an opportunity
to play in the U19 World Cup if selected'
Career highlights to date: 'Scoring 108 on my England U17 debut v New Zealand
U19. Making 54 in the second innings of the U19 Test v Bangladesh and the same
score on my ODI debut against the same opposition'
Cricket moments to forget: 'Top edging the ball into my face, breaking my nose
and eye socket. Getting a golden duck on my England U19 Test debut'
Cricket superstitions: 'Can't change kit if I'm batting well with it'
Cricketers particularly admired: Matthew Hayden, Graeme Hick
Young players to look out for: James Vince (Hampshire), Sam Northeast (Kent),
Nathan Buck (Leicestershire), Aneesh Kapil and Ben Cox (both Worcestershire)
Other sports played: 'None now, but I played as a striker for Tamworth & District
at football'
Other sports followed: Football (Manchester United)
Injuries: 'Facial injuries (see above) – out for 5 weeks'
Favourite band: Empire of the Sun
Relaxations: 'Spending time with my girlfriend, listening to music, playing on the
Wii'
Extras: Scored a festival record 137 v Durham at the Ampleforth U12s festival. Once
scored 203* in an U13 Twenty20 knockout match. Worcestershire Academy Player of
the Year 2008. Staffordshire Player of the Year 2008. Has played for both England
U17 and U19, making a century for the former against New Zealand U19

MARSHALL, H. J. H.   Gloucestershire

Name: <u>Hamish</u> John Hamilton Marshall
Role: Right-hand bat, right-arm
medium bowler
Born: 15 February 1979, Warkworth, Auckland,
New Zealand
Nickname: Marshy
County debut: 2006
County cap: 2006
Test debut: 2000
ODI debut: 2003
Twenty20 Int debut: 2004-05
1000 runs in a season: 1
Place in batting averages: 113th av. 35.16
(2008 122nd av. 30.35)
Place in bowling averages: 8th av. 22.50
Parents: Kate and Drew
Family links with cricket: Twin brother James Marshall also plays for Northern
Districts and has represented New Zealand
Education: Mahurangi College; King's College
Off-season: 'Training with Gloucestershire and playing some cricket for Northern
Districts in New Zealand'
Overseas tours: New Zealand U19 to South Africa (U19 World Cup) 1997-98; New
Zealand to South Africa 2000-01, to Pakistan (one-day series) 2003-04, to England
2004 (NatWest Series), to England (ICC Champions Trophy) 2004, to Bangladesh
2004-05, to Australia 2004-05, to Zimbabwe 2005-06, to South Africa 2005-06, to
India (ICC Champions Trophy) 2006-07, to Australia (C'wealth Bank Series) 2006-07,
to West Indies (World Cup) 2006-07
Overseas teams played for: Northern Districts 1998-99 – 2006-07 and 2008-09 – ;
Chandigarh Lions (ICL) 2007-08; Royal Bengal Tigers (ICL) 2008-09
Career highlights to date: '146 against Australia [Christchurch, March 2005]'
Cricket moments to forget: 'Any golden duck'
Cricketers particularly admired: Mark Waugh, Ricky Ponting, Stephen Fleming
Young players to look out for: Ian Saxelby (Gloucestershire), Kane Williamson
(Northern Districts)
Other sports followed: Rugby (North Harbour, Auckland Blues, Bristol),
football (Aston Villa)
Favourite band: U2
Relaxations: 'Golf, movies'
Extras: MCC Young Cricketer 1998. Attended New Zealand Cricket Academy 1999.
Played for Buckinghamshire in the 2004 C&G competition. Represented New Zealand
v FICA World XI 2004-05. One of *New Zealand Cricket Almanack*'s two Players of
the Year 2005. His match awards include Man of the Match v West Indies at Cardiff in

the NatWest Series 2004 (75*) and v Australia in the first ODI at Melbourne 2004-05 (50*). An overseas player with Gloucestershire 2006-07. Refused a contract with New Zealand 2007-08 to pursue his county career. Topped the county 40-over and Twenty20 batting averages in 2008. Is no longer considered an overseas player
Best batting: 168 Gloucestershire v Leicestershire, Cheltenham 2006
Best bowling: 4-24 Leicestershire v Gloucestershire, Grace Road 2009

2009 Season

	M	Inn	NO	Runs	HS	Avg	100	50	Ct	St	Balls	Runs	Wkts	Avg	BB	5I	10M
Test																	
FC	16	26	2	844	158	35.16	1	5	13	-	624	360	16	22.50	4-24	-	-
ODI																	
List A	18	18	2	411	57	25.68	-	3	6	-	91	78	2	39.00	2-21	-	
20/20 Int																	
20/20	9	9	0	201	42	22.33	-	-	4	-	0	0	0		-	-	

Career Performances

	M	Inn	NO	Runs	HS	Avg	100	50	Ct	St	Balls	Runs	Wkts	Avg	BB	5I	10M
Test	13	19	2	652	160	38.35	2	2	1	-	6	4	0		-	-	
FC	133	226	15	7391	168	35.02	16	35	69	-	2040	1083	27	40.11	4-24	-	-
ODI	66	62	9	1454	101*	27.43	1	12	18	-	0	0	0		-	-	
List A	223	214	24	5350	122	28.15	6	35	85	-	236	243	4	60.75	2-21	-	
20/20 Int	3	3	0	12	8	4.00	-	-	1	-	0	0	0		-	-	
20/20	36	36	1	797	100	22.77	1	2	19	-	0	0	0		-	-	

58. When England beat Pakistan by ten wickets at Trent Bridge in 1967, a total of only 509 runs was made. Which England batsman made 109 in the first innings?

MARTIN-JENKINS, R. S. C.   Sussex

Name: <u>Robin</u> Simon Christopher Martin-Jenkins
Role: Right-hand bat, right-arm
fast-medium bowler; all-rounder
Born: 28 October 1975, Guildford
Height: 6ft 5in **Weight:** 14st
Nickname: Tucker
County debut: 1995
County cap: 2000
Benefit: 2008
1000 runs in a season: 1
1st-Class 200s: 1
Place in batting averages: 214th av. 19.93
(2008 92nd av. 35.66)
Place in bowling averages: 76th av. 34.47
(2008 94th av. 32.87)

Parents: Christopher and Judy
Wife and date of marriage: Flora, 19 February 2000
Children: Isabella Mary, 26 December 2009
Family links with cricket: Father was *The Times* senior cricket columnist until
May 2008 and is a BBC *TMS* commentator. Brother James played for the Radley
Rangers
Education: Radley College, Oxon; Durham University
Qualifications: 10 GCSEs, 3 A-levels, 1 AS-level, Grade 3 bassoon (with merit),
BA (Hons) Social Sciences, Don MacKenzie School of Professional Photography
Certificate, SWPP (Society of Wedding and Portrait Photographers), BPPA (British
Professional Photographers Associates), Wine and Spirit Education Trust Intermediate
and Advanced Certificates
Career outside cricket: Land agent
Off-season: 'Work experience teaching in schools. Champions League in India. Wife
expecting in December!' [*Daughter Isabella arrived on Boxing Day 2009*]
Overseas tours: Radley College to Barbados 1992; Sussex U19 to Sri Lanka 1995;
Durham University to Vienna 1995; MCC to Kenya 1999; Sussex to Grenada 2001,
2002, to India (Champions League) 2009-10
Overseas teams played for: Lima CC, Peru 1994; Bellville CC, Cape Town 2000-01
Career highlights to date: 'Maiden first-class ton and double ton. Three
Championship titles. C&G Trophy final 2006 – any of the ten trophies Sussex has won
in the last few years. Either of my 7-fors'
Cricket superstitions: 'Never bowl first at Colwyn Bay'
Favourite sledging line: 'If I had a pound for every time someone had said to me
"Let's see what your dad writes about this in the paper…" – I'd be £53 richer!'
Young players to look out for: Joe Gatting and Will Beer (both Sussex)

Other sports played: Golf, tennis, Rugby fives
Other sports followed: Rugby, football (Liverpool)
Favourite band: Keane
Relaxations: 'Wine, food, guitar'
Extras: Played for ESCA U15-U19. European Player of the Year, Vienna 1995. Best Performance Award for Sussex 1998. NBC Denis Compton Award for the most promising young Sussex player 1998, 1999, 2000. Scored 205* v Somerset at Taunton 2002, in the process sharing with Mark Davis (111) in a record eighth-wicket stand for Sussex (291) – the stand fell one run short of the record eighth-wicket partnership in English first-class cricket, set in 1896. BBC South Cricketer of the Year 2002
Opinions on cricket: 'There's still too much county cricket played. I'm happy there's no more 50-over cricket, but ODIs need to be 40-over games, too.'
Best batting: 205* Sussex v Somerset, Taunton 2002
Best bowling: 7-51 Sussex v Leicestershire, Horsham 2002

2009 Season

	M	Inn	NO	Runs	HS	Avg	100	50	Ct	St	Balls	Runs	Wkts	Avg	BB	5I	10M
Test																	
FC	13	17	2	299	67	19.93	-	1	5	-	1666	793	23	34.47	5-43	1	-
ODI																	
List A	15	9	4	57	19*	11.40	-	-	4	-	582	460	12	38.33	3-49	-	
20/20 Int																	
20/20	8	4	1	18	15	6.00	-	-	1	-	138	158	6	26.33	3-17	-	

Career Performances

	M	Inn	NO	Runs	HS	Avg	100	50	Ct	St	Balls	Runs	Wkts	Avg	BB	5I	10M
Test																	
FC	175	263	38	6819	205*	30.30	3	36	51	-	23552	11660	354	32.93	7-51	7	-
ODI																	
List A	223	164	35	1922	68*	14.89	-	3	47	-	9686	6919	231	29.95	4-22	-	
20/20 Int																	
20/20	40	24	7	225	56*	13.23	-	1	11	-	775	953	30	31.76	4-20	-	

MASCARENHAS, A. D.   Hampshire

Name: Adrian <u>Dimitri</u> Mascarenhas
Role: Right-hand bat, right-arm
medium-fast bowler, county captain
Born: 30 October 1977, Chiswick, London
Height: 6ft 1in **Weight:** 12st 2lbs
Nickname: Dimi, D-Train
County debut: 1996
County cap: 1998
Benefit: 2007
ODI debut: 2007
Twenty20 Int debut: 2007
50 wickets in a season: 1
Place in batting averages: 157th av. 28.22
(2008 119th av. 30.59)
Place in bowling averages: 124th av. 47.53
(2008 29th av. 23.82)

Parents: Malik and Pauline
Marital status: Single
Family links with cricket: Uncle played in Sri Lanka and brothers both play for
Melville CC in Perth, Western Australia
Education: Trinity College, Perth
Qualifications: Level 2 coaching
Career outside cricket: Personal trainer
Overseas tours: England VI to Hong Kong 2004, 2005; England to New Zealand
2007-08 (one-day series), to South Africa (World Twenty20) 2007-08, to Sri Lanka
2007-08 (one-day series), to West Indies 2008-09 (one-day series). Otago to India
(Champions League) 2009-10
Overseas teams played for: Melville CC, Perth 1991 – ; Rajasthan Royals (IPL)
2007-08 – ; Otago 2008-09, 2009-10; Tasmania 2009-10
Cricketers particularly admired: Sir Viv Richards, Malcolm Marshall,
Shane Warne
Other sports followed: Australian Rules (Collingwood)
Favourite band: Red Hot Chili Peppers
Relaxations: Tennis, golf, Australian Rules
Extras: Played for Western Australia at U17 and U19 level as captain. Took 6-88 on
first-class debut, for Hampshire v Glamorgan at Southampton 1996, the best figures
for a Hampshire debutant for 97 years. Won NatWest Man of the Match awards in
semi-final v Lancashire at Southampton 1998 (3-28/73) and in quarter-final v
Middlesex at Lord's 2000 (4-25). Scorer of the first Championship century at The
Rose Bowl (104) v Worcestershire 2001. Took Hampshire competition best 5-14 v
Sussex at Hove in the Twenty20 2004, including the competition's first hat-trick
(Davis, Mushtaq Ahmed, Lewry). Struck 15-ball 36* in the sixth ODI v India at

The Oval 2007, including a six off each of the last five balls of the England innings. Played against New Zealand in ODI and Twenty20 games in 2008. Captained England to victory in the Hong Kong Sixes tournament 2008 – named Player of the Tournament. In 2008 became the first England player to sign with the IPL. Succeeded Shane Warne as county captain in 2008. Played for England in both one-day and Twenty20 fixtures 2009

Best batting: 131 Hampshire v Kent, Canterbury 2006
Best bowling: 6-25 Hampshire v Derbyshire, Rose Bowl 2004

2009 Season

	M	Inn	NO	Runs	HS	Avg	100	50	Ct	St	Balls	Runs	Wkts	Avg	BB	5I	10M
Test																	
FC	10	11	2	254	108	28.22	1	-	4	-	1446	618	13	47.53	2-46	-	-
ODI	4	3	0	30	19	10.00	-	-	1	-	198	165	2	82.50	1-49	-	
List A	14	9	2	242	76	34.57	-	1	4	-	672	528	15	35.20	4-39	-	
20/20 Int	3	3	2	42	25*	42.00	-	-	-	-	42	45	2	22.50	1-9	-	
20/20	11	11	5	227	45*	37.83	-	-	1	-	234	241	13	18.53	2-14	-	

Career Performances

	M	Inn	NO	Runs	HS	Avg	100	50	Ct	St	Balls	Runs	Wkts	Avg	BB	5I	10M
Test																	
FC	181	271	30	6185	131	25.66	8	22	72	-	26181	11818	418	28.27	6-25	16	-
ODI	20	13	2	245	52	22.27	-	1	4	-	822	634	13	48.76	3-23	-	
List A	244	205	43	4107	79	25.35	-	27	62	-	10389	7376	281	26.24	5-27	1	
20/20 Int	14	13	5	123	31 1	5.37	-	-	7	-	252	309	12	25.75	3-18	-	
20/20	63	61	18	948	57*	22.04	-	3	20	-	1261	1501	76	19.75	5-14	1	

59. Name the Pakistan bowler who took 7 for 40 in the Headingley Test in July 1987.

MASON, M. S. Worcestershire

Name: Matthew (<u>Matt</u>) Sean Mason
Role: Right-hand bat, right-arm
fast-medium bowler
Born: 20 March 1974, Claremont, Perth,
Western Australia
Height: 6ft 5in **Weight:** 16st
Nickname: Mase, Moose
County debut: 2002
County colours: 2002
50 wickets in a season: 3
Place in batting averages: 262nd av. 12.17
Place in bowling averages: 30th av. 27.58
(2008 69th av. 29.90)
Parents: Bill and Sue

Wife and date of marriage: Kellie, 8 October 2005
Children: Evie, 27 March 2007
Family links with cricket: Brother plays first-grade for Claremont-Nedlands in
Western Australia
Education: Mazenod College, Perth; Edith Cowan University, Perth
Qualifications: Level 1 ACB coach
Overseas tours: Worcestershire to South Africa 2003
Overseas teams played for: Western Australia 1996-97 – 1997-98; Wanneroo
District CC 1999-2001; Claremont-Nedlands CC, Perth 2007-08
Career highlights to date: 'Back-to-back Lord's finals 2003 and 2004'
Cricket moments to forget: 'Losing back-to-back Lord's finals 2003 and 2004'
Cricketers particularly admired: Dennis Lillee, Darren Gough, Justin Langer
Other sports played: Golf ('badly'), tennis, Australian Rules football
Other sports followed: Australian Rules football (West Coast Eagles), rugby union
(Worcester Warriors)
Favourite band: Snow Patrol
Relaxations: 'Love being at home with my family'
Extras: Scored maiden first-class fifty (50) from 27 balls v Derbyshire at Worcester
2002. Dick Lygon Award for the [Worcestershire] Clubman of the Year 2003. Took
up position of Worcestershire CC bowling coach 2008. Worcestershire's leading first-
class wicket-taker in the 2009 season. Is England-qualified
Best batting: 63 Worcestershire v Warwickshire, Worcester 2004
Best bowling: 8-45 Worcestershire v Gloucestershire, Worcester 2006

2009 Season

	M	Inn	NO	Runs	HS	Avg	100	50	Ct	St	Balls	Runs	Wkts	Avg	BB	5I	10M
Test																	
FC	14	23	6	207	28	§12.17	-	-	6	-	2512	1186	43	27.58	7-39	2	-
ODI																	
List A	8	5	2	13	9	4.33	-	-	1	-	322	220	6	36.66	2-23	-	
20/20 Int																	
20/20																	

Career Performances

	M	Inn	NO	Runs	HS	Avg	100	50	Ct	St	Balls	Runs	Wkts	Avg	BB	5I	10M
Test																	
FC	90	115	29	1183	63	13.75	-	3	21	-	16377	7561	280	27.00	8-45	10	1
ODI																	
List A	80	38	15	171	25	7.43	-	-	16	-	3636	2608	91	28.65	4-34	-	
20/20 Int																	
20/20	10	4	2	18	8*	9.00	-	-	2	-	220	290	9	32.22	3-42	-	

MASTERS, D. Leicestershire

Name: Daniel Masters
Role: Right-hand bat, right-arm
fast-medium bowler
Born: 7 December 1986, Chatham, Kent
County debut: 2009 (one-day)
Parents: Kevin and Tracey
Family links with cricket: Father Kevin played for
Kent. Brother David plays for Essex
Extras: Lordswood CC (Kent Premier League)
2002-09, Surrey 2nd XI 2006, Kent Academy 2006,
Kent 2nd XI 2006-08, Leicestershire 2nd XI 2009

2009 Season

	M	Inn	NO	Runs	HS	Avg	100	50	Ct	St	Balls	Runs	Wkts	Avg	BB	5I	10M
Test																	
FC																	
ODI																	
List A	1	0	0	0	0		-	-	-	-	46	49	1	49.00	1-49	-	
20/20 Int																	
20/20																	

Career Performances

	M	Inn	NO	Runs	HS	Avg	100	50	Ct	St	Balls	Runs	Wkts	Avg	BB	5I	10M
Test																	
FC																	
ODI																	
List A	1	0	0	0	0		-	-	-	-	46	49	1	49.00	1-49	-	
20/20 Int																	
20/20																	

MASTERS, D. D.   Essex

Name: <u>David</u> Daniel Masters
Role: Right-hand bat, right-arm
fast-medium bowler
Born: 22 April 1978, Chatham, Kent
Height: 6ft 4ins **Weight:** 12st 5lbs
Nickname: Hod, Race Horse, Hoddy
County debut: 2000 (Kent),
2003 (Leicestershire), 2008 (Essex)
County cap: 2007 (Leicestershire)
Place in batting averages: 200th av. 22.73
(2008 256th av. 10.50)
Place in bowling averages: 25th av. 26.93
(2008 27th av. 23.33)
Parents: Kevin and Tracey
Marital status: Single
Family links with cricket: Brother Daniel plays for Leicestershire. 'Dad was on staff at Kent 1983-86'
Education: Fort Luton High School, Chatham; Mid-Kent College
Qualifications: 8 GCSEs, GNVQ in Leisure and Tourism, qualified coach in cricket, football and athletics, bricklayer and plasterer
Career outside cricket: Builder
Overseas teams played for: Doubleview, Perth 1998-99

Cricketers particularly admired: Ian Botham
Other sports played: Football, boxing 'and most other sports'
Other sports followed: Football (Manchester United)
Relaxations: 'Going out with mates'
Extras: Joint Kent Player of the Year 2000 (with Martin Saggers). NBC Denis Compton Award for the most promising young Kent player 2000. Leicestershire Player of the Year 2005. Left Leicestershire at the end of the 2007 season and joined Essex for 2008
Best batting: 119 Leicestershire v Sussex, Hove 2003
Best bowling: 6-24 Essex v Leicestershire, Chelmsford 2008

2009 Season

	M	Inn	NO	Runs	HS	Avg	100	50	Ct	St	Balls	Runs	Wkts	Avg	BB	5I	10M
Test																	
FC	15	16	1	341	67	22.73	-	2	7	-	3344	1212	45	26.93	5-65	1	-
ODI																	
List A	13	3	3	12	7*		-	-	-	-	642	415	13	31.92	3-19	-	
20/20 Int																	
20/20	10	3	0	8	4	2.66	-	-	2	-	212	277	5	55.40	2-34	-	

Career Performances

	M	Inn	NO	Runs	HS	Avg	100	50	Ct	St	Balls	Runs	Wkts	Avg	BB	5I	10M
Test																	
FC	118	143	26	1683	119	14.38	1	4	37	-	20638	9669	323	29.93	6-24	11	-
ODI																	
List A	120	61	26	449	39	12.82	-	-	13	-	4953	3670	111	33.06	5-17	2	
20/20 Int																	
20/20	54	18	6	66	14	5.50	-	-	15	-	1007	1245	45	27.66	3-7	-	

MAUNDERS, J. K.   Essex

Name: <u>John</u> Kenneth Maunders
Role: Left-hand opening bat, right-arm
medium bowler
Born: 4 April 1981, Ashford, Middlesex
Height: 5ft 10in **Weight:** 13st
Nickname: Rod, Weaz
County debut: 1999 (Middlesex),
2003 (Leicestershire), 2008 (Essex)
Place in batting averages: 117th av. 34.50
Parents: Lynn and Kenneth
Marital status: Single
Family links with cricket: Grandfather and two
uncles club cricketers for Thames Valley Ramblers
Education: Ashford High School;
Spelthorne College

Qualifications: 10 GCSEs, coaching certificates
Career outside cricket: Cricket coach
Overseas tours: England U19 to New Zealand 1998-99, to Malaysia and (U19 World
Cup) Sri Lanka 1999-2000
Overseas teams played for: University CC, Perth 2001-02
Career highlights to date: 'Scoring maiden first-class hundred v Surrey at
Grace Road'
Cricket moments to forget: 'Not any one in particular – getting 0 and dropping
catches are not great moments!'
Cricket superstitions: 'Just a few small ones'
Cricketers particularly admired: Brad Hodge, Justin Langer
Other sports played: Football, hockey, squash
Other sports followed: Horse racing
Extras: Has been Seaxe Player of Year. Represented England U17 and U19. NBC
Denis Compton Award for most promising young Leicestershire player 1999.
Released by Leicestershire at the end of the 2007 season. Signed a new one-year
contract with Essex in October 2009
Best batting: 180 Leicestershire v Gloucestershire, Cheltenham 2006
Best bowling: 4-15 Leicestershire v Worcestershire, Worcester 2006

2009 Season

	M	Inn	NO	Runs	HS	Avg	100	50	Ct	St	Balls	Runs	Wkts	Avg	BB	5I	10M
Test																	
FC	11	18	0	621	150	34.50	1	3	12	-	0	0	0		-	-	-
ODI																	
List A	5	2	0	108	78	54.00	-	1	-	-	0	0	0		-	-	
20/20 Int																	
20/20																	

Career Performances

	M	Inn	NO	Runs	HS	Avg	100	50	Ct	St	Balls	Runs	Wkts	Avg	BB	5I	10M
Test																	
FC	83	147	3	4382	180	30.43	7	22	50	-	1525	928	24	38.66	4-15	-	-
ODI																	
List A	36	33	3	748	109*	24.93	1	2	9	-	139	103	4	25.75	2-16	-	
20/20 Int																	
20/20	14	7	3	24	10	6.00	-	-	2	-	12	14	2	7.00	2-14	-	

MAYNARD, T. L.   Glamorgan

Name: Thomas (<u>Tom</u>) Lloyd Maynard
Role: Right-hand bat, right-arm
medium bowler
Born: 25 March 1989, Cardiff
Height: 6ft 2in **Weight:** 15st
Nickname: George, Squirrel
County debut: 2007
Place in batting averages: 221st av. 19.16
(2008 251st av. 11.71)
Parents: Matthew and Sue
Marital status: Single
Family links with cricket: 'Dad used to play
[for Glamorgan and England]. Uncle plays'
Education: Millfield School; Whitchurch High
Qualifications: 11 GCSEs, 3 A-levels
Overseas tours: England U15 to South Africa 2003-04
Career highlights to date: 'Debut for Glamorgan'
Cricket moments to forget: 'None'
Cricket superstitions: 'None'
Cricketers particularly admired: Brian Lara, Kevin Pietersen
Other sports played: Rugby (Bath Youth/Cardiff Youth)
Other sports followed: Football (Man City)

Favourite band: Oasis
Relaxations: 'Golf'
Extras: Played for Wales Minor Counties 2006-07. Scored 75-ball 71 on List A debut v Gloucestershire at Colwyn Bay in the Friends Provident 2007
Best batting: 51* Glamorgan v Derbyshire, Cardiff 2009

2009 Season

	M	Inn	NO	Runs	HS	Avg	100	50	Ct	St	Balls	Runs	Wkts	Avg	BB	5I	10M
Test																	
FC	6	7	1	115	51*	19.16	-	1	6	-		0	0	0	-	-	-
ODI																	
List A	13	12	2	431	108	43.10	1	3	5	-		0	0	0		-	-
20/20 Int																	
20/20	8	8	1	102	49*	14.57	-	-	4	-		0	0	0		-	-

Career Performances

	M	Inn	NO	Runs	HS	Avg	100	50	Ct	St	Balls	Runs	Wkts	Avg	BB	5I	10M
Test																	
FC	13	17	1	232	51*	14.50	-	1	11	-	12	18	0		-	-	-
ODI																	
List A	30	29	2	824	108	30.51	1	6	9	-		0	0	0		-	-
20/20 Int																	
20/20	13	12	1	137	49*	12.45	-	-	8	-		0	0	0		-	-

60. Which Pakistan bowler took 9 for 56 against England in Lahore in November 1987?

McDONALD, A. B. Leicestershire

Name: <u>Andrew</u> Barry McDonald
Role: Right-hand bat, right-arm
fast-medium bowler
Born: 5 June 1981, Wodonga, Victoria, Australia
Height: 6ft 4ins
Nickname: Ronnie
Test debut: 2009
Overseas tours: Australia U19 to Sri Lanka
(ICC U19 World Cup) 1999-2000; Australia to South
Africa 2008-09, to England 2009
Overseas teams played for: Victoria Bushrangers
2002-03 – ; Delhi Daredevils (IPL) 2009
Extras: In 2006-07 became only the fifth player in
Sheffield Shield/Pura Cup history to score 750 runs
and take 25 wickets. Selected for the 2009 Ashes tour
to England, but did not play in any of the summer's Tests, ODIs or Twenty20
games despite a good showing in a warm-up game v Northamptonshire. Overseas
player with Leicestershire for 2010
Best batting: 150* Victoria v New South Wales, Melbourne 2006-07
Best bowling: 6-34 Queensland v Victoria, Brisbane 2006-07

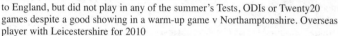

2009 Season

	M	Inn	NO	Runs	HS	Avg	100	50	Ct	St	Balls	Runs	Wkts	Avg	BB	5I	10M
Test																	
FC	1	2	0	107	75	53.50	-	1	-	-	96	38	4	9.50	4-15	-	-
ODI																	
List A																		
20/20 Int																		
20/20																		

Career Performances

	M	Inn	NO	Runs	HS	Avg	100	50	Ct	St	Balls	Runs	Wkts	Avg	BB	5I	10M
Test	4	6	1	107	68	21.40	-	1	2	-	732	300	9	33.33	3-25	-	-
FC	51	81	19	2318	150*	37.38	2	17	41	-	6946	3332	115	28.97	6-34	3	-
ODI																	
List A	60	50	17	1045	67	31.66	-	5	21	-	2287	1857	51	36.41	3-41	-	
20/20 Int																	
20/20	24	21	7	318	43	22.71	-	-	8	-	402	488	24	20.33	4-21	-	

McGRATH, A. Yorkshire

Name: Anthony McGrath
Role: Right-hand bat, right-arm medium bowler
Born: 6 October 1975, Bradford
Height: 6ft 2in **Weight:** 14st 7lbs
Nickname: Gripper, Mags, Terry
County debut: 1995
County cap: 1999
Benefit: 2009
Test debut: 2003
ODI debut: 2003
1st-class 200s : 1
1000 runs in a season: 2
Place in batting averages: 123rd av. 33.50

(2008 96th av. 34.66)
Parents: Terry and Kath
Marital status: Single
Education: Yorkshire Martyrs Collegiate School
Qualifications: 9 GCSEs, BTEC National Diploma in Leisure Studies, senior coaching award
Overseas tours: England U19 to West Indies 1994-95; England A to Pakistan 1995-96, to Australia 1996-97; MCC to Bangladesh 1999-2000; England to Bangladesh and Sri Lanka 2003-04 (one-day series), to West Indies 2003-04 (one-day series)
Overseas teams played for: Deep Dene, Melbourne 1998-99; Wanneroo, Perth 1999-2001
Cricket moments to forget: 'Losing semi-final to Lancashire 1996. Relegation to Division Two 2002'
Cricketers particularly admired: Darren Lehmann, Robin Smith
Other sports followed: 'Most sports', football (Manchester United)
Relaxations: 'Music, spending time with friends, eating out'
Extras: Captained Yorkshire Schools U13, U14, U15, U16. Captained English Schools U17. Bradford League Young Cricketer of the Year 1992 and 1993. Played for England U17 and U19. Captain of Yorkshire 2003; vice-captain of Yorkshire 2007, 2008. Captain again for 2009 season, but stepped down at the end of the year in order to concentrate on his playing. Signed a new three-year contract with the county in February 2009
Best batting: 211 Yorkshire v Warwickshire, Edgbaston 2009
Best bowling: 5-39 Yorkshire v Derbyshire, Derby 2004

2009 Season

	M	Inn	NO	Runs	HS	Avg	100	50	Ct	St	Balls	Runs	Wkts	Avg	BB	5I	10M
Test																	
FC	17	27	1	871	211	33.50	2	2	11	-	654	280	5	56.00	2-1	-	-
ODI																	
List A	14	14	3	298	67	27.09	-	2	5	-	66	44	0		-	-	
20/20 Int																	
20/20	7	7	1	132	34	22.00	-	-	5	-	54	70	2	35.00	1-17	-	

Career Performances

	M	Inn	NO	Runs	HS	Avg	100	50	Ct	St	Balls	Runs	Wkts	Avg	BB	5I	10M
Test	4	5	0	201	81	40.20	-	2	3	-	102	56	4	14.00	3-16	-	-
FC	215	360	26	12346	211	36.96	29	57	155	-	7986	4008	114	35.15	5-39	1	-
ODI	14	12	2	166	52	16.60	-	1	4	-	228	175	4	43.75	1-13	-	
List A	276	255	37	7058	148	32.37	7	40	90	-	2958	2473	75	32.97	4-41	-	
20/20 Int																	
20/20	45	44	8	1060	72*	29.44	-	7	17	-	391	564	17	33.17	3-27	-	

McGUIRE, B. T.   Nottinghamshire

Name: Ben Thomas McGuire
Role: Left-hand bat, right-arm medium bowler
Born: 31 December 1991, Ashington, Northumberland
County debut: 2009 (one-day)
Extras: Has played for Kidsgrove CC, Nottinghamshire 2nd XI and Staffordshire. Staffordshire U16 Player of the Year 2008. Represented the Midlands at U17 level. A key player for Nottinghamshire Academy in 2009, scoring 703 runs at an average of 70.30 including two centuries. Made his Nottinghamshire debut in the final Pro40 game of the 2009 season

2009 Season

	M	Inn	NO	Runs	HS	Avg	100	50	Ct	St	Balls	Runs	Wkts	Avg	BB	5I	10M
Test																	
FC																	
ODI																	
List A	1	1	0	0	0	0.00	-	-	-	-	0	0	0		-	-	
20/20 Int																	
20/20																	

Career Performances

	M	Inn	NO	Runs	HS	Avg	100	50	Ct	St	Balls	Runs	Wkts	Avg	BB	5I	10M
Test																	
FC																	
ODI																	
List A	1	1	0	0	0	0.00	-	-	-	-	0	0	0		-	-	
20/20 Int																	
20/20																	

McKENZIE, N. D. Hampshire

Name: Neil Douglas McKenzie
Role: Right-hand bat, right-arm medium bowler
Born: 24 November 1975, Johannesburg, South Africa
Nickname: Bertie
County debut: 2007 (Somerset), 2008 (Durham)
Test debut: 2000
ODI debut: 1999-2000
Twenty20 Int debut: 2005-06
1st-class 200s : 1
Wife: Kerry (McGregor, South African model)
Family links with cricket: Father Kevin played for North Eastern Transvaal and Transvaal
Education: King Edward VII School, Johannesburg; RAU, Johannesburg
Overseas tours: South Africa U19 to England 1995 (c); Transvaal to Australia 1997-98; South Africa to India 1999-2000 (one-day series), to Sri Lanka 2000, to West Indies 2000-01, to Zimbabwe 2001-02, to Australia 2001-02, to Bangladesh 2002-03, to England 2003, to Pakistan 2003-04, to New Zealand 2003-04, to Bangladesh 2007-08, to India 2007-08, to England 2008, to Australia 2008-09 plus other one-day tournaments in Sharjah, Australia and Singapore; South Africa A to

Zimbabwe 2002-03, 2004; South Africa Emerging Players to Australia (Cricket Australia Emerging Players Tournament) 2006 (c)

Overseas teams played for: Transvaal 1994-95 – 1996-97; Gauteng 1997-98 – 1998-99; Northerns 1999-2000 – 2003-04; Lions 2003-04 –

Extras: Captained South Africa Schools. One of *South African Cricket Annual*'s five Cricketers of the Year 2001. His match awards include Man of the Match in the second Test v New Zealand in Port Elizabeth 2000-01 (120) and in the second ODI v Sri Lanka in East London 2000-01 (120*). Captain of Highveld Lions. Was a temporary overseas player with Somerset during the 2007 season as a replacement for Cameron White. Man of the Match v Dolphins at Potchefstroom in the SuperSport Series 2007-08 (164). Recalled to South Africa Test side for the second Test v West Indies at Cape Town 2007-08. Joined Durham as an overseas player for 2008 as a locum for Shivnarine Chanderpaul. One of *Wisden*'s five Cricketers of the Year 2009. Has signed as a Kolpak player with Hampshire for 2010

Best batting: 226 South Africa v Bangladesh, Chittagong 2007-08
Best bowling: 2-13 Lions v Eagles, Kimberley 2007-08

2009 Season (Did not make any first-class or one-day appearances)

Career Performances

	M	Inn	NO	Runs	HS	Avg	100	50	Ct	St	Balls	Runs	Wkts	Avg	BB	5I	10M
Test	58	94	7	3253	226	37.39	5	16	54	-	90	68	0	-	-	-	-
FC	187	316	36	12079	226	43.13	30	61	159	-	672	369	7	52.71	2-13	-	-
ODI	64	55	10	1688	131*	37.51	2	10	21	-	46	27	0	-	-	-	
List A	207	185	28	5627	131*	35.84	7	38	59	-	255	248	4	62.00	2-19	-	
20/20 Int	2	1	1	7	7*	-	-	-	-	-	0	0	0	-	-	-	
20/20	28	27	8	665	85*	35.00	-	4	9	-	12	19	0	-	-	-	

McLAREN, R.   Kent

Name: Ryan McLaren
Role: Left-hand bat, right-arm
fast-medium bowler
Born: 9 February 1983, Kimberley,
South Africa
County debut: 2007
County cap: 2007
50 wickets in a season: 1
Place in batting averages: 229th av. 18.00
(2008 173rd av. 23.20)
Place in bowling averages: 60th av. 32.00
(2008 28th av. 23.58)

Family links with cricket: Father (Paul McLaren)
and uncle (Keith McLaren) played for Griqualand
West. Cousin (Adrian McLaren) currently plays for
Griqualand West
Overseas tours: South Africa U19 to New Zealand (U19 World Cup) 2001-02
Overseas teams played for: Free State 2003-04 – 2004-05; Eagles 2004-05 –
Extras: SuperSport Series Cricketer of the Year 2007. Took hat-trick (H. Marshall,
Adshead, Fisher) v Gloucestershire in the final of the Twenty20 Cup at Edgbaston
2007, winning Man of the Match award. His other awards include Man of the Match v
Canada U19 at Auckland in the U19 World Cup 2001-02 (4-9 – full figures 10-4-9-4),
v Warriors at Bloemfontein in the Supersport Series 2005-06 (140 and 3-31/4-50) and
v Dolphins at Bloemfontein in the SuperSport Series 2006-07 (53* and 5-57/4-59).
Selected for South Africa ODI squad to face Bangladesh and Kenya 2008, but was not
released by Kent. Signed to play in IPL 2008-09 by Mumbai Indians. Released by
Kent at the end of 2009 season to enable him to pursue his international career. Is not
considered an overseas player
Best batting: 140 Eagles v Warriors, Bloemfontein 2005-06
Best bowling: 8-38 Eagles v Cape Cobras, Stellenbosch (US) 2006-07

2009 Season

	M	Inn	NO	Runs	HS	Avg	100	50	Ct	St	Balls	Runs	Wkts	Avg	BB	5I	10M
Test																	
FC	7	8	1	126	43	18.00	-	-	1	-	989	608	19	32.00	4-51	-	-
ODI																	
List A																	
20/20 Int																	
20/20	10	6	4	100	31	50.00	-	-	5	-	214	288	11	26.18	4-37	-	

Career Performances

	M	Inn	NO	Runs	HS	Avg	100	50	Ct	St	Balls	Runs	Wkts	Avg	BB	5I	10M
Test																	
FC	78	112	18	2576	140	27.40	2	13	38	-	12325	6201	249	24.90	8-38	10	1
ODI																	
List A	88	64	25	1439	82*	36.89	-	8	29	-	3201	2644	88	30.04	5-46	1	
20/20 Int																	
20/20	67	45	20	509	46*	20.36	-	-	30	-	1255	1567	55	28.49	4-37	-	

MEAKER, S. C. Surrey

Name: <u>Stuart</u> Christopher Meaker
Role: Right-hand bat, right-arm fast bowler
Born: 21 January 1989, Durban, South Africa
Height: 5ft 11in **Weight:** 13st
Nickname: Meaksy, Herc
County debut: 2008
Place in batting averages: 170th av. 26.75
Place in bowling averages: 127th av. 49.80
Parents: Vivien White
Marital status: Single
Education: Cranleigh School
Qualifications: GCSEs, 4 A-levels
Overseas tours: England U16 to South Africa;
England U19 to Malaysia (U19 World Cup) 2007-08
Career highlights to date: 'Being given a contract
by Surrey, and making my first-class debut'
Cricket moments to forget: 'Playing against Kent for Surrey in a pre-season
friendly and going for an astonishing amount of runs. Being taken out of the attack
for bowling a couple of beamers'
Cricket superstitions: 'Wearing my helmet way before I go in to bat. Left pad
on first'
Cricketers particularly admired: Allan Donald, Mark Ramprakash
Young players to look out for: James Halton
Other sports played: Rugby, hockey, water polo, athletics, swimming, golf –
'as many sports as possible'
Other sports followed: Rugby (Natal Sharks, Sale Sharks)
Favourite band: Kings of Leon
Relaxations: 'Watching TV, stretching'
Extras: Lord's fielding award. Represented England U19 2007. NBC Denis
Compton Award for the most promising young Surrey player 2008. Selected for the
England Performance Fast Bowlng programme 2009-10
Opinions on cricket: 'Stick with local players. No need for Kolpaks.'

Best batting: 72 Surrey v Essex, Colchester 2009
Best bowling: 3-86 Surrey v Nottinghamshire, The Oval 2008

2009 Season

	M	Inn	NO	Runs	HS	Avg	100	50	Ct	St	Balls	Runs	Wkts	Avg	BB	5I	10M
Test																	
FC	5	9	1	214	72	26.75	-	2	-	-	664	498	10	49.80	3-114	-	-
ODI																	
List A	9	2	2	14	10*	-	-	-	3	-	300	315	8	39.37	2-21	-	
20/20 Int																	
20/20																	

Career Performances

	M	Inn	NO	Runs	HS	Avg	100	50	Ct	St	Balls	Runs	Wkts	Avg	BB	5I	10M
Test																		
FC	7	11	1	236	72	23.60	-	2	-	-	875	637	14	45.50	3-86	-	-
ODI																	
List A	11	2	2	14	10*		-	-	3	-	348	372	9	41.33	2-21	-	
20/20 Int																	
20/20																	

MENDIS, B. A. W. — Hampshire

Name: Balapuwaduge Ajantha Winslo Mendis
Role: Right-hand bat, right arm off-break/leg-break bowler
Born: 11 March 1985, Moratuwa, Sri Lanka
Test debut: 2008
ODI debut: 2008
Twenty20 Int debut: 2008
Education: St Anthony's College, Kadalana; Moratuwa Maha Vidyalaya
Overseas teams played for: Sri Lanka Army 2006-07 – 2007-08; Wayamba 2007-08 – ; Kolkata Night Riders (IPL)
Overseas tours: Sri Lanka to West Indies 2008 (one-day series), to Bangladesh 2008-09, to Pakistan 2008-09, to Canada (Al Barakah Twenty20) 2008-09, to England (ICC Twenty20) 2009, to India 2009-10
Extras: ICC Emerging Player of the Year 2008. Took 6-13 in Asia Cup Final against India in 2008, gaining him a Man of the Match award. His total of 17 wickets, at an average of 8.52 also won him the Man of the Tournament award. In his debut Test series against India 2008, took 26 wickets in the three match series which beat Alec Bedser's record by two. Signed as overseas player for Hampshire in August 2009

Best Batting: 37 Sri Lanka Army v Sri Lanka Air Force, Colombo 2006-07
Best bowling: 7-37 Sri Lanka Army v Lankan CC, Panagoda 2007-08

2009 Season

	M	Inn	NO	Runs	HS	Avg	100	50	Ct	St	Balls	Runs	Wkts	Avg	BB	5I	10M
Test																	
FC																	
ODI																	
List A																	
20/20 Int	7	1	1	4	4*	-	-	-	-	-	156	143	12	11.91	3-9	-	
20/20	7	1	1	4	4*	-	-	-	-	-	156	143	12	11.91	3-9	-	

Career Performances

	M	Inn	NO	Runs	HS	Avg	100	50	Ct	St	Balls	Runs	Wkts	Avg	BB	5I	10M
Test	9	9	3	31	17	5.16	-	-	1	-	2358	1136	42	27.04	6-117	2	1
FC	30	40	3	429	37	11.59	-	-	10	-	6312	2916	163	17.88	7-37	9	2
ODI	36	18	8	81	15*	8.10	-	-	5	-	1683	1162	71	16.36	6-13	3	
List A	55	33	11	408	71*	18.54	-	2	9	-	2477	1586	108	14.68	6-13	3	
20/20 Int	12	2	2	4	4*	-	-	-	1	-	276	244	25	9.76	4-15	-	
20/20	31	11	6	21	9	4.20	-	-	9	-	682	674	46	14.65	4-15	-	

MICKLEBURGH, J. C. Essex

Name: Jaik Charles Mickleburgh
Role: Right-hand bat, right-arm fast-medium bowler
Born: 30 March 1990, Norwich, Norfolk
County debut: 2008
Place in batting averages: 194th av. 23.75
Overseas tours: England U19 to South Africa 2008-09
Overseas teams played for: Newtown & Chilwell CC, Australia 2007-08
Extras: Made 2nd XI Championship debut 2006. Attended World Cricket Academy, Mumbai 2007. Played for Norfolk in Minor Counties competitions 2007. Played for Essex in the Twenty20 Floodlit Cup 2007. First-class debut 2008. Played for England U19 against Bangladesh U19 2009. Member of England Performance Programme squad 2009-10
Best batting: 72 Essex v Warwickshire, Chelmsford 2008

2009 Season

	M	Inn	NO	Runs	H	Avg	100	50	Ct	St	Balls	Runs	Wkts	Avg	BB	5I	10M
Test																	
FC	6	12	0	285	62	23.75	-	2	3	-	47	28	0		-	-	-
ODI																	
List A																		
20/20 Int																		
20/20																		

Career Performances

	M	Inn	NO	Runs	HS	Avg	100	50	Ct	St	Balls	Runs	Wkts	Avg	BB	5I	10M
Test																		
FC	9	16	0	435	72	27.18	-	4	6	-	71	39	0		-	-	-
ODI																		
List A																		
20/20 Int																		
20/20																		

MIDDLEBROOK, J. D.   Northamptonshire

Name: James Daniel Middlebrook
Role: Right-hand bat, off-spin bowler
Born: 13 May 1977, Leeds
Height: 6ft 1in **Weight:** 13st
Nickname: Midhouse, Midi, Midders
County debut: 1998 (Yorkshire),
2002 (Essex)
County cap: 2003 (Essex)
50 wickets in a season: 1
Place in batting averages: 188th av. 24.50
(2008 156th av. 25.87)
Place in bowling averages: 61st av. 32.07
(2008 104th av. 35.03)
Parents: Ralph and Mavis
Marital status: Single
Family links with cricket: 'Dad is a senior ECB staff coach'
Education: Crawshaw, Pudsey
Qualifications: NVQ Level 2 in Coaching Sport and Recreation, ECB senior coach
Off-season: 'Cape Town, January 2009'
Overseas tours: Yorkshire CCC to Guernsey
Overseas teams played for: Stokes Valley CC, New Zealand; Gold Coast
Dolphins, Brisbane; Surfers Paradise CC, Brisbane; Upper Valley CC,
Wellington, New Zealand 2006-07

Career highlights to date: 'Winning the Friends Provident, 2008. Pro40, 2008'
Cricket superstitions: 'Always put my batting gear on the same way'
Cricketers particularly admired: John Emburey, Ian Botham
Young players to look out for: Jaik Mickleburgh (Essex), Joe Denly (Kent)
Other sports played: Golf, tennis, squash, badminton
Other sports followed: Football (Leeds United), Formula One, golf
Favourite band: Hed Kandi, Ministry of Sound
Relaxations: 'Any music – MTV – sleeping, socialising, catching up with old friends'
Extras: Played for Yorkshire from U11 to 1st XI. His 6-82 v Hampshire at Southampton 2000 included a spell of four wickets in five balls. Took Championship hat-trick (Saggers, Muralitharan, Sheriyar) v Kent at Canterbury 2003. Released by Essex in August 2009 and joined Northamptonshire
Best batting: 127 Essex v Middlesex, Lord's 2007
Best bowling: 6-82 Yorkshire v Hampshire, Southampton 2000

2009 Season

	M	Inn	NO	Runs	HS	Avg	100	50	Ct	St	Balls	Runs	Wkts	Avg	BB	5I	10M
Test																	
FC	8	11	3	196	46	24.50	-	-	2	-	828	449	14	32.07	3-80	-	-
ODI																	
List A	7	2	1	21	17*	21.00	-	-	1	-	204	158	3	52.66	2-54	-	
20/20 Int																	
20/20	8	5	2	50	26	16.66	-	-	2	-	84	114	2	57.00	2-28	-	

Career Performances

	M	Inn	NO	Runs	HS	Avg	100	50	Ct	St	Balls	Runs	Wkts	Avg	BB	5I	10M
Test																	
FC	143	202	28	4405	127	25.31	4	16	72	-	23552	12310	319	38.58	6-82	8	1
ODI																	
List A	146	95	28	1256	47	18.74	-	-	42	-	5053	3898	112	34.80	4-27	-	
20/20 Int																	
20/20	47	36	9	353	43	13.07	-	-	10	-	504	706	15	47.06	3-13	-	

61. How many wickets did Abdul Kadir take in the three-match Test series against England in Pakistan in 1987-88?

MILLER, A. S.   Warwickshire

Name: <u>Andrew</u> Stephen Miller
Role: Right-hand bat, right-arm
fast-medium bowler
Born: 27 September 1987, Preston
Height: 6ft 4in **Weight:** 13st 3lbs
Nickname: Millsy
County debut: 2008
Parents: Steve and Sharon
Marital status: Single
Family links with cricket: 'Dad and brother played
club cricket at Longridge CC'
Education: St Cecilia's RC High School; Preston
College
Qualifications: 10 GCSEs, BTEC National Diploma
in Sport Fitness and Development, Levels 1 and 2
coaching
Off-season: 'Going to Tasmania to play club cricket for Clarence District CC, then
on a pre-season tour with Warwickshire'
Overseas tours: England U16 to South Africa 2004; England U19 to India 2004-05,
to Bangladesh 2005-06, to Sri Lanka (U19 World Cup) 2005-06, to Malaysia 2006-07
Overseas teams played for: Yarroweyah United CC, Melbourne 2007-08; Clarence
District CC, Tasmania 2009-10
Career highlights to date: 'Playing in an U19 Cricket World Cup and getting a full-
time contract at Warwickshire CCC. Making Championship debut v Hampshire 2009'
Cricket moments to forget: 'Being super-subbed for England U19 in the semi-final
of the U19 World Cup on TV after seven overs of the first innings of the match. Going
out to bat with two right-hand gloves'
Cricket superstitions: 'Never cross/stand on the line when going on or off the field,
always step over it'
Cricketers particularly admired: Glenn McGrath, Curtly Ambrose, Tim Munton
Young players to look out for: Richard Johnson and Chris Woakes
(both Warwickshire)
Other sports played: Golf
Other sports followed: Football (Preston North End)
Injuries: 'A tear in my left side – out for 8 weeks'
Favourite band: Arctic Monkeys
Relaxations: 'Watching TV, music, golf'
Extras: Represented England U19 2005, 2006, 2007. NBC Denis Compton Award
for the most promising young Warwickshire player 2006
Best batting: 4* Warwickshire v Bangladesh A, Edgbaston 2008
Best bowling: 4-76 Warwickshire v Lancashire, Old Trafford 2009

2009 Season

	M	Inn	NO	Runs	HS	Avg	100	50	Ct	St	Balls	Runs	Wkts	Avg	BB	5I	10M
Test																	
FC	3	3	1	1	1*	.50	-	-	-	-	498	249	8	31.12	4-76	-	-
ODI																	
List A																		
20/20 Int																		
20/20																		

Career Performances

	M	Inn	NO	Runs	HS	Avg	100	50	Ct	St	Balls	Runs	Wkts	Avg	BB	5I	10M
Test																		
FC	4	4	2	5	4*	2.50	-	-	-	-	618	294	11	26.72	4-76	-	-
ODI																		
List A																		
20/20 Int																		
20/20																		

MITCHELL, D. K. H. — Worcestershire

Name: <u>Daryl</u> Keith Henry Mitchell
Role: Right-hand bat, right-arm medium bowler; batting all-rounder; county vice-captain
Born: 25 November 1983, Evesham
Height: 5ft 10in **Weight:** 12st
Nickname: Mitch, Peggy, Toucan
County debut: 2005
County colours: 2005
1000 runs in a season: 1
1st-Class 200s: 1
Place in batting averages: 87th av. 38.73 (2008 64th av. 40.08)
Parents: Keith and Jane
Marital status: Single
Family links with cricket: 'Dad played club cricket and coaches WYC (Worcestershire Young Cricketers) U13'
Education: Prince Henry's High, Evesham; University of Worcester
Qualifications: 10 GCSEs, 4 A-levels, BSc (Hons) Sports Studies and Geography (2.2), Level 2 coaching
Career outside cricket: 'Coaching'
Off-season: 'Coaching, training, watching Aston Villa'
Overseas tours: Worcestershire to Guernsey 2007, to South Africa 2009

Overseas teams played for: Midland-Guildford, Perth 2005-06 – 2007-08
Career highlights to date: 'My first-class debut. 134* v Glamorgan – maiden first-class century 2006. Winning Pro40 2007'
Cricket moments to forget: 'Run out first ball by a Monty direct hit v Northants, Twenty20 2006. Bowling at Taunton! The 2009 Championship season'
Cricket superstitions: 'Put gloves on before helmet'
Cricketers particularly admired: Michael Atherton, Graeme Hick, Sir Ian Botham
Young players to look out for: Alexei Kervezee (Worcestershire)
Other sports played: Football, golf ('badly'), pool, darts, skittles
Other sports followed: Football (Aston Villa), rugby (Worcester), AFL (West Coast Eagles)
Favourite band: Oasis
Relaxations: 'Music, movies, PlayStation'
Extras: Scored 210* for Worcestershire v Bradford/Leeds UCCE at Harrogate 2006. Carried bat for 70* v Sussex at Hove 2007. Appointed county vice-captain in October 2009
Opinions on cricket: 'Our domestic cricket should mirror international formats of the game so as to provide cricketers for the England team.'
Best batting: 298 Worcestershire v Somerset, Taunton 2009
Best bowling: 4-49 Worcestershire v Yorkshire, Headingley 2009

2009 Season

	M	Inn	NO	Runs	HS	Avg	100	50	Ct	St	Balls	Runs	Wkts	Avg	BB	5I	10M
Test																	
FC	17	31	1	1162	298	38.73	2	5	18	-	540	252	9	28.00	4-49	-	-
ODI																	
List A	16	11	4	294	59	42.00	-	2	4	-	383	356	11	32.36	2-7	-	
20/20 Int																		
20/20	10	8	3	110	35	22.00	-	-	2	-	160	222	8	27.75	2-23	-	

Career Performances

	M	Inn	NO	Runs	HS	Avg	100	50	Ct	St	Balls	Runs	Wkts	Avg	BB	5I	10M
Test																	
FC	48	86	13	2822	298	38.65	5	14	43	-	1065	532	16	33.25	4-49	-	-
ODI																	
List A	42	31	7	747	92	31.12	-	6	12	-	911	915	24	38.12	4-42	-	
20/20 Int																		
20/20	36	20	8	193	35	16.08	-	-	11	-	639	846	31	27.29	4-11	-	

MONTGOMERY, G. S.   Lancashire

Name: <u>Gary</u> Stephen Montgomery
Role: Left-hand bat, left-arm medium bowler
Born: 10 August 1982, Leamington Spa, Warwickshire
Height: 6ft 2in
County debut: No first-team appearance
Extras: Goalkeeper with Coventry City, Rotherham United and Grimsby until released by the latter in March 2009. Played for Warwickshire and Leicestershire Second XIs before an appearance for Lancashire against Nottinghamshire at a similar level in August 2009. Took 7-29 in an eight over spell which led to the county offering him a contract for 2010

MOORE, S. C.   Lancashire

Name: <u>Stephen</u> Colin Moore
Role: Right-hand opening bat, right-arm medium bowler
Born: 4 November 1980, Johannesburg, South Africa
Height: 6ft 1in   **Weight:** 13st
Nickname: Mandy, Circles, Mork
County debut: 2003 (Worcestershire)
County colours: 2003
1000 runs in a season: 2
1st-Class 200s: 1
Place in batting averages: 140th av. 30.70 (2008 15th av. 55.80)
Parents: Shane and Carrol
Wife and date of marriage: Ruth, 4 October 2008
Education: St Stithians College, South Africa; Exeter University
Qualifications: MEng (Hons) Electronic Engineering
Overseas tours: England Performance Programme to India, 2008-09; England Lions to New Zealand 2009
Overseas teams played for: Midland-Guildford, Perth 2002-04; Northern Districts, Adelaide
Career highlights to date: 'First-class debut and Lord's final 2004'
Cricket moments to forget: 'Losing Lord's final 2004 and getting a duck!'

Cricket superstitions: 'Left pad first!'
Other sports played: Hockey, tennis (both Exeter University 1st team), golf, squash
Other sports followed: Tennis
Favourite band: Jack Johnson
Relaxations: 'My music (guitar and saxophone), watersports and wildlife'
Extras: Scored 1000 first-class runs in his first full season 2004. One of three Worcestershire batsmen to score over 1000 first-class runs in 2008. Played for England Lions against Australia 2009. Joined Lancashire from Worcestershire October 2009. Member of England Performance Programme squad 2009-10. Is not considered an overseas player
Opinions on cricket: 'These are exciting times. Hopefully the right decisions can be made to further the development of cricket in England and we can all benefit in the future.'
Best batting: 246 Worcestershire v Derbyshire, Worcester 2005
Best bowling: 1-13 Worcestershire v Lancashire, Worcester 2004

2009 Season

	M	Inn	NO	Runs	HS	Avg	100	50	Ct	St	Balls	Runs	Wkts	Avg	BB	5I	10M
Test																	
FC	17	32	1	952	120	30.70	2	5	6	-	0	0	0		-	-	-
ODI																	
List A	16	14	2	305	87*	25.41	-	2	7	-	0	0	0		-	-	
20/20 Int																	
20/20	10	10	1	294	62*	32.66	-	1	-	-	0	0	0		-	-	

Career Performances

	M	Inn	NO	Runs	HS	Avg	100	50	Ct	St	Balls	Runs	Wkts	Avg	BB	5I	10M
Test																	
FC	103	187	16	6862	246	40.12	15	33	49	-	342	321	5	64.20	1-13	-	-
ODI																	
List A	95	91	9	2199	105*	26.81	2	12	26	-	41	53	1	53.00	1-1	-	
20/20 Int																	
20/20	46	41	5	900	ß62*	25.00	-	3	12	-	0	0	0		-	-	

MORGAN, E. J. G. — Middlesex

Name: Eoin Joseph Gerard Morgan
Role: Left-hand bat, right-arm medium bowler
Born: 10 September 1986, Dublin
Height: 5ft 10in **Weight:** 11st 11lbs
Nickname: Moggie
County debut: 2005 (one-day), 2006 (first-class)
County cap: 2008
ODI debut: 2006
Twenty20 Int debut: 2009
1000 runs in a season: 1
1st-Class 200s: 1
Place in batting averages: 186th av. 24.72
(2008 29th av. 49.31)
Parents: Joseph and Olivia
Marital status: Single
Family links with cricket: 'My father, three brothers, two sisters, grandfather and great-grandfather all played'
Education: Catholic University School, Dublin
Overseas tours: Ireland U19 to Bangladesh (U19 World Cup) 2003-04, to Sri Lanka (U19 World Cup) 2005-06; Ireland to Namibia (ICC Inter-Continental Cup) 2005, to Scotland (European Championship) 2006, to Kenya (ICC World Cricket League) 2006-07, to West Indies (World Cup) 2006-07, plus Ireland age-group tours. England Performance Programme to India 2008-09; England Lions to New Zealand 2009; England to South Africa 2009-10 (one-day series)
Overseas teams played for: St Henry's Marist School U19, Durban 2003
Career highlights to date: 'Winning the Inter-Continental Cup with Ireland in Namibia [2005]'
Cricketers particularly admired: Ricky Ponting, Brian Lara
Other sports played: Rugby (Schools), Gaelic football
Other sports followed: Gaelic football (Dublin GAA), rugby, snooker, darts
Favourite band: Aslan
Relaxations: 'Watching sports and listening to music'
Extras: Capped for Ireland at every level from U13 up. Player of the Tournament at European U15 Championships 2000, 2002 and at European U17 Championships 2002. Became then youngest player to represent Ireland 2003. NBC Denis Compton Award for the most promising young Middlesex player 2003, 2004. C&G Man of the Match award for Ireland v Yorkshire in Belfast 2005 (59). Made ODI debut for Ireland v Scotland at Ayr in the European Championship 2006, winning Man of the Match award (99). Scored maiden first-class double century (209*) v UAE in Abu Dhabi in the 2006 ICC Inter-Continental Cup, winning Man of the Match award
Best batting: 209* Ireland v United Arab Emirates, Abu Dhabi (SZ) 2006-07
Best bowling: 2-24 Middlesex v Nottinghamshire, Lord's 2007

2009 Season

	M	Inn	NO	Runs	HS	Avg	100	50	Ct	St	Balls	Runs	Wkts	Avg	BB	5I	10M
Test																	
FC	11	20	2	445	114*	24.72	1	1	13	-	0	0	0		-	-	-
ODI	8	8	2	161	58	26.83	-	1	1	-	0	0	0		-	-	
List A	21	19	3	544	161	34.00	1	3	3	-	0	0	0		-	-	
20/20 Int	1	1	0	6	6	6.00	-	-	-	-	0	0	0		-	-	
20/20	8	8	0	94	31	11.75	-	-	2	-	0	0	0		-	-	

Career Performances

	M	Inn	NO	Runs	HS	Avg	100	50	Ct	St	Balls	Runs	Wkts	Avg	BB	5I	10M
Test																	
FC	48	81	11	2558	209*	36.54	6	11	43	1	79	46	2	23.00	2-24	-	-
ODI	35	35	5	1052	115	35.06	1	8	14	-	0	0	0		-	-	
List A	111	104	14	3195	161	35.50	4	20	34	-	42	49	0		-	-	
20/20 Int	1	1	0	6	6	6.00	-	-	-	-	0	0	0		-	-	
20/20	39	37	2	736	66	21.02	-	2	16	-	0	0	0		-	-	

MUCHALL, G. J.   Durham

Name: Gordon James Muchall
Role: Right-hand bat, right-arm medium bowler
Born: 2 November 1982, Newcastle upon Tyne
Height: 6ft 2in **Weight:** 13st
Nickname: Muchy
County debut: 2002
County cap: 2005
1st-Class 200s: 1
Place in batting averages: 145th av. 30.29
Parents: Mary and Arthur
Wife and date of marriage: Gemma, 8 November 2008
Children: Adam James, 10 November 2009
Family links with cricket: 'Grandad and brothers Matthew and Paul have all played for Northumberland. Dad played for Durham Over-50s. Paul will be joining the MCC in April.' (Paul has also played for Durham Academy)
Education: Durham School
Qualifications: 8 GCSEs, 2 A-levels, Level 2 coaching
Career outside cricket: Coaching
Overseas tours: England U19 to India 2000-01, to Australia and (U19 World Cup) New Zealand 2001-02; ECB National Academy to Australia and Sri Lanka 2002-03

Overseas teams played for: Fremantle 2001-02; Claremont-Nedlands, Perth 2005-06
Career highlights to date: '100 at Lord's. 200 against Kent. 250 for England U19. Winning Friends Provident Trophy [2007]. Winning the County Championship [2008, 2009] and being awarded my county cap'
Cricketers particularly admired: Dale Benkenstein, Mike Hussey, Jimmy Maher, Paul Collingwood, Jon Lewis
Young players to look out for: Paul Muchall (MCC)
Other sports played: Rugby (Durham School – played in *Daily Mail* Cup final at Twickenham)
Other sports followed: Rugby (Newcastle Falcons)
Favourite band: The Killers
Relaxations: 'Golf'
Extras: Represented England U19, scoring 254 in the first 'Test' v India U19 at Cardiff 2002. Cricket Society's Most Promising Young Cricketer of the Year Award 2002. NBC Denis Compton Award for the most promising young Durham player 2002. Durham Batsman of the Year 2004. Scored maiden first-class double century (219) v Kent at Canterbury 2006, in the process sharing with Phil Mustard (130) in a new Durham record partnership for the sixth wicket (249)
Opinions on cricket: 'Would like to see free hits in all forms of the game.'
Best batting: 219 Durham v Kent, Canterbury 2006
Best bowling: 3-26 Durham v Yorkshire, Headingley 2003

2009 Season

	M	Inn	NO	Runs	HS	Avg	100	50	Ct	St	Balls	Runs	Wkts	Avg	BB	5I	10M
Test																	
FC	13	19	2	515	106*	30.29	1	2	14	-	0	0	0		-	-	-
ODI																	
List A	9	9	0	186	61	20.66	-	1	3	-	0	0	0		-	-	
20/20 Int																	
20/20	5	4	2	98	50*	49.00	-	1	4	-	0	0	0		-	-	

Career Performances

	M	Inn	NO	Runs	HS	Avg	100	50	Ct	St	Balls	Runs	Wkts	Avg	BB	5I	10M
Test																	
FC	105	185	9	5056	219	28.72	8	25	74	-	890	615	15	41.00	3-26	-	-
ODI																	
List A	86	77	12	1835	101*	28.23	1	9	28	-	162	137	1	137.00	1-15	-	
20/20 Int																	
20/20	36	31	8	676	64*	29.39	-	2	15	-	12	8	1	8.00	1-8	-	

MULLANEY, S. J.   Nottinghamshire

Name: <u>Steven</u> John Mullaney
Role: Right-hand bat, right-arm medium bowler; all-rounder
Born: 19 November 1986, Warrington
Height: 5ft 8in **Weight:** 12st 1lb
Nickname: Mull, Mahoney
County debut: 2006 (Lancashire)
Parents: Andrew and Elaine
Marital status: Single – 'Girlfriend, Nicola'
Family links with cricket: 'Dad was club professional in 1980s and 1990s'
Education: St Mary's RC High School, Astley
Career outside cricket: 'PE teacher'
Qualifications: 9 GCSEs
Off-season: 'Staying at home – maybe go away after Christmas...'
Overseas tours: England U19 to India 2004-05, to Sri Lanka (U19 World Cup) 2005-06
Overseas teams played for: McKinnon, Melbourne 2006-08; South Caulfield, Melbourne, 2008-09
Career highlights to date: '165* for Lancashire v DUCCE 2007 (maiden first-class hundred)' (*Scored in his only first-class innings of 2007*)
Cricket moments to forget: 'Got a duck on my championship debut v Nottinghamshire'
Cricketers particularly admired: Andrew Flintoff, VVS Laxman
Young players to look out for: Karl Brown, Steven Croft, Tom Smith, Stephen Parry (all Lancashire)
Other sports played: Rugby league (formerly; 'toured France with England U15')
Other sports followed: Football (Manchester City), rugby league (St Helens)
Favourite band: Westlife
Relaxations: 'Watching football and rugby, socialising with mates'
Extras: Scored 208 for Lancashire U17. Represented England U19 2005, 2006. Signed for Nottinghamshire from Lancashire in October 2009
Best batting: 165* Lancashire v DUCCE, Durham 2007
Best bowling: 1-3 Lancashire v DUCCE, Durham 2008

2009 Season

	M	Inn	NO	Runs	HS	Avg	100	50	Ct	St	Balls	Runs	Wkts	Avg	BB	5I	10M
Test																	
FC																	
ODI																	
List A	2	1	0	10	10	10.00	-	-	3	-	66	61	4	15.25	3-36	-	
20/20 Int																	
20/20	1	0	0	0	0		-	-	-	-	18	21	1	21.00	1-21	-	

Career Performances

	M	Inn	NO	Runs	HS	Avg	100	50	Ct	St	Balls	Runs	Wkts	Avg	BB	5I	10M
Test																	
FC	4	5	1	257	165*	64.25	1	-	3	-	161	84	1	84.00	1-3	-	-
ODI																	
List A	8	4	1	36	12	12.00	-	-	4	-	182	158	10	15.80	3-13	-	
20/20 Int																	
20/20	3	1	0	5	5	5.00	-	-	1	-	18	21	1	21.00	1-21	-	

MUNDAY, M. K.   Somerset

Name: Michael Kenneth Munday
Role: Right-hand bat, leg-spin bowler
Born: 22 October 1984, Nottingham
Height: 5ft 8in **Weight:** 12st
County debut: 2005
Place in bowling averages: (2008 125th av. 41.00)
Parents: John and Maureen
Marital status: Single
Family links with cricket: 'Dad, brother and sister have played league cricket in Cornwall'
Education: Truro School; Corpus Christi College, Oxford University
Qualifications: 10 GCSEs, 3 A-levels, MChem (Oxon)
Overseas tours: Cornwall Schools U13 to South Africa 1998; ESCA West U15 to West Indies 2000
Overseas teams played for: Glenelg DCC, Adelaide 2006-08
Career highlights to date: 'Taking 8-55 on the last day of the 2007 season'
Cricket moments to forget: 'Being hit on the point of the elbow by Steffan Jones's "skiddy" bouncer, OUCCE v Derbyshire 2006'
Cricket superstitions: 'Always wear an arm guard'
Cricketers particularly admired: Shane Warne, Marcus Trescothick

Young players to look out for: Max Waller, Mark Turner, Jos Buttler (all Somerset)
Other sports played: Chess ('Yes, it is a sport')
Other sports followed: Football (Liverpool)
Favourite band: Coldplay, The Killers
Relaxations: 'Swimming, reading, crosswords'
Extras: Played for Cornwall in the C&G 2001. Played for OUCCE 2003-06. Oxford Blue 2003-06, returning match figures of 11-143 v Cambridge University in the Varsity Match at The Parks 2006. Represented England U19 2004. Returned match figures of 10-65 (2-10/8-55) v Nottinghamshire at Taunton 2007
Best batting: 21 Somerset v Lancashire, Old Trafford 2008
Best bowling: 8-55 Somerset v Nottinghamshire, Taunton 2007

2009 Season

	M	Inn	NO	Runs	HS	Avg	100	50	Ct	St	Balls	Runs	Wkts	Avg	BB	5I	10M
Test																	
FC	1	1	0	1	1	1.00	-	-	-	-	151	114	4	28.50	2-46	-	-
ODI																	
List A																	
20/20 Int																	
20/20																	

Career Performances

	M	Inn	NO	Runs	HS	Avg	100	50	Ct	St	Balls	Runs	Wkts	Avg	BB	5I	10M
Test																	
FC	28	25	10	107	21	7.13	-	-	11	-	3476	2296	80	28.70	8-55	4	2
ODI																	
List A	1	0	0	0	0		-	-	-	-	30	39	1	39.00	1-39	-	
20/20 Int																	
20/20																	

---

62. Name the 19 year-old who became the youngest Pakistan bowler to take 50 Test wickets.

MURPHY, D.

Northamptonshire

Name: <u>David</u> Murphy
Role: Right-hand bat, wicket-keeper
Born: 24 June 1989, Welwyn Garden City, Hertfordshire
Height: 6ft 1in **Weight:** 13st 1lb
Nickname: Murph, Spud
County debut: 2009
Parents: John and Mary
Marital status: 'In a relationship'
Family links with cricket: 'Dad played for a local club and coached for years'
Education: Richard Hale School, Hertford; Loughborough University
Qualifications: 12 GCSEs, 3 A Levels
Career outside cricket: Student
Off-season: 'Studying politics at Loughborough University'
Overseas teams played for: Merafong City, South Africa 2007-08
Career highlights to date: 'Making my first-team debut for Northamptonshire. Scoring 69* on my first-class debut'
Cricket moments to forget: 'Any duck or dropped catch'
Cricket superstitions: 'None'
Cricketers particularly admired: Steve Waugh, Jack Russell
Young players to look out for: Tom Brett (Northamptonshire), Alex Hales (Nottinghamshire)
Other sports played: Football, tennis
Other sports followed: Football (Tottenham Hotspur), 'Watford CC'
Favourite band: Muse
Relaxations: 'Enjoy watching sport, or relaxing with a movie or with friends'
Extras: Played for Hertfordshire U17 2005-06, Northamptonshire Cricket Board U19 2007-08, Northamptonshire Second XI 2006-08. Northamptonshire Academy Player of the Year 2008.
Opinions on cricket: 'There should be a Twenty20 competition in second-team cricket.'
Best batting: 69* LUCCE v Leicestershire, Grace Road 2009

2009 Season

	M	Inn	NO	Runs	HS	Avg	100	50	Ct	St	Balls	Runs	Wkts	Avg	BB	5I	10M
Test																	
FC	5	6	1	101	69*	20.20	-	1	11	1	0	0	0		-	-	-
ODI																	
List A																	
20/20 Int																	
20/20																	

Career Performances

	M	Inn	NO	Runs	HS	Avg	100	50	Ct	St	Balls	Runs	Wkts	Avg	BB	5I	10M
Test																	
FC	5	6	1	101	69*	20.20	-	1	11	1	0	0	0		-	-	-
ODI																	
List A																	
20/20 Int																	
20/20																	

MURTAGH, C. P. Surrey

Name: Christopher (<u>Chris</u>) Paul Murtagh
Role: Right-hand bat
Born: 14 October 1984, Lambeth, London
Height: 5ft 11in **Weight:** 11st 9lbs
Nickname: Murts, Baby, Brow
County debut: 2005 (one-day)
County cap: 2008
Parents: Dominic and Elizabeth
Marital status: Single
Family links with cricket: Elder brother Tim
played for Surrey and is now with Middlesex.
Uncle Andy (A. J. Murtagh) played for Hampshire
Education: John Fisher, Purley, Surrey;
Loughborough University
Qualifications: 10 GCSEs, 2 A-levels, BSc (Hons)
Sport and Exercise Science
Off-season: 'Playing for Parramatta in Sydney and training for the new season.'
Overseas tours: Surrey U19 to Sri Lanka 2002, to Perth 2004
Overseas teams played for: Parramatta, Sydney 2004 –
Cricket superstitions: 'Left pad on first'
Cricketers particularly admired: Sachin Tendulkar, Andrew Flintoff,
Curtly Ambrose

Other sports played: Rugby, football, golf
Other sports followed: Football (Liverpool FC)
Relaxations: 'Playing golf and watching sport'
Extras: Played for Surrey age groups and attended Surrey Academy. Made 2nd XI Championship debut 2002. Played for LUCCE 2005, 2006, 2007, scoring century (107) v Yorkshire at Headingley 2007. Released by Surrey at the end of the 2009 season
Best batting: 107 LUCCE v Yorkshire, Headingley 2007

2009 Season

	M	Inn	NO	Runs	HS	Avg	100	50	Ct	St	Balls	Runs	Wkts	Avg	BB	5I	10M
Test																	
FC	2	2	1	29	15	29.00	-	-	2	-	0	0	0		-	-	-
ODI																	
List A	3	3	0	14	8	4.66	-	-	1	-	0	0	0		-	-	
20/20 Int																	
20/20	2	2	1	33	28	33.00	-	-	-	-	0	0	0		-	-	

Career Performances

	M	Inn	NO	Runs	HS	Avg	100	50	Ct	St	Balls	Runs	Wkts	Avg	BB	5I	10M
Test																	
FC	14	20	3	316	107	18.58	1	-	9	-	6	8	0		-	-	-
ODI																	
List A	7	6	2	122	74	30.50	-	1	4	-	0	0	0		-	-	
20/20 Int																	
20/20	4	4	1	33	28	11.00	-	-	4	-	0	0	0		-	-	

MURTAGH, T. J. Middlesex

Name: Timothy (Tim) James Murtagh
Role: Left-hand bat, right-arm
fast-medium bowler
Born: 2 August 1981, Lambeth, London
Height: 6ft 2in **Weight:** 12st
County debut: 2000 (one-day, Surrey),
2001 (first-class, Surrey), 2007 (Middlesex)
50 wickets in a season: 2
Place in batting averages: 230th av. 17.78
(2008 211th av. 18.27)
Place in bowling averages: 20th av. 25.35
(2008 50th av. 27.09)
Parents: Dominic and Elizabeth
Marital status: Single

Family links with cricket: Younger brother Chris played for Surrey. Uncle Andy (A. J. Murtagh) played for Hampshire
Education: John Fisher, Purley, Surrey; St Mary's University, Twickenham
Qualifications: 10 GCSEs, 2 A-levels
Overseas tours: Surrey U17 to South Africa 1997; England U19 to Malaysia and (U19 World Cup) Sri Lanka 1999-2000; British Universities to South Africa 2002; Middlesex to Antigua 2008-09 to play in Stanford Super Series
Overseas teams played for: Eastern Suburbs, Sydney 2006-07
Cricketers particularly admired: Darren Gough, Glenn McGrath
Other sports played: Rugby (was captain of John Fisher 2nd XV), skiing ('in the past')
Other sports followed: Football (Liverpool FC), rugby
Relaxations: Playing golf, watching sport, films, reading
Extras: Represented British Universities 2000, 2001, 2002 and 2003. Represented England U19 2000. NBC Denis Compton Award for the most promising young Surrey player 2001. Took 6-24 v Middlesex at Lord's 2005, the best return in the history of the Twenty20 Cup
Best batting: 74* Surrey v Middlesex, The Oval 2004
74* Surrey v Warwickshire, Croydon 2005
Best bowling: 7-82 Middlesex v Derbyshire, Derby 2009

2009 Season

	M	Inn	NO	Runs	HS	Avg	100	50	Ct	St	Balls	Runs	Wkts	Avg	BB	5I	10M
Test																	
FC	13	20	6	249	51*	17.78	-	1	2	-	2658	1521	60	25.35	7-82	3	-
ODI																	
List A	9	4	1	4	3*	1.33	-	-	3	-	242	198	9	22.00	3-43	-	
20/20 Int																	
20/20																	

Career Performances

	M	Inn	NO	Runs	HS	Avg	100	50	Ct	St	Balls	Runs	Wkts	Avg	BB	5I	10M
Test																	
FC	82	114	32	1851	74*	22.57	-	7	25	-	12143	7117	242	29.40	7-82	10	1
ODI																	
List A	104	69	24	554	35*	12.31	-	-	30	-	4600	3944	148	26.64	4-14	-	
20/20 Int																	
20/20	51	26	10	176	40*	11.00	-	-	9	-	1039	1464	62	23.61	6-24	1	

MURTAZA HUSSAIN   Surrey

Name: Murtaza Hussain
Role: Right-hand bat, right-arm off-break bowler
Born: 20 December 1974, Bahawalpur, Pakistan
Height: 5ft 11in **Weight:** 12st 12lbs
Nickname: Murty
County debut: 2007
Place in batting averages: 242nd av. 15.85
Place in bowling averages: 113th av. 43.42
(2008 38th av. 25.63)
Parents: Sakina Begum and Mohammed
Mukhtiar Hussain
Wife and date of marriage: Christine, 29 July 1999
Education: Abbassia High School, Bahawalpur
Qualifications: ECB level 2 coaching
Off-season: Playing first-class cricket in Pakistan
Overseas teams played for: Several in Pakistan, including Bahawalpur 1990-91 –
1997-98, 2001-02, Khan Research Laboratories 1997-98 – 1999-2000, Pakistan
Customs 2004-05 – , Multan Tigers 2005-06
Career highlights to date: 'Taking 6 wickets for Surrey against Lancashire in the
2007 championship, helping us to win the game'
Cricket moments to forget: 'Breaking my thumb when playing for Walsall CC in
2001. It was broken in three places, and it was on my bowling hand. Thankfully, the
expertise of the doctors at Lister Hospital helped me to make a full recovery and
continue with my cricketing career.'
Cricketers particularly admired: Imran Khan, Wasim Akram
Young players to look out for: Chris Jordan, Jade Dernbach, Matthew Spriegel
(all Surrey)
Other sports followed: Football (Manchester United)
Favourite band: 'Indian music in general'
Relaxations: Watching Hindi films, listening to music
Extras: Prior to obtaining British Citizenship in 2007, played club cricket in the
UK as an overseas player for Vickers 1998-99, Stevenage 2000, 2002, Walsall 2001,
Pyrford 2003, 2004, Byfleet 2005, Welwyn Garden City 2006 and Londonderry 2007.
In Pakistani domestic cricket, held the record for the number of first-class wickets
taken in a season (105) from 1995-96 until 1998-99. Holds the record for the highest
number of wickets taken in the Qaid-i-Azam trophy (72 wickets in 10 matches,
1995-96). Represented Pakistan U19 1991-92. Played for Combined XI v New
Zealanders 1996-97, Dr Abdul Qadeer Khan's XI v West Indians 1997-98 and Pakistan
A v India A at Karachi 1997-98. Has played for Derbyshire 2nd XI and Middlesex
2nd XI. Released by Surrey at the end of the 2009 season. Now holds a British
passport and is no longer considered an overseas player

Best batting: 117 Pakistan Customs v Attock, Karachi (UBL) 2006-07
Best bowling: 9-54 Bahawalpur v Islamabad, Bahawalpur 1995-96

2009 Season

	M	Inn	NO	Runs	HS	Avg	100	50	Ct	St	Balls	Runs	Wkts	Avg	BB	5I	10M
Test																	
FC	7	8	1	111	34	15.85	-	-	-	-	1626	825	19	43.42	4-70	-	-
ODI																	
List A	1	0	0	0	0		-	-	-	-	60	60	1	60.00	1-60	-	
20/20 Int																	
20/20																	

Career Performances

	M	Inn	NO	Runs	HS	Avg	100	50	Ct	St	Balls	Runs	Wkts	Avg	BB	5I	10M
Test																	
FC	148	211	40	3571	117	20.88	1	12	72	-	34027	14305	573	24.96	9-54	36	7
ODI																	
List A	107	71	18	774	85	14.60	-	1	34	-	4875	3431	132	25.99	5-18	1	
20/20 Int																	
20/20																	

MUSTARD, P. Durham

Name: Philip (<u>Phil</u>) Mustard
Role: Left-hand bat, wicket-keeper
Born: 8 October 1982, Sunderland
Height: 5ft 11in **Weight:** 13st 3lbs
Nickname: Colonel
County debut: 2002
ODI debut: 2007-08
Twenty20 Int debut: 2007-08
Place in batting averages: 68th av. 41.80
(2008 191st av. 21.00)
Parents: Maureen
Marital status: Single
Children: Haydon Samuel, 12 July 2006
Education: Usworth Comprehensive,
Washington, Tyne and Wear
Overseas tours: England to Sri Lanka
2007-08, to New Zealand 2007-08
Overseas teams played for: Bulleen, Melbourne 2002; Glenorchy, Tasmania 2003;
Bankstown, Sydney 2004; Tea Tree Gully, South Australia
Career highlights to date: 'First century 2006. Playing for England U19

Cricket moments to forget: 'First ball against Jimmy Anderson on debut in C&G' *(Caught Flintoff, bowled Anderson)*
Cricketers particularly admired: Alec Stewart
Young players to look out for: Ben Harmison (Durham)
Other sports played: 'Golf, football' (he spent time as a schoolboy player with both Middlesbrough and Manchester United, and is still an enthusiastic participant)
Other sports followed: Football (Newcastle United)
Favourite band: Bee Gees
Relaxations: 'Socialising'
Extras: Scored 77-ball 75 on first-class debut v Sri Lankans at Riverside 2002. Represented England U19 2002. Scored maiden first-class century (130) v Kent at Canterbury 2006, in the process sharing with Gordon Muchall (219) in a new Durham record partnership for the sixth wicket (249). Made 50 (54) dismissals in a season for the first time and also scored 816 runs in first-class cricket 2006. Scored 21-ball fifty (ending with 40-ball 78) v Leicestershire at Riverside in the Pro40 2007, setting a new Durham record for fastest one-day fifty. Made ODI debut in the first ODI v Sri Lanka in Dambulla 2007-08. Top of Durham's Twenty20 batting averages in 2008
Best batting: 130 Durham v Kent, Canterbury 2006

2009 Season

	M	Inn	NO	Runs	HS	Avg	100	50	Ct	St	Balls	Runs	Wkts	Avg	BB	5I	10M
Test																	
FC	18	22	7	627	94*	41.80	-	5	69	1	0	0	0		-	-	-
ODI																	
List A	15	15	0	675	102	45.00	1	7	12	4	0	0	0		-	-	
20/20 Int																	
20/20	10	10	0	183	52	8.30	-	1	5	1	0	0	0		-	-	

Career Performances

	M	Inn	NO	Runs	HS	Avg	100	50	Ct	St	Balls	Runs	Wkts	Avg	BB	5I	10M
Test																	
FC	101	156	14	3956	130	27.85	2	22	346	13	0	0	0		-	-	-
ODI	10	10	0	233	83	23.30	-	1	9	2	0	0	0		-	-	
List A	117	103	6	2831	108	29.18	2	19	120	25	0	0	0		-	-	
20/20 Int	2	2	0	60	40	30.00	-	-	-	-	0	0	0		-	-	
20/20	52	52	2	1147	67*	22.94	-	6	19	14	0	0	0		-	-	

63. Which national side, other than Pakistan, did Abdul Kardar play for?

NAIK, J. K. H. Leicestershire

Name: Jigar Kumar Hakumatrai Naik
Role: Right-hand bat, right-arm off-break bowler
Born: 10 August 1984, Leicester
Height: 6ft 2in **Weight:** 14st
Nickname: Jigs, Jiggy, Jigsy
County debut: 2006
Place in batting averages: 155th av. 28.57
Parents: Hakumatrai and Daxa
Marital status: Single
Education: Rushey Mead; Gateway College;
Nottingham Trent University; Loughborough
University
Qualifications: BSc (Hons) Multimedia Technology,
MSc Computer Science
Career outside cricket: Technical systems engineer
Overseas tours: Leicestershire to India and Sri Lanka 2007
Career highlights to date: 'Making my Championship and Pro40 debuts'
Cricketers particularly admired: Sachin Tendulkar, Erapalli Prasanna
Other sports played: Golf, tennis, football
Other sports followed: Tennis, football (Liverpool FC)
Favourite band: Nickelback
Relaxations: 'Music, movies, going to the gym'
Extras: Played for Leicestershire Board XI in the 2003 C&G. Attended World Cricket
Academy 2007. Played for LUCCE 2007. First Leicester-born player of Asian origin
to represent the county
Opinions on cricket: 'The new ruling of having only one overseas player can only be
better for English cricket, so long as the overseas player has enough experience and
talent at the highest level to provide input to the club and be helpful to the younger
members of the squad.'
Best batting: 109* Leicestershire v Derbyshire, Grace Road, 2009
Best bowling: 3-70 Leicestershire v Bangladesh A, Grace Road 2008

2009 Season

	M	Inn	NO	Runs	HS	Avg	100	50	Ct	St	Balls	Runs	Wkts	Avg	BB	5I	10M
Test																	
FC	6	10	3	200	109*	28.57	1	-	1	-	725	367	9	40.77	2-32	-	-
ODI																	
List A	7	5	2	44	18	14.66	-	-	-	-	242	208	7	29.71	3-21	-	
20/20 Int																	
20/20	6	1	1	7	7*		-	-	1	-	90	103	3	34.33	2-22	-	

Career Performances

	M	Inn	NO	Runs	HS	Avg	100	50	Ct	St	Balls	Runs	Wkts	Avg	BB	5I	10M
Test																	
FC	13	17	6	260	109*	23.63	1	-	6	-	1457	881	16	55.06	3-70	-	
ODI																	
List A	13	8	3	59	18	11.80	-	-	1	-	502	415	14	29.64	3-21	-	
20/20 Int																	
20/20	11	4	3	13	7*	13.00	-	-	2	-	162	203	4	50.75	2-22	-	

NANNES, D. P.   Nottinghamshire

Name: <u>Dirk</u> Peter Nannes
Role: Right-hand bat, left-arm
fast-medium bowler
Born: 16 May 1976, Mount Waverley,
Melbourne, Australia
Height: 6ft 2in
Nickname: Digger, Dirty Dirk
County debut: 2008 (Middlesex)
County cap: 2008 (Middlesex)
ODI debut: 2009
Twenty20 Int debut: 2009
Education: Wesley College, Melbourne
Overseas tours: Netherlands to England (ICC
World Twenty20) 2009; Australia to England
(ICC World Twenty20) 2009, to Scotland
(one-day series) 2009
Overseas teams played for: Victoria 2005-06 – ; Delhi Daredevils (IPL) 2009
Other sports played: A former mogul ski racer who has competed in alpine skiing
World Cup competition
Extras: After an earlier sporting career as a skier, began playing club cricket for
Fitzroy-Doncaster (Victoria) in 1999. Made his first-class debut (for Victoria) in 2006
at the age of 29. Played club cricket in the UK for Netherfield CC (Northern Premier
League) 2006. Played only one match for Victoria in 2006-07 after sustaining an injury
during his time in the UK. Recovered to play a key role in Victoria's Twenty20 title
win in 2007-08 taking 22 Pura Cup wickets at an average of 28.54 in the same season.
Played for Middlesex and Middlesex 2nd XI 2008. Returned highly unusual figures of
1-2 off 0.1 overs for Victoria v Western Australia (Sheffield Shield, November 2008) –
after dismissing Shaun Marsh with his first ball, he bowled two successive beamers
and was banned from bowling for the rest of the innings. Has joined Nottinghamshire
for 2010.
Best batting: 31* Victoria v South Australia, Adelaide 2007-08
Best bowling: 7-50 Victoria v Queensland, Brisbane 2008-09

2009 Season

	M	Inn	NO	Runs	HS	Avg	100	50	Ct	St	Balls	Runs	Wkts	Avg	BB	5I	10M
Test																	
FC																	
ODI																	
List A																	
20/20 Int	3	1	0	6	6	6.00	-	-	-	-	48	56	1	56.00	1-26	-	
20/20	3	1	0	6	6	6.00	-	-	-	-	48	56	1	56.00	1-26	-	

Career Performances

	M	Inn	NO	Runs	HS	Avg	100	50	Ct	St	Balls	Runs	Wkts	Avg	BB	5I	10M
Test																	
FC	22	24	8	108	31*	6.75	-	-	6	-	3947	2205	89	24.77	7-50	2	1
ODI	1	1	0	1	1	1.00	-	-	-	-	42	20	1	20.00	1-20	-	
List A	21	10	5	18	5*	3.60	-	-	-	-	1104	865	28	30.89	4-38	-	
20/20 Int	3	1	0	6	6	6.00	-	-	-	-	48	56	1	56.00	1-26	-	
20/20	42	3	2	12	6	12.00	-	-	11	-	933	1067	63	16.93	4-11	-	

NAPIER, G. R. — Essex

Name: Graham Richard Napier
Role: Right-hand bat, right-arm medium bowler; all-rounder
Born: 6 January 1980, Colchester
Height: 5ft 9in **Weight:** 14st 2lbs
Nickname: George, Napes
County debut: 1997
Place in batting averages: 115th av. 34.80 (2008 197th av. 20.50)
Place in bowling averages: 78th av. 34.65 (2008 37th av. 25.77)
Parents: Roger and Carol
Marital status: Single
Family links with cricket: Father played for Palmers Boys School 1st XI (1965-68), Essex Police divisional teams, and Harwich Immigration CC
Education: Gilberd School, Colchester
Qualifications: City & Guilds Digital Imaging, NCA coaching award
Career outside cricket: 'I'm looking to further my career outside cricket, but it's difficult to decide what I want to do'
Off-season: 'Playing for Central Districts in the New Zealand domestic Twenty20 competition'

Overseas tours: England U17 to Bermuda (International Youth Tournament) 1997; England U19 to South Africa (including U19 World Cup) 1997-98; England A to Malaysia and India 2003-04; England VI to Hong Kong 2004; MCC to Namibia and Uganda 2004-05; England Lions to New Zealand 2008-09

Overseas teams played for: Campbelltown CC, Sydney 2000-01; North Perth, Western Australia 2001-02; Upper Valley CC, Wellington, New Zealand 2007-08; Wellington Firebirds, New Zealand 2008-09; Hutt District CC, New Zealand 2008-09; Mumbai Indians (IPL) 2009; Central Districts, New Zealand 2009-10

Career highlights to date: 'Testing myself against the world's best and scoring some runs. Winning the Friends Provident Trophy. Scoring 152*, including 16 sixes, in Twenty20 [Essex v Sussex, Chelmsford, 2008 – the 16 sixes set a new Twenty20 world record for a single innings]. Being included in the World Twenty20 squad. Playing in the IPL'

Cricket moments to forget: 'Being run out in a Lord's final'

Favourite sledging line: '"He who laughs last laughs the longest" – used against me!'

Young players to look out for: Adam Wheater (Essex)

Other sports played: Golf, fly fishing, tennis

Favourite band: Elton John, The Stereophonics

Relaxations: 'Fly fishing in New Zealand'

Extras: Represented England U19 1999. Man of the Match award for Essex Board XI v Lancashire Board XI in the NatWest 2000. ECB National Academy 2003-04. Included in preliminary England one-day squad of 30 for ICC Champions Trophy 2004. Took part in 'highest game of cricket ever played' at Everest base camp in 2007 in aid of the PCA's Benevolent Fund. Won the Walter Lawrence Trophy (for the season's fastest century) 2008 – in 44-balls v Sussex at Chelmsford, including nine sixes and nine fours. His innings finished at 152* off 58 balls, a Twenty20 Cup record score, and included 16 sixes, another Twenty20 Cup record. Scored 36 sixes from 327 deliveries in the 2008 season to win the Sky Sports Sixes League Trophy. Played for Mumbai Indians in the 2009 IPL. Completed the Three Peaks Challenge in 2009 for the PCA's Benevolent Fund. Scored 73 off 29 balls for Central Districts in a one-day win over Northern Districts in December 2009

Player website: www.grahamnapier.com

Opinions on cricket: 'The fixture schedule is becoming more and more crowded, with less chance for practice and rest. This will only end up in fatigue, which leads to injury.'

Best batting: 125 Essex v Nottinghamshire, Chelmsford 2007

Best bowling: 6-103 Essex v Glamorgan, Southend 2008

2009 Season

	M	Inn	NO	Runs	HS	Avg	100	50	Ct	St	Balls	Runs	Wkts	Avg	BB	5I	10M
Test																	
FC	10	16	6	348	64*	34.80	-	2	3	-	1628	1005	29	34.65	4-32	-	-
ODI																	
List A	15	13	1	295	63	24.58	-	1	2	-	672	605	22	27.50	4-33	-	
20/20 Int																	
20/20	7	6	1	59	47	11.80	-	-	4	-	134	179	9	19.88	3-21	-	

Career Performances

	M	Inn	NO	Runs	HS	Avg	100	50	Ct	St	Balls	Runs	Wkts	Avg	BB	5I	10M
Test																	
FC	99	136	29	3283	125	30.68	3	20	38	-	12686	7854	207	37.94	6-103	3	-
ODI																	
List A	185	143	18	2251	79	18.00	-	11	40	-	6002	5082	205	24.79	6-29	1	
20/20 Int																	
20/20	55	40	4	641	152*	17.80	1	-	14	-	1143	1386	70	19.80	4-10	-	

NASH, C. D. — Sussex

Name: Christopher (Chris) David Nash
Role: Right-hand bat, right-arm off-spin bowler
Born: 19 May 1983, Cuckfield
Height: 5ft 11½in **Weight:** 13st
Nickname: Nashy, Nashdog, Hero, Beaut, Pointless
County debut: 2002
County cap: 2008
Place in batting averages: 23rd av. 57.43
(2008 76th av. 37.69)
Parents: Nick and Jane
Marital status: Single ('girlfriend, Amy')
Family links with cricket: 'Brother played for
Sussex 2nd XI and Horsham 1st XI'
Education: Tanbridge House; Collyers Sixth Form
College; Loughborough University
Qualifications: 11 GCSEs, 4 A-levels, BSc (Hons) in Sports Science, Level 2 squash
and cricket coaching
Career outside cricket: 'Traveller, after-dinner speaker'
Overseas tours: England U17 to Northern Ireland (ECC Colts Festival) 1999; Sussex
U19 to Cape Town 1999; Horsham CC to Barbados 2005; Sussex to Dubai 2006-07

Overseas teams played for: Subiaco Marist, Perth 2004-05, 2005-06; Cornwall CC, Auckland 2007-08; Richmond CC, Melbourne 2008-09

Career highlights to date: 'Winning the Championship 2006. First championship century at Old Trafford, 2008.'

Cricket moments to forget: 'Every time I come on to bowl, I get a barrage of abuse from my team-mates (Lewry, Yardy, Hodd, Jenkins and everyone else). Getting a pair at Taunton, much to the amusement of the Swann brothers.'

Cricketers particularly admired: Murray Goodwin, Mushtaq Ahmed, Dr John Dew

Other sports played: Squash (county and national U11-15), football (Sussex CCC FC, PureTown FC, Horsham YMCA), tennis (county)

Other sports followed: Football (Brighton & Hove Albion, Horsham, PureTown)

Favourite band: Kings of Leon

Extras: 'Smallest ears in Sussex squad.' Represented England U15, U17, U18, U19, captaining at U17 and U18 levels. Sussex League Young Player of the Year 2001, 2003. Played for LUCCE 2002, 2003, 2004. Represented British Universities 2004. Man of the Match in the 2nd XI Trophy final v Nottinghamshire at Horsham 2005 (2-21/72*). Scored 82 v Warwickshire in the Pro40 at Hove 2006, winning Man of the Match award. Sussex Most Improved Player (Umer Rashid Memorial Award) 2006. Part of England Performance Programme squad in South Africa 2009-10 but had to return home early due to broken thumb

Opinions on cricket: 'Mirror international cricket in the domestic game. The game is in great shape. Overseas players play a key role, if they are committed to the county, in helping to produce future England players.'

Best batting: 157 Sussex v Somerset, Taunton 2009

Best bowling: 3-7 Sussex v Surrey, The Oval 2008

2009 Season

	M	Inn	NO	Runs	HS	Avg	100	50	Ct	St	Balls	Runs	Wkts	Avg	BB	5I	10M
Test																	
FC	15	26	3	1321	157	57.43	4	6	3	-	688	394	7	56.28	1-3	-	-
ODI																	
List A	10	9	0	217	41	24.11	-	-	4	-	159	138	7	19.71	4-40	-	
20/20 Int																	
20/20	10	8	3	216	56*	43.20	-	1	2	-	18	22	0			-	-

Career Performances

	M	Inn	NO	Runs	HS	Avg	100	50	Ct	St	Balls	Runs	Wkts	Avg	BB	5I	10M
Test																	
FC	62	105	9	3683	157	38.36	6	23	20	-	1602	1041	19	54.78	3-7	-	-
ODI																	
List A	39	36	0	835	82	23.19	-	3	8	-	380	340	13	26.15	4-40	-	
20/20 Int																	
20/20	32	30	5	535	56*	21.40	-	2	10	-	18	22	0			-	-

NASH, D. C. Middlesex

Name: <u>David</u> Charles Nash
Role: Right-hand bat, wicket-keeper
Born: 19 January 1978, Chertsey, Surrey
Height: 5ft 7in **Weight:** 11st 5lbs
Nickname: Nashy, Knocker
County debut: 1995 (one-day), 1997 (first-class)
County cap: 1999
Benefit: 2007
50 dismissals in a season: 1
Place in batting averages: 222nd av. 19.00
Parents: David and Christine
Marital status: Single
Family links with cricket: 'Father played club
cricket, and brother plays now and again for
Ashford CC. Mother is avid watcher and tea lady'
Education: Sunbury Manor; Malvern College
Qualifications: 9 O-levels, 1 A-level, Levels 1 and 2 cricket coaching,
qualified football referee
Career outside cricket: Qualified cricket coach
Overseas tours: England U15 to South Africa 1993; British Airways Youth Team
to West Indies 1993-94; England U19 to Zimbabwe 1995-96, to Pakistan 1996-97;
England A to Kenya and Sri Lanka 1997-98
Overseas teams played for: Fremantle, Perth 2000-01, 2002-03
Career highlights to date: 'Touring with England A and scoring first hundred for
Middlesex at Lord's v Somerset'
Cricket moments to forget: 'All golden ducks'
Cricket superstitions: 'Too many to mention'
Cricketers particularly admired: Angus Fraser
Other sports played: Rugby, football ('played for Millwall U15 and my district
side'), 'and most other sports'
Other sports followed: Rugby (London Irish), football (Chelsea)
Relaxations: 'Listening to music, watching sport and socialising with friends'
Extras: Represented Middlesex at all ages. Played for England U14, U15, U17 and
U19. Once took six wickets in six balls, aged 11 – 'when I could bowl!' Seaxe Young
Player of the Year 1993. Retired at end of 2009 season
Best batting: 114 Middlesex v Somerset, Lord's 1998
Best bowling: 1-8 Middlesex v Essex, Chelmsford 1997

2009 Season

	M	Inn	NO	Runs	HS	Avg	100	50	Ct	St	Balls	Runs	Wkts	Avg	BB	5I	10M
Test																	
FC	5	8	0	152	43	19.00	-	-	16	-	0	0	0		-	-	-
ODI																	
List A	1	1	0	20	20	20.00	-	-	1	-	0	0	0		-	-	
20/20 Int																	
20/20																	

Career Performances

	M	Inn	NO	Runs	HS	Avg	100	50	Ct	St	Balls	Runs	Wkts	Avg	BB	5I	10M
Test																	
FC	140	203	43	5684	114	35.52	11	27	297	23	90	105	2	52.50	1-8	-	-
ODI																	
List A	121	90	18	1500	67	20.83	-	6	92	18	0	0	0		-	-	
20/20 Int																	
20/20																	

NAVED-UL-HASAN   Yorkshire

Name: Rana Naved-ul-Hasan
Role: Right-hand bat, right-arm fast bowler
Born: 28 February 1978, Sheikhupura City, Pakistan
Height: 5ft 11in **Weight:** 12st 12lbs
County debut: 2005 (Sussex), 2008 (Yorkshire)
County cap: 2005 (Sussex)
Test debut: 2004-05
ODI debut: 2002-03
Twenty20 Int debut: 2006
50 wickets in a season: 2
Place in batting averages: 243rd av. 15.50
(2008 226th av. 16.28)
Place in bowling averages: 108th av. 41.20
(2008 117th av. 37.87)
Parents: Rana Mehdi Hassan Khan
Wife and date of marriage: Najma Naveed, 29 April 1997
Children: Aqsa, Rimsha, Naima, Maha
Education: Government High School, Sheikhupura
Career outside cricket: 'With family'
Overseas tours: Pakistan U19 to New Zealand 1994-95; Pakistan to Sharjah (Cherry Blossom Sharjah Cup) 2002-03, to England (ICC Champions Trophy) 2004, to Australia 2004-05, to India 2004-05, to West Indies 2004-05, to Sri Lanka 2005-06,

to UAE (DLF Cup) 2006, to England 2006, to India (ICC Champions Trophy) 2006-07, to South Africa 2006-07, to West Indies (World Cup) 2006-07, to Sri Lanka 2009 (one-day series), to Australia 2009-10 (one-day series), plus other one-day matches in England, India and Australia
Overseas teams played for: Lahore Division 1999-2000; Pakistan Customs 2000-01; Sheikhupura 2000-01 – 2001-02; Allied Bank 2001-02; WAPDA 2002-03 – 2003-04, 2006-07; Sialkot/Sialkot Stallions 2003-04 – 2006-07; Lahore Badshahs (ICL) 2008; Water and Power Development Authority 2009-10; Tasmania 2009-10
Cricket moments to forget: 'When we lost the World Cup match against Ireland'
Cricketers particularly admired: Brian Lara
Young players to look out for: Adil Rashid
Other sports played: Hockey
Other sports followed: Football (Manchester United)
Favourite band: 'Any music'
Relaxations: 'Music'
Extras: Played for Herefordshire in the 2003 C&G competition. Was selected in the World One-Day Team of the Year at the ICC Awards 2005. Has won several match and series awards, including Player of the [ODI] Series v India 2004-05 and Player of the [ODI] Series v West Indies 2006-07. An overseas player with Sussex 2005-07 and with Yorkshire in both 2008 and 2009. Played for a Pakistan XI against a World XI, November 2008. Returned to the Pakistan fold in 2009 after opting out of the ICL
Best batting: 139 Sussex v Middlesex, Lord's 2005
Best bowling: 7-49 Sheikhupura v Sialkot, Muridke 2001-02

2009 Season

	M	Inn	NO	Runs	HS	Avg	100	50	Ct	St	Balls	Runs	Wkts	Avg	BB	5I	10M
Test																	
FC	4	6	0	93	32	15.50	-	-	-	-	744	412	10	41.20	3-102	-	-
ODI																	
List A	8	8	1	163	53*	23.28	-	1	5	-	436	374	12	31.16	3-44	-	
20/20 Int																	
20/20	8	8	2	63	20*	10.50	-	-	2	-	163	159	11	14.45	4-23	-	

Career Performances

	M	Inn	NO	Runs	HS	Avg	100	50	Ct	St	Balls	Runs	Wkts	Avg	BB	5I	10M
Test	9	15	3	239	42*	19.91	-	-	3	-	1565	1044	18	58.00	3-30	-	-
FC	117	166	18	3352	139	22.64	4	9	56	-	21660	12229	503	24.31	7-49	27	4
ODI	69	46	17	448	33	15.44	-	-	15	-	3184	2931	104	28.18	6-27	1	
List A	161	122	33	1968	74	22.11	-	10	45	-	7576	6582	248	26.54	6-27	3	
20/20 Int	3	1	1	17	17*		-	-	2	-	61	74	4	18.50	3-19	-	
20/20	37	26	12	321	40*	22.92	-	-	19	-	754	839	38	22.07	4-23	-	

NEEDHAM, J. Derbyshire

Name: Jake Needham
Role: Right-hand bat, right-arm off-spin bowler; all-rounder
Born: 30 September 1986, Portsmouth, Hampshire
Height: 6ft 1in **Weight:** 11st 7lbs
County debut: 2005
Extras: Man of the Match playing for Ockbrook & Borrowash v Kibworth in the Cockspur Cup final at Lord's 2004 (51/4-27). Derbyshire Academy Player of the Year 2005. Represented England U19 2006. Is committed to Derbyshire until the end of the 2012 season
Best batting: 48 Derbyshire v Nottinghamshire, Chesterfield 2007
Best bowling: 6-49 Derbyshire v Leicestershire, Grace Road 2008

2009 Season

	M	Inn	NO	Runs	HS	Avg	100	50	Ct	St	Balls	Runs	Wkts	Avg	BB	5I	10M
Test																	
FC	5	7	3	55	20	13.75	-	-	3	-	610	353	7	50.42	3-47	-	-
ODI																	
List A	6	3	1	10	5	5.00	-	-	5	-	276	226	5	45.20	2-39	-	
20/20 Int																	
20/20	1	0	0	0	0		-	-	1	-	24	21	4	5.25	4-21	-	

Career Performances

	M	Inn	NO	Runs	HS	Avg	100	50	Ct	St	Balls	Runs	Wkts	Avg	BB	5I	10M
Test																	
FC	19	31	12	384	48	20.21	-	-	10	-	2263	1268	35	36.22	6-49	1	-
ODI																	
List A	34	24	11	213	42	16.38	-	-	13	-	1071	951	17	55.94	2-36	-	
20/20 Int																	
20/20	14	5	3	16	7*	8.00	-	-	4	-	159	212	8	26.50	4-21	-	

NEL, A.   Surrey

Name: Andre Nel
Role: Right-hand bat, right-arm
fast-medium bowler
Born: 15 July 1977, Germiston, Gauteng,
South Africa
County debut: 2003 (Northants),
2005 (Essex), 2009 (Surrey)
County cap: 2003 (Northants)
Test debut: 2001-02
ODI debut: 2000-01
Twenty20 Int debut: 2005-06
Place in batting averages: 249th av. 14.62
Place in bowling averages: 33rd av. 27.92
(2008 93rd av. 32.84)
Education: Hoërskool Dr E.G. Jansen, Boksburg
Overseas tours: South Africa Academy to Ireland and Scotland 1999; South Africa A
to Zimbabwe 2002-03, to Australia 2002-03, to Zimbabwe 2007-08; South Africa to
West Indies 2000-01, to Zimbabwe 2001-02, to England 2003 (NatWest Series), to
Pakistan 2003-04, to New Zealand 2003-04, to West Indies 2004-05, to India (one-day
series) 2005-06, to Australia 2005-06, to Sri Lanka 2006, to India (ICC Champions
Trophy) 2006-07, to West Indies (World Cup) 2006-07, to Ireland (one-day series v
India) 2007, to Pakistan 2007-08, to England 2008
Overseas teams played for: Easterns 1996-97 – 2005-06; Titans 2003-04 – 2007-08;
Mumbai Indians (IPL) 2008; Lions 2008-09
Extras: Was an overseas player with Northamptonshire 2003. One of *South African
Cricket Annual*'s five Cricketers of the Year 2004, 2005. His match awards include
Man of the Match in the fourth ODI v Pakistan at Rawalpindi 2003-04 (4-39) and in
the third Test v West Indies in Barbados 2004-05 (4-56/6-32). Was an overseas player
with Essex during the 2005 season as a locum for André Adams, taking a wicket
(Matthew Wood) with his first ball for the county, v Somerset at Colchester; returned
for part of the 2007 season. Represented South Africa in the Twenty20 World
Championship 2007-08. Released by Essex at the end of the 2008 season. Having
decided to retire from international cricket, signed for Surrey, March 2009. His season
came to a premature end when he injured his elbow on a door frame
Best batting: 56 South Africa v Bangladesh A, Worcester 2008
Best bowling: 6-25 Easterns v Gauteng, Johannesburg 2001-02

2009 Season

	M	Inn	NO	Runs	HS	Avg	100	50	Ct	St	Balls	Runs	Wkts	Avg	BB	5I	10M
Test																	
FC	9	10	2	117	32	14.62	-	-	3	-	1564	754	27	27.92	6-36	1	-
ODI																	
List A	7	4	2	21	8	10.50	-	-	-	-	346	291	10	29.10	3-39	-	
20/20 Int																	
20/20	9	6	4	48	19	24.00	-	-	2	-	210	243	4	60.75	1-22	-	

Career Performances

	M	Inn	NO	Runs	HS	Avg	100	50	Ct	St	Balls	Runs	Wkts	Avg	BB	5I	10M
Test	36	42	8	337	34	9.91	-	-	16	-	7630	3919	123	31.86	6-32	3	1
FC	123	140	42	1413	56	14.41	-	2	48	-	24097	11357	416	27.30	6-25	13	1
ODI	79	22	12	127	30*	12.70	-	-	21	-	3801	2935	106	27.68	5-45	1	
List A	204	81	43	473	58	12.44	-	1	48	-	10038	7198	281	25.61	6-27	4	
20/20 Int	2	1	1	0	0*		-	-	1	-	48	42	2	21.00	2-19	-	
20/20	32	18	7	110	19	10.00	-	-	9	-	726	758	24	31.58	2-13	-	

NELSON, M. A. G.　　　Northamptonshire

Name: <u>Mark</u> Anthony George Nelson
Role: Left-hand bat, right-arm
fast-medium bowler
Born: 24 September 1986, Milton Keynes
Height: 5ft 11in **Weight:** 11st 7lbs
Nickname: Nelo, Nelly
County debut: 2006 (one-day), 2007 (first-class)
Place in batting averages: 226th av. 18.71
Parents: George and Janet
Marital status: Single
Education: Lord Grey School, Milton Keynes;
Stowe School
Qualifications: 3 A-levels
Overseas tours: England U19 to Sri Lanka
(U19 World Cup) 2005-06
Cricket moments to forget: 'Batting for U19, the ball hit my bat and a piece of bat broke off, knocked on to a stump and I was declared out'
Cricket superstitions: 'Nobody can touch my bat before I go in'
Cricketers particularly admired: Brian Lara 'for his skill'
Young players to look out for: Alex Wakely, Ben Howgego (both Northamptonshire)
Other sports played: Football 'for recreational purposes only'
Other sports followed: Football (Manchester United)

Favourite band: Tupac, Notorious B.I.G.
Relaxations: 'Music and dancing'
Extras: NBC Denis Compton Award for the most promising young Northamptonshire player 2006. Represented England at U17, U18 and U19 levels. Released by Northamptonshire at the end of the 2009 season
Best batting: 42 Northamptonshire v Warwickshire, Edgbaston 2008
Best bowling: 2-62 Northamptonshire v Middlesex, Northampton 2007

2009 Season

	M	Inn	NO	Runs	HS	Avg	100	50	Ct	St	Balls	Runs	Wkts	Avg	BB	5I	10M
Test																	
FC	4	7	0	131	38	18.71	-	-	3	-	0	0	0		-	-	-
ODI																	
List A	4	4	0	100	74	25.00	-	1	-	-	0	0	0		-	-	
20/20 Int																	
20/20	6	4	1	23	13	7.66	-	-	2	-	0	0	0		-	-	

Career Performances

	M	Inn	NO	Runs	HS	Avg	100	50	Ct	St	Balls	Runs	Wkts	Avg	BB	5I	10M
Test																	
FC	7	11	0	195	42	17.72	-	-	4	-	96	124	2	62.00	2-62	-	-
ODI																	
List A	13	11	2	213	74	23.66	-	1	-	-	94	100	2	50.00	1-26	-	
20/20 Int																	
20/20	6	4	1	23	13	7.66	-	-	2	-	0	0	0		-	-	

NEW, T. J. Leicestershire

Name: Thomas (<u>Tom</u>) James New
Role: Left-hand bat, wicket-keeper, right-arm slow-medium bowler
Born: 18 January 1985, Sutton-in-Ashfield
Height: 5ft 10in **Weight:** 10st
Nickname: Newy, P
County debut: 2003 (one-day), 2004 (first-class)
Place in batting averages: 137th av. 31.26 (2008 154th av. 26.04)
Parents: Martin and Louise
Marital status: Engaged
Family links with cricket: 'Dad played local cricket'
Education: Quarrydale Comprehensive
Qualifications: GCSEs

Overseas tours: England U19 to Bangladesh (U19 World Cup) 2003-04
Overseas teams played for: Geelong Cement, Victoria 2001-02
Cricket moments to forget: 'Losing semi-final of Costcutter World Challenge 2000 to Pakistan'
Cricket superstitions: 'None'
Cricketers particularly admired: Ian Healy, Jack Russell
Other sports played: Golf, football
Other sports followed: Football (Mansfield Town)
Relaxations: 'Golf, music'
Extras: Played for Nottinghamshire U12, U13, U15, U16 and Midlands U13, U14, U15. Captained England U15 in Costcutter World Challenge [U15 World Cup] 2000. Sir John Hobbs Silver Jubilee Memorial Prize 2000. Represented England U19 2003 and 2004. NBC Denis Compton Award for the most promising young Leicestershire player 2003, 2004. On loan at Derbyshire for part of 2008 season
Best batting: 125 Leicestershire v OUCCE, The Parks 2007
Best bowling: 2-18 Leicestershire v Gloucestershire, Grace Road 2007

2009 Season

	M	Inn	NO	Runs	HS	Avg	100	50	Ct	St	Balls	Runs	Wkts	Avg	BB	5I	10M
Test																	
FC	18	30	4	813	85*	31.26	-	6	29	1	48	36	0		-	-	-
ODI																	
List A	10	8	1	190	50	27.14	-	1	8	2	0	0	0		-	-	
20/20 Int																	
20/20																	

Career Performances

	M	Inn	NO	Runs	HS	Avg	100	50	Ct	St	Balls	Runs	Wkts	Avg	BB	5I	10M
Test																	
FC	68	114	14	3180	125	31.80	2	23	95	6	229	211	5	42.20	2-18	-	-
ODI																	
List A	44	40	4	941	68	26.13	-	4	15	4	0	0	0		-	-	
20/20 Int																	
20/20	1	1	0	18	18	18.00	-	-	1	1	0	0	0		-	-	

64. Bangladesh's second series win, and only their second and third Test match victories, came in 2009. Who did they beat?

Name: <u>Oliver</u> James Newby
Role: Right-hand bat – 'aggressive!', right-arm
fast bowler; all-rounder
Born: 26 August 1984, Blackburn
Height: 6ft 5in **Weight:** 14st 7lbs
Nickname: Newbz, Strikers, Newbs, Hilfers
County debut: 2003 (Lancashire – *see Extras*)
Place in bowling averages: 85th av. 35.70
(2008 84th av. 31.72)
Parents: Frank and Carol
Marital status: Single
Family links with cricket: 'Dad played league
cricket for Read CC'
Education: Ribblesdale High School;
Myerscough College
Qualifications: 10 GCSEs, ND Sports Science, Level 1 coaching
Off-season: 'Going travelling to Third World countries and helping the
underprivileged. Also making Moroccan furniture'
Career highlights to date: 'My first contract, and my first-class debut'
Cricket moments to forget: 'Running in to bowl and my trousers falling down
around my ankles, making me fall over – very embarrassing'
Cricket superstitions: 'Always have to put on and take off my shirt three times
before going out'
Cricketers particularly admired: Alfonso Thomas, Zander de Bruyn
Young players to look out for: Adil Rashid (Yorkshire), Deb Newby (Lancashire)
Other sports followed: Darts, football (Blackburn Rovers)
Favourite band: Billy Joel
Relaxations: 'Ironing. Taking the girlfriend and the dog for walks'
Extras: Took a wicket in each of his first two overs on his one-day debut for
Lancashire v India A at Blackpool 2003. Played two Championship matches for
Nottinghamshire on loan 2005. Spent a month on loan at Gloucestershire, August
2008, during which he recorded his best bowling figures of 5-69 in a championship
game against Northamptonshire.
Opinions on cricket: 'Still think a lot of cricket is being played, but the professional
sportsman will always overcome this problem. I also think Kolpaks should be allowed
to come and play here'
Best batting: 38* Nottinghamshire v Kent, Trent Bridge 2005
Best bowling: 5-69 Gloucestershire v Northamptonshire, Bristol 2008

2009 Season

	M	Inn	NO	Runs	HS	Avg	100	50	Ct	St	Balls	Runs	Wkts	Avg	BB	5I	10M
Test																	
FC	13	11	1	64	15	6.40	-	-	2	-	1783	1107	31	35.70	4-21	-	-
ODI																	
List A	2	1	1	12	12*		-	-	1	-	84	86	5	17.20	4-41	-	
20/20 Int																	
20/20																	

Career Performances

	M	Inn	NO	Runs	HS	Avg	100	50	Ct	St	Balls	Runs	Wkts	Avg	BB	5I	10M
Test																	
FC	43	37	8	238	38*	8.20	-	-	8	-	5509	3505	105	33.38	5-69	1	-
ODI																	
List A	17	12	7	36	12*	7.20	-	-	3	-	644	632	15	42.13	4-41	-	
20/20 Int																	
20/20	10	4	2	14	6*	7.00	-	-	3	-	162	216	6	36.00	2-34	-	

NEWMAN, S. A. Middlesex

Name: <u>Scott</u> Alexander Newman
Role: Left-hand bat, right-arm
medium bowler
Born: 3 November 1979, Epsom
Height: 6ft 1in **Weight:** 13st 7lbs
Nickname: Ronaldo
County debut: 2001 (one-day, Surrey),
2002 (first-class, Surrey)
County cap: 2005
1000 runs in a season: 4
1st-Class 200s: 1
Place in batting averages: 187th av. 24.52
(2008 55th av. 41.76)
Parents: Ken and Sandy
Marital status: Married
Children: Lemoy, 1985; Brandon, 8 September 2002
Family links with cricket: 'Dad and brother both played'
Education: Trinity School, Croydon; Brighton University
Qualifications: 10 GCSEs, GNVQ (Advanced) Business Studies
Overseas tours: SCB to Barbados; England A to Malaysia and India 2003-04
Overseas teams played for: Mount Lawley CC, Perth

Career highlights to date: 'First one-day century'
Cricket moments to forget: 'Any time I fail'
Cricket superstitions: 'None'
Cricketers particularly admired: 'All of Surrey CCC'
Other sports played: 'Most sports'
Other sports followed: Football (Manchester Utd)
Favourite band: Nas
Relaxations: 'Music, relaxing with family'
Extras: Scored 99 on first-class debut v Hampshire at The Oval 2002. Scored 284 v Derbyshire 2nd XI at The Oval 2003, in the process sharing with Nadeem Shahid (266) in an opening partnership of 552, just three runs short of the English all-cricket record first-wicket stand of 555 set in 1932. Scored 117 and 219 v Glamorgan at The Oval 2005, becoming the first Surrey batsman to score a double hundred and a hundred in the same Championship match. ECB National Academy 2003-04. Spent the second half of 2009 season on loan to Nottinghamshire. In October 2009 he left Surrey to join Middlesex
Best batting: 219 Surrey v Glamorgan, The Oval 2005

2009 Season

	M	Inn	NO	Runs	HS	Avg	100	50	Ct	St	Balls	Runs	Wkts	Avg	BB	5I	10M
Test																	
FC	12	19	0	466	124	24.52	1	2	5	-	54	35	0		-	-	-
ODI																	
List A	8	7	0	463	177	66.14	2	2	1	-	0	0	0		-	-	
20/20 Int																	
20/20	8	8	1	200	81*	28.57	-	1	3	-	0	0	0		-	-	

Career Performances

	M	Inn	NO	Runs	HS	Avg	100	50	Ct	St	Balls	Runs	Wkts	Avg	BB	5I	10M
Test																	
FC	100	170	3	6771	219	40.54	14	40	75	-	78	57	0		-	-	-
ODI																	
List A	82	80	3	2280	177	29.61	3	13	18	-	0	0	0		-	-	
20/20 Int																	
20/20	39	37	4	740	81*	22.42	-	4	14	-	0	0	0		-	-	

NEWPORT, N. A.   Warwickshire

Name: <u>Nathan</u> Alexander Newport
Role: Right-hand opening bat, right-arm medium bowler**.**
Born: 10 May 1989, Worcester
County debut: 2009 (see *Extras*)
Family links with cricket: Father, Phil, played for Worcestershire and England
Extras: Former Worcestershire Academy player, released in 2007. Played club cricket for Barnt Green CC (Birmingham League) 2007-2009. Selected to play against Somerset in August 2009 but the match was postponed due to a waterlogged pitch. Although he started the rescheduled match, he participated only as a fielder before having to step down when Jonathan Trott returned from England duty

2009 Season

	M	Inn	NO	Runs	HS	Avg	100	50	Ct	St	Balls	Runs	Wkts	Avg	BB	5I	10M
Test																	
FC	1	0	0	0	0		-	-	-	-	0	0	0		-	-	-
ODI																	
List A																	
20/20 Int																	
20/20																	

Career Performances

	M	Inn	NO	Runs	HS	Avg	100	50	Ct	St	Balls	Runs	Wkts	Avg	BB	5I	10M
Test																		
FC	1	0	0	0	0		-	-	-	-	0	0	0		-	-	-
ODI																	
List A																	
20/20 Int																	
20/20																	

65. Who made a century in the Bangladesh second innings in the First Test in the West Indies in 2009?

NEWTON, R. I.   Northamptonshire

Name: Robert (Rob) Irving Newton
Role: Right-hand bat, leg break bowler.
Born: 18 January 1990, Taunton, Somerset
County debut: 2009 (one-day)
Education: Framlingham College, Suffolk
Extras: Played club cricket for Swardeston CC (East Anglian Premier League) 2003-08. Represented Norfolk at U15 level, and Midlands at U17 level. Northamptonshire Academy 2005-09. Northamptonshire 2nd XI 2006-09. One of 24 players selected for ECB trials as part of the selection process for the England U19 World Cup squad in August 2009. Made his first-team debut for Northamptonshire in the Pro40 game v Middlesex in September 2009

2009 Season

	M	Inn	NO	Runs	HS	Avg	100	50	Ct	St	Balls	Runs	Wkts	Avg	BB	5I	10M
Test																	
FC																	
ODI																	
List A	1	1	0	9	9	9.00	-	-	-	-	0	0	0		-	-	
20/20 Int																	
20/20																	

Career Performances

	M	Inn	NO	Runs	HS	Avg	100	50	Ct	St	Balls	Runs	Wkts	Avg	BB	5I	10M
Test																	
FC																	
ODI																	
List A	1	1	0	9	9	9.00	-	-	-	-	0	0	0		-	-	
20/20 Int																	
20/20																	

NIXON, P. A.   Leicestershire

Name: <u>Paul</u> Andrew Nixon
Role: Left-hand bat, wicket-keeper
Born: 21 October 1970, Carlisle
Height: 6ft **Weight:** 12st 10lbs
Nickname: Badger, Nico, Nobby
County debut: 1989 (Leicestershire), 2000 (Kent)
County cap: 1994 (Leicestershire), 2000 (Kent)
Benefit: 2007 (Leicestershire)
ODI debut: 2006-07
Twenty20 Int debut: 2006-07
1000 runs in a season: 1
Place in batting averages: 111th av. 35.40
(2008 19th av. 53.00)
Parents: Brian and Sylvia
Wife and date of marriage: Jen, 9 October 1999
Children: Isabella Rose, 13 May 2008
Family links with cricket: 'Grandad and father played local league cricket. Mum made the teas for Edenhall CC, Penrith'
Education: Ullswater High
Qualifications: 2 O-levels, 6 GCSEs, coaching certificates
Career outside cricket: Property development in the Bahamas (see *Player website*), and ethanol and waste interests
Overseas tours: Cumbria Schools U15 to Denmark 1985; Leicestershire to Barbados, to Jamaica, to Netherlands, to Johannesburg, to Bloemfontein; MCC to Bangladesh 1999-2000; England A to India and Bangladesh 1994-95; England to Pakistan and Sri Lanka 2000-01, to Australia 2006-07 (Commonwealth Bank Series), to West Indies (World Cup) 2006-07
Overseas teams played for: Melville, Western Australia; North Fremantle, Western Australia; Mitchells Plain, Cape Town 1993; Primrose CC, Cape Town 1995-96; Delhi Giants (ICL) 2008
Career highlights to date: 'Winning the Championship in 1996 with Leicestershire. Receiving phone call from David Graveney advising me of England [tour] selection'
Cricket moments to forget: 'Losing Lord's one-day finals. Walking off to the wrong exit at the MCG when out!'
Cricketers particularly admired: David Gower, Ian Botham, Ian Healy, Viv Richards
Young players to look out for: Josh Cobb, Nathan Buck and James Taylor (all Leicestershire)
Other sports played: Golf, football (played for Carlisle United)
Other sports followed: Football (Carlisle United), rugby (Leicester Tigers)
Injuries: 'Pulled calf and a burst varicose vein in the last game of the season when a throw missed the stumps and hit me whilst I was batting'

Favourite band: Stereophonics
Relaxations: Watching England rugby
Extras: Played for England U15. Played in Minor Counties Championship for Cumberland at 16. MCC Young Pro 1988. Took eight catches in debut match v Warwickshire at Hinckley 1989. Leicestershire Young Player of the Year two years running. In 1994 became only second Leicestershire wicket-keeper to score 1000 (1046) first-class runs in a season – also made 62 first-class dismissals to achieve double. Voted Cumbria Sports Personality of the Year 1994-95. Captained First-Class Counties Select XI v New Zealand A at Milton Keynes 2000. Released by Kent at the end of the 2002 season and rejoined Leicestershire for 2003. Took over as captain of county in the Championship in July 2007, scoring century (126) and taking eight catches in his first match in charge. Appointed captain of Leicestershire at the end of August 2007. Second-highest Leicestershire run-maker in 2008. Resigned as Leicestershire captain in August 2009
Player website: www.portstgeorge.com
Opinions on cricket: 'Too much cricket to keep the quality since staffs are getting smaller!'
Best batting: 173* Leicestershire v Kent, Canterbury 2009

2009 Season

	M	Inn	NO	Runs	HS	Avg	100	50	Ct	St	Balls	Runs	Wkts	Avg	BB	5I	10M
Test																	
FC	9	17	2	531	173*	35.40	1	2	10	-	7	9	0		-	-	-
ODI																	
List A	11	9	2	196	50	28.00	-	1	4	1	0	0	0		-	-	
20/20 Int																	
20/20	10	9	1	208	53*	26.00	-	1	9	-	0	0	0		-	-	

Career Performances

	M	Inn	NO	Runs	HS	Avg	100	50	Ct	St	Balls	Runs	Wkts	Avg	BB	5I	10M
Test																	
FC	335	499	110	13486	173*	34.66	20	65	885	67	112	150	0		-	-	-
ODI	19	18	4	297	49	21.21	-	-	20	3	0	0	0		-	-	
List A	401	344	71	7134	101	26.13	1	33	417	99	3	1	0		-	-	
20/20 Int	1	1	1	31	31*		-	-	-	1	0	0	0		-	-	
20/20	60	56	11	1095	65	24.33	-	4	33	13	0	0	0		-	-	

NOFFKE, A. A. Worcestershire

Name: <u>Ashley</u> Allan Noffke
Role: Right-hand bat, right-arm fast bowler;
all-rounder
Born: 30 April 1977, Sunshine Coast,
Queensland, Australia
Height: 6ft 3in **Weight:** 14st
Nickname: Noffers, Wombat
County debut: 2002 (Middlesex),
2005 (Durham), 2007 (Gloucestershire)
County cap: 2003 (Middlesex),
2007 (Gloucestershire)
Twenty20 Int debut: 2007
Place in batting averages: 154th av. 28.66
Place in bowling averages: 119th av. 45.20
Parents: Rob and Lesley Simpson, and Allan Noffke

Wife and date of marriage: Michelle, 8 April 2000
Family links with cricket: Father played club cricket
Education: Immanuel Lutheran College; Sunshine Coast University
Qualifications: Bachelor of Business, ACB Level 2 coaching certificate
Overseas tours: Commonwealth Bank [Australian] Cricket Academy to Zimbabwe
1998-99; Australia to England 2001, to West Indies 2002-03; Australia A to Pakistan
2007-08, to India 2008-09
Overseas teams played for: Queensland 1999-2000 – 2008-09; Bangalore Royal
Challengers (IPL) 2007-08; Western Australia 2009-10 –
Career highlights to date: 'Man of the Match in a winning Pura Cup final for
Queensland. Being selected for Australia for 2001 Ashes tour'
Cricket moments to forget: 'Rolling my ankle playing for Australia v Sussex,
forcing me home from the [2001] Ashes tour'
Cricket superstitions: 'None'
Cricketers particularly admired: Steve Waugh
Other sports played: Golf
Other sports followed: Rugby league, rugby union, 'enjoy all sports'
Favourite band: Powderfinger
Relaxations: Fishing
Extras: Queensland Academy of Sport Player of the Year 1998-99. Awarded an ACB
contract 2001-02 after just six first-class matches. Has represented Australia A.
Sunshine Coast Sportstar of the Year 2001. His awards include Man of the Match in
the Pura Cup final v Victoria 2000-01 for his 7-120 match return and 43 runs batting
as nightwatchman and v South Australia at Brisbane in the Pura Cup 2003-04 (4-48/2-
37 and 114*). Was Middlesex overseas player for two periods during the 2002 season;
returned as an overseas player for 2003. Was an overseas player with Durham in 2005
but was ruled out with a back injury from late July. Was a temporary overseas player

with Gloucestershire during the 2007 season. Made Twenty20 Int debut v New Zealand at Perth, December 2007. Man of the Match v Tasmania at Brisbane in the Pura Cup 2007-08 (5-33/2-114 and 100*). State Player of the Year award 2008. Played for Worcestershire as an overseas player in 2009 and released at the end of the season

Best batting: 114* Queensland v South Australia, Brisbane 2003-04
Best bowling: 8-24 Middlesex v Derbyshire, Derby 2002

2009 Season

	M	Inn	NO	Runs	HS	Avg	100	50	Ct	St	Balls	Runs	Wkts	Avg	BB	5I	10M
Test																	
FC	6	9	0	258	89	28.66	-	2	-	-	948	452	10	45.20	4-92	-	-
ODI																	
List A	6	4	0	79	29	19.75	-	-	1	-	240	140	7	20.00	3-37	-	
20/20 Int																	
20/20	10	10	2	169	34	21.12	-	-	3	-	210	250	11	22.72	2-25	-	

Career Performances

	M	Inn	NO	Runs	HS	Avg	100	50	Ct	St	Balls	Runs	Wkts	Avg	BB	5I	10M
Test																	
FC	112	155	23	3529	114*	26.73	2	16	41	-	21481	10766	375	28.70	8-24	18	1
ODI	1	0	0	0	0		-	-	-	-	54	46	1	46.00	1-46	-	
List A	114	62	19	752	58	17.48	-	1	27	-	5538	4172	129	32.34	4-32	-	
20/20 Int	2	1	0	0	0	0.00	-	-	-	-	45	41	4	10.25	3-18	-	
20/20	26	20	4	246	34	15.37	-	-	6	-	538	636	34	18.70	3-18	-	

66. What did the Pakistan team achieve for the first time in 1983-84?

NORMAN, A. J.   Glamorgan

Name: Aneurin (<u>Nye</u>) John Norman
Role: Right-hand bat, right-arm medium bowler
Born: 22 March 1991, Cardiff
Height: 6ft 1in **Weight:** 13st 5lbs
Nickname: Noddy, Mr Bean
County debut: No first team appearance
Parents: Carl Norman and Kristin Litton
Marital status: Single
Education: Millfield School
Qualifications: 4 A-levels
Off-season: 'Glamorgan Academy tour to Dubai.'
Overseas tours: Wales U16 to Jersey 2007;
Glamorgan and Wales Academy to UAE 2009
Career highlights to date: 'Glamorgan Academy
Player of the Year Award [2009]'
Cricket moments to forget: 'Being run out by a girl'
Cricket superstitions: 'None'
Favourite sledging line: '"Throw him a piano – see if he can play that"'
Cricketers particularly admired: Alan Jones
Young players to look out for: Daniel Bell-Drummond (Kent)
Other sports played: Football
Other sports followed: Football Cardiff City)
Favourite band: Stereophonics
Relaxations: 'Football Manager'
Extras: Captained Wales U12, 2003 and represented Wales at U13, U14, U15 and U16
level. Award for Best All-Rounder at the English Counties U15 Festival at
Ampleforth, 2005. Represented West of England U14 at the ECB National Academy,
Loughborough University, 2005. Played club cricket for Cardiff CC. Made debut for
Glamorgan Second X1 2008. Glamorgan Academy Player of the Year 2009. Awarded a
development contract for 2010
Opinions on cricket: 'One-day cricket played at weekends will attract more spectators
to support their county.'

NORTH, M. J.   Hampshire

Name: <u>Marcus</u> James North
Role: Left-hand bat, right-arm
off-spin bowler
Born: 28 July 1979, Pakenham,
Melbourne, Australia
Height: 6ft 1in **Weight:** 12st 10lbs
County debut: 2004 (Durham),
2005 (Lancashire), 2006 (Derbyshire),
2007 (Gloucestershire)
County cap: 2007 (Gloucestershire)
Test debut: 2008-09
ODI debut: 2009
Twenty20 Int debut: 2009
1st-Class 200s: 3
Place in batting averages: 15th av. 61.30
(2008 25th av. 50.00)
Place in bowling averages: (2008 137th av. 45.00)
Wife: Joanne
Overseas tours: Australia U19 to Pakistan 1996-97, to South Africa (U19 World Cup)
1997-98; Commonwealth Bank [Australian] Cricket Academy to Zimbabwe 1998-99;
Australia A to Pakistan 2005-06; Australia to South Africa 2008-09, to UAE (one-day
series) 2008-09, to England 2009
Overseas teams played for: Western Australia 1999-2000 –
Extras: Commonwealth Bank [Australian] Cricket Academy 1998. Won President's
Silver Trophy (season's best individual performance for Western Australia) for his
200* v Victoria at Melbourne in the Pura Cup 2001-02. Scored 200* and 132 in the
second 'Test' v Pakistan U19 at Sheikhupura 1996-97, winning Man of the Match
award (also Australia's Man of the 'Test' Series). Other awards include Man of the
Match for Australia A v Zimbabweans at Adelaide 2003-04 (115). An overseas player
with Durham 2004. A temporary overseas player with Lancashire during the 2005
season. A temporary overseas player with Derbyshire during the 2006 season. Was a
temporary overseas player with Gloucestershire during the 2007 season and returned
as overseas player for 2008. Won the Walter Lawrence Trophy 2007 for the season's
fastest first-class century for his 73-ball hundred (finishing with 106) v Leicestershire
at Bristol. Made 117 on his Test debut for Australia against South Africa in
Johannesburg, February 2009. Captain of Western Australia. Joined Hampshire as
overseas player for the first six weeks of 2009 in the place of Imran Tahir. Released
at the end of the 2009 season
Best batting: 239* Western Australia v Victoria, Perth 2006-07
Best bowling: 6-69 Australians v Board President's XI, Potschefstroom 2008-09

2009 Season

	M	Inn	NO	Runs	HS	Avg	100	50	Ct	St	Balls	Runs	Wkts	Avg	BB	5I	10M
Test	5	8	1	367	125*	52.42	2	1	3	-	405	204	4	51.00	4-98	-	-
FC	8	12	2	613	191*	61.30	3	1	4	-	507	249	5	49.80	4-98	-	-
ODI																	
List A																	
20/20 Int																	
20/20																	

Career Performances

	M	Inn	NO	Runs	HS	Avg	100	50	Ct	St	Balls	Runs	Wkts	Avg	BB	5I	10M
Test	7	12	1	527	125*	47.90	3	1	5	-	633	302	6	50.33	4-98	-	-
FC	137	240	24	9759	239*	45.18	27	52	105	-	8806	4515	105	43.00	6-69	1	-
ODI	2	2	0	6	5	3.00	-	-	1	-	18	16	0		-	-	
List A	130	123	15	3654	134*	33.83	6	25	40	-	2152	1837	58	31.67	4-26	-	
20/20 Int	1	1	0	20	20	20.00	-	-	-	-	0	0	0		-	-	
20/20	30	29	4	582	59	23.28	-	1	8	-	365	420	8	52.50	2-19	-	

NORTHEAST, S. A. — Kent

Name: <u>Sam</u> Alexander Northeast
Role: Right-hand top-order bat,
off-spin bowler
Born: 16 October 1989, Ashford, Kent
Height: 5ft 11in **Weight:** 11st
Nickname: North, Bam, Nick Knight
County debut: 2007
Place in batting averages: 84th av. 39.23
Parents: Allan and Diane
Marital status: Single
Family links with cricket: 'My brother played
Kent age-group as a kid'
Education: Harrow School
Qualifications: 10 GCSEs
Overseas tours: Harrow School to Sri Lanka 2004;
England U16 to South Africa; England U19 to Malaysia 2006-07, to Sri Lanka 2007-08, Under 19 World Cup in Malaysia 2007-08, to South Africa 2008-09
Cricket moments to forget: 'Not scoring many runs in first two appearances at Lord's, in the Eton v Harrow match'
Cricket superstitions: 'Right pad on first'
Cricketers particularly admired: Graham Thorpe, Steve Waugh
Young players to look out for: Alex Blake and Paul Dixey (both Kent)

Other sports played: Rackets, squash, cross-country running, football and rugby
Other sports followed: Football (Spurs), rugby (Bath)
Favourite band: Starsailor, Snow Patrol
Relaxations: 'Fishing, gardening – playing rackets releases stress'
Extras: Broke Graham Cowdrey's run record at Wellesley House (prep school). Captained England U15. *Daily Telegraph* Bunbury Scholarship 2005. BBC *Test Match Special* Young Cricketer of the Year 2005. Sir John Hobbs Silver Jubilee Memorial Prize for the outstanding U16 schoolboy cricketer 2005. Scored 96 on debut for Kent 2nd XI v Derbyshire 2nd XI at Beckenham 2005. Scored 62* for Sir JP Getty's XI v Sri Lankans in a 50-over game at Wormsley 2006. Top ten nominee for BBC Young Sports Personality of the Year 2006. Scored a century for Harrow v Eton at Lord's in July 2007. NBC Denis Compton Award for most promising young Kent player 2009. Scored a century in both innings for England U19 v Bangladesh U19 in second Test, Derby 2009. A few days later he followed up with another ton against the same opponents in the first ODI. Member of England Performance Programme squad 2009-10
Opinions on cricket: 'Young players are getting more of a chance to shine in the game. Hopefully that will help me.'
Best batting: 128* Kent v Gloucestershire, Bristol 2009

2009 Season

	M	Inn	NO	Runs	HS	Avg	100	50	Ct	St	Balls	Runs	Wkts	Avg	BB	5I	10M
Test																	
FC	11	19	2	667	128*	39.23	1	3	10	-	6	2	0		-	-	-
ODI																	
List A	6	6	0	144	69	24.00	-	1	1	-	0	0	0		-	-	
20/20 Int																	
20/20																	

Career Performances

	M	Inn	NO	Runs	HS	Avg	100	50	Ct	St	Balls	Runs	Wkts	Avg	BB	5I	10M
Test																	
FC	12	21	2	672	128*	35.36	1	3	10	-	6	2	0		-	-	-
ODI																	
List A	7	6	0	144	69	24.00	-	1	1	-	0	0	0		-	-	
20/20 Int																	
20/20																	

O'BRIEN, I. E.   Middlesex

Name: Iain Edward O'Brien
Role: Right-hand bat, right-arm
medium-fast bowler
Born: 10 July 1976, Lower Hutt, Wellington,
New Zealand
Height: 6ft 2in **Weight:** 13st 8lbs
Nickname: OB, Oba, Throb
County debut: 2009 (Leicestershire)
Test debut: 2004-05
ODI debut: 2007-08
Twenty20 Int debut: 2008-09
Place in batting averages: 253rd av. 13.75
Place in bowling averages: 21st av. 26.04
(2008 46th av. 28.80)
Parents: John and Heather
Wife and date of marriage: Rosie, 26 May 2007
Education: Hutt Valley Memorial College, Lower Hutt; Massey University,
Palmerston North
Qualifications: B. Ed., Dip. Tch.
Career outside cricket: 'Teaching'
Off-season: 'Back to New Zealand to play, and getting in as many holiday breaks to
the beach as I can'
Overseas tours: New Zealand A to Sri Lanka 2005, to India 2008; New Zealand to
South Africa 2007-08, to Australia 2007-08, to England 2008, to Australia 2008-09,
to Bangladesh 2008-09, to Sri Lanka 2009
Overseas teams played for: Wellington Firebirds 2000 –
Career highlights to date: '6-75 v West Indies at McLean Park with mum and
dad in the crowd'
Cricket moments to forget: 'Test toss v England at Old Trafford 2008!'
Cricket superstitions: 'I like to be organised and have everything I need in my bag'
Favourite sledging line: '"Have you got two broken legs?" as I walked out to bat
with my Aero pads on'
Cricketers particularly admired: Jacques Kallis, Dan Vettori, Shaun Polllock,
Glenn McGrath
Young players to look out for: James Taylor (Leicestershire), Steve Finn (Middlesex)
Other sports played: New Zealand indoor cricket ('three World Cups'), croquet
('Wellington U18')
Favourite band: Bon Jovi
Relaxations: 'Travelling, eating good food, drinking good wine, cooking…'
Extras: Wellington Bowler of the Year 2000-01 (third highest wicket-taker in a debut
season in New Zealand) and 2005-06. Wellington Player of the Year 2007-08. Played

the first part of the 2009 season with Leicestershire. Signed for Middlesex as an overseas player December 2009. He played his last Test for New Zealand against Pakistan that month

Player website: 'Write a blog – iainobrien.co.nz'
Best batting: 44 Wellington v Canterbury, Wellington, 2006-07
Best bowling: 8-55 Wellington v Auckland, Wellington, 2006-07

2009 Season

	M	Inn	NO	Runs	HS	Avg	100	50	Ct	St	Balls	Runs	Wkts	Avg	BB	5I	10M
Test																	
FC	7	9	1	110	31	13.75	-	-	1	-	1088	547	21	26.04	6-39	2	-
ODI																	
List A	7	2	1	11	8	11.00	-	-	2	-	298	243	7	34.71	2-32	-	
20/20 Int	1	0	0	0	0		-	-	-	-	6	16	0		-	-	
20/20	5	2	2	4	3*		-	-	3	-	90	129	6	21.50	5-23	1	

Career Performances

	M	Inn	NO	Runs	HS	Avg	100	50	Ct	St	Balls	Runs	Wkts	Avg	BB	5I	10M
Test	19	29	4	152	19*	6.08	-	-	6	-	3534	1981	58	34.15	6-75	1	-
FC	80	97	24	649	44	8.89	-	-	15	-	14484	7204	278	25.91	8-55	12	1
ODI	10	2	2	3	3*		-	-	1	-	453	488	14	34.85	3-68	-	
List A	56	20	16	89	19*	22.25	-	-	10	-	2718	2246	69	32.55	5-35	2	
20/20 Int	4	0	0	0	0		-	-	-	-	78	116	6	19.33	2-30	-	
20/20	17	4	3	5	3*	5.00	-	-	3	-	318	411	21	19.57	5-23	1	

67. How many matches did Pakistan win in the 2006 Test series in England?

O'BRIEN, K. J.   Nottinghamshire

Name: <u>Kevin</u> Joseph O'Brien
Role: Right-hand bat, right-arm medium-fast bowler
Born: 4 March 1984, Dublin, Ireland
County debut: 2009 (one-day)
ODI debut: 2006
Twenty20 Int debut: 2008
Parents: Brendan and Camilla
Family links with cricket: Father former captain of
Ireland. Older brother Niall is Ireland wicket-keeper
and plays for Northamptonshire
Overseas tours: Ireland A to UAE (EurAsia Cricket
Series) 2006, Ireland to Kenya (World Cricket League)
2006-07, to West Indies (Super Eights) 2006-07, to
Kenya (Kenya Tri-Series) 2008, to South Africa
(ICC World Cup Qualifiers) 2009
Extras: Scored close to 250 runs in U19 World Cup 2004. Played for Ireland in
ICC World Twenty20 tournament in England 2009. Had a trial period with
Nottinghamshire in 2009
Best batting: 171* Ireland v Kenya, Nairobi 2008-09
Best bowling: 4-38 Ireland v Scotland, Belfast 2007

2009 Season

	M	Inn	NO	Runs	HS	Avg	100	50	Ct	St	Balls	Runs	Wkts	Avg	BB	5I	10M
Test																	
FC	1	2	0	18	13	9.00	-	-	1	-	84	33	2	16.50	1-9	-	-
ODI																	
List A	14	13	2	299	94	27.18	-	2	4	-	246	276	4	69.00	1-14	-	
20/20 Int	5	5	1	69	39*	17.25	-	-	2	-	42	57	0		-	-	
20/20	10	8	2	100	39*	16.66	-	-	2	-	66	91	2	45.50	2-14	-	

Career Performances

	M	Inn	NO	Runs	HS	Avg	100	50	Ct	St	Balls	Runs	Wkts	Avg	BB	5I	10M
Test																	
FC	13	17	1	517	171*	32.31	1	3	10	-	568	238	11	21.63	4-38	-	-
ODI	35	31	3	884	142	31.57	1	4	18	-	858	757	18	42.05	3-30	-	
List A	74	68	11	1728	142	30.31	2	8	32	-	1865	1691	38	44.50	4-31	-	
20/20 Int	9	8	2	95	39*	15.83	-	-	2	-	102	115	4	28.75	2-15	-	
20/20	14	11	3	126	39*	15.75	-	-	2	-	126	149	6	24.83	2-14	-	

O'BRIEN, N. J.　Northamptonshire

Name: <u>Niall</u> John O'Brien
Role: Left-hand bat, leg-spin bowler,
wicket-keeper
Born: 8 November 1981, Dublin
Height: 5ft 9in **Weight:** 12st
Nickname: Nobby, Hornswoggle
County debut: 2004 (Kent),
2007 (Northamptonshire)
ODI debut: 2006
Twenty20 Int debut: 2008
Place in batting averages: 167th av. 27.12
(2008 43rd av. 45.85)
Parents: Brendan and Camilla
Marital status: Single

Family links with cricket: 'Dad is ex-captain of
Ireland. Brother Kevin is a current Irish international.
All the family played good club cricket.'
Education: Marian College, Ballsbridge, Dublin
Qualifications: 6 Leaving Certificates, Level 2 coaching
Career outside cricket: 'Property developer or footballer'
Overseas tours: Ireland U19 to Sri Lanka (U19 World Cup) 1999-2000; Ireland to
Namibia (ICC Inter-Continental Cup) 2005, to Scotland (European Championship)
2006, to Kenya (ICC World Cricket League) 2006-07, to West Indies (World Cup)
2006-07, to UAE (ICC World Twenty20 qualifiers) 2010 plus Ireland age-group
and A tours; Kent to Spain, France and Guernsey
Overseas teams played for: Railway Union CC, Dublin; Mosman DCC, Sydney
2000-02; University of Port Elizabeth Academy, South Africa 2002; North Sydney
DCC 2003-05
Career highlights to date: 'Playing in the Cricket World Cup. Getting Man of the
Match v Pakistan in World Cup [2006-07]'
Cricket moments to forget: 'Getting stumped v Pakistan in World Cup, needing
20 to win and having hit the previous ball for 6!'
Cricket superstitions: 'None'
Cricketers particularly admired: Steve Waugh, Adam Gilchrist
Young players to look out for: Paul Stirling
Other sports played: Hockey (Railway Union, Dublin), football, golf
Other sports followed: Football (Everton), rugby (Ireland)
Favourite band: Oasis
Relaxations: 'Music, walking my dog, socialising'
Extras: Made Ireland senior debut v Denmark 2002 and has played first-class and
one-day cricket for Ireland, including ODI (debut v Scotland at Ayr 2006) and C&G.

Ireland Cricketer of the Year 2002. Scored 58* as Ireland defeated West Indians in 50-over game in Belfast 2004, winning Man of the Match award. Man of the Match v Pakistan in Kingston in the World Cup 2006-07 (72 plus two catches)
Best batting: 176 Ireland v United Arab Emirates, Windhoek 2005-06
Best bowling: 1-4 Kent v CUCCE, Fenner's 2006

2009 Season

	M	Inn	NO	Runs	HS	Avg	100	50	Ct	St	Balls	Runs	Wkts	Avg	BB	5I	10M
Test																	
FC	9	16	0	434	128	27.12	1	1	34	1	0	0	0		-	-	-
ODI																	
List A	10	10	1	360	82	40.00	-	3	8	2	0	0	0		-	-	
20/20 Int	4	4	0	81	40	20.25	-	-	4	2	0	0	0		-	-	
20/20	9	9	1	231	48*	28.87	-	-	6	7	0	0	0		-	-	

Career Performances

	M	Inn	NO	Runs	HS	Avg	100	50	Ct	St	Balls	Runs	Wkts	Avg	BB	5I	10M
Test																	
FC	78	117	14	3618	176	35.12	9	14	225	25	3	4	1	4.00	1-4	-	-
ODI	33	33	3	815	72	27.16	-	7	24	6	0	0	0		-	-	
List A	106	85	11	2023	95	27.33	-	14	86	30	0	0	0		-	-	
20/20 Int	8	7	0	119	40	17.00	-	-	7	3	0	0	0		-	-	
20/20	44	34	8	545	69	20.96	-	1	19	15	0	0	0		-	-	

68. Name the Bangladesh bowler who took 3-59 and 5-70 in the Second Test in the West Indies in 2009.

ONIONS, G.   Durham

Name: Graham Onions
Role: Right-hand bat, right-arm
fast-medium bowler
Born: 9 September 1982, Gateshead
Height: 6ft 2in **Weight:** 11st 7lbs
Nickname: Wills
County debut: 2004
Test debut: 2009
50 wickets in a season: 2
Place in batting averages: (2008 241st av. 13.22)
Place in bowling averages: 3rd av. 19.95
(2008 47th av. 26.84)
Parents: Maureen and Richard
Marital status: Single
Education: St Thomas More RC Comprehensive
School, Blaydon
Qualifications: 10 GCSEs, GNVQ Advanced Science (Distinction), Level 2 coaching
Career outside cricket: 'Newcastle United manager'
Overseas tours: Durham to Dubai 2005, 2006; England A to Bangladesh 2006-07;
England Performance Programme to India 2007-08; England Lions to India 2007-08;
England to South Africa 2009-10 (one-day series)
Overseas teams played for: South Perth CC 2004
Career highlights to date: 'Being selected in squad for England's NatWest Series
against Pakistan [2006]. National Academy'
Cricket moments to forget: 'Getting out to my dad in a charity game!'
Cricket superstitions: 'Lick my fingers before I run in to bowl'
Cricketers particularly admired: Darren Gough, Paul Collingwood
Other sports played: Badminton (England U17 – now plays for Durham County)
Other sports followed: Football (Newcastle United)
Favourite band: 'No favourite – prefer R&B'
Relaxations: 'Sleep, music, the pub with mates'
Extras: Attended UPE International Cricket Academy, Port Elizabeth 2005. Durham
Young Player of the Year and Bowler of the Year 2006. ECB National Academy
2006-07. Represented England Lions 2007. Part of England's successful Ashes
winning team 2009. Match saviour in two Tests, the first at Centurion and the third at
Cape Town, against South Africa 2009-10 as he held on with nine wickets down to
secure drawn matches for England. England 12-month central contract 2009-10
Best batting: 41 Durham v Yorkshire, Headingley 2007
Best bowling: 8-101 Durham v Warwickshire, Edgbaston 2007

2009 Season

	M	Inn	NO	Runs	HS	Avg	100	50	Ct	St	Balls	Runs	Wkts	Avg	BB	5I	10M
Test	5	5	2	19	17*	6.33	-	-	-	-	739	503	20	25.15	5-38	1	-
FC	14	14	6	52	17*	6.50	-	-	5	-	2572	1377	69	19.95	7-38	5	-
ODI	1	0	0	0	0		-	-	-	-	54	28	1	28.00	1-28	-	
List A	2	1	0	4	4	4.00	-	-	1	-	96	64	2	32.00	1-28	-	
20/20 Int																	
20/20	6	4	3	17	13*	17.00	-	-	-	-	126	146	4	36.50	2-23	-	

Career Performances

	M	Inn	NO	Runs	HS	Avg	100	50	Ct	St	Balls	Runs	Wkts	Avg	BB	5I	10M
Test	5	5	2	19	17*	6.33	-	-	-	-	739	503	20	25.15	5-38	1	-
FC	69	88	27	747	41	12.24	-	-	17	-	10868	6557	222	29.53	8-101	9	-
ODI	4	1	0	1	1	1.00	-	-	1	-	204	185	4	46.25	2-58	-	
List A	52	21	5	107	19	6.68	-	-	8	-	2149	1872	58	32.27	3-39	-	
20/20 Int																	
20/20	19	8	3	54	31	10.80	-	-	4	-	408	437	15	29.13	3-25	-	

ORD, J. E.   Warwickshire

Name: <u>James</u> Edward Ord
Role: Right-hand middle-order bat, occasional right-arm medium/off-spin bowler
Born: 9 November 1987, Birmingham
Height: 5ft 10in **Weight:** 12st 8lbs
Nickname: Ordy, Johnny Bravo, Starters
County debut: 2009 (one-day)
Parents: Malcolm and Jennifer
Marital status: Single
Family links with cricket: 'Grandad, James Simpson Ord, played for Warwickshire and was a member of the Championship winning side of 1951'
Education: Solihull School; Loughborough University

Qualifications: 10 GCSEs, 3 A-levels
Career outside cricket: 'Student'
Overseas tours: Warwickshire Academy to Cape Town 2005-06
Career highlights to date: 'Signing for Warwickshire'
Cricket moments to forget: 'Being relegated with my former club Dorridge CC from Birmingham League division one'
Cricket superstitions: 'None. I'm still searching for one that works!'
Cricketers particularly admired: Mark Waugh, Brian Lara, Damien Martyn, Darren Lehmann

Other sports played: Tennis (Warwickshire Youth county cup squads. School national runners-up in HSBC tournament), rugby (school 1st XV and VII)
Other sports followed: 'Follow most sports, especially at the highest level, but unusually I don't have a team. I watch tennis, rugby (both codes), athletics and football, of course'
Favourite band: Kings of Leon
Relaxations: 'Gym, watching films, eating, wildlife documentaries, TV (*The Simpsons*, *Lost*)'
Extras: Played for ECB Schools v India U19 in 2006. Scored 188* for Warwickshire Academy v Glamorgan and Wales Academy at St Fagans 2006. Played for LUCCE 2007
Opinions on the game: 'Umpires should stand up against throwers/chuckers rather than turn a blind eye.'
Best batting: 9 LUCCE v Hampshire, Rose Bowl 2009

2009 Season

	M	Inn	NO	Runs	HS	Avg	100	50	Ct	St	Balls	Runs	Wkts	Avg	BB	5I	10M
Test																	
FC	1	2	0	10	9	5.00	-	-	-	-	0	0	0		-	-	-
ODI																	
List A	2	1	0	27	27	27.00	-	-	-	-	0	0	0		-	-	
20/20 Int																	
20/20																	

Career Performances

	M	Inn	NO	Runs	HS	Avg	100	50	Ct	St	Balls	Runs	Wkts	Avg	BB	5I	10M
Test																	
FC	1	2	0	10	9	5.00	-	-	-	-	0	0	0		-	-	-
ODI																	
List A	2	1	0	27	27	27.00	-	-	-	-	0	0	0		-	-	
20/20 Int																	
20/20																	

O'SHEA, M. P.   Glamorgan

Name: <u>Michael</u> Peter O'Shea
Role: Right-hand top-order bat,
'part-time' off-spin bowler
Born: 4 September 1987, Cardiff
Height: 5ft 11in **Weight:** 12st
Nickname: Chewey
County debut: 2005
Parents: Paul and June
Marital status: Single
Education: Barry Comprehensive School;
Millfield School
Qualifications: 13 GCSEs
Overseas tours: England U19 to India 2004-05, to
Bangladesh 2005-06; Glamorgan to India 2007-08
Career highlights to date: 'My Championship
debut v Kent'
Cricket moments to forget: 'Getting 0 on my Championship debut'
Cricket superstitions: 'Put left pad on first'
Cricketers particularly admired: Damien Martyn, Andrew Flintoff
Young players to look out for: Rory Hamilton-Brown (Surrey), Karl Brown
(Lancashire), Andy Miller (Warwickshire), Ben Wright (Glamorgan), Greg Wood
(Nottinghamshire)
Other sports played: Rugby (Millfield 1st XV – won national XVs competition)
Other sports followed: Rugby (Cardiff Blues, Wales)
Favourite band: Oasis, Westlife
Extras: Has represented England U15, U16, U17, U19. Played for Wales Minor
Counties in the C&G 2005 and in Minor Counties competitions 2005-07. Released
by Glamorgan at the end of the 2009 season
Best batting: 50 Glamorgan v Kent, Canterbury 2009

2009 Season

	M	Inn	NO	Runs	HS	Avg	100	50	Ct	St	Balls	Runs	Wkts	Avg	BB	5I	10M
Test																	
FC	1	2	0	75	50	37.50	-	1	-	-	0	0	0		-	-	-
ODI																	
List A	2	2	0	59	49	29.50	-	-	-	-	18	19	1	19.00	1-19	-	
20/20 Int																	
20/20	2	1	0	5	5	5.00	-	-	1	-	0	0	0		-	-	

	M	Inn	NO	Runs	HS	Avg	100	50	Ct	St	Balls	Runs	Wkts	Avg	BB	5I	10M
Test																	
FC	6	9	0	137	50	15.22	-	1	1	-	0	0	0		-	-	-
ODI																	
List A	9	9	1	149	49	18.62	-	-	3	-	198	213	4	53.25	2-37	-	
20/20 Int																	
20/20	2	1	0	5	5	5.00	-	-	1	-	0	0	0		-	-	

OSBORNE, M. Essex

Name: Max Osborne
Role: Right-hand bat, right-arm
medium-fast bowler
Born: 21 November 1990, Orsett, Essex
County debut: No first-team appearance
Education: Sawyers Hall College
Extras: Played club cricket for Horndon-on-the-Hill
2006-08 and Brentwood CC 2009. Has represented
Essex at U15, U17 and U19 levels. Played for Essex
2nd XI 2008-09. Essex Academy 2009. Signed a
two-year contract with Essex in September 2009

69. At which venue was a Test match awarded to England in 2006
when Pakistan refused to come out to play?

OWEN, W. T. Glamorgan

Name: William (<u>Will</u>) Thomas Owen
Role: Right-hand bat, right-arm
fast-medium bowler
Born: 2 September 1988, St Asaph,
North Wales
Height: 6ft **Weight:** 13st 11lbs
Nickname: Swillo
County debut: 2007 (*see Extras*)
Parents: Haydn and Stephanie
Marital status: Single
Education: Prestatyn High School; UWIC
Qualifications: GCSEs and A-levels,
Level 2 coaching
Off-season: 'Training'
Career highlights to date: 'My first-class debut
for Glamorgan against Gloucestershire 2007'
Cricketers particularly admired: Simon Jones
Young players to look out for: David Lloyd (Glamorgan Academy)
Other sports played: Rugby (represented North Wales at U12-U15)
Other sports followed: Football (Blackburn Rovers), rugby (Llanelli Scarlets)
Favourite band: Stereophonics
Relaxations: 'Going out with friends, Xbox, golf'
Extras: Played for Wales Minor Counties in Minor Counties competitions 2007.
Due to the truncated nature of his debut match against Gloucestershire (rain wiped out
days 2, 3 and 4) did not bat after having bowled eight overs.
Opinions on cricket: 'Cricket is changing rapidly, with the different formats of the
game encouraging players to improvise new techniques and strategies, making the
game more exciting for the spectators.'

2009 Season (Did not make any first-class or one-day appearances)

Career Performances

	M	Inn	NO	Runs	HS	Avg	100	50	Ct	St	Balls	Runs	Wkts	Avg	BB	5I	10M
Test																	
FC	1	0	0	0	0	-	-	-	-	-	48	37	0	-	-	-	-
ODI																	
List A																	
20/20 Int																	
20/20																	

PALLADINO, A. P.　　　　　　　　Essex

Name: Antonio (<u>Tony</u>) Paul Palladino
Role: Right-hand bat, right-arm fast-medium bowler; all-rounder
Born: 29 June 1983, Whitechapel, London
Height: 6ft **Weight:** 12st 8lbs
Nickname: Dino, TP, Freddie, Italian Stallion
County debut: 2003
Place in batting averages: (2008 234th av. 14.14)
Place in bowling averages: (2008 24th av. 22.88)
Parents: Antonio and Kathleen
Marital status: 'Attached'
Family links with cricket: 'Dad played cricket in the Kent League'
Education: Cardinal Pole Secondary School; Anglia Polytechnic University
Qualifications: 9 GCSEs, Advanced GNVQ Leisure and Tourism
Overseas teams played for: Mount Lawley CC, Perth 2005-06; Namibia 2009-10
Career highlights to date: '6-41 v Kent 2003; 6-68 v Leics 2006; 111 v Hampshire 2nd XI 2006'
Cricket moments to forget: 'Losing to Sussex 2006 in the C&G Trophy when defending nearly 300 and they were 30-4. Felt sick for about a week' (*Just for the record, the fourth Sussex wicket fell at 56 at Chelmsford 2006, but … Ed*)
Cricket superstitions: 'Try and get a corner spot in changing room'
Cricketers particularly admired: Ian Botham, Andy and Grant Flower, Kevin Brooks
Other sports played: Football, golf, snooker
Other sports followed: Football (Chelsea), baseball (Boston Red Sox)
Favourite band: 'Various artists'
Relaxations: 'Computer games, cinema, going out with the lads'
Extras: Represented England U17. Represented ECB U19 2000 and 2001. Played for CUCCE 2003, 2004, 2005. Recorded maiden first-class five-wicket return (6-41) v Kent at Canterbury 2003 in only his second Championship match. Represented British Universities 2005. His 6-68 v Leicestershire at Chelmsford 2006 included a spell of 5-9 in seven overs
Best batting: 53* Namibia v Boland, Windhoek 2009
Best bowling: 6-41 Essex v Kent, Canterbury 2003

2009 Season

	M	Inn	NO	Runs	HS	Avg	100	50	Ct	St	Balls	Runs	Wkts	Avg	BB	5I	10M
Test																	
FC	4	2	0	5	5	2.50	-	-	-	-	594	302	9	33.55	4-68	-	-
ODI																	
List A																	
20/20 Int																	
20/20																	

Career Performances

	M	Inn	NO	Runs	HS	Avg	100	50	Ct	St	Balls	Runs	Wkts	Avg	BB	5I	10M
Test																	
FC	41	46	16	351	41	11.70	-	-	19	-	5576	3118	80	38.97	6-41	2	-
ODI																	
List A	21	10	1	43	16	4.77	-	-	2	-	780	674	22	30.63	3-32	-	
20/20 Int																	
20/20	9	1	1	1	1*		-	-	-	-	162	202	10	20.20	2-3	-	

PANESAR, M. S. Sussex

Name: Mudhsuden (<u>Monty</u>) Singh Panesar
Role: Left-hand bat, slow left-arm bowler
Born: 25 April 1982, Luton
Height: 6ft 1in **Weight:** 12st 7lbs
Nickname: Monty
County debut: 2001 (Northamptonshire)
County cap: 2006 (Northamptonshire)
Test debut: 2005-06
ODI debut: 2006-07
Twenty20 Int debut: 2006-07
50 wickets in a season: 3
Place in batting averages: 264th av. 12.06
Place in bowling averages: 134th av. 54.31
(2008 119th av. 38.12)
Parents: Paramjit and Gursharan
Marital status: Single
Family links with cricket: 'Father used to play cricket'
Education: Stopsley High School, Luton; Bedford Modern School;
Loughborough University
Qualifications: 10 GCSEs, 3 A-levels, Computer Science degree
Overseas tours: Bedford Modern School to Barbados 1999; England U19 to
India 2000-01; Northamptonshire to Grenada 2001-02; British Universities to South

Africa 2002; ECB National Academy to Australia and Sri Lanka 2002-03; England to India 2005-06, to Australia 2006-07, to West Indies (World Cup) 2006-07, to Sri Lanka 2007-08, to New Zealand 2007-08, to India 2008-09, to West Indies 2008-09; England Lions to India 2007-08

Overseas teams played for: Highveld Lions 2009-10
Career highlights to date: 'Playing for England'
Cricketers particularly admired: Sachin Tendulkar
Other sports followed: Football (Luton, Arsenal)
Relaxations: 'Reading'
Player website: www.monty-panesar.com
Extras: Represented England U19. Had match figures of 8-131 on first-class debut v Leicestershire at Northampton 2001, including 4-11 in the second innings. NBC Denis Compton Award for the most promising young Northamptonshire player 2001. Played for LUCCE 2002, 2004. Represented British Universities 2002, 2004, 2005. Winner of the Beard Liberation Front's 'Beard of the Year' award 2006. Had first innings figures of 5-92 in the third Test v Australia 2006-07, becoming the first England spinner to record a five-wicket innings return in a Test at Perth. One of *Wisden*'s Five Cricketers of the Year 2007. Had match figures of 10-187 (4-50/6-137) in the third Test v West Indies at Old Trafford 2007, winning Man of the Match award. England's Man of the [Test] Series v West Indies 2007. His 6-126 in the third Test in Napier was a key contribution to England's 2-1 series win over New Zealand in 2008. Signed for Sussex November 2009

Best batting: 39* Northamptonshire v Worcestershire, Northampton 2005
Best bowling: 7-181 Northamptonshire v Essex, Chelmsford 2005

2009 Season

	M	Inn	NO	Runs	HS	Avg	100	50	Ct	St	Balls	Runs	Wkts	Avg	BB	5I	10M
Test	1	2	1	11	7*	11.00	-	-	-	-	210	115	1	115.00	1-115	-	-
FC	15	22	6	193	38	12.06	-	-	-	-	2705	1195	22	54.31	3-10	-	-
ODI																	
List A	10	4	1	28	17	9.33	-	-	3	-	349	302	8	37.75	2-27	-	
20/20 Int																	
20/20	9	3	1	1	1*	.50	-	-	1	-	162	167	1	167.00	1-22	-	

Career Performances

	M	Inn	NO	Runs	HS	Avg	100	50	Ct	St	Balls	Runs	Wkts	Avg	BB	5I	10M
Test	39	51	17	187	26	5.50	-	-	9	-	9042	4331	126	34.37	6-37	8	1
FC	110	142	48	789	39*	8.39	-	-	25	-	24591	11771	354	33.25	7-181	19	3
ODI	26	8	3	26	13	5.20	-	-	3	-	1308	980	24	40.83	3-25	-	
List A	54	22	10	126	17*	10.50	-	-	10	-	2437	1820	51	35.68	5-20	1	
20/20 Int	1	1	0	1	1	1.00	-	-	-	-	24	40	2	20.00	2-40	-	
20/20	19	6	2	7	3*	1.75	-	-	2	-	366	461	12	38.41	2-22	-	

PARDOE, M. G.   Worcestershire

Name: Matthew (<u>Matt</u>) Graham Pardoe
Role: Left-hand bat, left-arm medium bowler;
all-rounder
Born: 5 January 1991, Stourbridge, Worcestershire
Height: 6ft 1in **Weight:** 11st 2lbs
Nickname: Pards, Wedgey
County debut: No first team appearance
Parents: Allan and Elaine
Marital status: Single
Family links with cricket: Father and brother
both play
Education: Haybridge High School and Sixth
Form College
Qualifications: 11 GCSEs, 3 A Levels
Off-season: 'Playing cricket in Perth, Australia'
Overseas tours: Worcestershire U13 to South Africa 2003
Overseas teams played for: Swan Valley CC, Perth, 2009-10
Career highlights to date: 'Scoring an unbeaten century at New Road for
Worcestershire 2nd XI v Leicestershire 2nd XI'
Cricket moments to forget: 'A mis-field for 4 when 12th man v New Zealand in
front of a full house at New Road. What made it worse was that my mates were
behind me in the crowd and started jeering…'
Cricket superstitions: 'Always put my helmet on before my gloves'
Favourite sledging line: '"Bowl him a piano – see if he can play that!"'
Cricketers particularly admired: Matthew Hayden, Brian Lara, Graeme Hick,
Marcus Trescothick – 'to name a few'
Young players to look out for: Neil Pinner (Worcestershire), Sam Kelsall
(Nottinghamshire)
Other sports played: 'Used to play football and rugby for the school'
Other sports followed: Football (Wolverhampton Wanderers), rugby league
(St Helens)
Favourite band: Linkin Park, Oasis
Extras: MCC Young Player of the Year 2007. Worcestershire Academy Player of the
Year 2007.

PARK, G. T.   Derbyshire

Name: <u>Garry</u> Terence Park
Role: Right-hand bat, right-arm
medium bowler, wicket-keeper
Born: 19 April 1983, Empangeni,
South Africa
Height: 5ft 7in **Weight:** 10st 4lbs
Nickname: Parkie, Whippet
County debut: 2005 (Durham, one-day),
2006 (Durham, first-class), 2009 (Derbyshire)
Place in batting averages: 63rd av. 42.36
(2008 176th av. 25.28)
Parents: Mike Park and Christine Reeves
Marital status: Single
Family links with cricket: Brothers Sean and

Craig play for Cambridgeshire and Huntingdonshire
respectively
Education: Eshowe High School, South Africa; Anglia Ruskin University, Cambridge
Qualifications: Matric Exemption (South Africa), Levels 1 and 2 coaching
Career outside cricket: Coaching
Off-season: 'Playing cricket in KwaZulu-Natal, South Africa, for Zululand CC'
Overseas tours: CUCCE to Grenada 2003
Overseas teams played for: Eshow CC; Crusaders CC, Durban 2005;
Zululand CC 2006-07, 2009-10
Career highlights to date: 'Hitting Tino Best for 20 off the over. Maiden century
at Headingley to help Durham avoid dropping to Div 2. Reaching 1000 runs for
Derbyshire in 2009, and scoring a career-best 178* v Kent'
Cricket moments to forget: 'Being peppered by Tino Best at the Riverside,
Durham v West Indies A'
Cricket superstitions: 'None'
Cricketers particularly admired: Shivnarine Chanderpaul, Dale Benkenstein,
Jonty Rhodes, Ricky Ponting
Young players to look out for: Scott Borthwick (Durham)
Other sports played: Hockey (KwaZulu-Natal U15, U19), rugby
(KwaZulu-Natal U14), golf, tennis, squash, fishing
Other sports followed: Rugby (Natal Sharks)
Favourite band: Matchbox 20, Blink 182
Relaxations: 'Golf, music, travelling'
Extras: Played for CUCCE 2003-05. Durham 2nd XI Player of the Year 2006.
Durham 2nd XI Batsman of the Year 2007. Signed for Derbyshire in October 2008
Best batting: 178* Derbyshire v Kent, Derby 2009
Best bowling: 3-25 Derbyshire v Surrey, Derby 2009

2009 Season

	M	Inn	NO	Runs	HS	Avg	100	50	Ct	St	Balls	Runs	Wkts	Avg	BB	5I	10M
Test																	
FC	16	27	2	1059	178*	42.36	2	8	14	-	543	311	7	44.42	3-25	-	-
ODI																	
List A	13	11	2	297	64	33.00	-	1	2	-	353	328	6	54.66	2-40	-	
20/20 Int																	
20/20	10	9	0	172	50	19.11	-	1	1	-	162	195	11	17.72	3-23	-	

Career Performances

	M	Inn	NO	Runs	HS	Avg	100	50	Ct	St	Balls	Runs	Wkts	Avg	BB	5I	10M
Test																	
FC	34	57	8	1904	178*	38.85	3	12	35	-	933	631	9	70.11	3-25	-	-
ODI																	
List A	29	25	5	495	64	24.75	-	1	9	-	377	343	6	57.16	2-40	-	
20/20 Int																	
20/20	19	14	2	244	50	20.33	-	1	3	-	168	202	11	18.36	3-23	-	

PARNELL, W. D.   Kent

Name: <u>Wayne</u> Dillon Parnell
Role: Left-arm bat, left-arm medium-fast bowler
Born: 30 July 1989, Port Elizabeth
Nickname: Parny, Pigeon
County debut: 2009
Test debut: 2009-10
ODI debut: 2008-09
Twenty20 Int debut: 2008-09
Place in bowling averages: 54th av. 31.11
Education: Grey High School
Overseas teams played for: Eastern Province; Warriors
Overseas tours: South Africa U19 to Malaysia (U19 World Cup) 2008, South Africa Emerging Players to Australia (Emerging Players Tournament) 2008, South Africa to Australia 2008-09, to England (ICC Twenty20) 2009
Extras: Youngest player ever to be awarded a national contract by Cricket South Africa, early in 2009, Signed for Kent as an overseas player in April 2009. Dropped from South African squad for first two Tests against England 2009-10 but made Test debut Johannesburg, January, 2010. Signed for Delhi Daredevils (IPL) 2010
Best batting: 90 Kent v Glamorgan, Canterbury 2009
Best bowling: 4-7 Eastern Province v KwaZulu-Natal, Port Elizabeth, 2006-07

2009 Season

	M	Inn	NO	Runs	HS	Avg	100	50	Ct	St	Balls	Runs	Wkts	Avg	BB	5I	10M
Test																	
FC	5	6	1	183	90	36.60	-	2	-	-	999	529	17	31.11	4-78	-	-
ODI																	
List A	6	3	0	51	22	17.00	-	-	4	-	263	235	7	33.57	3-27	-	
20/20 Int	6	0	0	0	0		-	-	-	-	125	119	9	13.22	4-13	-	
20/20	8	1	1	0	0*		-	-	-	-	167	170	11	15.45	4-13	-	

Career Performances

	M	Inn	NO	Runs	HS	Avg	100	50	Ct	St	Balls	Runs	Wkts	Avg	BB	5I	10M
Test																	
FC	19	24	3	436	90	20.76	-	2	2	-	3113	1629	49	33.24	4-7	-	-
ODI	7	1	1	10	10*		-	-	1	-	384	384	17	22.58	5-57	1	
List A	30	18	8	219	26*	21.90	-	-	8	-	1408	1301	49	26.55	5-57	1	
20/20 Int	8	0	0	0	0		-	-	-	-	173	192	11	17.45	4-13	-	
20/20	23	7	5	32	11*	16.00	-	-	2	-	461	495	24	20.62	4-13	-	

PARRY, S. D. Lancashire

Name: Stephen David Parry
Role: Right-hand bat, slow left-arm bowler
Born: 12 January 1986, Manchester
Height: 6ft **Weight:** 11st 7lbs
Nickname: Pazza
County debut: 2007
Parents: David and Ann-Marie
Marital status: Single
Education: Audenshaw High School,
Greater Manchester
Qualifications: 9 GCSEs, 4 A-levels
Overseas teams played for: Eastern Suburbs,
Sydney 2005; Bundalaguah, Melbourne 2006, 2007;
Gosnells, Perth 2008
Career highlights to date: 'Getting first full-time
contract with Lancashire'
Cricket superstitions: 'None'
Cricketers particularly admired: Shane Warne
Other sports played: Football, table tennis
Other sports followed: Football (Man City), Australian Rules (St Kilda)
Favourite band: The Kooks

Extras: Lancashire Young Player of the Year. Played for Cumberland in Minor Counties competitions 2005, 2006. Recorded maiden first-class five-wicket return (5-23) on debut v DUCCE at Durham 2007. NBC Denis Compton Award for most promising young Lancashire player 2009
Best batting: 2 Lancashire v Durham, Old Trafford, 2009
Best bowling: 5-23 Lancashire v DUCCE, Durham 2007

2009 Season

	M	Inn	NO	Runs	HS	Avg	100	50	Ct	St	Balls	Runs	Wkts	Avg	BB	5I	10M
Test																	
FC	2	2	0	3	2	1.50	-	-	1	-	408	210	4	52.50	2-51	-	-
ODI																	
List A	9	4	0	44	31	11.00	-	-	1	-	396	252	13	19.38	2-12	-	
20/20 Int																	
20/20	9	1	0	4	4	4.00	-	-	2	-	198	223	10	22.30	3-20	-	

Career Performances

	M	Inn	NO	Runs	HS	Avg	100	50	Ct	St	Balls	Runs	Wkts	Avg	BB	5I	10M
Test																	
FC	3	2	0	3	2	1.50	-	-	1	-	523	256	9	28.44	5-23	1	-
ODI																	
List A	9	4	0	44	31	11.00	-	-	1	-	396	252	13	19.38	2-12	-	
20/20 Int																	
20/20	9	1	0	4	4	4.00	-	-	2	-	198	223	10	22.30	3-20	-	

PARSONS, T. W.   Hampshire

Name: Thomas (<u>Tom</u>) William Parsons
Role: Right-hand lower-order bat, right-arm fast-medium bowler
Born: 2 May 1987, Melbourne, Australia
Height: 6ft 3in **Weight:** 13st 5lbs
Nickname: Teeps, TP, Jonny Teepson
County debut: 2007 (one-day, Kent), 2008 (first-class, Kent)
Parents: Richard and Christine
Marital status: Single
Family links with cricket: 'Dad played Middlesex 2nd XI. Grandfathers, uncles and cousins have all played or play'
Education: Maidstone Grammar School; Loughborough University
Qualifications: 11 GCSEs, 3 A-levels, Level 2 cricket coach

Career highlights to date: 'First-class debut for LUCCE against Worcestershire. First-team debut for Kent v Sri Lanka A. Getting Vikram Solanki out for my first first-class wicket. Taking two wickets on debut for Kent – two players who have played Test match cricket for Sri Lanka.'

Cricket moments to forget: 'Getting hit on the head without a helmet in a school game, meaning I missed all my A-levels and was hospitalised for a while. Getting out needing two to win off the last ball for LUCCE against Yorkshire'

Cricket superstitions: 'Sliding my bat over the crease after every boundary'

Cricketers particularly admired: Glenn McGrath, Matthew Hoggard, Nick Knight, Ian Bell

Young players to look out for: Johan Malcolm, Arun Harinath, Jigar Naik, James Day, John Bowden, Dom O'Connell, Jonty Parsons, Robert Hulme

Other sports played: Hockey (Loughborough Town), rugby (Rutherford Hall 1st XV), squash, golf

Other sports followed: Football (Arsenal, Gillingham), rugby (Harlequins)

Favourite band: Bloc Party

Relaxations: 'Films, going out with friends, watching sport'

Extras: Kent Academy 2005. Played for LUCCE 2007. Awarded a development contract at Hampshire for 2009. Released by Hampshire at the end of the 2009 season

Opinions on cricket: 'Enjoy every minute of it!'

Best batting: 12 LUCCE v Worcestershire, Kidderminster 2008

Best bowling: 3-39 Hampshire v LUCCE, Rose Bowl 2009

2009 Season

	M	Inn	NO	Runs	HS	Avg	100	50	Ct	St	Balls	Runs	Wkts	Avg	BB	5I	10M
Test																	
FC	1	1	0	0	0	0.00	-	-	-	-	108	63	3	21.00	3-39	-	-
ODI																	
List A																	
20/20 Int																	
20/20																	

Career Performances

	M	Inn	NO	Runs	HS	Avg	100	50	Ct	St	Balls	Runs	Wkts	Avg	BB	5I	10M
Test																	
FC	6	6	1	24	12	4.80	-	-	-	-	707	375	11	34.09	3-39	-	-
ODI																	
List A	1	0	0	0	0		-	-	-	-	36	41	2	20.50	2-41	-	
20/20 Int																	
20/20																	

PATEL, A.   Nottinghamshire

Name: Akhil Patel
Role: Left-hand opening bat, left-arm wrist-spin
bowler; all-rounder
Born: 18 June 1990, Nottingham
Height: 5ft 10in **Weight:** 13st
Nickname: Shaq, Killer, Sneaky, Slidey
County debut: 2007 (Derbyshire), 2009
(Nottinghamshire)
Parents: Rohit and Sejal
Marital status: Single
Family links with cricket: 'Dad played a good
standard of club cricket in Leicestershire and
Derbyshire premier leagues. Brother Samit plays
first-class cricket for Nottinghamshire and England!'
Education: Trent College; Kimberley Comprehensive

Qualifications: 7 GCSEs, GNVQ in Leisure and Tourism, 2 A-levels (PE and
Business Studies)
Career outside cricket: 'Want to be a coach after cricket'
Off-season: 'I intend to go abroad to play some cricket – I'll also be training with
Nottinghamshire in the English winter!'
Overseas tours: Derbyshire Academy to South Africa 2008
Career highlights to date: 'Making my second-team debut against Lancashire, and
also in the same year making my first-class debut against CUCCE. Also making my
Championship debut v Sussex in 2009, a vital game for us to stay in second place.
Making my Pro40 debut, again v Sussex, which was on Sky.'
Cricket moments to forget: 'Dropping three catches against Dunstall CC in a
Derbyshire Premier League game. Being run out by my brother v Hampshire,
live on Sky!'
Cricket superstitions: 'Put right pad on first, and always run out to the crease
when batting'
Cricketers particularly admired: Sachin Tendulkar, Shane Warne, Stephen Fleming,
Brian Lara, Andrew Jackman, Kumar Sangakkara, Michael Clarke
Young players to look out for: Samit Patel, Alex Hales, Luke Fletcher (all
Nottinghamshire), James Vince (Hampshire)
Other sports played: 'Used to play rugby and hockey at a good standard at my old
school; try to play football'
Other sports followed: Football (Arsenal), American football (San Francisco 49ers)
Favourite band: Chris Brown, Lil Wayne, Oasis
Relaxations: 'Listening to music, watching films, going out with friends and team-
mates!'

Extras: Broke Trent College U13 record for the most runs in a season. Youngest player to appear for Trent College 1st XI. Third-youngest player to appear in first-class cricket for Derbyshire

Opinions on cricket: 'Cricket is getting to the stage where it's becoming more of an entertainment with the likes of Twenty20. Should play four-day cricket in the Second XI Championship!'

Best batting: 69* Nottinghamshire v OUCCE, The Parks 2009
Best bowling: 1-34 Nottinghamshire v OUCCE, The Parks 2009

2009 Season

	M	Inn	NO	Runs	HS	Avg	100	50	Ct	St	Balls	Runs	Wkts	Avg	BB	5I	10M
Test																	
FC	2	4	1	110	69*	36.66	-	1	2	-	89	46	1	46.00	1-34	-	-
ODI																	
List A	4	4	0	92	41	23.00	-	-	1	-	30	34	2	17.00	2-34	-	
20/20 Int																	
20/20																	

Career Performances

	M	Inn	NO	Runs	HS	Avg	100	50	Ct	St	Balls	Runs	Wkts	Avg	BB	5I	10M
Test																	
FC	3	6	2	153	69*	38.25	-	1	2	-	143	76	1	76.00	1-34	-	-
ODI																	
List A	4	4	0	92	41	23.00	-	-	1	-	30	34	2	17.00	2-34	-	
20/20 Int																	
20/20																	

70. Which Pakistan batsman was only 19 when he became the youngest player to score a Test double century?

PATEL, J. S.   Warwickshire

Name: <u>Jeetan</u> Shashi Patel
Role: Right-hand bat, right-arm offbreak bowler
Born: 7 May 1980, Wellington, New Zealand
County debut: 2009
Test debut: 2006
ODI debut: 2005
Twenty20 Int debut: 2005-06
Overseas tours: New Zealand to Zimbabwe
(Videocon Triangular Series) 2005, to South Africa
2005-06, to West Indies (World Cup) 2006-07, to
India (ICC Champions Trophy) 2006-07, to Australia
2007-08 (one-day series), to South Africa 2007-08,
to Australia 2008-09 (one-day series), to Bangladesh
2008-09, to Sri Lanka 2009, to South Africa (ICC
Champions Trophy) 2009

Overseas teams played for: Wellington, North Island
Extras: Signed for Warwickshire in March 2009
Best batting: 120 Warwickshire v Yorkshire, Edgbaston 2009
Best bowling: 6-32 Wellington v Otago, Queenstown Events Centre 2004-05

2009 Season

	M	Inn	NO	Runs	HS	Avg	100	50	Ct	St	Balls	Runs	Wkts	Avg	BB	5I	10M
Test																	
FC	3	4	1	131	120	43.66	1	-	1	-	564	399	6	66.50	3-112	-	-
ODI																	
List A	7	1	0	0	0	0.00	-	-	2	-	363	234	7	33.42	2-23	-	
20/20 Int																	
20/20	10	0	0	0	0		-	-	4	-	226	270	15	18.00	3-15	-	

Career Performances

	M	Inn	NO	Runs	HS	Avg	100	50	Ct	St	Balls	Runs	Wkts	Avg	BB	5I	10M
Test	9	12	2	131	27*	13.10	-	-	5	-	2556	1289	33	39.06	5-110	1	-
FC	81	95	33	1224	120	19.74	1	3	27	-	14656	7159	171	41.86	6-32	5	-
ODI	39	13	7	88	34	14.66	-	-	12	-	1804	1513	42	36.02	3-11	-	
List A	97	48	18	295	34	9.83	-	-	29	-	4639	3685	100	36.85	4-16	-	
20/20 Int	11	4	1	9	5	3.00	-	-	4	-	199	269	16	16.81	3-20	-	
20/20	33	10	3	40	12	5.71	-	-	12	-	676	790	42	18.80	3-15	-	

PATEL, S. R.   Nottinghamshire

Name: <u>Samit</u> Rohit Patel
Role: Right-hand bat, left-arm orthodox
spin bowler; all-rounder
Born: 30 November 1984, Leicester
Height: 5ft 8in
Nickname: Pilchy
County debut: 2002
County cap: 2008
ODI debut: 2008
Place in batting averages: 135th av. 31.57
(2008 20th av. 51.42)
Place in bowling averages: 123rd av. 47.21
(2008 118th av. 37.91)
Parents: Rohit and Sejal
Marital status: Single

Family links with cricket: Father local league cricketer and brother Akhil
is with Nottinghamshire
Education: Worksop College
Qualifications: 7 GCSEs, 2 A-levels
Career outside cricket: 'Want to be a coach'
Overseas tours: England U17 to Australia 2001; England U19 to Australia and (U19
World Cup) New Zealand 2001-02, to Australia 2002-03, to Bangladesh (U19 World
Cup) 2003-04; England to India (one-day series) 2008, to West Indies (one-day series)
2008-09; England Lions to New Zealand 2008-09
Cricket moments to forget: 'Playing at Headingley in the Twenty20 Cup against
Yorkshire, where I got hit for 28 in an over by Michael Lumb'
Cricket superstitions: 'Put my right pad on first'
Cricketers particularly admired: Sachin Tendulkar, Brian Lara
Young players to look out for: Akhil Patel (Nottinghamshire)
Other sports played: Rugby, hockey (both for Worksop College)
Other sports followed: Football (Nottingham Forest)
Favourite band: G-Unit
Relaxations: 'Listening to music; playing snooker; just generally relaxing'
Extras: Made Nottinghamshire 2nd XI debut in 1999, aged 14. Winner of inaugural
BBC *Test Match Special* U15 Young Cricketer of the Year Award 2000. Represented
England U19 2002, 2003 (captain in one-day series 2003) and 2004. Scored maiden
Championship hundred (156) v Middlesex at Lord's 2006, progressing from century
to 150 in 17 balls. Named in England's provisional squad for the Champions Trophy
2008. Part of England's ODI squad against South Africa 2008. Spent two months of
the 2009-10 winter at the Darren Lehmann Academy in Adelaide. Signed a new three-
year contract with Nottinghamshire in January 2010
Best batting: 176 Nottinghamshire v Gloucestershire, Bristol 2007

Best bowling: 6-84 Nottinghamshire v Sussex, Trent Bridge 2009

2009 Season

	M	Inn	NO	Runs	HS	Avg	100	50	Ct	St	Balls	Runs	Wkts	Avg	BB	5I	10M
Test																	
FC	17	26	0	821	95	31.57	-	4	11	-	2906	1558	33	47.21	6-84	2	-
ODI																	
List A	17	16	2	296	58	21.14	-	1	7	-	630	534	20	26.70	6-13	1	
20/20 Int																	
20/20	10	7	1	130	37	21.66	-	-	1	-	216	262	9	29.11	2-20	-	

Career Performances

	M	Inn	NO	Runs	HS	Avg	100	50	Ct	St	Balls	Runs	Wkts	Avg	BB	5I	10M
Test																	
FC	60	90	6	3680	176	43.80	9	20	32	-	5425	2761	67	41.20	6-84	2	-
ODI	11	5	0	116	31	23.20	-	-	4	-	340	319	11	29.00	5-41	1	
List A	102	85	14	2092	114	29.46	1	10	26	-	2664	2279	86	26.50	6-13	2	
20/20 Int																	
20/20	54	49	9	1003	84*	25.07	-	6	19	-	787	981	37	26.51	3-11	-	

PATTERSON, S. A.   Yorkshire

Name: <u>Steven</u> Andrew Patterson
Role: Right-hand bat, right-arm
fast-medium bowler
Born: 3 October 1983, Hull
Height: 6ft 4in **Weight:** 14st
Nickname: Dead
County debut: 2005
Place in bowling averages: (2008 35th av. 25.36)
Parents: Sue and Alan
Marital status: Single
Education: Malet Lambert School; St Mary's Sixth
Form College; Leeds University
Qualifications: 11 GCSEs, 3 A-levels, BSc Maths,
Level 2 coaching
Overseas tours: MCC A to UAE and Oman 2004
Overseas teams played for: Suburbs New Lynn CC, Auckland 2005-06
Career highlights to date: 'Making my first-class debut for Yorkshire'
Cricket moments to forget: 'Going in as nightwatchman and getting a
first-ball duck!'
Cricket superstitions: 'Not really'
Cricketers particularly admired: Glenn McGrath, Allan Donald

Young players to look out for: Adam Lyth, James Lee (both Yorkshire)
Other sports played: Football, golf, badminton, skiing, scuba diving
Favourite band: Coldplay
Relaxations: 'Playing guitar, travelling, reading'
Extras: Played for Yorkshire Board XI in the 2003 C&G. 2nd XI cap 2006.
Signed a new two-year contract in October 2008
Best batting: 46 Yorkshire v Lancashire, Old Trafford 2006
Best bowling: 4-41 Yorkshire v CUCCE, Fenner's 2009

2009 Season

	M	Inn	NO	Runs	HS	Avg	100	50	Ct	St	Balls	Runs	Wkts	Avg	BB	5I	10M
Test																	
FC	4	4	2	45	30*	22.50	-	-	-	-	661	409	7	58.42	4-41	-	-
ODI																	
List A	8	2	2	14	14*		-	-	-	-	317	255	7	36.42	3-35	-	
20/20 Int																	
20/20	2	1	0	0	0	0.00	-	-	-	-	36	57	1	57.00	1-42	-	

Career Performances

	M	Inn	NO	Runs	HS	Avg	100	50	Ct	St	Balls	Runs	Wkts	Avg	BB	5I	10M
Test																	
FC	15	16	5	166	46	15.09	-	-	3	-	1806	983	22	44.68	4-41	-	-
ODI																	
List A	26	13	12	83	25*	83.00	-	-	3	-	1125	943	23	41.00	3-11	-	
20/20 Int																	
20/20	2	1	0	0	0	0.00	-	-	-	-	36	57	1	57.00	1-42	-	

71. What is the highest Test match innings total made by Bangladesh to date?

PATTINSON, D. J.   Nottinghamshire

Name: <u>Darren</u> John Pattinson
Role: Right-hand bat, right-arm fast-medium bowler
Born: 2 August 1979, Grimsby, Lincolnshire
County debut: 2008
County cap: 2008
Test debut: 2008
Place in batting averages: 261st av. 12.75
Place in bowling averages: 142nd av. 87.20
(2008 36th av. 25.61)
Family links with cricket: Brother James was part
of Australia's U19 World Cup squad in 2008
Career outside cricket: Former roofer
Overseas teams played for: Dandenong, Melbourne,
Australia; Victoria 2006-07 –
Extras: Born in Grimsby, but raised in Australia.

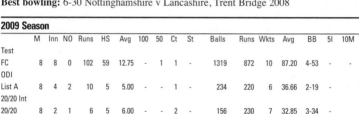

Holds a British passport and is not considered an overseas player. Surprise selection
for England's second Test match against South Africa, 2008. Brother made debut for
Victoria 2008-09
Best batting: 59 Nottinghamshire v Durham, Riverside 2009
Best bowling: 6-30 Nottinghamshire v Lancashire, Trent Bridge 2008

2009 Season

	M	Inn	NO	Runs	HS	Avg	100	50	Ct	St	Balls	Runs	Wkts	Avg	BB	5I	10M
Test																	
FC	8	8	0	102	59	12.75	-	1	1	-	1319	872	10	87.20	4-53	-	-
ODI																	
List A	8	4	2	10	5	5.00	-	-	1	-	234	220	6	36.66	2-19	-	
20/20 Int																	
20/20	8	2	1	6	5	6.00	-	-	2	-	156	230	7	32.85	3-34	-	

Career Performances

	M	Inn	NO	Runs	HS	Avg	100	50	Ct	St	Balls	Runs	Wkts	Avg	BB	5I	10M
Test	1	2	0	21	13	10.50	-	-	-	-	181	96	2	48.00	2-95	-	-
FC	29	34	3	326	59	10.51	-	1	3	-	4898	2793	78	35.80	6-30	5	-
ODI																	
List A	32	14	5	57	13*	6.33	-	-	10	-	1241	1046	40	26.15	4-29	-	
20/20 Int																	
20/20	17	4	2	14	5	7.00	-	-	3	-	309	419	15	27.93	3-18	-	

PAYNE, D. A.   Gloucestershire

Name: <u>David</u> Alan Payne
Role: Left-hand bat, left-arm fast-medium bowler
Born: 15 February 1991, Poole, Dorset
County debut: 2009 (one-day)
Overseas tours: England U19 to South Africa 2009, to Bangladesh 2009, to New Zealand (ICC World Cup) 2009-10

Extras: Ex-Academy player who signed a two-year development contract in August 2009. Has also represented Dorset at U13, U15 and U17 level, and in the Minor Counties Championship 2009. Played for Gloucestershire 2nd XI 2008-09, and for Bournemouth CC (Southern Premier League) 2008-09. Took 4-19 in England U19 World Cup quarter-final defeat to West Indies in January 2010 to round off an impressive run of performances in the tournament

2009 Season

	M	Inn	NO	Runs	HS	Avg	100	50	Ct	St	Balls	Runs	Wkts	Avg	BB	5I	10M
Test																	
FC																	
ODI																	
List A	3	2	2	4	3*		-	-	1	-	78	74	6	12.33	3-10	-	
20/20 Int																	
20/20																	

Career Performances

	M	Inn	NO	Runs	HS	Avg	100	50	Ct	St	Balls	Runs	Wkts	Avg	BB	5I	10M
Test																	
FC																	
ODI																	
List A	3	2	2	4	3*		-	-	1	-	78	74	6	12.33	3-10	-	
20/20 Int																	
20/20																	

PETERS, S. D.   Northamptonshire

Name: <u>Stephen</u> David Peters
Role: Right-hand bat, leg-break bowler
Born: 10 December 1978, Harold Wood, Essex
Height: 5ft 11in **Weight:** 11st 7lbs
Nickname: Pedro, Geezer
County debut: 1996 (Essex),
2002 (Worcestershire), 2006 (Northamptonshire)
County cap: 2002 (Worcestershire colours),
2007 (Northamptonshire)
1000 runs in a season: 3
Place in batting averages: 54th av. 43.75
(2008 59th av. 41.26)
Parents: Lesley and Brian
Marital status: Single
Family links with cricket: 'All family is linked
with Upminster CC'

Education: Coopers Company and Coborn School
Qualifications: 9 GCSEs, Level 2 coaching
Career outside cricket: 'Hopefully hard work and fun!'
Off-season: 'Golf, and working hard to push my career outside cricket'
Overseas tours: Essex U14 to Barbados; Essex U15 to Hong Kong; England U19
to Pakistan 1996-97, to South Africa (including U19 World Cup) 1997-98
Overseas teams played for: Cornwall CC, Auckland 2001-02; Willetton CC,
Perth 2002-03
Career highlights to date: 'Winning B&H Cup in 1998 with Essex.
Northamptonshire cap 2007, Every hundred I get'
Cricket moments to forget: 'Running myself out for a pair against Durham
in 2003. Any pair, or zero, or dropped catch!'
Cricket superstitions: 'Binned them all!'
Cricketers particularly admired: 'Anyone who has played at the top level'
Young players to look out for: James Taylor (Leicestershire)
Other sports played: Golf, football, badminton
Other sports followed: Football (West Ham United)
Injuries: 'Broken thumb – out for four weeks'
Favourite band: Rooster, Keane
Relaxations: 'Movies, wine'
Extras: Sir John Hobbs Silver Jubilee Memorial Prize 1994. Represented England at
U14, U15, U17 and U19. Scored century (110) on Essex first-class debut v Cambridge
University at Fenner's 1996, aged 17 years 194 days. Essex Young Player of the Year
1996. Man of the Match in the U19 World Cup final in South Africa 1997-98 (107)
Opinions on cricket: 'Too many for my own good, probably!'

Best batting: 178 Northamptonshire v Essex, Northampton 2006
Best bowling: 1-19 Essex v OUCCE, Chelmsford 1999

2009 Season

	M	Inn	NO	Runs	HS	Avg	100	50	Ct	St	Balls	Runs	Wkts	Avg	BB	5I	10M
Test																	
FC	14	25	1	1050	175	43.75	3	5	12	-	0	0	0		-	-	-
ODI																	
List A	8	8	1	148	69	21.14	-	1	3	-	0	0	0		-	-	
20/20 Int																	
20/20	2	2	1	61	61*	61.00	-	1	1	-	0	0	0		-	-	

Career Performances

	M	Inn	NO	Runs	HS	Avg	100	50	Ct	St	Balls	Runs	Wkts	Avg	BB	5I	10M
Test																	
FC	178	304	25	9365	178	33.56	21	46	137	-	35	31	1	31.00	1-19	-	-
ODI																	
List A	151	139	9	2832	107	21.78	2	16	43	-	0	0	0		-	-	
20/20 Int																	
20/20	15	12	2	143	61*	14.30	-	1	4	-	0	0	0		-	-	

PETERSON, R. J.   Derbyshire

Name: <u>Robin</u> John Peterson
Role: Left-hand bat, slow left-arm orthodox bowler
Born: 4 August 1979, Port Elizabeth, Cape Province
Test debut: 2002-03
ODI debut: 2002-03
Twenty20 Int debut: 2005-06
Overseas tours: South Africa to Sri Lanka (Champions Trophy) 2002; to Bangladesh 2002-03; to Pakistan 2003-04, to India 2004-05; to New Zealand 2007; to Bangladesh 2007-08, to Australia 2007-08 (one-day series), to Bangladesh 2008-09 (one-day series), to Australia 2008-09 (one-day series)
Overseas teams played for: Eastern Province; Warriors; Cape Cobras 2009-10
Extras: Played for South Africa U19 in 1998 World Cup. Was hit for 28 runs (four fours and two sixes, a Test match record) off a single over by Brian Lara (West Indies v South Africa, Johannesburg 2003-04). Signed for Derbyshire as a Kolpak player in November 2009
Best batting: 130 Eastern Province v Gauteng, Johannesburg 2002-03
Best bowling: 6-67 Eastern Province v Border, East London, 1999-2000

2009 Season (Did not make any first-class or one-day appearances)

Career Performances

	M	Inn	NO	Runs	HS	Avg	100	50	Ct	St	Balls	Runs	Wkts	Avg	BB	5I	10M
Test	6	7	1	163	61	27.16	-	1	5	-	959	497	14	35.50	5-33	1	-
FC	91	143	18	3164	130	25.31	5	10	40	-	16309	8271	240	34.46	6-67	11	1
ODI	35	15	4	147	36	13.36	-	-	7	-	1252	992	17	58.35	2-26	-	
List A	126	87	10	1893	101	24.58	1	11	40	-	5039	3715	130	28.57	7-24	4	
20/20 Int	5	2	0	42	34	21.00	-	-	2	-	65	86	6	14.33	3-30	-	
20/20	33	29	3	478	72*	18.38	-	2	6	-	592	647	33	19.60	3-24	-	

PETTINI, M. L. Essex

Name: <u>Mark</u> Lewis Pettini
Role: Right-hand bat, occasional
wicket-keeper, county captain
Born: 7 August 1983, Brighton
Height: 5ft 10in **Weight:** 11st 6lbs
Nickname: Swampy, the Carp
County debut: 2001
County cap: 2006
1000 runs in a season: 1
1st-Class 200s: 1
Place in batting averages: 83rd av. 39.54
(2008 78th av. 37.21)
Parents: Pauline and Max
Marital status: Single

Family links with cricket: 'Brother plays'
Education: Comberton Village College and Hills Road Sixth Form College,
Cambridge; Cardiff University
Qualifications: 10 GCSEs, 3 A-levels, Level 1 cricket coaching
Overseas tours: England U19 to Australia and (U19 World Cup) New Zealand
2001-02; MCC to Sierra Leone and Nigeria; Essex to Cape Town
Overseas teams played for: Rockingham-Mandurah CC, Perth 2005-07; Northern
Jets, Adelaide
Career highlights to date: 'Winning two Pro40 titles with Essex. Being made Essex
captain [2007]. Winning the Friends Provident Trophy 2008'
Cricket moments to forget: 'Relegation to division two of Pro40 2007'
Cricket superstitions: 'Hundreds'
Cricketers particularly admired: Graham Gooch, Andy Flower, Ronnie Irani
Young players to look out for: Tom Westley, Adam Wheater (both Essex)
Other sports played: Darts
Other sports followed: Football (Liverpool)

Favourite band: White Stripes, Foo Fighters, Editors
Relaxations: 'Fishing, surfing, travelling, music'
Extras: Captained Cambridgeshire U11-U16. Played for Development of Excellence XI (South) 2001. Represented England U19 2002. Essex 2nd XI Player of the Year 2002. Represented British Universities 2003 and 2004. Took over as captain of Essex during the 2007 season following the retirement of Ronnie Irani. Included in initial England squad of 30 for the Twenty20 World Championship 2007-08. County captain for 2010
Opinions on cricket: 'Great game but too much cricket in the season – 12 Championship games instead of 16. Twenty20 is great.'
Best batting: 208* Essex v Derbyshire, Chelmsford 2006

2009 Season

	M	Inn	NO	Runs	HS	Avg	100	50	Ct	St	Balls	Runs	Wkts	Avg	BB	5I	10M
Test																	
FC	15	28	6	870	101*	39.54	1	4	10	-	41	62	0		-	-	-
ODI																	
List A	16	15	1	299	101*	21.35	1	1	5	-	0	0	0		-	-	
20/20 Int																	
20/20	10	10	1	334	87	37.11	-	2	3	-	0	0	0		-	-	

Career Performances

	M	Inn	NO	Runs	HS	Avg	100	50	Ct	St	Balls	Runs	Wkts	Avg	BB	5I	10M
Test																	
FC	78	131	17	4064	208*	35.64	5	24	60	-	113	191	0		-	-	-
ODI																	
List A	100	91	6	2187	144	25.72	4	14	34	-	0	0	0		-	-	
20/20 Int																	
20/20	49	46	4	1111	87	26.45	-	6	17	-	0	0	0		-	-	

PHILLIPS, B. J.   Somerset

Name: <u>Ben</u> James Phillips
Role: Right-hand bat, right-arm
fast-medium bowler
Born: 30 September 1975, Lewisham, London
Height: 6ft 6in **Weight:** 15st
Nickname: Bennyphil, Bus
County debut: 1996 (Kent),
2002 (Northamptonshire), 2008 (Somerset)
County cap: 2005 (Northamptonshire)
Place in batting averages: 134th av. 31.66
(2008 179th av. 22.55)
Place in bowling averages: 92nd av. 38.00
(2008 83rd av. 31.66)
Parents: Glynis and Trevor

Wife and date of marriage: Sarah Jane,
20 January 2003
Family links with cricket: Father and brother both keen club cricketers for
Hayes CC (Kent)
Education: Langley Park School for Boys, Beckenham
Qualifications: 9 GCSEs, 3 A-levels
Overseas tours: Northamptonshire to Grenada 2002
Overseas teams played for: University of Queensland, Australia 1993-94; Cape
Technikon Green Point, Cape Town 1994-95, 1996-98; University of Western
Australia, Perth 1998-99; Valley, Brisbane 2001-02
Cricket superstitions: 'Arrive at the ground early – hate rushing!'
Cricketers particularly admired: Glenn McGrath, Jason Gillespie
Other sports followed: Football (West Ham United), rugby (Northampton Saints)
Relaxations: 'Enjoy swimming, watching a good movie, and just generally like
spending time with family and friends'
Extras: Set Langley Park School record for the fastest half-century, off 11 balls.
Represented England U19 Schools 1993-94
Best batting: 100* Kent v Lancashire, Old Trafford 1997
Best bowling: 6-29 Northamptonshire v CUCCE, Fenner's 2006

2009 Season

	M	Inn	NO	Runs	HS	Avg	100	50	Ct	St	Balls	Runs	Wkts	Avg	BB	5I	10M
Test																	
FC	7	8	2	190	84	31.66	-	1	4	-	949	456	12	38.00	4-46	-	-
ODI																	
List A	15	5	2	38	24	12.66	-	-	4	-	607	455	20	22.75	3-23	-	
20/20 Int																	
20/20	8	4	1	16	13*	5.33	-	-	3	-	180	260	6	43.33	2-19	-	

Career Performances

	M	Inn	NO	Runs	HS	Avg	100	50	Ct	St	Balls	Runs	Wkts	Avg	BB	5I	10M
Test																	
FC	97	135	23	2402	100*	21.44	1	13	26	-	13160	6460	209	30.90	6-29	4	-
ODI																	
List A	112	69	21	871	44*	18.14	-	-	30	-	4639	3700	128	28.90	4-25	-	
20/20 Int																	
20/20	41	32	9	420	41*	18.26	-	-	13	-	858	1179	40	29.47	4-18	-	

PHILLIPS, T. J.   Essex

Name: Timothy (<u>Tim</u>) James Phillips
Role: Left-hand bat, slow left-arm bowler
Born: 13 March 1981, Cambridge
Height: 6ft 2in **Weight:** 13st
Nickname: Pips
County debut: 1999
County cap: 2006
Parents: Carolyn and Martin (deceased)
Marital status: Single ('in a relationship')
Family links with cricket: 'Father played for various league sides in Lancashire and Essex. Brother Nick fancies himself as a bowling/batting/keeping all-rounder'
Education: Felsted School; Durham University
Qualifications: 10 GCSEs, 3 A-levels, BA (Hons) Sport in the Community
Career outside cricket: 'Running a player agency' (see *Player website*)
Off-season: 'Playing and training abroad'
Overseas tours: Felsted School to Australia 1995-96; England U19 to Malaysia and (U19 World Cup) Sri Lanka 1999-2000
Overseas teams played for: Gosnells CC 2004-05 – 2006-07, Northerns Goodwood CC, Cape Town, 2009-10

Career highlights to date: 'Receiving my first-team cap in 2006. Winning Totesport Pro40 competition with Essex. Lord's final in 2008. Being part of gaining promotion to CC Div 1 in 2009'

Cricket moments to forget: '2003 season' (*Out for the whole of the season with cartilage and ligament damage to a knee*)

Cricket superstitions: 'Plenty!'

Cricketers particularly admired: Phil Tufnell, Daniel Vettori

Young players to look out for: Adam Wheater and Jaik Mickleburgh (both Essex)

Other sports played: Golf

Other sports followed: Rugby union (Wasps), football (Arsenal)

Favourite band: The Libertines, Coldplay, The White Stripes

Relaxations: 'Music, gigs, socialising, fishing'

Player website: www.playerprovider.com

Extras: Holmwoods School Cricketer of the Year runner-up 1997 and 1998. Broke Nick Knight's and Elliott Wilson's record for runs in a season for Felsted School, scoring 1213 in 1999. NBC Denis Compton Award 1999. Played for DUCCE 2001 and 2002. Lost much of the 2008 season to injury

Best batting: 89 Essex v Worcestershire, Worcester 2005

Best bowling: 5-41 Essex v Derbyshire, Chelmsford 2006

2009 Season

	M	Inn	NO	Runs	HS	Avg	100	50	Ct	St	Balls	Runs	Wkts	Avg	BB	5I	10M
Test																	
FC	4	5	0	122	69	24.40	-	1	2	-	761	357	8	44.62	3-61	-	-
ODI																	
List A	8	4	1	64	41	21.33	-	-	3	-	270	252	12	21.00	5-38	1	
20/20 Int																	
20/20	1	0	0	0	0		-	-	2	-	18	25	0		-	-	

Career Performances

	M	Inn	NO	Runs	HS	Avg	100	50	Ct	St	Balls	Runs	Wkts	Avg	BB	5I	10M
Test																	
FC	51	69	8	1196	89	19.60	-	4	32	-	6914	4294	90	47.71	5-41	1	-
ODI																	
List A	42	25	10	260	41	17.33	-	-	13	-	1226	1006	46	21.86	5-34	2	
20/20 Int																	
20/20	17	8	2	65	31	10.83	-	-	7	-	195	236	7	33.71	2-11	-	

PIETERSEN, K. P.   Hampshire

Name: <u>Kevin</u> Peter Pietersen
Role: Right-hand bat, right-arm off-spin bowler
Born: 27 June 1980, Pietermaritzburg,
South Africa
Height: 6ft 4in **Weight:** 14st 9lbs
Nickname: KP, Kelv, Kapes
County debut: 2001 (Nottinghamshire),
2005 (Hampshire)
County cap: 2002 (Nottinghamshire),
2005 (Hampshire)
Test debut: 2005
ODI debut: 2004-05
Twenty20 Int debut: 2005
1000 runs in a season: 3
1st-Class 200s: 4
Place in batting averages: 175th av. 26.12 (2008 9th av. 58.91)
Parents: Jannie and Penny
Wife and date of marriage: Jessica, 29 December 2007
Education: Maritzburg College; University of South Africa
Qualifications: 3 A-levels
Overseas tours: Natal to Zimbabwe 1999-2000, to Australia 2000-01;
Nottinghamshire to South Africa 2001, 2002; England A to Malaysia and India
2003-04; England to Zimbabwe (one-day series) 2004-05, to South Africa 2004-05
(one-day series), to Pakistan 2005-06, to India 2005-06, to India (ICC Champions
Trophy) 2006-07, to Australia 2006-07, to West Indies (World Cup) 2006-07, to South
Africa (World 20/20) 2007-08, to Sri Lanka 2007-08, to New Zealand 2007-08, to
India 2008-09 (c), to West Indies 2008-09, to South Africa 2009-10, to Bangladesh
2009-10; ICC World XI to Australia (Super Series) 2005-06
Overseas teams played for: Berea Rovers, Durban 1997-98 – 2001-02;
KwaZulu-Natal 1997-98 – 2000-01; Sydney University 2002-03; Bangalore Royal
Challengers (IPL) 2009
Career highlights to date: 'Scoring the three centuries in South Africa for
England 2005'
Cricket moments to forget: 'Breaking my leg against Glamorgan in August 2002
in an NUL game'
Cricket superstitions: 'Left pad first'
Cricketers particularly admired: Shaun Pollock, Errol Stewart
Other sports played: Golf, swimming ('represented my state in 1992-93'), running
Other sports followed: Formula One (Ferrari), rugby (Natal Sharks)
Player website: www.kevinpietersen.com
Extras: Played for South Africa Schools B 1997. Scored 61* and had figures of 4-141
from 56 overs for KwaZulu-Natal v England XI 1999-2000. Scored 1275 first-class

runs in first season of county cricket 2001. Player of the [ODI] Series v South Africa 2004-05 (454 runs at 151.33, including the fastest hundred for England in ODIs, from 69 balls). Scored maiden Test century (158, including an Ashes record seven sixes) in the fifth Test v Australia at The Oval 2005, winning Man of the Match award. Scored maiden Test double century (226) in the second Test v West Indies at Headingley 2007, winning Man of the Match award. His other international awards include Man of the Match v Australia at Bristol in the NatWest Series 2005 (65-ball 91*), England's Man of the [Test] Series v Sri Lanka 2006, and Man of the Match in the first Test v India at Lord's 2007 (134). Scored 158 in the second Test v Australia at Adelaide 2006-07, in the process sharing with Paul Collingwood (206) in a record fourth-wicket partnership for England in Tests v Australia (310). ECB National Academy 2003-04, 2004-05. ICC Emerging Player of the Year and ICC ODI Player of the Year awards 2005. Appointed MBE in 2006 New Year Honours as part of 2005 Ashes-winning England team. One of *Wisden*'s Five Cricketers of the Year 2006. Autobiography *Crossing the Boundary: The Early Years in My Cricketing Life* published 2006. Succeeded Michael Vaughan as England captain in August 2008 – relinquished the post in January 2009. Bangalore Royal Challengers paid $1.55m for his services in the IPL in 2009. Was part of England's Ashes-winning side 2009 but after the second Test at Lord's underwent Achilles tendon surgery and missed the remainder of the series. England 12-month central contract 2009-10. Is married to Liberty X singer Jessica Taylor

Best batting: 254* Nottinghamshire v Middlesex, Trent Bridge 2002
Best bowling: 4-31 Nottinghamshire v DUCCE, Trent Bridge 2003

2009 Season

	M	Inn	NO	Runs	HS	Avg	100	50	Ct	St	Balls	Runs	Wkts	Avg	BB	5I	10M
Test	4	6	0	202	69	33.66	-	1	1	-	0	0	0		-	-	-
FC	5	8	0	209	69	26.12	-	1	1	-	0	0	0		-	-	-
ODI																	
List A																	
20/20 Int	4	4	0	154	58	38.50	-	1	-	-	6	9	0		-	-	
20/20	4	4	0	154	58	38.50	-	1	-	-	6	9	0		-	-	

Career Performances

	M	Inn	NO	Runs	HS	Avg	100	50	Ct	St	Balls	Runs	Wkts	Avg	BB	5I	10M
Test	54	97	4	4647	226	49.96	16	15	32	-	735	518	4	129.50	1-0	-	-
FC	140	233	16	11026	254*	50.81	38	44	112	-	5539	3229	61	52.93	4-31	-	-
ODI	92	82	15	3127	116	46.67	7	20	32	-	214	201	5	40.20	2-22	-	
List A	200	181	32	6562	147	44.04	12	41	74	-	2174	1920	39	49.23	3-14	-	
20/20 Int	19	19	1	529	79	29.38	-	2	7	-	6	9	0		-	-	
20/20	39	39	1	977	79	25.71	-	4	12	-	234	290	13	22.30	3-33	-	

PINNER, N. D.   Worcestershire

Name: <u>Neil</u> Douglas Pinner
Role: Right-hand bat, right-arm off-break bowler
Born: 28 September 1990, Wordsley, Stourbridge, Worcestershire
Height: 5ft 11in **Weight:** 12st 10lb
Nickname: Pins
County debut: No first team appearance
Parents: Brian and Gail
Marital status: Single
Family links with cricket: 'Father and grandfather played for Kidderminster CC'
Education: RGS Worcester
Qualifications: 10 GCSEs, 3 A-levels
Career outside cricket: 'Office assistant for my father's business'

Off-season: 'In Adelaide at the Darren Lehmann Academy'
Overseas tours: RGS to Sri Lanka, 2006
Overseas teams played for: Woodville District, Adelaide 2009-10
Career highlight to date: 'Representing England at U15 and U16 levels. Top scoring in a series for England U16 versus Australia'
Cricket moments to forget: 'Getting bowled out whilst not playing a shot, twice in one week'
Cricket superstitions: 'Tapping the boundary rope with my bat as I walk to the middle'
Favourite sledging line: '"Hey mate, I reckon if you turn the bat over there might be some instructions on the back for you."'
Cricketers particularly admired: Sachin Tendulkar, Ricky Ponting, Graeme Hick
Young players to look out for: Aneesh Kapil (Worcestershire)
Other sports played: Rugby ('school First XV'), golf
Other sports followed: Football (Manchester United)
Favourite band: Kanye West
Relaxations: Films, poker, listening to music, Facebook
Extras: Represented Midlands at U13 to U17 levels. Worcestershire Academy 2004-09; was Worcestershire Academy Player of the Year 2007. Played for England U16, 2006, and England U17, 2007. Plays club cricket for Kidderminster Victoria CC in the Birmingham League Premier Division; was Kidderminster Player of the Year 2008. Is qualified to play for both Canada and Ireland via his grandparents
Opinions on cricket: 'The game is moving forward very quickly, and may not be recognisable in the near future.'

PIOLET, S. A.   Warwickshire

Name: <u>Steffan</u> Andreas Piolet
Role: Right-hand bat, right-arm medium bowler
Born: 8 August 1988, Redhill
County debut: 2009
Place in bowling averages: 1st av. 4.30
Education: Millfield School; Oxford
Brookes University
Cricketers particularly admired: Jacques Kallis
Extras: Has played for Worcestershire 2nd XI (debut
v Gloucestershire 2nd XI, Bristol, May 2006) and
Sussex 2nd XI (debut v Yorkshire 2nd XI, Hove, June
2006). Made debut for Warwickshire 2nd XI v
Middlesex 2nd XI, Northwood, June 2008. His
remarkable ten-wicket haul on his first-class debut in
2009 – his only first-class match of the season – put
him at the top of the season's bowling averages
Best batting: 26* Warwickshire v DUCCE, Durham, 2009
Best bowling: 6-17 Warwickshire v DUCCE, Durham, 2009

2009 Season

	M	Inn	NO	Runs	HS	Avg	100	50	Ct	St	Balls	Runs	Wkts	Avg	BB	5I	10M
Test																	
FC	1	2	1	31	26*	31.00	-	-	-	-	162	43	10	4.30	6-17	1	1
ODI																	
List A	11	2	0	6	4	3.00	-	-	3	-	341	298	13	22.92	3-34	-	
20/20 Int																	
20/20	11	2	0	3	3	1.50	-	-	5	-	210	237	10	23.70	2-17	-	

Career Performances

	M	Inn	NO	Runs	HS	Avg	100	50	Ct	St	Balls	Runs	Wkts	Avg	BB	5I	10M
Test																	
FC	1	2	1	31	26*	31.00	-	-	-	-	162	43	10	4.30	6-17	1	1
ODI																	
List A	11	2	0	6	4	3.00	-	-	3	-	341	298	13	22.92	3-34	-	
20/20 Int																	
20/20	11	2	0	3	3	1.50	-	-	5	-	210	237	10	23.70	2-17	-	

PIPE, D. J.   Derbyshire

Name: David <u>James</u> Pipe
Role: Right-hand bat, wicket-keeper
Born: 16 December 1977, Bradford
Height: 5ft 11in **Weight:** 13st
Nickname: Pipey
County debut: 1998 (Worcestershire),
2006 (Derbyshire)
County cap: 2002 (Worcestershire colours),
2007 (Derbyshire)
50 dismissals in a season: 1
Place in batting averages: 91st av. 37.92
(2008 54th av. 42.00)
Parents: David and Dorothy
Marital status: Single
Family links with cricket: 'My dad and uncle
played in the local league'

Education: Queensbury Upper School; BICC
Qualifications: 8 GCSEs, BTEC National in Business and Finance, HND Leisure
Management, senior coaching award, Diploma in Personal Training, Diploma in
Sports Therapy
Overseas teams played for: Leeming Spartans CC/South Metropolitan Cricket
Association, Perth 1998-99; Manly CC, Australia 1999-2000 – 2003-04
Career highlights to date: 'Getting first hundred'
Cricket moments to forget: 'Any game we lose'
Cricket superstitions: 'None'
Cricketers particularly admired: Adam Gilchrist, Ian Healy
Young players to look out for: Brett D'Oliveira (Worcestershire Academy),
Gary Ballance (Yorkshire), Dan Redfern (Derbyshire)
Other sports followed: Rugby league (Bradford Bulls, Manly Sea Eagles), boxing
('all British fighters'), AFL (West Coast Eagles)
Relaxations: Training
Extras: MCC School of Merit Wilf Slack Memorial Trophy winner 1995. Took
eight catches v Hertfordshire at Hertford in the C&G 2001 to set a new NatWest/C&G
record for most dismissals in a match by a wicket-keeper. Dick Lygon Award 2002
(Worcestershire Club Man of the Year). Derbyshire Club Man of the Year 2006.
Retired as a player at the end of the 2009 season to take up a position as
Derbyshire physio
Best batting: 133* Derbyshire v Essex, Chelmsford 2007

2009 Season

	M	Inn	NO	Runs	HS	Avg	100	50	Ct	St	Balls	Runs	Wkts	Avg	BB	5I	10M
Test																	
FC	14	18	5	493	64*	37.92	-	3	36	2	6	5	0		-	-	-
ODI																	
List A	8	8	0	107	27	13.37	-	-	6	-	0	0	0		-	-	
20/20 Int																	
20/20	10	6	4	37	14*	18.50	-	-	4	2	0	0	0		-	-	

Career Performances

	M	Inn	NO	Runs	HS	Avg	100	50	Ct	St	Balls	Runs	Wkts	Avg	BB	5I	10M
Test																	
FC	82	121	22	2870	133*	28.98	4	12	225	21	6	5	0		-	-	-
ODI																	
List A	72	60	12	837	83	17.43	-	3	64	17	0	0	0		-	-	
20/20 Int																	
20/20	45	35	9	353	45	13.57	-	-	19	13	0	0	0		-	-	

PLUNKETT, L. E. Durham

Name: <u>Liam</u> Edward Plunkett
Role: Right-hand bat, right-arm fast bowler
Born: 6 April 1985, Middlesbrough
Height: 6ft 4in **Weight:** 13st
Nickname: Pudsey
County debut: 2003
Test debut: 2005-06
ODI debut: 2005-06
Twenty20 Int debut: 2006
50 wickets in a season: 3
Place in batting averages: 88th av. 38.63
(2008 146th av. 27.28)
Place in bowling averages: 13th av. 23.35
(2007 91st av. 32.50)
Parents: Alan and Marie
Family links with cricket: 'Father played a good standard of local cricket'
Education: Nunthorpe Comprehensive, Teesside Tertiary College
Qualifications: 9 GCSEs, volleyball coaching badge
Overseas tours: England U19 to Australia 2002-03, to Bangladesh (U19 World Cup) 2003-04; England to Pakistan 2005-06, to India 2005-06, to Australia 2006-07, to West Indies (World Cup) 2006-07, to South Africa (one-day series) 2009-10, to Bangladesh 2009-10; England Lions to India 2007-08, to New Zealand 2008-09; England Performance Programme to India 2008-09

Overseas teams played for: Adelaide University 2005; Durban Dolphins, South Africa 2007-08
Career highlights to date: 'England debut'
Cricket moments to forget: 'Injury (oblique)' (*Out from July to September 2006 with a damaged oblique muscle*)
Cricket superstitions: 'None'
Cricketers particularly admired: Glenn McGrath
Young players to look out for: Ben Harmison
Other sports played: Golf, swimming
Other sports followed: Football (Middlesbrough, Arsenal)
Favourite band: 'R&B'
Extras: Became only the second bowler to record a five-wicket innings return on Championship debut for Durham, 5-53 v Yorkshire at Headingley 2003. Represented England U19 2003. NBC Denis Compton Award for the most promising young Durham player 2003, 2005. ECB National Academy 2004-05 (part-time), 2005-06. Friends Provident Man of the Match award in the semi-final v Essex at Riverside 2007 (4-15/30*). Joint top wicket-taker in Twenty20 for Durham in 2008. Although not originally selected, called into England one-day squad in South Africa 2009-10 to cover injured players
Opinions on cricket: 'Twenty20 game loaded towards batsmen.'
Best batting: 94* Durham v Sussex, Hove 2009
Best bowling: 6-63 Durham v Worcestershire, Riverside 2009

2009 Season

	M	Inn	NO	Runs	HS	Avg	100	50	Ct	St	Balls	Runs	Wkts	Avg	BB	5I	10M
Test																	
FC	15	14	3	425	94*	38.63	-	3	13	-	2457	1401	60	23.35	6-63	3	1
ODI																	
List A	16	13	3	129	30	12.90	-	-	5	-	573	547	14	39.07	2-28	-	
20/20 Int																	
20/20	2	1	0	6	6	6.00	-	-	1	-	36	57	0		-	-	

Career Performances

	M	Inn	NO	Runs	HS	Avg	100	50	Ct	St	Balls	Runs	Wkts	Avg	BB	5I	10M
Test	9	13	2	126	44*	11.45	-	-	3	-	1538	916	23	39.82	3-17	-	-
FC	85	118	24	2067	94*	21.98	-	9	50	-	13219	8021	266	30.15	6-63	8	1
ODI	27	24	10	295	56	21.07	-	1	7	-	1291	1260	37	34.05	3-24	-	
List A	95	66	24	859	72	20.45	-	2	21	-	4153	3702	115	32.19	4-15	-	
20/20 Int	1	0	0	0	0		-	-	-	-	24	37	1	37.00	1-37	-	
20/20	25	14	8	73	13*	12.16	-	-	8	-	488	589	22	26.77	3-16	-	

POLLARD, K. A.   Somerset

Name: Kieron Adrian Pollard
Role: Right-hand bat, right-arm medium fast bowler
Born: 12 May 1987, Tacarigua, Trinidad
County debut: No first-team appearance
ODI debut: 2006-07
Twenty20 Int debut: 2008
Overseas tours: West Indies to New Zealand (one-day) 2008-09, to England (one-day and ICC World Twenty20) 2009, Trinidad & Tobago to India (Champions League) 2009
Overseas teams played for: Trinidad & Tobago; South Australia; Stanford Superstars; Mumbai Indians (IPL)
Extras: Scored 126 on his first-class debut for Trinidad & Tobago against Barbados. In January 2010 Somerset announced that they had signed him for Twenty20 action and Mumbai Indians bid $750,000 to secure his services for the IPL.
Best batting: 174 Trinidad & Tobago v Barbados, Pointe-a-Pierre 2008-09
Best bowling: 2-29 Trinidad & Tobago v Jamaica, Alpart Sports Club, St Elizabeth 2006-07

2009 Season

	M	Inn	NO	Runs	HS	Avg	100	50	Ct	St	Balls	Runs	Wkts	Avg	BB	5I	10M
Test																	
FC																	
ODI	2	2	0	20	12	10.00	-	-	1	-	72	80	2	40.00	2-63	-	
List A	2	2	0	20	12	10.00	-	-	1	-	72	80	2	40.00	2-63	-	
20/20 Int	6	4	1	37	19*	12.33	-	-	3	-	78	122	4	30.50	1-10	-	
20/20	6	4	1	37	19*	12.33	-	-	3	-	78	122	4	30.50	1-10	-	

Career Performances

	M	Inn	NO	Runs	HS	Avg	100	50	Ct	St	Balls	Runs	Wkts	Avg	BB	5I	10M
Test																	
FC	20	33	1	1199	174	37.46	3	5	32	-	571	313	6	52.16	2-29	-	-
ODI	15	13	0	147	42	11.30	-	-	5	-	356	336	12	28.00	2-16	-	
List A	30	26	3	644	87	28.00	-	5	16	-	764	671	34	19.73	4-32	-	
20/20 Int	10	7	2	86	38	17.20	-	-	5	-	126	188	7	26.85	2-29	-	
20/20	28	20	5	397	83	26.46	-	2	11	-	330	440	20	22.00	3-17	-	

POONIA, N. S.   Warwickshire

Name: Navdeep (<u>Navi</u>) Singh Poonia
Role: Right-hand bat, right-arm medium bowler
Born: 11 May 1986, Glasgow
Height: 6ft 3in **Weight:** 14st
Nickname: Nav, Sat Nav
County debut: 2006
ODI debut: 2006
Twenty20 Int debut: 2007-08
Place in batting averages: (2008 148th av. 27.15)
Parents: Jaipal and Bindy Poonia
Marital status: Single
Family links with cricket: 'Dad played club
cricket at Walsall CC'
Education: Moseley Park School;
Wolverhampton University

Qualifications: 10 GCSEs, 2 A-levels, Levels 1 and 2 coaching
Overseas tours: Warwickshire Academy to South Africa 2005; Scotland to
Bangladesh (one-day series) 2006-07, to Kenya (including ICC World Cricket
League) 2006-07, to West Indies (World Cup) 2006-07, to Ireland (Quadrangular
Series) 2007, to South Africa (World 20/20) 2007-08
Cricket superstitions: 'None'
Cricketers particularly admired: Sachin Tendulkar, Brian Lara, Allan Donald
Other sports played: Football, badminton
Other sports followed: Football (Manchester Utd and Glasgow Rangers)
Relaxations: 'Playing snooker with mates and cousins'
Extras: Played for Warwickshire Board XI in the 2003 C&G. Cyril Goodway
(Warwickshire Old County Cricketers' Association) Trophy U17. Top-scored with 59
on county one-day debut v Nottinghamshire at Edgbaston in the C&G 2006. Has
played one-day (including ODI and Twenty20 Int) cricket for Scotland
Best batting: 111 Warwickshire v CUCCE, Fenner's 2008

2009 Season

	M	Inn	NO	Runs	HS	Avg	100	50	Ct	St	Balls	Runs	Wkts	Avg	BB	5I	10M
Test																	
FC	1	2	0	6	6	3.00	-	-	-	-	0	0	0		-	-	-
ODI																	
List A	1	1	0	9	9	9.00	-	-	-	-	0	0	0		-	-	
20/20 Int	2	2	0	27	27	13.50	-	-	-	-	0	0	0		-	-	
20/20	2	2	0	27	27	13.50	-	-	-	-	0	0	0		-	-	

Career Performances

	M	Inn	NO	Runs	HS	Avg	100	50	Ct	St	Balls	Runs	Wkts	Avg	BB	5I	10M
Test																	
FC	14	22	0	557	111	25.31	1	2	5	-	0	0	0		-	-	-
ODI	21	21	0	237	67	11.28	-	1	7	-	0	0	0		-	-	
List A	42	41	1	732	79	18.30	-	4	13	-	0	0	0		-	-	
20/20 Int	7	6	2	95	38*	23.75	-	-	2	-	0	0	0		-	-	
20/20	11	10	2	127	38*	15.87	-	-	2	-	0	0	0		-	-	

POPE, J. I. Leicestershire

Name: <u>Joel</u> Ian Pope
Role: Right-hand bat, wicket-keeper
Born: 23 October 1988, Ashford, Middlesex
Height: 5ft 7in **Weight:** 10st 2lbs
Nickname: Popey
County debut: 2008 (one-day)
Parents: Tania and Ian
Marital status: Single
Family links with cricket: 'Uncle (Ben Scott) is wicket-keeper for Middlesex. Dad and Grandad played at club level for Wycombe House'
Education: Whitton Sports College
Qualifications: 9 GCSEs, Level 1 coaching
Overseas tours: MCC Young Cricketers to St Kitts and Nevis 2007
Overseas teams played for: Melville CC, Perth 2007-08
Career highlights to date: 'Fielding for England as thirteenth man at Lord's against the West Indies'
Cricket superstitions: 'Put left pad on first'
Cricketers particularly admired: Jack Russell, Alec Stewart, Mike Hussey
Other sports played: Golf, football
Other sports followed: Football (Manchester United)
Favourite band: Oasis
Relaxations: 'Art, music'
Extras: MCC Young Cricketers 2007. Played for Middlesex U10-19, Middlesex Academy and 2nd XI. Plays for Sunbury CC.
Opinions on cricket: '[Twenty20 is] quick and entertaining – good for the crowds.'

2009 Season (Did not make any first-class or one-day appearances)

Career Performances

	M	Inn	NO	Runs	HS	Avg	100	50	Ct	St	Balls	Runs	Wkts	Avg	BB	5I	10M
Test																	
FC																	
ODI																	
List A	1	1	0	9	9	9.00	-	-	2	1	0	0	0		-	-	
20/20 Int																	
20/20																	

PORTERFIELD, W. T. S.   Gloucestershire

Name: <u>William</u> Thomas Stuart Porterfield
Role: Left-hand bat, occasional right-arm off-break bowler
Born: 6 September 1984, Londonderry, Northern Ireland
Height: 5ft 11in **Weight:** 12st
Nickname: Purdy, Porty, Porters
County debut: 2008
ODI debut: 2006
Twenty20 Int debut: 2008
Place in batting averages: 201st av. 22.73 (2008 110th av. 31.79)
Parents: William and Alison
Marital status: Single
Family links with cricket: Father played for Killyclooney CC
Education: Strabane Grammar School; Leeds Metropolitan University
Qualifications: BA (Hons) Physical Education (2.1)
Overseas tours: Ireland U19 to Bangladesh (U19 World Cup) 2003-04; Ireland to Scotland (European Championship) 2006, to Kenya (ICC World Cricket League) 2006-07, to West Indies (World Cup) 2006-07, to South Africa 2008 (v Namibia), to UAE (ICC World Twenty20 qualifiers) 2010 (captain), plus various Ireland age-group and A tours
Overseas teams played for: Rush CC, Dublin
Career highlights to date: '2006-07 World Cup in West Indies with Ireland'
Cricket moments to forget: 'Not qualifying for the Twenty20 World Championship in South Africa (2007)'
Cricketers particularly admired: Brian Lara
Young players to look out for: Paul Stirling

Other sports played: 'Rugby at school; bit of football'
Other sports followed: Football (Manchester United and Northern Ireland)
Relaxations: 'Socialising'
Extras: Played for Bradford/Leeds UCCE in 2004 and 2006. Played for MCC YC 2004-06. Attended ICC Winter Training Camp in South Africa 2006-07. Has represented Ireland in first-class and one-day cricket, including ODIs and C&G/Friends Provident. Man of the Match v Bermuda in Nairobi in the ICC World Cricket League 2006-07 (112*) and v Bangladesh in Bridgetown in the World Cup 2006-07 (85). Played for MCC in 2007. NBC Denis Compton Award for the most promising young Gloucestershire player 2008. Captain of Ireland for Intercontinental Cup game against Afghanistan in Sri Lanka in 2010 a role he carried forward to the ICC World Twenty20 qualifiers in UAE
Best batting: 166 Ireland v Bermuda, Dublin 2007
Best bowling: 1-57 Gloucestershire v LUCCE, Bristol 2008

2009 Season

	M	Inn	NO	Runs	HS	Avg	100	50	Ct	St	Balls	Runs	Wkts	Avg	BB	5I	10M
Test																	
FC	9	16	1	341	81	22.73	-	2	17	-	0	0	0		-	-	-
ODI																	
List A	16	16	1	599	97*	39.93	-	4	8	-	0	0	0		-	-	
20/20 Int	5	5	0	100	40	20.00	-	-	-	-	0	0	0		-	-	
20/20	11	11	0	207	40	18.81	-	-	1	-	0	0	0		-	-	

Career Performances

	M	Inn	NO	Runs	HS	Avg	100	50	Ct	St	Balls	Runs	Wkts	Avg	BB	5I	10M
Test																	
FC	34	58	2	1807	166	32.26	2	11	38	-	36	57	1	57.00	1-57	-	-
ODI	37	37	3	1150	112*	33.82	4	4	19	-	0	0	0		-	-	
List A	80	79	4	2625	112*	35.00	4	15	32	-	0	0	0		-	-	
20/20 Int	9	8	0	111	40	13.87	-	-	1	-	0	0	0		-	-	
20/20	18	17	0	291	62	17.11	-	1	4	-	0	0	0		-	-	

72. What is the lowest Test match innings total made by Bangladesh to date?

POTHAS, N.   Hampshire

Name: Nicolas (<u>Nic</u>) Pothas
Role: Right-hand bat, wicket-keeper; county vice-captain
Born: 18 November 1973, Johannesburg, South Africa
Height: 6ft 1in **Weight:** 13st 7lbs
Nickname: Skeg
County debut: 2002
County cap: 2003
ODI debut: 2000
50 dismissals in a season: 3
Place in batting averages: 7th av. 74.18
(2008 18th av. 53.50)

Parents: Emmanuel and Penelope
Marital status: Single
Family links with cricket: 'Greek by nationality, therefore clearly none'
Education: King Edward VII High School; Rand Afrikaans University
Overseas tours: South Africa A to England 1996, to Sri Lanka 1998-99, to West Indies 2000-01; Gauteng to Australia 1997; South Africa to Singapore (Singapore Challenge) 2000-01
Overseas teams played for: Transvaal/Gauteng 1993-94 – 2001-02; Delhi Giants (ICL) 2008-09
Career highlights to date: 'First tour for South Africa A. Playing for South Africa'
Cricket superstitions: 'Too many to mention'
Cricketers particularly admired: Ray Jennings, Jimmy Cook, Robin Smith
Other sports played: Hockey (South Africa U21, Transvaal)
Other sports followed: Football (Manchester United)
Favourite band: Counting Crows, Gin Blossoms, Just Jinjer
Relaxations: 'Shopping; designing clothes; sleeping; gym'
Extras: Scored maiden first-class century (147) for South African Students v England tourists at Pietermaritzburg 1995-96. Benson and Hedges Young Player of the Year 1996. Transvaal Player of the Year 1996, 1998. C&G Man of the Match award v Glamorgan at Cardiff 2005 (114*). Scored 139 v Gloucestershire at Cheltenham 2005, in the process sharing with Andy Bichel (138) in a new Hampshire record partnership for the eighth wicket (257). Took seven catches in an innings v Lancashire at Old Trafford 2006, becoming the first Hampshire wicket-keeper to achieve the feat in a first-class match. Made 51 dismissals and scored 973 runs in first-class cricket 2005; 58 dismissals and 973 runs in first-class cricket 2006. Finished top of the Hampshire first-class run makers in 2008. Captain of Hampshire in the early part of the 2009 season in the absence of Dimitri Mascarenhas. Appointed county vice-captain for 2010. Is not considered an overseas player

Best batting: 165 Gauteng v KwaZulu-Natal, Johannesburg 1998-99
Best bowling: 1-16 Hampshire v Middlesex, Lord's 2006

2009 Season

	M	Inn	NO	Runs	HS	Avg	100	50	Ct	St	Balls	Runs	Wkts	Avg	BB	5I	10M
Test																	
FC	11	15	4	816	122*	74.18	1	6	24	-	0	0	0	-	-	-	
ODI																	
List A	11	9	5	220	57*	55.00	-	1	5	3	0	0	0		-	-	
20/20 Int																	
20/20	10	7	4	103	26*	34.33	-	-	1	3	0	0	0		-	-	

Career Performances

	M	Inn	NO	Runs	HS	Avg	100	50	Ct	St	Balls	Runs	Wkts	Avg	BB	5I	10M
Test																	
FC	201	310	59	10604	165	42.24	24	54	559	45	120	63	1	63.00	1-16	-	-
ODI	3	1	0	24	24	24.00	-	-	4	1	0	0	0		-	-	
List A	229	192	70	4456	114*	36.52	3	24	204	52	0	0	0		-	-	
20/20 Int																	
20/20	53	39	16	488	59	21.21	-	2	18	10	0	0	0		-	-	

POWELL, D. B. L. Lancashire

Name: <u>Daren</u> Brent Lyle Powell
Role: Right-hand bat, right-arm
fast-medium bowler
Born: 15 April 1978, St Elizabeth, Jamaica
County debut: 2004 (Derbyshire),
2007 (Hampshire)
Test debut: 2002
ODI debut: 2002-03
Twenty20 Int debut: 2007
Overseas tours: West Indies A to Ireland and
England 2002, to Canada 2002, to England 2006;
West Indies to India 2002-03, to Bangladesh 2002-03,
to Sri Lanka 2005, to Australia 2005-06, to New
Zealand 2005-06, to Pakistan 2006-07, to England
2007, to South Africa (World 20/20) 2007-08, to
South Africa 2007-08, to New Zealand 2008-09, plus other one-day series and
tournaments in India, Ireland and Zimbabwe and UAE
Overseas teams played for: Jamaica 2000-01 – ; Gauteng 2003-04
Extras: Represented West Indies in the 2006-07 World Cup. His match awards include
Man of the Match v Bangladesh A in Jamaica in the Busta Cup 2001-02 (3-39/5-37), v

West Indies B in Jamaica in the Carib Beer Cup 2002-03 (5-34/2-36) and v England in the third ODI at Trent Bridge 2007 (4-40). Was a temporary overseas player with Derbyshire during the 2004 season; was an overseas player with Hampshire during the 2007 season. Returned innings figures of 10-5-8-4 v Worcestershire at The Rose Bowl 2007. Signed as an overseas player for Lancashire in October 2009

Best batting: 69 Jamaica v Barbados, Bridgetown 2008-09
Best bowling: 6-49 Derbyshire v DUCCE, Derby 2004

2009 Season (Did not make any first-class or one-day appearances)

Career Performances

	M	Inn	NO	Runs	HS	Avg	100	50	Ct	St	Balls	Runs	Wkts	Avg	BB	5I	10M
Test	37	57	5	407	36*	7.82	-	-	8	-	7077	4068	85	47.85	5-25	1	-
FC	96	138	22	1477	69	12.73	-	4	31	-	15972	8829	267	33.06	6-49	6	-
ODI	55	25	3	118	48*	5.36	-	-	13	-	2850	2239	71	31.53	4-27	-	
List A	96	42	9	236	48*	7.15	-	-	23	-	4776	3783	138	27.41	5-23	1	
20/20 Int	5	1	1	1	1*		-	-	2	-	102	131	2	65.50	1-6	-	
20/20	12	3	3	2	1*		-	-	3	-	253	286	7	40.85	2-15	-	

POWELL, M. J.   Glamorgan

Name: <u>Michael</u> John Powell
Role: Right-hand bat, right-arm off-break bowler
Born: 3 February 1977, Crickhowell
Height: 6ft 1in   **Weight:** 14st 2lbs
Nickname: Powelly
County debut: 1997
County cap: 2000
1000 runs in a season: 5
1st-Class 200s: 3
Place in batting averages: 78th av. 40.60
(2008 113th av. 31.52)
Parents: Linda and John
Marital status: Single ('in a relationship')
Family links with cricket: 'Dad and Uncle Mike both played for Abergavenny'
Education: Crickhowell Secondary School; Pontypool College
Qualifications: 5 GCSEs, BTEC National Diploma in Sports Science, Level 1 coaching
Career outside cricket: 'Financial adviser'
Off-season: 'Studying to pass FPC's with Castle Court Consulting'
Overseas tours: Glamorgan to Cape Town 1999, 2002; England A to Sri Lanka 2004-05

Overseas teams played for: Wests, Brisbane 1996-97; Cornwall CC, Auckland 1998-99, 2000-01

Career highlights to date: 'Trophies I've won with Glamorgan over the years'

Cricket moments to forget: 'Missing the 2007 season due to illness'

Cricket superstitions: 'None'

Cricketers particularly admired: Matthew Elliott, Steve James

Other sports played: Rugby (Crickhowell RFC)

Other sports followed: Rugby (Cardiff)

Favourite band: Foo Fighters, Stereophonics

Relaxations: Eating and sleeping

Extras: Scored 200* on first-class debut v Oxford University at The Parks 1997. Second XI Championship Player of the Year 1997 (1210 runs at 75.63). NBC Denis Compton Award for the most promising young Glamorgan player 2000. Acted as 12th man in the third Test v Sri Lanka at Old Trafford 2002, taking the catch that ended Sri Lanka's second innings. Included in England one-day squad for NatWest Series 2004. ECB National Academy 2004-05. Glamorgan Player of the Year 2006. Had a serious operation to remove a rib in 2007

Opinions on cricket: 'If we lengthened the season by ten days at either end, this would create the extra days off the players need without losing any cricket'

Best batting: 299 Glamorgan v Gloucestershire, Cheltenham 2006

Best bowling: 2-39 Glamorgan v OUCCE, The Parks 1999

2009 Season

	M	Inn	NO	Runs	HS	Avg	100	50	Ct	St	Balls	Runs	Wkts	Avg	BB	5I	10M
Test																	
FC	17	25	2	934	108	40.60	2	7	8	-	0	0	0	-	-	-	
ODI																	
List A	9	9	0	115	33	12.77	-	-	1	-	0	0	0	-	-		
20/20 Int																	
20/20	10	10	2	176	39*	22.00	-	-	4	-	0	0	0	-	-		

Career Performances

	M	Inn	NO	Runs	HS	Avg	100	50	Ct	St	Balls	Runs	Wkts	Avg	BB	5I	10M
Test																	
FC	193	323	30	11511	299	39.28	25	58	121	-	164	132	2	66.00	2-39	-	-
ODI																	
List A	204	193	20	4665	114*	26.96	1	25	79	-	24	26	1	26.00	1-26	-	
20/20 Int																	
20/20	44	41	4	844	68*	22.81	-	5	16	-	0	0	0	-	-		

POYNTON, T. J. Derbyshire

Name: Thomas (<u>Tom</u>) James Poynton
Role: Right-hand bat, wicket-keeper
Born: 25 November 1989, Burton-on-Trent,
Staffordshire
Height: 5ft 10in **Weight:** 11st
Nickname: TP, Poynts
County debut: 2007
Parents: Keith and Sheena
Marital status: 'Long-term relationship –
Megan Jacobs'
Family links with cricket: 'Brother plays at same
club – Lullington Park CC. Both parents involved
in club cricket and keen county supporters'
Education: John Taylor High School;
Repton School (Sixth Form)

Qualifications: 11 GCSEs, 3 A-levels, Level 1 coaching
Career outside cricket: Part-time coach
Overseas tours: Derbyshire Academy to South Africa 2006; Repton School to
Grenada 2007; England U19 to South Africa 2008-09
Career highlights to date: 'Making first-class debut for Derbyshire v Middlesex in
2007, and being selected for England U19s to tour South Africa' (*see above*)
Cricket moments to forget: 'Pair on debut and Ant Botha dislocating my jaw
during first first-class innings'
Cricket superstitions: 'None'
Cricketers particularly admired: Ian Healy, Adam Gilchrist, Jack Russell
Other sports played: Football (Repton 1st XI), golf ('recreational')
Other sports followed: Football (Manchester Utd)
Favourite band: Usher, Ne-Yo ('Like all music')
Relaxations: 'Music, FIFA or PES, spending time with my girlfriend'
Extras: Played for Derbyshire U10-U17 and for Midlands U14, U15, U17. Derbyshire
Academy since 2004. Played in Bunbury Festival 2005. Derbyshire County Board
Young Player of the Year 2006. Represented England U17 2006, 2007. Attended ECB
National Skill Sets (wicket-keeping) 2006, 2007. Selected to tour South Africa with
England U19 2008-09. Youngest wicket-keeper to play first-class cricket for
Derbyshire
Opinions on cricket: 'Grateful that a number of first-class counties are giving young
players an opportunity to play at the highest level possible, reflecting the success of
the county academy set-ups.'
Best batting: 14 Derbyshire v Bangladesh A, Derby 2008

2009 Season

	M	Inn	NO	Runs	HS	Avg	100	50	Ct	St	Balls	Runs	Wkts	Avg	BB	5I	10M
Test																	
FC																	
ODI																	
List A	5	3	1	52	24	26.00	-	-	3	1	0	0	0		-	-	
20/20 Int																	
20/20																	

Career Performances

	M	Inn	NO	Runs	HS	Avg	100	50	Ct	St	Balls	Runs	Wkts	Avg	BB	5I	10M
Test																	
FC	3	5	0	17	14	3.40	-	-	7	2	0	0	0		-	-	-
ODI																	
List A	6	3	1	52	24	26.00	-	-	5	1	0	0	0		-	-	
20/20 Int																	
20/20	2	1	0	3	3	3.00	-	-	-	2	0	0	0		-	-	

PRINCE, A. G. Lancashire

Name: <u>Ashwell</u> Gavin Prince
Role: Left-hand bat
Born: 28 May 1977, Port Elizabeth, South Africa
County debut: 2008 (Nottinghamshire),
2009 (Lancashire)
Test debut: 2002
ODI debut: 2002
Twenty20 Int debut: 2005-06
Place in batting averages: 27th av. 52.60
(2008 17th av. 54.08)
Overseas tours: South Africa to West Indies
2004-05, to Australia 2005-06, to Sri Lanka 2006,
to West Indies (ICC World Cup) 2006-07, to Pakistan
2007-08, to Bangladesh 2007-08, to India 2007-08,
to England 2008

Overseas teams played for: Eastern Province B 1995-96 – 1997-98; Eastern Province 1995-96 – 1996-97; Western Province 1997-98 – 2003-04; Western Province Boland 2004-05; Cape Cobras 2006-07 – 2007-08; Warriors 2008-09
Extras: Joined Nottinghamshire as overseas player in August 2008, after the signing of Adam Voges as a replacement for Mike Hussey fell through. Smashed 162* against Bangladesh in the second Test at Centurion in November 2008. Signed by Lancashire as temporary replacement for VVS Laxman during the early part of 2009 season. Signed once more as an interim overseas player in January 2010

Best batting: 254 Warriors v Titans, Centurion 2008-09
Best bowling: 2-11 South Africans v Middlesex, Uxbridge 2008

2009 Season

	M	Inn	NO	Runs	HS	Avg	100	50	Ct	St	Balls	Runs	Wkts	Avg	BB	5I	10M
Test																	
FC	6	12	2	526	135*	52.60	1	3	9	-	0	0	0		-	-	-
ODI																	
List A	9	9	0	190	78	21.11	-	1	2	-	0	0	0		-	-	
20/20 Int																	
20/20	6	6	3	159	44	53.00	-	-	2	-	0	0	0		-	-	

Career Performances

	M	Inn	NO	Runs	HS	Avg	100	50	Ct	St	Balls	Runs	Wkts	Avg	BB	5I	10M
Test	48	77	12	3074	162*	47.29	11	8	29	-	96	47	1	47.00	1-2	-	-
FC	170	271	37	10402	254	44.45	26	48	113	-	276	166	4	41.50	2-11	-	-
ODI	52	41	12	1018	89*	35.10	-	3	26	-	12	3	0		-	-	
List A	196	171	34	4146	89*	30.26	-	22	90	-	91	86	0		-	-	
20/20 Int	1	1	0	5	5	5.00	-	-	-	-	0	0	0		-	-	
20/20	18	16	3	364	46	28.00	-	-	5	-	4	5	0		-	-	

PRIOR, M. J.   Sussex

Name: Matthew (Matt) James Prior
Role: Right-hand bat, wicket-keeper
Born: 26 February 1982, Johannesburg,
South Africa
Height: 5ft 11in **Weight:** 13st
Nickname: MP, Cheese
County debut: 2001
County cap: 2003
Test debut: 2007
ODI debut: 2004-05
Twenty20 Int debut: 2007
1000 runs in a season: 3
1st-Class 200s: 1
Place in batting averages: 71st av. 41.47
(2008 32nd av. 47.27)
Parents: Michael and Teresa
Wife: Emily
Children: Jonathan, February 2009
Education: Brighton College, East Sussex
Qualifications: 9 GCSEs, 3 A-levels, Level 1 coaching

Overseas tours: Brighton College to India 1997-98; Sussex Academy to Cape Town 1999; Sussex to Grenada 2001, 2002; England A to Malaysia and India 2003-04, to Sri Lanka 2004-05, to Bangladesh 2006-07; England to Zimbabwe (one-day series) 2004-05, to Pakistan 2005-06, to India 2005-06, to South Africa (World 20/20) 2007-08, to Sri Lanka 2007-08, to India (Test and one-day series) 2008-09, to West Indies (Test and one-day series) 2008-09, to South Africa 2009-10, to Bangladesh 2009-10
Cricket moments to forget: 'Falling on to the stumps at The Rose Bowl on Sky TV!'
Cricket superstitions: 'Too many to name all of them'
Cricketers particularly admired: Steve Waugh, Alec Stewart, Mushtaq Ahmed, Murray Goodwin
Other sports played: Golf
Other sports followed: Football (Arsenal), golf, rugby
Favourite band: Red Hot Chili Peppers
Relaxations: 'Gym, listening to music'
Extras: Has played for Sussex since U12. Represented England U14-U19, captaining England U17. NBC Denis Compton Award for the most promising young Sussex player 2001, 2002, 2003. Umer Rashid Award for Most Improved [Sussex] Player 2003. ECB National Academy 2003-04, 2004-05, 2006-07. Became first England wicket-keeper to score a century (126*) on Test debut in the first Test v West Indies at Lord's 2007. England 12-month central contract 2009-10
Best batting: 201* Sussex v LUCCE, Hove 2004

2009 Season

	M	Inn	NO	Runs	HS	Avg	100	50	Ct	St	Balls	Runs	Wkts	Avg	BB	5I	10M
Test	7	11	1	366	63	36.60	-	3	14	1	0	0	0	-	-	-	
FC	13	21	2	788	140	41.47	1	6	30	1	0	0	0	-	-	-	
ODI	9	9	0	210	87	23.33	-	1	7	-	0	0	0	-	-		
List A	12	12	0	263	87	21.91	-	2	10	-	0	0	0	-	-		
20/20 Int	1	0	0	0	0		-	-	-	1	0	0	0	-	-		
20/20	2	1	0	11	11	11.00	-	-	1	1	0	0	0	-	-		

Career Performances

	M	Inn	NO	Runs	HS	Avg	100	50	Ct	St	Balls	Runs	Wkts	Avg	BB	5I	10M
Test	23	37	7	1326	131*	44.20	2	10	51	2	0	0	0		-	-	-
FC	154	243	25	8785	201*	40.29	20	50	354	24	0	0	0		-	-	-
ODI	49	47	7	978	87	24.45	-	2	52	4	0	0	0		-	-	
List A	188	174	14	4303	144	26.89	4	23	162	26	0	0	0		-	-	
20/20 Int	6	5	0	116	32	23.20	-	-	4	2	0	0	0		-	-	
20/20	44	40	2	874	73	23.00	-	5	30	3	0	0	0		-	-	

PROCTER, L. A.   Lancashire

Name: <u>Luke</u> Anthony Procter
Role: Left-hand bat, right-arm medium fast bowler
Born: 24 June 1988, Oldham, Lancashire
County debut: 2009 (one-day)
Extras: Has played for Cumberland and MCC Young
Cricketers. Appeared for the county 2nd XI in 2009 as
well as his club side Royton in the Central Lancashire
League. Scored over 1400 runs in 2009 for the latter,
averaging 61.35, Has taken over 200 wickets in club
cricket

2009 Season

	M	Inn	NO	Runs	HS	Avg	100	50	Ct	St	Balls	Runs	Wkts	Avg	BB	5I	10M
Test																	
FC																	
ODI																	
List A	1	1	0	2	2	2.00	-	-	-	-	0	0	0		-	-	
20/20 Int																	
20/20																	

Career Performances

	M	Inn	NO	Runs	HS	Avg	100	50	Ct	St	Balls	Runs	Wkts	Avg	BB	5I	10M
Test																	
FC																	
ODI																	
List A	1	1	0	2	2	2.00	-	-	-	-	0	0	0		-	-	
20/20 Int																	
20/20																	

73. Which Pakistan cricketer was known as the 'Street Fighter'?

Name: Richard (Rich) Michael Pyrah
Role: Right-hand bat, right-arm
fast-medium bowler; all-rounder
Born: 1 November 1982, Dewsbury
Height: 6ft **Weight:** 12st 9lbs
Nickname: RP, Pyro
County debut: 2004
Place in batting averages: (2008 228th av. 16.00)
Parents: Mick and Lesley
Marital status: Single
Family links with cricket: 'Dad played local
cricket in the Central Yorkshire League for Ossett'
Education: Ossett High School; Wakefield College
Qualifications: 10 GCSEs, Level 2 coach
Overseas tours: Yorkshire to Mumbai 2005

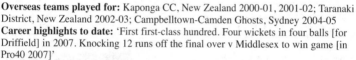

Overseas teams played for: Kaponga CC, New Zealand 2000-01, 2001-02; Taranaki
District, New Zealand 2002-03; Campbelltown-Camden Ghosts, Sydney 2004-05
Career highlights to date: 'First first-class hundred. Four wickets in four balls [for
Driffield] in 2007. Knocking 12 runs off the final over v Middlesex to win game [in
Pro40 2007]'
Cricket moments to forget: 'Dropping a dolly of a catch in front of full crowd at
Old Trafford and live on Sky Sports'
Cricket superstitions: 'None'
Cricketers particularly admired: Michael Vaughan, Darren Lehmann,
Anthony McGrath
Young players to look out for: Oliver Hannon-Dalby, Adil Rashid (both Yorkshire)
Other sports played: Golf, squash, football (had trials with Bradford City and
Sheffield Wednesday)
Other sports followed: Football (Leeds United), rugby league (Leeds Rhinos)
Favourite band: Take That, Girls Aloud
Extras: C&G Man of the Match award for his 5-50 (plus 26 runs) for Yorkshire Board
XI v Somerset at Scarborough in the third round 2002. His Bradford League awards
include the all-rounders' and bowling averages trophies 2006. Yorkshire Fielder of the
Year 2007. Has acted as 12th man for England
Opinions on cricket: 'Second XI cricket should mirror first-team competitions
and rules to feed young players into county cricket. There should be a minimum
number of English cricketers in each side who are eligible to play Test cricket,
e.g. seven or eight.'
Best batting: 106 Yorkshire v LUCCE, Headingley 2007
Best bowling: 2-53 Yorkshire v Nottinghamshire, Trent Bridge 2009

2009 Season

	M	Inn	NO	Runs	HS	Avg	100	50	Ct	St	Balls	Runs	Wkts	Avg	BB	5I	10M
Test																	
FC	3	4	1	59	50*	19.66	-	1	3	-	360	213	4	53.25	2-53	-	-
ODI																	
List A	15	12	5	233	67	33.28	-	1	3	-	540	538	22	24.45	4-54	-	
20/20 Int																	
20/20	6	5	1	35	26*	8.75	-	-	-	-	96	136	2	68.00	1-28	-	

Career Performances

	M	Inn	NO	Runs	HS	Avg	100	50	Ct	St	Balls	Runs	Wkts	Avg	BB	5I	10M
Test																		
FC	15	21	2	497	106	26.15	1	3	9	-	864	491	9	54.55	2-53	-	-
ODI																	
List A	69	50	13	742	67	20.05	-	1	25	-	2104	1975	80	24.68	5-50	1	
20/20 Int																	
20/20	31	21	6	161	33*	10.73	-	-	11	-	348	436	22	19.81	4-20	-	

RAMPRAKASH, M. R.   Surrey

Name: <u>Mark</u> Ravindra Ramprakash
Role: Right-hand bat, right-arm off-spin bowler
Born: 5 September 1969, Bushey, Herts
Height: 5ft 10in **Weight:** 12st 4lbs
Nickname: Ramps, Bloodaxe
County debut: 1987 (Middlesex), 2001 (Surrey)
County cap: 1990 (Middlesex), 2002 (Surrey)
Benefit: 2000 (Middlesex), 2008 (testimonial, Surrey)
Test debut: 1991
ODI debut: 1991
1000 runs in a season: 16
2000 runs in a season: 3
1st-Class 200s: 14
1st-Class 300s: 1
Place in batting averages: 1st av. 90.00 (2008 6th av. 61.75)
Parents: Deonarine and Jennifer
Wife and date of marriage: Van, 24 September 1993
Children: Cara, 1997; Anya, 2002

Family links with cricket: Father played club cricket in Guyana
Education: Gayton High School; Harrow Weald Sixth Form College
Qualifications: 6 O-levels, 2 A-levels, Level 3 cricket coach, Level 2 FA football coach
Overseas tours: England YC to Sri Lanka 1986-87, to Australia (U19 World Cup) 1987-88; England A to Pakistan 1990-91, to West Indies 1991-92, to India 1994-95 (vc); Lion Cubs to Barbados 1993; England to New Zealand 1991-92, to West Indies 1993-94, to Australia 1994-95, to South Africa 1995-96, to West Indies 1997-98, to Australia 1998-99, to South Africa 1999-2000, to Zimbabwe (one-day series) 2001-02, to India and New Zealand 2001-02
Overseas teams played for: Nairobi Jafferys, Kenya 1988; North Melbourne 1989; University of Perth 1996-97; Clico-Preysal, Trinidad 2004
Career highlights to date: 'My two Test hundreds, v West Indies and Australia'
Cricket moments to forget: 'Going up to receive an award I hadn't won!'
Cricket superstitions: 'Same piece of chewing gum in innings'
Cricketers particularly admired: 'All the great all-rounders'; Alec Stewart
Young players to look out for: Arun Harinath
Other sports played: Football (Corinthian Casuals FC, Arsenal Pro-Celeb XI)
Other sports followed: Football (Arsenal FC)
Extras: Voted Best U15 Schoolboy of 1985 by Cricket Society (Sir John Hobbs Silver Jubilee Memorial Prize) and Cricket Society's Most Promising Young Cricketer of the Year 1988. Man of the Match for his 56 in Middlesex's NatWest Trophy final win in 1988, on his debut in the competition. Represented England YC. Cricket Writers' Young Cricketer of the Year 1991. Middlesex captain May 1997 to the end of the 1999 season. Man of the Match in the fifth Test v West Indies at Bridgetown 1997-98 (154). Leading run-scorer in the single-division four-day era of the County Championship with 8392 runs (av. 56.32) 1993-99. Became first player to score a Championship century against all 18 first-class counties with his 110 v Middlesex at Lord's 2003. Surrey Players' Player of the Year 2003, 2004, 2005, 2006, 2007; Surrey Supporters' Player of the Year 2003, 2004. Vice-captain of Surrey 2004-05. In 2006 became the first English batsman to score 2000 first-class runs in a season since the start of the two-division Championship in 2000, reaching the landmark in a record 20 innings and finishing the season with 2278 runs at an average of 103.54. PCA Player of the Year 2006. Winner, with Karen Hardy, of *Strictly Come Dancing*, December 2006. One of *Wisden*'s Five Cricketers of the Year 2007. Scored century in each innings (196/130*) for the sixth time, v Lancashire at The Oval 2007 to become the first batsman to average more than 100 in consecutive English seasons, finishing with 2026 runs at an average of 101.30. In August 2008, he joined the select group of players who have completed one hundred first-class centuries when he scored a 'ton' against Yorkshire at Headingley on his way to topping the Surrey batting averages for the season. Missed the last month of the 2009 season due to a broken thumb. Topped the batting averages for the 2009 season (av. 90.00). Published his autobiography, *Strictly Me*, in 2009
Best batting: 301* Surrey v Northamptonshire, The Oval 2006
Best bowling: 3-32 Middlesex v Glamorgan, Lord's 1998

2009 Season

	M	Inn	NO	Runs	HS	Avg	100	50	Ct	St	Balls	Runs	Wkts	Avg	BB	5I	10M
Test																	
FC	11	17	2	1350	274	90.00	5	4	5	-	0	0	0		-	-	-
ODI																	
List A	8	7	1	397	121	66.16	3	-	3	-	0	0	0		-	-	
20/20 Int																	
20/20	8	8	1	225	73	32.14	-	2	1	-	0	0	0		-	-	

Career Performances

	M	Inn	NO	Runs	HS	Avg	100	50	Ct	St	Balls	Runs	Wkts	Avg	BB	5I	10M
Test	52	92	6	2350	154	27.32	2	12	39	-	895	477	4	119.25	1-2	-	-
FC	426	701	89	33244	301*	54.32	108	139	244	-	4171	2196	34	64.58	3-32	-	-
ODI	18	18	4	376	51	26.85	-	1	8	-	132	108	4	27.00	3-28	-	
List A	398	385	62	12947	147*	40.08	17	83	132	-	1734	1354	46	29.43	5-38	1	
20/20 Int																	
20/20	52	52	8	1388	85*	31.54	-	10	18	-	0	0	0		-	-	

RANKIN, W. B. — Warwickshire

Name: William Boyd Rankin
Role: Left-hand lower-order bat, right-arm fast-medium bowler
Born: 5 July 1984, Londonderry
Height: 6ft 8in **Weight:** 16st 7lbs
Nickname: Boydo, Stankin
County debut: 2006 (one-day, Derbyshire), 2007 (first-class, Derbyshire), 2008 (Warwickshire)
ODI debut: 2006-07
Twenty20 Int debut: 2009
Place in bowling averages: 77th av. 34.56 (2008 72nd av. 30.16)
Parents: Robert and Dawn
Marital status: Single
Family links with cricket: Both brothers (Robert and David) have played in Ireland age-group teams
Education: Strabane Grammar School; Harper Adams University College
Qualifications: 10 GCSEs, 3 A-levels, Level 1 cricket coaching
Career outside cricket: 'Student and work on home farm'
Overseas tours: Ireland U19 to Bangladesh (U19 World Cup) 2003-04; Ireland to Scotland (European Championship) 2006, to Kenya (ICC World Cricket League) 2006-07, to West Indies (World Cup) 2006-07, to South Africa (Intercontinental Cup)

2008, to South Africa (ICC World Cup Qualifiers) 2009, plus various Ireland age-group and A tours

Career highlights to date: 'Playing in 2006-07 Cricket World Cup, beating Pakistan and Bangladesh and tying with Zimbabwe'

Cricket moments to forget: 'U19 World Cup match against West Indies (2004)' (*Ireland U19 lost by just six runs*)

Cricket superstitions: 'None'

Cricketers particularly admired: Glenn McGrath, Curtly Ambrose

Young players to look out for: Gary Ballance, Daniel Redfern, Eoin Morgan

Other sports played: Rugby, football, badminton, snooker

Other sports followed: Football (Liverpool FC), rugby (Ulster)

Favourite band: Coldplay, Oasis

Relaxations: 'Shooting'

Extras: Attended European Cricket Academy in Spain. Formerly with Middlesex but made no first-team appearances. Has represented Ireland in first-class and ODI cricket. Left Derbyshire at the end of the 2007 season and joined Warwickshire for 2008. Part of the Ireland squad that faced Kenya in summer 2008. Took 4 wickets in Namibia's second innings during the Intercontinental Cup Final, which Ireland went on to win. Played for Ireland in ICC World Twenty20, England, 2009. Selected for the England Performance Fast Bowlng programme 2009-10. Selected in Ireland squad to tour Sri Lanka 2009-10 but had to withdraw due to a fractured foot

Opinions on cricket: 'Twenty20 cricket brings good crowds to games, which is good for cricket and clubs. I feel all 2nd XI cricket one-day matches should be coloured clothing and white ball, as this will help get young players used to playing in these conditions; otherwise it's completely new to them when they play first-team cricket.'

Best batting: 12* Warwickshire v Glamorgan, Edgbaston 2008

Best bowling: 5-39 Ireland v Namibia, Windhoek, 2007-08

2009 Season

	M	Inn	NO	Runs	HS	Avg	100	50	Ct	St	Balls	Runs	Wkts	Avg	BB	5I	10M
Test																	
FC	13	13	4	19	7	2.11	-	-	2	-	2042	1279	37	34.56	5-85	1	-
ODI																	
List A	8	1	0	9	9	9.00	-	-	1	-	246	196	8	24.50	2-18	-	
20/20 Int	4	1	1	5	5*		-	-	2	-	96	102	3	34.00	2-27	-	
20/20	5	2	2	8	5*		-	-	2	-	120	124	4	31.00	2-27	-	

Career Performances

	M	Inn	NO	Runs	HS	Avg	100	50	Ct	St	Balls	Runs	Wkts	Avg	BB	5I	10M
Test																	
FC	25	26	10	65	12*	4.06	-	-	9	-	3659	2273	79	28.77	5-39	2	-
ODI	20	6	4	16	7*	8.00	-	-	4	-	836	693	28	24.75	3-32	-	
List A	41	12	7	34	9	6.80	-	-	5	-	1627	1352	50	27.04	3-32	-	
20/20 Int	4	1	1	5	5*		-	-	2	-	96	102	3	34.00	2-27	-	
20/20	5	2	2	8	5*		-	-	2	-	120	124	4	31.00	2-27	-	

RASHID, A. U.   Yorkshire

Name: <u>Adil</u> Usman Rashid
Role: Right-hand bat, right-arm leg-break bowler; all-rounder
Born: 17 February 1988, Bradford
Nickname: Dilly
County debut: 2006
County cap: 2009
ODI debut: 2009
Twenty20 Int debut: 2009
50 wickets in a season: 1
Place in batting averages: 12th av. 68.12
(2008 171st av. 23.48)
Place in bowling averages: 86th av. 36.06
(2008 86th av. 31.83)
Family links with cricket: Brothers Amar and

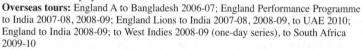

Haroon have both played for Bradford/Leeds UCCE
Overseas tours: England A to Bangladesh 2006-07; England Performance Programme to India 2007-08, 2008-09; England Lions to India 2007-08, 2008-09, to UAE 2010; England to India 2008-09; to West Indies 2008-09 (one-day series), to South Africa 2009-10
Extras: Has attended Terry Jenner spin-bowling courses in Australia. Played for Yorkshire Academy 2005. Recorded maiden first-class five-wicket return (6-67 from 28 successive overs) on debut v Warwickshire at Scarborough 2006. Scored 114 then took 8-157 in India U19's first innings in the second 'Test' at Taunton 2006 to become the first England player to score a century and record a five-wicket innings return in an U19 international. 2nd XI cap 2006. Represented England Lions 2007. Cricket Writers' Club Young Cricketer of the Year 2007. NatWest PCA Young Player of the Year 2007. Topped the Yorkshire first-class bowling averages in 2008, with a 65-wicket haul. England increment contract 2009-10
Best batting: 157* Yorkshire v Lancashire, Headingley 2009
Best bowling: 7-107 Yorkshire v Hampshire, Rose Bowl 2008

2009 Season

	M	Inn	NO	Runs	HS	Avg	100	50	Ct	St	Balls	Runs	Wkts	Avg	BB	5I	10M
Test																	
FC	10	12	4	545	157*	68.12	2	3	6	-	1840	1118	31	36.06	5-41	2	-
ODI	3	3	1	53	31*	26.50	-	-	1	-	162	148	2	74.00	1-55	-	
List A	13	12	4	130	35*	16.25	-	-	4	-	522	453	11	41.18	2-12	-	
20/20 Int	4	1	1	9	9*		-	-	-	-	78	95	3	31.66	1-11	-	
20/20	7	4	3	51	28*	51.00	-	-	2	-	138	176	5	35.20	1-11	-	

Career Performances

	M	Inn	NO	Runs	HS	Avg	100	50	Ct	St	Balls	Runs	Wkts	Avg	BB	5I	10M
Test																	
FC	53	73	13	2205	157*	36.75	4	13	23	-	9828	5809	171	33.97	7-107	10	-
ODI	4	4	1	60	31*	20.00	-	-	2	-	186	164	3	54.66	1-16	-	
List A	37	26	7	288	41*	15.15	-	-	15	-	1281	1108	29	38.20	3-37	-	
20/20 Int	4	1	1	9	9*		-	-	-	-	78	95	3	31.66	1-11	-	
20/20	15	10	5	69	28*	13.80	-	-	5	-	264	338	12	28.16	4-24	-	

RAYNER, O. P.   Sussex

Name: Oliver (<u>Ollie</u>) Philip Rayner
Role: Right-hand bat, right-arm off-spin bowler
Born: 1 November 1985, Walsrode, Germany
Height: 6ft 5¼in **Weight:** 16st
Nickname: Mervin, Rocket, Rain-cakes,
KP ('Kelvin Pietersen, not Kevin!')
County debut: 2006
Place in batting averages: 233rd av. 17.30
(2008 214th av. 22.17)
Place in bowling averages: 114th av. 43.50
(2008 97th av. 33.61)
Parents: Mark and Penny
Marital status: Single
Education: St Bede's, The Dicker, Hailsham,
East Sussex
Qualifications: 7 GCSEs, 2 A-levels, Level 1 coaching
Overseas tours: Sussex Academy to Sri Lanka 2001, to South Africa 2003;
England Performance Programme to India 2008-09
Overseas teams played for: University of Cape Town; Western Province
Cricket moments to forget: 'Chirping at Somerset, then getting a pair!'
Cricketers particularly admired: Andrew Flintoff, Shane Warne, Chris Gayle
Young players to look out for: Tom Smith, Krishna Singh
Other sports played: Football (Eastbourne Town Reserves; Eastbourne United 1st XI)
Other sports followed: Football (Brighton & Hove Albion)
Favourite band: Kanye West, Common, Talib Kwali
Relaxations: 'Bodyboarding, skiing, chilling with mates'
Extras: South of England U15. England Development Squad U19. Sussex 2nd XI
Player of the Year 2005. Scored century (101) on first-class debut v Sri Lankans
at Hove 2006, batting at No. 8. NBC Denis Compton award for most promising
young Sussex player 2006, 2008. Member of England Performance Programme
squad 2009-10

Best batting: 101 Sussex v Sri Lankans, Hove 2006
Best bowling: 5-49 Sussex v Hampshire, Arundel 2008

2009 Season

	M	Inn	NO	Runs	HS	Avg	100	50	Ct	St	Balls	Runs	Wkts	Avg	BB	5I	10M
Test																	
FC	11	11	1	173	60	17.30	-	1	15	-	1766	870	20	43.50	4-186	-	-
ODI																	
List A																		
20/20 Int																		
20/20																		

Career Performances

	M	Inn	NO	Runs	HS	Avg	100	50	Ct	St	Balls	Runs	Wkts	Avg	BB	5I	10M
Test																		
FC	31	35	7	526	101	18.78	1	1	32	-	5143	2674	71	37.66	5-49	3	-
ODI																		
List A	15	13	6	151	61	21.57	-	1	4	-	486	506	10	50.60	2-31	-	
20/20 Int																		
20/20	7	3	0	16	11	5.33	-	-	-	-	49	93	1	93.00	1-20	-	

READ, C. M. W. Nottinghamshire

Name: Christopher (<u>Chris</u>) Mark Wells Read
Role: Right-hand bat, wicket-keeper, county captain
Born: 10 August 1978, Paignton, Devon
Height: 5ft 8in **Weight:** 11st
Nickname: Readie, Reados
County debut: 1997 (one-day, Glos), 1998 (Notts)
County cap: 1999 (Notts)
Benefit: 2009
Test debut: 1999
ODI debut: 1999-2000
Twenty20 Int debut: 2006
1000 runs in a season: 2
1st-Class 200s: 1
Place in batting averages: 6th av. 75.18
(2008 44th av. 45.37)
Parents: Geoffrey and Carolyn
Wife and date of marriage: Louise, 2 October 2004
Education: Torquay Boys' Grammar School; University of Bath;
Loughborough University
Qualifications: 9 GCSEs, 4 A-levels, senior coaching award

Overseas tours: West of England U13 to Netherlands 1991; West of England U15 to West Indies 1992-93; England U17 to Netherlands (International Youth Tournament) 1995; England U19 to Pakistan 1996-97; England A to Kenya and Sri Lanka 1997-98, to Zimbabwe and South Africa 1998-99, to West Indies 2000-01, 2005-06; England to South Africa and Zimbabwe 1999-2000, to Australia 2002-03 (VB Series), to Bangladesh and Sri Lanka 2003-04, to West Indies 2003-04, to South Africa 2004-05, to India (ICC Champions Trophy) 2006-07, to Australia 2006-07; British Universities to South Africa 2002; ECB National Academy to Australia and Sri Lanka 2002-03; England VI to Hong Kong 2005

Career highlights to date: 'Winning Test series v West Indies 2004'

Cricket moments to forget: 'Ducking a slower ball from Chris Cairns in second Test v New Zealand at Lord's 1999'

Cricketers particularly admired: Adam Gilchrist, Bruce French, Alan Knott, Bob Taylor, Jack Russell, Ian Healy

Young players to look out for: James Hildreth

Other sports played: Hockey (Devon U18, U21; West of England U17; South Nottingham)

Other sports followed: Football (Torquay United)

Favourite band: Stereophonics

Relaxations: 'Reading, listening to music, keeping fit and going out with friends'

Player website: www.thechrisreadcricketacademy.com

Extras: Played for Devon 1995-97. Represented England U18 1996 and England U19 1997. NBC Denis Compton Award for most promising young Gloucestershire player 1997. Was selected for the England A tour to Kenya and Sri Lanka 1997-98 aged 18 and without having played a first-class game. Recorded eight dismissals on Test debut in the first Test v New Zealand at Edgbaston 1999. Man of the Match in the first ODI v West Indies at Georgetown 2003-04 after striking a match-winning 15-ball 27 including three sixes and a four. ECB National Academy 2005-06. Scored 165* v Essex at Trent Bridge 2007, in the process sharing with David Hussey (275) in a new record fifth-wicket partnership for Nottinghamshire (359). Scored 240 v Essex at Chelmsford 2007, becoming the first Nottinghamshire wicket-keeper to score a double century. Appointed captain of Nottinghamshire in 2008. Only Nottinghamshire player to pass 1000 runs in 2009

Opinions on cricket: 'Whilst new money being invested into the game in the short term is most welcome, administrators need to ensure that the longer-term future of the game is safeguarded. The balls we use in Championship cricket are not up to scratch. Choosing a ball can resemble a lottery, and many don't make it past 40 overs before they are changed.'

Best batting: 240 Nottinghamshire v Essex, Chelmsford 2007

2009 Season

	M	Inn	NO	Runs	HS	Avg	100	50	Ct	St	Balls	Runs	Wkts	Avg	BB	5I	10M
Test																	
FC	16	22	6	1203	125	75.18	4	6	46	4	6	2	0		-	-	-
ODI																	
List A	14	11	0	120	57	10.90	-	1	8	4	0	0	0		-	-	
20/20 Int																	
20/20	9	6	2	144	58*	36.00	-	1	7	-	0	0	0		-	-	

Career Performances

	M	Inn	NO	Runs	HS	Avg	100	50	Ct	St	Balls	Runs	Wkts	Avg	BB	5I	10M
Test	15	23	4	360	55	18.94	-	1	48	6	0	0	0		-	-	-
FC	222	328	56	9755	240	35.86	16	52	647	36	96	90	0		-	-	-
ODI	36	24	7	300	30*	17.64	-	-	41	2	0	0	0		-	-	
List A	250	199	48	4071	135	26.96	2	13	248	57	0	0	0		-	-	
20/20 Int	1	1	0	13	13	13.00	-	-	1	-	0	0	0		-	-	
20/20	46	41	11	799	58*	26.63	-	1	31	7	0	0	0		-	-	

REDFERN, D. J. Derbyshire

Name: Daniel (<u>Dan</u>) James Redfern
Role: Left-hand bat, occasional
right-arm off-spin bowler
Born: 18 April 1990, Shrewsbury, Shropshire
Height: 5ft 10in **Weight:** 11st
Nickname: Panda, Redders, Redskin
County debut: 2006 (one-day),
2007 (first-class)
Place in batting averages: 143rd av. 30.36
Parents: Michael and Shirley
Marital status: Single
Family links with cricket: 'Grandfathers, father
and brother all played for Leycett CC, Staffs.
Brother also plays Shropshire U21'
Education: Adams' Grammar School, Newport,
Shropshire
Qualifications: 10 GCSEs, 'A-levels'
Overseas tours: England U16 to South Africa 2005-06; Derbyshire Academy to
Port Elizabeth 2006-07; England U19 to Malaysia (U19 World Cup) 2007-08, to
South Africa 2008-09
Career highlights to date: 'Playing for Derbyshire 1st XI and for England U19
v Pakistan. Winning Man of the Match in a televised game against Yorkshire in which
I made 57 not out.'

Cricket moments to forget: 'Run out by Lou Vincent on Sky [on county one-day debut]'
Cricket superstitions: 'None'
Cricketers particularly admired: Graham Thorpe
Young players to look out for: Liam Dawson (Hampshire), Tom Poynton and Jake Needham (both Derbyshire)
Other sports played: 'A bit of golf'
Other sports followed: Football (Stoke City), rugby (Sale Sharks)
Favourite band: The Kooks
Relaxations: 'Watching telly, music, friends'
Extras: Has represented England U15, U16, U17 and U19. Neil Lloyd Memorial Trophy for Best Batsman at Bunbury Festival 2005. Made one-day debut for Derbyshire v Worcestershire at Worcester in Pro40 2006, aged 16. Made Minor Counties Trophy debut for Shropshire v Northumberland at Oswestry 2007, scoring 107. NBC Denis Compton Award for most promising young Derbyshire player 2009. Committed to Derbyshire until 2012
Opinions on cricket: 'Keep Pro40 – it's more exciting than 50-overs.'
Best batting: 95 Derbyshire v Northamptonshire, Northampton 2009
Best bowling: 1-7 Derbyshire v Somerset, Derby 2007
1-7 Derbyshire v Warwickshire, Edgbaston 2008

2009 Season

	M	Inn	NO	Runs	HS	Avg	100	50	Ct	St	Balls	Runs	Wkts	Avg	BB	5I	10M
Test																	
FC	14	23	1	668	95	30.36	-	5	8	-	192	117	2	58.50	1-26	-	-
ODI																	
List A	12	11	0	225	53	20.45	-	1	4	-	154	124	5	24.80	2-10	-	
20/20 Int																	
20/20																	

Career Performances

	M	Inn	NO	Runs	HS	Avg	100	50	Ct	St	Balls	Runs	Wkts	Avg	BB	5I	10M
Test																	
FC	23	36	3	1007	95	30.51	-	7	14	-	414	241	5	48.20	1-7	-	-
ODI																	
List A	23	20	1	410	57*	21.57	-	2	5	-	226	188	5	37.60	2-10	-	
20/20 Int																	
20/20	1	1	0	9	9	9.00	-	-	-	-	0	0	0		-	-	

74. This Pakistani took 93 Test match catches between 1976 and 1993. Who is he?

REED, M. T. Glamorgan

Name: <u>Michael</u> Thomas Reed
Role: Right-hand bat, right-arm
medium-fast bowler
Born: 10 September 1988, Leicester
Height: 6ft 7in **Weight:** 14st 3lbs
Nickname: Frank ('after Mike Reid, who
played Frank Butcher in *EastEnders*')
County debut: No first team appearance
Parents: Susan and Aidan
Marital status: Single
Education: De Lisle Catholic School;
Cardiff University
Qualifications: 4 A-levels
Career outside cricket: Student

Off-season: 'Studying for my maths degree (currently
in my second year), and training with Cardiff UCCE'
Overseas teams played for: Kensington CC, Adelaide, 2007-08
Career highlights to date: 'Debut for Wales Minor Counties – match figures of 7-83'
Cricket moments to forget: 'Welsh Cup quarter-final – I was last man out with just
two runs needed to win'
Cricket superstitions: 'None'
Cricketers particularly admired: Brett Lee
Other sports followed: 'BIG supporter of Leicester City Football Club – had
a season ticket for 10 years'
Favourite band: Maroon 5
Relaxations: 'Watching Leicester City'
Extras: Has played for Wales Minor Counties and Glamorgan Second X1 for whom
he made his debut in 2009. Also appeared regularly for the Usk club side. Awarded
a Development Contract for 2010
Opinions on cricket: 'There's too much Twenty20 cricket.'

---

75. In how many Test matches did Javed Miandad feature?

REES, G. P.   Glamorgan

Name: <u>Gareth</u> Peter Rees
Role: Left-hand opening bat, right-arm
fast-medium 'utility bowler'
Born: 8 April 1985, Swansea
Height: 6ft 1in   **Weight:** 15st
Nickname: Gums, Max Headroom, Lionheart,
Leg, Lego-hair, Worm
County debut: 2006
1000 runs in a season: 2
Place in batting averages: 43rd av. 46.13
(2008 62nd av. 40.29)
Parents: Peter and Diane
Marital status: Single
Education: Coedcae Comprehensive, Llanelli;
Coleg Sir Gar; Bath University

Qualifications: 10 GCSEs, 3 A-levels, Maths and Physics degree (First)
Overseas tours: Glamorgan to Guernsey 2006-07 ('and Mark Wallace's stag do,
Galway 2007!')
Career highlights to date: 'Getting my first first-class century against Essex, and
fielding short leg for Dean Cosker'
Cricket moments to forget: 'Getting run out by Ryan Watkins. Rooming with
Adam Shantry'
Cricket superstitions: 'There's no such thing as luck!'
Cricketers particularly admired: Brian Lara, David Hemp
Other sports played: Golf, rugby (Wales U17, Llanelli Scarlets U21, Bath University)
Other sports followed: Rugby (Llanelli Scarlets, Felinfoel RFC)
Favourite band: Oasis
Relaxations: 'Facebook, researching using the compact muon solenoid at CERN
searching for the "God" particle'
Extras: Played for Wales Minor Counties in the 2004 and 2005 C&G and in Minor
Counties competitions 2002-07. Topped the Glamorgan batting averages for 2008
Opinions on cricket: 'Grounds should provide more activities for supporters and
players for when it rains – for example, CHEERLEADERS!'
Best batting: 154 Glamorgan v Surrey, The Oval 2009

2009 Season

	M	Inn	NO	Runs	HS	Avg	100	50	Ct	St	Balls	Runs	Wkts	Avg	BB	5I	10M
Test																	
FC	17	25	2	1061	154	46.13	3	4	15	-	0	0	0		-	-	-
ODI																	
List A	10	10	1	327	123*	36.33	1	2	1	-	0	0	0		-	-	
20/20 Int																	
20/20	3	3	0	15	15	5.00	-	-	2	-	0	0	0		-	-	

Career Performances

	M	Inn	NO	Runs	HS	Avg	100	50	Ct	St	Balls	Runs	Wkts	Avg	BB	5I	10M
Test																	
FC	46	76	4	2662	154	36.97	8	13	44	-	0	0	0		-	-	-
ODI																	
List A	16	16	1	490	123*	32.66	1	3	3	-	0	0	0		-	-	
20/20 Int																	
20/20	3	3	0	15	15	5.00	-	-	2	-	0	0	0		-	-	

RIAZUDDIN, H.   Hampshire

Name: Hamza Riazuddin
Role: Right-hand bat, right-arm
fast-medium bowler
Born: 19 December 1989, Hendon, Middlesex
County debut: 2008
Education: Bradfield College, Reading
Overseas tours: England U19 to South Africa 2009
Extras: Hampshire Cricket Academy player. Has
also played for Hampshire 2nd XI. Awarded a
development contract for 2009
Best batting: 4 Hampshire v Somerset,
Taunton 2008
Best bowling: 1-21 Hampshire v Somerset,
Taunton 2008

2009 Season

	M	Inn	NO	Runs	HS	Avg	100	50	Ct	St	Balls	Runs	Wkts	Avg	BB	5I	10M
Test																	
FC	1	1	0	3	3	3.00	-	-	-	-	132	72	2	36.00	1-25	-	-
ODI																	
List A	9	2	2	2	2*		-	-	3	-	390	315	6	52.50	2-47	-	
20/20 Int																	
20/20	6	2	2	16	13*		-	-	-	-	114	148	7	21.14	3-15	-	

Career Performances

	M	Inn	NO	Runs	HS	Avg	100	50	Ct	St	Balls	Runs	Wkts	Avg	BB	5I	10M
Test																	
FC	2	2	0	7	4	3.50	-	-	-	-	306	171	3	57.00	1-21	-	-
ODI																	
List A	12	2	2	2	2*		-	-	3	-	534	402	8	50.25	2-47	-	
20/20 Int																	
20/20	11	4	3	16	13*	16.00	-	-	2	-	210	296	9	32.88	3-15	-	

RICHARDSON, A.   Worcestershire

Name: Alan Richardson
Role: Right-hand bat, right-arm medium bowler
Born: 6 May 1975, Newcastle-under-Lyme, Staffs
Height: 6ft 3in **Weight:** 14st
Nickname: Richo
County debut: 1995 (Derbyshire), 1999 (Warwickshire), 2005 (Middlesex)
County cap: 2002 (Warwickshire), 2005 (Middlesex)
50 wickets in a season: 1
Place in batting averages: (2008 243rd av. 13.16)
Place in bowling averages: 135th av. 56.18 (2008 25th av. 23.00)
Parents: Roy and Sandra
Marital status: Single
Family links with cricket: 'Dad captained Little Stoke 3rd XI and now patrols the boundary with pint in hand at the Sid Jenkins Cricket Ground'
Education: Alleyne's High School, Stone; Stafford College of Further Education
Qualifications: 8 GCSEs, 2 A-levels, 2 AS-levels, Level 2 coaching
Career outside cricket: 'Anything from coaching to spread betting to mowing lawns'
Off-season: 'Finishing my Level 3 coaching qualification'

Overseas tours: Derbyshire to Malaga 1995; Warwickshire to Bloemfontein 2000, to Cape Town 2001, 2002, to Portugal 2003; England Lions to India 2007-08
Overseas teams played for: Northern Natal, South Africa 1994-96; Hawkesbury CC, Sydney 1997-99; Northern Districts, Sydney 1999-2000, 2001-02, 2002-03, 2004-05 – 2006-07; Avendale, Cape Town 2000-01; Kyriang Mountains, Australia 2003-04
Career highlights to date: 'Winning NSCC league with Little Stoke in 1998. Getting capped by both Warwickshire and Middlesex. Doing well on my home debuts'
Cricket moments to forget: 'The whole 2006 season! (*Out for four weeks with a broken thumb; for the rest of the season with a floating bone in the elbow*); Being hooked by Jason Brown, rooming with David Nash and batting below Tim Murtagh'
Cricket superstitions: 'None'
Cricketers particularly admired: Angus Fraser, Tim Munton, Ed Reynolds
Young players to look out for: Will Speer (Middlesex), Ali Natkiel and Ian Carr (both Warwickshire)
Other sports followed: Football (Stoke City)
Favourite band: Maximo Park, Pete Murray, Jamie Scott and the Town, Josh Rouse
Relaxations: 'Cooking and reading'
Extras: *Cricket World* award for best bowling performance in Oxford U19 Festival (8-60 v Devon). Topped Minor Counties bowling averages with Staffordshire 1998 and won Minor Counties bowling award. Most Improved 2nd XI Player 1999. Outstanding Performance of the Year 1999 for his 8-51 v Gloucestershire on home debut. Scored 91 v Hampshire at Edgbaston 2002, in the process sharing with Nick Knight (255*) in a Warwickshire record tenth-wicket stand of 214. Had first innings figures of 7-113 on first-class debut for Middlesex v Nottinghamshire at Lord's 2005. Left Middlesex for Worcestershire September 2009
Opinions on cricket: 'Counties need to use 12-month contracts wisely. Invest and develop your players as much as possible.'
Best batting: 91 Warwickshire v Hampshire, Edgbaston 2002
Best bowling: 8-46 Warwickshire v Sussex, Edgbaston 2002

2009 Season

	M	Inn	NO	Runs	HS	Avg	100	50	Ct	St	Balls	Runs	Wkts	Avg	BB	5I	10M
Test																	
FC	6	7	4	40	18*	13.33	-	-	5	-	1334	618	11	56.18	3-52	-	-
ODI																	
List A	1	0	0	0	0		-	-	2	-	36	19	1	19.00	1-19	-	
20/20 Int																	
20/20	3	0	0	0	0		-	-	1	-	72	88	5	17.60	3-29	-	

Career Performances

	M	Inn	NO	Runs	HS	Avg	100	50	Ct	St	Balls	Runs	Wkts	Avg	BB	5I	10M
Test																	
FC	108	109	42	761	91	11.35	-	1	33	-	19612	9357	314	29.79	8-46	9	1
ODI																	
List A	62	27	17	104	21*	10.40	-	-	13	-	2716	2121	58	36.56	5-35	1	
20/20 Int																	
20/20	9	2	1	6	6*	6.00	-	-	2	-	186	223	9	24.77	3-13	-	

RICHARDSON, M. J. Durham

Name: <u>Michael</u> John Richardson
Role: Right-hand bat, wicket-keeper
Born: 4 October 1986, Port Elizabeth, South Africa
Height: 5ft 10in
Nickname: Richie
County debut: No first team appearance
Family links with cricket: Father, David, played for
South Africa 1991-98 and spent almost 20 years
playing for Eastern Province and Northern Trasvaal.
Grandfather, John, and uncle, Ralph, also played club
cricket in South Africa. Cousin Matthew currently
plays for Border CC

Overseas Teams played for: Western Province CC
2009-10
Cricketers particularly admired: Mark Boucher,
Jacques Kallis, Brian Lara, Neil McKenzie, JP Duminy
Extras: Scored 136* v Glamorgan 2nd XI 2008. Captained MCC Young Cricketers
2009

76. This Pakistan bowler took 414 Test match wickets between
1985 and 2002. Name him.

ROBERTS, A.   Leicestershire

Name: Alex Roberts
Role: Right-hand bat, right-arm fast
bowler; all-rounder
Born: 21 June 1983, Stockton-on-Tees, Co. Durham
Height: 6ft 3in **Weight:** 13st
Nickname: Robbo a rob fridge
County debut: 2008 (one-day, Essex),
2009 (one-day, Leicestershire)
Parents: Tony and Susan
Marital status: Single
Education: King's Manor Comprehensive
School, Middlesbrough; Teesside Tertiary
College (sports college)

Qualifications: 9 GCSEs, Sport & Recreation Level 1
Career outside cricket: Poker and male escort
Off-season: 'Playing for Springy (Springvale) South in Melbourne in the Dandenong
District Cricket Association competition'
Overseas tours: England U19 to Australia and New Zealand (World Cup) 2001-02
Overseas teams played for: Cornwall CC, Napier, New Zealand 2001-02 – 2003-04;
Berwick CC, Melbourne 2006-07, 2007-08; Springvale South CC, Melbourne 2009-10
Career highlights to date: 'Playing for Leicestershire and Essex in Twenty20, and
for England U19'
Cricket moments to forget: 'HD Ackerman dropping Michael Vaughan off me – it
was a dolly, and was just before he retired'
Cricket superstitions: 'Need chewing gum when batting. Left pad first'
Favourite sledging line: 'Being told I look like a baboon's a**e!'
Cricketers particularly admired: Andrew Flintoff, Darren Gough
Young players to look out for: Paul Goodchild and Brett Roberts (both Cleveland)
Other sports played: 'All sports – play golf off a 6 handicap – and poker'
Other sports followed: Football (Middlesbrough)
Injuries: 'Torn stomach muscle ended my season in June. A grade 2 tear that just
kept tearing more'
Favourite band: Westlife
Relaxations: 'Love playing poker and sunbathing and chasing nice-looking women
around nightclubs. Love playing hide and seek with my little brother Lee'
Extras: Has played for Cumberland, MCC Young Cricketers, England U19 and
Yorkshire Cricket board, as well as Worcestershire and Durham 2nd XIs. Teesside
Sports Personality of the Year 2005. Won *The Journal* Senior Cricketer of the Year
award for his performances with Berwick CC, Melbourne, 2007-08 (713 runs at an
average of 79.2 and 23 wickets at an average of 12.8; Highest score – 158; best
bowling – 6-24). Played club cricket with both Gidea Park and Romford in the Essex
Premier League

Opinions on cricket: 'Too many non-English players, and I hope there will be a stop to this at some point.'

2009 Season

	M	Inn	NO	Runs	HS	Avg	100	50	Ct	St	Balls	Runs	Wkts	Avg	BB	5I	10M
Test																	
FC																	
ODI																	
List A																	
20/20 Int																	
20/20	1	0	0	0	0	-	-	-	-	-	6	12	0		-	-	

Career Performances

	M	Inn	NO	Runs	HS	Avg	100	50	Ct	St	Balls	Runs	Wkts	Avg	BB	5I	10M
Test																	
FC																	
ODI																	
List A	1	1	0	1	1	1.00	-	-	-	-	24	22	1	22.00	1-22	-	
20/20 Int																	
20/20	2	0	0	0	0	-	-	-	-	-	6	12	0		-	-	

ROBSON, S. D.   *Middlesex*

Name: Samuel (<u>Sam</u>) David Robson
Role: Right-hand bat, left-arm leg-break bowler
Born: 1 July 1989, Paddington, NSW, Australia
Nickname: Robbo
County debut: 2008 (one-day), 2009 (first-class)
Place in batting averages: 118th av. 33.92
Overseas teams played for: University of NSW 2005-06; New South Wales 2008-09; Eastern Suburbs, Sydney 2009-10
Cricketers particularly admired: Shane Warne, Andrew Flintoff
Other sports followed: Football (Arsenal)
Favourite band: Coldplay
Extras: Has represented Australia at U19 level, and New South Wales at both U17 and U19 level, as well as playing for New South Wales Colts. Scored his maiden first-grade century at the age of 17 years 210 days, becoming the youngest player in 115 years of Sydney first-grade cricket to have both a century and a five-wicket haul to his name. Middlesex 2nd XI 2008. Made his one-day debut for the county in Pro40 v Worcestershire at the

end of the 2008 season. Made his Championship debut v Essex at Chelmsford, June 2009. He holds a UK passport and is not considered an oveseas player
Best batting: 110 Middlesex v Essex, Lord's 2009

2009 Season

	M	Inn	NO	Runs	HS	Avg	100	50	Ct	St	Balls	Runs	Wkts	Avg	BB	5I	10M
Test																	
FC	7	13	0	441	110	33.92	1	2	12	-	12	5	0		-	-	-
ODI																	
List A	3	1	0	48	48	48.00	-	-	-	-	0	0	0		-	-	
20/20 Int																	
20/20																	

Career Performances

	M	Inn	NO	Runs	HS	Avg	100	50	Ct	St	Balls	Runs	Wkts	Avg	BB	5I	10M
Test																	
FC	7	13	0	441	110	33.92	1	2	12	-	12	5	0		-	-	-
ODI																	
List A	4	2	0	69	48	34.50	-	-	-	-	0	0	0		-	-	
20/20 Int																	
20/20																	

ROGERS, C. J. L. Derbyshire

Name: Christopher (<u>Chris</u>) John Llewellyn Rogers
Role: Left-hand bat, leg-spin/right-arm medium bowler, county captain
Born: 31 August 1977, Sydney, Australia
Height: 5ft 11in **Weight:** 12st 8lbs
Nickname: Bucky
County debut: 2004 (Derbys), 2005 (Leics), 2006 (Northants)
County cap: 2008 (Derbyshire)
Test debut: 2007-08
1000 runs in a season: 3
1st-Class 200s: 6
1st-Class 300s: 1
Place in batting averages: 9th av. 73.05 (2008 12th av. 57.16)

Family links with cricket: Father played for New South Wales and became a cricket administrator
Overseas tours: Australia A to Pakistan 2007-08

Overseas teams played for: Western Australia 1998-99 – 2007-08; Victoria 2008-09
Extras: Represented Australia U19 1995-96. Has represented Australia A. Scored two centuries (101*/102*) in Pura Cup match v South Australia at Perth 2001-02, winning Man of the Match award. Won three Western Australia awards 2002-03 – Lawrie Sawle Medal (leading first-class and one-day player), President's Silver Trophy (season's best individual performance – for his 194 v NSW in the Pura Cup), and Excalibur Award (spirit of WA cricket). An overseas player with Derbyshire 2004 but forced to return home early injured; a temporary overseas player with Leicestershire during the 2005 season. Scored 209 v Australians at Leicester 2005, in the process sharing with Darren Robinson (81) in a record opening partnership for a county against an Australian touring side (247). An overseas player with Northamptonshire 2006-07. Scored century and double century (128/222*) in the same match, v Somerset at Taunton 2006, becoming the first Northants batsman to achieve the feat since Allan Lamb in 1992. Pura Cup Player of the Year 2006-07; also named State Player of the Year at the 2007 Allan Border Medal awards. Rejoined Derbyshire for 2008 and has continued as their overseas player since. Appointed county captain for 2010
Best batting: 319 Northamptonshire v Gloucestershire, Northampton 2006
Best bowling: 1-16 Northamptonshire v Leicestershire, Northampton 2006

2009 Season

	M	Inn	NO	Runs	HS	Avg	100	50	Ct	St	Balls	Runs	Wkts	Avg	BB	5I	10M
Test																	
FC	13	21	1	1461	222	73.05	6	4	21	-	0	0	0		-	-	-
ODI																	
List A	9	9	1	467	111*	58.37	1	3	5	-	0	0	0		-	-	
20/20 Int																	
20/20	10	10	0	256	58	25.60	-	3	10	-	0	0	0		-	-	

Career Performances

	M	Inn	NO	Runs	HS	Avg	100	50	Ct	St	Balls	Runs	Wkts	Avg	BB	5I	10M
Test	1	2	0	19	15	9.50	-	-	1	-	0	0	0		-	-	-
FC	149	263	17	12865	319	52.29	39	61	150	-	224	126	1	126.00	1-16	-	-
ODI																	
List A	109	105	7	3495	117*	35.66	3	26	55	-	24	26	2	13.00	2-22	-	
20/20 Int																	
20/20	21	17	0	350	58	20.58	-	3	15	-	0	0	0		-	-	

---

77. Which Pakistan bowler took 373 Test match wickets between 1989 and 2003?

ROLAND-JONES, T. S. Middlesex

Name: Tobias (<u>Toby</u>) Skelton Roland-Jones
Role: Right-hand bat, right-arm fast-medium bowler
Born: February 1988, Ashford, Middlesex
County debut: No first-team appearance
Family links with cricket: Older brother Oliver
has played for Middlesex 2nd XI, and plays club
cricket for Sunbury CC (1st XI captain 2010)
Education: Hampton School; University of Leeds
Extras: To date has played for Sunbury, Surrey
Second XI and Middlesex Second XI. Led the
Leeds/Bradford UCCE bowling attack as they won
the MCC Universities championship title in 2009.
Signed a full-time contract with Middlesex in
November 2009

ROOT, J. E. Yorkshire

Name: Joseph (<u>Joe</u>) Edward Root
Role: Right-hand bat, right arm
off-break bowler
Born: 30 December 1990, Sheffield, Yorkshire
Height: 6ft **Weight:** 12st 4lbs
Nickname: Rooty
County debut: 2009 (one-day)
Parents: Matt and Helen
Marital status: Single
Family links with cricket: Younger brother
Billy is with Yorkshire Academy
Education: Dore Primary; King Ecgbert's School;
Worksop College
Qualifications: 8 GCSEs
Off-season: 'England U19 to Bangladesh and New
Zealand for the World Cup'
Overseas tours: England U19 to Bangladesh 2009-10, to New Zealand (ICC U19
World Cup) 2009-10
Overseas teams played for: St Andrew's College, Bloemfontein
Career highlights to date: 'Making 63 on my first-team debut'
Cricket moments to forget: 'Losing in the final of the U17 two-day competition'
Cricket superstitions: 'Tidy kit'

Favourite sledging line: 'Aimed at me – "Shall I come off my short run to this one, skip?"'
Cricketers particularly admired: Michael Vaughan
Young players to look out for: Billy Root (Yorkshire)
Other sports played: Hockey ('School First XI, national semi-finalists')
Other sports followed: Football (Sheffield United)
Favourite band: Arctic Monkeys
Relaxations: 'Learning the guitar'
Extras: Was the youngest player ever to be offered a scholarship for Yorkshire. Signed a three year Junior Pro contract with Yorkshire November 2009 having previously played U17, Academy and Second XI.
Opinions on cricket: 'Love all the different forms, but Test cricket is the best.'

2009 Season

	M	Inn	NO	Runs	HS	Avg	100	50	Ct	St	Balls	Runs	Wkts	Avg	BB	5I	10M
Test																	
FC																	
ODI																	
List A	1	1	0	63	63	63.00	-	1	1	-	0	0	0		-	-	
20/20 Int																	
20/20																	

Career Performances

	M	Inn	NO	Runs	HS	Avg	100	50	Ct	St	Balls	Runs	Wkts	Avg	BB	5I	10M
Test																	
FC																	
ODI																	
List A	1	1	0	63	63	63.00	-	1	1	-	0	0	0		-	-	
20/20 Int																	
20/20																	

78. Bangladesh have played England in eight one-day internationals up until 2007. How many have they won?

ROY, J. J.   Surrey

Name: <u>Jason</u> Jonathan Roy
Role: Right-hand bat
Born: 21 July 1990, Reigate, Surrey
County debut: 2008 (one-day)
Education: Whitgift School
Qualifications: A-levels (Sports Science
and Business Studies)
Overseas teams played for: Port Adelaide CC
2008-09

Extras: Lived in South Africa until moving to
England at the age of 10. Represented Surrey at
U16, U17 and U19 level, as well as playing for
Surrey 2nd XI 2007-08. Scored 48 off 33 balls in
his 2nd XI debut against Hampshire to help Surrey
win by 3 runs. Represented the South at U17 level
in the ECB Regional Festival in Loughborough in July 2007. Appeared as a substitute
fielder for England's Test team against South Africa in the final Test of the 2008 series
at The Oval. Awarded the Easter Group scholarship at the end of the 2008 season,
allowing him to attend the Darren Lehmann Academy during the 2008-09 off-season.
Turned down the offer of a place at St Mary's University College to concentrate on
cricket. Awarded a 12-month Emerging Player contract in October 2009

2009 Season

	M	Inn	NO	Runs	HS	Avg	100	50	Ct	St	Balls	Runs	Wkts	Avg	BB	5I	10M
Test																	
FC																	
ODI																	
List A	1	1	0	6	6	6.00	-	-	-	-	0	0	0		-	-	
20/20 Int																	
20/20																	

Career Performances

	M	Inn	NO	Runs	HS	Avg	100	50	Ct	St	Balls	Runs	Wkts	Avg	BB	5I	10M
Test																	
FC																	
ODI																	
List A	3	3	0	12	6	4.00	-	-	1	-	6	12	0		-	-	
20/20 Int																	
20/20	1	1	0	4	4	4.00	-	-	-	-	0	0	0		-	-	

RUDOLPH, J. A.   Yorkshire

Name: Jacobus (<u>Jacques</u>) Andries Rudolph
Role: Left-hand bat, right-arm leg-spin bowler;
county vice-captain
Born: 4 May 1981, Springs, South Africa
Height: 5ft 10in **Weight:** 12st 4lbs
Nickname: Jakes
County debut: 2007
County cap: 2007
Test debut: 2003
ODI debut: 2003
Twenty20 Int debut: 2005-06
1000 runs in a season: 3
1st-Class 200s: 2
Place in batting averages: 40th av. 48.78
(2008 14th av. 56.17)
Parents: Johan and Monica
Wife and date of marriage: Elna, 5 November 2003
Family links with cricket: 'Dad coaches the Namibian national side – my brother Gerhard plays for them.'
Education: Afrikaanse Hoer Seunskool ('Affies')
Overseas tours: South Africa U19 to Pakistan 1998-99, to Sri Lanka (U19 World Cup) 1999-2000; South Africa A to Zimbabwe 2002-03, to Sri Lanka 2005-06; South Africa to Australia 2001-02, to Bangladesh 2003, to England 2003, to Pakistan 2003-04, to New Zealand 2003-04, to Sri Lanka 2004, to England (ICC Champions Trophy) 2004, to India 2004-05, to West Indies 2004-05, to Australia 2005-06, to Sri Lanka 2006
Overseas teams played for: Northerns B/Northerns 1997-98 – 2003-04; Titans 2003-04 – 2004-05; Eagles 2005-06 – 2008-09; Titans 2009-10
Career highlights to date: 'Making 222* on my Test debut.'
Cricketers particularly admired: Justin Langer
Young players to look out for: Adil Rashid
Other sports followed: Football (Manchester United)
Favourite band: U2, Dire Straits
Extras: Was twice on verge of Test debut – selected for the third Test v India at Centurion 2001-02, only for the match to be stripped of Test status due to the Denness Affair; chosen for the third Test v Australia in Sydney 2001-02, only for his selection to be overruled in favour of Justin Ontong. Man of the Match for his 222* on Test debut in the first Test v Bangladesh in Chittagong 2003; in the process shared with Boeta Dippenaar (177*) in the highest partnership for any wicket for South Africa in Tests (429*). One of *South African Cricket Annual*'s five Cricketers of the Year 2003. Scored second innings 102* to help save the first Test v Australia at Perth 2005-06.

Was due to join Derbyshire as an overseas player in 2006 but withdrew with a shoulder problem. Joined Yorkshire in 2007; is no longer considered an overseas player. Man of the Match v Cape Cobras at Cape Town in the SuperSport Series 2007-08 (94/5-80)

Relaxations: 'Fly fishing and adventure motorbiking (travelling)'
Best batting: 222* South Africa v Bangladesh, Chittagong 2003
Best bowling: 5-80 Eagles v Cape Cobras, Cape Town 2007-08

2009 Season

	M	Inn	NO	Runs	HS	Avg	100	50	Ct	St	Balls	Runs	Wkts	Avg	BB	5I	10M
Test																	
FC	17	29	1	1366	198	48.78	4	6	14	-	150	111	0	-	-	-	-
ODI																	
List A	15	15	1	685	118	48.92	1	6	11	-	0	0	0	-	-	-	
20/20 Int																	
20/20	10	8	0	166	61	20.75	-	1	-	-	18	22	0	-	-	-	

Career Performances

	M	Inn	NO	Runs	HS	Avg	100	50	Ct	St	Balls	Runs	Wkts	Avg	BB	5I	10M
Test	35	63	7	2028	222*	36.21	5	8	22	-	664	432	4	108.00	1-1	-	-
FC	163	275	18	11430	222*	44.47	33	52	149	-	4331	2440	58	42.06	5-80	3	-
ODI	45	39	6	1174	81	35.57	-	7	11	-	24	26	0	-	-	-	
List A	169	157	23	5922	134*	44.19	8	39	62	-	377	341	10	34.10	4-40	-	
20/20 Int	1	1	1	6	6*	-	-	-	-	-	0	0	0	-	-	-	
20/20	45	41	8	982	71	29.75	-	6	11	-	151	194	10	19.40	3-16	-	

79. What was the series result when England played three Tests in Pakistan in 1968-69?

RUSHWORTH, C.   Durham

Name: Christopher (Chris) Rushworth
Role: Right-hand bat, right-arm medium-fast bowler
Born: 11 July 1986, Sunderland
Height: 6ft 2in
Nickname: Rushy
County debut: No first-team appearance
(see *Extras*)
Parents: Joseph and Aileen
Marital status: Engaged
Family links with cricket: 'Cousin Phil
(Mustard) plays for Durham, brother Lee played
for England U19'
Education: Castle View, Sunderland
Qualifications: GCSEs, Level 2 coaching
Off-season: 'Work hard in the gym and possibly
go away somewhere in Australia after New Year'

Overseas teams played for: Doveton CC, Melbourne 2004-05; North Kalgoorlie,
Western Australia, 2005-06, 2006-07
Career highlights to date: 'Playing against Sri Lanka A in 2004 season, signing a
professional contract in 2009, and getting my brother out first ball in a cup final for
Durham Academy v Sunderland'
Cricket moments to forget: 'First team debut v Sri Lanka A – being hit for six off
the first ball'
Cricket superstitions: 'Left boot on first'
Cricketers particularly admired: Shaun Pollock, Darren Gough, Angus Fraser
Young players to look out for: Ben Stokes (Durham)
Other sports played: 5-a-side football
Other sports followed: Football (Sunderland AFC)
Favourite band: Keane, The Kooks, Coldplay
Extras: Is a Durham Academy player. Made 1st XI debut for Durham v Sri Lanka A
in a one-day fixture at Riverside 2004 but has yet to appear for the county in first-class
cricket or domestic competition
Opinions on cricket: 'Improving all the time – we need to keep Test cricket as
number one.'

2009 Season (Did not make any first-class or one-day appearances)

Career Performances

	M	Inn	NO	Runs	HS	Avg	100	50	Ct	St	Balls	Runs	Wkts	Avg	BB	5I	10M
Test																	
FC																	
ODI																	
List A	1	1	1	1	1*	-	-	-	-	-	42	36	0		-	-	
20/20 Int																	
20/20																	

RUSSELL, C. Worcestershire

Name: Chris Russell
Role: Right-hand bat, right-arm
fast-medium bowler
Born: 16 February 1989, Newport, Isle of Wight
Height: 6ft 1in **Weight:** 13st
Nickname: Goobs
County debut: No first team appearance
Education: Wroxall Primary School, Ventnor;
Medina High School
Career highlight to date: Playing first game for
Worcestershire 2nd XI
Qualifications: 11 GCSEs and 3 A-levels
Other sports followed: Football, tennis, rugby
Relaxations: Golf, music, surfing, socialising
Extras: Former Ventnor CC player. Moved to the

mainland in 2008, playing for Wolverhampton CC in the Birmingham League. After
a period on trial with the county, signed a one-year contract with Worcestershire in
October 2009

SADLER, J. L.   Derbyshire

Name: <u>John</u> Leonard Sadler
Role: Left-hand top-order bat,
right-arm off-spin bowler
Born: 19 November 1981, Dewsbury, Yorkshire
Height: 5ft 11in **Weight:** 13st 5lbs
Nickname: Sads, Chrome, Super
County debut: 2002 (one-day, Yorkshire),
2003 (Leicestershire), 2008 (Derbyshire)
1000 runs in a season: 1
Place in batting averages: (2008 189th av. 21.50)
Parents: Sue and Mike ('Baz')
Marital status: Engaged
Family links with cricket: 'Dad played cricket
for Ossett CC in the Yorkshire League for 30 years,
fielding round the corner with his sun hat on; now
coaches. Brothers Dave and Jamie represented Yorkshire Schools and
now play local league in Yorkshire CYCL. Mum did the teas...'
Education: St Thomas à Becket RC Comprehensive School, Wakefield
Qualifications: 9 GCSEs, Levels I and II coaching awards
Overseas tours: England U17 to Ireland; England U19 to Malaysia and (U19 World
Cup) Sri Lanka 1999-2000, to India 2000-01; Yorkshire to Grenada 2002
Overseas teams played for: Tuart Hill, Perth 2001-02 – 2003-04
Career highlights to date: 'My first first-class century. Winning Twenty20 with
Leicestershire 2004, 2006'
Cricket moments to forget: 'Being injured by Brett Lee (broken collarbone)
in 2005'
Cricketers particularly admired: Robin Smith, Brian Lara, Sachin Tendulkar,
Darren Lehmann
Other sports played: Five-a-side football, squash, golf – 'handicap 15'
Other sports followed: Football (Leeds United) – 'the Premier League in general'
Favourite band: Oasis
Extras: Played for Yorkshire Schools at all levels; attended Yorkshire Academy;
awarded Yorkshire 2nd XI cap. Yorkshire Supporters' Club Young Player of the Year
1998. Represented England U14, U15, U17, U18 and U19. Left Leicestershire at the
end of the 2007 season and joined Derbyshire for 2008
Relaxations: 'Walking the dog (Max)'
Opinions on cricket: 'The best game in the world... But still the hardest.'
Best batting: 145 Leicestershire v Surrey, Grace Road 2003
              145 Leicestershire v Sussex, Hove 2003
Best bowling: 1-5 Leicestershire v Middlesex, Southgate 2007

2009 Season

	M	Inn	NO	Runs	HS	Avg	100	50	Ct	St	Balls	Runs	Wkts	Avg	BB	5I	10M
Test																	
FC	3	4	3	71	27*	71.00	-	-	3	-	0	0	0		-	-	-
ODI																	
List A	5	4	1	105	38	35.00	-	-	-	-	0	0	0		-	-	
20/20 Int																	
20/20	9	8	5	123	29*	41.00	-	-	1	-	6	15	0		-	-	

Career Performances

	M	Inn	NO	Runs	HS	Avg	100	50	Ct	St	Balls	Runs	Wkts	Avg	BB	5I	10M
Test																	
FC	63	107	15	3002	145	32.63	3	16	43	-	231	250	3	83.33	1-5	-	-
ODI																	
List A	88	81	13	1821	113*	26.77	1	6	14	-	48	33	1	33.00	1-33	-	
20/20 Int																	
20/20	52	45	13	628	73	19.62	-	1	16	-	30	49	0		-	-	

SAGGERS, M. J.   Kent

Name: <u>Martin</u> John Saggers
Role: Right-hand bat, right-arm fast-medium bowler
Born: 23 May 1972, King's Lynn
Height: 6ft 2in   **Weight:** 14st
Nickname: Saggs, Jurgen
County debut: 1996 (Durham),
1999 (Kent) (see *Extras*)
County cap: 2001 (Kent)
Test debut: 2003-04
Benefit: 2009
50 wickets in a season: 4
Place in batting averages: 253rd av. 11.22
Place in bowling averages: 23rd av. 26.40
(2008 110th av. 36.37)
Parents: Brian and Edna
Wife and date of marriage: Samantha, 27 February 2004
Children: Ethan Patrick, 9 October 2005; Erin Savannah, 27 June 2008
Family links with cricket: Grandfather played in the Essex League
Education: Springwood High School; University of Huddersfield
Qualifications: BA (Hons) Architectural Studies International
Overseas tours: Kent to South Africa 2001; England VI to Hong Kong 2002;
England to Bangladesh 2003-04

Overseas teams played for: Randburg CC, Johannesburg 1996-98, 2000-04; Southern Suburbs CC, Johannesburg 1998-99
Career highlights to date: 'Winning the Norwich Union League 2001. Making my Test debut in Bangladesh. Taking a wicket with my first delivery in Test cricket on English soil'
Cricket moments to forget: 'Any form of injury'
Cricket superstitions: 'Getting a corner spot in the changing room'
Cricketers particularly admired: Neil Foster, Allan Donald, Brad Robinson
Young players to look out for: Sam Northeast, Ethan Saggers
Other sports played: Golf (10 handicap)
Other sports followed: Football (Spurs), 'any form of motor sport'
Favourite band: Metallica, Prime Circle, Puddle of Mudd, Creed
Extras: Won Most Promising Uncapped Player Award 2000. Joint Kent Player of the Year 2000 (with David Masters). Underwood Award (Kent leading wicket-taker) 2001, 2002, 2003. *Kent Messenger* Group Readers' Player of the Season 2002. Shepherd Neame Award for Best Bowler 2002. Cowdrey Award (Kent Player of the Year) 2002. Scored career best 64 as nightwatchman as Kent scored a then county fourth-innings record 429-5 to beat Worcestershire at Canterbury 2004. Took wicket (Mark Richardson) with his first delivery in Test cricket on English soil, in the second Test v New Zealand at Headingley 2004. Played two first-class, three List A and five Twenty20 matches for Essex on loan 2007. Retired at the end of the 2009 season
Opinions on cricket: 'Fantastic game! Twenty20 has brought a new lease of life to the game. Just hope we don't go on overkill for the one format of the game.'
Best batting: 64 Kent v Worcestershire, Canterbury 2004
Best bowling: 7-79 Kent v Durham, Riverside 2000

2009 Season

	M	Inn	NO	Runs	HS	Avg	100	50	Ct	St	Balls	Runs	Wkts	Avg	BB	5I	10M
Test																	
FC	4	4	2	5	5*	2.50	-	-	-	-	653	264	10	26.40	3-45	-	-
ODI																	
List A	1	1	0	11	11	11.00	-	-	-	-	30	32	0			-	-
20/20 Int																	
20/20																	

Career Performances

	M	Inn	NO	Runs	HS	Avg	100	50	Ct	St	Balls	Runs	Wkts	Avg	BB	5I	10M
Test	3	3	0	1	1	.33	-	-	1	-	493	247	7	35.28	2-29	-	-
FC	119	147	43	1165	64	11.20	-	2	27	-	20676	10513	415	25.33	7-79	18	-
ODI																	
List A	124	68	34	313	34*	9.20	-	-	23	-	5622	4229	166	25.47	5-22	2	
20/20 Int																	
20/20	10	1	0	5	5	5.00	-	-	2	-	186	256	6	42.66	2-14	-	

SALES, D. J. G.   Northamptonshire

Name: <u>David</u> John Grimwood Sales
Role: Right-hand bat, right-arm
medium bowler
Born: 3 December 1977, Carshalton, Surrey
Height: 6ft **Weight:** 14st 7lbs
Nickname: Jumble
County debut: 1994 (one-day),
1996 (first-class)
County cap: 1999
Benefit: 2007
1000 runs in a season: 56
1st-Class 200s: 6
1st-Class 300s: 1
Place in batting averages: (2008 27th av. 49.43)
Parents: Daphne and John
Wife and date of marriage: Abigail, 22 September 2001
Children: James, 11 February 2003; Benjamin David, 3 March 2005;
Charlie Matthew, 20 September 2006
Family links with cricket: Father played club cricket
Education: Caterham Boys' School, Surrey
Qualifications: 7 GCSEs, cricket coach
Overseas tours: England U15 to South Africa 1993; England U19 to West Indies
1994-95, to Zimbabwe 1995-96, to Pakistan 1996-97; England A to Kenya and Sri
Lanka 1997-98, to Bangladesh and New Zealand 1999-2000, to West Indies 2000-01;
Northamptonshire to Grenada 2000
Overseas teams played for: Wellington Firebirds, New Zealand 2001-02
Career highlights to date: '303 not out v Essex [1999]; 104 v Pakistan 2003'
Cricket moments to forget: 'Watching White and Powell for five hours, then getting
0' (*Rob White and Mark Powell shared in a new record Northamptonshire opening
partnership of 375 v Gloucestershire at Northampton 2002*)
Cricket superstitions: 'None'
Cricketers particularly admired: Graham Gooch, Steve Waugh
Young players to look out for: Alex Wakely, Graeme White
Other sports followed: Rugby (Northampton Saints), golf, football (Crystal Palace)
Favourite band: Coldplay
Relaxations: Fishing and golf
Extras: Sir John Hobbs Silver Jubilee Memorial Prize 1993. Scored 56-ball 70* v
Essex at Chelmsford in the Sunday League 1994, aged 16 years 289 days. Scored
210* on Championship debut v Worcs at Kidderminster 1996, aged 18 years 237 days.
NBC Denis Compton Award for the most promising young Northamptonshire player
1996. Became the youngest Englishman to score a first-class triple century (303*) v
Essex at Northampton 1999, aged 21 years 240 days. PCA/CGU Young Player of

the Year 1999. Man of the Match for Wellington v Canterbury in the final of New Zealand's State Shield at Wellington 2001-02 (62). Captain of Northamptonshire 2004-07. Northamptonshire's top-scoring batsman in 2008. Missed whole of 2009 season due to a knee injury that eventually necessitated surgery

Best batting: 303* Northamptonshire v Essex, Northampton 1999
Best bowling: 4-25 Northamptonshire v Sri Lanka A, Northampton 1999

2009 Season (Did not make any first-class or one-day appearances)

Career Performances

	M	Inn	NO	Runs	HS	Avg	100	50	Ct	St	Balls	Runs	Wkts	Avg	BB	5I	10M
Test																	
FC	188	299	28	11458	303*	42.28	23	57	167	-		339	174	9	19.33| 4-25	-	-
ODI																	
List A	229	217	30	6353	161	33.97	4	44	103	-		84	67	0		-	-
20/20 Int																	
20/20	44	41	10	1074	78*	34.64	-	10	25	-		12	23	1	23.00	1-10	-

SANDERSON, B. W.   Yorkshire

Name: <u>Ben</u> William Sanderson
Role: Right-hand bat, right-arm fast-medium bowler
Born: 3 January 1989, Sheffield
Height: 6ft **Weight:** 13st
Nickname: Sando
County debut: 2008
Parents: Roy and Lynne
Marital status: Single
Family links with cricket: 'Dad plays for Whitley Hall CC'
Education: Ecclesfield; Sheffield College
Qualifications: Plumber (trade)
Career highlights to date: 'Playing for Yorkshire 2nd XI. Winning U17 County Championship two years running'
Cricket moments to forget: 'Getting out on a hat-trick ball'
Cricketers particularly admired: Glenn McGrath, Darren Gough
Young players to look out for: Oliver Hannon-Dalby
Other sports played: Football (Hallam U19)
Other sports followed: Football (Sheffield Wednesday)
Favourite band: Milburn
Relaxations: 'Watching films'

Extras: Yorkshire Academy. Played for England U19 2008
Opinions on cricket: 'Glad to see the game moving forward and gaining interest with the public supporters.'
Best batting: 6 Yorkshire v Lancashire, Headingley 2008
Best bowling: 1-87 Yorkshire v Lancashire, Headingley 2008

2009 Season (Did not make any first-class or one-day appearances)

Career Performances

	M	Inn	NO	Runs	HS	Avg	100	50	Ct	St	Balls	Runs	Wkts	Avg	BB	5I	10M
Test																	
FC	2	2	1	6	6	6.00	-	-	-	-	222	140	1	140.00	1-87	-	-
ODI																	
List A																	
20/20 Int																	
20/20																	

SANDRI, P. S. E.   Sussex

Name: <u>Pepler</u> Sacto Emiliano Sandri
Role: Right-hand bat, right-arm medium-fast bowler
Born: 14 January 1983, Cape Town
County debut: 2009
Overseas teams played for: Cape Cobras: Boland
Extras: Had trials with Yorkshire in 2008, but was not signed after Yorkshire elected to retain Deon Kruis. Signed a 12-month contract with Sussex in March 2009. Took three wickets in nine overs during the first innings of Australia's opening tour match against the county. Played club cricket for Hastings (Sussex Premier League) 2009. Left Sussex at the end of the 2009 season. Holds an Italian passport and is not considered an overseas player

Best batting: 26* Boland v Western Province, Paarl 2007-08
Best bowling: 5-32 Boland v Eastern Province, Paarl 2005-06

2009 Season

	M	Inn	NO	Runs	HS	Avg	100	50	Ct	St	Balls	Runs	Wkts	Avg	BB	5I	10M
Test																	
FC	1	1	1	0	0*		-	-	-	-	84	80	0		-	-	-
ODI																	
List A																	
20/20 Int																	
20/20																	

Career Performances

	M	Inn	NO	Runs	HS	Avg	100	50	Ct	St	Balls	Runs	Wkts	Avg	BB	5I	10M
Test																	
FC	29	41	20	217	26*	10.33	-	-	4	-	3834	2126	72	29.52	5-32	1	-
ODI																	
List A	17	4	2	24	14*	12.00	-	-	5	-	690	545	16	34.06	2-18	-	
20/20 Int																	
20/20																	

SANGAKKARA, K. C.   Lancashire

Name: <u>Kumar</u> Chokshanada Sangakkara
Role: Left-hand bat, occasional offbreak bowler, wicketkeeper
Born: 27 October 1977, Matale, Sri Lanka
County debut: 2007 (Warwickshire)
Test debut: 2000
ODI debut: 2000
Twenty20 Int debut: 2006
1st-class 200s: 7
Overseas tours: Sri Lanka A to South Africa 1999-2000; Sri Lanka to Kenya (ICC Knockout Trophy) 2000-01, to South Africa 2000-01, to England 2002, to South Africa 2002-03, to Africa (World Cup) 2002-03, to West Indies 2003, Sri Lanka to Zimbabwe 2004, to Australia 2004, to

England (ICC Champions Trophy) 2004, to Pakistan 2004-05, to New Zealand 2004-05, to India 2005-06, to Bangladesh 2005-06, to England 2006, to New Zealand 2006-07, to India (ICC Champions Trophy) 2006-07, to West Indies (Super Eights & World Cup) 2006-07, to South Africa (World Twenty20) to Australia 2007-08, to India 2007-08, to Pakistan (Asia Cup) 2008, to Zimbabwe 2008-09, to Bangladesh 2008-09, to Pakistan 2009, to England (ICC World Twenty20) 2009, to South Africa (Champions Trophy) 2009-10, to India (Tri-series) 2009-10

Overseas teams played for: Central Province; Colombo District Cricket Association; Kandurata; Kings X1 Punjab (IPL); Nondescripts Cricket Club

Extras: In 2007 played in seven Test matches, accumulating 968 runs at an average of 138.28, finishing the year as the world's top Test batsman. Played as an overseas player for Warwickshire 2007. Signed for Lancashire December 2009 as an overseas player for 2010. Appointed captain of IPL side Kings X1 Punjab in January 2010

Best batting: 287 Sri Lanka v South Africa, Colombo 2006

Best bowling: 1-13 Sri Lankans v Zimbabwe A, Harare 2004

2009 Season

	M	Inn	NO	Runs	HS	Avg	100	50	Ct	St	Balls	Runs	Wkts	Avg	BB	5I	10M
Test																	
FC																	
ODI																	
List A																	
20/20 Int	7	7	2	177	64*	35.40	-	2	5	4	0	0	0		-	-	
20/20	7	7	2	177	64*	35.40	-	2	5	4	0	0	0		-	-	

Career Performances

	M	Inn	NO	Runs	HS	Avg	100	50	Ct	St	Balls	Runs	Wkts	Avg	BB	5I	10M
Test	85	142	10	7308	287	55.36	20	32	154	20	66	38	0		-	-	-
FC	170	271	20	11692	287	46.58	28	56	315	33	192	108	1	108.00	1-13	-	-
ODI	257	240	26	7660	138*	35.79	10	49	245	63	0	0	0		-	-	
List A	331	310	34	10497	156*	38.03	15	66	319	82	0	0	0		-	-	
20/20 Int	18	17	2	435	69	29.00	-	3	9	7	0	0	0		-	-	
20/20	51	48	4	1369	94	31.11	-	10	28	12	0	0	0		-	-	

80. Who was the first captain of Pakistan to score a Test century?

SAXELBY, I. D.   Gloucestershire

Name: <u>Ian</u> David Saxelby
Role: Right-hand bat, right-arm
fast-medium bowler
Born: 22 May 1989, Nottingham
County debut: 2008
Place in batting averages: 236th av. 16.80
Place in batting averages: 51st av. 31.00
Family links with cricket: Uncle Kevin played
for Nottinghamshire, and his late uncle Mark played
for Derbyshire, Durham and Nottinghamshire.
Overseas tours: England Performance Squad to
South Africa 2009-10 (*see Extras*)
Extras: Has represented England at U19 level, and
played for Gloucestershire 2nd XI. Signed his first
professional contract towards the end of the 2008

season. NBC Denis Compton Award for most promising young Gloucestershire player
2009. Member of England Performance Programme squad 2009-10, but was forced to
return home early from the squad's tour of South Africa after dislocating his shoulder.
Best batting: 60* Gloucestershire v Northamptonshire, Northampton 2009
Best bowling: 3-31 Gloucestershire v Essex, Southend-on-Sea 2009

2009 Season

	M	Inn	NO	Runs	HS	Avg	100	50	Ct	St	Balls	Runs	Wkts	Avg	BB	5I	10M
Test																	
FC	9	13	3	168	60*	16.80	-	1	5	-	1112	620	20	31.00	3-31	-	-
ODI																	
List A	6	5	2	25	7*	8.33	-	-	-	-	182	171	8	21.37	4-31	-	
20/20 Int																	
20/20	5	3	1	4	2	2.00	-	-	-	-	111	166	5	33.20	2-32	-	

Career Performances

	M	Inn	NO	Runs	HS	Avg	100	50	Ct	St	Balls	Runs	Wkts	Avg	BB	5I	10M
Test																	
FC	12	16	4	188	60*	15.66	-	1	6	-	1394	838	22	38.09	3-31	-	-
ODI																	
List A	6	5	2	25	7*	8.33	-	-	-	-	182	171	8	21.37	4-31	-	
20/20 Int																	
20/20	5	3	1	4	2	2.00	-	-	-	-	111	166	5	33.20	2-32	-	

SAYERS, J. J.   Yorkshire

Name: Joseph (Joe) John Sayers
Role: Left-hand bat, right-arm off-spin bowler
Born: 5 November 1983, Leeds, Yorkshire
Height: 6ft **Weight:** 13st
Nickname: Squirrel
County debut: 2003 (one-day), 2004 (first-class)
County cap: 2007
1000 runs in a season: 1
Place in batting averages: 60th av. 42.59
Place in bowling averages: 140th av. 61.68
Parents: Geraldine and Roger
Marital status: 'Engaged'
Family links with cricket: 'Father played at school, but otherwise none'
Education: St Mary's RC Comprehensive School, Menston; Worcester College, Oxford University
Qualifications: 12 GCSEs, 4 A-levels, BA Physics (Oxon)
Career outside cricket: 'Part-owner of Pongo Cricket, an online media platform especially for cricket. Also director of The Twentytwo Group Ltd., a company creating overseas opportunities for amateur and professional cricketers' (see *Player websites*)
Off-season: 'I'll be part of the England Performance Programme at the High Performance Centre, Pretoria, South Africa in November and December'
Overseas tours: Leeds Schools to South Africa 1998; Yorkshire U17 to South Africa 2001; England U17 to Australia 2001
Overseas teams played for: Manly-Warringah, Sydney 2004-05
Career highlights to date: 'Receiving my county cap for Yorkshire. Representing England Lions v Australia at Canterbury, 2009'
Cricketers particularly admired: Mark Ramprakash, Michael Vaughan, Marcus Trescothick, Steve Waugh
Young players to look out for: James Taylor (Leicestershire)
Other sports played: Football ('played as goalkeeper for Bradford City AFC for three years'), rowing (Worcester College)
Other sports followed: Rugby league (Leeds Rhinos), rugby union (Leeds Tykes), football
Favourite band: John Mayer
Relaxations: 'Managing my businesses; playing the guitar'
Extras: Captained England U17 v Australia U17 at Adelaide 2001. Played for OUCCE 2002, 2003, 2004 (captain 2003). Oxford Blue 2002, 2003, 2004. Represented England U19 2002, 2003 (captain in the third 'Test' 2003). Wrote a weekly column 'View from the Balcony' for *Yorkshire Post* during the 2006 season. Carried bat for 122* v Middlesex at Scarborough in 2006, and again for a 553-minute 149* v Durham at Headingley in 2007 when he was on the field of play for the

entire game. Member of England Performance Programme squad 2009-10
Player websites: www.pongocricket.com; www.twentytwointernational.com
Opinions on cricket: 'County championship cricket has become extremely
competitive, with any one side capable of beating any other and very few points
separating the eventual champions from those placed below them in the table.'
Best batting: 187 Yorkshire v Kent, Tunbridge Wells 2007
Best bowling: 3-20 Yorkshire v Warwickshire, Scarborough 2009

2009 Season

	M	Inn	NO	Runs	HS	Avg	100	50	Ct	St	Balls	Runs	Wkts	Avg	BB	5I	10M
Test																	
FC	17	29	2	1150	173	42.59	2	5	16	-	65	32	3	10.66	3-20	-	-
ODI																	
List A	7	7	0	166	55	23.71	-	2	1	-	0	0	0		-	-	
20/20 Int																	
20/20	2	2	0	6	5	3.00	-	-	-	-	0	0	0		-	-	

Career Performances

	M	Inn	NO	Runs	HS	Avg	100	50	Ct	St	Balls	Runs	Wkts	Avg	BB	5I	10M
Test																	
FC	76	125	10	3965	187	34.47	10	17	48	-	137	86	3	28.66	3-20	-	-
ODI																	
List A	20	20	2	415	62	23.05	-	4	1	-	54	71	1	71.00	1-31	-	
20/20 Int																	
20/20	5	3	0	18	12	6.00	-	-	2	-	0	0	0		-	-	

SCHOFIELD, C. P.   Surrey

Name: Christopher (<u>Chris</u>) Paul Schofield
Role: Left-hand bat, right-arm leg-spin bowler;
all-rounder
Born: 6 October 1978, Rochdale
Height: 6ft 2in **Weight:** 12st
Nickname: Schoey, Scho-boat
County debut: 1998 (Lancashire),
2006 (Surrey)
County cap: 2002 (Lancashire)
Test debut: 2000
Twenty20 Int debut: 2007-08
Place in batting averages: 107th av. 35.77
Parents: David and Judith
Marital status: Single

Family links with cricket: Father played with local club team Whittles and brother with local team Littleborough
Education: Wardle High School, Rochdale
Qualifications: 4 GCSEs, NVQ Levels 2 and 3 in Information Technology
Overseas tours: England U17 to Bermuda 1997; England U19 to South Africa (including U19 World Cup) 1997-98; England A to Bangladesh and New Zealand 1999-2000, to West Indies 2000-01, to India 2007-08; ECB National Academy to Australia 2001-02; England to South Africa (World 20/20) 2007-08; England Performance Programme to India 2007-08
Career highlights to date: 'Two Tests and four Twenty20 games for England'
Cricket moments to forget: 'Tribunal against Lancashire' (*2007-08 contract dispute*)
Cricketers particularly admired: Shane Warne
Young players to look out for: Adil Rashid
Other sports played: Football, golf, snooker ('highest break 124')
Other sports followed: Football (Liverpool FC)
Favourite band: Matchbox 20
Relaxations: Listening to music, playing snooker, socialising, internet poker
Extras: Was part of England U19 World Cup winning squad 1997-98. Won double twice in two years with Littleborough CC (Wood Cup and Lancashire Cup 1997; League and Wood Cup 1998). Won Sir Ron Brierley/Crusaders Scholarship 1998. NBC Denis Compton Award for the most promising young Lancashire player 1998, 1999, 2000. Leading first-class wicket-taker on England A tour to West Indies 2000-01 (22 wickets; av. 26.27). Represented England Lions 2007
Best batting: 144 Surrey v Essex, Colchester 2009
Best bowling: 6-120 England A v Bangladesh, Chittagong 1999-2000

2009 Season

	M	Inn	NO	Runs	HS	Avg	100	50	Ct	St	Balls	Runs	Wkts	Avg	BB	5I	10M
Test																	
FC	14	21	3	644	144	35.77	1	3	7	-	2183	1357	22	61.68	5-40	1	-
ODI																	
List A	16	14	5	276	66	30.66	-	1	4	-	694	573	25	22.92	5-32	1	
20/20 Int																	
20/20	9	7	0	66	17	9.42	-	-	2	-	209	298	12	24.83	3-21	-	

Career Performances

	M	Inn	NO	Runs	HS	Avg	100	50	Ct	St	Balls	Runs	Wkts	Avg	BB	5I	10M
Test	2	3	0	67	57	22.33	-	1	-	-	108	73	0		-	-	-
FC	92	130	18	3303	144	29.49	1	24	52	-	14598	7793	218	35.74	6-120	6	-
ODI																	
List A	129	97	26	1667	75*	23.47	-	7	35	-	4094	3526	133	26.51	5-31	2	
20/20 Int	4	4	3	24	9*	24.00	-	-	1	-	77	92	4	23.00	2-15	-	
20/20	38	27	8	220	27	11.57	-	-	8	-	610	756	44	17.18	4-12	-	

SCOTT, B. J. M.   Middlesex

Name: Benjamin (<u>Ben</u>) James Matthew Scott
Role: Right-hand bat, wicket-keeper
Born: 4 August 1981, Isleworth
Height: 'Small' (5ft 9in) **Weight:** 11st 7lbs
Nickname: Scotty
County debut: 2002 (one-day, Surrey), 2003
(first-class, Surrey), 2004 (Middlesex)
County cap: 2007 (Middlesex)
50 dismissals in a season: 1
Place in batting averages: 260th av. 12.84
(2008 101st av. 35.36)
Parents: Terry and Edna
Marital status: Single

Family links with cricket: Father played for the
Primitives; brother played local cricket. Nephew
Joel Pope is with Leicestershire
Education: Whitton School, Richmond; Richmond College
Qualifications: 9 GCSEs, 3 A-levels studied, ECB Level 1 coach, YMCA Fitness
Instructor's Award
Overseas tours: MCC YC to Cape Town 1999-2000; Middlesex to Mumbai, India
2005, 2006, to Antigua 2008-09 for Stanford Super Series; MCC to Uganda 2008;
England Lions to New Zealand 2008-09
Overseas teams played for: Portland CC, Victoria 1999-2000; Mt Gambia, South
Australia 2001-02; South Melbourne CC 2006
Career highlights to date: 'Scoring 101* at Lord's v Northants; just getting there
with Nantie Hayward down the other end'
Cricket moments to forget: 'Being the hat-trick for Billy Taylor v Hampshire'
(*At The Rose Bowl 2006*)
Cricket superstitions: 'None'
Cricketers particularly admired: Alec Stewart, Jack Russell, Nad Shahid
Young players to look out for: Eoin Morgan (Middlesex), Joel Pope (Leicestershire)
Other sports played: Golf
Favourite band: Michael Jackson, The Jacksons, Usher
Relaxations: Music, golf, TV
Extras: Middlesex YC cap. Represented ESCA U14 and U15. Played for
Development of Excellence XI 1999. Finchley CC Player of the Season 2000.
Will start the 2010 season on loan to Worcestershire for four weeks
Best batting: 164* Middlesex v Northamptonshire, Uxbridge 2008

2009 Season

	M	Inn	NO	Runs	HS	Avg	100	50	Ct	St	Balls	Runs	Wkts	Avg	BB	5I	10M
Test																	
FC	8	14	1	167	44	12.84	-	-	18	2	0	0	0		-	-	-
ODI																	
List A	15	10	7	120	30	40.00	-	-	10	4	0	0	0		-	-	
20/20 Int																	
20/20	11	8	3	55	21*	11.00	-	-	3	2	0	0	0		-	-	

Career Performances

	M	Inn	NO	Runs	HS	Avg	100	50	Ct	St	Balls	Runs	Wkts	Avg	BB	5I	10M
Test																	
FC	70	107	20	2397	164*	27.55	3	13	181	21	3	1	0		-	-	-
ODI																	
List A	95	58	20	759	73*	19.97	-	4	78	30	0	0	0		-	-	
20/20 Int																	
20/20	55	39	18	294	32*	14.00	-	-	17	24	0	0	0		-	-	

SHAFAYAT, B. M. — Nottinghamshire

Name: <u>Bilal</u> Mustapha Shafayat
Role: Right-hand bat, right-arm fast-medium bowler, occasional wicket-keeper
Born: 10 July 1984, Nottingham
Height: 5ft 7in **Weight:** 10st 7lbs
Nickname: Billy, Muzzy, Our Kid
County debut: 2001 (Nottinghamshire), 2005 (Northamptonshire)
1000 runs in a season: 1
Place in batting averages: 169th av. 26.81 (2008 56th av. 41.61)
Parents: Mohammad Shafayat and Mahfooza Begum
Marital status: Single
Family links with cricket: 'Brother Rashid played for Notts up to 2nd XI and is now playing in the Staffordshire Premier (took ten wickets in a game 2003). Uncle Nadeem played for PCC. Father just loves it!'
Education: Greenwood Dale; Nottingham Bluecoat School and Sixth Form College
Qualifications: 9 GCSEs, 2 A-levels, Level 1 coaching
Career outside cricket: 'Investing a little'
Overseas tours: ZRK to Pakistan 2000; 'Streets to Arena' ('Kadeer Ali's dad's academy') to Pakistan; England U17 to Australia 2000-01; England U19 to Australia

and (U19 World Cup) New Zealand 2001-02, to Australia 2002-03 (c); Nottinghamshire to South Africa 2002, 2003; England A to Malaysia and India 2003-04; MCC to Uganda 2008

Overseas teams played for: National Bank of Pakistan 2004-05; Pakistan Customs 2008-09

Career highlights to date: 'Making my first-class debut for Notts v Middlesex (scoring 72). Scoring a hundred and double hundred v India in final U19 "Test" 2002. Scoring crucial hundred v Worcestershire for promotion in Championship. Beating Australia U19 in first "Test" 2002-03, scoring 66, 108 and taking six wickets'

Cricket moments to forget: 'Losing U19 "Test" series to Australia'

Cricketers particularly admired: Sachin Tendulkar, Carl Hooper, Mark Ramprakash

Young players to look out for: Owais Walait

Other sports played: Football, badminton, squash, pool

Other sports followed: Football (Liverpool), boxing, snooker

Favourite band: Khalil Hussary, Ahmad Bukhatir

Relaxations: 'Voluntary work for SAS Trust charity'

Extras: Scored 72 on Championship debut v Middlesex at Trent Bridge 2001, aged 16 years 360 days. NBC Denis Compton Award for the most promising young Nottinghamshire player 2001, 2002. Scored record-equalling four 'Test' centuries for England U19. BBC East Midlands Junior Sportsman of the Year 2003. ECB National Academy 2003-04. Left Northamptonshire at the end of the 2006 season and rejoined Nottinghamshire for 2007. Kept wicket for Pakistan Customs during the 2008-09 off-season

Opinions on cricket: 'The game has moved rapidly forward due to Twenty20, which is good for the value of the players and the game.'

Best batting: 161 Northamptonshire v Derbyshire, Derby 2005

Best bowling: 2-25 Northamptonshire v Pakistanis, Northampton 2006

2009 Season

	M	Inn	NO	Runs	HS	Avg	100	50	Ct	St	Balls	Runs	Wkts	Avg	BB	5I	10M
Test																	
FC	14	23	1	590	90*	26.81	-	3	13	-	66	63	1	63.00	1-32	-	-
ODI																	
List A	5	4	0	35	22	8.75	-	-	4	3	0	0	0		-	-	
20/20 Int																	
20/20	3	2	0	36	29	18.00	-	-	-	-	0	0	0		-	-	

Career Performances

	M	Inn	NO	Runs	HS	Avg	100	50	Ct	St	Balls	Runs	Wkts	Avg	BB	5I	10M
Test																	
FC	112	190	7	5551	161	30.33	8	31	101	8	926	642	8	80.25	2-25	-	-
ODI																	
List A	105	98	8	2016	104	22.40	1	7	40	5	790	730	24	30.41	4-33	-	
20/20 Int																	
20/20	40	31	5	445	40	17.11	-	-	11	1	120	191	4	47.75	2-13	-	

SHAH, O. A.   Middlesex

Name: <u>Owais</u> Alam Shah
Role: Right-hand bat, right-arm off-spin bowler
Born: 22 October 1978, Karachi, Pakistan
Height: 6ft 1in **Weight:** 13st 7lbs
Nickname: Ace, The Mauler
County debut: 1995 (one-day),
1996 (first-class)
County cap: 1999
Benefit: 2008
Test debut: 2005-06
ODI debut: 2001
Twenty20 Int debut: 2007
1000 runs in a season: 8
1st-Class 200s: 1
Place in batting averages: 64th av. 42.21
(2008 53rd av. 42.16)

Parents: Jamshed and Mehjabeen
Wife and date of marriage: Gemma, 25 September 2004
Children: Maya, 13 October 2007
Family links with cricket: Father played for his college side
Education: Isleworth and Syon School; Lampton School, Hounslow; Westminster University, Harrow
Qualifications: 7 GCSEs, 2 A-levels
Overseas tours: England U19 to Zimbabwe 1995-96, to South Africa (including U19 World Cup) 1997-98 (c); England A to Australia 1996-97, to Kenya and Sri Lanka 1997-98, to Sri Lanka 2004-05, to West Indies 2005-06; ECB National Academy to Australia 2001-02; England to Zimbabwe (one-day series) 2001-02, to India and New Zealand 2001-02 (one-day series), to Sri Lanka (ICC Champions Trophy) 2002-03, to Australia 2002-03 (VB Series), to India 2005-06, to South Africa (World 20/20) 2007-08, to Sri Lanka 2007-08, to New Zealand 2007-08, to India 2008-09, to West Indies 2008-09, to South Africa 2009-10
Overseas teams played for: University of Western Australia, Perth; Delhi Daredevils (IPL) 2008-09; Wellington 2009-10
Career highlights to date: '[Debut] Test match against India in Mumbai'
Cricket moments to forget: 'Getting a pair in first-class cricket'
Cricketers particularly admired: Viv Richards, Sachin Tendulkar, Mark Waugh
Young players to look out for: Eoin Morgan, Sam Robson (both Middlesex)
Other sports played: Snooker
Other sports followed: Football ('like to watch Manchester United play')
Favourite band: 'Too many to mention'
Relaxations: 'Movies, eating out'

Extras: Man of the U17 'Test' series v India 1994. Captained England U19 to success in the 1997-98 U19 World Cup in South Africa, scoring 54* in the final; captain of England U19 v Pakistan U19 1998. Cricket Writers' Young Player of the Year 2001. Middlesex Player of the Year 2002. Vice-captain of Middlesex 2002 to June 2004. Leading run-scorer in English first-class cricket 2005 (1728 runs; av. 66.46). Made Test debut in the third Test v India at Mumbai 2005-06, scoring 88. Man of the Match in the second Twenty20 Int v West Indies at The Oval 2007 (55*). ECB National Academy 2004-05, 2005-06, 2006-07. Man of the Match in the second ODI v Sri Lanka in Dambulla 2007-08 (82). Signed by Delhi Daredevils for IPL 2009. England increment contract 2009-10

Best batting: 203 Middlesex v Derbyshire, Southgate 2001
Best bowling: 3-33 Middlesex v Gloucestershire, Bristol 1999

2009 Season

	M	Inn	NO	Runs	HS	Avg	100	50	Ct	St	Balls	Runs	Wkts	Avg	BB	5I	10M
Test																	
FC	8	16	2	591	159	42.21	2	2	5	-	6	1	0		-	-	-
ODI	9	9	0	273	75	30.33	-	1	5	-	48	26	1	26.00	1-14	-	
List A	19	18	1	727	130	42.76	1	4	8	-	68	37	5	7.40	4-11	-	
20/20 Int	6	5	0	106	38	21.20	-	-	2	-	0	0	0		-	-	
20/20	13	12	1	287	61*	26.09	-	1	6	-	0	0	0		-	-	

Career Performances

	M	Inn	NO	Runs	HS	Avg	100	50	Ct	St	Balls	Runs	Wkts	Avg	BB	5I	10M
Test	6	10	0	269	88	26.90	-	2	2	-	30	31	0		-	-	-
FC	209	356	33	13717	203	42.46	37	69	160	-	1974	1356	22	61.63	3-33	-	-
ODI	71	66	6	1834	107*	30.56	1	12	21	-	193	184	7	26.28	3-15	-	
List A	311	293	35	8879	134	34.41	12	56	103	-	852	824	26	31.69	4-11	-	
20/20 Int	17	15	1	347	55*	24.78	-	1	5	-	0	0	0		-	-	
20/20	59	57	10	1424	79	30.29	-	8	19	-	13	11	1	11.00	1-10	-	

SHAHID AFRIDI Hampshire

Name: Sahibzaha Mohammad <u>Shahid</u>
Khan Afridi
Role: Right-hand bat, leg-break bowler
Born: 1 March 1980, Kohat, Pakistan
County debut: 2001 (Leicestershire),
2003 (Derbyshire), 2004 (one-day, Kent)
Test debut: 1998-99
ODI debut: 1996-97
Twenty20 Int debut: 2006
Family links with cricket: Brother Tariq Afridi
played first-class cricket for Karachi 1999-2000.
Brother Ashfaq Afridi plays for Karachi Blues
Overseas tours: Pakistan U19 to West Indies
1996-97; Pakistan to Kenya (one-day series) 1996-97,
to Australia (one-day series) 1996-97, to India (one-
day series) 1996-97, to Zimbabwe and South Africa 1997-98 (one-day series), to
Bangladesh (Wills International Cup) 1998-99, to India 1998-99, to UK, Ireland and
Holland (World Cup) 1999, to Australia 1999-2000 (one-day series), to West Indies
1999-2000 (one-day series), to New Zealand 2000-01 (one-day series), to England
2001 (one-day series), to Sharjah (v West Indies) 2001-02, to Australia (Super
Challenge II) 2002, to Morocco (Morocco Cup) 2002, to Kenya (Nairobi Triangular)
2002, to Sri Lanka (ICC Champions Trophy) 2002-03, to Zimbabwe 2002-03, to South
Africa 2002-03 (one-day series), to Africa (World Cup) 2002-03, to England (ICC
Champions Trophy) 2004, to Australia 2004-05, to India 2004-05, to West Indies
2004-05, to Sri Lanka 2005-06, to England 2006, to India (ICC Champions Trophy)
2006-07, to South Africa 2006-07 (one-day series), to West Indies (ICC World Cup)
2006-07, to India 2007-08 (one-day series), to Bangladesh (Kitply Cup) 2008, to Sri
Lanka 2009 (one-day series), to England 2009 (one-day series), to South Africa (ICC
Champions Trophy) 2009-10, to Australia 2009-10 (one-day series), plus other one-
day tournaments in Toronto, Sharjah, UAE, India and Holland; Asian Cricket Council
XI to South Africa (Afro-Asia Cup) 2005-06; ICC World XI to Australia (Super
Series) 2005-06
Overseas teams played for: Karachi Whites 1995-96 – 2001-02; Habib Bank
1997-98 – 2002-03; Karachi Blues 1996-97; Karachi 2003-04; Griqualand
West 2003-04
Extras: Set record for fastest ODI century – 37 balls (out for 102) v Sri Lanka in
Kenya 1996-97 in his first ODI innings, aged 16 years 217 days; innings included a
record-equalling 11 sixes. Recorded his maiden Test five-wicket innings return (5-52)
on debut v Australia at Karachi 1998-99, going on to score his maiden Test century
(141) v India at Chennai (Madras) in his second match. Overseas player with
Leicestershire for part of the 2001 season. C&G Man of the Match awards for his 44-
ball 67 in the quarter-final v Worcestershire at Worcester and for his 58-ball 95 in the

semi-final v Lancashire at Leicester 2001. Has won numerous ODI awards, among them Man of the Finals in the CUB Series in Australia 1996-97 and Man of the Match v England at Lahore 2000-01 (5-40/61) and v Kenya at Edgbaston in the ICC Champions Trophy 2004 (5-11). Struck 18-ball 55* v Holland at Colombo in the ICC Champions Trophy 2002-03, equalling his own record for the second-fastest fifty in ODIs. His quicker ball was once timed at 86mph. Was an overseas player with Derbyshire April to May 2003. Was an overseas player with Kent in July 2004, pending the arrival of Ian Butler, absent on international duty. Signed as an overseas player with Hampshire for 2010

Best batting: 164 Leicestershire v Northamptonshire, Northampton 2001
Best bowling: 6-101 Habib Bank v KRL, Rawalpindi 1997-98

2009 Season

	M	Inn	NO	Runs	HS	Avg	100	50	Ct	St	Balls	Runs	Wkts	Avg	BB	5I	10M
Test																	
FC																	
ODI																	
List A																	
20/20 Int	7	7	2	176	54*	35.20	-	2	3	-	168	149	11	13.54	4-11	-	
20/20	7	7	2	176	54*	35.20	-	2	3	-	168	149	11	13.54	4-11	-	

Career Performances

	M	Inn	NO	Runs	HS	Avg	100	50	Ct	St	Balls	Runs	Wkts	Avg	BB	5I	10M
Test	26	46	1	1683	156	37.40	5	8	10	-	3092	1640	47	34.89	5-52	1	-
FC	109	180	4	5598	164	31.80	12	30	75	-	13391	6954	257	27.05	6-101	8	-
ODI	285	267	18	5755	109	23.11	4	29	97	-	11895	9162	264	34.70	6-38	3	
List A	375	354	21	8403	114	25.23	6	48	118	-	15930	12273	366	33.53	6-38	5	
20/20 Int	24	22	2	421	54*	21.05	-	3	7	-	561	535	34	15.73	4-11	-	
20/20	50	44	3	745	54*	18.17	-	3	16	-	1073	1090	62	17.58	4-11	-	

SHAHZAD, A. Yorkshire

Name: Ajmal Shahzad
Role: Right-hand bat, right-arm fast bowler; all-rounder
Born: 27 July 1985, Bradford
Height: 6ft **Weight:** 13st 8lbs
Nickname: The Dark Destroyer, AJ
County debut: 2004 (one-day), 2006 (first-class)
Place in batting averages: 93rd av. 37.58
Place in bowling averages: 74th av. 34.26
Parents: Parveen and Mohammed
Marital status: Single
Family links with cricket: 'Father played in Bradford League'

Education: Bradford Grammar School; Woodhouse Grove School; Leeds Metropolitan University
Qualifications: 9 GCSEs, 4 A-levels
Overseas tours: Schools tours to Scotland and Grenada; England U18 to Netherlands 2003
Career highlights to date: 'Making my debut for Yorkshire and being the first British-born Asian to play for YCCC'
Cricket moments to forget: 'Playing against Ireland in Holland – enough said. Also ripping my side (getting a side strain) in Twenty20 quarter-final in Essex'
Cricket superstitions: 'Put right pad on before left'
Cricketers particularly admired: Wasim Akram, Waqar Younis, Craig White, Anthony McGrath
Other sports played: Badminton (Yorkshire U15-U17), rugby (school), squash (school)
Other sports followed: Rugby league (Bradford Bulls)
Favourite band: Danny Bond, DJ Veteran, Jamie Duggan, DJ Leverton
Relaxations: 'Socialising, gym, study and Islam'
Extras: First British-born Asian to play for Yorkshire first team. Man of the Match in first match representing England – century and 3-22. Member of England Performance Programme squad 2009-10
Best batting: 88 Yorkshire v Sussex, Hove 2009
Best bowling: 4-22 Yorkshire v Sussex, Headingley 2007

2009 Season

	M	Inn	NO	Runs	HS	Avg	100	50	Ct	St	Balls	Runs	Wkts	Avg	BB	5I	10M
Test																	
FC	14	18	6	451	88	37.58	-	2	4	-	2537	1405	41	34.26	4-72	-	-
ODI																	
List A	6	5	1	66	43*	16.50	-	-	2	-	270	184	6	30.66	2-19	-	
20/20 Int																	
20/20	9	7	1	33	17*	5.50	-	-	3	-	180	219	4	54.75	1-18	-	

Career Performances

	M	Inn	NO	Runs	HS	Avg	100	50	Ct	St	Balls	Runs	Wkts	Avg	BB	5I	10M
Test																	
FC	22	27	9	553	88	30.72	-	2	4	-	3309	1857	53	35.03	4-22	-	-
ODI																	
List A	15	12	3	126	43*	14.00	-	-	2	-	678	518	18	28.77	5-51	1	
20/20 Int																	
20/20	10	8	2	35	17*	5.83	-	-	3	-	198	241	6	40.16	2-22	-	

SHAKIB AL HASAN   Worcestershire

Name: Shakib Al Hasan (also known as Saqibul Hasan)
Role: Left-hand bat, slow left-arm bowler
Born: 24 March 1987, Khulna, Bangladesh
County debut: No first-team appearance
Test debut: 2007
ODI debut: 2006
Twenty20 Int debut: 2006-07
Overseas tours: Bangladesh A to Zimabawe 2004-05, 2006, to England 2008; Bangladesh U19 to Sri Lanka (ICC U19 World Cup) 2005-06; Bangladesh to Kenya and Zimbabwe 2006 (one-day series), to Zimbabwe (one-day series) 2006-07, to West Indies (ICC World Cup) 2007, to Sri Lanka 2007, to Kenya 2007, to South Africa (ICC Twenty20 World Championship) 2007-08, to New Zealand 2007-08, to Pakistan 2007-08, to Australia (one-day series) 2008, to South Africa 2008-09, to England (ICC Twenty20 World Championship) 2009, to West Indies 2009, to New Zealand 2009-10
Overseas teams played for: Khulna Division 2004 –
Extras: Played for Bangladesh in all age groups from 15 upwards. Has captained his country on a number of occasions. Man of the Match (5-70/96) v Sri Lanka at Dhakar, December 2008; Man of the Match v West Indies at Port of Spain, July 2009 – later

named Man of the Series, the first Test series Bangladesh had won on foreign soil. *Wisden* World Test Player of the Year 2009. Signed for Worcestershire in November 2009. making him the first Bangladeshi contracted to play county cricket
Best batting: 129 Khulna Division v Dhaka Division, Khulna 2008-09
Best bowling: 7-36 Bangladesh v New Zealand, Chittagong (D) 2008/09

2009 Season

	M	Inn	NO	Runs	HS	Avg	100	50	Ct	St	Balls	Runs	Wkts	Avg	BB	5I	10M
Test																	
FC																	
ODI																	
List A																	
20/20 Int	2	2	0	15	8	7.50	-	-	1	-	42	47	2	23.50	1-23	-	
20/20	2	2	0	15	8	7.50	-	-	1	-	42	47	2	23.50	1-23	-	

Career Performances

	M	Inn	NO	Runs	HS	Avg	100	50	Ct	St	Balls	Runs	Wkts	Avg	BB	5I	10M
Test	14	26	2	715	96*	29.79	-	3	8	-	2991	1357	48	28.27	7-36	5	-
FC	38	70	7	2164	129	34.34	3	11	24	-	7024	3035	102	29.75	7-36	7	-
ODI	70	67	12	1904	134*	34.61	3	12	14	-	3489	2378	76	31.28	3-11	-	
List A	87	84	13	2271	134*	31.98	3	15	23	-	4201	2850	89	32.02	4-30	-	
20/20 Int	11	11	0	129	26	11.72	-	-	4	-	234	261	13	20.07	4-34	-	
20/20	11	11	0	129	26	11.72	-	-	4	-	234	261	13	20.07	4-34	-	

SHANKAR, A. A.   Lancashire

Name: Adrian Anton Shankar
Role: Right-hand bat, right-arm off-break bowler
Born: 7 May 1985, Ascot, Berkshire
County debut: No first-team appearance
Education: Bedford School;
Queen's College, Cambridge
Qualifications: Law degree
Other sports played: Football (was with Arsenal Academy), tennis
Extras: Former member of Middlesex Academy. Played for MCC against UCCE and for MCC Young Cricketers 2007. Has also played for CUCCE , Cambridge University (2002-05) and Bedfordshire (2000-06). Spent the first half of the 2008 season playing for Kent 2nd XI, and the second half for Lancashire 2nd XI. Signed for Lancashire in November 2008
Best batting: 143 Cambridge University v Oxford University, The Parks 2002

Career Performances

	M	Inn	NO	Runs	HS	Avg	100	50	Ct	St	Balls	Runs	Wkts	Avg	BB	5I	10M
Test																	
FC	12	20	0	384	143	19.20	1	-	5	-	0	0	0		-	-	-
ODI																	
List A	1	1	0	27	27	27.00	-	-	-	-	0	0	0		-	-	
20/20 Int																	
20/20																	

SHANTRY, A. J. Glamorgan

Name: <u>Adam</u> John Shantry
Role: Left-hand bat, left-arm
swing bowler; 'genuine all-rounder'
Born: 13 November 1982, Bristol
Height: 6ft 2in **Weight:** 14st 4lbs
Nickname: Shants, Cyril, Piece, Blue Steel, Bruno
County debut: 2003 (Northamptonshire),
2005 (one-day, Warwickshire),
2006 (first-class, Warwickshire), 2008 (Glamorgan)
Place in batting averages: 203rd av. 22.42
Place in bowling averages: 50th av. 30.96
(2008 4th av. 18.16)
Parents: Brian and Josephine
Marital status: Single. 'Future husband of Hayley
Williams or Fearne Cotton – ideally both'
Family links with cricket: 'Father played for Gloucestershire. Brother Jack plays
for Worcestershire. Mother is fourth in the world-wide rankings for the most cricket
whites ever washed'
Education: The Priory School, Shrewsbury; Shrewsbury Sixth Form College
Qualifications: 11 GCSEs, 4 A-levels, Level 2 coaching
Career outside cricket: 'Centre back for Bristol City – strong tackle, good engine,
don't really like heading'
Off-season: 'Dividing my time between the driving range, Ashton Gate, moshpits, the
gym, the pool, any river bank, and making sure my ducks are well fed'
Overseas tours: England U19 to India 2004-05; Warwickshire to Grenada 2007;
Glamorgan to Cape Town 2009
Overseas teams played for: Balwyn, Melbourne 2001-02; Subiaco-Floreat,
Perth 2004-05 – 2006-07
Career highlights to date: 'Five-fors against New Zealanders and West Indies A. Ten
wickets against Warwickshire 2008. My maiden first-class century v Leicestershire'

Cricket moments to forget: 'Any time I get stuck behind Gareth Rees in the lunch queue. Any time I break Dean Conway's 6-inch rule. Umpires in league cricket not giving me LBWs to batsmen shouldering arms because "it hit him in line, but it just pitched outside off stump"'

Cricket superstitions: 'Never wear underwear when fielding. Every changing room must contain the current issues of *Nuts*, *Zoo* and *Front* magazines'

Cricketers particularly admired: Jason Gillespie, Wasim Akram

Young players to look out for: Jack Shantry (Worcestershire)

Other sports played: Football, table tennis, golf

Other sports followed: Football (Bristol City)

Favourite band: Feeder, Escape The Fate, Funeral For A Friend, InMe

Relaxations: 'Fishing, moshing, crowd surfing'

Extras: England U17 squad. Represented ESCA U18 2001. Radio Shropshire Young Player of the Year 2001. Took 3-8 (including spell of three wickets in five balls before conceding a run) on Championship debut v Somerset at Northampton 2003. Took 5-37 v New Zealanders in 50-over match at Northampton 2004, winning Carlsberg Man of the Match award. His 5-15 v Warwickshire 2nd XI at Kenilworth 2004 included four wickets in four balls (bowled, bowled, lbw, bowled). Took 5-49 on first-class debut for Warwickshire v West Indies A at Edgbaston 2006. Took four wickets in his first four overs on Championship debut for Warwickshire v Sussex at Hove 2007 for innings figures of 4-31. Left Warwickshire at the end of the 2007 season and joined Glamorgan for 2008, Took 10-129 (5-77/5-52) for Glamorgan v Warwickshire in the County Championship at Edgbaston in September 2008

Opinions on cricket: 'Bowlers should be allowed to roll the covers off the ground when the groundsmen have gone home three times a season.'

Best batting: 100 Glamorgan v Leicestershire, Colwyn Bay 2009

Best bowling: 5-49 Warwickshire v West Indies A, Edgbaston 2006

2009 Season

	M	Inn	NO	Runs	HS	Avg	100	50	Ct	St	Balls	Runs	Wkts	Avg	BB	5I	10M
Test																	
FC	13	17	3	314	100	22.42	1	-	-	-	1668	898	29	30.96	5-62	1	-
ODI																	
List A	3	2	2	22	19*		-	-	-	-	114	97	2	48.50	1-29	-	
20/20 Int																	
20/20																	

Career Performances

	M	Inn	NO	Runs	HS	Avg	100	50	Ct	St	Balls	Runs	Wkts	Avg	BB	5I	10M
Test																		
FC	28	36	12	422	100	17.58	1	-	6	-	3600	1882	80	23.52	5-49	4	1
ODI																	
List A	12	6	3	48	19*	16.00	-	-	6	-	408	325	13	25.00	5-37	1	
20/20 Int																	
20/20	1	0	0	0	0		-	-	-	-	12	31	0		-	-	

SHANTRY, J. D.   Worcestershire

Name: <u>Jack</u> David Shantry
Role: Left-hand bat, left-arm medium bowler
Born: 29 January 1988, Shrewsbury, Shropshire
Height: 6ft 4in **Weight:** 13st
Nickname: Shants, Mincer, Tripod
County debut: 2009
Parents: Brian and Josephine
Marital status: Single
Family links with cricket: Dad played for
Gloucestershire, brother Adam plays for Glamorgan
Education: The Priory School, Shrewsbury;
Shrewsbury Sixth Form College
Qualifications: 12 GCSEs, 3 A-levels,
Level 1 coaching
Off-season: 'Watching Bristol City FC, eating'
Overseas teams played for: Claremont Nedlands 2006-07
Career highlights to date: 'Taking a wicket (Bopara) on my debut, and being left on
my own with the pudding table at Taunton'
Cricket moments to forget: 'Sky Sports passing my brother's photo off as me in
three successive televised games, much to the delight of my team-mates'
Cricket superstitions: 'Eat as much lunch and tea as possible'
Favourite sledging line: 'Whilst batting for a long time trying to save a game, the
opposition wicket-keeper, an ex-teammate of my brother, said: "Come on boys, he's
gotta be out soon – I've never seen a Shantry go this long without texting a girl."'
Cricketers particularly admired: Adam Gilchrist
Young players to look out for: Jack Manuel (Worcestershire)
Other sports played: Football – 'Played in goal for university and Hyde
United reserves'
Other sports followed: Football (Bristol City). 'Manchester University netball 1st XI'
Favourite band: Fightstar, Dashboard Confessional, The Wurzels
Relaxations: 'Reading – favourite authors Richard Dawkins and
Christopher Hitchens'
Extras: Has played for Shropshire and Minor Counties U25s
Opinions on cricket: 'Keeps improving and is more exciting to watch.
Introduce away kits in one-day games to avoid colour clashes.'
Best batting: 6 Worcestershire v Durham, Worcester 2009
Best bowling: 2-53 Worcestershire v Nottinghamshire, Worcester 2009

2009 Season

	M	Inn	NO	Runs	HS	Avg	100	50	Ct	St	Balls	Runs	Wkts	Avg	BB	5I	10M
Test																	
FC	4	5	1	12	6	3.00	-	-	2	-	763	382	8	47.75	2-53	-	-
ODI																	
List A	5	1	1	7	7*		-	-	-	-	204	212	5	42.40	2-43	-	
20/20 Int																	
20/20																	

Career Performances

	M	Inn	NO	Runs	HS	Avg	100	50	Ct	St	Balls	Runs	Wkts	Avg	BB	5I	10M
Test																		
FC	4	5	1	12	6	3.00	-	-	2	-	763	382	8	47.75	2-53	-	-
ODI																	
List A	5	1	1	7	7*		-	-	-	-	204	212	5	42.40	2-43	-	
20/20 Int																	
20/20																	

SHEIKH, A.   Derbyshire

Name: Atif Sheikh
Role: Right-hand bat, left-arm medium-fast bowler
Born: 18 February 1991, Nottingham
County debut: No first-team appearance
Overseas tours: England U19 to South Africa 2008-09
Extras: Has represented England at U17 and U19 level. Played for Nottinghamshire at U13 and U15 level. Derbyshire Academy 2007-2008. Derbyshire 2nd XI 2008-09. Signed a professional contract at the end of the 2008 season

81. So far, only one Bangladesh batsman averages more than 30 in Test matches. Name him.

SHRECK, C. E.   Nottinghamshire

Name: Charles (<u>Charlie</u>) Edward Shreck
Role: Right-hand bat, right-arm
fast-medium bowler
Born: 6 January 1978, Truro
Height: 6ft 7in **Weight:** 15st 7lbs
Nickname: Shrecker, Ogre, Stoat, Chough
County debut: 2002 (one-day), 2003 (first-class)
County cap: 2006
50 wickets in a season: 1
Place in bowling averages: 139th av. 61.00
(2008 68th av. 29.78)
Parents: Peter and Sheila
Marital status: Single
Family links with cricket: 'Grandfather
watched Southampton'
Education: Truro School
Qualifications: Level 1 coaching
Overseas tours: Cornwall U17 to South Africa 1997; England Lions to India 2007-08
Overseas teams played for: Merewether District CC, NSW 1997-98;
Hutt District CC, New Zealand 2000-03; Wellington, New Zealand 2005-06
Cricket moments to forget: 'Being run out off the last ball of the game against
Shropshire, walking off – we lost!'
Cricket superstitions: 'None'
Cricketers particularly admired: Viv Richards, Michael Holding, Ian Botham
Young players to look out for: Michael Munday, Carl Gazzard
Relaxations: 'Swimming, music'
Extras: C&G Man of the Match award for his 5-19 for Cornwall v Worcestershire
at Truro 2002. Took wicket (Vikram Solanki) with his third ball in county cricket v
Worcestershire at Trent Bridge in the NUL 2002, going on to record maiden one-day
league five-wicket return (5-35). Took four wickets in six balls, including hat-trick
(Smith, Morgan, Weekes), v Middlesex at Lord's 2006. Took 61 first-class wickets in
2006 (including 12-129 v Middlesex at Trent Bridge), having missed the entire 2005
season after undergoing back surgery. Nottinghamshire Player of the Year 2006, 2008.
Called up to squad for England Lions tour of India 2007-08
Best batting: 19 Nottinghamshire v Essex, Chelmsford 2003
Best bowling: 8-31 Nottinghamshire v Middlesex, Trent Bridge 2006

2009 Season

	M	Inn	NO	Runs	HS	Avg	100	50	Ct	St	Balls	Runs	Wkts	Avg	BB	5I	10M
Test																	
FC	11	12	7	28	12*	5.60	-	-	1	-	2180	1281	21	61.00	4-63	-	-
ODI																	
List A	2	1	0	1	1	1.00	-	-	-	-	59	83	1	83.00	1-47	-	
20/20 Int																	
20/20																	

Career Performances

	M	Inn	NO	Runs	HS	Avg	100	50	Ct	St	Balls	Runs	Wkts	Avg	BB	5I	10M
Test																	
FC	80	90	53	144	19	3.89	-	-	27	-	16171	8813	289	30.49	8-31	18	2
ODI																	
List A	50	19	12	45	9*	6.42	-	-	12	-	2278	1973	63	31.31	5-19	2	
20/20 Int																	
20/20	22	6	5	10	6*	10.00	-	-	4	-	457	597	23	25.95	4-22	-	

SIDEBOTTOM, R. J.   Nottinghamshire

Name: <u>Ryan</u> Jay Sidebottom
Role: Left-hand bat, left-arm fast bowler
Born: 15 January 1978, Huddersfield
Height: 6ft 4in **Weight:** 14st 7lbs
Nickname: Siddy, Sexual, Jazz
County debut: 1997 (Yorkshire),
2004 (Nottinghamshire)
County cap: 2000 (Yorkshire),
2004 (Nottinghamshire)
Benefit: 2010
Test debut: 2001
ODI debut: 2001-02
Twenty20 Int debut: 2007
50 wickets in a season: 2
Place in batting averages: 237th av. 16.66
(2008 255th av. 10.83)
Place in bowling averages: 16th av. 24.51 (2008 21st av. 22.72)
Parents: Arnie and Gillian
Marital status: Single
Family links with sport: Father played cricket for Yorkshire and England and football for Manchester United and Huddersfield Town

Education: King James Grammar School, Almondbury
Qualifications: 5 GCSEs
Overseas tours: England U17 to Netherlands 1995; MCC to Bangladesh 1999-2000; England A to West Indies 2000-01; England to Zimbabwe (one-day series) 2001-02, to Sri Lanka 2007-08, to New Zealand 2007-08, to India (one-day series) 2008-09, to West Indies (Test and one-day series) 2008-09, to South Africa 2009-10; ECB National Academy to Australia 2001-02
Overseas teams played for: Ringwood, Melbourne 1998
Cricketers particularly admired: Darren Gough, Chris Silverwood, Glenn McGrath
Other sports played: Football (once with Sheffield United), 'all sports'
Other sports followed: 'Love rugby league (any team)', football (Manchester United)
Relaxations: 'Music (R&B), films, clubbing, going out with my team-mates'
Extras: NBC Denis Compton Award for the most promising young Yorkshire player 1999, 2000. Took 5-31 (8-65 in match) for England A v Jamaica at Kingston in the Busta Cup 2000-01, winning the Man of the Match award; topped tour first-class bowling averages (16 wickets; av. 16.81). Made Test debut in the first Test v Pakistan at Lord's 2001 (England's 100th Test at the ground), becoming the tenth player to follow his father into the England Test team. Recalled to Test side after six years for the second Test v West Indies at Headingley 2007, returning match figures of 8-86 (4-42/4-44). Man of the [ODI] Series v Sri Lanka 2007-08. Named as one of *Wisden*'s Five Cricketers of the Year 2008. England 12-month central contract 2009-10. Benefit year 2010
Best batting: 54 Yorkshire v Glamorgan, Cardiff 1998
Best bowling: 7-47 England v New Zealand, Napier 2007-08

2009 Season

	M	Inn	NO	Runs	HS	Avg	100	50	Ct	St	Balls	Runs	Wkts	Avg	BB	5I	10M
Test																	
FC	7	9	3	100	46	16.66	-	-	1	-	1562	760	31	24.51	5-59	2	-
ODI	6	6	2	57	24	14.25	-	-	3	-	312	281	3	93.66	1-45	-	
List A	10	9	3	69	24	11.50	-	-	3	-	486	393	6	65.50	2-39	-	
20/20 Int	4	0	0	0	0		-	-	1	-	80	100	3	33.33	2-31	-	
20/20	8	1	1	17	17*		-	-	2	-	176	186	11	16.90	3-16	-	

Career Performances

	M	Inn	NO	Runs	HS	Avg	100	50	Ct	St	Balls	Runs	Wkts	Avg	BB	5I	10M
Test	21	29	11	298	31	16.55	-	-	5	-	4626	2133	77	27.70	7-47	5	1
FC	137	175	52	1511	54	12.28	-	1	46	-	24302	11378	443	25.68	7-47	19	2
ODI	24	18	8	133	24	13.30	-	-	6	-	1231	993	28	35.46	3-19	-	
List A	166	80	36	498	32	11.31	-	-	36	-	7388	5330	169	31.53	6-40	2	
20/20 Int	8	1	1	5	5*		-	-	3	-	172	202	11	18.36	3-16	-	
20/20	28	7	6	45	17*	45.00	-	-	8	-	593	636	37	17.18	3-16	-	

SILVERWOOD, C. E. W.   Middlesex

Name: Christopher (<u>Chris</u>) Eric
Wilfred Silverwood
Role: Right-hand bat, right-arm fast bowler
Born: 5 March 1975, Pontefract
Height: 6ft 1in **Weight:** 12st 9lbs
Nickname: Spoons, Silvers, Chubby
County debut: 1993 (Yorkshire), 2006 (Middlesex)
County cap: 1996 (Yorkshire), 2006 (Middlesex)
Benefit: 2004 (Yorkshire)
Test debut: 1996-97
ODI debut: 1996-97
50 wickets in a season: 3
Place in batting averages: 240th av. 16.14
Parents: Brenda
Wife and date of marriage: Victoria, 2006

Family links with cricket: 'Dad played a bit'
Education: Garforth Comprehensive
Qualifications: 8 GCSEs, City and Guilds in Leisure and Recreation
Overseas tours: England A to Kenya and Sri Lanka 1997-98, to Bangladesh and New Zealand 1999-2000, to West Indies 2000-01; England to Zimbabwe and New Zealand 1996-97, to West Indies 1997-98, to Bangladesh (Wills International Cup) 1998-99, to South Africa 1999-2000, to Zimbabwe (one-day series) 2001-02, to Australia 2002-03; England VI to Hong Kong 2002, 2003
Overseas teams played for: Wellington, Cape Town 1993-94, 1995-96
Career highlights to date: 'Making Test debut. Winning the Championship [2001]'
Cricketers particularly admired: Ian Botham, Allan Donald
Other sports played: Karate (black belt), rugby league, athletics
(represented Yorkshire)
Other sports followed: Rugby league (Castleford)
Extras: NBC Denis Compton Award for the most promising young Yorkshire player 1996. Attended Yorkshire Academy. Represented England U19. C&G Man of the Match awards v Northamptonshire at Northampton 2002 (61/2-35) and v Dorset at Dean Park 2004 (4-18). Took 500th first-class wicket (Andrew Gale) against his old county, Yorkshire, at Southgate 2006, finishing with match figures of 8-64. Released by Middlesex at the end of the 2009 season
Best batting: 80 Yorkshire v Durham, Riverside 2005
Best bowling: 7-93 Yorkshire v Kent, Headingley 1997

2009 Season

	M	Inn	NO	Runs	HS	Avg	100	50	Ct	St	Balls	Runs	Wkts	Avg	BB	5I	10M
Test																	
FC	5	8	1	113	46	16.14	--	-	2	-	690	355	4	88.75	1-23	-	-
ODI																	
List A	9	4	0	44	26	11.00	-	-	2	-	372	301	9	33.44	3-26	-	
20/20 Int																	
20/20	6	4	3	25	18*	25.00	-	-	-	-	132	152	2	76.00	1-27	-	

Career Performances

	M	Inn	NO	Runs	HS	Avg	100	50	Ct	St	Balls	Runs	Wkts	Avg	BB	5I	10M
Test	6	7	3	29	10	7.25	-	-	2	-	828	444	11	40.36	5-91	1	-
FC	184	243	49	3075	80	15.85	-	9	43	-	29917	15819	577	27.41	7-93	25	1
ODI	7	4	0	17	12	4.25	-	-	-	-	306	244	6	40.66	3-43	-	
List A	202	114	37	1046	61	13.58	-	4	32	-	9046	6488	259	25.05	5-28	1	
20/20 Int																	
20/20	20	12	7	69	18*	13.80	-	-	4	-	438	550	14	39.28	2-22	-	

SIMPSON, J. A.　　　　　　　　　Middlesex

Name: <u>John</u> Andrew Simpson
Role: Left-hand bat, wicket-keeper
Born: 13 July 1988, Ramsbottom,
Bury, Lancashire
Height: 5ft 10in **Weight:** 10st 5lbs
Nickname: Simmo, Gags
County debut: 2008
Place in batting averages: 156th av. 28.33
Parents: Jack and Karen
Marital status: Single
Family links with sport: Father, Jack, played cricket
in the Lancashire 2nd XI, the Lancashire League and
for England Amateurs. Grandad played, uncle and
cousin still play. Dad also played lacrosse for England,
and grandad and great grandad played rugby league
for Great Britain
Education: St Gabriel's RC High School
Qualifications: Level 1 coaching
Off-season: In Australia and Sri Lanka
Overseas tours: England U17 to South Africa; England U19 to India and Malaysia
2004-05, to Sri Lanka and Bangladesh (U19 World Cup) 2005-06

Overseas teams played for: South Caulfield CC, Victoria, Australia 2005-06, 2006-07; Adelaide University 2007-08

Career highlights to date: 'Pro40 and Twenty20 debuts for Middlesex at Lord's. Scoring a century in the last game of cricket my grandad watched before passing away'

Cricketers particularly admired: Adam Gilchrist, Jack Russell, Ian Healy, Ricky Ponting, Brian Lara, Warren Hegg – 'Dad was a massive influence'

Young players to look out for: Adam London, Dawid Malan, Dan Housego and Sam Robson (all Middlesex)

Other sports played: Golf, football

Other sports followed: Golf, football (Newcastle United)

Favourite band: Kings of Leon

Relaxations: 'Gym, chilling with mates, visiting family'

Extras: Played in the Lancashire league for Haslingden CC first team when only ten years old, the youngest player ever to make his Lancashire league debut. Represented Lancashire in every age group from U11 upwards. NBC Denis Compton Award for the most promising young Lancashire player 2004. Lancashire Academy 2004-07. Joined Lancashire on a scholarship in 2007. Played for the 2nd XI at Lancashire, Durham and Nottinghamshire during the 2007 season. MCC Young Cricketer 2008. Signed a two-year contract with Middlesex in June 2008. Came on as substitute wicket-keeper when Ben Scott injured his ankle during the Middlesex v Northamptonshire match in September 2008, taking two catches (not his first-class debut). Middlesex 2nd XI Player of the Year 2008. Received the Betfair Scholarship Award, which affords the recipient a place at the Darren Lehmann Academy, at the end of the 2008 season. Member of England Performance Programme squad 2009-10

Best batting: 87 Middlesex v Northamptonshire, Northampton 2009

2009 Season

	M	Inn	NO	Runs	HS	Avg	100	50	Ct	St	Balls	Runs	Wkts	Avg	BB	5I	10M
Test																	
FC	3	6	0	170	87	28.33	-	1	5	-	0	0	0		-	-	-
ODI																	
List A	6	5	0	108	32	21.60	-	-	3	1	0	0	0		-	-	
20/20 Int																	
20/20	1	1	0	13	13	13.00	-	-	-	-	0	0	0		-	-	

Career Performances

	M	Inn	NO	Runs	HS	Avg	100	50	Ct	St	Balls	Runs	Wkts	Avg	BB	5I	10M
Test																	
FC	3	6	0	170	87	28.33	-	1	5	-	0	0	0		-	-	-
ODI																	
List A	6	5	0	108	32	21.60	-	-	3	1	0	0	0		-	-	
20/20 Int																	
20/20	1	1	0	13	13	13.00	-	-	-	-	0	0	0		-	-	

SMITH, B. F.   Worcestershire

Name: Benjamin (<u>Ben</u>) Francis Smith
Role: Right-hand bat, right-arm medium bowler
Born: 3 April 1972, Corby, Northamptonshire
Height: 5ft 9in **Weight:** 11st
Nickname: Smudge
County debut: 1990 (Leicestershire),
2002 (Worcestershire)
County cap: 1995 (Leicestershire),
2002 (Worcestershire colours)
Benefit: 2009
1000 runs in a season: 8
1st-Class 200s: 3
Place in batting averages: 177th av. 26.08
(2008 46th av. 44.79)

Parents: Keith and Janet
Wife and date of marriage: Lisa, 10 October 1998
Children: Ruby, 6 November 2005
Family links with cricket: Father, grandfather and uncles all played club and representative cricket
Education: Kibworth High School; Robert Smyth, Market Harborough
Qualifications: 5 O-levels, 8 GCSEs, NCA coaching certificate
Off-season: 'Finishing off my benefit year, and in Worcestershire preparing for next season on a 12-month contract.'
Overseas tours: England YC to New Zealand 1990-91; MCC to Bangladesh 1999-2000; Worcestershire to South Africa 2009-10 and 'numerous pre-season tours to South Africa, Caribbean and Sri Lanka'
Overseas teams played for: Alexandria, Zimbabwe 1990; Bankstown-Canterbury, Sydney 1993-96; Central Hawke's Bay CC, New Zealand 1997-98; Central Districts, New Zealand 2000-02
Career highlights to date: 'Winning 1996 County Championship'
Cricket moments to forget: 'Lord's finals'
Cricketers particularly admired: Viv Richards, David Gower, Steve Waugh
Young players to look out for: Ben Cox (Worcestershire)
Other sports played: Tennis (Leicestershire aged 12), golf, touch rugby
Other sports followed: Rugby union (Leicester Tigers)
Favourite band: Paul Weller, Muse
Relaxations: Family time, golf
Extras: Cricket Society Young Player of the Year 1991. Vice-captain of Leicestershire 2001. Scored century (137) on first-class debut for Worcestershire v OUCCE at The Parks and another (129) on Championship debut for the county v Gloucestershire at Worcester 2002 to become the first player to achieve this 'double' for Worcestershire.

Worcestershire Supporters' Player of the Year 2002. Worcestershire Player of the Year 2003. Scored 187 v Gloucestershire at Worcester 2004, in the process sharing with Graeme Hick (262) in the highest first-class partnership ever made at New Road (417). Scored 203 v Somerset at Taunton 2006, in the process sharing with Graeme Hick (182) in a Worcestershire record partnership for the fourth wicket (330). Captain of Worcestershire 2003 until standing down in August 2004

Player website: www.bensmithbenefit.com
Best batting: 204 Leicestershire v Surrey, The Oval 1998
Best bowling: 1-5 Leicestershire v Essex, Ilford 1991

2009 Season

	M	Inn	NO	Runs	HS	Avg	100	50	Ct	St	Balls	Runs	Wkts	Avg	BB	5I	10M
Test																	
FC	14	27	3	626	80*	26.08	-	4	9	-	0	0	0	-	-	-	-
ODI																	
List A	15	12	2	288	70	28.80	-	2	5	-	0	0	0	-	-	-	
20/20 Int																	
20/20	10	10	3	171	44	24.42	-	-	3	-	0	0	0	-	-		

Career Performances

	M	Inn	NO	Runs	HS	Avg	100	50	Ct	St	Balls	Runs	Wkts	Avg	BB	5I	10M
Test																		
FC	326	515	56	18495	204	40.29	40	98	205	-	653	488	4	122.00	1-5	-	-
ODI																	
List A	394	377	54	9869	115	30.55	3	61	140	-	127	121	2	60.50	1-2	-	
20/20 Int																	
20/20	51	49	6	866	105	20.13	1	1	23	-	0	0	0	-	-		

82. Which Bangladesh batsman has scored the most Test centuries?

SMITH, D. R.   Sussex

Name: <u>Dwayne</u> Romel Smith
Role: Right-hand bat, right-arm medium bowler, occasional wicket-keeper; all-rounder
Born: 12 April 1983, St Michael, Barbados
Height: 6ft 1in **Weight:** 13st 3lbs
Nickname: Agent Smith
County debut: 2008 (one-day)
County cap: 2009
Test debut: 2004
ODI debut: 2004
Twenty20 Int debut: 2006
Place in batting averages: 227th av. 18.64
Place in bowling averages: 65th av. 32.56
Parents: Lorraine Smith and Wilbur Bruce
Marital status: Single
Family links with cricket: 'My dad'

Education: Garrison Secondary School, Barbados
Overseas tours: West Indies to South Africa (Test and one-day series) 2003-04, to England 2004 (one-day series), to Sri Lanka (Indian Oil Cup) 2005, to New Zealand 2005-06 (one-day series), to Malaysia (DLF Cup) 2006-07, to India (one-day series) 2006-07, to Pakistan 2006-07 (one-day series), to England 2007 (one-day series), to Ireland (Quadrangular series) 2007, to South Africa (ICC Twenty20 World Championship) 2007-08, to Australia 2009-10 (one-day series)
Overseas teams played for: Barbados 2001-02 – ; Mumbai Indians (IPL) 2007-08, 2008-09
Career highlights to date: 'Scoring a hundred on my Test debut against South Africa'
Cricket moments to forget: 'Losing to Australia in the 2006 Champions Trophy Final'
Cricketers particularly admired: Brian Lara, Jonty Rhodes
Young players to look out for: Jonathan Carter (Barbados)
Other sports played: 'None'
Other sports followed: Football (Manchester United)
Favourite band: Square One
Relaxations: 'Partying and the beach'
Extras: Scored 105* on his Test debut against South Africa in Cape Town in January 2004, his 93-ball century being the fastest ever by a debutant in Test cricket. Joined Sussex as a replacement for the injured Mushtaq Ahmed in June 2008. Played for Sussex as a Kolpak in 2009; released at the end of the season when his Kolpak status expired. Re-signed with Sussex as an overseas player for Twenty20 matches in 2010
Best batting: 155 Barbados v Combined Campuses & Colleges, Crab Hill 2008-09
Best bowling: 4-22 Barbados v Trinidad & Tobago, Pointe-a-Pierre 2007

2009 Season

	M	Inn	NO	Runs	HS	Avg	100	50	Ct	St	Balls	Runs	Wkts	Avg	BB	5I	10M
Test																	
FC	9	14	0	261	80	18.64	-	2	1	-	1806	814	25	32.56	4-58	-	-
ODI																	
List A	10	9	1	237	60*	29.62	-	3	-	-	222	167	9	18.55	6-29	1	
20/20 Int																	
20/20	13	13	3	338	69*	33.80	-	3	6	-	144	165	8	20.62	3-19	-	

Career Performances

	M	Inn	NO	Runs	HS	Avg	100	50	Ct	St	Balls	Runs	Wkts	Avg	BB	5I	10M
Test	10	14	1	320	105*	24.61	1	-	9	-	651	344	7	49.14	3-71	-	
FC	80	132	9	3656	155	29.72	7	14	77	-	7840	3907	121	32.28	4-22	-	-
ODI	71	56	3	791	68	14.92	-	2	24	-	2264	1813	49	37.00	5-45	1	
List A	124	105	8	2130	96	21.95	-	13	41	-	3497	2771	83	33.38	6-29	2	
20/20 Int	5	5	0	49	29	9.80	-	-	-	-	80	108	5	21.60	3-24	-	
20/20	46	44	4	877	72*	21.92	-	4	17	-	693	876	37	23.67	4-9	-	

SMITH, G. M.   Derbyshire

Name: Gregory (<u>Greg</u>) Marc Smith
Role: Right-hand bat, right-arm medium/
off-spin bowler; all-rounder
Born: 20 April 1983, Johannesburg, South Africa
Height: 5ft 8½in **Weight:** 11st 5lbs
Nickname: Smithy, Smudge
County debut: 2006
County cap: 2009
Place in batting averages: 62nd av. 42.47
(2008 100th av. 33.25)
Place in bowling averages: 75th av. 34.31
(2008 139th av. 45.63)
Parents: Ian and Nadine
Wife and date of marriage: Bethany,
10 October 2008
Family links with cricket: 'Dad used to be financial
adviser of the UCB [United Cricket Board of South Africa]'
Education: St Stithians College; UNISA (University of South Africa)
Qualifications: Matriculation, Level 2 coaching certificate
Overseas tours: South Africa U19 to New Zealand (U19 World Cup) 2001-02
Overseas teams played for: Old Edwardians, Johannesburg; Griqualand West
2003-04; Frankston (Melbourne) 2007-08

Career highlights to date: 'Scoring half-century in U19 World Cup final v Australia. Scoring a century in Twenty20 v Yorkshire in 2008'
Cricket moments to forget: 'Getting my first pair.'
Cricketers particularly admired: Ashley Smith, Nyan Doshi, Jon Lewis
Other sports played: Golf, tennis
Other sports followed: Football (Arsenal), rugby (Sharks)
Favourite band: Coldplay
Extras: Represented Gauteng U13, U15, U19. South Africa Academy 2003-04. Most Improved Derbyshire player 2007
Opinions on cricket: 'Too many flat wickets – not enough turning ones for me to turn it on! More Twenty20 – I really love it, because I'm good at it.'
Best batting: 126 Derbyshire v Gloucestershire, Cheltenham 2009
Best bowling: 5-65 Derbyshire v Middlesex, Uxbridge 2009

2009 Season

	M	Inn	NO	Runs	HS	Avg	100	50	Ct	St	Balls	Runs	Wkts	Avg	BB	5I	10M
Test																	
FC	16	27	4	977	126	42.47	1	6	5	-	1982	1098	32	34.31	5-65	1	-
ODI																	
List A	13	13	3	334	77	33.40	-	1	8	-	582	532	21	25.33	4-53	-	
20/20 Int																	
20/20	10	10	1	259	56	28.77	-	2	4	-	143	202	3	67.33	1-14	-	

Career Performances

	M	Inn	NO	Runs	HS	Avg	100	50	Ct	St	Balls	Runs	Wkts	Avg	BB	5I	10M
Test																	
FC	55	95	9	2587	126	30.08	2	18	15	-	4847	2722	71	38.33	5-65	1	-
ODI																	
List A	51	51	5	1155	88	25.10	-	5	22	-	1363	1309	42	31.16	4-53	-	
20/20 Int																	
20/20	25	25	2	658	100*	28.60	1	4	7	-	167	239	3	79.66	1-14	-	

SMITH, G. P. Leicestershire

Name: Greg Phillip Smith
Role: Right-hand bat, occasional slow left-arm orthodox bowler
Born: 16 November 1988, Leicester
County debut: 2008
Place in batting averages: 232nd av. 17.76 (2008 188th av. 21.50)
Education: Durham University
Career highlights to date: 'Scoring back-to-back 150s in an England U19 Test series against New Zealand in 2008'
Cricketers particularly admired: Russell Spiers, Aravinda de Silva, Matthew Boyce
Relaxations: Darts, eating out
Extras: Has played for England U19, Leicestershire 2nd XI and Kibworth CC (Leicestershire Premier League). Leicestershire Academy 2005-08. Won the 2008 Leicestershire 2nd XI Outstanding Performance Award for his 146 runs v Northamptonshire. A broken thumb sustained whilst fielding for DUCCE earlier in the year delayed his return to county action in 2009. Signed a three-year deal in October 2009
Best batting: 54 Leicestershire v Derbyshire, Grace Road 2008
Best bowling: 1-64 Leicestershire v Gloucestershire, Grace Road 2008

2009 Season

	M	Inn	NO	Runs	HS	Avg	100	50	Ct	St	Balls	Runs	Wkts	Avg	BB	5I	10M
Test																	
FC	7	14	1	231	51	17.76	-	1	3	-	0	0	0		-	-	-
ODI																	
List A	1	1	0	1	1	1.00	-	-	-	-	0	0	0		-	-	
20/20 Int																	
20/20																	

Career Performances

	M	Inn	NO	Runs	HS	Avg	100	50	Ct	St	Balls	Runs	Wkts	Avg	BB	5I	10M
Test																	
FC	13	24	1	446	54	19.39	-	2	5	-	30	64	1	64.00	1-64	-	-
ODI																	
List A	3	3	0	72	58	24.00	-	1	-	-	0	0	0		-	-	
20/20 Int																	
20/20																	

SMITH, T. C. P.   Lancashire

Name: Thomas (<u>Tom</u>) Christopher Pascoe Smith
Role: Left-hand bat, right-arm fast-medium bowler; all-rounder
Born: 26 December 1985, Liverpool
Height: 6ft 3in   **Weight:** 14st 7lbs
Nickname: Smudger, Tommy Canoeshoe, Plank
County debut: 2005
Place in batting averages: 130th av. 32.50
(2008 102nd av. 32.77)
Place in bowling averages: 109th av. 41.53
(2008 77th av. 31.12)

Parents: Mark and Jacqui
Marital status: Single
Family links with cricket: Brother Lancashire U19.
Father and stepfather play for local village teams
Education: Parklands High School; Runshaw College
Qualifications: 10 GCSEs, 4 A-levels
Off season: 'Perth, playing cricket'
Overseas tours: England U19 to India 2004-05; England A to Bangladesh 2006-07
Overseas teams played for: St Kilda CC, Melbourne 2007-08; Gosnells CC, Perth 2009-10
Career highlights to date: 'Contract with Lancashire. Being picked for National Academy 2005-06. 6-46 v Yorkshire (County Championship) 2009'
Cricket moments to forget: 'First-ball duck on my first-class debut'
Cricket superstitions: 'Right pad on first'
Cricketers particularly admired: Andrew Flintoff, Ricky Ponting
Young players to look out for: Karl Brown (Lancashire), James Vince (Hampshire)
Other sports played: Football, golf, swimming
Other sports followed: Football (Liverpool FC)
Favourite band: Foo Fighters
Relaxations: 'Watching films and socialising with friends'
Extras: Lancashire Academy 2003, 2004. NBC Denis Compton Award for the most promising young Lancashire player 2005, 2006, 2007. Represented England U19 2005. ECB National Academy 2005-06, 2006-07. On loan to Leicestershire for part of the 2008 season. Lancashire One-Day Player of the Year 2009
Opinions on cricket: 'More Twenty20!'
Best batting: 104* Lancashire v DUCCE, Durham 2009
Best bowling: 6-46 Lancashire v Yorkshire, Old Trafford 2009

2009 Season

	M	Inn	NO	Runs	HS	Avg	100	50	Ct	St	Balls	Runs	Wkts	Avg	BB	5I	10M
Test																	
FC	9	15	3	390	104*	32.50	1	2	7	-	1198	623	15	41.53	6-46	1	-
ODI																	
List A	11	11	1	389	87*	38.90	-	4	4	-	487	401	15	26.73	3-52	-	
20/20 Int																	
20/20	6	6	2	143	57*	35.75	-	1	3	-	84	74	5	14.80	3-20	-	

Career Performances

	M	Inn	NO	Runs	HS	Avg	100	50	Ct	St	Balls	Runs	Wkts	Avg	BB	5I	10M
Test																	
FC	42	53	13	1050	104*	26.25	1	3	36	-	5909	2879	84	34.27	6-46	1	-
ODI																	
List A	37	27	7	567	87*	28.35	-	5	10	-	1442	1128	44	25.63	3-8	-	
20/20 Int																	
20/20	21	15	6	222	57*	24.66	-	1	9	-	328	384	15	25.60	3-15	-	

SMITH, T. M. J.   Middlesex

Name: Thomas Michael John Smith
Role: Right-hand bat, slow left-arm orthodox bowler
Born: 29 August 1987, Eastbourne, Sussex
Height: 5ft 9in **Weight:** 11st 7lbs
Nickname: Smudge
County debut: 2006 (one-day, Sussex),
2007 (first-class, Sussex)
Parents: Michael and Claudine
Marital status: Single
Education: Seaford Head Community College;
Sussex Downs College
Qualifications: NVQ Level 2 in plumbing
Overseas tours: Sussex Academy to Cape
Town 2003, 2005
Overseas teams played for: Police CC, Cape
Town 2007-08; North Shore CC, Auckland,
New Zealand 2008-09
Career highlights to date: 'Captaining Sussex 2nd XI to the 2nd XI Championship'
Cricket moments to forget: 'Semi-dislocating my shoulder in a net a week before I
went to Cape Town on a cricket tour'
Cricket superstitions: 'None'
Cricketers particularly admired: Daniel Vettori, Monty Panesar, Mike Yardy

Young players to look out for: Matt Machan, Ben Brown, Will Beer (all Sussex)
Other sports played: Football (Seaford Town FC), golf
Favourite band: The Subways
Relaxations: 'Watching *Lost*!'
Extras: Sussex 2nd XI Player of the Year 2006. Sussex League Young Player of the Year 2006. Spent a short period on loan at Surrey at the end of the 2009 season, playing two Pro40 matches for the county; shared a Pro40 record 126-run 6th wicket partnership with Matt Spriegel v Leicestershire in September 2009. Released by Sussex at end of 2009 season. Member of England Performance Programme squad 2009-10. Will play for Middlesex in 2010
Opinions on cricket: 'Good that younger players are getting more opportunity and also Twenty20 is a great competition.'
Best batting: 10 Sussex v Lancashire, Hove 2009
Best bowling: 1-52 Sussex v Sri Lanka A, Hove 2007

2009 Season

	M	Inn	NO	Runs	HS	Avg	100	50	Ct	St	Balls	Runs	Wkts	Avg	BB	5I	10M
Test																	
FC	1	2	0	11	10	5.50	-	-	-	-	76	70	0		-	-	-
ODI																	
List A	2	1	0	65	65	65.00	-	1	-	-	54	52	2	26.00	1-25	-	
20/20 Int																	
20/20																	

Career Performances

	M	Inn	NO	Runs	HS	Avg	100	50	Ct	St	Balls	Runs	Wkts	Avg	BB	5I	10M
Test																	
FC	2	3	0	13	10	4.33	-	-	-	-	154	149	1	149.00	1-52	-	-
ODI																	
List A	10	3	0	87	65	29.00	-	1	7	-	366	364	7	52.00	2-45	-	
20/20 Int																	
20/20	2	1	1	3	3*		-	-	-	-	12	14	0		-	-	

SMITH, W. R. Durham

Name: William (<u>Will</u>) Rew Smith
Role: Right-hand top-order bat, right-arm off-break
bowler, occasional wicket-keeper; county captain
Born: 28 September 1982, Luton, Bedfordshire
Height: 5ft 9in **Weight:** 11st 7lbs
Nickname: Smudge, Jiggy
County debut: 2002 (Nottinghamshire),
2007 (Durham)
1st-Class 200s: 1
Place in batting averages: 92nd av. 37.90
(2008 21st av. 51.38)
Parents: Jim and Barbara
Marital status: Engaged to Katherine Trick
Family links with cricket: 'Brother Ben played a
lot of youth cricket; father a cricket "statto". Both
are keen followers of the game'
Education: Bedford School; Durham University; Staffordshire University
Qualifications: 11 GCSEs, 3 A-levels, BSc Molecular Biology and Biochemistry,
Level 2 cricket coach
Career outside cricket: Sports journalism
Off-season: 'Hibernating…'
Overseas tours: British Universities to South Africa 2004; Nottinghamshire to
Cape Town; Durham to Cape Town. 'Various pre-season tours to South Africa'
Overseas teams played for: Gordon DCC, Sydney 2001-02, 2006-07, 2008-09
Career highlights to date: 'Being part of Durham's Friends Provident Trophy
winning side 2007. Maiden Championship century against Surrey (*he went on to
make 201**). Regaining the Championship title as Durham captain'
Cricket moments to forget: 'None – embrace every moment'
Cricket superstitions: 'None'
Favourite sledging line: 'Usually about hitting my small pads…'
Cricketers particularly admired: Michael DiVenuto, Dale Benkenstein,
Steve Harmison, Geoff Cook, Graeme Fowler
Young players to look out for: Scott Borthwick, Ben Stokes, Luke Evans
(all Durham)
Other sports played: 'Golf, football'
Other sports followed: Football (Rushden & Diamonds, Newcastle United),
rugby (Bedford), horse racing, golf
Favourite band: White Lies
Relaxations: 'Reading, socialising, people-watching in cafes or wine bars,
going to music festivals and gigs'
Extras: Represented England U16-U18. Played for DUCCE 2003-05 (captain 2004-
05). Represented British Universities 2004, 2005 (captain 2005). Nottinghamshire

2nd XI Player of the Year 2005. Took over the county captaincy from Dale Benkenstein in November 2008. Durham Player of the Year 2008

Opinions on cricket: 'The integrity of Championship cricket must be upheld, while the development of the one-day game should be closely monitored. Both can be allowed to flourish independently if handled carefully.'

Best batting: 201* Durham v Surrey, Guildford 2008

Best bowling: 3-34 DUCCE v Leicestershire, Grace Road 2005

2009 Season

	M	Inn	NO	Runs	HS	Avg	100	50	Ct	St	Balls	Runs	Wkts	Avg	BB	5I	10M
Test																	
FC	17	25	3	834	150	37.90	2	5	6	-	60	31	0		-	-	-
ODI																	
List A	16	16	0	338	77	21.12	-	2	4	-	48	45	1	45.00	1-29	-	
20/20 Int																	
20/20	10	10	3	69	20	9.85	-	-	11	-	0	0	0		-	-	

Career Performances

	M	Inn	NO	Runs	HS	Avg	100	50	Ct	St	Balls	Runs	Wkts	Avg	BB	5I	10M
Test																	
FC	70	112	8	3433	201*	33.00	8	11	33	-	705	525	8	65.62	3-34	-	-
ODI																	
List A	65	60	3	1439	103	25.24	1	10	24	-	53	51	2	25.50	1-6	-	
20/20 Int																	
20/20	45	39	8	583	55	18.80	-	3	30	-	24	39	1	39.00	1-31	-	

SNELL, S. D.   Gloucestershire

Name: <u>Steven</u> David Snell
Role: Right-hand bat, wicket-keeper
Born: 27 February 1983, Winchester
Height: 6ft **Weight:** 12st 12lbs
Nickname: Snelly
County debut: 2005
County cap: 2005
Place in batting averages: 238th av. 16.53
2008 34th av. 47.20)
Parents: Jonathan and Sandra
Marital status: Single
Family links with cricket: 'Grandad and Dad both keen amateur cricketers. Brothers Rob and Peter both play at Ventnor Cricket Club (the real home of cricket!) on the Isle of Wight'

Education: Sandown High School, Isle of Wight
Qualifications: 10 GCSEs, 2 A-levels, ECB Level 2 cricket coach, FA Level 1 football coach, EBA basketball coach, YMCA fitness instructor
Career outside cricket: 'Coaching or something else involved in the game to pay the bills!'
Off-season: 'Studying for ECB Level 4 coaching and following Bristol North West FC'
Overseas tours: MCC Young Cricketers to Cape Town 2002, to Lanzarote 2003, to Sri Lanka 2004; MCC B to USA 2004
Overseas teams played for: Hermanus, Cape Town 2002-03; Brighton, Melbourne 2003-04 – 2005-06
Career highlights to date: 'Ventnor first-team debut; 83* on first-class debut against Bangladesh A'
Cricket moments to forget: 'Breaking my jaw in three places during nets at Lord's. Any dropped catch or missed chance…'
Cricket superstitions: 'No'
Favourite sledging line: '"Are you left-handed?"'
Cricketers particularly admired: Jack Russell, Adam Gilchrist, Charlie Freestone, Ian Healy, Jonty Rhodes
Young players to look out for: Chris Dent (Gloucestershire), Danny Briggs (Hampshire)
Other sports played: Football ('played in the youth team for AFC Bournemouth'), squash ('thought I was half-decent till I played Matt Windows')
Other sports followed: Football (Portsmouth FC)
Favourite band: The Pigeon Detectives. 'Anything by John Mayer'
Relaxations: 'Watching any live sport, going to the beach on the Isle of Wight, visiting Ventnor cricket ground, having a drink with Ray Herridge'
Extras: Played for Hampshire Board XI in the 2002 C&G. Attended World Cricket Academy, Mumbai 2003; International Cricket Academy, Port Elizabeth 2005. NBC Denis Compton Award for most promising young Gloucestershire player 2005
Opinions on cricket: 'The "performance"/age-related fee payments that have been introduced for 2010 are a terrible idea for the game.'
Best batting: 127 Gloucestershire v Worcestershire, Worcester 2008

2009 Season

	M	Inn	NO	Runs	HS	Avg	100	50	Ct	St	Balls	Runs	Wkts	Avg	BB	5I	10M
Test																	
FC	9	14	1	215	85	16.53	-	1	28	2	0	0	0		-	-	-
ODI																	
List A	1	1	0	19	19	19.00	-	-	1	-	0	0	0		-	-	
20/20 Int																	
20/20	2	2	1	13	11	13.00	-	-	1	-	0	0	0		-	-	

Career Performances

	M	Inn	NO	Runs	HS	Avg	100	50	Ct	St	Balls	Runs	Wkts	Avg	BB	5I	10M
Test																	
FC	31	50	6	1357	127	30.84	1	11	78	3	18	15	0		-	-	-
ODI																	
List A	13	10	0	61	19	6.10	-	-	19	-	0	0	0		-	-	
20/20 Int																	
20/20	2	2	1	13	11	13.00	-	-	1	-	0	0	0		-	-	

SOLANKI, V. S. Worcestershire

Name: Vikram Singh Solanki
Role: Right-hand bat, right-arm
off-spin bowler, county captain
Born: 1 April 1976, Udaipur, India
Height: 6ft **Weight:** 12st
Nickname: Vik
County debut: 1993 (one-day),
1995 (first-class)
County cap: 1998; colours, 2002
Benefit: 2007
ODI debut: 1999-2000
Twenty20 Int debut: 2005
1000 runs in a season: 5
1st-Class 200s: 4
Place in batting averages: 120th av. 33.86
(2008 37th av. 46.95)
Parents: Mr Vijay Singh and Mrs Florabel Solanki
Marital status: Single
Family links with cricket: 'Father played in India. Brother Vishal is a keen cricketer'
Education: Regis School, Wolverhampton; Open University
Qualifications: 9 GCSEs, 3 A-levels
Overseas tours: England U18 to South Africa 1992-93, to Denmark (ICC Youth
Tournament) 1994; England U19 to West Indies 1994-95; Worcestershire CCC
to Barbados 1996, to Zimbabwe 1997; England A to Zimbabwe and South Africa
1998-99, to Bangladesh and New Zealand 1999-2000, to West Indies 2000-01, to Sri
Lanka 2004-05, to West Indies 2005-06 (c); England to South Africa and Zimbabwe
1999-2000 (one-day series), to Kenya (ICC Knockout Trophy) 2000-01, to Pakistan
2000-01 (one-day series), to Bangladesh and Sri Lanka 2003-04 (one-day series), to
Zimbabwe (one-day series) 2004-05, to South Africa 2004-05 (one-day series), to
Pakistan 2005-06 (one-day series), to India 2005-06 (one-day series), to South Africa
(World 20/20) 2007-08

Overseas teams played for: Midland-Guildford, Perth; Rajasthan, India 2006-07; Mumbai Champs (ICL) 2007-08
Career highlights to date: 'Playing for England'
Cricket moments to forget: 'Losing to Scotland (NatWest 1998)'
Cricketers particularly admired: Sachin Tendulkar, Graeme Hick
Other sports played: 'Enjoy most sports'
Relaxations: 'Reading; spending time with family and friends'
Extras: NBC Denis Compton Award for most promising young Worcestershire player 1995. Scored more first-class runs (1339) in 1999 season than any other English player. Scored 106 v South Africa at The Oval in the NatWest Series 2003, winning the Man of the Match award and sharing with Marcus Trescothick (114*) in a record England opening partnership in ODIs (200). Man of the Match in the third ODI v Zimbabwe at Bulawayo 2004-05 (100*). C&G Man of the Match awards for his 127 (plus three catches and a run-out) in the semi-final v Warwickshire at Edgbaston 2004 and for his 115 in the final v Gloucestershire at Lord's 2004. Captain of Worcestershire since 2005. His 270 v Gloucestershire in July 2008 was the season's highest individual score in Division Two. Took on the role of chief executive of the Professional Cricketers' Association after Sean Morris stepped down in October 2009 until a permanent replacement could be appointed
Best batting: 270 Worcestershire v Gloucestershire, Cheltenham 2008
Best bowling: 5-40 Worcestershire v Middlesex, Lord's 2004

2009 Season

	M	Inn	NO	Runs	HS	Avg	100	50	Ct	St	Balls	Runs	Wkts	Avg	BB	5I	10M
Test																	
FC	17	31	1	1016	206*	33.86	1	4	14	-	102	68	1	68.00	1-32	-	-
ODI																	
List A	16	15	3	386	82*	32.16	-	2	5	-	6	9	1	9.00	1-9	-	
20/20 Int																	
20/20	10	10	0	269	100	26.90	1	1	3	-	0	0	0			-	-

Career Performances

	M	Inn	NO	Runs	HS	Avg	100	50	Ct	St	Balls	Runs	Wkts	Avg	BB	5I	10M
Test																	
FC	252	418	25	14322	270	36.44	26	75	258	-	6931	4024	85	47.34	5-40	4	1
ODI	51	46	5	1097	106	26.75	2	5	16	-	111	105	1	105.00	1-17	-	
List A	350	322	28	9339	164*	31.76	13	53	131	-	1049	934	27	34.59	4-14	-	
20/20 Int	3	3	0	76	43	25.33	-	-	3	-	0	0	0			-	
20/20	41	40	0	1110	100	27.75	1	7	23	-	66	100	3	33.33	1-9	-	

SPEARMAN, C. M. Gloucestershire

Name: <u>Craig</u> Murray Spearman
Role: Right-hand opening bat
Born: 4 July 1972, Auckland, New Zealand
Height: 6ft **Weight:** 13st 7lbs
Nickname: Spears
County debut: 2002
County cap: 2002
Benefit: 2008
Test debut: 1995-96
ODI debut: 1995-96
1000 runs in a season: 3
1st-Class 200s: 2
1st-Class 300s: 1
Place in batting averages: 199th av. 22.88
(2008 186th av. 21.62)
Parents: Murray and Sandra
Wife and date of marriage: Maree, 4 March 2004
Education: Kelston Boys High School, Auckland; Massey University, Palmerston North, New Zealand
Qualifications: Bachelor of Business Studies (BBS; Finance major)
Overseas tours: New Zealand to India and Pakistan (World Cup) 1995-96, to West Indies 1995-96, to Sharjah (Singer Champions Trophy) 1996-97, to Pakistan 1996-97, to Zimbabwe 1997-98, to Australia 1997-98 (CUB Series), to Sri Lanka 1998, to India 1999-2000, to Zimbabwe 2000-01, to Kenya (ICC Knockout Trophy) 2000-01, to South Africa 2000-01; FICA World XI to New Zealand 2004-05
Overseas teams played for: Auckland 1993-96; Central Districts 1996-97 – 2000-01, 2002-03 – 2004-05
Career highlights to date: 'Playing international cricket; Test century. Winning ICC Knockout Trophy with New Zealand. Winning two C&G finals with Gloucestershire. Scoring 341 for Gloucestershire v Middlesex (highest score for Gloucestershire)'
Cricket moments to forget: 'Misfielding on the boundary at the SCG in the fifth over and hearing about it for the next 45 overs'
Cricket superstitions: 'None'
Cricketers particularly admired: Gordon Greenidge
Other sports played: Golf, tennis
Other sports followed: Rugby, golf, football
Favourite band: U2
Relaxations: 'Sleeping'
Extras: Gloucestershire Players' Player of the Year 2002. Scored 123-ball 153 v Warwickshire at Gloucester in the NCL 2003 to set a new individual record score for Gloucestershire in the one-day league. Vice-captain of Gloucestershire 2003. Scored 341, the highest individual score for Gloucestershire in first-class cricket, v Middlesex

at Gloucester 2004. C&G Man of the Match award for his 122-ball 143* in the semi-final v Yorkshire at Bristol 2004. Struck century (100) before lunch on first day v Surrey at Bristol 2006. Released by Gloucestershire at the end of the 2009 season. Is England-qualified

Best batting: 341 Gloucestershire v Middlesex, Gloucester 2004
Best bowling: 1-37 Central Districts v Wellington, New Plymouth 1999-2000

2009 Season

	M	Inn	NO	Runs	HS	Avg	100	50	Ct	St	Balls	Runs	Wkts	Avg	BB	5I	10M
Test																	
FC	6	9	0	206	57	22.88	-	1	9	-	0	0	0		-	-	-
ODI																	
List A	9	9	2	339	92	48.42	-	4	3	-	0	0	0		-	-	
20/20 Int																	
20/20	8	8	0	133	51	16.62	-	1	7	-	0	0	0		-	-	

Career Performances

	M	Inn	NO	Runs	HS	Avg	100	50	Ct	St	Balls	Runs	Wkts	Avg	BB	5I	10M
Test	19	37	2	922	112	26.34	1	3	21	-	0	0	0		-	-	-
FC	201	360	16	13021	341	37.85	30	56	197	-	78	55	1	55.00	1-37	-	-
ODI	51	50	0	936	86	18.72	-	5	15	-	3	6	0		-	-	
List A	285	282	11	8058	153	29.73	8	52	104	-	33	43	0		-	-	
20/20 Int																	
20/20	50	46	3	830	88	19.30	-	5	20	-	0	0	0		-	-	

SPRIEGEL, M. N. W. Surrey

Name: Matthew Neil William Spriegel
Role: Left-hand bat, right-arm
off-spin bowler; all-rounder
Born: 4 March 1987, Epsom, Surrey
Height: 6ft 3in **Weight:** 13st 8lbs
Nickname: Spriegs
County debut: 2008
Place in batting averages: 171st av. 26.72
(2008 172nd av. 23.22)
Parents: Geoff and Julie
Marital status: Single
Education: Whitgift School, South Croydon;
Loughborough University
Qualifications: 11 GCSEs, 1 AS-level, 3 A-levels,
degree in Sports and Exercise Science,
Level 1 coaching

Overseas tours: Surrey Academy to Perth 2004, to Cape Town 2005, 2006; British Universities to Pretoria 2007; MCC Universities to Cape Town 2008
Overseas teams played for: Subiaco Marist CC, Perth 2005-06; Perth CC 2009-10
Career highlights to date: 'Taking 7-85 and scoring 96 in the same game for Surrey v Kent in the 2nd XI Championship 2006. Making my Championship debut for Surrey'
Cricket moments to forget: 'Scoring three ducks in six innings on tour in Perth in 2004'
Cricketers particularly admired: Steve Waugh, Mark Ramprakash, Alec Stewart
Other sports played: Golf, football
Favourite band: The Wombats
Relaxations: 'Golf'
Extras: Captained LUCCE 2007. Shared a Pro40 record 126-run 6th wicket partnership with Tom Smith v Leicestershire in September 2009
Opinions on cricket: 'Preparation is the most important thing.'
Best batting: 100 Surrey v Glamorgan, The Oval 2009
Best bowling: 2-28 Surrey v Hampshire, The Oval 2008

2009 Season

	M	Inn	NO	Runs	HS	Avg	100	50	Ct	St	Balls	Runs	Wkts	Avg	BB	5I	10M
Test																	
FC	6	11	0	294	100	26.72	1	2	7	-	268	205	2	102.50	1-22	-	-
ODI																	
List A	15	14	3	337	81*	30.63	-	3	8	-	474	410	10	41.00	2-23	-	
20/20 Int																	
20/20	10	8	0	100	25	12.50	-	-	3	-	192	257	11	23.36	4-33	-	

Career Performances

	M	Inn	NO	Runs	HS	Avg	100	50	Ct	St	Balls	Runs	Wkts	Avg	BB	5I	10M
Test																	
FC	21	36	2	812	100	23.88	1	3	13	-	862	560	12	46.66	2-28	-	-
ODI																	
List A	25	23	9	526	81*	37.57	-	4	13	-	816	676	15	45.06	2-23	-	
20/20 Int																	
20/20	19	16	7	152	25	16.88	-	-	4	-	354	449	17	26.41	4-33	-	

SREESANTH   Warwickshire

Name: Sreesanth (see *Extras*)
Role: Right-hand bat, right-arm
fast-medium bowler
Born: 6 February 1983, Kothamangalam,
Kerala, India
Nickname: Sree, Gopu
County debut: 2009
Test debut: 2005-06
ODI debut: 2005-06
Twenty20 Int debut: 2006-07
Place in bowling averages: 62nd av. 32.15
Overseas tours: India to Pakistan 2005-06 (one-day
series), to West Indies 2006, to South Africa 2006-07,
to South Africa (ICC Twenty20 World Championship)
2007, to Australia 2007-08, to Bangladesh 2009-10
Overseas teams played for: Kerala; Kings XI Punjab (IPL)
Extras: In the past he has been known variously as Sri Sreesanth, Sree Sreesanth,
Shantha Sreesanth and Shanthakumaran Sreesanth; in September 2007, he announced
that his real name was simply Sreesanth, and all other variations were incorrect.
Joined Warwickshire in July 2009 to play out the rest of the season. Suffered a stress
fracture in his lower back early in 2009, missing part of the IPL season
Best batting: 35 India v England, The Oval 2007
Best bowling: 5-40 India v South Africa, Johannesburg 2006-07

2009 Season

	M	Inn	NO	Runs	HS	Avg	100	50	Ct	St	Balls	Runs	Wkts	Avg	BB	5I	10M
Test																	
FC	5	7	2	74	30*	14.80	-	-	3	-	658	418	13	32.15	5-93	1	-
ODI																	
List A	5	0	0	0	0		-	-	-	-	219	174	9	19.33	3-36	-	
20/20 Int																	
20/20																	

Career Performances

	M	Inn	NO	Runs	HS	Avg	100	50	Ct	St	Balls	Runs	Wkts	Avg	BB	5I	10M
Test	14	21	7	217	35	15.50	-	-	2	-	2873	1573	50	31.46	5-40	1	-
FC	51	70	21	493	35	10.06	-	-	10	-	9113	5071	159	31.89	5-40	4	-
ODI	41	16	8	34	10*	4.25	-	-	6	-	1925	1856	59	31.45	6-55	1	
List A	68	29	13	103	33	6.43	-	-	8	-	3233	2957	87	33.98	6-55	1	
20/20 Int	10	3	2	20	19*	20.00	-	-	2	-	204	288	7	41.14	2-12	-	
20/20	36	11	6	44	19*	8.80	-	-	5	-	727	1043	35	29.80	3-29	-	

STAYT, T. P. Gloucestershire

Name: Thomas (<u>Tom</u>) Patrick Stayt
Role: Right-hand bat, right-arm
fast-medium bowler
Born: 20 January 1986, Salisbury
Height: 6ft 2in **Weight:** 11st
Nickname: Staytie, Stick
County debut: 2007
County cap: 2007
Parents: Patrick and Jane
Marital status: Single
Family links with cricket: 'Dad plays occasionally
for Erlestoke and Coulston Cricket Club and is part-
time groundsman'
Education: Lavington School, Market Lavington;
St Augustine's Catholic College, Trowbridge;
University of Exeter
Qualifications: 1 AS-Level, 3 A-Levels, BA (Hons) Accounting and Finance
Career highlights to date: 'Making first-class debut at Lord's, August 2007'
Cricket moments to forget: 'Being run out by Chris Taylor without facing a ball on
first-class debut at Lord's'
Cricket superstitions: 'Get to the ground early'
Cricketers particularly admired: Jon Lewis, Allan Donald, Courtney Walsh
Other sports played: 'Will try anything'
Other sports followed: Rugby union (Gloucester)
Favourite band: John Legend
Relaxations: 'Spending time with mates and girlfriend; watching sport'
Extras: Released by Gloucestershire at the end of the 2009 season
Best batting: 36 Gloucestershire v Leicestershire, Bristol 2009
Best bowling: 3-51 Gloucestershire v Middlesex, Lord's 2007

2009 Season

	M	Inn	NO	Runs	HS	Avg	100	50	Ct	St	Balls	Runs	Wkts	Avg	BB	5I	10M
Test																	
FC	1	1	0	36	36	36.00	-	-	-	-	204	77	2	38.50	1-19	-	-
ODI																	
List A	3	3	1	1	1	.50	-	-	1	-	84	96	3	32.00	2-51	-	
20/20 Int																	
20/20																	

Career Performances

	M	Inn	NO	Runs	HS	Avg	100	50	Ct	St	Balls	Runs	Wkts	Avg	BB	5I	10M
Test																	
FC	4	4	1	45	36	15.00	-	-	2	-	558	295	6	49.16	3-51	-	-
ODI																	
List A	4	3	1	1	1	.50	-	-	1	-	113	130	3	43.33	2-51	-	
20/20 Int																	
20/20																	

STEVENS, D. I. Kent

Name: Darren Ian Stevens
Role: Right-hand top-order bat, right-arm
medium bowler
Born: 30 April 1976, Leicester
Height: 5ft 11in **Weight:** 13st 7lbs
Nickname: Stevo
County debut: 1997 (Leicestershire), 2005 (Kent)
County cap: 2002 (Leicestershire), 2005 (Kent)
1000 runs in a season: 2
1st-Class 200s: 2
Place in batting averages: 38th av. 50.00
(2008 174th av. 23.15)
Place in bowling averages: (2008 88th av. 32.20)
Parents: Maddy and Bob
Marital status: Single
Family links with cricket: Father and grandfather played league cricket
in Leicestershire
Education: Mount Grace High School; John Cleveland College, Hinckley;
Hinckley Tech; Charles Klein College
Qualifications: 5 GCSEs, BTEC National in Sports Studies
Overseas tours: Leicestershire U19 to South Africa 1994-95; Leicestershire to
Barbados 1998, to Sri Lanka 1999, to Potchefstroom 2001; ECB National Academy
to Australia and Sri Lanka 2002-03; London CCC to West Indies 2007-08
Overseas teams played for: Wanderers CC, Johannesburg, South Africa 1996-97;
Rhodes University, Grahamstown, South Africa 1997-98; Fairfield CC, Sydney
1998-99; Hawthorn-Waverley, Melbourne 1999-2000; Taita CC, Wellington,
New Zealand 2000-01; Ringwood CC, Melbourne 2001-02
Career highlights to date: 'Winning the 2007 Twenty20'
Cricket moments to forget: 'Losing in my first final in the C&G against
Somerset 2001'
Cricket superstitions: 'Left pad first'

Cricketers particularly admired: Ricky Ponting
Other sports played: Golf, squash
Other sports followed: Rugby union (Leicester Tigers), football (Dover FC)
Favourite band: Snow Patrol
Relaxations: 'Spending time with friends'
Extras: Received painting from Sir Colin Cowdrey on day of maiden first-class 100 (130 in fourth Championship match), v Sussex at Arundel 1999. Won Sir Ron Brierley/Crusaders Scholarship 1999. Included in provisional England squad of 30 for the 2002-03 World Cup. Kent Player of the Year 2005
Best batting: 208 Kent v Glamorgan, Canterbury 2005
Best bowling: 4-36 Kent v Yorkshire, Canterbury 2006

2009 Season

	M	Inn	NO	Runs	HS	Avg	100	50	Ct	St	Balls	Runs	Wkts	Avg	BB	5I	10M
Test																	
FC	17	24	3	1050	208	50.00	4	2	11	-	408	256	2	128.00	1-42	-	-
ODI																	
List A	10	10	2	286	75*	35.75	-	2	2	-	96	108	4	27.00	2-25	-	
20/20 Int																	
20/20	11	11	5	356	77	59.33	-	4	4	-	96	96	5	19.20	2-21	-	

Career Performances

	M	Inn	NO	Runs	HS	Avg	100	50	Ct	St	Balls	Runs	Wkts	Avg	BB	5I	10M
Test																	
FC	155	250	17	7857	208	33.72	17	40	122	-	5105	2639	66	39.98	4-36	-	-
ODI																	
List A	202	190	19	5003	133	29.25	4	32	78	-	1925	1580	48	32.91	5-32	1	
20/20 Int																	
20/20	65	60	13	1275	77	27.12	-	6	21	-	348	413	19	21.73	4-14	-	

83. Name the Pakistan batsman who made double centuries in England in both 1971 and 1974.

STIFF, D. A. Somerset

Name: <u>David</u> Alexander Stiff
Role: Right-hand bat, right-arm fast bowler
Born: 20 October 1984, Dewsbury
Height: 6ft 6in **Weight:** 16st
Nickname: Stiffy, Goat
County debut: 2004 (Kent), 2007 (Leicestershire), 2009 (Somerset)
Place in batting averages: 208th av. 21.44
Place in bowling averages: 87th av. 36.12
Parents: Christine and Ian
Marital status: Single
Family links with cricket: 'Eldest and youngest brothers as well as one of my sisters have all played cricket at various levels'
Education: Batley Grammar School; Leeds Technical College
Qualifications: 9 GCSEs, Level 2 coach
Off-season: 'Training, and playing for South Brisbane District CC, Queensland'
Overseas tours: England U17 to Australia 2001; Yorkshire to Grenada 2002; England U19 to Australia 2002-03, to Bangladesh (U19 World Cup) 2003-04
Overseas teams played for: Adelaide University 2006; South Brisbane District CC 2009-10
Career highlights to date: 'Five wickets in the third U19 "Test" v Australia 2003'
Cricket moments to forget: 'Being booed at Canterbury for no-balling, Kent v Middlesex, September 2004'
Cricket superstitions: 'Left pad, boot and glove first'
Cricketers particularly admired: Allan Donald, Brett Lee, Courtney Walsh
Other sports played: 'A bit of 5-a-side now and then (badly) '
Other sports followed: 'F1 – motorsport in general '
Favourite band: Radiohead
Extras: Yorkshire Cricket Academy 1999-2003. Took 5-35 for England U19 in the third 'Test' v Australia U19 at Bankstown Oval, Sydney 2002-03. Represented England U19 2004. ECB National Academy 2004-05 (part-time). Released by Kent at the end of the 2006 season and spent a year with Leicestershire in 2007. Joined Somerset for the 2009 season
Best batting: 49 Somerset v York, Taunton 2009
Best bowling: 5-91 Somerset v Hampshire, Taunton 2009

2009 Season

	M	Inn	NO	Runs	HS	Avg	100	50	Ct	St	Balls	Runs	Wkts	Avg	BB	5I	10M
Test																	
FC	10	14	5	193	49	21.44	-	-	-	-	1610	1120	31	36.12	5-91	1	-
ODI																	
List A																	
20/20 Int																	
20/20																	

Career Performances

	M	Inn	NO	Runs	HS	Avg	100	50	Ct	St	Balls	Runs	Wkts	Avg	BB	5I	10M
Test																	
FC	18	20	8	250	49	20.83	-	-	1	-	2333	1699	41	41.43	5-91	1	-
ODI																	
List A	1	0	0	0	0		-	-	-	-	30	27	1	27.00	1-27	-	
20/20 Int																	
20/20																	

STIRLING, P. R.　　　　　　Middlesex

Name: <u>Paul</u> Robert Stirling
Role: Right-hand bat, right-arm off-break bowler
Born: 3 September 1990, Ireland
County debut: No first-team appearance
ODI debut: 2008
Twenty20 Int debut: 2009
Family links with cricket: Brother Richard has played for Ireland at U19 level
Overseas tours: Ireland U19 to South Africa (ICC U19 World Cup Qualifiers) 2009, to New Zealand (ICC U19 World Cup) 2009-10; Ireland to Bangladesh 2007-08, to Sri Lanka 2009-10
Extras: Has played for Ireland at U13, U15, U17, U19 and U23 level. Middlesex 2nd XI 2008. Played for Ireland in ICC World Twenty20 in England 2009.

Has a central contract with Ireland, to whom he has committed his international future. Signed a three-year deal with Middlesex in December 2009
Best batting: 100 Ireland v Kenya, Eglinton, 2009-10

2009 Season

	M	Inn	NO	Runs	HS	Avg	100	50	Ct	St	Balls	Runs	Wkts	Avg	BB	5I	10M
Test																	
FC																	
ODI																	
List A	6	6	0	180	80	30.00	-	2	2	-	0	0	0		-	-	
20/20 Int	1	1	0	17	17	17.00	-	-	-	-	0	0	0		-	-	
20/20	1	1	0	17	17	17.00	-	-	-	-	0	0	0		-	-	

Career Performances

	M	Inn	NO	Runs	HS	Avg	100	50	Ct	St	Balls	Runs	Wkts	Avg	BB	5I	10M
Test																	
FC	5	8	0	201	100	25.12	1	-	3	-	12	12	0		-	-	-
ODI	6	6	1	128	84	25.60	-	1	2	-	0	0	0		-	-	
List A	20	20	1	426	84	22.42	-	4	8	-	0	0	0		-	-	
20/20 Int	1	1	0	17	17	17.00	-	-	-	-	0	0	0		-	-	
20/20	2	2	0	37	20	18.50	-	-	2	-	0	0	0		-	-	

STOKES, B. A.   Durham

Name: Benjamin (Ben) Andrew Stokes
Role: Left-hand bat, right-arm medium bowler; all-rounder
Born: 4 June 1991, Christchurch, Canterbury, New Zealand
County debut: 2009 (one-day)
Parents: Ged and Deb
Overseas tours: England U19 to New Zealand (ICC U19 World Cup) 2009-10
Extras: Represented Cumbria at U13, U15 and U17 levels. Played for Durham 2nd XI in 2007 and 2009 and Durham Academy 2007-09. Claimed the wicket of Mark Ramprakash with his third delivery in senior cricket (in the Friends Provident Trophy, May 2009). Played for England U19 in home Test series against Bangladesh U19 2009. In December 2009, signed a two-year professional contract with Durham. Scored a century against India U19 in England U19 final group game, ICC World Cup, 2009-10

2009 Season

	M	Inn	NO	Runs	HS	Avg	100	50	Ct	St	Balls	Runs	Wkts	Avg	BB	5I	10M
Test																	
FC																	
ODI																	
List A	3	3	1	22	11*	11.00	-	-	1	-	36	36	2	18.00	2-22	-	
20/20 Int																	
20/20																	

Career Performances

	M	Inn	NO	Runs	HS	Avg	100	50	Ct	St	Balls	Runs	Wkts	Avg	BB	5I	10M
Test																	
FC																	
ODI																	
List A	3	3	1	22	11*	11.00	-	-	1	-	36	36	2	18.00	2-22	-	
20/20 Int																	
20/20																	

STONEMAN, M. D.   Durham

Name: <u>Mark</u> Daniel Stoneman
Role: Left-hand top-order bat, 'right-arm variations'
Born: 26 June 1987, Newcastle upon Tyne
Height: 5ft 11in **Weight:** 12st 5lbs
Nickname: Rocky
County debut: 2007
Place in batting averages: 197th av. 23.30
(2008 198th av. 20.42)
Parents: Ian and Pauline
Marital status: Single
Family links with cricket: 'Father played.
Grandfather played and was also an umpire'
Education: Marley Hill Primary; Whickham
Comprehensive School, Gateshead, Whickham
Sixth Form
Qualifications: 11 GCSEs, 3 A-levels
Career outside cricket: 'Socialite!'
Off-season: 'Five months in Sydney playing for St George District CC'
Overseas tours: Durham Development Squad to Mumbai 2004-05; England U19
to Malaysia and Sri Lanka (U19 World Cup) 2005-06; Durham pre-season tours
to Dubai, Cape Town and Johannesburg

Overseas teams played for: St George DCC, Sydney 2006-07, 2008-09, 2009-10; Mulgrave CC, Melbourne
Cricket moments to forget: 'Numerous run-outs with Michael DiVenuto'
Cricket superstitions: 'Right pad on first'
Cricketers particularly admired: Michael DiVenuto, Brian Lara, Matthew Hayden, Neil McKenzie, Shiv Chanderpaul, Marcus Trescothick
Young players to look out for: Ben Stokes (Durham)
Other sports played: Golf
Other sports followed: Football (Newcastle United FC)
Injuries: 'Thigh strain – out for three weeks'
Favourite band: Eminem
Relaxations: 'Shooting, fishing, movies'
Extras: Has represented England at U17 and U19 level. Attended Darren Lehmann Talent Squad, Adelaide, January-March 2006
Best batting: 101 Durham v Sussex, Riverside 2007

2009 Season

	M	Inn	NO	Runs	HS	Avg	100	50	Ct	St	Balls	Runs	Wkts	Avg	BB	5I	10M
Test																	
FC	13	21	1	466	64	23.30	-	1	14	-		0	0	0	-	-	-
ODI																	
List A																		
20/20 Int																		
20/20																		

Career Performances

	M	Inn	NO	Runs	HS	Avg	100	50	Ct	St	Balls	Runs	Wkts	Avg	BB	5I	10M
Test																		
FC	34	58	2	1264	101	22.57	1	5	23	-		0	0	0	-	-	-
ODI																		
List A	1	1	0	21	21	21.00	-	-	-	-		0	0	0	-	-	
20/20 Int																		
20/20																		

84. How many times did Imran Khan take ten or more wickets in a Test match?

STRAUSS, A. J. Middlesex

Name: <u>Andrew</u> John Strauss
Role: Left-hand bat, left-arm medium bowler
Born: 2 March 1977, Johannesburg, South Africa
Height: 5ft 11in **Weight:** 13st
Nickname: Straussy, Johann, Levi,
Mareman, Muppet, Lord Brocket
County debut: 1997 (one-day),
1998 (first-class)
County cap: 2001
Benefit: 2009
Test debut: 2004
ODI debut: 2003
Twenty20 Int debut: 2005
1000 runs in a season: 4
Place in batting averages: 33rd av. 50.94
(2008 35th av. 47.03)
Parents: David and Dawn
Wife and date of marriage: Ruth, 18 October 2003
Children: Samuel David, December 2005; Luca, July 2008
Education: Radley College; Durham University
Qualifications: 4 A-levels, BA (Hons) Economics
Overseas tours: Durham University to Zimbabwe 1997-98; Middlesex to South
Africa 2000; ECB National Academy to Australia 2001-02; England to Bangladesh
and Sri Lanka 2003-04 (one-day series), to West Indies 2003-04, to Zimbabwe (one-
day series) 2004-05, to South Africa 2004-05, to Pakistan 2005-06, to India 2005-06,
to India (ICC Champions Trophy) 2006-07, to Australia 2006-07, to West Indies
(World Cup) 2006-07, to New Zealand 2007-08, to India 2008-09, to West Indies
2008-09 (captain for Tests, ODIs and Twenty20s), to South Africa 2009-10 (captain
for Tests, ODIs and Twenty20s)
Overseas teams played for: Sydney University 1998-99; Mosman, Sydney
1999-2001; Northern Districts, New Zealand 2007-08
Cricketers particularly admired: Allan Donald, Brian Lara, Saqlain Mushtaq
Other sports played: Golf (Durham University 1998), rugby (Durham
University 1996-97)
Other sports followed: 'Anything with a ball'
Extras: Middlesex Player of the Year 2001. Scored century (112) plus 83 in second
innings on Test debut in the first Test v New Zealand at Lord's (his home ground)
2004, winning Man of the Match award. Scored century (100) v West Indies, also at
Lord's, in the NatWest Series 2004, in the process sharing with Andrew Flintoff (123)
in a new record partnership for England in ODIs (226). Wombwell Cricket Lovers'
Society George Spofforth Cricketer of the Year 2004. Captain of Middlesex 2002-04.

Scored 126 in the first Test v South Africa at Port Elizabeth 2004-05, achieving feat of scoring a Test century on home and away debuts and becoming first player to score a Test century in his first innings against each of first three opponents. His other series and match awards include Man of the [Test] Series v South Africa 2004-05 (656 runs at 72.88) and England's Man of the [Test] Series v Pakistan 2006. Vodafone England Cricketer of the Year 2004-05. One of *Wisden*'s Five Cricketers of the Year 2005. Appointed MBE in 2006 New Year Honours as part of 2005 Ashes-winning England team. Man of the Series v New Zealand, summer 2008. First England batsman to score two centuries in a Test v India in that country, 2008-09. Captained England's 2009 Ashes-winning side. Captained England in the drawn Test series v South Africa 2009-10. England 12-month central contract 2009-10

Best batting: 177 England v New Zealand, Napier 2007-08
Best bowling: 1-16 Middlesex v Nottinghamshire, Lord's 2007

2009 Season

	M	Inn	NO	Runs	HS	Avg	100	50	Ct	St	Balls	Runs	Wkts	Avg	BB	5I	10M
Test	7	12	1	530	161	48.18	1	3	8	-	0	0	0		-	-	-
FC	11	19	1	917	161	50.94	2	5	12	-	12	10	0		-	-	-
ODI	9	9	0	323	63	35.88	-	3	3	-	0	0	0		-	-	
List A	9	9	0	323	63	35.88	-	3	3	-	0	0	0		-	-	
20/20 Int																	
20/20																	

Career Performances

	M	Inn	NO	Runs	HS	Avg	100	50	Ct	St	Balls	Runs	Wkts	Avg	BB	5I	10M
Test	67	123	5	5266	177	44.62	18	17	75	-	0	0	0		-	-	-
FC	181	321	16	13090	177	42.91	35	56	148	-	102	89	2	44.50	1-16	-	-
ODI	96	95	8	2814	152	32.34	3	18	35	-	6	3	0		-	-	
List A	217	210	14	6036	163	30.79	7	38	67	-	6	3	0		-	-	
20/20 Int	4	4	0	73	33	18.25	-	-	1	-	0	0	0		-	-	
20/20	28	28	0	519	60	18.53	-	2	12	-	0	0	0		-	-	

STUBBINGS, S. D.   Derbyshire

Name: <u>Stephen</u> David Stubbings
Role: Left-hand bat, right-arm bowler 'all
disciplines', occasional wicket-keeper
Born: 31 March 1978, Huddersfield
Height: 6ft 4in **Weight:** 15st 5lbs
Nickname: Stubbo, Hollywood, Wilton Shagpile,
The Plank
County debut: 1997
County cap: 2001
Benefit: 2008
1000 runs in a season: 3
Place in batting averages: 150th av. 29.60
(2008 112th av. 31.62)
Parents: Marie and David
Marital status: Single

Family links with cricket: 'Father and brother both played, as I did, for Delacombe
Park Cricket Club in Melbourne, Australia'
Education: Frankston High School; Swinburne University – both in
Melbourne, Australia
Qualifications: Victorian Certificate of Education (VCE), Level 2 coaching
Career outside cricket: Coach, journalist
Overseas tours: Derbyshire to Portugal 2000
Overseas teams played for: Delacombe Park CC, Melbourne 1989-90 – 1993-94;
Frankston Peninsula CC, Victoria 1994-95 – 1999-2000, 2002-03 – 2005-06;
Kingborough CC, Tasmania 2000-01 – 2001-02
Career highlights to date: '2006 Championship season at Derbyshire'
Cricket moments to forget: '2005 Championship season at Derbyshire'
Cricket superstitions: 'No shaving on first day of a game'
Cricketers particularly admired: Michael DiVenuto
Other sports played: Golf, Aussie Rules, football
Other sports followed: AFL (Essendon Bombers), football (Cambridge United FC)
Favourite band: Powderfinger
Extras: Represented Victoria at all junior levels. Spent two years on the cricket
programme at the Victorian Institute of Sport. Scored 135* v Kent at Canterbury 2000,
taking part in an unbroken opening partnership of 293 with Steve Titchard (141*); it
was the first occasion on which Derbyshire had batted all day without losing a wicket.
Derbyshire Player of the Year 2001 and 2006. Released at the end of the 2009 season
Best batting: 151 Derbyshire v Somerset, Taunton 2005

2009 Season

	M	Inn	NO	Runs	HS	Avg	100	50	Ct	St	Balls	Runs	Wkts	Avg	BB	5I	10M
Test																	
FC	7	11	1	296	83	29.60	-	1	4	-	0	0	0		-	-	-
ODI																	
List A	3	3	0	83	50	27.66	-	1	-	-	0	0	0		-	-	
20/20 Int																	
20/20																	

Career Performances

	M	Inn	NO	Runs	HS	Avg	100	50	Ct	St	Balls	Runs	Wkts	Avg	BB	5I	10M
Test																	
FC	139	251	14	7557	151	31.88	12	38	64	-	96	121	0		-	-	-
ODI																	
List A	117	109	6	2707	110	26.28	1	16	20	-	0	0	0		-	-	
20/20 Int																	
20/20	9	9	1	186	57	23.25	-	2	4	-	0	0	0		-	-	

SUPPIAH, A. V.   Somerset

Name: Arul Vivasvan Suppiah
Role: Right-hand bat, left-arm orthodox
spin bowler; all-rounder
Born: 30 August 1983, Kuala Lumpur, Malaysia
Height: 6ft **Weight:** 12st 12lbs
Nickname: Ruley
County debut: 2002
County cap: 2009
1000 runs in a season: 1
Place in batting averages: 42nd av. 48.04
Place in bowling averages: 121st av. 45.46
Parents: Suppiah and Baanumathi
Marital status: Single
Family links with cricket: Brother Rohan
Vishnu Suppiah has played cricket for Malaysia
Education: Millfield School; Exeter University
Qualifications: 9 GCSEs, 4 A-levels,
BA (Hons) in Accounting and Finance, Level 1 coaching qualification
Overseas tours: Millfield School to South Africa 1997, to Sri Lanka 1999; West of
England U15 to West Indies 1998; Malaysia to Sharjah (Asian Cricket Council
Trophy) 2000-01, to Nepal (ACC Fast Track Countries Tournament) 2005; Somerset
to India (ICC Champions League) 2009

Overseas teams played for: Doubleview Carine CC, Perth 2005-06; Old Edwardians, Johannesburg 2006-07

Career highlights to date: 'Making my first-class debut v West Indies A for Somerset 2002; making my debut in the NUL for Somerset v Durham 2002; being the youngest ever cricketer to play for Malaysia; playing for England through the age groups; maiden first-class hundred for Somerset against Derbyshire 2005'

Cricket moments to forget: 'Being bowled out for a golden duck off the seventh ball of the over'

Cricket superstitions: 'Right pad first'

Cricketers particularly admired: Sachin Tendulkar, Wasim Akram, Marcus Trescothick

Young players to look out for: Calum Haggett (Somerset)

Other sports played: Hockey (Somerset U16), badminton (Millfield School 1st team), squash

Other sports followed: Football (Manchester United)

Favourite band: Black Eyed Peas

Relaxations: 'Starbucks'

Extras: Made debut for Malaysia aged 15. Represented England U14, U15, U17 and U18. Somerset U15 Player of the Year 1998. West of England U15 Player of the Year 1998. Most Promising Sportsman for Malaysia 2000. NBC Denis Compton Award for the most promising young Somerset player 2002. Was refused permanent residency in the UK in January 2009, forcing him to return to Malaysia to apply for a work permit

Best batting: 151 Somerset v Nottinghamshire, Taunton 2009

Best bowling: 3-46 Somerset v West Indies A, Taunton 2002

2009 Season

	M	Inn	NO	Runs	HS	Avg	100	50	Ct	St	Balls	Runs	Wkts	Avg	BB	5I	10M
Test																	
FC	16	26	1	1201	151	48.04	3	6	18	-	1277	682	15	45.46	3-58	-	-
ODI																	
List A	17	11	7	234	52*	58.50	-	1	4	-	110	125	5	25.00	2-12	-	
20/20 Int																	
20/20	11	6	2	30	10*	7.50	-	-	5	-	103	124	7	17.71	3-25	-	

Career Performances

	M	Inn	NO	Runs	HS	Avg	100	50	Ct	St	Balls	Runs	Wkts	Avg	BB	5I	10M
Test																	
FC	44	73	2	2525	151	35.56	4	14	29	-	2682	1632	29	56.27	3-46	-	-
ODI																	
List A	59	52	10	1174	79	27.95	-	6	22	-	1145	1093	34	32.14	4-39	-	
20/20 Int																	
20/20	38	25	7	212	32*	11.77	-	-	16	-	343	435	20	21.75	3-25	-	

Name: <u>Luke</u> David Sutton
Role: Right-hand bat, wicket-keeper, 'right-arm rubbish'
Born: 4 October 1976, Keynsham
Height: 5ft 11in   **Weight:** 12st 13lbs
Nickname: Sutts
County debut: 1997 (Somerset), 2000 (Derbyshire), 2006 (Lancashire)
County cap: 2002 (Derbyshire), 2007 (Lancashire)
Place in batting averages: 162nd av. 27.37 (2008 149th av. 27.11)
Parents: David and Molly
Wife and date of marriage: Jude, 7 October 2006
Education: Millfield School; Durham University
Qualifications: 9 GCSEs, 4 A-levels, 2.1 degree in Economics, CeMAP 1, 2 and 3, Level 1 coaching
Career outside cricket: 'Running Activate Sport camps (see *Player website*)'
Off-season: 'Running Activate Sport and preparing hard for the 2010 season'
Overseas tours: Various Somerset Schools tours to Netherlands; West of England U15 to West Indies 1991; Millfield School to Zimbabwe 1993, to Sri Lanka 1994; Durham University to Zimbabwe 1997
Overseas teams played for: UNSW, Sydney 1998-99; Northville, Port Elizabeth, South Africa 1999-2000; Subiaco Marist, Perth 2000-01
Career highlights to date: 'Scoring my highest first-class score to date of 151* in the Roses match at Old Trafford in 2006'
Cricket moments to forget: 'Losing the C&G final and the Championship to Sussex in 2006'
Cricket superstitions: 'Plenty!'
Cricketers particularly admired: Ian Healy, Jack Russell, Alec Stewart, Steve Waugh
Young players to look out for: James Vince (Hampshire)
Other sports followed: Football (Derby County), rugby (Bath)
Favourite band: Kings of Leon
Relaxations: 'Spending time with my family and friends'
Extras: Captained England U15 and also represented England U18 and U19. Won Sir John Hobbs Silver Jubilee Memorial Prize for the U16 Cricketer of the Year in 1992 and the Gray-Nicolls Award for the English Schools Cricketer of the Year in 1995. Voted Derbyshire 2nd XI Player of the Year 2000. NBC Denis Compton Award for the most promising young Derbyshire player 2000, 2001, 2002. Captain of Derbyshire 2004-05. Scored 151* v Yorkshire at Old Trafford 2006, setting a new

record for the highest Championship score by a Lancashire wicket-keeper. 'Set up a charity with my brother Noel called Freddie Fight, which raises money for CAH research; CAH (congenital adrenal hyperplasia) is a condition suffered by my nephew Freddie.'

Player website: www.activatesport.co.uk

Opinions on cricket: 'Why doesn't domestic cricket mirror international cricket?'

Best batting: 151* Lancashire v Yorkshire, Old Trafford 2006

2009 Season

	M	Inn	NO	Runs	HS	Avg	100	50	Ct	St	Balls	Runs	Wkts	Avg	BB	5I	10M
Test																	
FC	17	23	7	438	53*	27.37	-	1	56	3	0	0	0		-	-	-
ODI																	
List A	10	6	3	115	31*	38.33	-	-	13	2	0	0	0		-	-	-
20/20 Int																	
20/20																	

Career Performances

	M	Inn	NO	Runs	HS	Avg	100	50	Ct	St	Balls	Runs	Wkts	Avg	BB	5I	10M
Test																	
FC	147	233	37	6250	151*	31.88	9	19	371	17	0	0	0		-	-	-
ODI																	
List A	149	125	26	1911	83	19.30	-	6	168	21	0	0	0		-	-	
20/20 Int																	
20/20	16	14	4	306	61*	30.60	-	1	9	7	0	0	0		-	-	

85. How many times has Danish Kaneria taken ten or more wickets in a Test match?

SWANN, G. P. Nottinghamshire

Name: <u>Graeme</u> Peter Swann
Role: Right-hand bat, right-arm off-spin bowler
Born: 24 March 1979, Northampton
Height: 6ft **Weight:** 13st
Nickname: G-spot, Besty
County debut: 1997 (one-day, Northants),
1998 (first-class, Northants), 2005 (Notts)
County cap: 1999 (Northants)
Test debut: 2008-09
ODI debut: 1999-2000
Twenty20 Int debut: 2007-08
50 wickets in a season: 1
Place in batting averages: 112th av. 35.20
(2008 84th av. 36.62)
Place in bowling averages: 46th av. 30.51
(2008 70th av. 29.96)

Parents: Ray and Mavis
Marital status: Single
Family links with cricket: Father played Minor Counties cricket for Bedfordshire
and Northumberland and also for England Amateurs. Brother Alec played for
Northamptonshire and Lancashire. 'Cat is named after Gus Logie'
Education: Sponne School, Towcester
Qualifications: 10 GCSEs, 4 A-levels, Levels 1 and 2 coaching awards, 'London
Marathon sub 2hr 45min certificate'
Career outside cricket: 'After-dinner speaking, journalism'
Overseas tours: England U19 to South Africa (including U19 World Cup) 1997-98;
England A to Zimbabwe and South Africa 1998-99, to West Indies 2000-01, to Sri
Lanka 2004-05; England to South Africa 1999-2000, to Sri Lanka 2007-08 (one-day
series), to New Zealand 2007-08, to India (one-day series) 2008-09, to West Indies
2008-09, to South Africa 2009-10; ECB National Academy to Australia 2001-02
Overseas teams played for: Old Colts, Christchurch 2002-03
Career highlights to date: 'Winning County Championship [2005]'
Cricket moments to forget: 'Being hit for an enormous six by Peter Such'
Cricketers particularly admired: Neil Foster, Devon Malcolm
Other sports played: Golf, rugby (Northants U14, U15, U16), football
(Old Northamptonians Chenecks FC)
Other sports followed: Football (Newcastle United)
Favourite band: Oasis, The Fratellis, The Stone Roses, The Charlatans
Extras: Played for England U14, U15, U17 and U19. Gray-Nicolls Len Newbery
Schools Cricketer of the Year 1996. Took 8-118 for England U19 in second 'Test' v
Pakistan U19 1998, the best ever figures for England in an U19 'Test'. Cricket
Society's Leading Young All-rounder award 1999, 2002. Man of the Match for

England A v Windward Islands in St Lucia in the Busta Cup 2000-01. ECB National Academy 2004-05. Scored 33-ball 59, then took 5-17 v Gloucestershire at Trent Bridge in the Pro40 2007. Man of the Match in the third ODI v Sri Lanka in Dambulla 2007-08 (4-34/25). During 2009 took 54 wickets in eleven Tests which saw him in third place in the world rankings by year end. Took five wickets in South Africa's second innings of the second Test 2009-10 to help secure the England win. England 12-month central contract 2009-10

Best batting: 183 Northamptonshire v Gloucestershire, Bristol 2002
Best bowling: 7-33 Northamptonshire v Derbyshire, Northampton 2003

2009 Season

	M	Inn	NO	Runs	HS	Avg	100	50	Ct	St	Balls	Runs	Wkts	Avg	BB	5I	10M
Test	7	9	2	312	63*	44.57	-	3	4	-	1256	686	21	32.66	4-38	-	-
FC	10	12	2	352	63*	35.20	-	3	6	-	1616	824	27	30.51	4-38	-	-
ODI	7	4	0	33	14	8.25	-	-	3	-	336	235	11	21.36	5-28	1	
List A	8	4	0	33	14	8.25	-	-	3	-	388	259	14	18.50	5-28	1	
20/20 Int	5	3	1	15	10*	7.50	-	-	-	-	102	121	5	24.20	2-28	-	
20/20	7	5	2	111	90*	37.00	-	1	2	-	150	193	7	27.57	2-28	-	

Career Performances

	M	Inn	NO	Runs	HS	Avg	100	50	Ct	St	Balls	Runs	Wkts	Avg	BB	5I	10M
Test	12	14	4	354	63*	35.40	-	3	7	-	2941	1459	48	30.39	5-57	2	-
FC	187	258	21	6440	183	27.17	4	34	134	-	32002	15978	486	32.87	7-33	17	3
ODI	27	19	2	221	34	13.00	-	-	12	-	1110	864	31	27.87	5-28	1	
List A	212	166	17	2871	83	19.26	-	14	70	-	8250	6089	225	27.06	5-17	3	
20/20 Int	8	5	3	33	15*	16.50	-	-	-	-	162	188	10	18.80	2-21	-	
20/20	46	41	7	708	90*	20.82	-	3	13	-	978	1117	53	21.07	3-16	-	

86. Who is the only Bangladesh bowler to have taken 100 Test wickets?

TAHIR, N. S. Warwickshire

Name: <u>Naqaash</u> Sarosh Tahir
Role: Right-hand bat, right-arm fast bowler
Born: 14 November 1983, Birmingham
Height: 5ft 10in **Weight:** 11st
Nickname: Naq, Naqy
County debut: 2004
Place in batting averages: 245th av. 15.20
Place in bowling averages: 6th av. 22.18
Parents: Mohammed Amin and Ishrat Nasreen
Marital status: Single
Family links with cricket: 'Dad played club cricket and brother played for Worcestershire and Warwickshire'
Education: Moseley School; Spring Hill College
Qualifications: 3 GCSEs, Level 1 coaching
Overseas tours: Warwickshire U15 to South Africa 1999
Overseas teams played for: Mirpur, Pakistan; Subiaco-Floreat, Perth
Cricket superstitions: 'Putting my pads on in a certain way'
Cricketers particularly admired: Waqar Younis, Wasim Akram, Brett Lee, Darren Gough
Other sports played: Football
Other sports followed: Football (Manchester United)
Relaxations: 'Watching TV; PlayStation 2'
Extras: Has been Moseley Ashfield U15 Player of the Year, Warwickshire U15 Youth Player of the Year, Warwickshire U19 Players' Player of the Year and Warwickshire U19 Player of the Year (Coney Edmonds Trophy). Had match figures of 8-90 (4-47/4-43) on Championship debut v Worcestershire at Edgbaston 2004
Best batting: 49 Warwickshire v Worcestershire, Worcester 2004
Best bowling: 7-107 Warwickshire v Lancashire, Blackpool 2006

2009 Season

	M	Inn	NO	Runs	HS	Avg	100	50	Ct	St	Balls	Runs	Wkts	Avg	BB	5I	10M
Test																	
FC	12	14	4	152	24	15.20	-	-	2	-	1646	843	38	22.18	5-67	1	-
ODI																	
List A	1	0	0	0	0		-	-	-	-	42	52	0		-	-	
20/20 Int																	
20/20																	

Career Performances

	M	Inn	NO	Runs	HS	Avg	100	50	Ct	St	Balls	Runs	Wkts	Avg	BB	5I	10M
Test																	
FC	49	53	16	589	49	15.91	-	-	5	-	6465	3577	123	29.08	7-107	2	-
ODI																	
List A	14	5	3	19	13*	9.50	-	-	1	-	486	390	5	78.00	2-47	-	
20/20 Int																	
20/20																	

TAIT, S. W. Glamorgan

Name: Shaun William Tait
Role: Right-hand bat, right-arm fast bowler
Born: 22 February 1983, Bedford Park,
Adelaide, Australia
Height: 6ft 4in
Nickname: Sloon
County debut: 2004 (Durham)
Test debut: 2005
ODI debut: 2007
Twenty20 Int debut: 2007-08
Overseas tours: Australia to Sri Lanka 2003-04,
to England 2005, to South Africa 2005-06, to West
Indies (World Cup) 2007; Australia A to India 2008
Overseas teams played for: Rajasthan Royals (IPL);
South Australia 2002-03 –
Extras: Commonwealth Bank [Australian] Cricket Academy 2003. Represented
Australia A v Indians and Zimbabweans 2003-04. Took 8-43 v Tasmania at Adelaide
in the ING Cup 2003-04, becoming the first bowler to return eight wickets in a match
in the Australian domestic one-day competition. ING Cup Best New Talent award
2003-04. Named Bradman Young Cricketer of the Year at the 2004 Allan Border
Medal awards. Called up for Australia tour to Sri Lanka 2003-04 as a replacement for
the injured Brett Lee. Bradman Young Cricketer of the Year 2004. Was an overseas
player with Durham August 2004 as a replacement for Shoaib Akhtar. Named South
Australia's Player of the Season 2006-07. ICC Emerging Player of the Year 2007.
Battled with injury problems throughout 2008 and 2009. Signed for Glamorgan in
December 2009 as an overseas player in Twenty20 Cup competition
Best batting: 68 South Australia v Victoria, Adelaide 2005-06
Best bowling: 7-29 South Australia v Queensland, Brisbane 2007-08

Career Performances

	M	Inn	NO	Runs	HS	Avg	100	50	Ct	St	Balls	Runs	Wkts	Avg	BB	5I	10M
Test	3	5	2	20	8	6.66	-	-	1	-	414	302	5	60.40	3-97	-	-
FC	50	70	29	509	68	12.41	-	2	15	-	9263	5661	198	28.59	7-29	7	1
ODI	22	4	2	24	11	12.00	-	-	2	-	1080	961	38	25.28	4-39	-	
List A	79	30	15	106	22*	7.06	-	-	16	-	3974	3339	145	23.02	8-43	3	
20/20 Int	3	1	1	1	1*		-	-	1	-	72	95	4	23.75	2-22	-	
20/20	12	6	3	43	14*	14.33	-	-	3	-	272	324	23	14.08	4-14	-	

TAYLOR, B. V. Hampshire

Name: <u>Billy</u> Victor Taylor
Role: Left-hand bat, right-arm
fast-medium bowler
Born: 11 January 1977, Southampton
Height: 6ft 3in **Weight:** 13st 4lbs
Nickname: Tav, Crusty
County debut: 1999 (Sussex),
2004 (Hampshire)
County cap: 2006 (Hampshire)
Parents: Jackie and Victor
Marital status: Single
Family links with cricket: 'Learnt from and played
cricket with both my brothers, Martin and James'
Education: Bitterne Park; Southampton Technical
College; Sparsholt Agricultural College, Hampshire
Qualifications: 10 GCSEs, NVQ Level 2 Carpentry and Joinery, NTPC Tree
Surgery, Level 2 coaching
Career outside cricket: 'Hopefully falconry'
Overseas tours: Sussex/Hampshire to Cyprus 1999; Sussex to Grenada 2002
Overseas teams played for: Central Hawke's Bay, New Zealand 1996-97;
Manawatu Foxton CC and Horowhenua rep team, New Zealand 1998-99, 2000-01;
Te Puke 2002
Career highlights to date: 'Winning the County Championship in 2003 [with
Sussex]. Being capped for Hampshire. All my three hat-tricks'
Cricket moments to forget: 'Don't want to forget any moments as it's such a great
career and too short a one'
Cricket superstitions: 'Have a towel hanging out of back of trousers, and wearing
sweat band and wristwatch'
Cricketers particularly admired: Malcolm Marshall, Robin Smith, Mushtaq Ahmed

Young players to look out for: Liam Dawson (Hampshire)
Other sports played: Golf and falconry
Other sports followed: Football (Havant & Waterlooville) – 'follow my brother playing football for Totton FC'
Favourite band: Dido, Black Eyed Peas
Relaxations: Falconry
Extras: Took 98 wickets in New Zealand club cricket in 1998-99. Sussex 2nd XI Player of the Year 1999, 2000. Took hat-trick (Ormond, Sampson, Giddins) v Surrey at Hove in the B&H and another (G. Flower, Maddy, Malcolm) v Leicestershire at Leicester in the C&G, both in 2002. Took Championship hat-trick (Compton, Weekes, Scott) v Middlesex at The Rose Bowl 2006, finishing with 6-32. Appeared only in limited-over competitions in 2007 and 2008; made a single County Championship appearance in April 2009, his first first-class game for almost three years. Released by Hampshire at the end of the 2009 season. Is an ambassador for the charity Honeypot, which provides respite holidays and support to young carers and vulnerable children
Opinions on cricket: 'Should play more Twenty20 and one-day matches.'
Best batting: 40 Hampshire v Essex, Rose Bowl 2004
Best bowling: 6-32 Hampshire v Middlesex, Rose Bowl 2006

2009 Season

	M	Inn	NO	Runs	HS	Avg	100	50	Ct	St	Balls	Runs	Wkts	Avg	BB	5I	10M
Test																	
FC	1	0	0	0	0		-	-	-	-	126	52	1	52.00	1-52	-	-
ODI																	
List A	10	2	1	5	4	5.00	-	-	1	-	500	414	18	23.00	3-37	-	
20/20 Int																	
20/20	7	1	1	2	2*		-	-	-	-	143	183	7	26.14	2-24	-	

Career Performances

	M	Inn	NO	Runs	HS	Avg	100	50	Ct	St	Balls	Runs	Wkts	Avg	BB	5I	10M
Test																	
FC	54	68	26	431	40	10.26	-	-	6	-	8412	4535	136	33.34	6-32	4	-
ODI																	
List A	142	58	28	191	21*	6.36	-	-	26	-	6311	4699	182	25.81	5-28	1	
20/20 Int																	
20/20	37	9	8	22	12*	22.00	-	-	3	-	713	883	30	29.43	2-9	-	

---

87. Zaheer Abbas made the highest individual score by a Pakistan batsman in a Test match against England. He did it at Edgbaston in 1971.
What was his total?

TAYLOR, C. G. — Gloucestershire

Name: Christopher (<u>Chris</u>) Glyn Taylor
Role: Right-hand bat, right-arm
off-spin bowler
Born: 27 September 1976, Bristol
Height: 5ft 8in **Weight:** 10st
Nickname: Tales, Tootsie
County debut: 2000
County cap: 2001
1000 runs in a season: 2
Place in batting averages: 122nd av. 33.57
(2008 52nd av. 42.34)
Parents: Chris and Maggie
Wife and date of marriage: Sarah,
8 December 2001
Children: Harriet, 2003; Alexandra, 2004;
Jonty 2007

Family links with cricket: Father and grandfather both played local club cricket
Education: Colston's Collegiate School, Bristol
Qualifications: GCSEs and A-levels
Overseas teams played for: Harbord CC, Manly, Australia 2000
Cricket moments to forget: 'B&H loss to Surrey at Lord's [2001]'
Cricketers particularly admired: Jonty Rhodes, Mark Waugh
Other sports played: Rugby, hockey (both county level); squash, tennis
Other sports followed: Rugby
Relaxations: Fishing
Extras: Represented England Schools U18. In 1995 won the Cricket Society's
A. A. Thomson Fielding Prize and Wetherell Award for Leading All-rounder in English
Schools Cricket. Scored maiden first-class century (104) v Middlesex 2000, becoming
the first player to score a century at Lord's on Championship debut; also the first
player to score a century for Gloucestershire in match that was both first-class and
Championship debut. NBC Denis Compton Award for the most promising young
Gloucestershire player 2000. Four-day captain of Gloucestershire 2004-05. Became
a member of the English Academy coaching staff in 2008
Best batting: 196 Gloucestershire v Nottinghamshire, Trent Bridge 2001
Best bowling: 4-52 Gloucestershire v Northamptonshire, Northampton 2007

2009 Season

	M	Inn	NO	Runs	HS	Avg	100	50	Ct	St	Balls	Runs	Wkts	Avg	BB	5I	10M
Test																	
FC	15	22	1	705	111	33.57	1	5	11	-	518	242	6	40.33	1-6	-	-
ODI																	
List A	18	16	3	477	71	36.69	-	3	8	-	296	232	4	58.00	1-13	-	
20/20 Int																	
20/20	7	7	0	72	23	10.28	-	-	4	-	18	34	1	34.00	1-22	-	

Career Performances

	M	Inn	NO	Runs	HS	Avg	100	50	Ct	St	Balls	Runs	Wkts	Avg	BB	5I	10M
Test																	
FC	129	223	16	7141	196	34.49	17	31	85	-	2183	1280	24	53.33	4-52	-	-
ODI																	
List A	157	141	20	2998	93	24.77	-	18	65	1	574	490	12	40.83	2-5	-	
20/20 Int																	
20/20	50	46	10	923	83	25.63	-	4	20	-	24	45	1	45.00	1-22	-	

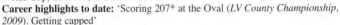

TAYLOR, J. W. A.   Leicestershire

Name: <u>James</u> William Arthur Taylor
Role: Right-hand bat, leg-spin bowler
Born: 6 January 1990, Nottingham
Height: 5ft 7in **Weight:** 10st 6lbs
Nickname: Jimmy, Titch
County debut: 2008
1000 runs in a season: 1
1st-Class 200s: 1
Place in batting averages: 22nd av. 57.47
Parents: Stephen and Carol
Marital status: Single
Education: Shrewsbury School
Qualifications: 9 GCSEs, 4 AS-Levels, 3 A- Levels
Overseas tours: England U19 to Malaysia (U19 World Cup) 2007-08, to South Africa 2008-09
Career highlights to date: 'Scoring 207* at the Oval (*LV County Championship, 2009*). Getting capped'
Cricketers particularly admired: Sachin Tendulkar
Young players to look out for: Shiv Thakor (Leicestershire)
Favourite band: Pussycat Dolls
Relaxations: Fishing, shooting, hunting

Extras: Played for Worcestershire 2nd XI 2006, 2007. Played one match for Shropshire in the Minor Counties Championship 2007. Played for Midlands U17 at ECB U17 Regional Festival at Loughborough 2007. *Wisden* Schools Cricketer of the Year 2008. Included in the England U19 squad to South Africa 2008-09; scored 85 in the third ODI, helping England to their first win of the series. Cricket Writers' Young Player of the Year 2009. Cricket Society's Most Promising Player 2009. Member of England Performance Programme squad 2009-10

Best batting: 207* Leicestershire v Surrey, The Oval 2009

2009 Season

	M	Inn	NO	Runs	HS	Avg	100	50	Ct	St	Balls	Runs	Wkts	Avg	BB	5I	10M
Test																	
FC	17	28	7	1207	207*	57.47	3	6	9	-	139	82	0		-	-	-
ODI																	
List A	15	14	2	556	101	46.33	1	3	-	-	72	72	0		-	-	
20/20 Int																	
20/20	10	10	3	205	41*	29.28	-	-	2	-	62	84	2	42.00	1-10	-	

Career Performances

	M	Inn	NO	Runs	HS	Avg	100	50	Ct	St	Balls	Runs	Wkts	Avg	BB	5I	10M
Test																	
FC	21	33	7	1271	207*	48.88	3	7	13	-	139	82	0		-	-	-
ODI																	
List A	19	16	3	636	101	48.92	1	3	-	-	72	72	0		-	-	
20/20 Int																	
20/20	13	12	3	237	41*	26.33	-	-	2	-	62	84	2	42.00	1-10	-	

88. Apart from Zaheer Abbas, which Pakistan batsman has made more than 250 in a Test innings against England?

TELO, F. D.

Name: Filipe <u>Dominic</u> Telo
Role: Right-hand bat, right-arm fast-medium bowler
Born: 4 March 1986, Cape Town, South Africa
County debut: 2008
Place in batting averages: (2008 213th av. 18.13)
Overseas teams played for: Western Province
2005-06 – 2007-08, Cape Cobras 2005-06 – 2007-08
Extras: Signed for Derbyshire in April 2008.
Released at the end of the 2009 season
Best batting: 134* Western Province v Boland,
Paarl 2007-08
Best bowling: 1-36 Derbyshire v Essex,
Derby 2008

2009 Season

	M	Inn	NO	Runs	HS	Avg	100	50	Ct	St	Balls	Runs	Wkts	Avg	BB	5I	10M
Test																	
FC																	
ODI																	
List A	1	1	0	25	25	25.00	-	-	-	-	0	0	0		-	-	
20/20 Int																	
20/20																	

Career Performances

	M	Inn	NO	Runs	HS	Avg	100	50	Ct	St	Balls	Runs	Wkts	Avg	BB	5I	10M
Test																	
FC	25	45	3	1401	134*	33.35	3	6	8	-	47	48	1	48.00	1-36	-	-
ODI																	
List A	23	21	2	501	90	26.36	-	4	3	-	0	0	0		-	-	
20/20 Int																	
20/20	16	13	0	256	48	19.69	-	-	4	-	0	0	0		-	-	

TEN DOESCHATE, R. N.　　　　　Essex

Name: <u>Ryan</u> Neil ten Doeschate
Role: Right-hand bat, right-arm
fast-medium bowler; all-rounder
Born: 30 June 1980, Port Elizabeth,
South Africa
Height: 5ft 11in　**Weight:** 13st 5lbs
Nickname: Tendo
County debut: 2003
County cap: 2006
ODI debut: 2006
Twenty20 Int debut: 2008
1st-Class 200s: 1
Place in batting averages: 44th av. 45.72
(2008 69th av. 39.09)
Place in bowling averages: 117th av. 44.09
(2008 26th av. 23.06)
Parents: Boudewyn and Ingrid
Marital status: Single
Education: Fairbairn College; University of Cape Town
Qualifications: Business science degree
Overseas tours: Netherlands to Ireland (ICC Trophy) 2005, to Scotland (European
Championship) 2006, to South Africa (ICC Associates Tri-Series) 2006-07, to Kenya
(ICC World Cricket League) 2006-07, to West Indies (World Cup) 2006-07, to Ireland
(Quadrangular Series) 2007, to England (ICC World Twenty20), to South Africa (ICC
World Cup Qualifiers) 2009
Overseas teams played for: Western Province, South Africa; Bloemendaal,
Netherlands; Rockingham-Mandurah, Australia
Career highlights to date: 'Winning Totesport in 2005. Getting my county cap'
Cricket moments to forget: 'My county debut at Chelmsford'
Cricketers particularly admired: Jacques Kallis, Kepler Wessels
Other sports played: Rugby
Other sports followed: Football (Arsenal), rugby (Stormers)
Favourite band: Phil Collins
Relaxations: Golf, tennis, reading
Extras: Has played first-class and one-day cricket (including ODIs and Twenty20
Internationals) for Netherlands. Scored 686 runs (av. 228.66) in the ICC Inter-
Continental Cup 2006, recording four consecutive centuries, including twin hundreds
(138/100) v Bermuda and a competition record 259* (plus match figures of 6-20/3-92)
v Canada, both in Pretoria. His match awards include Man of the Match v Bermuda in
Nairobi in the ICC World Cricket League 2006-07 (3-37/109*). Shortlisted for the ICC
Associate ODI Player of the Year 2007; ICC Associate Player of the Year 2008.
Leading first-class wicket-taker for Essex 2008. Is not considered an overseas player

Best batting: 259* Netherlands v Canada, Pretoria (SCC) 2006
Best bowling: 6-20 Netherlands v Canada, Pretoria (SCC) 2006

2009 Season

	M	Inn	NO	Runs	HS	Avg	100	50	Ct	St	Balls	Runs	Wkts	Avg	BB	5I	10M
Test																	
FC	14	22	4	823	159*	45.72	2	2	5	-	1476	970	22	44.09	5-62	1	-
ODI																	
List A	14	8	3	242	88	48.40	-	2	3	-	447	463	6	77.16	1-28	-	
20/20 Int	2	2	1	36	22*	36.00	-	-	-	-	48	77	3	25.66	2-35	-	
20/20	9	8	2	155	43	25.83	-	-	2	-	66	103	5	20.60	2-26	-	

Career Performances

	M	Inn	NO	Runs	HS	Avg	100	50	Ct	St	Balls	Runs	Wkts	Avg	BB	5I	10M
Test																	
FC	69	97	12	4132	259*	48.61	15	12	35	-	6539	4368	124	35.22	6-20	5	-
ODI	24	23	7	1026	109*	64.12	2	7	11	-	1136	918	44	20.86	4-31	-	
List A	113	89	26	2848	134*	45.20	3	17	38	-	3146	2841	111	25.59	5-50	1	
20/20 Int	5	5	2	120	56	40.00	-	1	1	-	120	144	9	16.00	3-23	-	
20/20	53	44	13	740	56	23.87	-	1	16	-	486	595	29	20.51	4-24	-	

THOMAS, A. C.   Somerset

Name: Alfonso Clive Thomas
Role: Right-hand bat, right-arm fast-medium bowler
Born: 9 February 1977, Cape Town, South Africa
County debut: 2007 (Warwickshire), 2008 (Somerset)
Twenty20 Int debut: 2006-07
Place in batting averages: 159th av. 28.16 (2008 209th av. 19.25)
Place in bowling averages: 90th av. 37.62 (2008 51st av. 27.23)
Overseas tours: South Africa VI to Hong Kong 2001; South Africa A to Zimbabwe 2004, 2006-07; South Africa to India 2004-05; South Africa Emerging Players to Australia (Cricket Australia Emerging Players Tournament) 2006; Somerset to India (ICC Champions League) 2009
Overseas teams played for: Western Province B 1998-99; North West 2000-01 – 2002-03; Northerns 2003-04 – 2005-06; Titans 2003-04 – 2006-07; Dolphins 2003-04 –

Extras: Played for South African Board President's XI v India A 2001-02, for South Africa A v India A 2001-02 and v England XI 2004-05, and for Rest of South Africa v Indians 2006-07. His match awards include Man of the Match v Dolphins at Pietermaritzburg in the SuperSport Series 2006-07 (5-55/2-46) and v Lions at Potchefstroom in the SuperSport Series 2006-07 (4-43/3-67 plus 54). Played for Staffordshire in the C&G 2005. Was a temporary overseas player with Warwickshire during August and September 2007. Signed for Somerset in February 2008
Best batting: 119* North West v Northerns, Centurion 2002-03
Best bowling: 7-54 Titans v Cape Cobras, Cape Town 2005-06

2009 Season

	M	Inn	NO	Runs	HS	Avg	100	50	Ct	St	Balls	Runs	Wkts	Avg	BB	5I	10M
Test																	
FC	14	15	3	338	70	28.16	-	3	2	-	2407	1317	35	37.62	5-53	1	-
ODI																	
List A	15	4	2	31	28*	15.50	-	-	3	-	625	555	33	16.81	4-18	-	
20/20 Int																	
20/20	12	3	1	10	10*	5.00	-	-	4	-	242	310	18	17.22	3-31	-	

Career Performances

	M	Inn	NO	Runs	HS	Avg	100	50	Ct	St	Balls	Runs	Wkts	Avg	BB	5I	10M
Test																	
FC	97	138	29	2830	119*	25.96	2	11	31	-	17921	8453	304	27.80	7-54	14	1
ODI																	
List A	110	59	28	461	28*	14.87	-	-	20	-	4879	4002	141	28.38	4-18	-	
20/20 Int	1	0	0	0	0		-	-	-	-	24	25	3	8.33	3-25	-	
20/20	60	19	10	124	30*	13.77	-	-	19	-	1105	1374	63	21.80	4-27	-	

THOMPSON, C. E. J.   Leicestershire

Name: Christopher (Chris) Everton Junior Thompson
Role: Right-hand bat, right-arm fast-medium bowler
Born: 26 June 1987, Lambeth, London
Height: 5ft 7in **Weight:** 12st 8lbs
Nickname: Thommo
County debut: 2009
Parents: Bery Roberts and Everton Thompson
Family links with cricket: 'Dad plays club cricket. Brother played Surrey U19'
Education: Archbishop Tenison School; South Thames College
Qualifications: 3 GCSEs
Career outside cricket: 'Musician'
Overseas tours: Surrey Academy to Perth 2004, to Cape Town 2005;
England U19 to Bangladesh 2005-06

Career highlights to date: '118 [for South] v West at Loughborough [in ECB U19 tournament]. 186 v Glamorgan at The Oval for Surrey 2nds'
Cricket superstitions: 'Don't have any'
Cricketers particularly admired: Brian Lara, Courtney Walsh, Curtly Ambrose, Sachin Tendulkar
Other sports played: Football, basketball, table tennis
Other sports followed: Football (Manchester United)
Favourite band: 'Too many to list'
Relaxations: 'Listening to music, playing drums, sleeping, chilling with friends, walking the dog, going to church'

Extras: Represented England U19 2005-06. Girdlers Award (Young Player of the Year). Played for Surrey 2nd XI 2004-07, and Derbyshire and Kent 2nd XIs in 2008. Played for both Leicestershire and Worcestershire in the 2nd XI Championship during 2009; both counties were later fined and deducted points after it emerged that Thompson was ineligible because he was still registered to Surrey at the time. He was subsequently loaned to Leicestershire and played for them legitimately in August and September 2009
Best batting: 16 Leicestershire v Glamorgan, Colwyn Bay 2009
Best bowling: 1-45 Leicestershire v Glamorgan, Colwyn Bay 2009

2009 Season

	M	Inn	NO	Runs	HS	Avg	100	50	Ct	St	Balls	Runs	Wkts	Avg	BB	5I	10M
Test																	
FC	1	2	0	16	16	8.00	-	-	-	-	92	45	1	45.00	1-45	-	-
ODI																	
List A	3	3	2	56	39*	56.00	-	-	1	-	36	51	1	51.00	1-22	-	
20/20 Int																	
20/20																	

Career Performances

	M	Inn	NO	Runs	HS	Avg	100	50	Ct	St	Balls	Runs	Wkts	Avg	BB	5I	10M
Test																	
FC	1	2	0	16	16	8.00	-	-	-	-	92	45	1	45.00	1-45	-	-
ODI																	
List A	3	3	2	56	39*	56.00	-	-	1	-	36	51	1	51.00	1-22	-	
20/20 Int																	
20/20																	

THORNELY, M. A.   Sussex

Name: <u>Michael</u> Alistair Thornely
Role: Right-hand top-order bat, right-arm
fast-medium bowler
Born: 19 October 1987, London
Height: 6ft 1in **Weight:** 13st 5lbs
Nickname: Thorners, Major
County debut: 2007
Parents: Richard and Jan
Marital status: Single
Family links with cricket: 'Uncle played for
Cambridgeshire; father played at Cambridge,
once claiming the wicket of David Gower'
Education: Pennthorpe Prep School;
Brighton College

Qualifications: 8 GCSEs, 3 A-levels, Level 2
coaching
Off-season: 'Around training, fit in some part-time work and attend some
photography classes'
Overseas tours: Brighton College to Sri Lanka; Sussex Academy to Cape
Town 2003, 2005; Sussex to Mumbai 2004
Overseas teams played for: Subiaco Marist CC, Perth 2007-08; Subiaco
Floreat CC, Perth 2008-09
Career highlights to date: '150 v Essex 2nd XI for Sussex 2nd XI 2007. Winning
the 2nd XI Championship 2007. Debuting v India'
Cricket moments to forget: 'Forgetting my whites for my first county game (U11)
and getting a first-ball duck. Dropping a catch at Lord's in the National Club
Championship final in front of all the opposition fans'
Cricket superstitions: 'Not superstitious'
Cricketers particularly admired: Mark Waugh, Michael Vaughan, Kevin Pietersen,
Alec Stewart
Young players to look out for: Jack Parsons (Sussex Academy)
Other sports played: Squash
Other sports followed: Football (Manchester United), rugby (Harlequins)
Favourite band: Red Hot Chili Peppers
Relaxations: 'Playing the guitar and photography'
Extras: Scored 1350 runs for Brighton College 2005, including six centuries.
Scored more than 800 runs for Sussex 2nd XI in 2007
Opinions on cricket: 'The impact of Twenty20 on the modern game has been
enormous, and has only benefited the sport with the injection of vast sums of money
from India and the IPL in particular. As a result, cricket is as popular as it has ever
been around the world. With Twenty20 being as popular as it is now, it will be

interesting to see how the game will develop further over the next 20 years. Despite the popularity of Twenty20, I still believe that Test cricket is the pinnacle of the sport, and the true test of a player's ability.'

Best batting: 19 Sussex v Yorkshire, Headingley 2009

2009 Season

	M	Inn	NO	Runs	HS	Avg	100	50	Ct	St	Balls	Runs	Wkts	Avg	BB	5I	10M
Test																	
FC	1	2	0	27	19	13.50	-	-	1	-	0	0	0		-	-	-
ODI																	
List A																	
20/20 Int																	
20/20																	

Career Performances

	M	Inn	NO	Runs	HS	Avg	100	50	Ct	St	Balls	Runs	Wkts	Avg	BB	5I	10M
Test																	
FC	5	9	1	55	19	6.87	-	-	7	-	24	25	0		-	-	-
ODI																	
List A	1	0	0	0	0		-	-	-	-	0	0	0		-	-	
20/20 Int																	
20/20																	

THORP, C. D.   Durham

Name: <u>Callum</u> David Thorp
Role: Right-hand bat, right-arm fast-medium bowler
Born: 11 January 1975, Perth, Western Australia
Height: 6ft 3in **Weight:** 13st 5lbs
County debut: 2005
50 wickets in a season: 1
Place in batting averages: 234th av. 17.25 (2008 242nd av. 13.18)
Place in bowling averages: 18th av. 24.88 (2008 10th av. 19.62)
Parents: Annette and David
Marital status: Single
Education: Servite College, Western Australia
Overseas teams played for: Western Warriors 2002-03 – 2003-04; Wanneroo DCC
Cricket superstitions: 'Left shoe on first'
Cricketers particularly admired: Mike Hussey

Other sports followed: AFL (West Coast Eagles), football (West Ham United)
Relaxations: 'Golf'
Extras: Took 4-58 for Western Australia v England XI in two-day match at Perth 2002-03. Attended Commonwealth Bank [Australian] Cricket Academy 2003. Took 6-17 v Scotland at The Grange in the C&G 2006, the best one-day figures for Durham since the county gained first-class status, following up with 100 runs (75/28) and ten wickets (6-55/5-42) in the Championship match v Hampshire at The Rose Bowl later that week. His second-innings figures of 7-88 v Kent in September 2008 made a major contribution to the win that confirmed Durham as 2008 County Champions. Has British parents and is not considered an overseas player
Best batting: 75 Durham v Hampshire, Rose Bowl 2006
Best bowling: 7-88 Durham v Kent , Canterbury 2008

2009 Season

	M	Inn	NO	Runs	HS	Avg	100	50	Ct	St	Balls	Runs	Wkts	Avg	BB	5I	10M
Test																	
FC	13	12	0	207	42	17.25	-	-	15	-	1925	846	34	24.88	5-49	2	-
ODI																	
List A	3	3	1	25	20*	12.50	-	-	1	-	132	110	2	55.00	2-47	-	
20/20 Int																	
20/20																	

Career Performances

	M	Inn	NO	Runs	HS	Avg	100	50	Ct	St	Balls	Runs	Wkts	Avg	BB	5I	10M
Test																	
FC	50	66	7	833	75	14.11	-	2	30	-	7466	3716	143	25.98	7-88	7	1
ODI																	
List A	38	25	8	286	52	16.82	-	1	7	-	1765	1286	47	27.36	6-17	1	
20/20 Int																	
20/20	9	6	0	63	13	10.50	-	-	1	-	162	266	3	88.66	2-32	-	

89. Which Bangladesh batsman has scored the most centuries
in one-day internationals?

TOMLINSON, J. A.   Hampshire

Name: <u>James</u> Andrew Tomlinson
Role: Left-hand lower-order bat, left-arm
fast-medium bowler
Born: 12 June 1982, Winchester
Height: 6ft 1in **Weight:** 12st 7lbs
Nickname: Tommo, T-Bird, Mr T, Dangerous Dave
County debut: 2002
County cap: 2008
Place in batting averages: 257th av. 13.14
(2008 233rd av. 14.50)
Place in bowling averages: 101st av. 39.76
(2008 33rd av. 24.76)
Parents: Ian and Janet
Marital status: Single
Family links with cricket: 'Both grandads played
at a high level in Yorkshire leagues. Brothers Ralph (Dulwich CC) and Hugh
(Winterslow CC) both play, and have given me great support throughout my career'
Education: Harrow Way Community School, Andover; Cricklade College, Andover;
Cardiff University
Qualifications: 3 A-levels, 2.1 degree in Education and Psychology
Career outside cricket: 'Patient!'
Overseas teams played for: South Perth 2004-05, 2006-07
Career highlights to date: '35* v Lancashire 2008; 8-46 v Somerset 2008. Being
leading wicket-taker with 67 championship victims in 2008. The last two months of
the 2008 season were an amazing experience.'
Cricket moments to forget: 'Tearing a rib muscle on the first day of the 2005 season.
Any dropped catch'
Cricketers particularly admired: Wasim Akram, Shane Warne, Darren Gough,
Dimitri Mascarenhas, Malcolm Marshall, Robin Smith, Ryan Sidebottom
Young players to look out for: Chris Wood, James Vince (both Hampshire)
Other sports played: Golf, darts
Other sports followed: Football (West Ham United)
Favourite band: U2
Relaxations: 'Ornithology, wildlife in general'
Extras: Played for Development of Excellence XI (South) 2001. Played for Cardiff
UCCE 2002-03. Represented British Universities 2002-03. NBC Denis Compton
Award for the most promising young Hampshire player 2003. Cardiff University
Sportsperson of the Year award 2003. Leading first-class wicket-taker for his county
in 2008. Hampshire Player of the Season 2008
Opinions on cricket: 'Keep limiting Kolpak and non-English qualified players.
Encourage home-grown talent. 2nd XI cricket should be four-day and Twenty20, not
three-day.'

Best batting: 35* Hampshire v Lancashire, Rose Bowl 2008
Best bowling: 8-46 Hampshire v Somerset, Taunton 2008

2009 Season

	M	Inn	NO	Runs	HS	Avg	100	50	Ct	St	Balls	Runs	Wkts	Avg	BB	5I	10M
Test																	
FC	12	14	7	92	23	13.14	-	-	3	-	1909	1193	30	39.76	3-53	-	-
ODI																	
List A																		
20/20 Int																		
20/20																		

Career Performances

	M	Inn	NO	Runs	HS	Avg	100	50	Ct	St	Balls	Runs	Wkts	Avg	BB	5I	10M
Test																		
FC	50	64	30	332	35*	9.76	-	-	13	-	8019	5111	144	35.49	8-46	6	1
ODI																		
List A	22	12	4	18	6	2.25	-	-	3	-	887	715	20	35.75	4-47	-	
20/20 Int																		
20/20	2	1	0	5	5	5.00	-	-	-	-	42	48	1	48.00	1-20	-	

TOOR, K. S.   Middlesex

Name: <u>Kabir</u> Singh Toor
Role: Right-hand bat, leg-spin bowler
Born: 30 April 1990, Watford, Hertfordshire
County debut: 2009 (one-day)
Education: John Lyon School, Harrow
Extras: Made 2nd XI Championship debut 2006.
Played for Middlesex U17. Played for South U17
in ECB U17 Regional Festival at Loughborough
2007. Plays for Radlett CC. Signed to Middlesex in
October 2009. Spent the winter of 2009-10 at the
Darren Lehmann Academy in Adelaide

2009 Season

	M	Inn	NO	Runs	HS	Avg	100	50	Ct	St	Balls	Runs	Wkts	Avg	BB	5I	10M
Test																	
FC																	
ODI																	
List A	2	2	1	8	5	8.00	-	-	-	-	24	32	1	32.00	1-25	-	
20/20 Int																	
20/20																	

Career Performances

	M	Inn	NO	Runs	HS	Avg	100	50	Ct	St	Balls	Runs	Wkts	Avg	BB	5I	10M
Test																	
FC																	
ODI																	
List A	2	2	1	8	5	8.00	-	-	-	-	24	32	1	32.00	1-25	-	
20/20 Int																	
20/20																	

TREDWELL, J. C.   Kent

Name: <u>James</u> Cullum Tredwell
Role: Left-hand bat, right-arm
off-spin bowler
Born: 27 February 1982, Ashford, Kent
Height: 5ft 11in **Weight:** 14st 2lbs
Nickname: Tredders, Pingu, Chad
County debut: 2001
County cap: 2007
50 wickets in a season: 1
Place in batting averages: 144th av. 30.31
(2008 178th av. 22.57)
Place in bowling averages: 24th av. 26.63
(2008 142nd av. 49.14)
Parents: John and Rosemary
Marital status: Single
Family links with cricket: Father played for Ashford and Folkestone in Kent League
Education: Southlands Community Comprehensive
Qualifications: 10 GCSEs, 2 A-levels, ECB Level 1 coach
Overseas tours: Kent U17 to Sri Lanka 1998-99; Kent to Port Elizabeth 2002;
England A to Malaysia and India 2003-04; England Performance Programme to
India 2007-08; England to New Zealand 2007-08 (one-day series); England Lions
to UAE 2009-10

Overseas teams played for: Redlands Tigers, Brisbane 2000-02

Cricket moments to forget: 'Being hit for six in a crucial B&H Cup match v Essex, which probably cost Kent's qualification to next stage'

Cricketers particularly admired: 'All the great spinners'

Extras: Represented England U19 2001 (captain in second 'Test'). Kent Most Improved Player Award 2003. NBC Denis Compton Award for the most promising young Kent player 2003. ECB National Academy 2003-04. Took over captaincy of England A in India 2003-04 after Alex Gidman was forced to return home with a hand injury. Chosen for the MCC team that played champions Sussex in the opening fixture of the 2008 season

Best batting: 123* Kent v New Zealand, Canterbury 2008

Best bowling: 8-66 Kent v Glamorgan, Canterbury 2009

2009 Season

	M	Inn	NO	Runs	HS	Avg	100	50	Ct	St	Balls	Runs	Wkts	Avg	BB	5I	10M
Test																	
FC	17	21	5	485	86*	30.31	-	4	12	-	4091	1838	69	26.63	8-66	4	2
ODI																	
List A	14	11	2	121	45	13.44	-	-	1	-	630	505	14	36.07	6-27	1	
20/20 Int																	
20/20	12	0	0	0	0		-	-	2	-	252	271	13	20.84	3-18	-	

Career Performances

	M	Inn	NO	Runs	HS	Avg	100	50	Ct	St	Balls	Runs	Wkts	Avg	BB	5I	10M
Test																	
FC	88	124	17	2479	123*	23.16	2	12	84	-	15381	8202	223	36.78	8-66	7	3
ODI																	
List A	136	101	35	1229	88	18.62	-	4	57	-	5418	4276	130	32.89	6-27	1	
20/20 Int																	
20/20	62	27	6	252	34	12.00	-	-	21	-	1104	1317	57	23.10	4-21	-	

90. Name the Pakistan opener who made a double century at
Old Trafford in his first Test series.

TREGO, P. D.   Somerset

Name: <u>Peter</u> David Trego
Role: Right-hand bat, right-arm fast-medium/
occasional leg-break bowler; all-rounder
Born: 12 June 1981, Weston-super-Mare
Height: 6ft **Weight:** 13st 7lbs
Nickname: Tregs
County debut: 2000 (Somerset), 2003 (Kent),
2005 (Middlesex)
County cap: 2007 (Somerset)
Place in batting averages: 119th av. 33.88
(2008 51st av. 42.45)
Place in bowling averages: 122nd av. 46.78
(2008 34th av. 24.78)
Parents: Carol and Paul
Wife and date of marriage: Claire, 8 May 2000
Children: Amelia Ann, 9 July 2001; Davis Paul, 8 February 2005;
Dexter Gerard, 15 November 2007
Family links with cricket: 'Brother on staff at Somerset 1997; unlucky not to get a
better go – batter and off-spin bowler'
Education: Wyvern Comprehensive, Weston-super-Mare
Qualifications: 'School of Life'
Career outside cricket: 'Being a dad, and *still* thinking about life after cricket'
Off-season: 'Trying to play overseas somewhere'
Overseas tours: Somerset to Cape Town 2000, 2001, 2006, to India 2007, to Abu
Dhabi 2008. England VIs to Hong Kong 2009; Somerset to India (ICC Champions
League) 2009; England Lions to UAE 2009-10
Career highlights to date: 'County cap, 10 June 2007; 54-ball 103* v Yorkshire,
chasing 485; 65 off 14 balls v Sri Lanka in Hong Kong 2009'
Cricket moments to forget: 'All of 2003'
Cricket superstitions: 'None'
Cricketers particularly admired: Ian Botham, Graham Rose, Justin Langer,
Andrew Caddick, Marcus Trescothick, Ian Blackwell
Young players to look out for: 'Davis and Dexter Trego (Somerset)'
Other sports played: Football (semi-professional with Weston-super-Mare and
Margate FC), golf (Weston-super-Mare first team; 2 handicap)
Other sports followed: Football (Manchester United), golf (Tiger Woods), snooker
Favourite band: Oasis
Relaxations: 'Shopping, watches and cars'
Extras: Represented England U19. NBC Denis Compton Award for the most
promising young Somerset player 2000. Scored 140 at Taunton 2002 as Somerset,
chasing 454 to win, tied with West Indies A. 'I'm very proud of being the first player
ever to incur a five-run penalty for replacing Jamie Cox and nobody thinking to tell

Mr Dudleston.' 'Played football in the FA Cup on *Match of the Day* – that was cool up until the part where I was 'megged to let in the goal to send us out; but still got Star Man in the paper.' Left Middlesex at the end of the 2005 season and rejoined Somerset for 2006. Scored 63-ball 78 and took 4-61 v Middlesex at Lord's in the Friends Provident 2007. Wetherall All-rounder of the Year 2007

Opinions on cricket: 'Just hope that the long form of the game is looked after as much as the short. I will personally be as proud, if not more proud, of my first-class record when I hang my boots up. It's the true test of your skill...'

Player website: www.eurocams.co.uk
Best batting: 140 Somerset v West Indies A, Taunton 2002
Best bowling: 6-59 Middlesex v Nottinghamshire, Trent Bridge 2005

2009 Season

	M	Inn	NO	Runs	HS	Avg	100	50	Ct	St	Balls	Runs	Wkts	Avg	BB	5I	10M
Test																	
FC	16	23	5	610	103*	33.88	1	5	5	-	1545	889	19	46.78	3-53	-	-
ODI																	
List A	17	12	4	272	74*	34.00	-	2	6	-	710	632	22	28.72	4-17	-	
20/20 Int																	
20/20	12	8	3	241	58*	48.20	-	1	3	-	216	280	6	46.66	2-18	-	

Career Performances

	M	Inn	NO	Runs	HS	Avg	100	50	Ct	St	Balls	Runs	Wkts	Avg	BB	5I	10M
Test																	
FC	83	120	18	3659	140	35.87	7	22	25	-	8462	5527	144	38.38	6-59	1	-
ODI																	
List A	87	70	14	1030	78	18.39	-	4	24	-	3014	2830	91	31.09	5-44	1	
20/20 Int																	
20/20	39	34	6	691	79	24.67	-	2	8	-	470	642	21	30.57	2-17	-	

91. Three Bangladesh bowlers have taken more than 100 wickets in one-day internationals. Name them.

TREMLETT, C. T.   Surrey

Name: Christopher (<u>Chris</u>) Timothy Tremlett
Role: Right-hand bat, right-arm fast-medium bowler
Born: 2 September 1981, Southampton
Height: 6ft 7in **Weight:** 16st 1lb
Nickname: Twiggy, Goober
County debut: 2000 (Hampshire)
County cap: 2004 (Hampshire)
Test debut: 2007
ODI debut: 2005
Twenty20 Int debut: 2007-08
Place in batting averages: (2008 215th av. 17.58)
Place in bowling averages: 102nd av. 40.28 (2008
103rd av. 34.54)
Parents: Timothy and Carolyn
Marital status: Single
Family links with cricket: Grandfather [Maurice] played for Somerset and in
three Tests for England. Father played for Hampshire and is now director of
cricket at the county
Education: Thornden School, Chandlers Ford; Taunton's College, Southampton
Qualifications: 5 GCSEs, BTEC National Diploma
in Sports Science, Level 2 coach
Overseas tours: West of England U15 to West Indies 1997; Hampshire U16 to Jersey;
England U17 to Northern Ireland (ECC Colts Festival) 1999; England U19 to India
2000-01; ECB National Academy to Australia 2001-02, to Australia and Sri Lanka
2002-03; England VI to Hong Kong 2004; England to Australia 2006-07 (C'wealth
Bank Series), to South Africa (World 20/20) 2007-08, to Sri Lanka 2007-08 (one-day
series), to New Zealand 2007-08 (one-day series); England Performance Programme to
India 2007-08
Cricketers particularly admired: Glenn McGrath, Mark Waugh, Shane Warne
Other sports played: Basketball, volleyball
Other sports followed: Football (Arsenal)
Relaxations: 'Socialising with friends; cinema'
Extras: Took wicket (Mark Richardson) with first ball in first-class cricket v New
Zealand A at Portsmouth 2000; finished with debut match figures of 6-91. Represented
England U19. NBC Denis Compton Award for the most promising young Hampshire
player 2000, 2001. Hampshire Young Player of the Year 2001. Took Championship
hat-trick (Ealham, Swann, G. Smith) v Nottinghamshire at Trent Bridge 2005. ECB
National Academy 2006-07. Played against New Zealand in the 2008 ODI series.
Moved from Hampshire to Surrey in January 2010
Best batting: 64 Hampshire v Gloucestershire, Rose Bowl 2005
Best bowling: 6-44 Hampshire v Sussex, Hove 2005

2009 Season

	M	Inn	NO	Runs	HS	Avg	100	50	Ct	St		Balls	Runs	Wkts	Avg	BB	5I	10M
Test																		
FC	7	8	0	75	36	9.37	-	-	2	-		1038	564	14	40.28	4-49	-	-
ODI																		
List A	8	5	5	26	8*		-	-	2	-		370	337	9	37.44	3-76	-	
20/20 Int																		
20/20	4	1	0	0	0	0.00	-	-	1	-		95	129	4	32.25	2-28	-	

Career Performances

	M	Inn	NO	Runs	HS	Avg	100	50	Ct	St		Balls	Runs	Wkts	Avg	BB	5I	10M
Test	3	5	1	50	25*	12.50	-	-	1	-		859	386	13	29.69	3-12	-	-
FC	92	122	31	1638	64	18.00	-	6	27	-		15381	8283	289	28.66	6-44	7	-
ODI	9	6	2	38	19*	9.50	-	-	2	-		479	419	9	46.55	4-32	-	
List A	112	66	22	415	38*	9.43	-	-	23	-		5195	4081	156	26.16	4-25	-	
20/20 Int	1	0	0	0	0		-	-	-	-		24	45	2	22.50	2-45	-	
20/20	25	12	4	58	13	7.25	-	-	5	-		531	654	32	20.43	4-25	-	

TRESCOTHICK, M. E. Somerset

Name: <u>Marcus</u> Edward Trescothick
Role: Left-hand bat, right-arm swing bowler, reserve wicket-keeper; county vice-captain
Born: 25 December 1975, Keynsham, Bristol
Height: 6ft 3in **Weight:** 14st 7lbs
Nickname: Banger, Tres
County debut: 1993
County cap: 1999
Benefit: 2008
Test debut: 2000
ODI debut: 2000
Twenty20 Int debut: 2005
1000 runs in a season: 3
1st-Class 200s: 2
Place in batting averages: 5th av. 75.70
(2008 38th av. 46.59)
Parents: Martyn and Lin
Wife and date of marriage: Hayley, 24 January 2004
Children: Ellie, April 2005
Family links with cricket: Father played for Somerset 2nd XI; uncle played club cricket

Education: Sir Bernard Lovell School, Bristol
Qualifications: 7 GCSEs
Overseas tours: England U18 to South Africa 1992-93; England U19 to Sri Lanka 1993-94, to West Indies 1994-95 (c); England A to Bangladesh and New Zealand 1999-2000; England to Kenya (ICC Knockout Trophy) 2000-01, to Pakistan and Sri Lanka 2000-01, to Zimbabwe (one-day series) 2001-02, to India and New Zealand 2001-02, to Sri Lanka (ICC Champions Trophy) 2002-03, to Australia 2002-03, to Africa (World Cup) 2002-03, to Bangladesh and Sri Lanka 2003-04, to West Indies 2003-04, to South Africa 2004-05, to Pakistan 2005-06, to India 2005-06, to Australia 2006-07
Overseas teams played for: Melville CC, Perth 1997-99
Cricketers particularly admired: Adam Gilchrist, Andy Caddick
Other sports followed: Golf, football (Bristol City FC)
Relaxations: 'Spending time at home, playing golf'
Extras: Scored more than 1000 runs for England U19. Took hat-trick (Gilchrist, Angel, McIntyre) for Somerset v Young Australia at Taunton 1995. NBC Denis Compton Award for the most promising young Somerset player 1996, 1997. PCA Player of the Year 2000. Sports.com Cricketer of the Year 2001. BBC West Country Sports Sportsman of the Year 2001. One of *Indian Cricket*'s five Cricketers of the Year 2002. Scored 114* v South Africa at The Oval in the NatWest Series 2003, sharing with Vikram Solanki (106) in a record England opening partnership in ODIs (200). Scored century in each innings (105/107) in the second Test v West Indies at Edgbaston 2004. Man of the Match in his 100th ODI v Bangladesh at The Oval in the NatWest Series 2005 (100*). His Test awards include England's Man of the Series v Bangladesh 2005 and Man of the Match in the fifth Test v South Africa at The Oval 2003 (219/69*). His other ODI awards include Man of the Series v West Indies 2003-04 and Man of the Match v Australia at Headingley in the NatWest Challenge 2005 (104*). One of *Wisden*'s Five Cricketers of the Year 2005. Appointed MBE in 2006 New Year Honours as part of 2005 Ashes-winning England team. Announced his retirement from international cricket in March 2008. Topped the Somerset batting averages in all forms of cricket in 2008. His autobiography, *Coming Back To Me*, won the William Hill Sports Book of the Year Award in November 2008
Best batting: 284 Somerset v Northamptonshire, Northampton 2007
Best bowling: 4-36 Somerset v Young Australia, Taunton 1995

2009 Season

	M	Inn	NO	Runs	HS	Avg	100	50	Ct	St	Balls	Runs	Wkts	Avg	BB	5I	10M
Test																	
FC	16	26	2	1817	146	75.70	8	9	21	-	30	10	0		-	-	-
ODI																	
List A	17	17	2	794	144	52.93	1	5	11	-	6	8	0		-	-	
20/20 Int																	
20/20	12	11	1	323	69*	32.30	-	3	1	-	0	0	0		-	-	

Career Performances

	M	Inn	NO	Runs	HS	Avg	100	50	Ct	St	Balls	Runs	Wkts	Avg	BB	5I	10M
Test	76	143	10	5825	219	43.79	14	29	95	-	300	155	1	155.00	1-34	-	-
FC	255	438	23	16645	284	40.10	39	85	314	-	2704	1551	36	43.08	4-36	-	-
ODI	123	122	6	4335	137	37.37	12	21	49	-	232	219	4	54.75	2-7	-	
List A	320	307	25	10770	184	38.19	27	51	123	-	2010	1644	57	28.84	4-50	-	
20/20 Int	3	3	0	166	72	55.33	-	2	2	-	0	0	0		-	-	
20/20	32	31	1	1041	107	34.70	1	8	14	-	0	0	0		-	-	

TROT, I. J. L.   Warwickshire

Name: Ian <u>Jonathan</u> Leonard Trott
Role: Right-hand bat, right-arm medium
bowler; all-rounder
Born: 22 April 1981, Cape Town, South Africa
Height: 6ft **Weight:** 13st 5lbs
Nickname: Booger
County debut: 2003
County cap: 2005
Test debut: 2009
ODI debut: 2009
Twenty20 Int debut: 2007
1000 runs in a season: 5
1st-Class 200s: 1
Place in batting averages: 8th av. 73.68
(2008 5th av. 62.00)
Place in bowling averages: 140th av. 46.30
Parents: Ian and Donna
Marital status: Single
Family links with cricket: Father a professional cricket coach. Brother (Kenny
Jackson) played for Western Province and Boland. Is related to the late-19th-century
Test cricketers Albert (Australia and England) and Harry Trott (Australia)
Education: Rondebosch Boys' High School; Stellenbosch University
Qualifications: Level 2 coaching
Overseas tours: South Africa U15 to England (U15 World Cup) 1996; South
Africa U19 to Pakistan 1998-99, to Sri Lanka (U19 World Cup) 1999-2000;
England Performance Programme to India 2007-08; England Lions to India 2007-08,
to New Zealand 2008-09; England to South Africa 2009-10, to Bangladesh 2009-10
Overseas teams played for: Boland 1999-2000 – 2000-01; Western Province
2001-02; Otago 2005-06
Cricket superstitions: 'Personal'
Cricketers particularly admired: Sachin Tendulkar, Adam Hollioake, Steve Waugh

Other sports played: Hockey (Western Province U16, U18, U21), golf
Other sports followed: Football (Tottenham Hotspur)
Favourite band: Roxette, Robbie Williams
Relaxations: 'Music, watching sport'
Extras: Represented South Africa A. Struck 245 on debut for Warwickshire 2nd XI v Somerset 2nd XI at Knowle & Dorridge 2002. Scored century (134) on Championship debut for Warwickshire v Sussex at Edgbaston 2003. Became the first player to bat for the full 20 overs in the Twenty20, for a 54-ball 65* v Gloucestershire at Edgbaston 2003. Represented England Lions 2007. Called up to England's ODI squad, June 2007. Scored over 2000 runs in all competitions during the 2008 season and again in 2009. England increment contract 2009-10
Best batting: 210 Warwickshire v Sussex, Edgbaston 2005
Best bowling: 7-39 Warwickshire v Kent, Canterbury 2003

2009 Season

	M	Inn	NO	Runs	HS	Avg	100	50	Ct	St	Balls	Runs	Wkts	Avg	BB	5I	10M
Test	1	2	0	160	119	80.00	1	-	1	-	0	0	0		-	-	-
FC	17	25	6	1400	184*	73.68	5	5	13	-	590	355	5	71.00	2-26	-	-
ODI																	
List A	15	12	2	544	120	54.40	1	4	4	-	150	132	8	16.50	3-36	-	
20/20 Int	1	1	1	0	0*		-	-	-	-	0	0	0		-	-	
20/20	12	12	4	525	86*	65.62	-	5	2	-	0	0	0		-	-	

Career Performances

	M	Inn	NO	Runs	HS	Avg	100	50	Ct	St	Balls	Runs	Wkts	Avg	BB	5I	10M
Test	1	2	0	160	119	80.00	1	-	1	-	0	0	0		-	-	-
FC	135	225	29	8773	210	44.76	20	44	131	-	4130	2314	51	45.37	7-39	1	-
ODI	1	1	0	0	0	0.00	-	-	-	-	0	0	0		-	-	
List A	149	137	28	4705	125*	43.16	9	29	48	-	1357	1284	52	24.69	4-55	-	
20/20 Int	3	3	1	11	9	5.50	-	-	-	-	0	0	0		-	-	
20/20	58	53	14	1617	86*	41.46	-	10	15	-	144	234	8	29.25	2-19	-	

---

92. Which Bangladesh bowler took 12 wickets in the second Test against Zimbabwe in 2005?

TROUGHTON, J. O.   Warwickshire

Name: Jamie (<u>Jim</u>) Oliver Troughton
Role: Left-hand bat, slow left-arm bowler
Born: 2 March 1979, London
Height: 5ft 11in **Weight:** 13st
Nickname: Troughts
County debut: 2001
County cap: 2002
ODI debut: 2003
1000 runs in a season: 1
1st-Class 200s: 1
Place in batting averages: 105th av. 36.00
(2008 26th av. 49.80)
Parents: Ali and David
Wife and date of marriage: Naomi,
28 September 2002
Children: Eva, 15 February 2007; Rosie, 1 April 2009
Family links with cricket: Father was a Middlesex Colt. Great-grandfather Henry Crichton played for Warwickshire. 'Younger brother, Wigsy, is a Stratford Panther'
Education: Trinity School, Leamington Spa; Birmingham University
Qualifications: 3 A-levels, BSc Sport & Exercise Psychology, Level 3 coaching
Career outside cricket: 'Coaching and freelance illustration'
Off-season: 'Time abroad, training, sketching and time with the family.'
Overseas tours: Warwickshire Development of Excellence squad to Cape Town; MCC to Australia and Singapore 2001; ECB National Academy to Australia and Sri Lanka 2002-03
Overseas teams played for: Harvinia CC, Bloemfontein, South Africa 2000; Avendale CC, Cape Town 2001-02; Belville CC, Cape Town 2003-04; Claremont-Nedlands CC, Perth 2004-05
Career highlights to date: 'B&H final 2002, England call-up 2003, County champions 2004, highest first-class score 2009
Cricket superstitions: 'Don't leave straight ones'
Cricketers particularly admired: Brian Lara, Graham Thorpe, Nick Knight, Ashley Giles
Young players to look out for: Chris Woakes, Ateeq Javid (both Warwickshire)
Other sports played: Football (Stoke City youth player)
Other sports followed: 'Hooked on Manchester United since going to their soccer school aged five'
Favourite band: Stone Roses, Beatles, Red Hot Chili Peppers
Relaxations: 'Going abroad, time with the family, sketching for AOC (*All Out Cricket* magazine)'

Extras: Is grandson of *Dr Who* actor Patrick Troughton. Acting runs in the family – 'Dad's a fantastic Shakespearean actor, older brother Sam is playing Romeo at the RSC (2009-10), little brother Wigsy (William) is in a horror film, *Warhouse*, coming soon...' County colours U12-U19. Has represented England U15, U16 and U17. Represented ECB Midlands U19 1998. Has won the Alec Hastilow Trophy and the Coney Edmonds Trophy (Warwickshire awards). Warwickshire 2nd XI Player of the Year 2001. Scored 1067 first-class runs in his first full season 2002. NBC Denis Compton Award for the most promising young Warwickshire player 2002. Warwickshire Young Player and Most Improved Player of the Year 2002. Produced an illustrated book, *The Push For Promotion 2008*, recording Warwickshire's second division-winning season

Opinions on cricket: '[Should have] three main competitions – 50-over, Twenty20, four-day. Fewer games, therefore more intensity in those games.'

Best batting: 223 Warwickshire v Hampshire, Edgbaston 2009

Best bowling: 3-1 Warwickshire v CUCCE, Fenner's 2004

2009 Season

	M	Inn	NO	Runs	HS	Avg	100	50	Ct	St	Balls	Runs	Wkts	Avg	BB	5I	10M
Test																	
FC	17	23	0	828	223	36.00	2	3	10	-	0	0	0	-	-	-	-
ODI																	
List A	16	11	1	394	77	39.40	-	5	5	-	0	0	0	-	-	-	
20/20 Int																	
20/20	11	11	0	280	62	25.45	-	4	8	-	0	0	0	-	-	-	

Career Performances

	M	Inn	NO	Runs	HS	Avg	100	50	Ct	St	Balls	Runs	Wkts	Avg	BB	5I	10M
Test																	
FC	110	166	14	5913	223	38.90	16	30	53	-	2359	1416	22	64.36	3-1	-	-
ODI	6	5	1	36	20	9.00	-	-	1	-	0	0	0	-	-	-	
List A	123	107	10	2805	115*	28.91	2	16	43	-	736	644	25	25.76	4-23	-	
20/20 Int																	
20/20	51	46	2	926	62	21.04	-	6	24	-	96	127	6	21.16	2-10	-	

TUDOR, A. J.   Surrey

Name: Alexander (<u>Alex</u>) Jeremy Tudor
Role: Right-hand bat, right-arm fast bowler
Born: 23 October 1977, West Brompton, London
Height: 6ft 4in **Weight:** 13st 7lbs
Nickname: Big Al, Bambi, Tudes
County debut: 1995 (Surrey), 2005 (Essex)
County cap: 1999 (Surrey)
Test debut: 1998-99
ODI debut: 2002
Place in batting averages: (2008 206th av. 19.71)
Place in bowling averages: (2008 143rd av. 52.57)
Parents: Daryll and Jennifer
Marital status: Engaged to Francesca
Children: Sienna
Family links with cricket: Brother was on the
staff at The Oval

Education: St Mark's C of E, Fulham; City of Westminster College
Overseas tours: England U15 to South Africa 1992-93; England U19 to Zimbabwe
1995-96, to Pakistan 1996-97; England to Australia 1998-99, to South Africa 1999-
2000, to Pakistan 2000-01, to Australia 2002-03; England A to West Indies 2000-01;
ECB National Academy to Australia 2001-02, 2002-03
Cricketers particularly admired: Curtly Ambrose, Brian Lara
Other sports followed: Basketball, football (QPR)
Relaxations: Listening to music
Extras: Played for London Schools at all ages from U8. Represented England U17.
MCC Young Cricketer. Took 4-89 in Australia's first innings on Test debut at Perth
1998-99; his victims included both Waugh twins. Scored 99* in second innings of the
first Test v New Zealand at Edgbaston 1999, bettering the highest score by a
nightwatchman for England (Harold Larwood's 98 v Australia at Sydney 1932-33)
and winning Man of the Match award. Cricket Writers' Club Young Cricketer of the
Year 1999. Recorded match figures of 7-109 in the third Test v Sri Lanka at Old
Trafford 2002, winning Man of the Match award. Rejoined Surrey from Essex in
October 2008. Released by Surrey at the end of the 2009 season
Best batting: 144 Essex v Derbyshire, Chelmsford 2006
Best bowling: 7-48 Surrey v Lancashire, The Oval 2000

	M	Inn	NO	Runs	HS	Avg	100	50	Ct	St	Balls	Runs	Wkts	Avg	BB	5I	10M
Test																	
FC	4	6	2	83	33	20.75	-	-	1	-	600	417	4	104.25	2-109	-	-
ODI																	
List A	3	2	0	6	6	3.00	-	-	2	-	114	122	2	61.00	1-20	-	
20/20 Int																	
20/20																	

Career Performances

	M	Inn	NO	Runs	HS	Avg	100	50	Ct	St	Balls	Runs	Wkts	Avg	BB	5I	10M
Test	10	16	4	229	99*	19.08	-	1	3	-	1512	963	28	34.39	5-44	1	-
FC	129	169	34	2960	144	21.92	2	9	36	-	18191	11023	351	31.40	7-48	14	-
ODI	3	2	1	9	6	9.00	-	-	1	-	127	136	4	34.00	2-30	-	
List A	82	55	16	470	56	12.05	-	1	23	-	3451	2785	111	25.09	4-26	-	
20/20 Int																	
20/20																	

TURNER, M. L. Somerset

Name: <u>Mark</u> Leif Turner
Role: Right-hand lower-order bat, right-arm fast-medium bowler
Born: 23 October 1984, Sunderland
Height: 6ft **Weight:** 12st 12lbs
Nickname: Tina, Racing Pigeon, Gimp
County debut: 2005 (Durham), 2007 (Somerset)
Parents: Kenny and Eileen
Marital status: 'Living with partner'
Family links with cricket: 'Brother Ian played county juniors and was a well-respected local player'
Education: Thornhill Comprehensive School
Qualifications: 7 GCSEs, Level 2 coaching
Overseas tours: England U19 to Bangladesh (U19 World Cup) 2003-04; Durham to India 2004, to South Africa 2005, to Dubai 2005
Career highlights to date: 'Being part of the Somerset team that achieved double promotion'
Cricket moments to forget: 'Dropping a dolly on Sky for England U19'
Cricketers particularly admired: Allan Donald, Andrew Caddick, Marcus Trescothick, Sachin Tendulkar, Dale Benkenstein, Keith Parsons

Other sports played: Football (junior with Manchester United and Sunderland), golf, fishing
Other sports followed: Football (Sunderland AFC)
Favourite band: 'Anything that is neo-soul, old school R&B (Maxwell, Keith Sweat etc.)'
Extras: Represented England U19 2003 and 2004, returning match figures of 9-104 (5-57/4-47) in the second 'Test' v Bangladesh U19 at Taunton 2004. ECB Elite Fast Bowler Development Programme to Florida, 2008-09
Opinions on cricket: 'Two-division format is good and the difference between the two divisions is becoming stronger.'
Best batting: 57 Somerset v Derbyshire, Taunton 2007
Best bowling: 4-30 Somerset v LUCCE, Taunton 2007

2009 Season

	M	Inn	NO	Runs	HS	Avg	100	50	Ct	St	Balls	Runs	Wkts	Avg	BB	5I	10M
Test																	
FC	1	0	0	0	0		-	-	1	-	180	111	2	55.50	2-82	-	-
ODI																	
List A	6	1	1	15	15*		-	-	2	-	182	175	8	21.87	3-27	-	
20/20 Int																	
20/20	5	1	1	1	1*		-	-	2	-	90	128	6	21.33	2-20	-	

Career Performances

	M	Inn	NO	Runs	HS	Avg	100	50	Ct	St	Balls	Runs	Wkts	Avg	BB	5I	10M
Test																	
FC	9	8	2	89	57	14.83	-	1	3	-	1323	853	17	50.17	4-30	-	-
ODI																	
List A	15	6	4	38	15*	19.00	-	-	2	-	557	534	19	28.10	3-27	-	
20/20 Int																	
20/20	18	7	3	13	7	3.25	-	-	3	-	312	465	16	29.06	2-20	-	

93. Three Pakistan batsmen have made more than 20 Test centuries. Inzamam-ul-Haq and Javed Miandad are two of them. Who is the third?

UDAL, S. D.   Middlesex

Name: <u>Shaun</u> David Udal
Role: Right-hand bat, off-spin bowler;
county captain
Born: 18 March 1969, Farnborough, Hampshire
Height: 6ft 2in **Weight:** 14st 2lbs
Nickname: Shaggy
County debut: 1989 (Hampshire)
County cap: 1992 (Hampshire)
Benefit: 2002 (Hampshire)
Test debut: 2005-06
ODI debut: 1994
50 wickets in a season: 7
Place in batting averages: 216th av. 19.90
(2008 66th av. 39.71)
Place in bowling averages: 27th av. 27.21
(2008 96th av. 33.00)
Parents: Robin and Mary
Wife and date of marriage: Emma, 4 October 1991
Children: Katherine Mary, 26 August 1992; Rebecca Jane, 17 November 1995;
Jack David, 23 August 2004
Family links with cricket: 'Great-grandfather [J. S. Udal] – MCC; grandfather
[G. F. Udal] – Middlesex and Leicestershire; father – Camberley CC for 40 years;
brother [Gary] – captain of Camberley CC'
Education: Tower Hill infant and junior schools; Cove Comprehensive, Farnborough
Qualifications: 8 CSEs, print finisher, company director
Off-season: 'Family holiday, work, South African tour with Warren Rumsey over
Christmas, and training'
Career outside cricket: 'Media – printing company; Masuri helmets; clothing –
graphics and embroidery'
Overseas tours: England to Australia 1994-95, to Pakistan 2005-06, to India 2005-06;
England A to Pakistan 1995-96; England XI to New Zealand (Cricket Max) 1997;
Hampshire to Anguilla 1998, to Cape Town 2001; Middlesex to Antigua for Stanford
Super Series 2008-09
Overseas teams played for: Hamilton Wickham, Newcastle, NSW 1989-90
Career highlights to date: 'Captain of Hants in C&G final 2005 – and being the
only ever Hampshire born and bred captain to lift a trophy. Being picked for England
again aged 36. Twenty20 win, 2008.'
Cricket moments to forget: 'Getting out twice as nightwatchman, hooking'
Cricket superstitions: 'Left everything on first'
Favourite sledging line: 'Received from Shane Warne – "You bat two places too
high and bowl throw downs!"'

Cricketers particularly admired: Sir Ian Botham, Shane Warne, Robin Smith, Tim Murtagh
Young players to look out for: David Malan, Steve Finn (both Middlesex)
Other sports played: Golf (12 handicap), football
Other sports followed: Football (West Ham Utd, Aldershot Town)
Injuries: 'Sore knee – out for a week'
Favourite band: Take That
Relaxations: 'My three children, pubs, good food and alcohol'
Extras: Scored double hundred for Camberley CC in 40-over game. Man of the Match on NatWest debut against Berkshire 1991. Hampshire Cricket Association Player of the Year 1993. Vice-captain of Hampshire 1998-2000. Hampshire Players' Player of the Year 2001, 2002. Skipper of Hampshire in C&G final at Lord's 2005, becoming the first Hampshire-born captain to lift silverware for the county. Had second innings figures of 4-14 as England defeated India in the third Test at Mumbai 2005-06. Leading wicket-taker for Hampshire in one-day cricket; all-time sixth-highest wicket-taker for Hampshire. President of Camberley CC. Retired at the end of the 2007 season but later accepted an invitation to join Middlesex for 2008. Captained Middlesex in the Stanford Series 2008; appointed county captain in September 2008. Scored 79 off 46 balls in Friends Provident Trophy match against Scotland, May 2009
Opinions on cricket: 'Authorities, stop messing around with the formats every year! County cricket has to replicate the highest level'
Best batting: 117* Hampshire v Warwickshire, Southampton 1997
Best bowling: 8-50 Hampshire v Sussex, Southampton 1992

2009 Season

	M	Inn	NO	Runs	HS	Avg	100	50	Ct	St	Balls	Runs	Wkts	Avg	BB	5I	10M
Test																	
FC	14	24	4	398	55	19.90	-	1	4	-	2213	1007	37	27.21	6-36	2	1
ODI																	
List A	16	10	4	182	79*	30.33	-	1	9	-	648	487	20	24.35	3-32	-	
20/20 Int																	
20/20	11	8	2	87	26*	14.50	-	-	4	-	210	302	7	43.14	2-23	-	

Career Performances

	M	Inn	NO	Runs	HS	Avg	100	50	Ct	St	Balls	Runs	Wkts	Avg	BB	5I	10M
Test	4	7	1	109	33*	18.16	-	-	1	-	596	344	8	43.00	4-14	-	-
FC	288	411	78	7715	117*	23.16	1	33	121	-	52214	25778	795	32.42	8-50	36	5
ODI	11	7	4	35	11*	11.66	-	-	1	-	612	400	9	44.44	2-37	-	
List A	400	257	81	2884	79*	16.38	-	9	133	-	18325	13515	452	29.90	5-43	1	
20/20 Int																	
20/20	52	35	13	379	40*	17.22	-	-	14	-	1029	1211	45	26.91	3-19	-	

VAN DER WATH, J. J.   Northamptonshire

Name: Johannes (<u>Johan</u>) Jacobus van der Wath
Role: Right-hand bat, right-arm fast-medium
bowler; all-rounder
Born: 10 January 1978, Newcastle, Natal,
South Africa
County debut: 2005 (Sussex),
2007 (Northamptonshire)
ODI debut: 2005-06
Twenty20 Int debut: 2005-06
50 wickets in a season: 1
Place in batting averages: 182nd av. 25.11
(2008 190th av. 21.14)
Place in bowling averages: 17th av. 24.74
(2008 13th av. 20.30)
Education: Ermelo High School

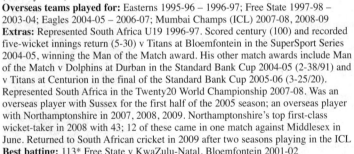

Overseas tours: South Africa A to Sri Lanka 2005-06, to Zimbabwe 2006-07;
South Africa to Australia 2005-06 (VB Series), to Sri Lanka 2006, to Zimbabwe
(one-day series) 2007-08
Overseas teams played for: Easterns 1995-96 – 1996-97; Free State 1997-98 –
2003-04; Eagles 2004-05 – 2006-07; Mumbai Champs (ICL) 2007-08, 2008-09
Extras: Represented South Africa U19 1996-97. Scored century (100) and recorded
five-wicket innings return (5-30) v Titans at Bloemfontein in the SuperSport Series
2004-05, winning the Man of the Match award. His other match awards include Man
of the Match v Dolphins at Durban in the Standard Bank Cup 2004-05 (2-38/91) and
v Titans at Centurion in the final of the Standard Bank Cup 2005-06 (3-25/20).
Represented South Africa in the Twenty20 World Championship 2007-08. Was an
overseas player with Sussex for the first half of the 2005 season; an overseas player
with Northamptonshire in 2007, 2008, 2009. Northamptonshire's top first-class
wicket-taker in 2008 with 43; 12 of these came in one match against Middlesex in
June. Returned to South African cricket in 2009 after two seasons playing in the ICL
Best batting: 113* Free State v KwaZulu-Natal, Bloemfontein 2001-02
Best bowling: 7-60 Northamptonshire v Middlesex, Uxbridge 2008
Stop press: Despite the county's appeal, both Johan van der Wath and Riki Wessels
will be prevented from playing for Northamptonshire in 2010 after the introduction by
the ECB of tighter regulations governing work permits means thay have lost their
Kolpak status

2009 Season

	M	Inn	NO	Runs	HS	Avg	100	50	Ct	St	Balls	Runs	Wkts	Avg	BB	5I	10M
Test																	
FC	13	19	1	452	85	25.11	-	3	4	-	2187	1237	50	24.74	5-71	1	-
ODI																	
List A	6	4	1	76	35*	25.33	-	-	1	-	252	211	6	35.16	3-55	-	
20/20 Int																	
20/20	12	10	5	176	29*	35.20	-	-	2	-	240	311	13	23.92	3-23	-	

Career Performances

	M	Inn	NO	Runs	HS	Avg	100	50	Ct	St	Balls	Runs	Wkts	Avg	BB	5I	10M
Test																	
FC	94	139	23	2828	113*	24.37	2	17	29	-	15772	7937	310	25.60	7-60	15	1
ODI	10	8	2	89	37*	14.83	-	-	3	-	526	551	13	42.38	2-21	-	
List A	131	103	31	1985	91	27.56	-	11	31	-	5703	4600	164	28.04	4-31	-	
20/20 Int	8	4	1	46	21	15.33	-	-	-	-	186	231	8	28.87	2-31	-	
20/20	60	42	14	494	48*	17.64	-	-	5	-	1187	1479	56	26.41	3-23	-	

VAN JAARSVELD, M.   Kent

Name: Martin van Jaarsveld
Role: Right-hand top-order bat, right-arm
off-spin bowler
Born: 18 June 1974, Klerksdorp, South Africa
Height: 6ft 2in **Weight:** 12st 12lbs
Nickname: Jarre
County debut: 2004 (Northamptonshire),
2005 (Kent)
County cap: 2005 (Kent)
Test debut: 2002-03
ODI debut: 2002-03
1000 runs in a season: 5
1st-Class 200s: 3
Place in batting averages: 11th av. 68.59
(2008 31st av. 47.91)
Place in bowling averages: (2008 12th av. 20.00)
Parents: Leon and Isobel
Wife and date of marriage: Jill, 6 May 2005
Education: Warmbads High School; University of Pretoria
Qualifications: BComm (Financial Management)
Overseas tours: South Africa A to Sri Lanka 1998, to Zimbabwe 2002-03, to
Australia 2002-03; South Africa Academy to Zimbabwe 1998-99; South Africa to

England 2003, to New Zealand 2003-04, to Sri Lanka 2004, to England (ICC Champions Trophy) 2004, to India 2004-05

Overseas teams played for: Northern Transvaal/Northerns Titans 1994-95 – 2003-04; Titans 2004-05 –

Career highlights to date: 'Playing for South Africa. Being chosen as one of the five Cricketers of the Year in South Africa 2002'

Cricket moments to forget: 'Losing the NatWest Series final [playing for South Africa] at Lord's, July 2003'

Cricket superstitions: 'Left pad first when padding up'

Cricketers particularly admired: Gary Kirsten, Michael Atherton

Young players to look out for: Neil Dexter, Joe Denly

Other sports played: Golf, tennis

Other sports followed: Rugby (Blue Bulls), football (Blackburn Rovers)

Favourite band: Snow Patrol

Relaxations: 'Spending time with friends and family'

Extras: Scored 182* and 158* v Griqualand West at Centurion 2001-02, becoming only the second batsman to record two 150s in the same match in South Africa. Player of the SuperSport Series 2001-02 (934 runs at 84.90); also topped South African first-class averages 2001-02 (1268 runs at 74.58). One of *South African Cricket Annual*'s five Cricketers of the Year 2002. Was an overseas player with Northamptonshire 2004. Scored a century in each innings (118/111) on first-class debut for Kent, v Warwickshire at Canterbury 2005, becoming the first Kent debutant to achieve the feat. Scored 168 v Surrey at Tunbridge Wells 2005, in the process sharing with Robert Key (189) in a new Kent record third-wicket partnership (323). Retired from international cricket in February 2005. Leading run-scorer in the SuperSport Series 2006-07 with 828 runs (av. 55.20). Finished top of the Kent first-class batting averages for 2008 with 1150 runs. PCA Player of the Year 2008. Is no longer considered an overseas player

Opinions on cricket: 'I think the standard of county cricket, with the inclusion of overseas players and the odd Kolpak player is very strong and although there is a lot of resistance I do think the English game has benefited from it.'

Best batting: 262* Kent v Glamorgan, Cardiff 2005

Best bowling: 5-33 Kent v Surrey, The Oval, 2008

2009 Season

	M	Inn	NO	Runs	HS	Avg	100	50	Ct	St	Balls	Runs	Wkts	Avg	BB	5I	10M
Test																	
FC	16	25	3	1509	182	68.59	7	7	30	-	427	241	4	60.25	2-15	-	-
ODI																	
List A	9	9	1	262	132*	32.75	1	-	5	-	192	191	3	63.66	2-25	-	
20/20 Int																	
20/20	12	10	1	326	75*	36.22	-	3	5	-	6	11	0		-	-	

Career Performances

	M	Inn	NO	Runs	HS	Avg	100	50	Ct	St	Balls	Runs	Wkts	Avg	BB	5I	10M
Test	9	15	2	397	73	30.53	-	3	11	-	42	28	0		-	-	-
FC	222	373	34	15587	262*	45.97	48	75	329	-	2940	1516	42	36.09	5-33	1	-
ODI	11	7	1	124	45	20.66	-	-	4	-	31	18	2	9.00	1-0	-	
List A	250	232	37	7973	132*	40.88	14	48	144	-	1389	1228	30	40.93	3-13	-	
20/20 Int																	
20/20	80	71	10	1573	76*	25.78	-	11	52	-	78	116	4	29.00	2-19	-	

VAUGHAN, M. P. Yorkshire

Name: Michael Paul Vaughan
Role: Right-hand bat, off-spin bowler
Born: 29 October 1974, Eccles, Manchester
Height: 6ft 2in **Weight:** 11st 7lbs
Nickname: Frankie, Virgil
County debut: 1993
County cap: 1995
Benefit: 2005
Test debut: 1999-2000
ODI debut: 2000-01
Twenty20 Int debut: 2005
1000 runs in a season: 4
Place in batting averages: 222nd av. 19.87
(2008 161st av. 25.00)
Parents: Graham John and Dee
Wife and date of marriage: Nichola, September 2003
Children: Tallulah Grace, 4 June 2004; Archie, December 2005
Family links with cricket: Father played league cricket for Worsley CC. Brother plays for Sheffield Collegiate. Mother is related to the famous Tyldesley family (Lancashire and England)
Education: Silverdale Comprehensive, Sheffield
Qualifications: 7 GCSEs
Overseas tours: Yorkshire to West Indies 1994, to South Africa 1995, to Zimbabwe 1996; England U19 to India 1992-93, to Sri Lanka 1993-94 (c); England A to India 1994-95, to Australia 1996-97, to Zimbabwe and South Africa 1998-99 (c); England to South Africa 1999-2000, to Pakistan and Sri Lanka 2000-01, to India and New Zealand 2001-02, to Australia 2002-03, to Africa (World Cup) 2002-03, to Bangladesh and Sri Lanka 2003-04 (c), to West Indies 2003-04 (c), to Zimbabwe (one-day series) 2004-05 (c), to South Africa 2004-05 (c), to Pakistan 2005-06 (c), to India 2005-06 (c), to Australia 2006-07 (C'wealth Bank Series; c), to West Indies (World Cup) 2006-07 (c), to Sri Lanka 2007-08 (Test c), to New Zealand 2007-08 (Test c)

Cricketers particularly admired: Darren Lehmann, 'all the Yorkshire and England squads'
Other sports played: Football (Baslow FC), golf (10 handicap)
Other sports followed: Football (Sheffield Wednesday), all golf
Relaxations: Most sports. 'Enjoy a good meal with friends'
Extras: Maurice Leyland Batting Award 1990; Cricket Society's Most Promising Young Cricketer 1993; A. A. Thompson Memorial Trophy 1993. Scored 1066 runs in first full season of first-class cricket 1994. Captained England U19. PCA Player of the Year 2002. Highest-scoring batsman in Test cricket for the calendar year 2002 (1481 runs). One of *Wisden*'s Five Cricketers of the Year 2003. Topped Pricewaterhouse Coopers rankings for Test batsmen in early summer 2003. Vodafone Cricketer of the Year 2002-03. Scored century in each innings (103/101*) in the first Test v West Indies at Lord's 2004. His international awards include England's Man of the [Test] Series v India 2002 (615 runs at 102.50) and Man of the [Test] Series v Australia 2002-03 (633 runs at 63.30), as well as Man of the Match v Australia at Edgbaston in the ICC Champions Trophy 2004 (86/2-42 plus run-out). England one-day captain from May 2003 to June 2007 and England Test captain from July 2003; led England to a Test series win over Australia in 2005, their first Ashes success for 18 years, and was appointed OBE in 2006 New Year Honours. Book *A Year in the Sun* published 2003. Scored century (103) in the second Test v West Indies at his home ground of Headingley 2007 on his return to Test cricket after 18 months out through injury. England 12-month central contract 2007-08. Resigned England captaincy before the final Test v South Africa in 2008, England having already lost the series. Announced his immediate retirement from all forms of professional cricket at the end of June 2009
Best batting: 197 England v India, Trent Bridge 2002
Best bowling: 4-39 Yorkshire v Oxford University, The Parks 1994

2009 Season

	M	Inn	NO	Runs	HS	Avg	100	50	Ct	St	Balls	Runs	Wkts	Avg	BB	5I	10M
Test																	
FC	6	8	0	159	43	19.87	-	-	-	-	0	0	0		-	-	-
ODI																	
List A	6	6	0	280	82	46.66	-	3	1	-	78	66	0		-	-	
20/20 Int																	
20/20	9	9	1	188	41*	23.50	-	-	1	-	6	9	0		-		-

Career Performances

	M	Inn	NO	Runs	HS	Avg	100	50	Ct	St	Balls	Runs	Wkts	Avg	BB	5I	10M
Test	82	147	9	5719	197	41.44	18	18	44	-	978	561	6	93.50	2-71	-	-
FC	268	468	27	16295	197	36.95	42	68	117	-	9342	5245	114	46.00	4-39	-	-
ODI	86	83	10	1982	90*	27.15	-	16	25	-	796	649	16	40.56	4-22	-	
List A	282	273	25	7238	125*	29.18	3	46	88	-	3381	2604	78	33.38	4-22	-	
20/20 Int	2	2	0	27	27	13.50	-	-	-	-	0	0	0		-	-	
20/20	18	18	1	319	41*	18.76	-	-	2	-	54	81	1	81.00	1-21	-	

VINCE, J. M.　　　　　　　　　　　Hampshire

Name: <u>James</u> Michael Vince
Role: Right-hand bat, right-arm medium/
off-spin bowler
Born: 14 March 1991, Cuckfield, Sussex
County debut: 2009
Place in batting averages: 183rd av. 25.08
Education: St Mary's CE Primary School,
Warminster Secondary School
Overseas tours: England U19 to Bangladesh 2009
Overseas teams played for: Melville CC,
Australia 2008-09
Other sports played: Football (former Reading FC
Academy player)
Extras: Has played for Chippenham CC and
Wiltshire CCC; has represented Wiltshire at U15 and
U17 level, as well as representing West of England at U17 level. Scored a century for
Hampshire Academy v Portsmouth aged 14. First century for Hampshire 2nd XI 2007.
Scored a career-best 210, including 33 boundaries, for Melville v Midland-Guildford
in October 2008. Awarded a development contract at Hampshire for 2009; signed a
new two-year contract with the county in November 2009
Best batting: 75 Hampshire v Nottinghamshire, Rose Bowl 2009

2009 Season

	M	Inn	NO	Runs	HS	Avg	100	50	Ct	St	Balls	Runs	Wkts	Avg	BB	5I	10M
Test																	
FC	9	13	1	301	75	25.08	-	1	3	-	60	37	0		-	-	-
ODI																	
List A	6	6	1	257	93	51.40	-	2	1	-	0	0	0		-	-	
20/20 Int																	
20/20																	

Career Performances

	M	Inn	NO	Runs	HS	Avg	100	50	Ct	St	Balls	Runs	Wkts	Avg	BB	5I	10M
Test																	
FC	9	13	1	301	75	25.08	-	1	3	-	60	37	0		-	-	-
ODI																	
List A	6	6	1	257	93	51.40	-	2	1	-	0	0	0		-	-	
20/20 Int																	
20/20																	

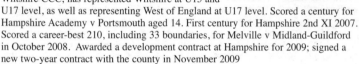

VOGES, A. C.   Nottinghamshire

Name: <u>Adam</u> Charles Voges
Role: Right-hand bat, left-arm wrist-spin bowler
Born: 4 October 1979, Subiaco, Perth, Australia
Height: 6ft 1in
Nickname: Kenny, Hank
County debut: 2007 (one-day, Hampshire),
2008 (first-class, Nottinghamshire)
ODI debut: 2006-07
Twenty20 Int debut: 2007-08
Place in batting averages: 4th av. 77.44
(2008 82nd av. 36.88)

Overseas tours: Australia U19 to England 1999;
Australian Cricket Academy to Bangladesh 2000-01,
to South Africa 2006-07, to Zimbabwe 2006-07 (c);
University of Western Australia to India 2006-07;
Australia to New Zealand (one-day series) 2006-07, to South Africa (ICC Champions Trophy) 2009-10, to India (one-day) 2009-10; Australia A to Pakistan 2007-08, to India 2008-09
Overseas teams played for: Western Australia 2002-03 –
Extras: Played for the Prime Minister's XI v West Indians 2005-06 and v England XI 2006-07. Represented Australia Centre of Excellence in Cricket Australia Emerging Players Tournament 2006. Scored 62-ball 100* v New South Wales at Sydney in the ING Cup 2004-05, the then fastest century in the competition's history, winning Man of the Match award. His other match awards include Man of the Match v Victoria at Perth in the ING Cup 2006-07 (82). Was a temporary overseas player with Hampshire during the 2007 season as a replacement for Stuart Clark. Made Twenty20 Int debut v New Zealand at Perth 2007-08. Overseas player with Nottinghamshire since 2008
Best batting: 180 Western Australia v Tasmania, Hobart 2007-08
Best bowling: 4-92 Western Australia v South Australia, Adelaide 2006-07

2009 Season

	M	Inn	NO	Runs	HS	Avg	100	50	Ct	St	Balls	Runs	Wkts	Avg	BB	5I	10M
Test																	
FC	8	10	1	697	139	77.44	1	6	8	-	201	100	3	33.33	1-2	-	-
ODI																	
List A	11	10	2	194	48	24.25	-	-	4	-	164	143	6	23.83	3-25	-	
20/20 Int	1	1	1	11	11*		-	-	-	-	0	0	0		-	-	
20/20	7	7	3	209	82*	52.25	-	1	1	-	24	44	0		-	-	

Career Performances

	M	Inn	NO	Runs	HS	Avg	100	50	Ct	St	Balls	Runs	Wkts	Avg	BB	5I	10M
Test																	
FC	74	123	15	4184	180	38.74	8	22	96	-	2297	1251	34	36.79	4-92	-	-
ODI	2	2	1	88	72	88.00	-	1	1	-	36	51	0		-	-	
List A	81	77	16	2626	104*	43.04	2	21	30	-	1070	937	20	46.85	3-25	-	
20/20 Int	4	3	1	63	26	31.50	-	-	2	-	12	5	2	2.50	2-5	-	
20/20	44	43	8	1184	82*	33.82	-	7	19	-	203	304	12	25.33	2-4	-	

WAGG, G. G. Derbyshire

Name: Graham Grant Wagg
Role: Right-hand bat, left-arm fast-medium bowler
Born: 28 April 1983, Rugby
Height: 6ft **Weight:** 13st
Nickname: Waggy, GG
County debut: 2002 (Warwickshire), 2006 (Derbyshire)
County cap: 2007
50 wickets in a season: 2
Place in batting averages: 209th av. 21.00 (2008 152 av. 26.90)
Place in bowling averages: 91st av. 37.72 (2008 48th av. 26.98)
Parents: John and Dawn
Marital status: Single, 'but getting close to the special day'
Children: Brayden Grant, 28 September 2008
Family links with cricket: 'Dad played for Warwickshire Seconds, and coached in local leagues in Rugby'
Education: Ashlawn School, Rugby; Warwickshire College
Qualifications: Level 1 cricket coach ('coached in South Africa and Holland')
Off-season: 'Spend as much time as possible with my little boy and my girlfriend Jade'
Overseas tours: Warwickshire Development tour to South Africa 1998, to West Indies 2000; England A to Malaysia and India 2003-04; England Sixes to Hong Kong 2008-09, 2009-10
Overseas teams played for: Hams Tech, East London, South Africa 1999; HBS, Netherlands
Career highlights to date: 'Winning our first match for Derby at Derby for four years. Getting 6-38 against Somerset [at Taunton 2006] to win us the game. My first first-class century in 2008. Taking ten wickets and scoring 100 runs in the same

game.'

Cricket moments to forget: 'Bowling at Cameron White at Derby when he made 260 in no time. Ravi Bopara getting dropped on 0, then smacking me all around the ground afterwards (thanks, Birchy!)'

Cricketers particularly admired: Brett Lee, Ravi Bopara

Young players to look out for: Dan Redfern (Derbyshire)

Other sports played: Snooker, fishing, football, rugby

Other sports followed: Football (Manchester United), snooker (Ronnie O'Sullivan)

Relaxations: 'Casino, snooker, partying'

Extras: Represented England U16, U17, U18, U19 as well as Development of Excellence (Midlands) XI. Scored 42* from 50 balls, 51 from 57 balls and took 4-43 on first-class debut v Somerset at Edgbaston 2002. NBC Denis Compton Award for the most promising young Warwickshire player 2003. ECB National Academy 2003-04. Took over 50 wickets in 2008 for the second season in succession

Best batting: 108 Derbyshire v Northamptonshire, Northampton 2008

Best bowling: 6-35 Derbyshire v Surrey, Derby 2009

2009 Season

	M	Inn	NO	Runs	HS	Avg	100	50	Ct	St	Balls	Runs	Wkts	Avg	BB	5I	10M
Test																	
FC	14	14	1	273	71	21.00	-	1	4	-	3129	1773	47	37.72	6-35	3	-
ODI																	
List A	9	9	3	141	35	23.50	-	-	2	-	420	331	8	41.37	2-51	-	
20/20 Int																	
20/20	10	9	1	94	62	11.75	-	1	3	-	204	282	8	35.25	2-41	-	

Career Performances

	M	Inn	NO	Runs	HS	Avg	100	50	Ct	St	Balls	Runs	Wkts	Avg	BB	5I	10M
Test																	
FC	64	87	11	1942	108	25.55	1	10	22	-	11140	6778	206	32.90	6-35	8	1
ODI																	
List A	71	56	6	764	45	15.28	-	-	19	-	2699	2472	77	32.10	4-35	-	
20/20 Int																	
20/20	45	38	8	455	62	15.16	-	1	13	-	724	989	34	29.08	3-23	-	

94. This Pakistan Test wicketkeeper took 201 catches and effected 27 stumpings between 1967 and 1984. Name him.

WAGH, M. A.   Nottinghamshire

Name: <u>Mark</u> Anant Wagh
Role: Right-hand bat, off-spin bowler
Born: 20 October 1976, Birmingham
Height: 6ft 2in **Weight:** 13st
Nickname: Waggy
County debut: 1997 (Warwickshire), 2007
(Nottinghamshire)
County cap: 2000 (Warwickshire)
1000 runs in a season: 6
1st-Class 200s: 1
1st-Class 300s: 1
Place in batting averages: 98th av. 37.00
(2008 36th av. 46.95)
Parents: Mohan and Rita
Marital status: Single

Education: King Edward's School, Birmingham; Keble College, Oxford
Qualifications: BA degree, Level 2 coaching
Overseas tours: Warwickshire U19 to South Africa 1992; ECB National Academy
to Australia 2001-02; MCC to Uganda 2007-08
Career highlights to date: '315 at Lord's 2001'
Cricket moments to forget: 'Too many to mention'
Cricketers particularly admired: Andy Flower
Favourite band: Dido
Extras: Oxford Blue 1996-98; Oxford University captain 1997. Scored maiden first-
class century (116) for Oxford University v Glamorgan at The Parks 1997, following
up with another hundred (101) in the second innings. His 315 v Middlesex at Lord's
2001 is the equal second highest individual Championship score made at Lord's
behind Jack Hobbs's 316* in 1926 (although Percy Holmes's 315 in 1925 was
unbeaten). C&G Man of the Match award for his 102* v Kent at Edgbaston 2004.
Included in preliminary England one-day squad of 30 for ICC Champions Trophy
2004
Best batting: 315 Warwickshire v Middlesex, Lord's 2001
Best bowling: 7-222 Warwickshire v Lancashire, Edgbaston 2003

	M	Inn	NO	Runs	HS	Avg	100	50	Ct	St	Balls	Runs	Wkts	Avg	BB	5I	10M
Test																	
FC	15	24	2	814	147	37.00	3	2	4	-		0	0	0		-	-	-
ODI																	
List A	13	13	1	372	85	31.00	-	4	2	-		0	0	0		-	-
20/20 Int																	
20/20																	

Career Performances

	M	Inn	NO	Runs	HS	Avg	100	50	Ct	St	Balls	Runs	Wkts	Avg	BB	5I	10M
Test																	
FC	187	308	26	11234	315	39.83	28	55	80	-	8697	4611	100	46.11	7-222	2	-
ODI																	
List A	111	107	9	2715	102*	27.70	1	21	21	-	1096	862	25	34.48	4-35	-
20/20 Int																	
20/20	18	15	0	288	56	19.20	-	1	5	-	75	106	5	21.20	2-16	-

WAINWRIGHT, D. J. Yorkshire

Name: <u>David</u> John Wainwright
Role: Left-hand bat, left-arm orthodox
spin bowler
Born: 21 March 1985, Pontefract
Height: 5ft 9in **Weight:** 9st 6lbs
Nickname: Wainers
County debut: 2004
Place in batting averages: 66th av. 42.00
Place in bowling averages: 57th av. 31.69
Parents: Paul and Debbie
Marital status: Single
Family links with cricket: 'Grandfather (Harry
Heritage) represented Yorkshire Schoolboys 1950-51
and played for Yorkshire 2nd XI. He was also a left-
arm orthodox spinner'
Education: Hemsworth High School; Hemsworth Arts and Community College;
Loughborough University
Qualifications: 10 GCSEs, 3 A-levels, Sports Science and Physics degree,
Level 2 coaching
Off-season: 'Part of the England Performance Programme tour to South Africa'
Overseas tours: Yorkshire U15 to South Africa 2000; Yorkshire to Abu Dhabi 2008,
2009; England Lions to UAE 2010

Overseas teams played for: Grovedale CC, Geelong, Melbourne 2006-07
Career highlights to date: 'Winning at Lord's in BUSA final for Loughborough. My first first-class century at Hove [September 2008]'
Cricketers particularly admired: Brian Lara, Daniel Vettori
Young players to look out for: Oliver Hannon-Dalby (Yorkshire)
Other sports played: Football, golf
Other sports followed: Football (Liverpool FC)
Injuries: 'Split webbing between fingers – out for three weeks'
Favourite band: Akon
Relaxations: Listening to music
Extras: Best bowling award at Bunbury Festival for North of England U15. Played for LUCCE 2005-06. Represented British Universities 2005-06. Member of England Performance Programme squad 2009-10
Opinions on cricket: 'Twenty20 cricket is becoming more popular and an extension of that competition is good for the game to get more people interested in cricket. I feel a 50-over competition would be more beneficial to players than a 40-over competition because that is what is played at international level. Also, as a spin bowler, I think spinners would benefit from this as there is less chance of them bowling in a 40-over competition because of all the powerplays that have been introduced. The longer format of the game is still the one at the top of the players' priorities as the best team in the country will come out top.'
Best batting: 104* Yorkshire v Sussex, Hove 2008
Best bowling: 5-134 Yorkshire v Sussex, Hove 2009

2009 Season

	M	Inn	NO	Runs	HS	Avg	100	50	Ct	St	Balls	Runs	Wkts	Avg	BB	5I	10M
Test																	
FC	10	13	4	378	102*	42.00	1	1	-	-	1502	824	26	31.69	5-134	1	-
ODI																	
List A	12	6	4	55	15*	27.50	-	-	6	-	516	358	10	35.80	3-33	-	
20/20 Int																	
20/20	6	2	2	3	3*		-	-	3	-	90	115	5	23.00	2-21	-	

Career Performances

	M	Inn	NO	Runs	HS	Avg	100	50	Ct	St	Balls	Runs	Wkts	Avg	BB	5I	10M
Test																	
FC	24	31	8	817	104*	35.52	2	2	9	-	3392	1836	56	32.78	5-134	1	-
ODI																	
List A	31	13	8	117	26	23.40	-	-	7	-	1062	817	22	37.13	3-33	-	
20/20 Int																	
20/20	15	5	3	9	3*	4.50	-	-	5	-	251	288	13	22.15	3-6	-	

WAKELY, A. G.   Northamptonshire

Name: Alexander (<u>Alex</u>) George Wakely
Role: Right-hand bat, right-arm off-spin bowler;
batting all-rounder
Born: 3 November 1988, Hammersmith, London
Height: 6ft 2in **Weight:** 14st 1lbs
Nickname: Baby Seal, Wakers, Pup, Hologram,
Allan, 'The Hof'
County debut: 2007
Place in batting averages: 192nd av. 24.05
(2008 223rd av. 16.85)
Parents: Jan and John
Marital status: Single
Family links with cricket: 'Father played club
and representative cricket for 30 years. Uncle
umpired first-class cricket for ten years'
Education: Bedford School
Qualifications: 11 GCSEs, 3 A-levels, Level 2 coaching
Career outside cricket: 'Golf, pilot'
Off-season: 'Play cricket abroad, relax and spend some time with my girlfriend
and family'
Overseas tours: Bedford School to Australia 2003, 2005-06; England U16 to
South Africa 2004; England U19 to Malaysia 2006-07, to Malaysia (U19 World
Cup) 2007-08 (c), to Sri Lanka 2007-08
Career highlights to date: '108 for England U19 to beat Sri Lanka 2007' (*HSBC
Invitational 1st Tri-Series 2006-07, Kuala Lumpur*); 63 on my debut for Somerset in
2007. Marcus Trescothick as my first wicket. 113* v Glamorgan (2009) and bowling
a double wicket maiden in my first over in one-day cricket v Lancashire'
Cricket moments to forget: 'Diving for a ball on Championship debut and losing my
trousers (still get letters about it). First-ball duck on my TV debut v Sussex. Being
knocked out of the Twenty20 Cup at finals day in the semi-final'
Cricket superstitions: 'Always chew gum when I bat'
Favourite sledging line: 'The best sledging against me was on a televised game
abroad – me and the other player were going at it but forgot he was on stump mic,
so he ended up with a ban!'
Cricketers particularly admired: Ricky Ponting, David Sales, Michael Clarke,
Herschelle Gibbs
Young players to look out for: James Kettleborough (Middlesex),
Rob Newton (Northamptonshire)
Other sports played: Golf (6 handicap), hockey (regional and GB trials),
football (Meppershall FC), rugby (school 1st XV, VIIs finalist), tennis (LTA
junior competitions)
Other sports followed: Rugby (Northampton Saints)

Favourite band: Elvis, The Beach Boys

Relaxations: 'Love watching DVDs, love seeing my friends, but most of all enjoy going home to spend time with my girlfriend, Tasha'

Extras: *Daily Telegraph* Bunbury Scholarship for Batting 2004. Played for Bedfordshire in the 2005 C&G. Northamptonshire Young Player of the Year 2006, 2007. Represented England U19 2007. Scored 66 on first-class debut v Somerset at Taunton, following up with 55 in second match v Nottinghamshire at Northampton 2007. NBC Denis Compton Award for the most promising young Northamptonshire player 2008

Opinions on cricket: 'Twenty20 should be introduced to players at a young age so they can perfect the skills needed to take it to the next level.'

Best batting: 113* Northamptonshire v Glamorgan, Cardiff 2009

Best bowling: 2-62 Northamptonshire v Somerset, Taunton 2007

2009 Season

	M	Inn	NO	Runs	HS	Avg	100	50	Ct	St	Balls	Runs	Wkts	Avg	BB	5I	10M
Test																	
FC	12	20	1	457	113*	24.05	1	2	10	-	66	64	0		-	-	-
ODI																	
List A	8	7	2	85	32	17.00	-	-	1	-	0	0	0		-	-	
20/20 Int																	
20/20	6	5	1	86	29*	21.50	-	-	1	-	0	0	0		-	-	

Career Performances

	M	Inn	NO	Runs	HS	Avg	100	50	Ct	St	Balls	Runs	Wkts	Avg	BB	5I	10M
Test																	
FC	21	36	2	744	113*	21.88	1	5	15	-	246	195	3	65.00	2-62	-	-
ODI																	
List A	12	11	2	103	32	11.44	-	-	2	-	18	14	2	7.00	2-14	-	
20/20 Int																	
20/20	6	5	1	86	29*	21.50	-	-	1	-	0	0	0		-	-	

WALKER, G. W. Leicestershire

Name: <u>George</u> William Walker
Role: Left-hand bat, slow left-arm bowler
Born: 12 May 1984, Norwich
Height: 5ft 10in **Weight:** 12st 8lbs
Nickname: Walks, Walksy
County debut: 2002
Parents: John and Sarah
Marital status: Single
Family links with cricket: 'Just a family interest'
Education: Norwich School; Loughborough
University ('studying Geography')
Qualifications: 9 GCSEs, 1 AS-level,
3 A-levels, ECB Level II coaching award
Career highlights to date: 'First-class debut v
Kent 2002. First first-class wicket – Chris Adams –
v Sussex 2003'
Cricket moments to forget: 'Any dropped catch'
Cricketers particularly admired: Brian Lara, Jacques Kallis
Young players to look out for: David Thomas, Rod Bunting (both Norfolk)
Other sports played: Football ('only socially for fun')
Other sports followed: Football ('mighty Norwich City FC')
Favourite band: 50 Cent, Eminem, Groove Armada, JT
Relaxations: 'Socialising, films, chilling with friends'
Extras: Played for Norfolk from U12 to 1st XI. Represented Midlands U13 and U14
and England U14, U15 and U17. LUCCE 2004.
Opinions on cricket: 'Enjoy the Twenty20 game – was a good way to increase
spectators and fans as, without these, cricket as a business would fail.'
Best batting: 37* Leicestershire v Kent, Canterbury 2002
Best bowling: 1-75 Leicestershire v Derby, Derby 2009

2009 Season

	M	Inn	NO	Runs	HS	Avg	100	50	Ct	St	Balls	Runs	Wkts	Avg	BB	5I	10M
Test																	
FC	3	4	0	21	13	5.25	-	-	-	-	300	159	2	79.50	1-75	-	-
ODI																	
List A																	
20/20 Int																	
20/20																	

Career Performances

	M	Inn	NO	Runs	HS	Avg	100	50	Ct	St	Balls	Runs	Wkts	Avg	BB	5I	10M
Test																	
FC	7	9	2	95	37*	13.57	-	-	2	-	594	349	3	116.33	1-75	-	-
ODI																	
List A																	
20/20 Int																	
20/20																	

WALKER, M. J. Essex

Name: Matthew (<u>Matt</u>) Jonathan Walker
Role: Left-hand bat
Born: 2 January 1974, Gravesend
Height: 5ft 6in **Weight:** 13st
Nickname: Walks, Pumba
County debut: 1992-93 (Kent)
County cap: 2000 (Kent)
Benefit: 2008 (Kent)
1000 runs in a season: 4
1st-Class 200s: 1
Place in batting averages: 106th av. 35.85
(2008 257th av. 10.44)
Parents: Richard and June
Wife and date of marriage: Claudia,
25 September 1999

Children: Charlie Jack, 20 November 2002; Lexie, 19 January 2007
Family links with cricket: 'Dad played Kent and Middlesex 2nd XIs and was on Lord's groundstaff. Grandfather kept wicket for Kent. Mum was women's cricket coach.'
Education: King's School, Rochester
Qualifications: 9 GCSEs, 2 A-levels, advanced cricket coaching certificate
Career outside cricket: PE teacher
Overseas tours: Kent U17 to New Zealand 1990-91; England U19 to Pakistan 1991-92, to India 1992-93 (c); Kent to Zimbabwe 1993
Career highlights to date: 'Captaining England U19. Winning Norwich Union League 2001'
Cricket moments to forget: 'Losing Lord's B&H final v Surrey 1997'
Cricket superstitions: 'None'
Cricketers particularly admired: Darren Lehmann, Nick Knight, Mark Ramprakash
Other sports played: Hockey (England U14-U21 – captain U15-U17), rugby (Kent U18)

Other sports followed: Football (Charlton Athletic), hockey (Gore Court HC)
Favourite band: Razorlight, Arctic Monkeys, Jeff Buckley
Relaxations: 'Music and films'
Extras: Captained England U16 cricket and hockey teams in same year. Sir John Hobbs Silver Jubilee Memorial Prize for outstanding U16 cricketer 1989. Captained England U19 1993. Woolwich Kent League's Young Cricketer of the Year 1994. Scored 275* against Somerset in 1996 – the highest ever individual score by a Kent batsman at Canterbury. Ealham Award for Fielding Excellence 2003, 2004, 2005. Cowdrey Award (Kent Player of the Year) 2004, 2006. Vice-captain of Kent 2005. Denness Award (Kent leading run-scorer) 2006. Scored century in each innings (142/157) v Lancashire at Canterbury 2007. Signed for Essex for the 2009 season. Became an Eminent Roffensian 1995
Best batting: 275* Kent v Somerset, Canterbury 1996
Best bowling: 2-21 Kent v Middlesex, Canterbury 2004

2009 Season

	M	Inn	NO	Runs	HS	Avg	100	50	Ct	St	Balls	Runs	Wkts	Avg	BB	5I	10M
Test																	
FC	17	31	3	1004	150	35.85	2	3	13	-	20	22	0		-	-	-
ODI																	
List A	14	12	3	256	69*	28.44	-	1	2	-	18	19	0		-	-	
20/20 Int																	
20/20	10	9	1	157	50	19.62	-	1	-	-	0	0	0		-	-	

Career Performances

	M	Inn	NO	Runs	HS	Avg	100	50	Ct	St	Balls	Runs	Wkts	Avg	BB	5I	10M
Test																	
FC	200	332	35	10772	275*	36.26	27	43	134	-	1896	1143	22	51.95	2-21	-	-
ODI																	
List A	271	246	37	5921	117	28.33	3	35	72	-	904	759	30	25.30	4-24	-	
20/20 Int																	
20/20	50	47	7	922	58*	23.05	-	2	4	-	0	0	0		-	-	

WALLACE, M. A.　　　　　　　　Glamorgan

Name: <u>Mark</u> Alexander Wallace
Role: Left-hand bat, wicket-keeper; county
vice-captain
Born: 19 November 1981, Abergavenny
Height: 5ft 10in **Weight:** 11st 13lbs
Nickname: Wally, Wash, Grommit,
Screech, Marcellus
County debut: 1999
County cap: 2003
50 dismissals in a season: 2
Place in batting averages: 152nd av. 29.31
(2008 140th av. 27.83)
Parents: Ryland and Alvine
Wife and date of marriage: Lucy, 28 October 2007
Children: Harry Alexander, 30 October 2008
Family links with cricket: 'Father plays for Wales Over 50s and club cricket
at Abergavenny'
Education: Crickhowell High School; Staffordshire University; University Wales
Institute, Cardiff (UWIC)
Qualifications: 10 GCSEs, 2 A-levels, Level 2 coach, BA (Hons) Journalism
Career outside cricket: 'Journalist'
Off-season: 'Studying for a Masters Degree and covering local rugby for
a newspaper'
Overseas tours: England U19 to New Zealand 1998-99, to Malaysia and (U19 World
Cup) Sri Lanka 1999-2000, to India 2000-01; ECB National Academy to Australia
2001-02, to Australia and Sri Lanka 2002-03; MCC to New Zealand and Papua New
Guinea 2007
Overseas teams played for: Port Adelaide, South Australia 2002-03; Redlands Tigers,
Brisbane 2004-05, 2005-06
Career highlights to date: 'Academy tours. Winning one-day league with Glamorgan
2002 and 2004. Captaining Glamorgan. Scoring a century at Lord's (*LV County
Championship v Middlesex, April 2009*)'
Cricket moments to forget: 'Summer 2007. Getting caught at slip off Robert Croft
in a league game this year (2009) – should have slogged him'
Cricket superstitions: 'Too many'
Cricketers particularly admired: Ian Healy, Adam Gilchrist, Chris Read,
Brendon McCullum, Steve James, David Hemp, Matt Elliott, Keith Piper
Young players to look out for: James Harris, Gareth Rees and Tom Maynard
(all Glamorgan), James Taylor (Leicestershire)
Other sports played: Golf
Other sports followed: Football (Merthyr Tydfil FC), rugby (Cardiff Blues)

Injuries: 'Cracked thumb – no time out'
Favourite band: Stereophonics, Shania Twain
Relaxations: 'Most sports, reading and time with the family'
Extras: Represented England U17. Represented England U19 1998, 1999 and 2000 (captain for second 'Test' 2000). Made first-class debut v Somerset at Taunton 1999 aged 17 years 287 days – youngest ever Glamorgan wicket-keeper. NBC Denis Compton Award 1999. Captained ECB National Academy to innings victory over Commonwealth Bank [Australian] Cricket Academy at Adelaide 2001-02. Glamorgan Young Player of the Year 2002. Byron Denning Glamorgan Clubman of the Year Award 2003. Captained Glamorgan v Somerset at Taunton 2007 in the absence of David Hemp, Glamorgan One-day Player of the Year 2008. Glamorgan Supporters' Player of the Year 2008
Opinions on cricket: 'Age-related fee payments to counties is only going to harm the domestic game when it's widely considered to be at its strongest level ever. Age should neither be a barrier, nor a pink ticket, to selection. Using a different ball in divisions one and two of the County Championship is a ridiculous situation.'
Best batting: 139 Glamorgan v Surrey, The Oval 2009

2009 Season

	M	Inn	NO	Runs	HS	Avg	100	50	Ct	St	Balls	Runs	Wkts	Avg	BB	5I	10M
Test																	
FC	17	22	0	645	139	29.31	2	-	31	6	0	0	0		-	-	-
ODI																	
List A	14	12	3	173	60	19.22	-	1	10	7	0	0	0		-	-	
20/20 Int																	
20/20	10	10	0	96	26 9	.60	-	-	4	5	0	0	0		-	-	

Career Performances

	M	Inn	NO	Runs	HS	Avg	100	50	Ct	St	Balls	Runs	Wkts	Avg	BB	5I	10M
Test																	
FC	151	241	16	6222	139	27.65	8	28	375	33	0	0	0		-	-	-
ODI																	
List A	142	113	26	1689	85	19.41	-	3	138	36	0	0	0		-	-	
20/20 Int																	
20/20	52	42	12	587	35*	19.56	-	-	18	12	0	0	0		-	-	

WALLER, M. T. C.   Somerset

Name: Maximilian (<u>Max</u>) Thomas Charles Waller
Role: Right-hand bat, right-arm leg-break bowler
Born: 3 March 1988, Salisbury, Wiltshire
Height: 6ft **Weight:** 12st
Nickname: Maxi, Gecko, Walz
County debut: 2009
Parents: Ian and Julie
Marital status: Single
Family links with cricket: 'Dad – playing
member of the MCC'
Education: Millfield School; Bournemouth University
Qualifications: 10 GCSEs, 3 A-levels
Off-season: 'ECB Performance Programme, and
training in South Africa in January and February'
Overseas tours: Millfield School to South Africa
2002; West of England to West Indies 2002, 2003
Overseas teams played for: Gosnells CC, Perth 2007-08
Career highlights to date: 'Twenty20 finals day 2009. Twenty20 Champions
League in India'
Cricket moments to forget: 'Being caught and bowled by Scott Styris in the
final over v Deccan Chargers (Twenty20 Champions League) in Hyderabad, 2009'
Cricket superstitions: 'None'
Favourite sledging line: '"Knock his floppy off!"'
Cricketers particularly admired: Shane Warne, Brian Lara
Young players to look out for: Jos Buttler (Somerset), Adam Wheater (Essex)
Other sports played: 'Tennis, county hockey, golf, darts'
Other sports followed: Football (Arsenal)
Favourite band: Kings of Leon, Duffy, Lily Allen, Kanye West
Relaxations: 'Listening to music, travelling, Starbucks and playing "Steve
Bucknor Says…"'
Extras: Member of England Performance Programme squad 2009-10
Opinions on cricket: 'Twenty20 – fast, exciting, explosive!'
Best batting: 28 Somerset v Hampshire, Rose Bowl 2009
Best bowling: 2-27 Somerset v Sussex, Hove 2009

2009 Season

	M	Inn	NO	Runs	HS	Avg	100	50	Ct	St	Balls	Runs	Wkts	Avg	BB	5I	10M
Test																	
FC	4	6	1	67	28	13.40	-	-	1	-	496	320	5	64.00	2-27	-	-
ODI																	
List A	7	2	2	3	2*		-	-	1	-	240	219	7	31.28	2-34	-	
20/20 Int																	
20/20	10	2	0	0	0	0.00	-	-	3	-	162	208	10	20.80	3-17	-	

Career Performances

	M	Inn	NO	Runs	HS	Avg	100	50	Ct	St	Balls	Runs	Wkts	Avg	BB	5I	10M
Test																	
FC	4	6	1	67	28	13.40	-	-	1	-	496	320	5	64.00	2-27	-	-
ODI																	
List A	7	2	2	3	2*		-	-	1	-	240	219	7	31.28	2-34	-	
20/20 Int																	
20/20	13	5	1	1	1 . 25		-	-	4	-	210	263	13	20.23	3-17	-	

WALTERS, S. J. Surrey

Name: Stewart Jonathan Walters
Role: Right-hand bat, right-arm
slow-medium/leg-spin bowler
Born: 25 June 1983, Mornington, Victoria, Australia
Height: 6ft **Weight:** 12st 12lbs
Nickname: Steve
County debut: 2005 (one-day), 2006 (first-class)
Place in batting averages: 132nd av. 31.83
(2008 229th av. 15.87)
Parents: Stewart and Sue
Wife and date of marriage: Jacki,
24 February 2006
Children: Maddison Summer, 19 February 2008
Family links with cricket: 'Father played'
Education: Guildford Grammar School, Perth
Career outside cricket: Fitness trainer
Off-season: 'Perth CC in Western Australia'
Overseas teams played for: Midland-Guildford CC, Perth; Perth CC 2007-08 –
Career highlights to date: 'Scoring 91 v Northamptonshire in Pro40, 2008. Scoring 142 v Essex at Guildford, 2009. The Surrey captaincy' (*he was appointed acting captain for the latter part of the 2009 season in Mark Butcher's absence through injury*)

Cricket moments to forget: 'Mushtaq Ahmed! Any dropped catch off Jade Dernbach'
Cricket superstitions: 'Right pad first'
Cricketers particularly admired: Justin Langer, Alistair Brown
Young players to look out for: Alistair Brown (Nottinghamshire)
Other sports played: Australian Rules football (AFL)
Other sports followed: Australian Rules (Collingwood)
Injuries: 'Mental frustration!'
Favourite band: Mark Butcher's band
Relaxations: 'Family time is always relaxing'
Extras: Captain of Western Australia U17 for two years. Signed a new contract with Surrey 2009
Opinions on cricket: 'If you do the same you will get the same results – the game is moving forward and it doesn't wait for anybody.'
Best batting: 188 Surrey v Leicestershire, The Oval 2007
Best bowling: 1-4 Surrey v Durham, Riverside 2007

2009 Season

	M	Inn	NO	Runs	HS	Avg	100	50	Ct	St	Balls	Runs	Wkts	Avg	BB	5I	10M
Test																	
FC	11	18	0	573	188	31.83	2	1	15	-	114	75	0		-	-	-
ODI																	
List A	10	10	1	346	85	38.44	-	3	3	-	24	36	1	36.00	1-36	-	
20/20 Int																	
20/20	10	9	0	143	34	15.88	-	-	5	-	6	9	1	9.00	1-9	-	

Career Performances

	M	Inn	NO	Runs	HS	Avg	100	50	Ct	St	Balls	Runs	Wkts	Avg	BB	5I	10M
Test																	
FC	28	44	1	1094	188	25.44	2	3	30	-	408	224	3	74.66	1-4	-	-
ODI																	
List A	35	33	5	729	91	26.03	-	4	16	-	165	179	3	59.66	1-12	-	
20/20 Int																	
20/20	21	15	2	192	34	14.76	-	-	12	-	18	26	1	26.00	1-9	-	

95. How many runs did Younis Khan and Mohammad Yousuf put on for the third wicket versus England at Headingley in August 2006?

WARNER, D. A.   Durham

Name: <u>David</u> Andrew Warner
Role: Left-hand bat, occasional off/leg-spin bowler
Born: 27 October 1986, Paddington, NSW
Height: 5ft 7in
Nickname: Lloyd
County debut: 2009 (one-day)
ODI debut: 2008-09
Twenty20 Int debut: 2008-09
Education: Matraville Public School; Randwick
Boys High School
Overseas tours: Australia U19 to India 2005-06, to
Sri Lanka (U19 World Cup) 2005-06; Australia Sixes
to Hong Kong 2008-09; Australia to England 2009
(one-day series); New South Wales to India (ICC
Champions League) 2009-10

Overseas teams played for: New South Wales 2007 – ; Delhi Daredevils 2009-10
Extras: Made his first-grade debut with Eastern Suburbs CC at the age of 15. Made
his one-day international debut against South Africa in Melbourne, January 2009,
becoming the first man in 132 years to debut for Australia in any form of the game
without a first-class appearance to his name; he made 89 from only 43 balls, including
seven fours and six sixes; his 19-ball half-century was the second fastest ever in
Twenty20 internationals. Signed for Durham in February 2009 as their overseas
player in the Twenty20 Cup. Will continue with Durham in 2010
Best batting: 42 New South Wales v Western Australia, Sydney 2008-09

2009 Season

	M	Inn	NO	Runs	HS	Avg100	50	Ct	St	Balls	Runs	Wkts	Avg	BB	5I	10M
Test																
FC																
ODI																
List A																
20/20 Int	3	3	0	96	63	32.00	-	1	1	-	0	0	0		-	-
20/20	7	7	0	209	63	29.85	-	2	1	-	0	0	0		-	-

Career Performances

	M	Inn	NO	Runs	HS	Avg100	50	Ct	St	Balls	Runs	Wkts	Avg	BB	5I	10M
Test																
FC	1	1	0	42	42	42.00	-	-	2	-	12	7	0		-	-	-
ODI	7	7	0	106	69	15.14	-	1	1	-	0	0	0		-	-
List A	20	20	2	627	165*	34.83	1	3	5	-	66	60	1	60.00	1-32	-
20/20 Int	8	8	0	273	89	34.12	-	2	1	-	0	0	0		-	-
20/20	36	36	1	1005	89	28.71	-	6	7	-	0	0	0		-	-

WATERS, H. T.   Glamorgan

Name: <u>Huw</u> Thomas Waters
Role: Right-hand bat, right-arm
medium-fast bowler
Born: 26 September 1986, Cardiff
Height: 6ft 2in **Weight:** 14st
Nickname: Muddy
County debut: 2005
Parents: Valerie and Donald
Marital status: Single
Family links with cricket: 'Long line of club
cricketers, most notably Big Don, a stalwart of
the old Three Counties League'
Education: Llantarnam CS;

Monmouth School
Qualifications: 8 GCSEs, 'a couple of
A-levels – somehow!', Level 2 coaching
Overseas tours: West Region to West Indies 2002; Wales U16 to Jersey 2002;
Monmouth School to St Lucia 2003; England U19 to Bangladesh 2005-06, to
Sri Lanka (U19 World Cup) 2005-06
Overseas teams played for: Westmeadows CC, Melbourne 2007-08
Career highlights to date: 'Making debut. Taking my first five-for'
Cricket moments to forget: 'Running Matt Elliott out on 96 when I was
batting with him!'
Cricketers particularly admired: Glenn McGrath
Young players to look out for: 'Our academy boys'
Other sports played: Football ('mainly during warm-ups')
Other sports followed: Football (Manchester United)
Favourite band: Coldplay, 'any indie rock'
Relaxations: 'Listening to music, watching Manchester United'
Extras: Played for Wales Minor Counties in the C&G 2005 and in Minor
Counties competitions 2004-07
Opinions on cricket: 'Gaining more interest due to Twenty20. Should just have
one one-day competition. Glad only one overseas – means youngsters get more
of a chance.'
Best batting: 34 Glamorgan v Kent, Canterbury 2005
Best bowling: 5-86 Glamorgan v Somerset, Taunton 2006

2009 Season

	M	Inn	NO	Runs	HS	Avg	100	50	Ct	St	Balls	Runs	Wkts	Avg	BB	5I	10M
Test																	
FC																	
ODI																	
List A	3	1	0	2	2	2.00	-	-	-	-	108	92	3	30.66	2-42	-	
20/20 Int																	
20/20																	

Career Performances

	M	Inn	NO	Runs	HS	Avg	100	50	Ct	St	Balls	Runs	Wkts	Avg	BB	5I	10M
Test																	
FC	23	37	18	145	34	7.63	-	-	6	-	2532	1479	39	37.92	5-86	1	-
ODI																	
List A	15	8	3	24	8	4.80	-	-	-	-	624	622	11	56.54	3-47	-	
20/20 Int																	
20/20																	

WATERS, S. R. Surrey

Name: <u>Seren</u> Robert Waters
Role: Right-hand bat, legbreak bowler
Born: 11 April 1990, Nairobi, Kenya
Height: 6ft
Nickname: Burundi
County debut: No first team appearance
ODI debut: 2008-09
Family links with cricket: Father David is a stalwart of cricket in Kenya, former Chairman of selectrors of the Kenyan national cricket team and current Chairman and club cricket captain of Kenya Kongonis CC
Education: Cranleigh School
Overseas tours: Kenya to South Africa (one-day series) 2008-09, to South Africa (ICC World Cup Qualifiers) 2008-09; to Canada (ICC Intercontinental Cup) 2009
Extras: Has played for Surrey at U17 and U19 level; on his debut for Surrey U17 he scored a double century. Made his debut for Surrey Second X1 in 2008. Also plays for the Old Cranleighan CC and Weybridge CC. Awarded Emerging Player contract for 12 months from October 2009
Best batting: 157* Kenya v Canada, King City, Canada 2009-10

Career Performances

	M	Inn	NO	Runs	HS	Avg	100	50	Ct	St	Balls	Runs	Wkts	Avg	BB	5I	10M
Test																	
FC	3	6	1	294	157*	58.80	1	1	2	-	6	3	0		-	-	-
ODI	12	12	0	261	74	21.75	-	1	3	-	0	0	0		-	-	
List A	14	14	1	326	74	25.07	-	2	4	-	0	0	0		-	-	
20/20 Int																	
20/20																	

WATKINS, R. E. Glamorgan

Name: Ryan Edward Watkins
Role: Left-hand bat, right-arm medium-fast bowler, occasional wicket-keeper; all-rounder
Born: 9 June 1983, Abergavenny, Monmouthshire
Height: 6ft **Weight:** 13st 12lbs
Nickname: Tets, Maverick, Big Red, Commando, Roider
County debut: 2003 (one-day), 2005 (first-class)
Place in batting averages: (2008 239th av. 13.42)
Parents: Huw and Gaynor
Wife and date of marriage: Lisa, 16 October 2005
Family links with cricket: 'Father was captain of Abergavenny 4ths; brother all-rounder for Blackwood CC'
Education: Pontllanfraith Comprehensive School; Crosskeys College
Qualifications: Numerous academic qualifications; Level 2 coaching, qualified tyre and exhaust fitter, 'Working Safely' Level 1 qualified
Career outside cricket: 'Police officer'
Off-season: 'In Adelaide, playing for the Buffalos'
Overseas tours: Glamorgan to Guernsey 2006, 2007, Mumbai 2008; Commandos tour to Egypt 2007
Overseas teams played for: North Balwyn CC, Victoria, Australia 2003; Adelaide CC 2009-10
Career highlights to date: 'Being voted Man of the Match in the Glamorgan v Nottinghamshire end-of-season football victory. Glamorgan Young Player of the Year 2006. Every time I play for Glamorgan.'
Cricket moments to forget: None. 'I thoroughly enjoy every moment I play cricket'

Cricket superstitions: 'Right pad on first'
Cricketers particularly admired: Brian Lara, Matt Hayden, Jason Gillespie, Gareth Rees
Other sports played: Football (Clydach Wasps AFC – Gwent County Div 1)
Other sports followed: Football (Tottenham Hotspur), rugby (Cardiff Blues), 'Markham Tigers'
Favourite band: Westlife
Relaxations: 'Playing golf. Walking my dog, Missy'
Extras: Played for Wales Minor Counties in Minor Counties competitions 2003-07. Took five catches in an innings v Gloucestershire at Cheltenham 2006, equalling Glamorgan record. Glamorgan Young Player of the Year 2006. Glamorgan's leading wicket-taker in the 2008 season, Released at the end of the 2009 season
Opinions on cricket: 'Love it!'
Best batting: 87 Glamorgan v Essex, Cardiff 2006
Best bowling: 4-40 Glamorgan v Worcestershire, Worcester 2006

2009 Season

	M	Inn	NO	Runs	HS	Avg	100	50	Ct	St	Balls	Runs	Wkts	Avg	BB	5I	10M
Test																	
FC																	
ODI																	
List A	4	4	1	54	28	18.00	-	-	1	-	66	95	0		-	-	
20/20 Int																	
20/20	10	9	0	82	18	9.11	-	-	3	-	180	214	11	19.45	5-16	1	

Career Performances

	M	Inn	NO	Runs	HS	Avg	100	50	Ct	St	Balls	Runs	Wkts	Avg	BB	5I	10M
Test																	
FC	33	56	4	951	87	18.28	-	2	18	-	2932	1927	39	49.41	4-40	-	-
ODI																	
List A	24	20	4	269	39	16.81	-	-	2	-	676	745	16	46.56	2-25	-	
20/20 Int																	
20/20	27	13	3	93	18	9.30	-	-	8	-	456	603	31	19.45	5-16	1	

WELLS, L. W. P. Sussex

Name: <u>Luke</u> William Peter Wells
Role: Left-hand bat, right-arm, offbreak bowler
Born: 29 December 1990, Eastbourne
County debut: No first team appearance
Family links with cricket: Father Alan played for
both Sussex and England, as did his uncle Colin
Education: St Bede's School, Upper Dicker;
Loughborough University
Extras: Sussex Academy 2009. Sussex 2nd XI 2009;
on the strength of his performances with the 2nd XI
Sussex signed him on a three-year summer contract
in October 2009. Represented England U19 v
Bangladesh in "Test" and ODI matches, July 2009.
Plays club cricket for Brighton & Hove CC (Sussex
Premier League)

WESSELS, M. H. Northamptonshire

Name: Mattheus Hendrik (<u>Riki</u>) Wessels
Role: Right-hand bat, wicket-keeper
Born: 12 November 1985, Nambour, Australia
Height: 5ft 10½in **Weight:** 11st 7lbs
Nickname: Weasel, Blood
County debut: 2005
Place in batting averages: 110th av. 35.48
(2008 109th av. 32.00)
Parents: Kepler and Sally
Marital status: Engaged
Family links with cricket: 'Dad' (*Kepler Wessels
played Test and ODI cricket for Australia and
South Africa between 1982-83 and 1994-95*)
Education: Woodridge College, Port Elizabeth

Overseas teams played for: Pirates CC, Port
Elizabeth; Mid West Rhinos 2009-10
Cricket moments to forget: 'Getting my first and last pair; tearing my hamstring
going for a run'
Cricket superstitions: 'None'
Cricketers particularly admired: Justin Langer
Young players to look out for: Alex Wakely (Northamptonshire)

Other sports played: Hockey, archery
Other sports followed: Football (Spurs)
Favourite band: Linkin Park
Extras: Northamptonshire Academy Players' Player of the Year 2004. Northamptonshire Young Player of the Year (Frank Rudd Trophy) 2004. Made first-class debut for MCC v West Indians at Arundel 2004. Scored maiden first-class century (102) v Somerset at Northampton 2005 after coming to the wicket on a hat-trick ball
Best batting: 109 Northamptonshire v Surrey, The Oval 2009
Stop press: Despite the county's appeal, both Johan van der Wath and Riki Wessels will be prevented from playing for Northamptonshire in 2010 after the introduction by the ECB of tighter regulations governing work permits means thay have lost their Kolpak status

2009 Season

	M	Inn	NO	Runs	HS	Avg	100	50	Ct	St	Balls	Runs	Wkts	Avg	BB	5I	10M
Test																	
FC	15	25	0	887	109	35.48	1	7	27	1	6	0	0		-	-	-
ODI																	
List A	12	12	1	266	57	24.18	-	1	9	-	0	0	0		-	-	
20/20 Int																	
20/20	12	11	2	261	66*	29.00	-	2	2	3	0	0	0		-	-	

Career Performances

	M	Inn	NO	Runs	HS	Avg	100	50	Ct	St	Balls	Runs	Wkts	Avg	BB	5I	10M
Test																	
FC	66	108	7	3037	109	30.06	4	20	127	11	18	13	0		-	-	-
ODI																	
List A	69	65	7	1565	100	26.98	1	8	53	-	0	0	0		-	-	
20/20 Int																	
20/20	46	37	8	668	66*	23.03	-	2	11	12	0	0	0		-	-	

WESTFIELD, M. S. Essex

Name: <u>Mervyn</u> Simon Westfield
Role: Right-hand bat, right-arm fast bowler
Born: 5 May 1988, Romford
Height: 6ft 1in **Weight:** 12st
Nickname: Swerve
County debut: 2005
Parents: Pamela and Mervyn
Marital status: Single
Family links with cricket: 'Dad used to play cricket and my older brother played for Essex for a couple of years'
Education: The Chafford School, Rainham; Havering College
Qualifications: 8 GCSEs, Level 1 coaching
Overseas tours: England U16 to South Africa 2004-05; England U19 to Malaysia 2006-07
Career highlights to date: 'Taking four wickets against Somerset and scoring 32 runs as well in 2006'
Cricketers particularly admired: Andy Flower, Andy Bichel
Other sports followed: Football (Manchester United)
Favourite band: TOK
Relaxations: 'Socialising with friends, listening to music'
Extras: Wanstead U11 Young Player of the Year 1997. Wanstead U11 All-Rounder of 1998. Havering District U13 Best Innings 2000. MCC Cricketer of the Year 2003, 2004. *Daily Telegraph* Bunbury Scholar 2003 (Best Fast Bowler; scholarship entailed a week's training with England A)
Best batting: 32 Essex v Somerset, Southend 2006
Best bowling: 4-72 Essex v Somerset, Southend 2006

96. Name the Bangladesh wicket-keeper who made 87 dismissals (78 caught, nine stumped) between 2000 and 2007.

2009 Season

	M	Inn	NO	Runs	HS	Avg	100	50	Ct	St	Balls	Runs	Wkts	Avg	BB	5I	10M
Test																	
FC	2	1	0	1	1	1.00	-	-	-	-	211	82	4	20.50	3-25	-	-
ODI																	
List A	6	2	1	25	17	25.00	-	-	1	-	210	205	5	41.00	2-32	-	
20/20 Int																	
20/20																	

Career Performances

	M	Inn	NO	Runs	HS	Avg	100	50	Ct	St	Balls	Runs	Wkts	Avg	BB	5I	10M
Test																	
FC	7	8	3	46	32	9.20	-	-	1	-	655	416	11	37.81	4-72	-	-
ODI																	
List A	8	4	3	31	17	31.00	-	-	2	-	246	243	5	48.60	2-32	-	
20/20 Int																	
20/20																	

WESTLEY, T.   Essex

Name: Thomas (Tom) Westley
Role: Right-hand top-order bat, right-arm off-spin bowler
Born: 13 March 1989, Cambridge
Height: 6ft 2in
Nickname: Spongebob, Pup
County debut: 2006 (one-day), 2007 (first-class)
Place in batting averages: 86th av. 39.07 (2008 183rd av. 21.92)
Parents: Ade and Mags
Family links with cricket: 'Dad has played village club cricket in Cambridgeshire, along with uncle and brother'
Education: Linton Village College; Hills Road Sixth Form College (both Cambridge)
Overseas tours: England U16 to South Africa 2004-05; England U19 to Malaysia (U19 World Cup) 2007-08
Cricket moments to forget: 'King pair against Surrey 2nd XI 2005'
Cricket superstitions: 'Mark my crease three times before every over and after every boundary'
Cricketers particularly admired: Steve Waugh, Sachin Tendulkar, Andy Flower, Alastair Cook

Young players to look out for: Mervyn Westfield, Adam Wheater (both Essex)
Other sports followed: Football (Newcastle United)
Extras: Played for MCC 2007. Represented England U19 2007 and 2008 (captain).
NBC Denis Compton Award for most promising young Essex Player 2008, 2009
Best batting: 132 Essex v Derbyshire, Derby 2009
Best bowling: 2-33 Essex v Glamorgan, Cardiff 2009

2009 Season

	M	Inn	NO	Runs	HS	Avg	100	50	Ct	St	Balls	Runs	Wkts	Avg	BB	5I	10M
Test																	
FC	10	17	3	547	132	39.07	1	2	6	-	174	104	2	52.00	2-33	-	-
ODI																	
List A	1	1	0	0	0	0.00	-	-	-	-	0	0	0		-	-	
20/20 Int																	
20/20																	

Career Performances

	M	Inn	NO	Runs	HS	Avg	100	50	Ct	St	Balls	Runs	Wkts	Avg	BB	5I	10M
Test																	
FC	25	43	8	1077	132	30.77	1	5	14	-	294	186	4	46.50	2-33	-	-
ODI																	
List A	4	3	0	37	36	12.33	-	-	-	-	0	0	0		-	-	
20/20 Int																	
20/20																	

WESTWOOD, I. J.   Warwickshire

Name: Ian James Westwood
Role: Left-hand opening bat, right-arm
off-spin bowler; county captain
Born: 13 July 1982, Birmingham
Height: 5ft 8in **Weight:** 11st
Nickname: Westy, Wezzo
County debut: 2003
Place in batting averages: 161st av. 27.81
(2008 127th av. 29.76)
Parents: Ann and Dave
Marital status: Single
Family links with cricket: 'Brother
played Warwickshire Youth cricket'
Education: Wheelers Lane, Kings Heath;
Solihull Sixth Form College
Qualifications: 10 GCSEs, BTEC Sports Science, Level 2 cricket coaching

Overseas tours: Warwickshire Development squad to Cape Town 1998
Overseas teams played for: Hawkesbury CC, Sydney 2001-02; University CC, Perth 2004-05, 2005-06
Career highlights to date: 'First Championship century for Warwickshire'
Cricket moments to forget: 'Too many to mention'
Cricket superstitions: 'None'
Cricketers particularly admired: Brian Lara
Young players to look out for: Chris Woakes (Warwickshire)
Other sports played: Football (Coleshill Town FC)
Other sports followed: Football (Birmingham City)
Favourite band: Fleetwood Mac
Relaxations: 'Music, poker, TV'
Extras: Scored 250* v Worcestershire 2nd XI at Barnt Green 2003, sharing with Jonathan Trott (248) in an opening partnership of 429; also took 6-104 in Worcestershire 2nd XI's only innings. NBC Denis Compton Award for most promising young Warwickshire player 2007. County captain since November 2008
Opinions on cricket: 'Too many Kolpaks.'
Best batting: 178 Warwickshire v West Indies A, Edgbaston 2006
Best bowling: 2-39 Warwickshire v Hampshire, Rose Bowl 2009

2009 Season

	M	Inn	NO	Runs	HS	Avg	100	50	Ct	St	Balls	Runs	Wkts	Avg	BB	5I	10M
Test																	
FC	15	25	3	612	133	27.81	1	4	10	-	114	49	2	24.50	2-39	-	-
ODI																	
List A	14	10	1	125	33	13.88	-	-	-	-	18	17	0		-	-	
20/20 Int																	
20/20	11	8	3	143	49*	28.60	-	-	2	-	0	0	0		-	-	

Career Performances

	M	Inn	NO	Runs	HS	Avg	100	50	Ct	St	Balls	Runs	Wkts	Avg	BB	5I	10M
Test																	
FC	66	112	12	3423	178	34.23	7	18	34	-	371	222	6	37.00	2-39	-	-
ODI																	
List A	48	40	5	762	65	21.77	-	3	4	-	210	167	2	83.50	1-28	-	
20/20 Int																	
20/20	28	18	11	239	49*	34.14	-	-	5	-	54	91	5	18.20	3-29	-	

WHARF, A. G. B.　　　　　Glamorgan

Name: Alexander (<u>Alex</u>) George Busfield Wharf
Role: Right-hand bat, right-arm fast-
medium bowler; all-rounder
Born: 4 June 1975, Bradford
Height: 6ft 4in **Weight:** 15st
Nickname: Gangster
County debut: 1994 (Yorkshire),
1998 (Nottinghamshire), 2000 (Glamorgan)
County cap: 2000 (Glamorgan)
ODI debut: 2004
50 wickets in a season: 1
Place in batting averages: (2008 187th av. 21.54)
Place in bowling averages: (2008 133rd av. 42.66)
Parents: Jane and Derek
Wife and date of marriage: Shelley Jane,
1 December 2001

Children: Tristan Jack Busfield Wharf, 15 November 1997;
Alf Alexander Busfield Wharf, 30 June 2001
Family links with cricket: Father played local cricket and brother Simon plays
local cricket
Education: Buttershaw Upper School, Bradford; Thomas Danby College, Leeds
Qualifications: 6 GCSEs, City & Guilds in Sports Management, NCA coaching
award, junior football coaching award
Overseas tours: England to Zimbabwe (one-day series) 2004-05, to South Africa
2004-05 (one-day series); England VI to Hong Kong 2005; England A to West Indies
2005-06; various pre-season tours with Yorkshire, Nottinghamshire and Glamorgan;
MCC to Uganda 2007-08
Overseas teams played for: Somerset West, Cape Town 1993-95; Johnsonville CC,
Wellington, New Zealand 1996-97; Universities, Wellington 1998-99
Cricket moments to forget: 'Too many to mention'
Cricket superstitions: 'None'
Cricketers particularly admired: Ian Botham
Other sports played: Football
Other sports followed: Football (Manchester United, Bradford City)
Relaxations: 'Spending time with family and friends, movies, PlayStation 2,
eating (too much), TV, gym, football'
Extras: Took hat-trick (Wagg, Knight, Pretorius) v Warwickshire at Edgbaston in the
totesport League 2004. Had figures of 6-5 v Kent at Cardiff in the totesport League
2004 (match reduced to 25 overs a side). Made ODI debut v India at Trent Bridge in
the NatWest Challenge 2004, taking a wicket in each of his first three overs, finishing
with 3-30 and winning Man of the Match award. Retired at the end of the 2009 season

Best batting: 128* Glamorgan v Gloucestershire, Bristol 2007
Best bowling: 6-59 Glamorgan v Gloucestershire, Bristol 2005

2009 Season

	M	Inn	NO	Runs	HS	Avg	100	50	Ct	St	Balls	Runs	Wkts	Avg	BB	5I	10M
Test																	
FC																	
ODI																	
List A	1	0	0	0	0		-	-	-	-	0	0	0		-	-	
20/20 Int																	
20/20	5	4	0	20	15	5.00	-	-	-	-	83	115	3	38.33	2-23	-	

Career Performances

	M	Inn	NO	Runs	HS	Avg	100	50	Ct	St	Balls	Runs	Wkts	Avg	BB	5I	10M
Test																	
FC	121	184	29	3570	128*	23.03	6	14	63	-	16825	10941	293	37.34	6-59	5	1
ODI	13	5	3	19	9	9.50	-	-	1	-	584	428	18	23.77	4-24	-	
List A	155	109	22	1411	72	16.21	-	1	42	-	6497	5552	192	28.91	6-5	1	
20/20 Int																	
20/20	34	20	7	157	19	12.07	-	-	5	-	650	1045	39	26.79	4-39	-	

WHEATER, A. J.   Essex

Name: Adam Jack Wheater
Role: Right-hand bat, left-arm spin bowler, wicket-keeper
Born: 13 February 1990, Whipps Cross, London
Height: 5ft 6in **Weight:** 9st 12lbs
Nickname: Wheates
County debut: 2008
Parents: Phillip and Nikki
Marital status: Single
Family links with cricket: 'Father loves cricket'
Education: Millfield School; Cambridge Anglia Ruskin University
Career outside cricket: 'Entrepreneur'
Off-season: 'In education'
Overseas tours: England U19 to South Africa 2008-09; Essex to India

Overseas teams played for: Midland Guildford CC, Perth 2008-09
Cricketers particularly admired: James Foster, Adam Gilchrist
Young players to look out for: Rishabh Shah (Essex Academy)

Other sports played: Hockey, golf
Other sports followed: Hockey (Old Loughtonians)
Injuries: 'Hamstring tendonitis – out for a month'
Favourite band: Kings of Leon
Relaxations: 'FTSE 100'
Extras: Played for Essex U17. Made 2nd XI Championship debut 2006. Played for South U17 in ECB U17 Regional Festival at Loughborough 2007. Has played for England U19. Plays club cricket for Saffron Walden CC. Member of England Performance Programme squad 2009-10
Opinions on cricket: 'The game is becoming more scientific and more professional which means it will evolve quicker.'
Best batting: 36 Essex v CUCCE, Fenner's 2009

2009 Season

	M	Inn	NO	Runs	HS	Avg	100	50	Ct	St	Balls	Runs	Wkts	Avg	BB	5I	10M
Test																	
FC	2	2	0	36	36	18.00	-	-	6	-	0	0	0		-	-	-
ODI																	
List A																		
20/20 Int																		
20/20	3	2	1	7	4	7.00	-	-	1	-	0	0	0		-	-	

Career Performances

	M	Inn	NO	Runs	HS	Avg	100	50	Ct	St	Balls	Runs	Wkts	Avg	BB	5I	10M
Test																		
FC	4	3	0	58	36	19.33	-	-	9	-	0	0	0		-	-	-
ODI																		
List A																		
20/20 Int																		
20/20	3	2	1	7	4	7.00	-	-	1	-	0	0	0		-	-	

---

97. Who, in 1984, became the 100th player to play Test cricket for Pakistan?

WHEELDON, D. A. Worcestershire

Name: <u>David</u> Antony Wheeldon
Role: Top order left-hand bat, right-arm
off-spin bowler
Born: 12 April 1989, Stoke-on-Trent, Staffordshire
Height: 5ft 7in **Weight:** 11st
Nickname: Wheels
County debut: 2009
County colours: 2009
Place in batting averages: 172nd av. 26.66
Parents: Angela and Terry
Education: St Giles Primary School; Painsley
Catholic High School; Moorlands 6th Form;
Worcester University
Qualifications: 12 GCSEs, 3 A-levels
Off-season: 'Training at Worcestershire'
Overseas tours: England U16 to South Africa 2005
Career highlights to date: 'Being named as England U15 player of the year.
Receiving my first-team colours for Worcestershire'
Cricket moments to forget: 'My second first-class game v Durham, scoring 0 and 8'
Cricketers particularly admired: Brian Lara
Young players to look out for: Aneesh Kapil (Worcestershire)
Other sports played: Football
Other sports followed: Football (Stoke City)
Favourite band: Oasis
Relaxations: 'Watching television, sleeping'
Extras: Named Best All-rounder at Bunbury Festival, 2004. England U15 Player of
the Year 2004. Made 2nd XI Championship debut 2006. Played for Staffordshire in the
Minor Counties Championship 2006. Worcestershire Young Cricketer of the Year 2009
Best batting: 87 Worcestershire v Somerset, Taunton 2009

2009 Season

	M	Inn	NO	Runs	HS	Avg	100	50	Ct	St	Balls	Runs	Wkts	Avg	BB	5I	10M
Test																	
FC	5	6	0	160	87	26.66	-	1	3	-	0	0	0		-	-	-
ODI																	
List A																	
20/20 Int																	
20/20																	

Career Performances

	M	Inn	NO	Runs	HS	Avg	100	50	Ct	St	Balls	Runs	Wkts	Avg	BB	5I	10M
Test																	
FC	5	6	0	160	87	26.66	-	1	3	-	0	0	0		-	-	-
ODI																	
List A																	
20/20 Int																	
20/20																	

WHELAN, C. D.

Worcestershire

Name: Christopher (Chris) David Whelan
Role: Right-hand bat, right-arm fast bowler
Born: 8 May 1986, Liverpool
Height: 6ft 2in **Weight:** 12st 8lbs
Nickname: R-Kid, Wheelo, Scouse, Juan
County debut: 2004 (one-day, Middlesex),
2005 (first-class, Middlesex), 2008 (Worcestershire)
Place in batting averages: 248th av. 14.64
(2008 123rd av. 40.10)
Place in bowling averages: 125th av. 48.50
Parents: Sue and Dave
Marital status: Single
Family links with cricket: 'Dad was an
accomplished left-hand opening bat'
Education: St Margaret's High School, Liverpool;
St Margaret's 6th Form
Qualifications: 11 GCSEs, 3 A-levels, Level 1 coaching
Career outside cricket: 'Property'
Overseas tours: Middlesex to Mumbai 2004-05, 2005-06, to Perth, WA 2007-08
Overseas teams played for: Randwick-Petersham, Sydney 2005-06; Fairfield
Liverpool CC, Sydney 2007-08
Career highlights to date: 'Playing at Lord's – Pro40 debut'
Cricket superstitions: 'Clean socks every session'
Cricketers particularly admired: Brett Lee
Young players to look out for: Alexei Kervezee
Other sports played: Football, golf
Other sports followed: Football (Everton)
Favourite band: Fall-out Boy
Relaxations: 'Internet poker; DVDs'
Extras: Merseyside Young Sports Personality of the Year 2004-05. Left Middlesex at
the end of the 2007 season and joined Worcestershire for 2008

Opinions on cricket: 'Cricket is moving in the right direction with emphasis on four-day cricket and Twenty20. Reduce the number of Kolpaks to help English players gain more experience at the top level. '
Best batting: 58 Worcestershire v Middlesex, Kidderminster 2008
Best bowling: 5-95 Worcestershire v Lancashire, Worcester 2009

2009 Season

	M	Inn	NO	Runs	HS	Avg	100	50	Ct	St	Balls	Runs	Wkts	Avg	BB	5I	10M
Test																	
FC	12	17	3	205	47	14.64	-	-	2	-	1392	1067	22	48.50	5-95	1	-
ODI																	
List A	11	5	2	25	11	8.33	-	-	3	-	372	313	14	22.35	4-27	-	
20/20 Int																	
20/20	10	1	1	2	2*		-	-	1	-	200	242	9	26.88	2-27	-	

Career Performances

	M	Inn	NO	Runs	HS	Avg	100	50	Ct	St	Balls	Runs	Wkts	Avg	BB	5I	10M
Test																	
FC	21	25	6	297	58	15.63	-	1	3	-	2182	1681	43	39.09	5-95	1	-
ODI																	
List A	22	11	2	40	11	4.44	-	-	4	-	684	674	23	29.30	4-27	-	
20/20 Int																	
20/20	16	3	2	4	2*	4.00	-	2	-	302	407	16	25.43	2-24	-		

WHITE, C. L. Somerset

Name: <u>Cameron</u> Leon White
Role: Right-hand bat, leg-break bowler
Born: 18 August 1983, Bairnsdale, Victoria, Australia
Height: 6ft 2in **Weight:** 14st 2lbs
Nickname: Bear, Whitey
County debut: 2006
County cap: 2007
Test debut: 2008
ODI debut: 2005-06
Twenty20 Int debut: 2006-07
1000 runs in a season: 2
1st-Class 200s: 2
Overseas tours: Australia U19 to New Zealand

(U19 World Cup) 2001-02; Australia A to Pakistan 2005-06, 2007-08; Australia to Zimbabwe (one-day series) 2003-04; to India 2004-05, to New Zealand (one-day series) 2005-06, to West Indies 2008, to India 2008-09, to England 2009, to India 2009-10

Overseas teams played for: Victoria 2000-01 – ; Royal Challengers Bangalore (IPL)
Extras: Appointed captain of Victoria one-day side 2003-04 (and deputy in Pura Cup) at age 20, becoming the youngest captain in the state's cricket history; overall captain of Victoria since 2004-05. Has won several match awards, including Man of the Match v Queensland at Brisbane in the Pura Cup 2003-04 and v Tasmania at Devonport in the ING Cup 2003-04. Scored 53-ball 116* v Gloucestershire at Taunton 2006, in the process sharing with Justin Langer (90) in a Twenty20 world-record any-wicket partnership of 186 as Somerset reached 250-3 (also then a Twenty20 world record). Scored a world record individual score of 141* (out of 198) from 70 balls v Worcestershire at Worcester 2006. An overseas player with Somerset 2006-07; acting captain of Somerset from late May to mid-August 2006 in the absence of the injured Ian Blackwell. Made Twenty20 International debut v England at Sydney 2006-07, winning Man of the Match award. Will rejoin Somerset for 2010 Twenty20 Cup
Best batting: 260* Somerset v Derbyshire, Derby 2006
Best bowling: 6-66 Victoria v Western Australia, Melbourne 2002-03

2009 Season

	M	Inn	NO	Runs	HS	Avg	100	50	Ct	St	Balls	Runs	Wkts	Avg	BB	5I	10M
Test																	
FC																	
ODI	7	6	1	260	105	52.00	1	1	3	-	0	0	0		-	-	
List A	7	6	1	260	105	52.00	1	1	3	-	0	0	0		-	-	
20/20 Int	1	1	0	55	55	55.00	-	1	-	-	0	0	0		-	-	
20/20	1	1	0	55	55	55.00	-	1	-	-	0	0	0		-	-	

Career Performances

	M	Inn	NO	Runs	HS	Avg	100	50	Ct	St	Balls	Runs	Wkts	Avg	BB	5I	10M
Test	4	7	2	146	46	29.20	-	-	1	-	558	342	5	68.40	2-71	-	-
FC	103	172	21	6351	260*	42.05	15	28	97	-	11556	6773	170	39.84	6-66	2	1
ODI	41	30	8	700	105	31.81	1	2	20	-	325	345	12	28.75	3-5	-	
List A	145	121	19	3412	126*	33.45	4	19	63	-	3688	3276	92	35.60	4-15	-	
20/20 Int	8	8	3	207	55	41.40	-	1	6	-	24	25	1	25.00	1-11	-	
20/20	51	51	12	1389	141*	35.61	2	8	21	-	316	458	22	20.81	4-10	-	

WHITE, G. G. — Nottinghamshire

Name: <u>Graeme</u> Geoffrey White
Role: Right-hand bat, slow left-arm bowler; all-rounder
Born: 18 April 1987, Milton Keynes
Height: 5ft 11in **Weight:** 10st
Nickname: Whitey, Chalky, Pony
County debut: 2006 (Northamptonshire)
Parents: David and Sophie
Marital status: Single
Family links with cricket: Sister Rachel played England Women U17. Father played good standard club cricket and is also a Level 2 coach. Brother Russell played county U11

Education: Stowe School, Buckingham
Qualifications: 9 GCSEs, 1 AS-level, 3 A-levels, Level 2 coaching
Overseas tours: Stowe School to India 2004; England U19 to Sri Lanka (U19 World Cup) 2005-06
Career highlights to date: 'Representing my country at the U19 World Cup in Sri Lanka in 2006 and reaching the semi-finals'
Cricket moments to forget: 'Getting hit for five sixes in one over playing for Stowe School (they kept going further!)'
Cricket superstitions: 'Putting pads on from the top down'
Cricketers particularly admired: Bishan Bedi, Phil Tufnell, Daniel Vettori
Other sports played: Badminton, hockey, football
Other sports followed: Football ('big Manchester United fan')
Favourite band: Kings of Leon, Bloc Party
Relaxations: 'Like listening to music. Playing PS2'
Extras: Represented England U15, U17 and U19. Dorothy Radd Shield (Northamptonshire) 2003. Colin Shillington Award (Stowe School) 2005. NBC Denis Compton Award for the most promising young Northamptonshire player 2004, 2005, 2007. Moved from Northamptonshire to Nottinghamshire in October 2009
Best batting: 65 Northamptonshire v Glamorgan, Colwyn Bay 2007
Best bowling: 2-35 Northamptonshire v CUCCE, Fenner's 2007

2009 Season

	M	Inn	NO	Runs	HS	Avg	100	50	Ct	St	Balls	Runs	Wkts	Avg	BB	5I	10M
Test																	
FC	2	4	2	32	29*	16.00	-	-	-	-	168	110	2	55.00	1-48	-	-
ODI																	
List A	2	2	1	7	4*	7.00	-	-	1	-	95	72	6	12.00	3-30	-	
20/20 Int																	
20/20	2	1	0	8	8	8.00	-	-	-	-	18	21	0			-	-

Career Performances

	M	Inn	NO	Runs	HS	Avg	100	50	Ct	St	Balls	Runs	Wkts	Avg	BB	5I	10M
Test																	
FC	8	10	2	140	65	17.50	-	1	1	-	810	394	5	78.80	2-35	-	-
ODI																	
List A	8	5	1	23	14	5.75	-	-	4	-	305	246	10	24.60	3-30	-	
20/20 Int																	
20/20	6	1	0	8	8	8.00	-	-	1	-	48	91	1	91.00	1-10	-	

WHITE, R. A.   Northamptonshire

Name: Robert (Rob) Allan White
Role: Right-hand bat, leg-spin bowler
Born: 15 October 1979, Chelmsford, Essex
Height: 5ft 11in **Weight:** 13st 7lbs
Nickname: Whitey, Toff
County debut: 2000
1st-Class 200s: 1
1000 runs in a season: 1
Place in batting averages: 102nd av. 36.74
(2008 28th av. 49.38)
Parents: Dennis and Ann
Wife and date of marriage: Emma,
20 December 2008
Family links with cricket: 'Grandfather on Essex
committee for many years. Dad flailed the willow
and brother travels the local leagues high and low'
Education: Stowe School, Buckingham;
St John's College, Durham University; Loughborough University
Qualifications: 9 GCSEs, 3 A-levels, degree in Politics
Overseas tours: British Universities to South Africa 2001
Overseas teams played for: Mount Lawley, Perth, WA 2002-03

Career highlights to date: 'Scoring 277 v Gloucestershire in 2002, the highest maiden century by an Englishman.'
Cricket moments to forget: 'Franklyn Rose telling me my mates had bet £10 that he couldn't injure me, as I walked out to play Lashings. Brother-in-law Ryan Cummings getting me out.'
Cricketers particularly admired: Viv Richards
Young players to look out for: Alex Wakeley
Other sports played: Badminton, squash, golf, kabaddi
Other sports followed: Football (West Ham), rugby (Northampton Saints)
Extras: Northamptonshire League Young Player of the Year and Youth Cricketer of the Year 1999. Northamptonshire Young Player of the Year (Frank Rudd Trophy) 2001. Played for Loughborough UCCE 2001, 2002 and 2003. Recorded the highest maiden century in the history of English first-class cricket (277, including a hundred before lunch on the first day), v Gloucestershire at Northampton 2002 in his fifth first-class match. NBC Denis Compton Award for the most promising young Northamptonshire player 2002. Represented British Universities 2003
Opinions on cricket: 'The structure of cricket has been moving in the right direction over the last five years'
Best batting: 277 Northamptonshire v Gloucestershire, Northampton 2002
Best bowling: 2-30 Northamptonshire v Gloucestershire, Northampton 2002

2009 Season

	M	Inn	NO	Runs	HS	Avg	100	50	Ct	St	Balls	Runs	Wkts	Avg	BB	5I	10M
Test																	
FC	17	31	4	992	193	36.74	1	7	11	-	0	0	0		-	-	-
ODI																	
List A	12	11	1	337	70*	33.70	-	2	4	-	0	0	0		-	-	
20/20 Int																	
20/20	12	12	1	240	59	21.81	-	1	2	-	0	0	0		-	-	

Career Performances

	M	Inn	NO	Runs	HS	Avg	100	50	Ct	St	Balls	Runs	Wkts	Avg	BB	5I	10M
Test																	
FC	87	150	15	4682	277	34.68	7	24	55	-	1120	800	14	57.14	2-30	-	-
ODI																	
List A	76	72	3	1534	111	22.23	2	7	16	-	54	55	2	27.50	2-18	-	
20/20 Int																	
20/20	43	40	4	845	94*	23.47	-	4	8	-	0	0	0		-	-	

WHITE, W. A.   Leicestershire

Name: <u>Wayne</u> Andrew White
Role: Right-hand bat, right-arm
fast-medium bowler; all-rounder
Born: 22 April 1985, Derby
Height: 6ft 2in **Weight:** 13st
Nickname: Chalky, Stix, Philip Schofield
County debut: 2005 (Derbyshire)
Place in batting averages: 213th av. 20.00
Place in bowling averages: 118th av. 44.84
Parents: John and Sharon
Marital status: Single
Family links with cricket: 'Brother plays for
Midlands/Derbyshire'
Education: John Port School, Etwall;
Nottingham University

Qualifications: 11 GCSEs, 4 A-levels, BA Politics
Career outside cricket: 'Semi-professional footballer;
internet business – www.darts-store.com'
Career highlights to date: 'First wicket for Derbyshire – Anthony McGrath.
5-87 v Northamptonshire [2007]'
Cricket moments to forget: '0-107 in the first innings of my debut against Yorkshire'
Cricketers particularly admired: Mike Hendrick, Graeme Welch, Andy Caddick
Other sports played: Football (Gresley Rovers, Burton Albion, Mickleover Sports,
Derby County), golf
Other sports followed: Football (Derby County, LA Galaxy)
Favourite band: Arctic Monkeys, Stone Roses
Relaxations: 'Internet, Xbox 360, spread betting'
Extras: Scored 76 and took 7-18 on club cricket debut for Swarkestone. NBC Denis
Compton Award for the most promising young Derbyshire player 2006. Released at
the end of the 2008 season. Spent a period on trial at Leicestershire prior to the county
signing him for the 2009 season. Signed a new two-year contract with Leicestershire
in October 2009
Best batting: 68 Leicestershire v Glamorgan, Grace Road, 2009
Best bowling: 5-87 Derbyshire v Northamptonshire, Northampton 2007

	M	Inn	NO	Runs	HS	Avg	100	50	Ct	St	Balls	Runs	Wkts	Avg	BB	5I	10M
Test																	
FC	12	19	2	340	68	20.00	-	1	5	-	1185	852	19	44.84	3-91	-	-
ODI																	
List A	15	11	5	140	46*	23.33	-	-	4	-	449	466	13	35.84	4-36	-	
20/20 Int																	
20/20	10	6	1	33	12	6.60	-	-	8	-	188	243	10	24.30	3-27	-	

Career Performances

	M	Inn	NO	Runs	HS	Avg	100	50	Ct	St	Balls	Runs	Wkts	Avg	BB	5I	10M
Test																	
FC	23	35	5	486	68	16.20	-	1	10	-	2930	2052	50	41.04	5-87	1	-
ODI																	
List A	29	21	9	219	46*	18.25	-	-	8	-	994	1004	23	43.65	4-36	-	
20/20 Int																	
20/20	10	6	1	33	12	6.60	-	-	8	-	188	243	10	24.30	3-27	-	

WHITELEY, R. A.   Derbyshire

Name: <u>Ross</u> Andrew Whiteley
Role: Left-hand bat, left-arm medium-fast bowler, wicket-keeper; all-rounder
Born: 13 September 1988, Sheffield, Yorkshire
Height: 6ft 2in **Weight:** 13st 5lbs
Nickname: Rossco
County debut: 2008
Parents: Sue and Steve
Marital status: Single
Family links with cricket: 'Brother, Adam, played Derbyshire age-groups and some Derbyshire 2nd XI games.'
Education: Westfield School, Sheffield; Repton School 6th form; Leeds Metropolitan University
Qualifications: 10 GCSEs, 3 A-levels
Career outside cricket: 'Student'
Off-season: 'Training with the squad in Derby, and also with the University side. Tours to South Africa and Jamaica with Leeds Met.'
Overseas tours: Repton to Sri Lanka 2005; Derbyshire Academy to South Africa 2006
Career highlights to date: 'Making my first-team debut against Glamorgan at Cardiff in a floodlit Pro40 game on Sky.'

Cricket moments to forget: 'Breaking my nose and getting knocked unconscious in winter nets 2005, attempting to pull the triallists'
Cricket superstitions: 'When batting, scrape the mark three times when I come on strike.'
Cricketers particularly admired: Michael Bevan, Ryan Sidebottom
Young players to look out for: Dan Redfern, Edward Jones
Other sports played: Football (Repton 1st XI), rugby (Repton 1st XV)
Other sports followed: Football (Sheffield United)
Favourite band: Oasis – 'but more into funky electro house'
Relaxations: Gym, socialising with friends, DJ-ing, sleep
Extras: Played for Chesterfield CC. Made Derbyshire 2nd XI debut in 2006.
Opinions on cricket: 'The introduction of Twenty20 cricket has had an effect on the way teams go about structuring an innings in all the other forms of cricket, resulting in higher-scoring games and much more interesting run chases.'
Best batting: 27 Derbyshire v Leicestershire, Grace Road 2008

2009 Season

	M	Inn	NO	Runs	HS	Avg	100	50	Ct	St	Balls	Runs	Wkts	Avg	BB	5I	10M
Test																	
FC																	
ODI																	
List A	3	2	0	17	17	8.50	-	-	1	-		12	16	0		-	-
20/20 Int																	
20/20																	

Career Performances

	M	Inn	NO	Runs	HS	Avg	100	50	Ct	St	Balls	Runs	Wkts	Avg	BB	5I	10M
Test																	
FC	1	2	0	45	27	22.50	-	-	-	-	66	38	0		-	-	-
ODI																	
List A	4	3	0	41	24	13.66	-	-	2	-	24	28	0		-	-	
20/20 Int																	
20/20																	

98. Mohammad Ashraful and Mushfiqur Rahim enjoyed a partnership of 191 against Sri Lanka in a Test match played in 2007. For which wicket?

WIGLEY, D. H.   Northamptonshire

Name: <u>David</u> Harry Wigley
Role: Right-hand bat, right-arm
fast-medium bowler
Born: 26 October 1981, Bradford, Yorkshire
Height: 6ft 3in   **Weight:** 14st
Nickname: Wiggy, Wiggers, Wigs
County debut: 2002 (Yorkshire), 2003
(Worcestershire), 2006 (Northamptonshire)
County colours: 2003 (Worcestershire)
Place in batting averages: 269th av. 10.57
Place in bowling averages: 93rd av. 38.43
(2008 106th av. 35.16)
Parents: Max and Judith
Marital status: Single

Family links with cricket: Father played league
cricket in Liverpool Competition, Bradford League and Durham Senior League
Education: St Mary's RC Comprehensive, Menston; Loughborough University
Qualifications: 9 GCSEs, 3 A-levels, degree in Sport and Exercise Science,
Level 1 coaching
Overseas tours: British Universities to Cape Town 2004
Overseas teams played for: Gormandale CC, Victoria 2001; Mount Lawley CC,
Perth 2004-05
Career highlights to date: 'Taking my first five-for in first-class cricket
against Pakistan'
Cricket moments to forget: 'Losing Uni final at Lord's 2004 in last over'
Cricket superstitions: 'Must turn to left to run in and bowl'
Cricketers particularly admired: Darren Gough, Andrew Flintoff
Other sports played: Golf, rugby ('used to play to decent standard; gave up at 16')
Other sports followed: Football (Leeds United), rugby (Llanelli Scarlets)
Relaxations: 'Music, films, golf'
Extras: Played for ECB Schools v Sri Lanka U19 2000. Yorkshire U19 Bowling
Award 2000. Played for Loughborough UCCE 2002-04 (captain 2004), taking 5-52 v
Oxford in the UCCE One-Day Challenge at Lord's and 5-71 v Hampshire at The Rose
Bowl 2002. Represented British Universities 2003 and (as captain) 2004
Best batting: 70 Northamptonshire v Middlesex, Northampton 2007
Best bowling: 6-72 Northamptonshire v Gloucestershire, Northampton 2009

2009 Season

	M	Inn	NO	Runs	HS	Avg	100	50	Ct	St	Balls	Runs	Wkts	Avg	BB	5I	10M
Test																	
FC	12	15	8	74	16	10.57	-	-	5	-	1885	1230	32	38.43	6-72	2	-
ODI																	
List A	1	1	0	2	2	2.00	-	-	3	-	30	38	1	38.00	1-38	-	
20/20 Int																	
20/20																	

Career Performances

	M	Inn	NO	Runs	HS	Avg	100	50	Ct	St	Balls	Runs	Wkts	Avg	BB	5I	10M
Test																	
FC	50	62	22	532	70	13.30	-	2	22	-	7249	4932	136	36.26	6-72	4	-
ODI																	
List A	24	12	0	34	10	2.83	-	-	7	-	822	870	16	54.37	4-37	-	
20/20 Int																	
20/20	2	1	0	1	1	1.00	-	-	-	-	30	33	1	33.00	1-8	-	

WILLEY, D. J.   Northamptonshire

Name: <u>David</u> Jonathan Willey
Role: Left-hand bat, slow left-arm orthodox
spin bowler
Born: 28 February 1990, Northampton
County debut: 2009
Parents: Peter and Charmaine
Place in batting averages: 211th av. 20.68
Family links with cricket: Father Peter played
for England and became an umpire after his
playing days were over
Extras: Played for England U19 in 2009. Made a
half-century (60) on his Championship debut v
Leicestershire in 2009. Part of England Performance
Programme squad 2009-10
Best batting: 60 Northamptonshire v Leicestershire,
Grace Road 2009
Best bowling: 2-21 Northamptonshire v Kent, Canterbury 2009

2009 Season

	M	Inn	NO	Runs	HS	Avg	100	50	Ct	St	Balls	Runs	Wkts	Avg	BB	5I	10M
Test																	
FC	10	17	1	331	60	20.68	-	1	3	-	412	295	6	49.16	2-21	-	-
ODI																	
List A	12	9	2	75	21	10.71	-	-	3	-	108	126	3	42.00	2-44	-	
20/20 Int																	
20/20	12	6	2	57	18*	14.25	-	-	3	-	132	113	10	11.30	3-9	-	

Career Performances

	M	Inn	NO	Runs	HS	Avg	100	50	Ct	St	Balls	Runs	Wkts	Avg	BB	5I	10M
Test																	
FC	10	17	1	331	60	20.68	-	1	3	-	412	295	6	49.16	2-21	-	-
ODI																	
List A	12	9	2	75	21	10.71	-	-	3	-	108	126	3	42.00	2-44	-	
20/20 Int																	
20/20	12	6	2	57	18*	14.25	-	-	3	-	132	113	10	11.30	3-9	-	

WILLIAMS, R. E. M.   Middlesex

Name: Robert (Robbie) Edward Morgan Williams
Role: Right-hand bat, right-arm fast-medium bowler
Born: 19 January 1987, Pembury, Kent
Height: 6ft **Weight:** 14st 2lbs
County debut: 2007
Parents: Gail and Tim
Marital status: Single
Education: Marlborough College; Durham University
Qualifications: 3 A-levels, BA in Economics
Off-season: 'Work experience in the City'
Overseas tours: Marlborough College to South Africa 2003; Durham University to Cape Town 2007; British Universities to South Africa 2008
Overseas teams played for: Corrimal, Wollongong 2005-06
Career highlights to date: 'Taking five wickets on Championship debut'
Cricket moments to forget: 'Leaving a ball and getting stumped at the Bunbury Festival when nine down and three balls from a draw'
Cricket superstitions: 'None'
Cricketers particularly admired: Brett Lee, Glenn McGrath, Malcolm Marshall
Other sports played: Rugby (Marlborough College 1st XV), hockey (Marlborough College 1st XI), tennis

Other sports followed: Rugby union (Leicester Tigers)
Injuries: 'Stress fracture in my back – out from June till September'
Favourite band: Florence and the Machine
Relaxations: 'Table tennis, yoga, losing the game'
Extras: Played for Durham UCCE 2007, taking 5-70 v Lancashire at Durham. Played for MCC 2007. Took 5-112 on Championship debut v Essex at Chelmsford 2007. Played for Durham UCCE in 2008 and 2009. Missed much of the 2009 season due to a back injury
Best batting: 31 DUCCE v Lancashire, Durham, 2009

2009 Season

	M	Inn	NO	Runs	HS	Avg	100	50	Ct	St	Balls	Runs	Wkts	Avg	BB	5I	10M
Test																	
FC	3	6	1	85	31	17.00	-	-	2	-	367	192	6	32.00	3-51	-	-
ODI																	
List A																	
20/20 Int																	
20/20																	

Career Performances

	M	Inn	NO	Runs	HS	Avg	100	50	Ct	St	Balls	Runs	Wkts	Avg	BB	5I	10M
Test																	
FC	9	15	5	119	31	11.90	-	-	4	-	1241	755	23	32.82	5-70	2	-
ODI																	
List A	1	0	0	0	0		-	-	-	-	36	49	0		-	-	
20/20 Int																	
20/20																	

99. By what name was the country of Bangladesh known prior to 1972?

WILLOUGHBY, C. M.   Somerset

Name: <u>Charl</u> Myles Willoughby
Role: Left-hand bat, left-arm
fast-medium bowler
Born: 3 December 1974, Cape Town,
South Africa
Height: 6ft 3in **Weight:** 12st 12lbs
Nickname: Puppy, Harry
County debut: 2005 (Leicestershire),
2006 (Somerset)
County cap: 2005 (Leicestershire),
2007 (Somerset)
Test debut: 2003
ODI debut: 1999-2000
50 wickets in a season: 4
Place in batting averages: (2008 252nd av. 11.66)
Place in bowling averages: 44th av. 30.01 (2008 38th av. 25.90)
Parents: David and Belinda
Wife and date of marriage: Nicky, 17 April 2004
Children: Cole, 18 October 2006
Family links with cricket: 'Father played club cricket'
Education: Wynberg Boys' High School; Stellenbosch University and UNISA
Overseas tours: South Africa Academy to Zimbabwe 1998-99; South Africa A to
West Indies 2000, to Zimbabwe 2004; South Africa to Sharjah (Coca-Cola Sharjah
Cup) 1999-2000, to Bangladesh 2003, to England 2003; Somerset to India (ICC
Champions League) 2009
Overseas teams played for: Boland 1994-95 – 1999-2000; Western Province
2000-01 – 2003-04; Western Province Boland 2003-04 – 2004-05; Cape Cobras
2005-06 – 2006-07
Career highlights to date: 'Test and ODI debuts. Four wickets in four balls in
first-class match v Dolphins'
Cricket moments to forget: 'Dislocating my shoulder diving on boundary'
Cricketers particularly admired: Graeme Smith, Andrew Flintoff, Wasim Akram
Young players to look out for: JP Duminy, Stuart Broad
Other sports followed: Rugby (Stormers)
Favourite band: Coldplay
Relaxations: 'Movies and time with my wife'
Extras: Played for Berkshire in the NatWest 2000. Took four wickets in four balls v
Dolphins at Durban in the Supersport Series 2005-06; the feat was spread over two
innings and consisted of a hat-trick (Mhlongo, Gobind, Hayward) plus the wicket of
Watson with his first ball of the second innings. Has won several match awards,
including Man of the Match for South Africa A v Barbados at Bridgetown 2000 (6-24)

·

and for Leicestershire v Somerset at Leicester in the C&G 2005 (6-16; the best one-day return by a Leicestershire bowler). An overseas player with Leicestershire 2005. Joined Somerset in 2006. Is no longer considered an overseas player

Best batting: 47 Somerset v Worcestershire, Taunton 2006
Best bowling: 7-44 Somerset v Gloucestershire, Taunton 2006

2009 Season

	M	Inn	NO	Runs	HS	Avg	100	50	Ct	St	Balls	Runs	Wkts	Avg	BB	5I	10M
Test																	
FC	16	13	4	40	23	4.44	-	-	4	-	3334	1621	54	30.01	5-56	3	-
ODI																	
List A	13	2	0	15	15	7.50	-	-	-	-	586	458	14	32.71	3-36	-	
20/20 Int																	
20/20	11	2	1	4	4	4.00	-	-	1	-	252	303	10	30.30	4-29	-	

Career Performances

	M	Inn	NO	Runs	HS	Avg	100	50	Ct	St	Balls	Runs	Wkts	Avg	BB	5I	10M
Test	2	0	0	0	0		-	-	-	-	300	125	1	125.00	1-47	-	-
FC	193	215	96	716	47	6.01	-	-	41	-	38860	18064	716	25.22	7-44	30	3
ODI	3	2	0	0	0	0.00	-	-	-	-	168	148	2	74.00	2-39	-	
List A	206	59	32	147	15	5.44	-	-	26	-	10026	6957	254	27.38	6-16	5	
20/20 Int																	
20/20	65	15	11	26	11	6.50	-	-	11	-	1439	1691	70	24.15	4-9	-	

WILSON, G. C.   Surrey

Name: <u>Gary</u> Craig Wilson
Role: Right-hand bat, wicket-keeper, very occasional right-arm medium bowler
Born: 5 February 1986, Dundonald, Co Roscommon, Ireland
Height: 5ft 10in **Weight:** 13st 2lbs
Nickname: Gaz, Wils
County debut: 2008 (one-day)
ODI debut: 2007
Twenty20 Int debut: 2008
Parents: George and Iris
Marital status: 'Unmarried'
Family links with cricket: 'Dad played league cricket in Ireland'
Education: Methodist College, Belfast

Qualifications: 10 GCSEs, 3 A-levels, gym instructor Level 2, FA Level 1
Career outside cricket: 'Bit of coaching'

Overseas tours: Ireland U19 to Bangladesh (U19 World Cup) 2003-04, to Sri Lanka (U19 World Cup) 2005-06; Ireland A to UAE (EurAsia Series) 2006, to UAE (ICC World Twenty20 qualifiers) 2010, plus various Ireland age-group and Ireland A tours
Overseas teams played for: Portland Colts CC, Melbourne 2004-05; Durbanville CC, Cape Town 2006-07
Career highlights to date: 'Playing first game of U19 World Cup in Bangladesh; beating Scotland in the Inter-Continental Cup by three runs; being signed by Surrey'
Cricket moments to forget: 'Being beaten by three wickets by New Zealand in U19 World Cup 2005-06 after scoring 304; being beaten by four runs by England in the same World Cup; pair on debut for Surrey 2nd XI'
Cricket superstitions: 'Left pad first'
Cricketers particularly admired: Alec Stewart, Brian Lara, Mark Boucher
Young players to look out for: Gary Kidd, William Porterfield, Paul Stirling
Other sports played: Rugby, football, golf ('badly')
Other sports followed: Football (Man United), rugby (Ireland)
Favourite band: 'Any really'
Extras: Player of the Tournament at European U19 Championship 2003 and 2004. MCC Young Cricketer 2005-06. Has represented Ireland in first-class and one-day cricket, including an ODI and the 2006 C&G and 2007 Friends Provident; has also represented Ireland A in one-day (List A) cricket
Opinions on cricket: 'A lot of cricket being played in England – good for the advertising of the game; wouldn't fancy being a quick bowler, though.'
Best batting: 38 Ireland v Kenya, Eglinton 2009-10

2009 Season

	M	Inn	NO	Runs	HS	Avg	100	50	Ct	St	Balls	Runs	Wkts	Avg	BB	5I	10M
Test																	
FC																	
ODI																	
List A	15	12	2	164	42	16.40	-	-	12	4	0	0	0		-	-	
20/20 Int	3	3	0	52	23	17.33	-	-	1	-	0	0	0		-	-	
20/20	12	9	2	100	23	14.28	-	-	3	3	0	0	0		-	-	

Career Performances

	M	Inn	NO	Runs	HS	Avg	100	50	Ct	St	Balls	Runs	Wkts	Avg	BB	5I	10M
Test																	
FC	7	10	1	127	38	14.11	-	-	13	-	0	0	0		-	-	
ODI	16	16	1	290	51*	19.33	-	2	10	4	0	0	0		-	-	
List A	56	51	4	976	61	20.76	-	7	42	11	0	0	0		-	-	
20/20 Int	7	6	0	73	23	12.16	-	-	1	-	0	0	0		-	-	
20/20	18	14	2	122	23	10.16	-	-	6	3	0	0	0		-	-	

WOAKES, C. R.   Warwickshire

Name: Christopher (<u>Chris</u>) Roger Woakes
Role: Right-hand bat, right-arm
fast-medium bowler; all-rounder
Born: 2 March 1989, Birmingham
Height: 6ft 1in **Weight:** 12st 8lbs
Nickname: Woakesy, Jokes, Cheetah, Woaka
County debut: 2006
Place in batting averages: 127th av. 33.00
(2008 144th av. 27.44)
Place in bowling averages: 70th av. 33.53
(2008 14th av. 20.48)

Parents: Roger and Elaine
Family links with cricket: 'Stepbrothers played
club cricket'
Education: Barr Beacon Language College, Walsall
Qualifications: 7 GCSEs, 3 A-levels, Level 1 coaching
Off-season: 'England Performance Programme and Fitness Camp in Florida,
November to December.'
Career outside cricket: 'Have not got a clue'
Overseas tours: Warwickshire Academy to Cape Town 2005; England U19 to
Malaysia (U19 World Cup) 2007-08, to Sri Lanka 2007-08; Warwickshire pre-season
to Bloemfontein 2008; England Lions to UAE 2009-10
Career highlights to date: 'Making Championship debut and representing England
U19 v Pakistan 2007. Maiden 5-wicket haul v Glamorgan at Cardiff in the County
Championship. Maiden century v Hampshire at the Rose Bowl, 2009. Taking 6-49 for
the England Lions v West Indies'
Cricket moments to forget: 'Bowling two beamers in an over'
Cricket superstitions: 'Always turn to my left at end of bowling run-up'
Cricketers particularly admired: Allan Donald, Glenn McGrath, Jacques Kallis
Young players to look out for: Liam Dawson, Tom Lewis, James Harris
Other sports played: Golf, snooker
Other sports followed: Football (Aston Villa)
Favourite band: John Mayer
Relaxations: 'Listening to music, cinema, chilling with friends'
Extras: Played for Herefordshire in Minor Counties competitions 2006-07. England
U17 squad 2006. Represented England U19 2007. Achieved a ten-wicket match haul
(6-68, 4-94) in the final Championship game of the season v Glamorgan at Edgbaston
in September 2008. NBC Denis Compton Award for the most promising young
Warwickshire player 2008, 2009. Member of England Performance Programme
squad 2009-10

Opinions on cricket: 'Twenty20 is a good game and is improving the sport and its popularity, but Test cricket and four-day cricket should always play the major role in the cricket arena.'
Best batting: 131* Warwickshire v Hampshire, Rose Bowl 2009
Best bowling: 6-43 England A v West Indians, Derby 2009

2009 Season

	M	Inn	NO	Runs	HS	Avg	100	50	Ct	St	Balls	Runs	Wkts	Avg	BB	5I	10M
Test																	
FC	19	23	8	495	131*	33.00	1	1	5	-	2939	1576	47	33.53	6-43	2	-
ODI																	
List A	10	3	1	31	25	15.50	-	-	4	-	386	303	9	33.66	2-28	-	
20/20 Int																	
20/20	4	3	2	15	11*	15.00	-	-	1	-	64	115	1	115.00	1-38	-	

Career Performances

	M	Inn	NO	Runs	HS	Avg	100	50	Ct	St	Balls	Runs	Wkts	Avg	BB	5I	10M
Test																	
FC	32	38	12	769	131*	29.57	1	2	16	-	5043	2690	96	28.02	6-43	5	1
ODI																	
List A	20	9	3	99	31*	16.50	-	-	4	-	638	535	12	44.58	2-28	-	
20/20 Int																	
20/20	15	6	5	19	11*	19.00	-	-	3	-	234	382	8	47.75	4-21	-	

WOOD, C. P.   Hampshire

Name: Christopher (<u>Chris</u>) Philip Wood
Role: Right-hand bat, left-arm medium-fast bowler
Born: 27 June 1990, Basingstoke, Hampshire
County debut: No first team appearance
Education: Alton College
Overseas tours: England U19 to South Africa 2008-09
Extras: Has played for Hampshire U13 and U17, Hampshire Academy and Hampshire 2nd XI. Awarded a development contract for 2010

WOOD, M. J.   Nottinghamshire

Name: <u>Matthew</u> James Wood
Role: Right-hand bat, right-arm
off-spin bowler
Born: 30 September 1980, Exeter
Height: 5ft 11in   **Weight:** 12st 6lbs
Nickname: Woody, Gran, Moo
County debut: 2001 (Somerset),
2008 (Nottinghamshire)
County cap: 2005 (Somerset)
1000 runs in a season: 1
1st-Class 200s: 1
Place in batting averages: 168th av. 27.00
(2008 151st av. 26.95)
Parents: James and Trina
Marital status: Single
Family links with cricket: Father is chairman of Devon Cricket Board
Education: Exmouth College; Exeter University
Qualifications: 10 GCSEs, 2 A-levels, ECB Level 3 coach
Career outside cricket: Coach
Overseas tours: West of England U15 to West Indies 1995
Overseas teams played for: Doubleview CC, Perth 2001, 2002
Career highlights to date: 'Winning the Twenty20 Cup and scoring 297 v Yorkshire'
Cricket moments to forget: 'Getting a pair v Essex 2005'
Cricket superstitions: 'None'
Cricketers particularly admired: Marcus Trescothick
Other sports followed: Football (Liverpool FC), horse racing
Relaxations: Golf
Extras: NBC Denis Compton Award for the most promising young Somerset player
2001. Scored century in each innings (106/131) v Surrey at Taunton 2002. Somerset
Player of the Year 2002. Scored 297 v Yorkshire at Taunton 2005, the fifth highest
individual score in Somerset's history. Vice-captain of Somerset July 2005-2006.
Left Somerset at the end of the 2007 season and joined Nottinghamshire for 2008
Best batting: 297 Somerset v Yorkshire, Taunton 2005

2009 Season

	M	Inn	NO	Runs	HS	Avg	100	50	Ct	St	Balls	Runs	Wkts	Avg	BB	5I	10M
Test																	
FC	7	11	1	270	86	27.00	-	1	-	-	0	0	0		-	-	-
ODI																	
List A	8	7	0	157	91	22.42	-	1	2	-	0	0	0		-	-	
20/20 Int																	
20/20	4	4	1	137	45	45.66	-	-	-	-	0	0	0		-	-	

Career Performances

	M	Inn	NO	Runs	HS	Avg	100	50	Ct	St	Balls	Runs	Wkts	Avg	BB	5I	10M
Test																	
FC	97	164	8	5184	297	33.23	9	32	30	-	85	68	0		-	-	-
ODI																	
List A	91	86	4	2229	129	27.18	2	15	14	-	0	0	0		-	-	
20/20 Int																	
20/20	34	34	1	1006	94	30.48	-	5	5	-	0	0	0		-	-	

WOODMAN, R. J. Gloucestershire

Name: <u>Robert</u> James Woodman
Role: Left-hand bat, left-arm medium-fast bowler
Born: 12 October 1986, Taunton, Somerset
Height: 5ft 11in
Nickname: Woody
County debut: 2005 (Somerset), 2008 (Gloucestershire)
Place in batting averages: 241st av. 16.00
Education: The Castle School, Taunton; Richard Huish College
Overseas tours: West of England U15 to West Indies; England U19 to Bangladesh 2005-06, to Sri Lanka (U19 World Cup) 2005-06
Overseas teams played for: Valley DCC, Brisbane, Australia 2008-09
Other sports played: Football (Bristol City Academy), basketball (Taunton Tigers Basketball Academy), tennis (South West Tennis Academy)
Other sports followed: Football (Tottenham Hotspur)
Extras: Played for Somerset in 2005; Somerset 2nd XI 2005-07; Devon 2007; MCC Young Cricketers 2008, as well as club cricket in the West of England. Played for MCC v Bangladesh A at Durham in a 50-over match in 2008. Has represented England at U15 and U17 level. Signed for Gloucestershire in September 2008, a week after scoring a century for MCC Young Cricketers v Gloucestershire 2nd XI
Best batting: 46* Somerset v Worcestershire, Worcester 2005
Best bowling: 4-65 Gloucestershire v Essex, Bristol 2008

2009 Season

	M	Inn	NO	Runs	HS	Avg	100	50	Ct	St	Balls	Runs	Wkts	Avg	BB	5I	10M
Test																	
FC	6	10	1	144	32	16.00	-	-	3	-	30	8	1	8.00	1-4	-	-
ODI																	
List A																	
20/20 Int																	
20/20																	

Career Performances

	M	Inn	NO	Runs	HS	Avg	100	50	Ct	St	Balls	Runs	Wkts	Avg	BB	5I	10M
Test																	
FC	10	16	2	213	46*	15.21	-	-	3	-	495	341	7	48.71	4-65	-	
ODI																	
List A	5	1	0	14	14	14.00	-	-	2	-	150	163	1	163.00	1-38	-	
20/20 Int																	
20/20	2	2	2	1	1*		-	-	-	-	42	63	2	31.50	2-37	-	

WRIGHT, B. J. Glamorgan

Name: <u>Ben</u> James Wright
Role: Right-hand bat, right-arm medium bowler
Born: 5 December 1987, Fulwood, Preston
Height: 5ft 8in **Weight:** 11st
Nickname: Kevin, Space, Bej
County debut: 2006
Place in batting averages: 215th av. 19.92
Parents: Julia and Peter
Marital status: Single
Education: Cowbridge Comprehensive
Qualifications: 11 GCSEs
Overseas tours: West of England U15 to West Indies 2003; England U16 to South Africa 2004; England U19 to Bangladesh 2005-06, to Sri Lanka (U19 World Cup) 2005-06, to Malaysia 2006-07
Cricket moments to forget: 'Watching my dad bat and get a not out'
Cricket superstitions: 'All left kit goes on before right'
Cricketers particularly admired: Matthew Maynard
Young players to look out for: 'All the Glamorgan youngsters'
Other sports played: Rugby (Wales U16)
Other sports followed: Football (Manchester United), rugby (Leicester Tigers)

Favourite band: 'All R&B'
Relaxations: 'Spending time with girlfriend and watching TV'
Extras: Sir John Hobbs Memorial Prize 2003. A.A. Thomson Fielding Prize 2003.
BBC *Test Match Special* U15 Young Cricketer of the Year Award 2003. Played for
Wales Minor Counties in Minor Counties competitions 2005-06. Represented England
U19 2006, 2007. NBC Denis Compton Award for the most promising young
Glamorgan player 2006. Scored maiden first-class century (108) v Leicestershire at
Leicester 2007 aged 19, becoming the youngest Glamorgan centurion since Matthew
Maynard in 1985
Best batting: 108 Glamorgan v Leicestershire, Grace Road 2007
Best bowling: 1-14 Glamorgan v Essex, Chelmsford 2007

2009 Season

	M	Inn	NO	Runs	HS	Avg	100	50	Ct	St	Balls	Runs	Wkts	Avg	BB	5I	10M
Test																	
FC	9	14	0	279	81	19.92	-	1	3	-	48	41	0		-	-	-
ODI																	
List A	10	9	2	202	65	28.85	-	1	2	-	60	57	1	57.00	1-19	-	
20/20 Int																	
20/20	8	8	2	179	55*	29.83	-	1	2	-	24	22	1	22.00	1-16	-	

Career Performances

	M	Inn	NO	Runs	HS	Avg	100	50	Ct	St	Balls	Runs	Wkts	Avg	BB	5I	10M
Test																	
FC	21	33	2	680	108	21.93	1	3	18	-	180	130	2	65.00	1-14	-	-
ODI																	
List A	38	36	4	749	65	23.40	-	4	9	-	132	126	1	126.00	1-19	-	
20/20 Int																	
20/20	20	18	8	311	55*	31.10	-	1	7	-	24	22	1	22.00	1-16	-	

WRIGHT, C. J. C. Essex

Name: Christopher (<u>Chris</u>) Julian
Clement Wright
Role: Right-hand bat, right-arm
fast-medium bowler
Born: 14 July 1985, Chipping Norton, Oxfordshire
Height: 6ft 3in **Weight:** 12st
Nickname: Wrighty, Baron, Jesus, Gyppo
County debut: 2004 (Middlesex), 2008 (Essex)
Place in batting averages: 250th av. 14.44
(2008 203rd av. 20.11)
Place in bowling averages: 94th av. 38.45
(2008 53rd av. 27.31)
Parents: Alan and Nikki
Marital status: Single

Children: George, 1 June 2009
Family links with cricket: 'Dad plays for Hampshire Over 50s'
Education: Eggars School, Alton; Alton College; Anglia Polytechnic
University, Cambridge
Qualifications: 11 GCSEs, 4 A-levels, HND in Sports Science
Career outside cricket: 'Family business – Hygienics Limited'
Off-season: 'In the gym at Chelmsford, and resting and spending time with
my family'
Overseas tours: Cambridge UCCE to Grenada 2004; Essex to Dubai 2008
Overseas teams played for: Tamil Union C&AC, Colombo 2005-06; Bayswater
Morley, Perth 2008-09
Career highlights to date: 'Middlesex debut v Yorkshire. First match at Lord's.
70-odd not out v Middlesex (*71* at Chelmsford, April 2008*) chasing 280 to win.
Friends Provident Trophy win 2008. 6-22 v Leicestershire. Watching the lads chase
and beat Northamptonshire and then Derbyshire to gain promotion to Division 1
in 2009.'
Cricket moments to forget: 'Relegation for Middlesex. Any dropped catch.
Conceding 12 off the final over v Worcestershire and losing the match'
Cricket superstitions: 'Not really; they make people crazy'
Cricketers particularly admired: Jason Gillespie, Courtney Walsh. 'Any pro – it's
hard work. Especially senior bowlers who aren't grumpy'
Young players to look out for: Jaik Mickleburgh, Adam Wheater, Billy Godleman
(all Essex)
Other sports played: Basketball, table football, poker
Other sports followed: Football (Arsenal), basketball (Dallas Mavericks)
Favourite band: 'At the moment, Linkin Park'
Relaxations: 'Movies, eating out, gambling and watches'

Extras: Played for Cambridge UCCE 2004-05. Represented British Universities 2005. Left Middlesex at the end of the 2007 season and joined Essex for 2008
Opinions on cricket: 'It's good, so don't tamper too much.'
Best batting: 76 CUCCE v Essex, Fenner's 2005
Best bowling: 6-22 Essex v Leicestershire, Grace Road 2008

2009 Season

	M	Inn	NO	Runs	HS	Avg	100	50	Ct	St	Balls	Runs	Wkts	Avg	BB	5I	10M
Test																	
FC	14	16	7	130	24*	14.44	-	-	2	-	2623	1538	40	38.45	4-43	-	-
ODI																	
List A	15	3	1	16	14*	8.00	-	-	3	-	594	587	14	41.92	3-22	-	
20/20 Int																	
20/20	8	3	3	12	6*		-	-	-	-	152	197	7	28.14	4-24	-	

Career Performances

	M	Inn	NO	Runs	HS	Avg	100	50	Ct	St	Balls	Runs	Wkts	Avg	BB	5I	10M
Test																	
FC	43	53	13	755	76	18.87	-	3	11	-	6286	3954	92	42.97	6-22	1	-
ODI																	
List A	48	21	8	118	23	9.07	-	-	10	-	1836	1676	38	44.10	3-3	-	
20/20 Int																	
20/20	12	4	4	13	6*		-	-	2	-	230	306	10	30.60	4-24	-	

WRIGHT, D. G.   Sussex

Name: <u>Damien</u> Geoffrey Wright
Role: Right-hand bat, right-arm
fast-medium bowler
Born: 25 July 1975, Casino, New South
Wales, Australia
Height: 6ft 2in
Nickname: Moves
County debut: 2003 (Northamptonshire),
2007 (Glamorgan), 2009 (Sussex)
50 wickets in a season: 1
Overseas tours: Australia A to South Africa 2002-03
Overseas teams played for: Tasmania 1997-98 –
2007-08; Victoria 2008-09 –
Extras: Played for Scotland in the 2002 C&G,
winning two Man of the Match awards. Has also won
several match awards in Australia, including Man of the Match v Victoria at
Melbourne in the ING Cup 2001-02 (4-23/40) and v Queensland at Brisbane

in the Pura Cup 2003-04 (4-30/3-33 plus 60). Has represented Australia A. Tasmania's leading wicket-taker in the Pura Cup 2002-03 (31 wickets – av. 27.25) and (jointly with Andrew Downton) 2003-04 (37 – 26.49). Tasmanian Player of the Year 2002-03. Named in Australia's initial squad of 30 for the 2002-03 World Cup. Was a member of Tasmania's first Pura Cup winning side 2006-07, taking 5-13 in NSW's second innings in the final in Hobart (having also taken 3-38 in the first innings and scored 67 and 47). Was an overseas player with Northamptonshire in 2003 (temporary) and 2005. Was an overseas player with Glamorgan during the 2007 season but was forced to return home early through injury. Signed for Sussex as an overseas player in April 2009

Best batting: 111 Tasmania v Victoria, Hobart 2004-05
Best bowling: 8-60 Northamptonshire v Yorkshire, Headingley 2005

2009 Season

	M	Inn	NO	Runs	HS	Avg	100	50	Ct	St	Balls	Runs	Wkts	Avg	BB	5I	10M
Test																	
FC	3	4	1	88	42	29.33	-	-	-	-	503	187	5	37.40	3-64	-	-
ODI																	
List A	3	2	0	18	13	9.00	-	-	-	-	132	80	3	26.66	2-24	-	
20/20 Int																	
20/20																	

Career Performances

	M	Inn	NO	Runs	HS	Avg	100	50	Ct	St	Balls	Runs	Wkts	Avg	BB	5I	10M
Test																	
FC	97	146	22	3059	111	24.66	1	16	45	-	19793	9120	300	30.40	8-60	9	-
ODI																	
List A	99	77	23	924	55	17.11	-	4	23	-	5053	3481	121	28.76	5-37	1	
20/20 Int																	
20/20	22	16	3	174	38*	13.38	-	-	4	-	412	513	17	30.17	3-17	-	

100. Who, totally innocently, once referred to Pakistani bowler Asif Massood as Massif Arsood?

WRIGHT, L. J. Sussex

Name: <u>Luke</u> James Wright
Role: Right-hand bat, right-arm
medium-fast bowler; all-rounder
Born: 7 March 1985, Grantham
Height: 6ft **Weight:** 13st
Nickname: Wrighty
County debut: 2003 (Leicestershire),
2004 (Sussex)
County cap: 2007 (Sussex)
ODI debut: 2007
Twenty20 Int debut: 2007-08
Place in batting averages: 39th av. 49.00
(2008 85th av. 36.52)
Place in bowling averages: 79th av. 34.72
(2008 147th av. 61.66)
Parents: Keith and Anna

Marital status: Single
Family links with cricket: 'Father very keen cricketer (Level 2 coach).' Brother
Ashley played for Leicestershire
Education: Belvoir High School, Bottesford; Ratcliffe College, Leicester;
Loughborough University
Qualifications: 8 GCSEs, National Diploma in Sports Science and Sports Massage,
Level 1 coaching
Overseas tours: Leicestershire U13 to South Africa; Leicestershire U15 to South
Africa; England U19 to Australia 2002-03, to Bangladesh (U19 World Cup) 2003-04;
England A to West Indies 2005-06; England to South Africa (World 20/20) 2007-08, to
Sri Lanka 2007-08 (one-day series), to New Zealand 2007-08 (one-day series), to India
(one-day series) 2008-09, to South Africa 2009-10; England Performance Programme
to India 2007-08 (*see Extras*); England Lions to New Zealand 2008-09
Cricket superstitions: 'Too many to name'
Cricketers particularly admired: Andrew Flintoff, Jacques Kallis
Other sports played: Football, hockey, squash, tennis
Other sports followed: Football (Newcastle United)
Relaxations: Music, cinema, going out
Extras: NBC Denis Compton Award for the most promising young Leicestershire
player 2002. Took the first ever hat-trick for England U19 in one-day cricket, v South
Africa U19 at Hove 2003. Scored maiden first-class century (100) on Sussex debut v
Loughborough UCCE at Hove 2004. NBC Denis Compton Award for most promising
young Sussex player 2004, 2005, 2007. ECB National Academy 2004-05 (part-time),
2005-06. Leading run-scorer in the Twenty20 2007 with 346 runs (av. 43.25),
including 45-ball 103 v Kent at Canterbury and 48-ball 98 v Hampshire at Hove.

ODI debut in the sixth ODI v India at The Oval 2007, scoring 50. Was forced to return home from England Performance Programme in India 2007-08 with a foot injury. Although part of both one-day and Test squads in South Africa 2009-10 he played only in the one-day games. England increment contract 2009-10

Best batting: 155* Sussex v MCC, Lord's 2008
Best bowling: 5-66 Sussex v Worcestershire, Hove 2009

2009 Season

	M	Inn	NO	Runs	HS	Avg	100	50	Ct	St	Balls	Runs	Wkts	Avg	BB	5I	10M
Test																	
FC	10	15	2	637	118*	49.00	3	3	1	-	1345	764	22	34.72	5-66	2	-
ODI	4	4	0	79	38	19.75	-	-	1	-	144	103	3	34.33	2-52	-	
List A	16	15	1	381	95*	27.21	-	1	5	-	660	563	14	40.21	3-50	-	
20/20 Int	6	5	0	113	71	22.60	-	1	4	-	48	64	1	64.00	1-24	-	
20/20	15	14	0	312	71	22.28	-	2	7	-	204	259	7	37.00	2-28	-	

Career Performances

	M	Inn	NO	Runs	HS	Avg	100	50	Ct	St	Balls	Runs	Wkts	Avg	BB	5I	10M
Test																	
FC	57	81	14	2402	155*	35.85	7	12	26	-	5742	3351	78	42.96	5-66	2	-
ODI	25	19	1	404	52	22.44	-	2	8	-	414	343	7	49.00	2-34	-	
List A	116	88	13	1630	125	21.73	1	4	31	-	3666	3197	85	37.61	4-12	-	
20/20 Int	14	13	0	211	71	16.23	-	1	7	-	78	109	2	54.50	1-24	-	
20/20	56	45	3	864	103	20.57	1	3	23	-	696	910	35	26.00	3-17	-	

WYATT, A. C. F.   Leicestershire

Name: Alexander (<u>Alex</u>) Charles Frederick Wyatt
Role: Right-hand bat, right-arm fast bowler
Born: 23 July 1990, Roehampton, London
Height: 6ft 7in **Weight:** 15st
Nickname: Waz, Goober, Dave
County debut: 2009
Parents: John and Sue
Marital status: Single
Family links with cricket: 'Grandfather (C.E.N. Wyatt) played first-class cricket in 1932, but moved on to play for, and captain, the England hockey team'
Education: Oakham School, Rutland
Qualifications: 12 GCSEs, 1 AS-level, 3 A-levels, Level 1 coaching
Off-season: 'Visiting Potchefstroom, South Africa, in the New Year'

Overseas tours: Leicestershire YC to South Africa 2004-05; Oakham School 1st XI to South Africa 2005-06
Overseas teams played for: Potchdorp CC, Potchefstroom 2008-09
Career highlights to date: 'Taking the wicket of Ramnaresh Sarwan in West Indies tour match (at Grace Road, April 2009), and getting a wicket maiden in my Twenty20 debut (*v Durham, May 2009*) – 4-1-14-3'
Cricket moments to forget: 'Bowling backwards (in terms of pace) v Lancashire on Sky Sports (*Twenty20 Cup, May 2009*)'
Cricketers particularly admired: Glenn McGrath
Young players to look out for: James Taylor, Josh Cobb, Nathan Buck, Sam Cliff, Harry Gurney (all Leicestershire), Keiron Garside (MCC YC)
Other sports played: Golf
Other sports followed: Rugby union (Leicester Tigers)
Injuries: 'Back injury (stress reaction) – out for 12 weeks'
Favourite band: Bob Marley and the Wailers
Extras: Former Leicestershire Academy player. Leicestershire Second XI 2007-09. Played for Leicestershire & Rutland U17 2007. Followed in Stuart Broad's footsteps at Oakham School, the educational establishment whose Director of Cricket, Frank Hayes, is a former England batsman. Took a gap year to allow him to accept a twelve-month contract with Leicestershire for 2009. Spent winter 2008-09 in Potchefstroom in South Africa, working with former Leicestershire player Gordon Parsons, who now works as a performance coach
Best batting: 3 Leicestershire v West Indians, Grace Road 2009
Best bowling: 3-42 Leicestershire v West Indians, Grace Road 2009

2009 Season

	M	Inn	NO	Runs	HS	Avg	100	50	Ct	St	Balls	Runs	Wkts	Avg	BB	5I	10M
Test																	
FC	3	3	1	4	3	2.00	-	-	1	-	366	159	7	22.71	3-42	-	-
ODI																	
List A	2	0	0	0	0		-	-	1	-	66	62	2	31.00	1-31	-	
20/20 Int																	
20/20	2	0	0	0	0		-	-	1	-	42	36	3	12.00	3-14	-	

Career Performances

	M	Inn	NO	Runs	HS	Avg	100	50	Ct	St	Balls	Runs	Wkts	Avg	BB	5I	10M
Test																	
FC	3	3	1	4	3	2.00	-	-	1	-	366	159	7	22.71	3-42	-	-
ODI																	
List A	2	0	0	0	0		-	-	1	-	66	62	2	31.00	1-31	-	
20/20 Int																	
20/20	2	0	0	0	0		-	-	1	-	42	36	3	12.00	3-14	-	

YARDY, M. H.   Sussex

Name: Michael (Mike) Howard Yardy
Role: Left-hand bat, left-arm
medium/spin bowler, county captain
Born: 27 November 1980, Pembury, Kent
Height: 6ft **Weight:** 14st 2lbs
Nickname: Yards, Paolo
County debut: 1999 (one-day),
2000 (first-class)
County cap: 2005
ODI debut: 2006
Twenty20 Int debut: 2006
1000 runs in a season: 1
1st-Class 200s: 1
Place in batting averages: 65th av. 42.15
(2008 83rd av. 36.69)
Parents: Beverly and Howard
Wife and date of marriage: Karin, October 2005
Children: Syenna Lucienne, 24 December 2006
Family links with cricket: 'Brother plays for local team'
Education: William Parker School, Hastings
Qualifications: 5 GCSEs, 2 A-levels, ECB Level 1 coach, Sports Psychology diploma
Overseas tours: Sussex Academy to Barbados 1997; Sussex to Grenada 2001, 2002;
England A to West Indies 2005-06, to Bangladesh 2006-07 (c); England to India (ICC
Champions Trophy) 2006-07; England Lions to India 2007-08 (c); Sussex to India
(Champions League Twenty20) 2009-10
Overseas teams played for: Cape Town CC 1999
Cricket superstitions: 'Loads – all secret'
Cricketers particularly admired: 'All those who have reached the pinnacle of
their careers'
Other sports followed: Football (West Ham)
Favourite band: Bluetones
Relaxations: 'Watching West Ham; relaxing with my wife'
Extras: Played for Sussex U15, U16 and U19. Represented England U17. Attended
Sussex Academy. Sussex Most Improved Player 2001. His 257 v Bangladeshis at
Hove 2005 is the highest individual score for Sussex against a touring side; also
took 5-83 in Bangladeshis' second innings. Scored 159* v Warwickshire at Hove
2006, in the process sharing with Murray Goodwin (214*) in a new Sussex record
partnership for the third wicket (385*). ECB National Academy 2005-06, 2006-07.
Vice-captain of Sussex 2007; took over from Chris Adams as county captain in
September 2008. Despite Sussex's relegation led them to both the Twenty20 Cup and
Pro40 title in the 2009 season

Best batting: 257 Sussex v Bangladeshis, Hove 2005
Best bowling: 5-83 Sussex v Bangladeshis, Hove 2005

2009 Season

	M	Inn	NO	Runs	HS	Avg	100	50	Ct	St	Balls	Runs	Wkts	Avg	BB	5I	10M
Test																	
FC	17	29	3	1096	152	42.15	2	6	13	-	414	320	4	80.00	3-15	-	-
ODI																	
List A	18	15	2	515	92*	39.61	-	5	7	-	556	509	10	50.90	4-54	-	
20/20 Int																	
20/20	13	8	4	107	26*	26.75	-	-	6	-	283	254	13	19.53	3-21	-	

Career Performances

	M	Inn	NO	Runs	HS	Avg	100	50	Ct	St	Balls	Runs	Wkts	Avg	BB	5I	10M
Test																	
FC	120	204	19	7261	257	39.24	14	37	87	-	3442	2003	26	77.03	5-83	1	-
ODI	6	5	1	49	19	12.25	-	-	1	-	252	135	4	33.75	3-24	-	
List A	146	129	17	2556	98*	22.82	-	16	61	-	3959	3252	87	37.37	6-27	1	
20/20 Int	3	2	2	47	24*		-	-	2	-	60	85	2	42.50	1-20	-	
20/20	47	36	15	568	68*	27.04	-	1	17	-	805	868	32	27.12	3-21	-	

YASIR ARAFAT   Sussex

Name: Yasir Arafat Satti
Role: Right-hand bat, right-arm fast bowler
Born: 12 March 1982, Rawalpindi,
Punjab, Pakistan
Height: 5ft 9½in **Weight:** 11st 11lbs
Nickname: Yas
County debut: 2006 (Sussex), 2007 (Kent)
County cap: 2006 (Sussex), 2007 (Kent)
Test debut: 2007-08
ODI debut: 1999-2000
Twenty20 Int debut: 2007-08
Place in batting averages: (2008 36th av. 28.21)
Place in bowling averages: 129th av. 51.75
(2008 66th av. 29.07)
Parents: M. Idrees (father)
Marital status: Single
Family links with cricket: 'Father plays club cricket'
Education: Gordon College, Rawalpindi
Overseas tours: Pakistan U15 to England (U15 World Cup) 1996; Pakistan U19 to Australia 1997-98, to Sri Lanka (U19 World Cup) 1999-2000; Pakistan A to UAE

(UAE National Day Tournament) 1999-2000, to Kenya 2000, to Sri Lanka 2001, 2004-05, to UAE (EurAsia Cricket Series) 2006; Pakistan to Sharjah (ARY Gold Cup) 2000-01, to India (ICC Champions Trophy) 2006-07, to West Indies (World Cup) 2006-07, to South Africa (World 20/20) 2007-08, to India 2007-08

Overseas teams played for: Rawalpindi 1997-98, 2000-01 – 2001-02, 2003-04 – 2005-06; Pakistan Reserves 1999-2000; Khan Research Laboratories 1999-2000 – 2004-05, 2006-07 – ; REDCO 1999-2000; National Bank of Pakistan 2005-06; Federal Areas 2008-09; Otago 2009-10
Career highlights to date: 'Playing for Pakistan'
Cricket moments to forget: 'Nil'
Cricket superstitions: 'Nil'
Other sports played: Football
Other sports followed: Football (Real Madrid)
Relaxations: 'Watching movies and music'
Extras: Pakistan domestic Player of the Year 2003-04. Played for Clydesdale CC, Scotland 2001-06 and for Scotland in the totesport and C&G 2004-05. Became fourth bowler in history of first-class cricket to take five wickets in six balls, for Rawalpindi v Faisalabad at Rawalpindi in the Quaid-e-Azam Trophy 2004-05; his feat, spread across two innings, included a hat-trick. Made Test debut in the third Test v India at Bangalore 2007-08. Was an overseas player with Sussex from June to September 2006; was an overseas player with Kent 2007 and 2008; signed at the end of the 2008 season to return to Sussex as overseas player for 2009; retained by Sussex as overseas player for 2010
Best batting: 122 Kent v Sussex, Canterbury 2007
Best bowling: 9-35 Khan Research Laboratories v Sui Southern Gas, Rawalpindi 2008-09

2009 Season

	M	Inn	NO	Runs	HS	Avg	100	50	Ct	St	Balls	Runs	Wkts	Avg	BB	5I	10M
Test																	
FC	5	5	0	108	37	21.60	-	-	-	-	906	621	12	51.75	3-83	-	-
ODI																	
List A	14	10	4	107	24*	17.83	-	-	8	-	714	620	24	25.83	3-30		
20/20 Int	1	1	0	4	4	4.00	-	-	-	-	24	42	0		-	-	
20/20	11	7	1	87	43	14.50	-	-	1	-	231	252	15	16.80	2-13	-	

Career Performances

	M	Inn	NO	Runs	HS	Avg	100	50	Ct	St	Balls	Runs	Wkts	Avg	BB	5I	10M
Test	3	3	1	94	50*	47.00	-	1	-	-	627	438	9	48.66	5-161	1	-
FC	157	237	35	5476	122	27.10	4	29	44	-	26135	15098	628	24.04	9-35	36	5
ODI	11	8	3	74	27	14.80	-	-	2	-	414	373	4	93.25	1-28	-	
List A	196	142	38	2158	87	20.75	-	7	46	-	9492	7629	317	24.06	6-24	5	
20/20 Int	5	5	2	50	17	16.66	-	-	1	-	102	145	2	72.50	1-31	-	
20/20	59	42	11	536	49	17.29	-	-	8	-	1189	1541	78	19.75	4-17	-	

THE UMPIRES

BAILEY, R. J.

Name: Robert (<u>Rob</u>) John Bailey
Born: 28 October 1963, Biddulph,
Stoke-on-Trent
Height: 6ft 3in
Nickname: Bailers
Wife and date of marriage: Rachel,
11 April 1987
Children: Harry, 7 March 1991;
Alexandra, 13 November 1993
Family links with cricket: 'Son Harry plays
for Northampton Saints CC'
Education: Biddulph High School
Career outside cricket: Rob Bailey
Ceramics ('promotional mugs etc.')
Other sports played: Badminton
(county schools)
Other sports followed: 'All football clubs
that I supply mugs to!'
Appointed to 1st-Class list: 2006
Umpiring honours: Stood at Twenty20 Cup finals day 2008 and 2009
Counties as player: Northamptonshire, Derbyshire
Role: Right-hand bat, off-spin bowler
County debut: 1982 (Northamptonshire), 2000 (Derbyshire)
County cap: 1985 (Northamptonshire), 2000 (Derbyshire)
Benefit: 1993 (Northamptonshire)
Test debut: 1988
ODI debut (matches): 1984-85 (4)
1000 runs in a season: 13
1st-Class 200s: 4
One-Day 100s: 9
One-Day 5 w. in innings: 1
Overseas tours: England to Sharjah 1984-85, 1986-87, to India 1988-89 (cancelled),
to West Indies 1989-90
Overseas teams played for: Rhodes University, Grahamstown, South Africa 1982-83;
Uitenhage CC, South Africa 1983-85; Fitzroy CC, Melbourne 1985-86; Gosnells CC,
Perth 1987-88
Highlights of playing career: 'Loved all of it'
Extras: Won three consecutive NatWest Man of the Match awards 1995 and three
consecutive B&H Gold Awards 1996. Northamptonshire captain 1996-97. In 1999
became sixth player to pass 20,000 first-class runs for Northamptonshire
Best batting: 224* Northamptonshire v Glamorgan, Swansea 1986
Best bowling: 5-54 Northamptonshire v Nottinghamshire, Northampton 1993

	M	Inn	NO	Runs	HS	Avg	100	Ct	St	Runs	Wkts	Avg	BB	5I	10M
Test	4	8	0	119	43	14.87	-	-	-						
FC	374	628	89	21844	224*	40.52	47	272	-	5144	121	42.51	5-54	2	-

BAINTON, N. L.

Name: Neil Laurence Bainton
Born: 2 October 1970, Romford, Essex
Height: 5ft 8in
Wife and date of marriage: Kay,
25 October 1997
Family links with cricket: Father played and
umpired club cricket in Essex
Education: Ilford County High School
Career outside cricket: 'Postman'
Off-season: 'Postman in Braintree, Essex'
Other sports played: Golf ('very badly')
Other sports followed: Football (West Ham
'and whichever local team my mate
plays for!')
Appointed to 1st-Class list: 2006
Umpiring honours: MCC tour to
Mozambique, 2009
Highlights of umpiring career:
'Being appointed to first-class list'
Players to watch for the future:
Jaik Mickleburgh (Essex), Nathan Buck (Leicestershire)
Highlights of playing career: 'Playing for South of England U15 at England Schools
Festival 1986. Still hold record for number of catches in an innings (6) in an Essex
Schools match.'

Did not play first-class cricket

BENSON, M. R.

Name: <u>Mark</u> Richard Benson
Born: 6 July 1958, Shoreham, Sussex
Height: 5ft 10in
Nickname: Benny
Wife and date of marriage: Sarah Patricia, 20 September 1986
Children: Laurence, 16 October 1987; Edward, 23 June 1990
Education: Sutton Valence School
Other sports played: Bridge, golf, swimming, cycling
Relaxations: Bridge, golf
Appointed to 1st-Class list: 2000
International panel: 2004-2006
Elite panel: 2006-2010
Tests umpired: 27 (plus 9 as TV umpire)
ODIs umpired: 72 (plus 25 as TV umpire)
Twenty20 Ints umpired: 19 (plus 6 as TV umpire)

Other umpiring honours: Stood in the C&G Trophy final 2003. Umpired in the 2006-07 World Cup and the Twenty20 World Championship 2007-08
County as player: Kent
Role: Left-hand bat
County debut: 1980
County cap: 1981
Benefit: 1991
Test debut: 1986
ODI debut (matches): 1986 (1)
1000 runs in a season: 11
1st-Class 200s: 1
One-Day 100s: 5
Overseas tours: None
Highlights of playing career: '257 v Hampshire. Winning Sunday League as captain of Kent. Two 90s to win a game against Hampshire with Malcolm Marshall bowling. One of only four cricketers in the history of Kent to have scored more than 10,000 runs and have an average in excess of 40 [in a completed career]'
Extras: Scored 1000 runs in first full season. Kent captain 1991-95
Best batting: 257 Kent v Hampshire, Southampton 1991
Best bowling: 2-55 Kent v Surrey, Dartford 1986
Stop press: On 5 February 2010, it was announced that Mark Benson was retiring from international umpiring, but would continue to umpire domestic cricket in England.

	M	Inn	NO	Runs	HS	Avg	100	Ct	St	Runs	Wkts	Avg	BB	5I	10M
Test	1	2	0	51	30	25.50	-	-	-						
FC	292	491	34	18387	257	40.23	48	140	-	493	5	98.60	2-55	-	-

BODENHAM, M. J. D.

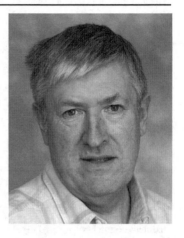

Name: <u>Martin</u> John Dale Bodenham
Born: 23 April 1950, Brighton
Height: 6ft 1in
Marital status: Single
Family links with cricket: 'Father was a qualified cricket umpire'
Education: Goring Hall School
Career outside cricket: Football Association referee coach: '12 designated referees assigned to me for the whole of the football season'
Other sports played: Golf
Other sports followed: Horse racing
Relaxations: Veteran car enthusiast – 'owner of a car which is over 100 years old'
Appointed to 1st-Class list: 2009
Umpiring honours: Umpired 2 Sussex League Cup finals
Highlights of umpiring career:
'Initially being appointed to the ECB Reserve List (3 seasons) and then on to the Full List for season 2009'
Players to watch for the future: Joe Denly, Luke Wright, Ben Brown
County as player: 'Played for Sussex in a number of 2nd XI Championship matches'
Role: Batsman, wicket-keeper
Cricket moments to forget: 'Being out to the first ball of a Sussex League match'
Extras: Ex-FIFA International Football Referee. Football League Referee 1978-1992 and FA Premier League Referee 1992-1998; refereed the 1997 League Cup final and three FA Cup semi-finals. Reserve referee European Cup final AC Milan v Barcelona 1994. Took up umpiring following retirement as football referee in 1998; Sussex League; in 2006 added by ECB to its reserve list; first first-class game Essex v Loughborough UCCE, Chelmsford, 15-17 April 2006
Opinions on cricket: 'Competitive but must always be played in the right spirit. Attendance at all types of matches (particularly one-day games) on the increase so the game must be in a healthy state.'

Did not play first-class cricket

COOK, N.G.B.

Name: Nicholas (<u>Nick</u>) Grant Billson Cook
Born: 17 June 1956, Leicester
Height: 6ft
Nickname: Beast, Rag'ead
Wife and date of marriage: Shan, 20
September 1991
Children: None
Education: Lutterworth High
Career outside cricket: Cricket pro at Rugby
School
Other sports followed: Football (Leicester
City), rugby (Leicester Tigers), National Hunt
racing
Relaxations: See above
Appointed to 1st-Class list: 2009
Highlights of umpiring career:
'Being appointed to the first-class panel'
Counties as player: Leicestershire,
Northamptonshire

Role: Right-hand bat, slow left-arm leg-spin bowler
County debut: 1978 (Leics), 1986 (Northants)
County cap: 1982 (Leics), 1987 (Northants)
Test debut: 1983
ODI debut (matches): 1983-84 (3)
50 wickets in a season: 8
1st-Class 10w in match: 4
Overseas tours: England to New Zealand (1984), to Pakistan (1984), to Pakistan
(1987)
Cricket moments to forget: 'When David Boon swept me in 1989 to win the Ashes
back for Australia'
Extras: Played 15 Tests and 3 ODIs for England
Best batting: 75 Leicestershire v Somerset, Taunton 1980
Best bowling: 7-34 Northamptonshire v Essex, Chelmsford 1992
Opinions on cricket: 'The game is in a pretty healthy state, both internationally and
countywise... I disagree entirely with the bandwagon that says we play too much
cricket.'

First-Class Career Performances

	M	Inn	NO	Runs	HS	Avg	100	Ct	St	Runs	Wkts	Avg	BB	5I	10M
Test	15	25	4	179	31	8.52	-	5		1689	52	32.48	6-65	4	1
FC	356	365	96	3138	75	11.67	-	197		25507	879	29.02	7-34	31	4

COWLEY, N. G. C.

Name: <u>Nigel</u> Geoffrey Charles Cowley
Born: 1 March 1953, Shaftesbury, Dorset
Height: 5ft 6½in
Marital status: Divorced
Children: Mark Antony, 14 June 1973;
Darren James, 30 October 1976
Family links with cricket: Son Darren
played Hampshire Schools U11, U12, U13;
Natal Schools 1993, 1994, 1995; and toured
India with South Africa U19 1996
Education: Duchy Manor, Mere, Wiltshire
Other sports played: Golf (8 handicap)
Other sports followed: Football
(Liverpool FC)
Appointed to 1st-Class list: 2000
Counties as player: Hampshire, Glamorgan
Role: Right-hand bat, off-spin bowler
County debut: 1974 (Hampshire),
1990 (Glamorgan)
County cap: 1978 (Hampshire)

Benefit: 1988 (Hampshire)
1000 runs in a season: 1
50 wickets in a season: 2
One-Day 5 w. in innings: 1
Overseas tours: Hampshire to Barbados 1985, 1986, 1987, to Dubai 1989
Overseas teams played for: Paarl CC 1982-83; Amanzimtoti 1984-96
(both South Africa)
Extras: Played for Dorset 1972. NatWest Man of the Match award
Best batting: 109* Hampshire v Somerset, Taunton 1977
Best bowling: 6-48 Hampshire v Leicestershire, Southampton 1982

First-Class Career Performances

	M	Inn	NO	Runs	HS	Avg	100	Ct	St	Runs	Wkts	Avg	BB	5I	10M
Test															
FC	271	375	62	7309	109*	23.35	2	105	-	14879	437	34.04	6-48	5	-

DULESTON, B.

Name: Barry Dudleston
Born: 16 July 1945, Bebington, Cheshire
Height: 5ft 9in
Nickname: Danny
Wife and date of marriage: Louise Wendy, 19 October 1994
Children: Sharon Louise, 29 October 1968; Matthew Barry, 12 September 1988; Jack Nicholas, 29 April 1998
Family links with cricket: 'Dad was a league cricketer'
Education: Stockport School
Career outside cricket: Managing director of Sunsport Ltd
Other sports played: Golf
Other sports followed: All sports
Relaxations: Bridge, red wine
Appointed to 1st-Class list: 1984
First appointed to Test panel: 1991
Tests umpired: 2 (plus 4 as TV umpire)
ODIs umpired: 4 (plus 6 as TV umpire)

Other umpiring honours: Stood in C&G final 2001 and B&H final 2002; also officiated at the inaugural Twenty20 finals day at Trent Bridge 2003, including standing in the final, and at Twenty20 finals day 2006 at Trent Bridge
Highlight of umpiring career: 'A Lord's Test match'
Players to watch for the future: Chris Woakes
Counties as player: Leicestershire, Gloucestershire
Role: Right-hand opening bat, slow left-arm bowler, occasional wicket-keeper
County debut: 1966 (Leicestershire), 1981 (Gloucestershire)
County cap: 1969 (Leicestershire)
Benefit: 1980 (Leicestershire)
1000 runs in a season: 8
1st-Class 200s: 1
One-Day 100s: 4
Overseas tours: Kent (as guest player) to West Indies 1972; D.H. Robins' XI to West Indies 1973; Wisden XI to West Indies 1984; MCC to Kenya 1993
Overseas teams played for: Rhodesia/Zimbabwe-Rhodesia 1976-80
Highlights of playing career: 'Winning County Championship [with Leicestershire]'
Extras: Played for England U25. Holder with John Steele of the highest first-wicket partnership for Leicestershire, 390 v Derbyshire at Leicester in 1979. Fastest player in Rhodesian cricket history to 1000 first-class runs in Currie Cup; second fastest ever in Currie Cup

Best batting: 202 Leicestershire v Derbyshire, Leicester 1979
Best bowling: 4-6 Leicestershire v Surrey, Leicester 1972

First-Class Career Performances

	M	Inn	NO	Runs	HS	Avg	100	Ct	St	Runs	Wkts	Avg	BB	5I	10M
Test															
FC	295	501	47	14747	202	32.48	32	234	7	1365	47	29.04	4-6	-	-

EVANS, J. H.

Name: Jeffrey (<u>Jeff</u>) Howard Evans
Born: 7 August 1954, Llanelli
Height: 5ft 8in
Children: Rhian; Siân
Education: Llanelli Boys Grammar School;
Dudley College of Education
Career outside cricket: Teacher
Off-season: 'Supply teaching. Ski-ing. Coach
driving to the Alps.'
Other sports played: Rugby, squash
Other sports followed: 'Most sports, rugby
in particular'
Relaxations: 'Walking, keeping fit'
Appointed to 1st-Class list: 2001
Other umpiring honours: Toured Namibia
and Uganda 2004-05 with MCC (as umpire)
Highlights of umpiring career: 'Indian
Cricket League, 2008, MCC Tour to Namibia
and Uganda 2005'
Players to watch for the future: Azeem Rafiq (Yorkshire), James Harris (Glamorgan)
Cricket moments to forget: 'Any error of judgement'
County as player: Did not play first-class cricket. Played league cricket in South
Wales as a right-hand bat
Extras: Coach to Welsh Schools Cricket Association team on tour to Australia 1993.
Taught in the Gwendraeth Grammar School – 'the old "outside-half factory"'
Opinions on cricket: 'Would like to see more honesty throughout the game.'

Did not play first-class cricket

GARRATT, S. A.

Name: Stephen (<u>Steve</u>) Arthur Garratt
Born: 5 July 1953, Nottingham
Height: 6ft 2in
Nickname: Trigger
Wife and date of marriage: Marion, 1975
Children: Mark, 27; Chris, 25;
Farris (grandson), 5
Family links with cricket: 'Father Arthur
played local club cricket in Nottingham'
Education: Arnold County High School,
Nottingham
Career outside cricket: Retired police
officer
Off-season: 'Taking holidays with my wife'
Other sports played: Rugby union, football
Other sports followed: 'All sports'
Relaxations: 'Walk on the beach at Whitby'
Appointed to 1st-Class list: 2008
Highlights of umpiring career: 'MCC tour to Argentina, 2008'
Players to watch for the future: Adam Lyth, Chris Woakes, Liam Dawson
County as player: Did not play first-class cricket

Did not play first-class cricket

GOUGH, M.A.

Name: <u>Michael </u>Andrew Gough
Born: 18 December 1979, Hartlepool
Height: 6ft 5in
Nickname: Goughy
Wife and date of marriage: Charlotte Rae, 3 February 2006
Children: None
Education: English Martyrs School and Sixth Form College, Hartlepool
Family links with cricket: 'Father Michael played minor counties for Durham'
Other sports played: Football
Other sports followed: Football (Hartlepool United), rugby, golf
Off-season: 'Keeping fit – jogging, walking, swimming, gym'
Relaxations: 'Eating out, sport on TV, reading, sudoku'
Umpiring career: Started 2005 after retirement from first-class game; appointed to
ECB reserve list 2006. Believed to be the youngest first-class umpire in the history of

the game, a year younger than either David Constant or the legendary inter-war umpire Frank Chester.

Appointed to 1st-Class list: 2009
Counties as player: Durham
Role: Right-hand bat; right-arm off-spin bowler
County debut: 1998
1st-Class 50s: 15
1st-Class 100s: 2
1st-Class 5 w. in innings: 1
1st-Class catches: 57
One-Day 100s: 1
Place in batting averages: 202nd av. 23.36 (2002 31st av. 51.33)
Strike rate: 57.33 (career 82.86)
Overseas tours: England U17 to Bermuda (international youth tournament winners) 1997; England U19 to South Africa (1997), to New Zealand (1998-99); England A to Bangladesh (1999), to New Zealand (1999-2000)
Overseas teams played for: Claremont Nedlands, Perth, Australia 2001 – 2003

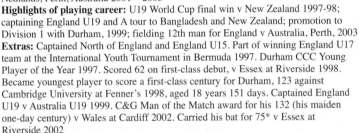

Highlights of playing career: U19 World Cup final win v New Zealand 1997-98; captaining England U19 and A tour to Bangladesh and New Zealand; promotion to Division 1 with Durham, 1999; fielding 12th man for England v Australia, Perth, 2003
Extras: Captained North of England and England U15. Part of winning England U17 team at the International Youth Tournament in Bermuda 1997. Durham CCC Young Player of the Year 1997. Scored 62 on first-class debut, v Essex at Riverside 1998. Became youngest player to score a first-class century for Durham, 123 against Cambridge University at Fenner's 1998, aged 18 years 151 days. Captained England U19 v Australia U19 1999. C&G Man of the Match award for his 132 (his maiden one-day century) v Wales at Cardiff 2002. Carried his bat for 75* v Essex at Riverside 2002
Best batting: 123 Durham v Cambridge University, Fenner's 1998
Best bowling: 5-66 Durham v Middlesex, Riverside 2001

First-Class Career Performances

	M	Inn	NO	Runs	HS	Avg	100	Ct	St	Runs	Wkts	Avg	BB	5I	10M
Test															
FC	67	119	3	2952	123	25.44	2	58		1350	30	45.00	5-66	1	-

GOULD, I. J.

Name: <u>Ian</u> James Gould
Born: 19 August 1957, Taplow, Bucks
Height: 5ft 7in
Nickname: Gunner
Wife and date of marriage: Joanne,
27 September 1986
Children: Gemma; Michael; George
Education: Westgate Secondary Modern,
Slough
Other sports played: Golf
Other sports followed: Football (Arsenal),
racing
Appointed to 1st-Class list: 2002
International panel: 2006 –
Elite panel: 2010 –
Tests umpired: 11 (plus 8 as TV umpire)
ODIs umpired: 42 (plus 12 as TV umpire)
Twenty20 Ints umpired: 7 (plus 4 as TV
umpire)

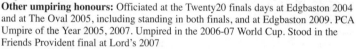

Other umpiring honours: Officiated at the Twenty20 finals days at Edgbaston 2004 and at The Oval 2005, including standing in both finals, and at Edgbaston 2009. PCA Umpire of the Year 2005, 2007. Umpired in the 2006-07 World Cup. Stood in the Friends Provident final at Lord's 2007
Players to watch for the future: Ollie Rayner
Counties as player: Middlesex, Sussex
Role: Left-hand bat, wicket-keeper
County debut: 1975 (Middlesex), 1981 (Sussex)
County cap: 1977 (Middlesex), 1981 (Sussex)
Benefit: 1990 (Sussex)
ODI debut (matches): 1982-83 (18)
Overseas tours: England YC to West Indies 1976; D.H. Robins' XI to Canada 1978-79; International XI to Pakistan 1980-81; England to Australia and New Zealand 1982-83; MCC to Namibia
Overseas teams played for: Auckland 1979-80
Highlights of playing career: 'Playing in the World Cup'
Extras: Represented England in the 1983 World Cup. Retired from county cricket in 1991
Best batting: 128 Middlesex v Worcestershire, Worcester 1978
Best bowling: 3-10 Sussex v Surrey, The Oval 1989

	M	Inn	NO	Runs	HS	Avg	100	Ct	St	Runs	Wkts	Avg	Best	5I	10M
Test															
FC	297	399	63	8756	128	26.06	4	536	67	365	7	52.14	3-10	-	-

HARTLEY, P. J.

Name: Peter John (<u>Jack</u>) Hartley
Born: 18 April 1960, Keighley, Yorkshire
Height: 6ft
Nickname: Jack
Wife and date of marriage: Sharon,
12 March 1988
Children: Megan, 25 April 1993;
Courtney, 25 July 1995
Family links with cricket: Father and
brother played local league cricket
Education: Greenhead Grammar School,
Keighley; Bradford College
Off-season: 'Playing golf and skiing as often
as possible'
Other sports played: Golf (2 handicap)
Other sports followed: Football (Chelsea)
Relaxations: 'Walking'
Appointed to 1st-Class list: 2003
International panel: 2006 –
Tests umpired: 9 as TV umpire
ODIs umpired: 6 (plus 10 as TV umpire)
Twenty20 Ints umpired: 3 (plus 3 as TV umpire)
Other umpiring honours: Officiated at Twenty20 finals day 2006 at Trent Bridge,
including standing in the final. Umpired his first ODI in 2007 – England v India,
The Oval. Umpired U19 World Cup final 2008 in Malaysia
Highlights of umpiring career: 'Above [ODI], and umpired Friends Provident
final 2007, plus the U19 World Cup final'
Counties as player: Warwickshire, Yorkshire, Hampshire
Role: Right-hand bat, right-arm fast-medium bowler
County debut: 1982 (Warwickshire), 1985 (Yorkshire), 1998 (Hampshire)
County cap: 1987 (Yorkshire), 1998 (Hampshire)
Benefit: 1996 (Yorkshire)
50 wickets in a season: 7
One-Day 5 w. in innings: 5
Overseas tours: Yorkshire pre-season tours to Barbados 1986-87, to South Africa

1991-92, 1992-93, to Zimbabwe
Overseas teams played for: Melville, New Zealand 1983-84; Adelaide, Australia
1985-86; Harmony and Orange Free State, South Africa 1988-89
Highlights of playing career: 'Hat-trick and taking 9-41 in same game'
Extras: His 9-41 v Derbyshire at Chesterfield 1995 contained a spell of five wickets
in nine balls, including a hat-trick (DeFreitas, Harrison, Cork). Returned 8-65, his best
figures for Hampshire, against Yorkshire, his former county, at Basingstoke 1999.
Recorded his highest B&H score (32*) and best one-day analysis (5-20) v Sussex at
Hove 2000. Retired from county cricket at the end of the 2000 season
Opinions on cricket: 'Game in good shape; let's not let four-day cricket decline.
Twenty20 has some yards to go yet.'
Best batting: 127* Yorkshire v Lancashire, Old Trafford 1988
Best bowling: 9-41 Yorkshire v Derbyshire, Chesterfield 1995

First-Class Career Performances

	M	Inn	NO	Runs	HS	Avg	100	Ct	St	Runs	Wkts	Avg	BB	5I	10M
Test															
FC	232	283	66	4321	127*	19.91	2	68	-	20635	683	30.21	9-41	23	3

HOLDER, V. A.

Name: <u>Vanburn</u> Alonza Holder
Born: 8 October 1945, St Michael, Barbados
Height: 6ft 3in
Nickname: Vanny
Wife and date of marriage: Chris,
19 July 1980
Children: James, 2 September 1981
Education: St Leonard's Secondary Modern;
Community High
Off-season: 'Relaxing'
Other sports followed: Football (Liverpool)
Relaxations: Music, doing crosswords
Appointed to 1st-Class list: 1992
ODIs umpired: 2 as TV umpire
County as player: Worcestershire
Role: Right-hand bat, right-arm
fast-medium bowler
County debut: 1968
County cap: 1970
Benefit: 1979
Test debut: 1969

ODI debut (matches): 1973 (12)
50 wickets in a season: 9
One-Day 5 w. in innings: 3
Overseas tours: West Indies to England 1969, 1973, 1975 (World Cup), 1976, to India, Sri Lanka and Pakistan 1974-75, to Australia 1975-76, to India and Sri Lanka 1978-79 (vc); Rest of the World to Pakistan 1973-74
Overseas teams played for: Barbados 1966-78
Extras: Made his debut for Barbados in the Shell Shield competition in 1966-67. Won John Player League 1973 and County Championship 1974 with Worcestershire. Played in West Indies 1975 World Cup-winning side
Best batting: 122 Barbados v Trinidad, Bridgetown 1973-74
Best bowling: 7-40 Worcestershire v Glamorgan, Cardiff 1974

First-Class Career Performances

	M	Inn	NO	Runs	HS	Avg	100	Ct	St	Runs	Wkts	Avg	BB	5I	10M
Test	40	59	11	682	42	14.20	-	16	-	3627	109	33.27	6-28	3	-
FC	311	354	81	3559	122	13.03	1	98	-	23183	948	24.45	7-40	38	3

ILLINGWORTH, R. K.

Name: Richard Keith Illingworth
Born: 23 August 1963, Greengates, near Bradford, Yorkshire
Height: 5ft 11in
Nickname: Harry, Lucy
Wife and date of marriage: Anne Louise, 20 September 1985
Children: Miles, 28 August 1987; Thomas, 20 April 1989
Family links with cricket: Father and mother involved around Bradford League
Education: Salts GS
Off-season: 'Coaching'
Other sports played: Golf, cycling, running
Other sports followed: Football (Leeds), rugby league (Bradford Bulls), rugby union (Worcester)
Relaxations: 'Watching my two sons playing sport; cooking; wine tasting'

Appointed to 1st-Class list: 2006
Highlights of umpiring career: Stood at Twenty20 finals day in 2008 and at Edgbaston 2009, including the final
Players to watch for the future: 'Sam Northeast (Kent), Jonathan Bairstow

(Yorkshire), Dan Redfern (Derbyshire). Never seen James Taylor score a run but my colleagues say he is one to watch'

Counties as player: Worcestershire, Derbyshire
Role: Right-hand bat, left-arm orthodox spin bowler
County debut: 1982 (Worcestershire), 2001 (Derbyshire)
County cap: 1986 (Worcestershire)
Benefit: 1997 (Worcestershire)
Test debut: 1991
ODI debut (matches): 1991 (25)
50 wickets in a season: 5
One-Day 5 w. in innings: 2
Overseas tours: England A to Kenya and Zimbabwe 1989-90, to Pakistan and Sri Lanka 1990-91; England to New Zealand and Australia (World Cup) 1991-92, to South Africa 1995-96, to India and Pakistan (World Cup) 1995-96
Overseas teams played for: Brisbane Colts 1982-83; Zingari, Pietermaritzburg, South Africa 1984-85, 1988-89; University/St Heliers, New Zealand 1986-88; Natal 1988-89; Abahani, Bangladesh 1994
Highlights of playing career: 'Playing for England. Being part of many Worcestershire trophy wins. Wicket [Phil Simmons of West Indies] with first ball in Test cricket'
Cricket moments to forget: 'None, apart from getting out for nought or dropping catches (of which there were a few)'
Extras: Scored three centuries batting as a nightwatchman. First Worcestershire bowler to take a one-day hat-trick, v Sussex at Hove in the Sunday League 1993. Retired from county cricket at the end of the 2001 season
Best batting: 120* Worcestershire v Warwickshire, Worcester 1987
Best bowling: 7-50 Worcestershire v Oxford University, The Parks 1985

First-Class Career Performances

	M	Inn	NO	Runs	HS	Avg	100	Ct	St	Runs	Wkts	Avg	BB	5I	10M
Test	9	14	7	128	28	18.28	-	5	-	615	19	32.36	4-96	-	-
FC	376	435	122	7027	120*	22.45	4	161	-	26213	831	31.54	7-50	27	6

JESTY, T. E.

Name: <u>Trevor</u> Edward Jesty
Born: 2 June 1948, Gosport, Hampshire
Height: 5ft 9in
Nickname: Jets
Wife and date of marriage: Jacqueline, 12 September 1970
Children: Graeme Barry, 27 September 1972; Lorna Samantha, 7 November 1976
Family links with cricket: Daughter played for England XI 2000
Education: Privett County Secondary Modern, Gosport
Other sports followed: Football (Arsenal)
Relaxations: Gardening, reading
Appointed to 1st-Class list: 1994
ODIs umpired: 3 as TV umpire
Counties as player: Hampshire, Surrey, Lancashire
Role: Right-hand bat, right-arm medium bowler
County debut: 1966 (Hampshire), 1985 (Surrey), 1988 (Lancashire)
County cap: 1971 (Hampshire), 1985 (Surrey), 1990 (Lancashire)
Benefit: 1982 (Hampshire)
ODI debut (matches): 1982-83 (10)
1000 runs in a season: 10
50 wickets in a season: 2
1st-Class 200s: 2
One-Day 100s: 7
Overseas tours: International XI to West Indies 1982; joined England tour to Australia 1982-83; Lancashire to Zimbabwe 1989
Overseas teams played for: Border, South Africa 1973-74; Griqualand West 1974-76, 1980-81; Canterbury, New Zealand 1979-80
Highlights of playing career: 'Winning Championship with Hampshire in 1973. Playing against Australia for England in one-day match on 1982-83 tour'
Extras: One of *Wisden*'s Five Cricketers of the Year 1983
Best batting: 248 Hampshire v Cambridge University, Fenner's 1984
Best bowling: 7-75 Hampshire v Worcestershire, Southampton 1976

First-Class Career Performances

	M	Inn	NO	Runs	HS	Avg	100	Ct	St	Runs	Wkts	Avg	BB	5I	10M
Test															
FC	490	777	107	21916	248	32.71	35	265	1	16075	585	27.47	7-75	19	-

KETTLEBOROUGH, R. A.

Name: <u>Richard</u> Allan Kettleborough
Born: 15 March 1973, Sheffield
Height: 5ft 10in
Nickname: Ketts
Wife and date of marriage: Lucy,
6 October 2007
Children: Millie Hannah, 16 October 2008
Family links with cricket: 'Dad played
league cricket'
Education: Worksop College; Airedale and
Wharfdale College
Career outside cricket: Groundsman
Other sports played: Football, golf
Other sports followed: Football (Sheffield
Wednesday FC)
Relaxations: 'Socialising with friends'
Appointed to 1st-Class list: 2006
International panel: 2008 –
Tests umpired: 3 as TV umpire
ODIs umpired: 5 (5 as TV umpire)
Twenty20 Ints umpired: 1 (1 as TV umpire)
Other umpiring honours: Stood in the International 20:20 Club Championship 2005.
Stood at Twenty20 finals day at Edgbaston 2009, including the final
Highlights of umpiring career: 'Any major match appointment'
Players to watch for the future: Adil Rashid, Liam Dawson
Counties as player: Yorkshire, Middlesex
Role: Left-hand bat
County debut: 1994 (Yorkshire), 1998 (Middlesex)
Overseas tours: England U18 to Canada 1991; Yorkshire to South Africa 1994, to
Zimbabwe 1995, to West Indies 1996; MCC to Hong Kong 2000, to Kenya 2001, to
Australia 2002-03, to UAE 2004, to Namibia and Uganda 2005, to India 2006
Overseas teams played for: Somerset West, Cape Town 1993-94; Constantia,
Cape Town 2003
Highlights of playing career: 'Yorkshire debut 1994. Maiden first-class hundred v
Essex 1996. Winning National Club Knockout with Sheffield Collegiate 2000'
Cricket moments to forget: '1998 and 1999 in London'
Extras: MCC Young Cricketer of the Year 1988. Yorkshire Young Player of the
Year 1996
Opinions on cricket: 'Reduce the number of non-English-qualified players in
county cricket.'
Best batting: 108 Yorkshire v Essex, Headingley 1996
Best bowling: 2-26 Yorkshire v Nottinghamshire, Scarborough 1996

First-Class Career Performances

	M	Inn	NO	Runs	HS	Avg	100	Ct	St	Runs	Wkts	Avg	BB	5I	10M
Test															
FC	33	56	6	1258	108	25.16	1	20	-	243	3	81.00	2-26	-	-

LLONG, N. J.

Name: Nigel James Llong
Born: 11 February 1969, Ashford, Kent
Height: 6ft
Nickname: Nidge
Wife and date of marriage: Melissa,
20 February 1999
Children: Andrew Stuart, 30 August 2002;
Matthew James, 14 December 2004
Family links with cricket: Father and
brother played local club cricket
Education: North School for Boys, Ashford
Off-season: Coaching – Duke of York
School, Dover
Other sports followed: Football (Arsenal),
'generally most sports'
Relaxations: Fishing
Appointed to 1st-Class list: 2002
International panel: 2004-2006 as TV
umpire; 2006 –
Tests umpired: 8 (plus 12 as TV umpire)
ODIs umpired: 32 (plus 21 as TV umpire)
Twenty20 Ints umpired: 12 (plus 6 as TV umpire)
Other umpiring honours: Officiated at Twenty20 finals day at Edgbaston 2004,
including standing in the final, and 2007, and at Edgbaston 2009. Stood in his first
Test match in January 2008 – the first Test between New Zealand and Bangladesh at
Dunedin
Highlights of umpiring career: 'Umpired at Twenty20 World Championship, South
Africa 2007-08'
County as player: Kent
Role: Left-hand bat, right-arm off-spin bowler
County debut: 1991
County cap: 1993
One-Day 100s: 2
Overseas tours: Kent to Zimbabwe 1993
Overseas teams played for: Ashburton, Melbourne 1988-90, 1996-97; Green Point,
Cape Town 1990-95

Highlights of playing career: 'B&H final 1997. Sunday League winners 1995. First Championship hundred, Lord's 1993'

Cricket moments to forget: 'Sunday League [1993], last match against Glamorgan at Canterbury – lost the match and were runners-up. Plus not making the most of my ability'

Extras: Kent Young Player of the Year 1992. Man of the Match in 2nd XI Trophy semi-final and final 1999. Retired from county cricket in September 1999 and played for Norfolk in 2000

Opinions on cricket: 'Umpires watch every ball of a game. It's amazing how little their opinions are valued!'

Best batting: 130 Kent v Hampshire, Canterbury 1996

Best bowling: 5-21 Kent v Middlesex, Canterbury 1996

First-Class Career Performances

	M	Inn	NO	Runs	HS	Avg	100	Ct	St	Runs	Wkts	Avg	BB	5I	10M
Test															
FC	68	108	11	3024	130	31.17	6	59	-	1259	35	35.97	5-21	2	-

LLOYDS, J. W.

Name: <u>Jeremy</u> William Lloyds
Born: 17 November 1954, Penang, Malaya
Height: 5ft 11in
Nickname: Jerry
Wife and date of marriage: Janine, 16 September 1997
Children: Kaeli, 16 November 1991
Family links with cricket: Father played cricket in Malaya. Brother Chris played for Somerset 2nd XI
Education: Blundell's School, Tiverton
Career outside cricket: Coaching and setting up Western Province Youth Programme 1992-95 in South Africa
Off-season: 'Getting a job'
Other sports played: Golf (6 handicap)
Other sports followed: Golf, football (Tottenham Hotspur), American football (San Francisco 49ers), Formula One and saloon car racing, rugby (Gloucester)
Relaxations: 'Reading, music and spending time at home with my family'
Appointed to 1st-Class list: 1998
International panel: 2002-2004 as TV umpire; 2004-2006

Tests umpired: 5 (plus 10 as TV umpire)
ODIs umpired: 18 (plus 22 as TV umpire)
Twenty20 Ints umpired: 1
Other umpiring honours: Stood in the C&G final 2006. Officiated at Twenty20 finals day 2007 and 2008
Counties as player: Somerset, Gloucestershire
Role: Left-hand bat, off-spin bowler
County debut: 1979 (Somerset), 1985 (Gloucestershire)
County cap: 1982 (Somerset), 1985 (Gloucestershire)
1000 runs in a season: 3
Overseas tours: Somerset to Antigua 1982; Gloucestershire to Barbados 1985, to Sri Lanka 1987
Overseas teams played for: St Stithian's Old Boys, Johannesburg 1978-79; Toombull DCC, Brisbane 1980-82; North Sydney District 1982-83; Alberton, Johannesburg 1984; Preston CC, Melbourne 1986; Orange Free State 1987; Fish Hoek CC, Cape Town 1988-92
Highlights of playing career: 'Winning 1983 NatWest final'
Extras: Highest score in Brisbane Premier League 1980-81 (165). Britannic Player of the Month July 1987. Gloucestershire Player of the Year 1987. Leading run-scorer in Western Province Cricket League 1988, 1989
Opinions on cricket: 'Would take too long. I would suggest that by having central contracts we are creating elitism. Batsmen must be allowed to bat and bowlers to bowl whenever possible. Net bowling/batting is never quite the same.'
Best batting: 132* Somerset v Northamptonshire, Northampton 1982
Best bowling: 7-88 Somerset v Essex, Chelmsford 1982

First-Class Career Performances

	M	Inn	NO	Runs	HS	Avg	100	Ct	St	Runs	Wkts	Avg	BB	5I	10M
Test															
FC	267	408	64	10679	132*	31.04	10	229	-	12943	333	38.86	7-88	13	1

MALLENDER, N. A.

Name: Neil Alan Mallender
Born: 13 August 1961, Kirk Sandall, Doncaster
Height: 6ft
Nickname: Ghostie
Marital status: Divorced
Children: Kirstie, 20; Dominic, 17; Jacob, 12
Education: Beverley Grammar School
Off-season: Training
Other sports played: Golf (2 handicap)
Other sports followed: 'Most sports'
Relaxations: 'Watching sport; music'
Appointed to 1st-Class list: 1999
International panel: 2002-2004
Tests umpired: 3 (plus 5 as TV umpire)
ODIs umpired: 22 (plus 10 as TV umpire)
Other umpiring honours: Went with MCC to umpire in Namibia March/April 2001.

PCA Umpire of the Year 2001, 2002, 2003, 2004, 2006, 2008. Stood in the 2002-03 World Cup. Umpired the 2004, 2005 and 2006 C&G Trophy finals. Officiated at Twenty20 finals day at Edgbaston 2007, including standing in the final; in 2008, and 2009, including the final
Highlights of umpiring career: 'First ODI at Lord's, Twenty20 finals day 2007, 2008, 2009'
Players to watch for the future: James Tomlinson, Adil Rashid, Chris Jordan, Chris Woakes, Liam Dawson
Counties as player: Northamptonshire, Somerset
Role: Right-hand bat, right-arm fast-medium bowler
County debut: 1980 (Northamptonshire), 1987 (Somerset)
County cap: 1984 (Northamptonshire), 1987 (Somerset)
Benefit: 1994 (Somerset)
Test debut: 1992
50 wickets in a season: 6
One-Day 5 w. in innings: 3
Overseas tours: England YC to West Indies 1979-80
Overseas teams played for: Kaikorai, Dunedin, New Zealand; University, Wellington, New Zealand; Otago, New Zealand 1983-84 – 1992-93
Highlights of playing career: 'Test debut at Headingley'
Extras: Represented England YC 1980-81. Took 5-50 on Test debut v Pakistan at Headingley in 1992. Retired from county cricket in 1996

Best batting: 100* Otago v Central Districts, Palmerston North 1991-92
Best bowling: 7-27 Otago v Auckland, Auckland 1984-85

First-Class Career Performances

	M	Inn	NO	Runs	HS	Avg	100	Ct	St	Runs	Wkts	Avg	BB	5I	10M
Test	2	3	0	8	4	2.66	-	-	-	215	10	21.50	5-50	1	-
FC	345	396	122	4709	100*	17.18	1	111	-	24654	937	26.31	7-27	36	5

MILLNS, D. J.

Name: <u>David</u> James Millns
Born: 27 February 1965, Mansfield
Height: 6ft 3in
Nickname: Rocket Man
Marital status: Divorced
Children: Dylan, 17 April 1998; Lucas, 10
October 2000; Jessica, 16 October 2001
Education: Samuel Barlow Junior; Garibaldi
Comprehensive; North Notts College of
Further Education; Nottingham Trent
Polytechnic
Off-season: 'Director of marketing
company'
Other sports played: Golf
Other sports followed: 'Football
(Manchester City), American football (New
England Patriots), baseball (Boston
Redsocks)
Relaxations: 'Trying to play better golf, and gym, which means drinking tea in the
bar!'
Umpiring career: First first-class match Glamorgan v Oxford UCCE, The Parks
2007; ECB reserve list 2007
Appointed to 1st-Class list: 2009
Players to watch for the future: Joe Root, Alex Hales
Counties as player: Nottinghamshire 1988-89, Leicestershire 1990-1999,
Nottinghamshire 2000
Role: Left-hand bat; right-arm fast-medium bowler
County debut: 1988 (Nottinghamshire), 1990 (Leicestershire)
County cap: 1991 (Leicestershire), 2000 (Nottinghamshire – *see Extras*)
Benefit: 1999 (Leicestershire)
50 wickets in a season: 4
1st-Class 50s: 8
1st-Class 100s: 3

1st-Class 5 w. in innings: 23
1st-Class 10 w. in match: 4
1st-Class catches: 76
Overseas tours: Leicestershire to South Africa 1994, 1995, to Holland 1994, 1996, to Barbados 1998
Overseas teams played for: Uitenhage, Port Elizabeth, South Africa 1988-89; Birkenhead, Auckland 1989-91; Tasmania, Australia 1994-95; Boland, South Africa 1996-97
Highlights of playing career: 'Last player in Championship cricket to score a century (103) and take 10 wickets in match (10 for 128), Leicestershire versus Essex 1996'
Cricket moments to forget: 'Batting at the other end to Phil Whitticase when he lost 13 teeth after being hit by Neil Williams.'
Extras: Harold Larwood Bowling Award 1984. Asked to be released by Nottinghamshire at the end of the 1989 season and joined Leicestershire in 1990. Finished third in national bowling averages in 1990. Britannic Assurance Player of the Month in August 1991 after taking 9-37 v Derbyshire, the best Leicestershire figures since George Geary's 10-18 v Glamorgan in 1929. Was players' representative on Cricketers' Association Executive for Leicestershire. Leicestershire Cricketer of the Year 1992. Leicestershire Bowling Award 1990, 1991, 1992 and 1994. Left Leicestershire at the end of the 1999 season and rejoined Nottinghamshire for 2000, taking 5-58 v Northamptonshire at Trent Bridge in his first match. Retired during the 2001 season
Opinions on cricket: 'As every old pro will tell you, "We were better in our day!" It's still a great game.'
Best batting: 121 Leicestershire v Northamptonshire, Northampton 1997
Best bowling: 9-37 Leicestershire v Derbyshire, Derby 1991

First-Class Career Performances

	M	Inn	NO	Runs	HS	Avg	100	Ct	St	Runs	Wkts	Avg	BB	5I	10M
Test															
FC	171	203	63	3082	121	22.01	3	76	-	15129	553	27.36	9-37	23	4

ROBINSON, R. T.

Name: Robert Timothy (Tim) Robinson
Born: 21 November 1958, Sutton-in-Ashfield, Nottinghamshire
Height: 6ft
Nickname: Robbo
Marital status: Divorced
Children: Philip; Alex
Family links with cricket: 'Father, uncles all played local cricket'
Education: Dunstable GS; High Pavement GS; Sheffield University
Career outside cricket: 'Accountancy. Sports promotions'

Off-season: 'Working for sports retail/promotions company'
Other sports played: Golf, squash
Other sports followed: Golf, rugby, football
Appointed to 1st-Class list: 2007
Players to watch for the future: Eoin Morgan, Will Smith
County as player: Nottinghamshire
Role: Right-hand opening bat
County debut: 1978
County cap: 1983
Benefit: 1992
Test debut: 1984-85
ODI debut (matches): 1984-85 (26)
1000 runs in a season: 14
1st-Class 200s: 3
One-Day 100s: 9
Overseas tours: England to India and Sri Lanka 1984-85, to West Indies 1985-86, to India and Pakistan (World Cup) 1987-88, to Pakistan 1987-88, to New Zealand and Australia 1987-88, plus two one-day tournaments in Sharjah; unofficial England XI to South Africa 1989-90
Highlights of playing career: '175 v Aussies, home Test debut 1985' (*In the first Test at Headingley*)
Cricket moments to forget: 'Retiring from first-class cricket'
Extras: One of *Wisden*'s Five Cricketers of the Year 1986. Second in the list of Nottinghamshire first-class run-scorers behind George Gunn. Captain of Nottinghamshire 1988-95. Retired from county cricket at the end of the 1999 season
Opinions on cricket: 'Do not let money spoil it!'
Best batting: 220* Nottinghamshire v Yorkshire, Trent Bridge 1990
Best bowling: 1-22 Nottinghamshire v Northamptonshire, Northampton 1982

First-Class Career Performances

	M	Inn	NO	Runs	HS	Avg	100	Ct	St	Runs	Wkts	Avg	BB	5I	10M
Test	29	49	5	1601	175	36.38	4	8	-	0	0		-	-	-
FC	425	739	85	27571	220*	42.15	63	257	-	289	4	72.25	1-22	-	-

SHARP, G.

Name: George Sharp
Born: 12 March 1950, West
Hartlepool,**Height:** 5ft 11in
Nickname: Sharpy
Wife and date of marriage: Audrey,
14 September 1974
Children: Gareth James, 27 June 1984
Education: Elwick Road Secondary Modern,
Hartlepool
Career outside cricket: Watching all sports
Off-season: Working as joint director of
GSB Loams Ltd for soils and top dressing
Other sports played: Golf (8 handicap)
Other sports followed: Football (Newcastle
Utd and Middlesbrough), rugby
(Northampton Saints)
Relaxations: Golf; 'spend a lot of time in the
gym during the off-season'
Appointed to 1st-Class list: 1992
International panel: 1996-2002
Tests umpired: 15 (plus 1 as TV umpire)
ODIs umpired: 31 (plus 13 as TV umpire)
Other umpiring honours: Has umpired three B&H finals and one NatWest final and
stood in the inaugural C&G final 2001 and the 2002 final; also officiated at the
inaugural Twenty20 finals day at Trent Bridge 2003, at finals day 2005 at The Oval
and at finals day 2006 at Trent Bridge. Has stood in four overseas tournaments,
including the Singer Cup (India, Sri Lanka, Pakistan) in Singapore 1995-96 and the
Singer Champions Trophy (Pakistan, Sri Lanka, New Zealand) in Sharjah 1996-97
County as player: Northamptonshire
Role: Right-hand bat, wicket-keeper
County debut: 1967
County cap: 1973
Benefit: 1982
Overseas tours: England Counties XI to Barbados and Trinidad 1975
Best batting: 98 Northamptonshire v Yorkshire, Northampton 1983
Best bowling: 1-47 Northamptonshire v Yorkshire, Northampton 1980

First-Class Career Performances

	M	Inn	NO	Runs	HS	Avg	100	Ct	St	Runs	Wkts	Avg	BB	5I	10M
Test															
FC	306	396	81	6254	98	19.85	-	565	90	70	1	70.00	1-47	-	-

STEELE, J. F.

Name: <u>John</u> Frederick Steele
Born: 23 July 1946, Stafford
Height: 5ft 10in
Nickname: Steely
Wife and date of marriage: Susan,
17 April 1977
Children: Sarah Jane, 2 April 1982;
Robert Alfred, 10 April 1985
Family links with cricket: Uncle Stan
played for Staffordshire. Brother David
played for Northamptonshire, Derbyshire and
England. Cousin Brian Crump played for
Northamptonshire and Staffordshire
Education: Endon School, Stoke-on-Trent;
Stafford College
Other sports followed: Football (Stoke City,
Port Vale), golf
Relaxations: Music and walking
Appointed to 1st-Class list: 1997
Counties as player: Leicestershire, Glamorgan
Role: Right-hand bat, slow left-arm bowler
County debut: 1970 (Leicestershire), 1984 (Glamorgan)
County cap: 1971 (Leicestershire), 1984 (Glamorgan)
Benefit: 1983 (Leicestershire)
1000 runs in a season: 6
One-Day 100s: 1
One-Day 5 w. in innings: 4
Overseas teams played for: Springs HSOB, Northern Transvaal 1971-73;
Pine Town CC, Natal 1973-74, 1982-83; Natal 1975-76, 1978-79
Extras: Played for England U25. Was voted Natal's Best Bowler in 1975-76. First-wicket record partnership for Leicestershire of 390 with Barry Dudleston v Derbyshire at Leicester 1979. Won two Man of the Match Awards in the Gillette Cup and four in the Benson and Hedges Cup. Won the award for the most catches in a season in 1984
Best batting: 195 Leicestershire v Derbyshire, Leicester 1971
Best bowling: 7-29 Natal B v Griqualand West, Umzinto 1973-74
        7-29 Leicestershire v Gloucestershire, Leicester 1980

First-Class Career Performances

	M	Inn	NO	Runs	HS	Avg	100	Ct	St	Runs	Wkts	Avg	BB	5I	10M
Test															
FC	379	605	85	15053	195	28.94	21	414	-	15793	584	27.04	7-29	16	-

WILLEY, P.

Name: Peter Willey
Born: 6 December 1949, Sedgefield, County Durham
Height: 6ft 1in
Nickname: Will, 'many unprintable'
Wife and date of marriage: Charmaine, 23 September 1971
Children: Heather Jane, 11 September 1985; David, 28 February 1990
Family links with cricket: Father played local club cricket in County Durham
Education: Seaham Secondary School, County Durham
Other sports followed: All sports
Relaxations: 'Dog-walking, keeping fit (?), fishing'
Appointed to 1st-Class list: 1993
International panel: 1996-2003
Tests umpired: 25 (plus 7 as TV umpire)
ODIs umpired: 34 (plus 16 as TV umpire)

Other umpiring honours: Stood in the 1999 and 2002-03 World Cups, in the 1999 Benson and Hedges Super Cup final and in the 2004 C&G Trophy final. Officiated at Twenty20 finals days at The Oval 2005 and Edgbaston 2007, including standing in both finals. Chairman of the First-Class Umpires' Association
Counties as player: Northamptonshire, Leicestershire
Role: Right-hand bat, off-break bowler
County debut: 1966 (Northamptonshire), 1984 (Leicestershire)
County cap: 1971 (Northamptonshire), 1984 (Leicestershire)
Benefit: 1981 (Northamptonshire)
Test debut: 1976
ODI debut (matches): 1977 (26)
1000 runs in a season: 10
50 wickets in a season: 2
1st-Class 200s: 1
One-Day 100s: 9
Overseas tours: England to Australia and India 1979-80, to West Indies 1980-81, 1985-86; unofficial England XI to South Africa 1981-82
Overseas teams played for: Eastern Province, South Africa 1982-85
Cricket moments to forget: 'First ball in first-class cricket (v Cambridge University), bowled – thought it can only get better'
Extras: Became youngest player ever to play for Northamptonshire, at 16 years 180

days, v Cambridge University in 1966. Leicestershire captain 1987. Played for Northumberland in 1992. Offered membership of the ICC Elite Panel of umpires in 2002 but declined because of the amount of time the appointment would require away from his family

Opinions on cricket: 'Too much "robot" coaching from nine-year-olds to county standard. Players don't seem to be allowed individual batting styles or bowling actions. Bowling actions changed in case of injury. Too much time spent looking at video analysis and training instead of more time spent in nets. Seems bowling length and line (Pollock, McGrath) is a thing of the past.'

Best batting: 227 Northamptonshire v Somerset, Northampton 1976
Best bowling: 7-37 Northamptonshire v Oxford University, The Parks 1975

First-Class Career Performances

	M	Inn	NO	Runs	HS	Avg	100	Ct	St	Runs	Wkts	Avg	BB	5I	10M
Test	26	50	6	1184	102*	26.90	2	3	-	456	7	65.14	2-73	-	-
FC	559	918	121	24361	227	30.56	44	235	-	23400	756	30.95	7-37	26	3

APPENDICES

Roll of Honour 2009
First-class Averages 2009
Index of Players by County

ROLL OF HONOUR 2009

LV COUNTY CHAMPIONSHIP

Division One

		P	W	L	D	T	Bt	Bl	Pts
1	Durham (I/1)	16	8	0	8	0	49	48	240
2	Nottinghamshire (I/2)	16	4	2	10	0	56	41	193
3	Somerset (I/4)	16	3	1	12	0	50	43	182
4	Lancashire (I/5)	16	4	2	10	0	35	44	175
5	Warwickshire (II/1)	16	3	3	10	0	54	38	174
6	Hampshire (I/3)	16	3	3	10	0	50	40	169
7	Yorkshire (I/7)	16	2	2	12	0	46	44	166
8	Sussex (I/6)	16	2	6	8	0	45	39	143
9	Worcestershire (II/2)	16	0	10	6	0	30	40	94

The bottom two counties were relegated to Division Two for the 2010 season.
Positions in 2008 in brackets.

Division Two

		P	W	L	D	T	Bt	Bl	Pts
1	Kent (I/8)	16	8	3	5	0	43	44	219
2	Essex (II/5)	16	6	3	7	0	40	43	194
3	Northamptonshire (II/4)	16	6	4	6	0	40	45	193
4	Gloucestershire (II/9)	16	6	6	4	0	39	46	185
5	Glamorgan (II/8)	16	2	2	12	0	56	43	175
6	Derbyshire (II/6)	16	2	3	11	0	55	45	172
7	Surrey (I/9)	16	1	4	11	0	54	36	148
8	Middlesex (II/3)	16	2	7	7	0	43	41	140
9	Leicestershire (II/7)	16	2	3	11	0	31	35	138

The top two counties were promoted to Division One for the 2010 season. Positions in
2008 in brackets.

The following sides incurred points deductions for slow over rates in 2009:
Durham, Sussex, Somerset, Essex 1, Hampshire 3.

NATWEST PRO40 LEAGUE

Division One

		P	W	L	NR	T	Pts
1	Sussex (I/1)	8	6	2	0	0	12
2	Somerset (I/6)	8	5	2	1	0	11
3	Worcestershire (I/7)	8	5	2	1	0	11
4	Essex (II/1)	8	5	3	0	0	10
5	Hampshire (I/2)	8	4	4	0	0	8
6	Durham (I/3)	8	4	4	0	0	8
7	Yorkshire (II/2)	8	2	5	1	0	5
8	Gloucestershire (I/5)	8	2	5	1	0	5
9	Nottinghamshire (I/4)	8	0	6	2	0	2

Positions in 2008 in brackets.

Division Two

		P	W	L	NR	T	Pts
1	Warwickshire (II/6)	8	5	0	2	1	13
2	Middlesex (I/9)	8	5	1	2	0	12
3	Kent (II/4)	8	5	3	0	0	9
4	Northamptonshire (II/9)	8	3	2	1	1	9
5	Lancashire (I/8)	8	3	3	1	0	8
6	Glamorgan (II/3)	8	2	4	1	0	6
7	Leicestershire (II/7)	8	2	4	0	0	6
8	Derbyshire (II/8)	8	2	5	1	0	5
9	Surrey (II/5)	8	2	6	0	0	4

Positions in 2008 in brackets.

FRIENDS PROVIDENT TROPHY

Winners: Hampshire   **Runners-up:** Sussex

In the 2010 season, there will be a 40-overs per innings tournament replacing both the Pro40 League and the Friends Provident Trophy.

TWENTY20 CUP

Winners: Sussex   **Runners-up:** Somerset
Semi-finalists: Northamptonshire, Kent

2009 AVERAGES (all first-class matches)

BATTING AVERAGES
Qualifying requirements: 6 completed innings and an average of over 10.00

	Name	M	Inn	NO	Runs	HS	Avg	SR	100	50
1	MR Ramprakash	11	17	2	1350	274	90.00	54.02	5	4
2	S Chanderpaul	9	13	5	683	201*	85.37	52.21	3	2
3	MJ Di Venuto	17	27	6	1654	254*	78.76	65.97	6	6
4	AC Voges	8	10	1	697	139	77.44	54.07	1	6
5	ME Trescothick	16	26	2	1817	146	75.70	60.95	8	9
6	CMW Read	16	22	6	1203	125	75.18	68.50	4	6
7	N Pothas	11	15	4	816	122*	74.18	52.40	1	6
8	IJL Trott	17	25	6	1400	184*	73.68	61.02	5	5
9	CJL Rogers	13	21	1	1461	222	73.05	64.67	6	4
10	MA Carberry	12	21	3	1251	204	69.50	62.30	4	8
11	M van Jaarsveld	16	25	3	1509	182	68.59	64.95	7	7
12	AU Rashid	10	12	4	545	157*	68.12	56.83	2	3
13	VVS Laxman	11	16	3	857	135	65.92	51.53	4	4
14	PJ Hughes	7	12	1	724	195	65.81	70.35	3	3
15	MJ North	8	12	2	613	191*	61.30	54.29	3	1
16	MJ Cosgrove	10	15	2	780	175	60.00	65.87	3	5
17	RS Bopara	9	15	2	772	201	59.38	58.00	4	1
18	C Kieswetter	16	24	3	1242	153	59.14	68.73	4	7
19	MJ Clarke	6	10	1	532	136	59.11	57.51	2	3
20	WL Madsen	9	16	2	809	170*	57.78	52.66	3	3
21	U Afzaal	16	28	6	1269	204*	57.68	56.50	3	7
22	JWA Taylor	17	28	7	1207	207*	57.47	48.18	3	6
23	CD Nash	15	26	3	1321	157	57.43	67.60	4	6
24	MEK Hussey	7	12	2	572	150	57.20	55.75	2	4
25	MB Loye	14	22	4	996	151*	55.33	45.73	2	6
26	SR Watson	4	7	0	374	84	53.42	65.84	0	5
27	AG Prince	6	12	2	526	135*	52.60	64.14	1	3
28	MJ Chilton	16	23	6	891	114	52.41	42.61	2	6
29	JHK Adams	17	30	4	1350	147	51.92	44.88	3	10
30	RJ Hamilton-Brown	5	8	2	311	171*	51.83	77.94	2	0
31	GO Jones	17	26	0	1345	156	51.73	62.26	5	6
32	JS Gatting	4	6	0	310	152	51.6	70.93	1	1
33	AJ Strauss	11	19	1	917	161	50.94	56.18	2	5
34	AJ Hall	16	25	2	1161	159	50.47	59.84	2	6
35	JWM Dalrymple	17	23	3	1009	128	50.45	53.98	3	5
36	RWT Key	17	28	4	1209	270*	50.37	65.52	4	3
37	JEC Franklin	14	22	4	904	109	50.22	51.13	3	4
38	DI Stevens	17	24	3	1050	208	50.00	71.72	4	2
39	LJ Wright	10	15	2	637	118*	49.00	64.73	3	3

	Name	M	Inn	NO	Runs	HS	Avg	SR	100	50
40	JA Rudolph	17	29	1	1366	198	48.78	55.10	4	6
41	DM Benkenstein	18	24	0	1168	181	48.66	49.80	5	4
42	AV Suppiah	16	26	1	1201	151	48.04	50.76	3	6
43	GP Rees	17	25	2	1061	154	46.13	45.89	3	4
44	RN ten Doeschate	14	22	4	823	159*	45.72	66.31	2	2
45	JM Bairstow	12	19	6	592	84*	45.53	52.95	0	6
46	SM Katich	7	11	0	498	122	45.27	56.20	1	2
47	ID Blackwell	18	24	3	949	158	45.19	70.24	2	6
48	CC Benham	6	9	2	316	111	45.14	50.31	2	1
49	APR Gidman	15	23	0	1028	176	44.69	62.45	4	4
50	JC Hildreth	15	23	2	934	303*	44.47	67.29	2	4
51	BJ Haddin	5	8	1	310	121	44.28	70.29	1	1
52	GL Brophy	14	22	5	748	99	44.00	51.33	0	6
53	IR Bell	19	30	3	1185	172	43.88	50.10	4	6
54	SD Peters	14	25	1	1050	175	43.75	56.39	3	5
55	MJ Lumb	16	24	1	1006	219	43.73	50.73	2	5
56	JL Langer	15	21	2	831	122*	43.73	56.30	2	4
57	JM Kemp	14	21	3	780	183	43.33	63.51	2	2
58	AN Cook	17	30	3	1168	160	43.25	53.11	2	6
59	HH Dippenaar	17	31	5	1121	143	43.11	43.63	2	8
60	JJ Sayers	17	29	2	1150	173	42.59	35.81	2	5
61	JL Denly	11	17	1	680	123	42.50	55.10	3	2
62	GM Smith	16	27	4	977	126	42.47	61.75	1	6
63	GT Park	16	27	2	1059	178*	42.36	48.84	2	8
64	OA Shah	8	16	2	591	159	42.21	63.41	2	2
65	MH Yardy	17	29	3	1096	152	42.15	47.92	2	6
66	DJ Wainwright	10	13	4	378	102*	42.00	49.93	1	1
67	MA Butcher	5	8	2	251	65	41.83	49.21	0	2
68	P Mustard	18	22	7	627	94*	41.80	57.20	0	5
69	NJ Dexter	10	19	2	709	146	41.70	57.83	2	2
70	SM Ervine	15	22	2	832	114	41.60	74.35	3	3
71	MJ Prior	13	21	2	788	140	41.47	75.98	1	6
72	J Allenby	12	18	2	662	137	41.37	65.09	1	6
73	HD Ackerman	12	21	1	827	180	41.35	67.23	1	5
74	EC Joyce	15	24	1	945	183	41.08	49.86	3	3
75	SM Davies	15	28	3	1023	126	40.92	65.32	2	5
76	SJ Adshead	7	10	1	367	156*	40.77	56.28	2	0
77	AD Hales	7	12	1	447	78	40.63	47.91	0	4
78	MJ Powell	17	25	2	934	108	40.60	44.22	2	7
79	AD Brown	16	24	3	849	148	40.42	58.59	1	6
80	RT Ponting	6	10	0	401	150	40.10	66.39	1	2
81	N Boje	15	25	5	801	98	40.05	51.84	0	8
82	JB Hockley	5	8	2	240	72	40.00	57.97	0	2
83	ML Pettini	15	28	6	870	101*	39.54	43.60	1	4
84	SA Northeast	11	19	2	667	128*	39.23	52.31	1	3
85	JS Foster	17	27	2	980	103*	39.20	49.92	1	6

Name	M	Inn	NO	Runs	HS	Avg	SR	100	50
86 T Westley	10	17	3	547	132	39.07	48.15	1	2
87 DKH Mitchell	17	31	1	1162	298	38.73	44.16	2	5
88 LE Plunkett	15	14	3	425	94*	38.63	45.02	0	3
89 SCJ Broad	9	13	3	382	61	38.20	75.49	0	3
90 MA Ealham	14	20	7	493	70*	37.92	63.20	0	2
91 DJ Pipe	14	18	5	493	64*	37.92	79.26	0	3
92 WR Smith	17	25	3	834	150	37.90	38.36	2	5
93 A Shahzad	14	18	6	451	88	37.58	44.43	0	2
94 PD Collingwood	8	13	2	413	79*	37.54	47.47	0	5
95 DJ Malan	15	28	3	930	88	37.20	51.09	0	8
96 R Clarke	14	18	1	631	112	37.11	65.72	1	5
97 TR Ambrose	18	24	2	814	153	37.00	58.14	3	4
98 MA Wagh	15	24	2	814	147	37.00	53.87	3	2
99 HH Gibbs	5	7	0	259	96	37.00	65.56	0	2
100 CDHopkinson	9	13	1	443	139	36.91	53.69	2	0
101 AW Gale	17	26	1	921	121	36.84	49.27	2	5
102 RA White	17	31	4	992	193	36.74	64.29	1	7
103 MJ Brown	16	28	1	992	120	36.74	48.55	2	4
104 JN Batty	16	26	0	937	120	36.03	40.30	2	1
105 JO Troughton	17	23	0	828	223	36.00	48.90	2	3
106 MJ Walker	17	31	3	1004	150	35.85	43.44	2	3
107 CP Schofield	14	21	3	644	144	35.77	52.96	1	3
108 GM Andrew	10	16	5	391	92*	35.54	49.93	0	3
109 KJ Coetzer	6	9	1	284	107	35.50	38.74	1	0
110 MH Wessels	15	25	0	887	109	35.48	68.92	1	7
111 PA Nixon	9	17	2	531	173*	35.40	38.47	1	2
112 GP Swann	10	12	2	352	63*	35.20	74.73	0	3
113 HJH Marshall	16	26	2	844	158	35.16	62.01	1	5
114 WW Hinds	16	26	2	841	148	35.04	55.88	2	2
115 GR Napier	10	16	6	348	64*	34.80	62.36	0	2
116 K Ali	16	28	4	834	90	34.75	39.98	0	4
117 JK Maunders	11	18	0	621	150	34.50	50.90	1	3
118 SD Robson	7	13	0	441	110	33.92	40.64	1	2
119 PD Trego	16	23	5	610	103*	33.88	76.15	1	5
120 VS Solanki	17	31	1	1016	206*	33.86	52.72	1	4
121 RDB Croft	17	21	4	574	121	33.76	51.80	1	1
122 CG Taylor	15	22	1	705	111	33.57	59.24	1	5
123 A McGrath	17	27	1	871	211	33.50	52.53	2	2
124 PJ Franks	5	6	0	201	64	33.50	52.48	0	2
125 MW Goodwin	16	27	3	800	344*	33.33	55.36	1	2
126 NRD Compton	14	28	2	860	178	33.07	56.72	2	3
127 CR Woakes	19	23	8	495	131*	33.00	57.69	1	1
128 LMP Simmons	5	8	1	228	102*	32.57	51.35	1	1
129 G Chapple	11	14	2	390	89	32.50	66.10	0	3
130 TC Smith	9	15	3	390	104*	32.50	47.33	1	2
131 BP Nash	5	8	1	227	81	32.42	43.82	0	2

Name	M	Inn	NO	Runs	HS	Avg	SR	100	50
132 SJ Walters	11	18	0	573	188	31.83	48.64	2	1
133 GK Berg	13	23	2	668	98	31.80	72.21	0	7
134 BJ Phillips	7	8	2	190	84	31.66	56.54	0	1
135 SR Patel	17	26	0	821	95	31.57	61.91	0	4
136 PJ Horton	17	30	2	881	173	31.46	49.63	2	4
137 TJ New	18	30	4	813	85*	31.26	54.74	0	6
138 F du Plessis	13	20	3	531	86*	31.23	53.15	0	5
139 Z de Bruyn	16	25	3	686	106	31.18	49.60	1	6
140 SC Moore	17	32	1	952	120	30.70	60.90	2	5
141 WD Bragg	9	12	0	367	92	30.58	51.69	0	2
142 CJ Jordan	8	10	3	213	42	30.42	52.46	0	0
143 DJ Redfern	14	23	1	668	95	30.36	48.79	0	5
144 JC Tredwell	17	21	5	485	86*	30.31	37.92	0	4
145 GJ Muchall	13	19	2	515	106*	30.29	48.35	1	2
146 WI Jefferson	4	6	0	181	133	30.16	49.05	1	0
147 LA Dawson	15	23	4	571	69	30.05	50.62	0	4
148 SJ Croft	9	14	2	360	79	30.00	52.47	0	2
149 A Lyth	5	8	0	240	71	30.00	48.97	0	2
150 SD Stubbings	7	11	1	296	83	29.60	33.48	0	1
151 PP Chawla	6	10	3	206	102*	29.42	100.48	1	0
152 MA Wallace	17	22	0	645	139	29.31	66.83	2	0
153 MM Ali	17	30	2	803	153	28.67	46.52	2	3
154 AA Noffke	6	9	0	258	89	28.66	48.86	0	2
155 JKH Naik	6	10	3	200	109*	28.57	39.37	1	0
156 JA Simpson	3	6	0	170	87	28.33	46.19	0	1
157 AD Mascarenhas	10	11	2	254	108	28.22	57.46	1	0
158 JGE Benning	7	12	2	282	72	28.20	71.39	0	1
159 AC Thomas	14	15	3	338	70	28.16	47.27	0	3
160 JP Crawley	8	14	3	308	81*	28.00	36.57	0	2
161 IJ Westwood	15	25	3	612	133	27.81	44.34	1	4
162 LD Sutton	17	23	7	438	53*	27.37	37.21	0	1
163 MAG Boyce	15	29	2	738	98	27.33	40.23	0	5
164 AN Kervezee	8	14	0	381	66	27.21	56.11	0	2
165 T Frost	15	23	1	598	105	27.18	45.16	1	2
166 AB London	4	8	1	190	68	27.14	40.16	0	2
167 NJ O'Brien	9	16	0	434	128	27.12	55.78	1	1
168 MJ Wood	7	11	1	270	86	27.00	41.99	0	1
169 BM Shafayat	14	23	1	590	90*	26.81	43.12	0	3
170 SC Meaker	5	9	1	214	72	26.75	40.83	0	2
171 MNW Spriegel	6	11	0	294	100	26.72	41.76	1	2
172 DA Wheeldon	5	6	0	160	87	26.66	48.19	0	1
173 RR Sarwan	4	7	0	184	100	26.28	71.87	1	0
174 A Flintoff	7	12	1	288	74	26.18	70.24	0	2
175 KP Pietersen	5	8	0	209	69	26.12	54.28	0	1
176 AG Botha	14	19	2	444	64	26.11	44.48	0	2
177 BF Smith	14	27	3	626	80*	26.08	46.54	0	4

Name	M	Inn	NO	Runs	HS	Avg	SR	100	50
178 TT Bresnan	14	17	2	386	97	25.73	50.00	0	1
179 KW Hogg	14	15	2	333	69	25.61	48.68	0	2
180 V Chopra	12	21	0	537	88	25.57	51.78	0	5
181 RKJ Dawson	7	10	0	254	50	25.40	51.41	0	1
182 JJ van der Wath	13	19	1	452	85	25.11	54.45	0	3
183 JM Vince	9	13	1	301	75	25.08	50.00	0	1
184 AR Adams	11	13	1	300	84	25.00	105.26	0	1
185 AJ Hodd	16	23	3	499	101	24.95	37.88	1	2
186 EJG Morgan	11	20	2	445	114*	24.72	50.74	1	1
187 SA Newman	12	19	0	466	124	24.52	55.67	1	2
188 JD Middlebrook	8	11	3	196	46	24.50	36.84	0	0
189 NM Carter	9	13	0	318	67	24.46	99.06	0	2
190 SJ Cook	13	13	4	220	60*	24.44	53.39	0	1
191 A Harinath	6	9	0	219	57	24.33	45.81	0	1
192 AG Wakely	12	20	1	457	113*	24.05	40.84	1	2
193 M Kartik	10	19	5	336	62*	24.00	65.75	0	2
194 JC Mickleburgh	6	12	0	285	62	23.75	42.72	0	2
195 PG Dixey	3	6	0	142	103	23.66	51.63	1	0
196 D Ramdin	4	7	0	165	61	23.57	59.13	0	2
197 MD Stoneman	13	21	1	466	64	23.30	46.60	0	1
198 RA Jones	7	11	2	209	53*	23.22	53.58	0	1
199 CM Spearman	6	9	0	206	57	22.88	50.86	0	1
200 DD Masters	15	16	1	341	67	22.73	53.36	0	2
201 WTS Porterfield	9	16	1	341	81	22.73	39.46	0	2
202 PS Jones	12	13	3	225	54*	22.50	73.52	0	2
203 AJ Shantry	13	17	3	314	100	22.42	45.63	1	0
204 J Lewis	15	22	6	358	61*	22.37	76.65	0	2
205 DG Cork	12	15	2	290	52	22.30	44.20	0	1
206 CW Henderson	10	13	2	241	79*	21.90	50.84	0	1
207 BHN Howgego	6	11	1	219	47	21.90	39.89	0	0
208 DA Stiff	10	14	5	193	49	21.44	80.41	0	0
209 GG Wagg	14	14	1	273	71	21.00	66.58	0	1
210 MG Johnson	7	8	0	166	63	20.75	61.71	0	1
211 DJ Willey	10	17	1	331	60	20.68	33.74	0	1
212 JER Gallian	7	13	1	245	125	20.41	43.75	1	0
213 WA White	12	19	2	340	68	20.00	45.27	0	1
214 RSC Martin-Jenkins	13	17	2	299	67	19.93	47.84	0	1
215 BJ Wright	9	14	0	279	81	19.92	39.51	0	1
216 SD Udal	14	24	4	398	55	19.90	60.57	0	1
217 MP Vaughan	6	8	0	159	43	19.87	42.17	0	0
218 JAR Harris	14	16	3	256	76*	19.69	47.85	0	1
219 JJ Cobb	14	26	0	510	95	19.61	44.85	0	4
220 TD Groenewald	9	11	1	194	50	19.40	39.35	0	1
221 TL Maynard	6	7	1	115	51*	19.16	57.21	0	1
222 DC Nash	5	8	0	152	43	19.00	44.05	0	0
223 DS Smith	5	8	0	151	46	18.87	56.98	0	0

Name	M	Inn	NO	Runs	HS	Avg	SR	100	50
224 Imran Tahir	12	15	4	206	77*	18.72	86.19	0	1
225 GJ Kruis	9	9	2	131	37	18.71	99.24	0	0
226 MAG Nelson	4	7	0	131	38	18.71	47.63	0	0
227 DR Smith	9	14	0	261	80	18.64	92.55	0	2
228 DS Lucas	16	24	7	312	55*	18.35	41.32	0	1
229 R McLaren	7	8	1	126	43	18.00	50.80	0	0
230 TJ Murtagh	13	20	6	249	51*	17.78	38.72	0	1
231 B-A Godleman	5	9	0	160	48	17.77	25.76	0	0
232 GP Smith	7	14	1	231	51	17.76	37.31	0	1
233 OP Rayner	11	11	1	173	60	17.30	56.16	0	1
234 CD Thorp	13	12	0	207	42	17.25	52.53	0	0
235 A Khan	11	12	3	153	62*	17.00	62.70	0	1
236 ID Saxelby	9	13	3	168	60*	16.80	51.37	0	1
237 RJ Sidebottom	7	9	3	100	46	16.66	34.60	0	0
238 SD Snell	9	14	1	215	85	16.53	40.71	0	1
239 PRA Johnston	3	6	0	99	73	16.50	59.63	0	1
240 CEW Silverwood	5	8	1	113	46	16.14	77.39	0	0
241 RJ Woodman	6	10	1	144	32	16.00	36.00	0	0
242 Murtaza Hussain	7	8	1	111	34	15.85	29.05	0	0
243 Naved-ul-Hasan	4	6	0	93	32	15.50	76.22	0	0
244 JM Anderson	9	11	3	123	29	15.37	49.39	0	0
245 NS Tahir	12	14	4	152	24	15.20	36.19	0	0
246 GJP Kruger	13	13	7	91	28*	15.16	43.33	0	0
247 MJ Hoggard	16	17	4	195	56*	15.00	41.66	0	1
248 CD Whelan	12	17	3	205	47	14.64	45.65	0	0
249 A Nel	9	10	2	117	32	14.62	56.25	0	0
250 CJC Wright	14	16	7	130	24*	14.44	37.90	0	0
251 SJ Benn	4	7	1	86	35	14.33	54.08	0	0
252 DM Housego	3	6	0	86	34	14.33	43.87	0	0
253 IE O'Brien	7	9	1	110	31	13.75	50.92	0	0
254 Imran Arif	9	13	7	81	35	13.50	54.00	0	0
255 K Ali	5	8	2	81	30*	13.50	36.00	0	0
256 DA Cosker	8	11	3	107	46*	13.37	41.31	0	0
257 JA Tomlinson	12	14	7	92	23	13.14	25.27	0	0
258 TG Burrows	6	7	1	78	32	13.00	46.70	0	0
259 Azhar Mahmood	4	6	0	78	35	13.00	65.54	0	0
260 BJM Scott	8	14	1	167	44	12.84	46.77	0	0
261 DJ Pattinson	8	8	0	102	59	12.75	58.95	0	1
262 MS Mason	14	23	6	207	28	12.17	53.35	0	0
263 Danish Kaneria	11	15	2	158	37	12.15	110.48	0	0
264 MS Panesar	15	22	6	193	38	12.06	44.67	0	0
265 SP Kirby	16	22	8	157	27	11.21	34.27	0	0
266 JEL Buttleman	3	6	0	67	33	11.16	44.07	0	0
267 GJ Batty	11	16	0	175	46	10.93	41.96	0	0
268 JW Dernbach	14	19	6	138	19	10.61	37.19	0	0
269 DH Wigley	12	15	8	74	16	10.57	32.31	0	0

Name	M	Inn	NO	Runs	HS	Avg	SR	100	50
270 ME Claydon	12	12	1	110	38	10.00	48.03	0	0
271 CT Tremlett	7	8	0	75	36	9.37	39.47	0	0
272 A Javid	3	6	0	55	21	9.16	23.91	0	0
273 AJ Harris	16	19	3	143	22*	8.93	39.17	0	0
274 JD Lewry	6	10	4	51	25	8.50	46.78	0	0
275 PJ Foster	3	6	0	48	24	8.00	31.37	0	0
276 SJ Harmison	17	15	5	79	25*	7.90	55.24	0	0
277 V Banerjee	7	12	3	71	16	7.88	22.32	0	0
278 SI Mahmood	14	14	1	100	30*	7.69	47.16	0	0
279 CD Collymore	14	17	5	89	23	7.41	24.25	0	0
280 G Keedy	17	16	7	63	18	7.00	27.51	0	0
281 G Onions	14	14	6	52	17*	6.50	38.51	0	0
282 OJ Newby	13	11	1	64	15	6.40	32.65	0	0
283 ST Finn	14	22	4	107	24*	5.94	28.60	0	0
284 JE Taylor	3	6	0	35	15	5.83	70.00	0	0
285 DA Griffiths	10	13	4	45	20*	5.00	29.03	0	0
286 JC Glover	3	6	0	27	14	4.50	19.01	0	0
287 CD Paget	3	6	0	27	18	4.50	21.95	0	0
288 CM Willoughby	16	13	4	40	23	4.44	43.95	0	0
289 WB Rankin	13	13	4	19	7	2.11	16.66	0	0

BOWLING AVERAGES
Qualifying requirements: 10 wickets taken

	Name	M	Balls	Runs	Wkts	Avg	RPO	BB	5I
1	SA Piolet	1	162	43	10	4.30	1.59	6-17	1
2	Azhar Mahmood	4	783	382	21	18.19	2.92	5-39	1
3	G Onions	14	2572	1377	69	19.95	3.21	7-38	5
4	J Lewis	15	2559	1146	57	20.10	2.68	5-73	1
5	DS Lucas	16	2487	1299	60	21.65	3.13	7-24	3
6	NS Tahir	12	1646	843	38	22.18	3.07	5-67	1
7	SP Kirby	16	2836	1420	64	22.18	3.00	5-44	1
8	HJH Marshall	16	624	360	16	22.50	3.46	4-24	0
9	ID Blackwell	18	2741	1064	47	22.63	2.32	7-85	3
10	JM Anderson	9	1743	886	39	22.71	3.04	6-56	5
11	AJ Hall	16	1862	911	40	22.77	2.93	5-29	1
12	M Kartik	10	1903	755	33	22.87	2.38	5-65	1
13	LE Plunkett	15	2457	1401	60	23.35	3.42	6-63	3
14	Danish Kaneria	11	3587	1777	75	23.69	2.97	8-116	6
15	SJ Harmison	17	3080	1503	63	23.85	2.92	6-20	4

Name	M	Balls	Runs	Wkts	Avg	RPO	BB	5I
16 RJ Sidebottom	7	1562	760	31	24.51	2.91	5-59	2
17 JJ van der Wath	13	2187	1237	50	24.74	3.39	5-71	1
18 CD Thorp	13	1925	846	34	24.88	2.63	5-49	2
19 G Chapple	11	2014	884	35	25.25	2.63	6-19	2
20 TJ Murtagh	13	2658	1521	60	25.35	3.43	7-82	3
21 IE O'Brien	7	1088	547	21	26.04	3.01	6-39	2
22 SCJ Broad	9	1611	887	34	26.08	3.30	6-91	3
23 MJ Saggers	4	653	264	10	26.40	2.42	3-45	0
24 JC Tredwell	17	4091	1838	69	26.63	2.69	8-66	4
25 DD Masters	15	3344	1212	45	26.93	2.17	5-65	1
26 TD Groenewald	9	1640	921	34	27.08	3.36	6-50	2
27 SD Udal	14	2213	1007	37	27.21	2.73	6-36	2
28 PP Chawla	6	2051	981	36	27.25	2.86	6-52	4
29 BW Hilfenhaus	5	1085	604	22	27.45	3.34	4-60	0
30 MS Mason	14	2512	1186	43	27.58	2.83	7-39	2
31 LJ Fletcher	8	1473	800	29	27.58	3.25	4-38	0
32 J Allenby	12	1144	471	17	27.70	2.47	3-70	0
33 A Nel	9	1564	754	27	27.92	2.89	6-36	1
34 ID Hunter	7	1090	593	21	28.23	3.26	5-46	2
35 DG Cork	12	1722	767	27	28.40	2.67	5-14	1
36 AR Adams	11	2454	1224	43	28.46	2.99	4-39	0
37 JEC Franklin	14	1755	904	31	29.16	3.09	5-30	1
38 KW Hogg	14	2030	1000	34	29.41	2.95	4-22	0
39 PM Siddle	6	1051	680	23	29.56	3.88	5-21	1
40 DA Cosker	8	1873	769	26	29.57	2.46	6-91	2
41 M Davies	9	1303	562	19	29.57	2.58	4-87	0
42 N Boje	15	1890	891	30	29.70	2.82	4-59	0
43 RDB Croft	17	4421	1727	58	29.77	2.34	5-65	1
44 CM Willoughby	16	3334	1621	54	30.01	2.91	5-56	3
45 SR Clark	4	564	301	10	30.10	3.20	3-18	0
46 GP Swann	10	1616	824	27	30.51	3.05	4-38	0
47 ST Finn	14	2511	1624	53	30.64	3.88	5-57	1
48 SJ Cook	13	2245	1047	34	30.79	2.79	5-22	3
49 A Flintoff	7	1160	586	19	30.84	3.03	5-92	1
50 AJ Shantry	13	1668	898	29	30.96	3.23	5-62	1
51 ID Saxelby	9	1112	620	20	31.00	3.34	3-31	0
52 ME Claydon	12	1404	777	25	31.08	3.32	4-90	0
53 RH Joseph	4	584	373	12	31.08	3.83	6-55	1
54 WD Parnell	5	999	529	17	31.11	3.17	4-78	0
55 PT Collins	5	824	504	16	31.50	3.66	5-75	1
56 AJ Ireland	7	1002	664	21	31.61	3.97	6-31	1
57 DJ Wainwright	10	1502	824	26	31.69	3.29	5-134	1
58 V Banerjee	7	1203	667	21	31.76	3.32	4-58	0

	Name	M	Balls	Runs	Wkts	Avg	RPO	BB	5I
59	A Khan	11	2035	1146	36	31.83	3.37	5-113	1
60	R McLaren	7	989	608	19	32.00	3.68	4-51	0
61	JD Middlebrook	8	828	449	14	32.07	3.25	3-80	0
62	S Sreesanth	5	658	418	13	32.15	3.81	5-93	1
63	MJ Hoggard	16	2875	1486	46	32.30	3.10	5-56	2
64	DA Griffiths	10	1700	1039	32	32.46	3.66	4-48	0
65	DR Smith	9	1806	814	25	32.56	2.70	4-58	0
66	Imran Tahir	12	2926	1711	52	32.90	3.50	7-140	4
67	RMR Brathwaite	4	856	428	13	32.92	3.00	5-54	1
68	JWM Dalrymple	17	1395	726	22	33.00	3.12	3-11	0
69	CD Collymore	14	2376	1104	33	33.45	2.78	4-66	0
70	CR Woakes	19	2939	1576	47	33.53	3.21	6-43	2
71	RA Jones	7	1044	745	22	33.86	4.28	6-100	1
72	SI Mahmood	14	2277	1394	41	34.00	3.67	6-30	2
73	G Keedy	17	3263	1540	45	34.22	2.83	6-50	3
74	A Shahzad	14	2537	1405	41	34.26	3.32	4-72	0
75	GM Smith	16	1982	1098	32	34.31	3.32	5-65	1
76	RSC Martin-Jenkins	13	1666	793	23	34.47	2.85	5-43	1
77	WB Rankin	13	2042	1279	37	34.56	3.75	5-85	1
78	GR Napier	10	1628	1005	29	34.65	3.70	4-32	0
79	LJ Wright	10	1345	764	22	34.72	3.40	5-66	2
80	JAR Harris	14	2636	1498	43	34.83	3.40	4-69	0
81	MA Chambers	7	850	526	15	35.06	3.71	4-62	0
82	MA Ealham	14	2322	983	28	35.10	2.54	5-31	1
83	SJ Benn	4	720	353	10	35.30	2.94	4-31	0
84	PS Jones	12	2388	1210	34	35.58	3.04	5-35	1
85	OJ Newby	13	1783	1107	31	35.70	3.72	4-21	0
86	AU Rashid	10	1840	1118	31	36.06	3.64	5-41	2
87	DA Stiff	10	1610	1120	31	36.12	4.17	5-91	1
88	TT Bresnan	14	2662	1168	32	36.50	2.63	4-116	0
89	GJ Kruis	9	1513	816	22	37.09	3.23	3-51	0
90	AC Thomas	14	2407	1317	35	37.62	3.28	5-53	1
91	GG Wagg	14	3129	1773	47	37.72	3.39	6-35	3
92	BJ Phillips	7	949	456	12	38.00	2.88	4-46	0
93	DH Wigley	12	1885	1230	32	38.43	3.91	6-72	2
94	CJC Wright	14	2623	1538	40	38.45	3.51	4-43	0
95	DS Harrison	8	1243	770	20	38.50	3.71	4-60	0
96	MG Johnson	7	1292	924	24	38.50	4.29	5-69	1
97	GK Berg	13	1495	886	23	38.52	3.55	5-55	2
98	JW Dernbach	14	2372	1436	37	38.81	3.63	6-47	2
99	GJP Kruger	13	2122	1283	33	38.87	3.62	6-93	1
100	PJ Franks	5	819	428	11	38.90	3.13	3-52	0
101	JA Tomlinson	12	1909	1193	30	39.76	3.74	3-53	0

Name	M	Balls	Runs	Wkts	Avg	RPO	BB	5I
102 CT Tremlett	7	1038	564	14	40.28	3.26	4-49	0
103 JL Clare	5	714	407	10	40.70	3.42	3-64	0
104 T Lungley	6	797	531	13	40.84	3.99	3-56	0
105 AG Botha	14	1899	941	23	40.91	2.97	5-51	1
106 NM Hauritz	5	928	492	12	41.00	3.18	3-63	0
107 AJ Harris	16	2371	1439	35	41.11	3.64	5-26	1
108 Naved-ul-Hasan	4	744	412	10	41.20	3.32	3-102	0
109 TC Smith	9	1198	623	15	41.53	3.12	6-46	1
110 LA Dawson	15	582	421	10	42.10	4.34	2-3	0
111 M Hayward	5	740	472	11	42.90	3.82	4-99	0
112 GM Andrew	10	1545	991	23	43.08	3.84	5-117	1
113 Murtaza Hussain	7	1626	825	19	43.42	3.04	4-70	0
114 OP Rayner	11	1766	870	20	43.50	2.95	4-186	0
115 NM Carter	9	1140	704	16	44.00	3.70	5-37	1
116 K Ali	5	702	485	11	44.09	4.14	6-68	1
117 RN ten Doeschate	14	1476	970	22	44.09	3.94	5-62	1
118 WA White	12	1185	852	19	44.84	4.31	3-91.	0
119 AA Noffke	6	948	452	10	45.20	2.86	4-92	0
120 CW Henderson	10	2369	1044	23	45.39	2.64	6-152	1
121 AV Suppiah	16	1277	682	15	45.46	3.20	3-58	0
122 PD Trego	16	1545	889	19	46.78	3.45	3-53	0
123 SR Patel	17	2906	1558	33	47.21	3.21	6-84	2
124 AD Mascarenhas	10	1446	618	13	47.53	2.56	2-46	0
125 CD Whelan	12	1392	1067	22	48.50	4.59	5-95	1
126 Azeem Rafiq	4	747	487	10	48.70	3.91	3-34	0
127 SC Meaker	5	664	498	10	49.80	4.50	3-114	0
128 RKJ Dawson	7	952	610	12	50.83	3.84	4-76	0
129 Yasir Arafat	5	906	621	12	51.75	4.11	3-83	0
130 HF Gurney	10	1373	829	16	51.81	3.62	5-82	1
131 AR Caddick	5	787	525	10	52.50	4.00	3-53	0
132 Imran Arif	9	1109	899	17	52.88	4.86	5-93	1
133 JD Lewry	6	955	535	10	53.50	3.36	2-53	0
134 MS Panesar	15	2705	1195	22	54.31	2.65	3-10	0
135 A Richardson	6	1334	618	11	56.18	2.77	3-52	0
136 R Clarke	14	985	640	11	58.18	3.89	2-15	0
137 CJ Jordan	8	1250	764	13	58.76	3.66	4-84	0
138 SM Ervine	15	1401	793	13	61.00	3.39	3-22	0
139 CE Shreck	11	2180	1281	21	61.00	3.52	4-63	0
140 CP Schofield	14	2183	1357	22	61.68	3.72	5-40	1
141 GJ Batty	11	1363	724	10	72.40	3.18	2-71	0
142 DJ Pattinson	8	1319	872	10	87.20	3.96	4-53	0

INDEX OF PLAYERS BY COUNTY

*denotes not registered for the 2010 season. Where a player is known to have moved in the off-season he is listed under his new county.

DERBYSHIRE

BORRINGTON, P.M.
CLARE, J.L.
GODDARD, L.J.
FOOTITT, M.H.A.
GROENWALD, T.D.
HINDS, W.W.*
HUGHES, C.F.
HUNTER, I.D.
JONES, E.P.
JONES, P.S.
KLOKKER, F.A.
LAW, S.G.*
LAWSON, M.A.K.*
LUNGLEY, T.
MADSEN, W.L.
NEEDHAM, J.
PARK, G.T.
PETERSON, R.J.
PIPE, D.J.*
POYNTON, T.J.
REDFERN, D.J.
ROGERS, C.J.L.
SADLER, J.L.
SHEIKH, A.
SMITH, G.M.
STUBBINGS, S.D.*
TELO, F.D.*
WAGG, G.G.
WHITELEY, R.A.

DURHAM

BENKENSTEIN, D.M.
BLACKWELL, I.D.
BORTHWICK, S.G.
BREESE, G.R.
CHANDERPAUL, S.
CLAYDON, M.E.
COETZER, K.J.
COLLINGWOOD, P.D.
DAVIES, M.A.
DIVENUTO, M.J.
EVANS, L.
GIDMAN, W.R.S.
HARMISON, B.W.
HARMISON, S.J.
KILLEEN, N.
MUCHALL, G.J.
MUSTARD, P.
ONIONS, G.
PLUNKETT, L.E.
RICHARDSON, M.J.
RUSHWORTH, C.
SMITH, W.R.
STOKES, B.A.
STONEMAN, M.D.
THORP, C.D.
WARNER, D.A.

ESSEX

AHMED, J.S.*
BOPARA, R.S.
CHAMBERS, M.A.
COMBER, M.A.
COOK, A.N.
DANISH KANERIA
FLOWER, G.W.
FOSTER, J.S.
GALLIAN, J.E.R.*
GODLEMAN, B-A.
HARDINGES, M.A.
MASTERS, D.D.
MAUNDERS, J.K.
MICKLEBURGH, J.C.
NAPIER, G.R.
OSBORNE, M.
PALLADINO, A.P.
PETTINI, M.L.
PHILLIPS, T.J.
TEN DOESCHATE, R.N.
WALKER, M.J.
WESTFIELD, M. S.
WESTLEY, T.
WHEATER, A.J.
WRIGHT, C.J.C.

GLAMORGAN

ALLENBY, J.
ASHLING, C.P.
BRAGG, W.D.
BROWN, D.O.
COSGROVE, M.J.
COSKER, D.A.
CROFT, R.D.B.
DALRYMPLE, J.W.M.
GLOVER, J.C.
HARRIS, J.A.R.
HARRISON, D.S.
JAMES, N.A.
JONES, A.J.
KRUGER, G.J-P.*
MAYNARD, T.L.
NORMAN, A.J.
O'SHEA, M.P.*
OWEN, W.T.
POWELL, M.J.
REED, M.T.

754

INDEX OF PLAYERS BY COUNTY

REES, G.P.
SHANTRY, A.J.
TAIT, S.W.
WATERS, H.T.
WALLACE, M.A.
WRIGHT, B.J.

GLOUCESTERSHIRE

ADSHEAD, S.J.
ALI, KADEER
BANERJEE, V.
BATTY, J.N.
DAWSON, R.K.J.
DENT, C.D.J.
FRANKLIN, J.E.C.
GIDMAN, A.P.R.
HODNETT, G.P.*
HUSSAIN, G.M.
IRELAND, A.J.
KIRBY, S.P.
LEWIS, J.
MARSHALL, H.J.H.
PAYNE, D.A.
PORTERFIELD, W.T.S.
SAXELBY, I.J.
SNELL, S.D.
SPEARMAN, C.M.*
STAYT, T.P.
TAYLOR, C.G.
WOODMAN, R.J.

HAMPSHIRE

ADAMS, J.H.K.
BALCOMBE, D.J.
BATES, A.M.
BENHAM, C.C.
BRIGGS, D.R.

BURROWS, T.G.*
CARBERRY, M.A.
CORK, D.G.
CRAWLEY, J.P.
DAWSON, L.A.
ERVINE, S.M.
GRIFFITHS, D.A.
HAYWARD, N.
HOWELL, B.A.C.
JONES, S.P.
LUMB, M.J.
MASCARENHAS, A.D.
MCKENZIE, N.D.
MENDIS, B.A.W.
NORTH, M.J.*
PARSONS, T.W.*
PIETERSEN, K.P.
POTHAS, N.
RIAZUDDIN, H.
SHAHID AFRIDI
TAYLOR, B.V.*
TOMLINSON, J.A.
VINCE, J.M.
WOOD, C.P.

KENT

AZHAR MAHMOOD
BANDARA, C.M.
BLAKE, A.J.
CLARK, S.R.
COLES, M.T.
COOK, S.J.
DENLY, J.L.
DIXEY, P.G.
EDWARDS, P.D.
FERLEY, R.S.
GOODMAN, J.E.
HOCKLEY, J.B.

JONES, G.O.
JOSEPH, R.H.
KEMP, J.M.
KEY, R.W.T.
KHAN, A.
LEE, W.W.
MCLAREN, R.*
NORTHEAST, S.A.
PARNELL, W.D.
SAGGERS, M.J.*
STEVENS, D.I.
TREDWELL, J.C.
TUFFEY, D.
VAN JAARSVELD, M.

LANCASHIRE

ANDERSON, J.M.
BROWN, K.R.
CHAPPLE, G.
CHEETHAM, S.P.
CHILTON, M.J.
CROFT, S.J.
CROSS, G.D.
DU PLESSIS, F.
FLINTOFF, A.
HOGG, K.W.
HORTON, P.J.
KEEDY, G.
KERRIGAN, S.C.
LAXMAN, V.V.S.
MAHMOOD, S.I.
MONTGOMERY, G.S.
MOORE, S.C.
NEWBY, O.J.
PARRY, S.D.
POWELL, D.B.L.
PRINCE, A.G.
PROCTER, L.A.

INDEX OF PLAYERS BY COUNTY

SANGAKKARA, K.C.
SHANKAR, A.A.
SMITH, T.C.P.
SUTTON, L.D.

LEICESTERSHIRE

ACKERMAN, H.D.
BENNING, J.G.E.
BOYCE, M.A.G.
BUCK, N.L.
CLIFF, S.J.
COBB, J.J.
CROWE, C.D.
DAGNALL, C.E.
DIPPENAAR, H.H.
DU TOIT, J.
GURNEY, H.F.
HARRIS, A.J.
HENDERSON, C.W.
HODGE, B.J.
HOGGARD, M.J.
JEFFERSON, W.I.
MALIK, M.N.
MASTERS, D.
MCDONALD, A.B.
NAIK, J.K.H.
NEW, T.J.
NIXON, P.A.
POPE, J.I.
ROBERTS, A.
SMITH, G.P.
TAYLOR, J.W.A.
THOMPSON, C.E.J.
WALKER, G.W.
WHITE, W.A.
WYATT, A.C.F.

MIDDLESEX

BERG, G.K.
BURTON, D.A.*
DAVEY, J.H.
DEXTER, N.J.
EVANS, D.
FINN, S.T.
GILCHRIST, A.
HENDERSON, T.*
HOUSEGO, D.M.
HUGHES, P.J.
LONDON, A.B.
MALAN, D.J.
MORGAN, E.J.G.
MURTAGH, T.J.
NASH, D.C.*
NEWMAN, S.A.
O'BRIEN, I.E.
ROBSON, S.D.
ROLAND-JONES, T.S.
SCOTT, B.J.M.
SHAH, O.A.
SILVERWOOD, C.E.W.*
SIMPSON, J.A.
SMITH, T.M.J.
STIRLING, P.R.
STRAUSS, A.J.
TOOR, K.S.
UDAL, S.D.
WILLIAMS, R.E.M.

NORTHAMPTONSHIRE

BOJE, N.
BROOKS, J.A.
CROOK, S.P.
CUMMINS, R.A.G.*
DAGGETT, L.M.
HALL, A.J.
HARRISON, P.W.
HARVEY, I.J.*
HOWGEGO, B.H.N.
LOYE, M.B.
LUCAS, D.S.
MURPHY, D.
MIDDLEBROOK, J.D.
NELSON, M.A.G.*
NEWTON, R.I.
O'BRIEN, N.J.
PETERS, S.D.
SALES, D.J.G.
WAKELY, A.G.
WHITE, R.A.
WIGLEY, D.H.
WILLEY, D.J

NOTTINGHAMSHIRE

ADAMS, A.R.
AMLA, H.M.
BALL, J.T.
BROAD, S.C.J.
BROWN, A.D.
BROWN, J.F.*
CARTER, A.
EALHAM, M.A.*
EDWARDS, N.J.
FLETCHER, L.J.
FRANKS, P.J.
HALES, A.D.
HUSSEY, D.J.
MCGUIRE, B.T.
MULLANEY, S.J.
NANNES, D.P.
O'BRIEN, K.J.
PATEL, A.

INDEX OF PLAYERS BY COUNTY

PATEL, S.R.
PATTINSON, D.J.
READ, C.M.W.
SHAFAYAT, B.M.
SHRECK, C.E.
SIDEBOTTOM, R.J.
SWANN, G.P.
VOGES, A.C.
WAGH, M.A.
WHITE, G.G.
WOOD, M.J.

SOMERSET

BANKS, O.A.C.
BURKE, J.E.
BUTTLER, J.C.
CADDICK, A.R.*
COMPTON, N.R.D.
DE BRUYN, Z.
DIBBLE, A.J.
DURSTON, W.J.*
GAZZARD, C.M.*
HAGGETT, C.J.
HILDRETH, J.C.
JONES, C.R.
KARTIK, M.
KIESWETTER, C.
LANGER, J.L.*
LETT, R.J.H.
MUNDAY, M.K.
PHILLIPS, B.J.
POLLARD, K.A.
STIFF, D.A.
SUPPIAH, A.V.
THOMAS, A.C.
TREGO, P.D.
TRESCOTHICK, M.E.
TURNER, M.L.

WALLER, M.T.C.
WHITE, C.L.
WILLOUGHBY, C.M.

SURREY

AFZAAL, U.
BATTY, G.J.
BROWN, M.J.
BUTCHER, M.A.*
CHAWLA, P.P.
COLLINS, P.T.*
DAVIES, S.M.
DERNBACH, J.W.
EDWARDS, G.A.
ELLIOTT, G.D.*
EVANS, L.J.
HAMILTON-BROWN, R.J.
HARINATH, A.
HARINATH, M.
HERATH, H.M.R.K.B.
JEWELL, T.M.
JORDAN, C.J.
KING, S.J.
LANCEFIELD, T.J.
LINLEY, T.E.
LOGAN, R.J.*
MEAKER, S.C.
MURTAGH, C.P.*
MURTAZA HUSSAIN*
NEL, A.
RAMPRAKASH, M.R.
ROY, J.J.
SCHOFIELD, C.P.
SPRIEGEL, M.N.W.
TREMLETT, C.T.
TUDOR, A.J.*
WALTERS, S.J.
WATERS, S.R.
WILSON, G.C.

SUSSEX

AGA, R.G.
ANYON, J.E.
BEER, W.A.T.
BROWN, B.C.
COLLYMORE, C.D.
GATTING, J.S.
GOODWIN, M.W.
HODD, A.J.
HOPKINSON, C.D.*
JOYCE, E.C.
KEEGAN, C.B.
KIRTLEY, R.J.
LEWRY, J.D.*
LIDDLE, C.J.
MARTIN-JENKINS, R.S.C.
NASH, C.D.
PANESAR, M.S.
PRIOR, M.J.
RAYNER, O.P.
SANDRI, P.S.E.
SMITH, D.R.
THORNELY, M.A.
WELLS, L.W.P.
WRIGHT, D.G..
WRIGHT, L.J.
YARDY, M.H.
YASIR ARAFAT

WARWICKSHIRE

AMBROSE, T.R.
BARKER, K.H.D.
BELL, I.R.
BOTHA, A.G.
CARTER, N.M.
CHOPRA, V.
CHOUDHRY, S.H.

INDEX OF PLAYERS BY COUNTY

CLARKE, R.
FROST, T.*
IMRAN TAHIR
JAVID, A.
JOHNSON, R.M.
MACLEOD, C.S.
MADDY, D.L.
MILLER, A.S.
NEWPORT, N.A.
ORD, J.E.
PATEL, J.S.
PIOLET, S.A.
POONIA, N.S.
RANKIN, W.B.
SREESANTH
TAHIR, N. S.
TROTT, I.J.L.
TROUGHTON, J.O.
WESTWOOD, I.J.
WOAKES, C.R.

WORCESTERSHIRE

AHMED, M.*
ALI, KABIR
ALI, M.M.
ANDREW, G.M.
ANEESH KAPIL
COX, O.B.
FISHER, I.D.*
IMRAN ARIF
JAQUES, P.A.
JONES, R.A.
KERVEZEE, A.N.
KNAPPETT, J.P.T.*
LEACH, J.
MANUEL, J.K.
MASON, M.S.
MITCHELL, D.K.H.

NOFFKE, A.A.*
PARDOE, M.G.
PINNER, N.D.
RICHARDSON, A.
RUSSELL, C.
SHAKIB AL HASAN
SHANTRY, J.D.
SMITH, B.F.
SMITH, S.
SOLANKI, V.S.
WHEELDON, D.A.
WHELAN, C.D.

YORKSHIRE

AZEEM RAFIQ
BAIRSTOW, J.M.
BALLANCE, G.S.
BLAIN, J.A.R.
BRESNAN, T.T.
BROPHY, G.L.
GALE, A.W.
GIBBS, H.H.
GUY, S.M.*
HANNON-DALBY, O.J.
HARRIS, R.J.
HODGSON, L.J.
KRUIS, G.J.*
LEE, J.E.
LYTH, A.
MCGRATH, A.
NAVED-UL-HASAN
PATTERSON, S.A.
PYRAH, R.M.
RASHID, A.U.
ROOT, J.E.
RUDOLPH, J.A.
SANDERSON, B.W.
SAYERS, J.J.

SHAHZAD, A.
VAUGHAN, M.P.*
WAINWRIGHT, D.J.

QUIZ ANSWERS

1. 1-1 with 2 matches drawn
2. 88
3. 48
4. Javed Miandad
5. 1979
6. 2005
7. Intikhab Alam
8. 1983
9. Imtiaz Ahmed
10. An innings and 261 runs
11. Waqar Younis
12. Javed Miandad
13. 108
14. Fazal Mahmood
15. Ramiz and Wasim Raja
16. 87 and 90
17. Mudassar Nazar
18. Saeed Anwar
19. Habibul Bashar (18 Tests, 69 one-day internationals, between 2004 and 2007)
20. Rashid Latif
21. Nine
22. Hanif Mohammad
23. Trescothick (192) and Vaughan (120)
24. Riverside, Chester-le-Street
25. 23
26. Wasim Bari
27. Delhi
28. Hasan Raza
29. Headingley
30. Javed Miandad and Inzamam-ul-Haq
31. 202
32. Imran Khan
33. Trescothick (151) and Bell (162*)
34. Zaheer Abbas
35. 1996
36. Mohammad Wasim
37. Australia
38. Mohammad Ashraful (100 exactly)
39. Javed Miandad
40. Asif Iqbal and Intikhab Alam
41. England
42. Iqbal Qasim
43. Mohsin Khan
44. 400
45. Aminul Islam (145)
46. Mushtaq Mohammad
47. He was the nightwatchman
48. Four; Pakistan won the other
49. 1983-84 (1-0)
50. 708
51. Javed Miandad
52. Mike Gatting
53. 100
54. Zimbabwe
55. Pakistan (2003) and Sri Lanka (2007)
56. Rashid Latif
57. Intikhab Alam
58. Ken Barrington
59. Imran Khan
60. Abdul Qadir
61. 30
62. Waqar Younis
63. India (1946) under the name of Abdul Hafeez
64. West Indies
65. Tamim Iqbal (128)
66. A series win over England
67. None
68. Shakib Al Hasan
69. The Oval
70. Javed Miandad
71. 488 (v Zimbabwe in January 2005)
72. 62 (v Sri Lanka in July 2007)
73. Javed Miandad
74. Javed Miandad
75. 124
76. Wasim Akram
77. Waqar Younis
78. None
79. All three matches were drawn
80. Javed Burki
81. Habibul Bashar
82. Mohammad Ashraful (5)
83. Zaheer Abbas
84. Six
85. Twice
86. Mohammad Rafique
87. 274
88. Javed Miandad (260 at The Oval in 1987)
89. Shahriar Nafees (4)
90. Aamir Sohail
91. Mashrafe Mortaza, Mohammad Rafique and Abdur Razzak
92. Enamul Haque Jr (12 for 200)
93. Mohammad Yousuf
94. Wasim Bari
95. 363
96. Khaled Mashud
97. Mohsin Kamal
98. The Sixth
99. East Pakistan
100. Brian Johnston